BAND OF BRIGANDS

By the same author

THE MAHARAJAH'S BOX
An Imperial Story of Conspiracy, Love and a Guru's Prophecy

FENIAN FIRE
The British Government Plot to Assassinate Queen Victoria

PHYLLOXERA
How Wine was Saved for the World

BAND
OF BRIGANDS

The First Men in Tanks

CHRISTY CAMPBELL

HarperPress

An Imprint of HarperCollins*Publishers*

Harper Press
An Imprint of HarperCollins*Publishers*
77–85 Fulham Palace Road,
Hammersmith, London W6 8JB

www.harpercollins.co.uk
Visit our authors' blog: www.fifthestate.co.uk

Published by Harper Press 2007

1 3 5 7 9 8 6 4 2

A catalogue record for this book is available
from the British Library

ISBN 13 978-0-00-721459-4

Maps by John Gilkes

Set in PostScript Linotype Meridien
with Castellar display by
Rowland Phototypesetting Ltd,
Bury St Edmunds, Suffolk

Printed and bound in Great Britain
by Clays Ltd, St Ives plc

For Bill and Frank – who liked this sort of thing

CONTENTS

ILLUSTRATIONS

Lt Daniel Hickey *National Army Museum*
Capt. Clement Robertson, VC www.haileybury.herts.sch.uk
British tanks in German hands *Library of Congress*

Log bundles called fascines, used for trench crossing *Tank Museum*
    Collection, Bovington
Captured German machine gunners *Imperial War Museum*

Highlanders of the 51st Division *Imperial War Museum*
Pigeons take the blame *Australian War Memorial Negative Number H09572*

Advertisement for shaving foam, by Daivd Langdon *Tank Museum*
    Collection, Bovington
Christmas card, 1917 *Liddell Hart Centre for Military Archives*

Poster for 'Hero Land' pageant in Manhattan *Library of Congress*
Capt. George S. Patton *Virginia Military Institute Archives*
Col. Samuel D. Rockenbach *Virginia Military Institute Archives*

Mk V's equipped with trench-crossing cribs *Imperial War Museum*
Winston Churchill inspecting Mk V's *Liddell Hart Centre for Military*
    Archives, King's College, London
The cumbersome A7V Sturmpanzerwagen *Imperial War Museum*

2/Lt Frank Heap *Philippe Gorckzynski/Solo Syndication*
Battlefield clearance team inters tank D.51 Deborah [two photographs]
    Tank Museum Collection, Bovington
Men of the Royal Tank Regiment move D.51 Deborah to new home *Solo*
    Syndication

TANK TIPS

Remember your orders.
Shoot quick.
Shoot low. A miss which throws dust in the enemy's eyes is better than one
        which whistles in his ear.
Shoot cunning.
Shoot the enemy while they are rubbing their eyes.
Economise ammunition and don't kill a man three times.
Remember that trenches are curly and dug-outs deep – look round the
        corners.

Watch the progress of the fight and your neighbouring Tanks.
Watch your infantry whom you are helping.
Remember the position of your own line.
Smell out the enemy's machine guns and other small guns and kill them first
        with your 6-pdrs.
You will not see them for they will be cunningly hidden;
You must ferret out where they are, judging by the following signs:–
      Sound.
      Dust.
      Smoke.
      A shadow in a parapet.
      A hole in a wall, haystack, rubbish heap, woodstack, pile of bricks.
      They will usually be placed to fire slantways across the front and to
        shoot along wire.
      One 6-pdr. shell that hits the loophole of a m.g. emplacement will do
        it in.

Use the 6-pdr. with care; shoot to hit and not to make a noise.
Never have any gun, even when unloaded, pointing at your own infantry, or
        a 6-pdr. gun pointed at another Tank.
It is the unloaded gun that kills the fool's friends.

Never mind the heat.
Never mind the noise.
Never mind the dust.
Think of your pals in the infantry.
Thank God you are bullet proof and can help the infantry, who are not.

Have your mask always handy.

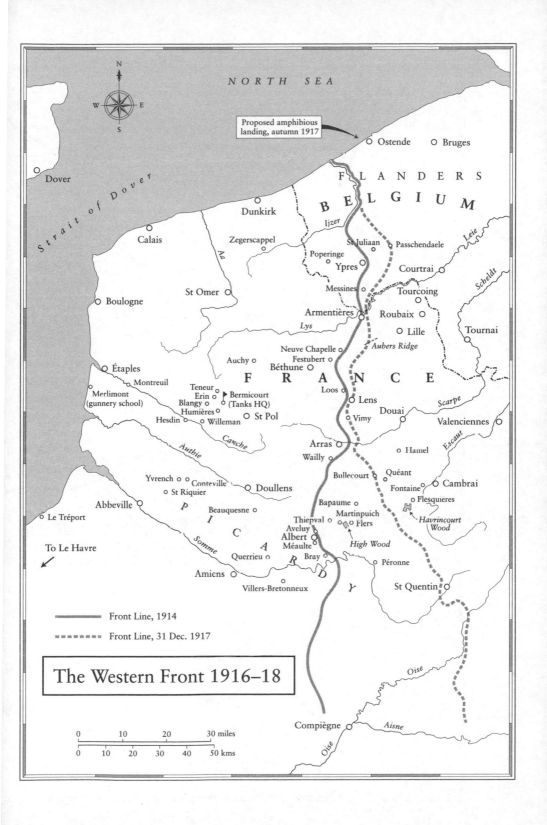

The Western Front 1916–18

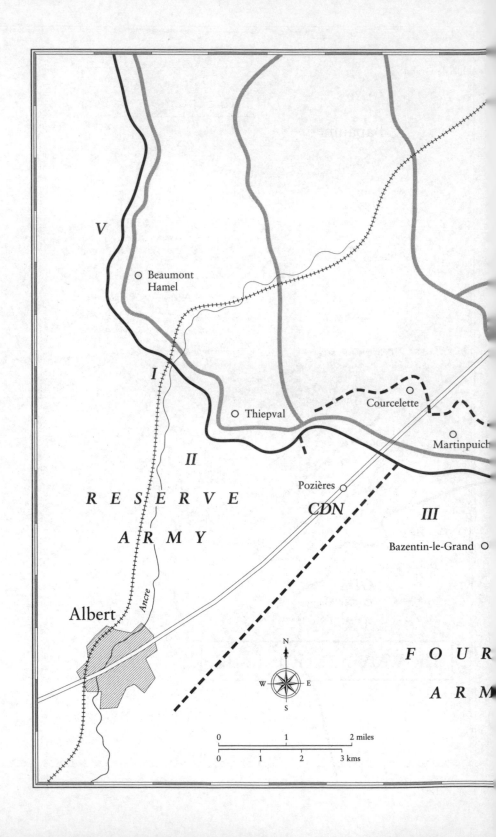

V

Beaumont
Hamel ○

I

Thiepval ○

Courcelette ○

Martinpuich ○

II

R E S E R V E

Pozières ○

CDN

III

A R M Y

Bazentin-le-Grand ○

Ancre

Albert

F O U R

A R M

N
W   E
S

0   1   2 miles

0   1   2   3 kms

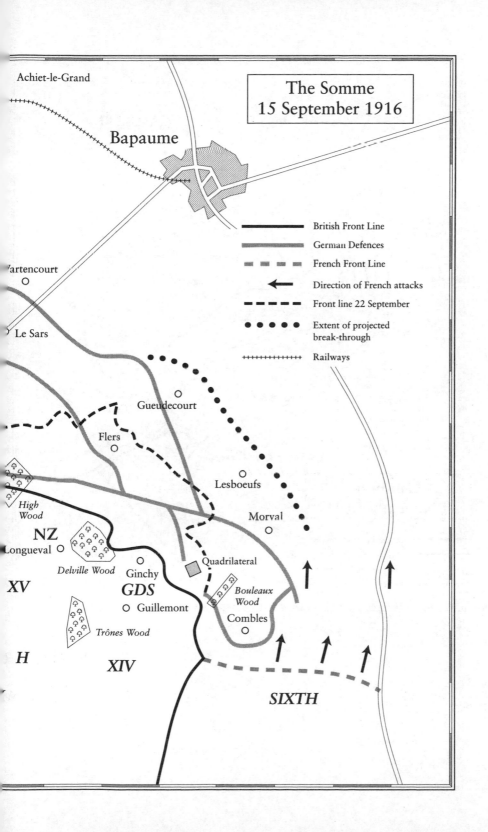

Achiet-le-Grand

Bapaume

The Somme
15 September 1916

━━━━━━ British Front Line

▰▰▰▰▰ German Defences

▰ ▰ ▰ ▰ French Front Line

← Direction of French attacks

▬ ▬ ▬ ▬ Front line 22 September

● ● ● ● ● Extent of projected
break-through

+++++++++++ Railways

Martencourt

Le Sars

Gueudecourt

Flers

Lesboeufs

High
Wood

Morval

NZ

Longueval

Quadrilateral

Delville Wood   Ginchy

XV

GDS

Bouleaux
Wood

Guillemont

Combles

Trônes Wood

H

XIV

SIXTH

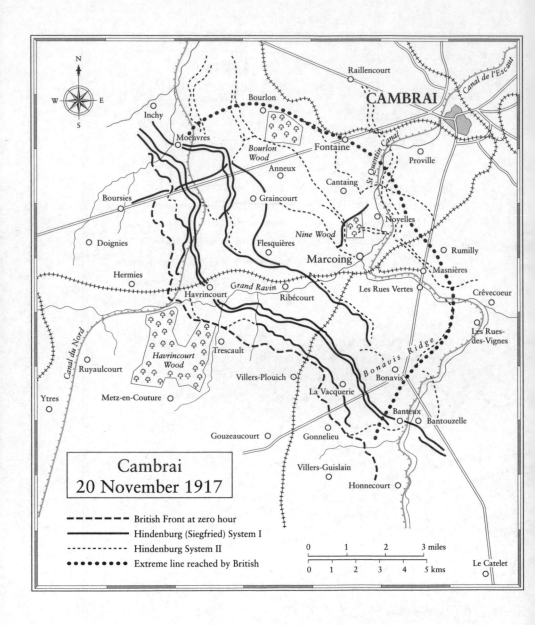

N
W • E
S

Raillencourt

Canal de l'Escaut

CAMBRAI

Bourlon

Inchy

Moeuvres

*Bourlon
Wood*

Fontaine

Proville

Anneux

Cantaing

St Quentin Canal

Boursies

Graincourt

Noyelles

Doignies

Nine Wood

Flesquières

Rumilly

Marcoing

Masnières

Hermies

Grand Ravin

Havrincourt

Ribécourt

Les Rues Vertes

Crêvecoeur

Canal du Nord

Les Rues-
des-Vignes

*Havrincourt
Wood*

Trescault

Bonavis Ridge

Ruyaulcourt

Villers-Plouich

Bonavis

Ytres

Metz-en-Couture

La Vacquerie

Banteux

Bantouzelle

Gouzeaucourt

Gonnelieu

Villers-Guislain

Honnecourt

Cambrai
20 November 1917

– – – – – – British Front at zero hour
————— Hindenburg (Siegfried) System I
- - - - - - Hindenburg System II
•••••••• Extreme line reached by British

| 0 | 1 | 2 | 3 miles |

| 0 | 1 | 2 | 3 | 4 | 5 kms |

Le Catelet

In no man's land one early morn at sixty in the shade
From out the British lines came the famous tank brigade
The Huns began to shake, couldn't make it out at all
Exactly when the tanks began their caterpillar crawl.

'The Tanks that Broke the Ranks out in Picardy',
sung by Fred Curran

I'd like to see a Tank come down the stalls,
Lurching to rag-time tunes, or 'Home, sweet Home',
And there'd be no more jokes in Music-halls
To mock the riddled corpses round Bapaume.

'Blighters', Siegfried Sassoon, February 1917

A wistful face in a faded photo.
Under the stairs is a khaki cap;
That was Dad's . . .

Autumn Journal,
Louis MacNeice, October 1938

PREFACE

On a cold day in November I stood behind a farmer's tractor and plough in a muddy field in north-east France watching bits of metal come out of the ground. I always enjoyed this sort of thing. Every so often my employers would allow me, as defence correspondent of the *Sunday Telegraph*, to hare off to some old battlefield to look for stories from the past. War stories: I had been captivated by them from TV-watching childhood.

At home, my parents' war was rarely mentioned. It had killed my mother's brother and her first husband. For me, growing up in the 1960s, Hitler's war was still dark and dangerous. I glued together model Messerschmitts in secrecy. The Kaiser's war was another matter. My grandfather gave me a bayonet he had taken off a dead Turk at Gaza – wherever that might have been. There was a picture of him on a camel. My father admitted sheepishly that a great-uncle had been a general. My mother took us all to see Joan Littlewood's *Oh! What a Lovely War* at the Theatre Royal, Stratford, which, it seemed, had a suitably pacifist message. My mother's father, once long ago an RAMC stretcher-bearer, was not keen on the production. 'It wasn't all songs, you know.'

Thirty years on and my grandfather was long dead. The Great War was fading rapidly from living memory. How men fought and endured and for what reasons seemed beyond comprehension. Asinine generals, tousle-haired subalterns, courageous tommies – mud, wire and machine guns. The presiding narrative was by now long enshrined. Historians and novelists tampered with it at their peril. At the same time the popular hunger for the period was stronger than ever. On any day the National Archives at Kew was thronged with amateur researchers looking for what they might find about Uncle Jack. Whenever I had touched on the subject as a journalist I was rewarded with a sheaf of letters.

A flurry of anniversaries in the 1990s afforded me the privilege of meeting more veterans. Some were as frail as ash, others robust enough to cross the Channel for a last centenarian hurrah. Sometimes there was nobody left.

Hence my outing with the tractor. We were a few miles south-east of the French city of Cambrai where eighty years earlier, on 20 November 1917, British 'tanks' had rumbled out of the dawn mist in the first mass, armoured attack in history. They got further in one morning than the British Army had done in four months in the mires of Flanders to the north. A great victory was announced. Church bells rang out across England, but it all ended in disaster. The upcoming eightieth anniversary would make a good Poppy Day newspaper story.

But what happened at Cambrai was interesting for more than that. The Great War myth was turned upside down. Commanders were clever. There was not much mud. Surprise and deception were paramount. The enemy crumbled – for the most part. For one day the Western Front siege of wire and trenches was broken. Soldiers were courageous, devious and cowardly by turn. There was widespread looting. Large amounts of alcohol were evidently consumed. The generals seemed astonished at their own success and did not know what to do next. A new, technocratic force of men in tanks had at last used intelligence and cunning to minimize the casualties.

My eightieth anniversary guide to the battlefield was a thirty-six-year-old hotelier named Philippe Gorczynski, who declared himself to have been 'obsessed with the battle since he found his first piece of British tank at the age of six'. He had been prying into every corner ever since, interviewing elderly villagers, collecting remnants – bullet cases, fragments of metal, huge stoneware flagons of British Army-issue rum.

His barn was full of such stuff. 'Farmers tell me they've found something and I come and take it away,' he explained. 'Most French people think we are crazy. They are amazed when you English wear poppies. Only the very old here wear *les bleuets*, cornflowers, our soldiers' sign of remembrance.'

We went to see M. Xavier Leriche, a farmer and mayor of the nearby village of Ribecourt. His tractor had returned from its morning work to his farmyard, sagging under a strange burden. A torrent of oxidized metal tumbled out with the shiny wet sugar beet.

There was a clutch of Mills bombs, their firing pins fused with rust, fragments of gas mask, a huge artillery shell. The farm workers shrugged. 'They are live and extremely dangerous,' M. Leriche said as the crop was neatly separated by hand. I instinctively shuffled backwards. French army engineers, I was assured, would arrive within a few days to blow them up.

And there were bodies. The mayor's tractor had come back loaded with bones a few months before. 'We found fragments of an Englishman. We worked out his name from badges and an engraved knife: Sgt Paul Kitto, of the RAMC.'

'What about tanks?' I asked. 'Are there any left here?' Many were carted away by the Germans in 1918, I was informed – and those that were left were blown up where they stood on the battlefield by a special British commission at the end of the war. There were rumours, however, which had never gone away.

Philippe told me something tantalizing. 'I know where a complete tank is buried – on an old lady's farm,' he said. 'She remembers the Germans ordering Russian prisoners to push it into a shell hole near the café owned by her parents – but she won't let anyone dig it up.'

Mme Bouleux would not be moved. She was almost as old as the century and perhaps had seen too many invading armies fight over her farm at the southern edge of the village of Flesquières to be disturbed again. The house was shuttered and dark. 'It's no use knocking,' said Philippe, 'she will just shoo us away.'

Marthe Bouleux died in spring 1998. The little farm's new owners were more accommodating. Philippe Gorczynski moved in with contemporary battle maps, aerial photographs, an infrared imaging camera and a mine detector. Something very large was buried beneath the spinach plot.

A dozen volunteers began digging on the morning of 8 November 1998. Whatever was in the ground was buried about a metre down in some sort of existing excavation, crudely back-filled with rubble and chalky subsoil. Within an hour it appeared. A metal hulk – with a roof hatch plainly discernible. It was a British tank of the First World War, interred in the very spot where, apparently, it had been stopped in its tracks by a German shell over eight decades before.

The British military attaché rushed from Paris. That evening a ceremony was conducted around the floodlit pit. A poppy wreath was solemnly laid and two bagpipers played a lament in memory of the infantrymen of the 51st Highland Division who had fought and died in the wake of the advancing tanks.

Eight flares were fired into the wintry sky, one for each of the British Army divisions involved in the battle and one for the Tank Corps. Mark IV tanks had eight-man crews.

Busloads of curious Britons crossed the Channel to see the tank that somehow stayed behind – and to watch it being lifted from its pit by crane like a mammoth from the permafrost to be placed in a barn. British soldiers still come reverentially to spray her with oil to keep the rust at bay.

The unearthed machine, meanwhile, was as enigmatic as the Unknown Soldier. No markings had survived except a barely discernible figure '1' on an oxidized petrol tank. There were no bodies inside, no badges or uniforms just a jumble of bullet cases, jam tins, Johnny Walker whisky and anonymous clear-glass bottles. One especially baffled French investigators. I identified it as HP Sauce.

The machine's interment beneath the spinach patch was equally mysterious. Why was it here? Who were its crew? What happened to them? There were no bodies but there were ghosts in the machine.

The anonymous tank did have a name. Research and happy accident would identify her. That faint '1' on the rear petrol tank. It could be one of many. The Tank Museum at Bovington, Dorset, received some family photographs dating from 1917. One showed a disabled tank with the number 51 on the petrol tank. The damage was identical – on the back was written 'Heap's bus'.

One member of the crew at least had been identified – the tank's commander, 2/Lt Heap. In D Battalion's order of battle he was listed as commander of tank D.51 Deborah. The tank had a name.

She (tanks, like warships, tend to be feminine), it would turn out, was named thus in August 1917 by her first commander, 2/Lt George Ranald Macdonald, a New Zealander who had taken her into battle in the mires of Flanders. Deborah had survived that dismal campaign. Three months later her commander was 2/Lt Frank Gustave Heap, aged twenty-three, the son of a Blackpool businessman, who had enlisted as a private in the Royal Engineers from Cambridge in 1915 before joining the Heavy Branch Machine Guns Corps. Tall and bespectacled, even in his Tank Corps uniform he looks more like a parson than the Hun-crushing hero who won an MC that day.

Four men were killed and four survived her end. The dead were eventually reburied in the nearby Flesquières Hill war cemetery (it's just at the end of the village street on the D92 road heading north-east towards Cantaing) – F. W. Tipping, gunner 110380, born and enlisted in Nottingham; Walter George Robinson, private 94838, enlisted in Lambeth, Surrey; George Foot, private 40342, born in London and enlisted in Aylesbury, Buckinghamshire; and Joseph Cheverton, private 92960, enlisted in Cambridge. Their average age was twenty-one.

Clambering inside Deborah in her barn it is hard to see how anyone survived. Clearly battered by machine-gun fire, her front is blown out by some internal explosion. Frank Heap's grandson, William Heap, himself a civilian ordnance expert, went to see her in Flesquières and formed a theory. 'It looks as if they were hit by something first, shell fragments perhaps. My grandfather ordered evacuation. Then the fatal shell struck – went through the side and blew up inside. Either some of the crew did not get out quickly enough – or they all did but four of them were picked off by machine-guns.

'He was quite an athlete. Nobody could have run faster on the battlefield. He became a keen mountain climber after the war. I only knew him as a small child – he died in the early fifties – he was pretty reticent about telling war stories – that was that generation's style.'

A photograph from the Heap family album showed the disabled tank outside a shattered house in the centre of the village. There was no explanation as to how it came to be taken. The place remained clearly identifiable. Its present-day occupant, M. Gilbert Guidez, aged sixty-seven, would tell me: 'My grandmother Katrine was in the cellar but she was killed by an *obus* [shell] that came through the window. My mother survived. She remembered that four bodies from the tank were hastily buried in the garden.' They were taken away and reinterred later.

Deborah's crew were young men both of the volunteer New Armies of 1915–16 and conscripts. As I pieced together their truncated biographies, I wondered what had led them here. They were not the first soldiers to go to war like this. The first pioneers had been trained in a secret camp in Suffolk and had gone into action on the Somme the year before in dramatic and controversial circumstances. Where had 'tanks' come from? Who was their first commander? A line in a rumbustious, irreverent book by a Tank Corps veteran published in 1920 called *The Tank in Action* immediately struck me: 'The curious might spend a profitable week or so at the British Museum investigating the origins of the landship . . .' It seemed an appropriate place to start.

Some Abbreviations and Military Expressions

AEF   American Expeditionary Force

Alpaca   First two companies of HSMGC, sent to France
   August 1916

AP   Armour-piercing

APM   Assistant Provost Marshal

Armstrong   Collapsible wood and canvas hut

ASC   Army Service Corps

Autovac Vacuum   Fuel feed device

BEF   British Expeditionary Force

'Bitch' Infantry   Expression for 'female' tank

'Bull' Infantry   Expression for 'male' tank

'Bus'   Tank (current from mid-1917)

'Car'   Tank (current in 1916–17)

CID   Committee of Imperial Defence

CIGS   Chief of the Imperial General Staff

C-in-C   Commander-in-Chief

'Crump'   Large shell, also the resulting crater

DAD   Director Air Division (Admiralty)

DCGS   Deputy Chief of the General Staff

DNC   Director of Naval Construction

DORA   Defence of the Realm Act

DSO   Distinguished Service Order

Field ambulance   First line medical unit, not a vehicle

Female   Machine-gun armed tank

'France'   GHQ Headquarters BEF

FT   *Faible tonnage*, lightweight

GHQ   General Headquarters

GQG   *Grand Quartier Général*, French field headquarters

GSO   General Staff Officer

HE   High explosive

HSMGC   Heavy Section Machine Guns Corps

KuK   Imperial and royal – Austro-Hungarian

LGOC   London General Omnibus Company

Male   Cannon- (and machine gun-) armed

MET   Metropolitan Electric Tramways

MMGS   Motor Machine Gun Service

MG '08   Machine gun Model 1908

MGC   Machine Gun Corps

MO   Medical Officer

MO5   Military Operations fifth directorate (intelligence)

MWSD   Mechanical Warfare Supply Department

OC   Officer Commanding

OHL   Oberste Heeresleitung, German field headquarters

Osprey   Codeword for tank (from mid-1917)

Point d'appui   Base for military operations

PSC   Passed staff college

QF   Quick-firer

'Red tab', 'red hat'   Staff officer

RAC   Royal Automobile Club, (also, from 1939)
   Royal Armoured Corps

RAMC   Royal Army Medical Corps

RFC   Royal Flying Corps

RNAS   Royal Naval Air Service

RTC   Royal Tank Corps (from 1923)

RTR   Royal Tank Regiment (from 1939)

RUSI   Royal United Services Institute

Saa   Small arms ammunition

'Sapper'   Royal Engineer

'The Senior'   Army and Navy Club

SIW   Self-inflicted wound

SmK   German armour-piercing bullet

SRD   Supply reserve depot (rum ration)

S-round   Reversed bullet (more effective against armour)

Willie   Tank

WO   War Office

WP   Wire pulling

AUTHOR'S NOTE

Who invented the tank? In May 1941, as German panzers romped across the North African desert and were running the British Army out of Greece, H. G. Wells got into trouble considering the same question. The author and seer was told that someone had been on the wireless claiming that he was the inventor of the famous fighting machine.

He knew exactly who the claimant was – an old literary rival from decades ago, now a Fellow of All Souls and Chichele Professor of the History of War at the University of Oxford – Major-General Sir Ernest Dunlop Swinton, KBE, CB, DSO.

It would have been better if Mr Wells had heard the broadcast himself. He wrote a cross letter to *The Listener*, the BBC's cerebral journal, claiming Sir Ernest had invented nothing. Indeed, he had 'lifted' the idea from a short story he himself had written almost four decades before – 'The Land Ironclads'. But the speaker had made no such claim; he had mildly puffed his own record as a long-ago prophet who had been ignored and at the end been justified. Wells's attack would land him and the BBC with a hefty libel suit.

The great author was accused of falsely claiming that Sir Ernest 'was too stupid and self-satisfied to understand the tank . . . and that he was a dishonest, arrogant and unimaginative person who only became enterprising when he was seeking to secure for himself the rewards to which he knew he was not entitled'. It was not a bad precis of the article. 'It has been left to the Germans to inflict one disaster after another upon us with our own native invention,' said Wells in his piece. No one could argue with that.

The defendants settled out of court for a large sum. Why such a fuss at such a time of national crisis? Because 'Who invented the tank?' was a big question, one that had already been picked over for years in the law courts with a great deal of money in contention.

H. G. Wells had published his science-romance story in 1903. The French author Albert Robida had introduced the idea of 'mobile blockhouses' into his 1887 fantasy novel *La Guerre au vingtième siècle*. Various inventors had been inspired by both or either pieces of fiction, and proposals were sent to War Offices in London, Berlin and Vienna to be filed and forgotten. An Australian corporal named Lancelot de Mole sent something looking very similar to a tank to the War Office in 1912. It was ignored. Around the same time a Leeds electrician sent a plan to the Admiralty for land battleships to 'fight off an invasion'. It looked plain mad. An Austrian engineer called Günther Burstyn designed a tracked armoured vehicle in 1911 carrying a light gun in a rotating turret. The War Ministry in Vienna said it would be interested if its originator could secure commercial backing. An approach to the German government was no more successful.

But in Britain something did happen under the spur of conflict and in 1915–16 a vehicle that might certainly be recognized as a tank was built and successfully tested. Then it went to war . . .

There was money at stake. A year after the Armistice the 'Royal Commission on Awards to Inventors' began its hearings; they would last for a decade and a half, reviewing 1834 proposals for weapons of war from improved nose bags for horses to air-launched torpedoes. In November 1919 the commission considered the question of 'tanks' – before Mr Justice Sargant in Lincoln's Inn Hall. The proceedings were formal and judicial. The Crown was represented by the attorney-general, solicitor-general and two eminent counsels. Their aim was to protect the Treasury from monster payouts (the standard sum demanded by various individuals was £100,000). Winston Churchill was the first witness called by the Crown. He was not a claimant but a highly interested party. The six days of closely argued testimony and cross-examination provide fascinating glimpses into the story of the birth of the tank (some follows in this narrative) referred to as the 'Inventions Commission'.

Churchill thought that no single man was its inventor although he acknowledged H. G. Wells as the literary inspiration. That is what the Inventions Commission eventually decided. The tank had many inventors, although some had been more inventive than others.

PART ONE

A Shadow in a Parapet

He put a bullet through his brain
No one spoke of him again

'Suicide in the Trenches',
Siegfried Sassoon, 1918

1

The colonel's body was discovered on a high summer's morning in a roadside ditch. It was lying face down, half-hidden by bushes. It was a sergeant of the Glosters who found him – a day and a night since the alarm was raised. The missing officer had a gunshot wound to the head. A big Webley revolver was clenched in his hand. He was clearly dead. As L/Sgt J. C. Gibbs had been instructed when the search party was mustered, he did not touch a thing.

The death of a British soldier, however senior, on the Western Front in the baleful year of 1917 might seem wholly unremarkable. But this was altogether a different affair. No enemy bullet had claimed him. The sound of heavy gunfire could be borne at any time on the wind from the east – but farmers still worked the fields in this corner of northern France up close to the border with Belgium. This was a 'quiet' area, twenty miles behind the Ypres salient.

It was all rather curious. In the full light of day, Lieutenant-Colonel (temporary) John Brough, MVO, CGM, late of 'special service with the Heavy Section, Machine Gun Corps', had walked up a country lane, clambered into a thicket in an apparent attempt to hide himself, pressed the muzzle of his Webley service revolver to his temple and pulled the trigger. The first round misfired. He tried again. The second bullet, according to the army doctor who would examine the body, killed him instantly.

The colonel's self-immolation obliterated him from history. The divisional war diary does not mention it. His name is all but forgotten even by those who care obsessively about such things. *The History of the Great War Based on Official Documents* (otherwise known as the *Official History*) mentions him once in passing. The Tank Museum at Bovington, Dorset, has no personal or official papers – not even an obituary notice. The index to the Liddell Hart collection at King's College London, a splendid depository of all things to do with warfare in the twentieth century, spells his name incorrectly – 'Burgh'. They did not speak of him again.

But Lt-Col. John Brough occupies a certain place in the annals of war. In the summer of 1916, the forty-three-year-old former Royal Marine was responsible for the very first mechanized, armoured fighting force ever to take the field. He had helped raise and train it, then taken it to France to do what he might in preparing it for action. On the eve of its going into battle on the Somme he was dismissed after some sort of row with General Headquarters. Nobody really knew what it was about.

After his abrupt departure from the front, the colonel had sought new employment. He had hung around the War Office, another 'dud' posted home. He had got a desk job in London – to be posted at last in the spring of 1917 as second General Staff Officer (GSO2) of the 61st (2nd South Midlands) Division, a second-line unit of Territorials. After its own shaky combat debut in July 1916 the division had been deemed to have certain 'command confidence' problems. In the summer of 1917 it had just arrived in a training area a few miles due south of Dunkirk still trying to sort them out.

The search party of L/Sgt Gibbs and Pte W. P. Venton found the 'missing divisional officer' at 9.00 a.m. on 30 July – two shiny boots sticking out of a hedge. Officers were summoned. No one touched the body until the Medical Officer and the Assistant Provost Marshal arrived from Division: there was a procedure for these things. A casualty wire must be sent, next of kin informed of the cause of death – an enquiry convened. Bloody man seemed to have shot himself. This was going to be a sticky business. Self-inflicted wounds, fatal or otherwise, always were.

It was the paperwork, you see. Army Form W.3428 (Report on Accidental or Self-inflicted Injuries) had to be filled in with its check boxes. It was configured on the premise that a soldier who shot himself intended to survive. There was item 2, for example: 'Nature, location and severity of injury. NB Field Ambulance to be notified at once if wound is believed to be self-inflicted.' And there was item 4 which invited the: 'Commanding Officer's opinion whether man was injured (a) in the performance of military duty – (b) was to blame.'

If it was (b) it meant trouble. A soldier who shot himself in the foot or stuck a bayonet through his thigh (the usual despairing methods of finding a ticket home) could expect to face a field court martial and a long term of imprisonment if found guilty. Lieutenant-Colonel Brough was dead but an official decision, self-inflicted injury or not, must be reached. Officers were not meant to do this sort of thing. If they did, they must be mad.

On 31 July the court of enquiry opened at divisional HQ, Zegerscappel, Lt-Col. Leonard Bilton, divisional staff officer, in the chair.

Captain Murray Phillips, the division's Assistant Provost Marshal (more used to handling prisoners of war but in this case the nearest thing in the British Army to a police detective in uniform), had examined the body where it lay.

The colonel's powder-stained fingers still gripped his .445-calibre Webley army pattern pistol. He seemed to have made some effort to conceal himself in the undergrowth before committing what appeared to be an obvious act of suicide. There was nothing to suggest he had consumed alcohol. Boots, belt and buttons were all highly polished. Examination of the gun told the story of the first round which was still in the chamber, struck by the hammer but misfired.

The MO, Capt. L. A. Scanlon, RAMC, was clearly relieved to have retrieved the second and fatal bullet.* He told the enquiry:

> I was asked to make an examination of the body . . . I did so and found a small hole about one inch behind the outer angle of the right orbit. I found another, lacerated, about two inches above and behind the left ear. The skull was fractured, the skin surrounding the wound near the right orbit was blackened as if by powder. I formed the opinion that death was due to laceration of the brain as the result of a bullet wound, death must have been instantaneous.

---

* Self-inflicted wounds were a very serious and theoretically capital offence in the British Army, but although men were sentenced to many years of penal servitude, no executions were actually carried out in the course of the war. It was up to MOs to determine whether the wound (usually by gunshot in the foot or hand) was the result of enemy action or not, hence the obligatory search for the bullet and determination of the angle of entry. Suicide was much rarer but the investigative procedure was the same. Without the convenience of an officer's sidearm, infantry rankers who sought death as a final way out would usually place the muzzle of a .303 rifle in their mouths and pull the trigger with a toe.

I found a revolver bullet and small pieces of bone in the deceased's cap. There were no other signs of injury to the body.

No suicide note was found on the body or in the colonel's billet in the village of Zegerscappel. He had left no documents at all except 'a letter from his aunt'. Captain Phillips took statements from those who had last seen the deceased alive.

The colonel's batman, Pte H. Trussler, had been ordered by Mr Brough a little before midday on the 29th to summon a staff car and driver to 'go to the brigade training area'. He told how the colonel had gone first to his billet to collect his revolver, something he had never done before. The gun appeared to be loaded which was unusual anyway, but its owner was 'as normal'.

Army Service Corps driver Pte A. Searle said: 'I took him as far as I might until the road to Eringhem got too bad . . . Colonel Brough got out – told me to go back to the village and walked on . . .'

Then he shot himself. The court of enquiry met at divisional headquarters on 31 July, the opening day of the great offensive that Field Marshal Sir Douglas Haig, Commander-in-Chief of the British Armies in France, planned would sweep the Germans from the Flanders coast. The 61st Division was part of the Fifth Army reserve – waiting for the day (it would come in mid-August) when it was its turn to go into the line. More than two hundred tanks had been assembled to support the infantry in the promised breaking of the German defences and the capture of Passchendaele Ridge. They were supposed to reach it in a day. It would take three months. Most of the tanks would drown in a bog. John Brough had been working on the 61st Division's place in the plan of attack for weeks.

Why had he killed himself? Was he 'windy'? Was it what the MOs were calling 'NYD(M)'.* There had been no nerve-shattering shelling, no more than the usual discomforts of life in a training area behind the front. Anyway, Brough was a desk-wallah. The division had seen some small-scale action in the spring. Since then it had been in reserve, billeted in the village of Willeman near Hesdin

---

* 'Not Yet Diagnosed (Mental).' 'Shell shock' had been discussed in the medical literature since early 1916 and it was by now common currency among the rank and file. Some MOs though it was a malingerers' ticket. Others were much more sympathetic.

through July. It was all rather jolly. The weather had been sweltering
– shirtsleeves order – too hot to train sometimes.

The divisional 'horse show and sports day' was on the 10th. There
was an inter-regimental cricket match. Sergeant Dobbs performed
his famous acrobatic routine. The band played selections from *Iolanthe*
and *The Bing Boys are Here*, with an uplifting interlude performed by
the Glosters' concert party, the Cheeriohs. A full afternoon card of
point-to-pointing followed. Even an unfashionable division like the
61st could be show-offs sometimes.

Colonel Brough on Ginger Nut had snatched the fourth race, the
Willeman Plate, 'open to officers of twelve stone and up over five
furlongs'. Captain J. H. Bevan came second on Signoretta. In the open
handicap Brough had triumphed again on Snodgrass. The divisional
commander, Maj.-Gen. Colin Mackenzie, was chief judge and
Brough his deputy. The colonel seemed as dashing as ever, his work
in the past few weeks no less conscientious. But there was a melancholy about him. Lieutenant-Colonel Brough had had something to
do with 'tanks' in the last show on the Somme, although he did not
talk about it much. Tanks had been having a rough time of it. At a
place called Bullecourt in April they had been all but wiped out and
the infantry they were supposed to be leading massacred.

On 25 July the division had moved to Flanders. It was Brough's
job to draft the training schedule – 'trench attack under barrage',
followed by 'open warfare advance against enemy rearguards'. Open
warfare – the Fifth Army plan was disarmingly optimistic. On the
morning of the 27th Brough had drafted final instructions and presented them to the divisional conference. They ended: 'The discipline
of sleep must be insisted upon . . . there is nothing more important
than insisting on rest during fighting.'

The colonel was himself clearly weary. Captain Bevan, the divisional GSO3, told the tribunal how his superior had been 'exceedingly conscientious' – but had become 'more and more worried about
his work' since joining the division two and a half months before.
An old friend, Lt-Col. Singleton, the divisional quartermaster, testified how Brough had lately become 'morose and dejected to an
extraordinary degree'.

The tribunal, a kind of military inquest, did not take long to reach
its verdict. The MO was not asked for any expert opinion on the

deceased's state of mind. It did not require much discussion. According to the members of the court, Lt-Col. Brough had 'shot himself
with his revolver in a fit of temporary insanity caused by mental
worry'.*

A blank Form W.3428 was put into the typewriter. The words
were tapped out in blue ink: 'Bullet-wound – Head – Self-Inflicted –
Fatal.'

There was no need for the tribunal chairman's opinion on
whether 'the man was to blame'. It was all rather obvious. Box (b)
stayed unticked. So did Box (a). But if Lt-Col. Brough had not been
injured in the course of military duty, what had led to his death?
That little unchecked box was the problem.

The divisional commander, Maj.-Gen. Colin Mackenzie, concurred with the insanity verdict. But madness was not an excuse.
Suicide was a coward's trick. A certain Capt. Roberts signed off the
W.3428 on behalf of the GOC Fifth Army, Gen. Sir Hubert Gough.
'This casualty should be reported as killed – self-inflicted,' it stated
starkly. HQ Fifth Army applied their stamp.† On 3 August the report
was forwarded to the Adjutant-General's central registry in London.

But the casualty wire had already been sent. The War Office's
vast mechanism for informing relatives that their son/husband/
brother had been killed was clanking forward. Brough was a bachelor. His father was next of kin. The day the court of enquiry's verdict
was signed off, the OHMS telegram arrived at the Junction Hotel,
Dorchester – 'deeply regret . . . died of wounds . . . Army Council
express their sympathy'. Hundreds got the same knock on the door
and flimsy piece of paper every day. On some days there had been
thousands.

Two days later the heartbroken Col. William Brough received a

---

* Captain E. Fryer Ballard, RAMC(T), an army psychiatrist, published a paper in the
July 1917 *Journal of Mental Science* which gave a glimpse of new humane thinking in the
origins and treatment of what he called 'battle psycho-neuroses': 'Severe types that
exhibit well-marked symptoms after six months do not recover well in the army. A
considerable proportion of those who recover in hospital, break down again at their
depots or command depots . . . These soldiers ought therefore to be given not less than
three months' leave, then be sent to a convalescent home and from there to a command
depot. If they subsequently break down they will be no use for the field and never will be.'

† It was the 1889th case of accidental or self-inflicted injury in Fifth Army since its
establishment nine months before.

typewritten letter. 'The Military Secretary deeply regrets to inform you that a report has just been received from General Headquarters that Lt-Col. J. Brough died of wounds (self-inflicted) . . . No further details have been received.' His son would not be listed among the fallen. It was a death without honour.*

The baffled, grieving father, a veteran artilleryman of the Indian Army, 'could not imagine why . . . save that perhaps his mind must have given way under the long strain of active service'. By return of post he begged the 'merciful kindness' of the War Office to publish the fact of his son's death and its manner as 'died of wounds'. The request was turned down. 'No – he can place his own notice in the papers' is scribbled in the margin of the old man's letter.

As in so many Anglo-Irish families†, his sons, born in Sialkot in the Punjab, had never considered anything other than following their father into the army. The fate of his eldest son was beyond endurance.

The colonel's body was taken from Zegerscappel by a concerned party to be buried at Longuenesse (St Omer) Souvenir Cemetery a few miles inland from the Channel coast. It was not the end of the affair.

It came out this way. Under the Death Duties (Killed in War) Act passed by Parliament in a patriotic rush in September 1914, it was determined that the Inland Revenue should grant relief on the taxable estates of officers killed in action. But Lt-Col. Brough had killed himself. Insane or not, suicide was not tax-deductible.‡

* There was a kind of residual respect among front-line soldiers. Captain Charles McMoran Wilson RAMC (later Lord Moran), who had been a regimental MO, cited the case of 'the sergeant at Armentières who shot himself . . . it was plain enough then that he could not face war . . . and had taken the matter into his own hands before he did something dreadful that might bring disgrace on himself and his regiment . . .' A Tank Corps veteran recalled many years later that his company commander always carried a pistol – 'to shoot himself should he be terribly maimed'.

† Col. W. R. C. Brough, b. 1841, had served in the Madras Artillery, then the Royal Marine Artillery. India Office records show him marrying Anne Maria Irwin of Rathcore, Enfield, co. Meath, Ireland, on 18 September 1873.

‡ It remained a fine point of law. In November 1917 in a fit of conscience after the Passchendaele offensive the War Cabinet agreed that 'pensions to dependants for those soldiers shot for cowardice or other crimes . . . should be paid in the same manner as to soldiers who died on active service and that the same should apply as regards officers' – and further that 'communications to dependants should not convey that the man had been shot, rather that he had died on service.'

A similar move was thereafter made for widows and dependants of those who

The colonel's estate passed to his sister, Miss Elizabeth Brough, of the Convent, Ashford, Kent. Tax was levied. The deceased had not been killed in performance of military duty. In 1919 the heartbroken father requested relief as a way of exonerating his shamed son. The Revenue was unmoved and remained so for years. The father was ailing. John's younger brother, Lt-Col. Alan Brough, took up the correspondence. He was an informed witness.

In July 1917 he had been on the staff at General Headquarters, the field command of the British forces in France (with a rather grand job – Deputy Director of Transport, British Expeditionary Force). On the late afternoon of the 29th he had been telegrammed at St Omer with the news that his brother had apparently disappeared. He rushed to Zegerscappel overnight. He met an old friend, Col. Singleton, who told him that lately John had been profoundly 'melancholy . . . depressed' and appeared to be 'brooding over some grievance'.

The next morning his brother's body was found. It was Alan Brough who had himself taken it in a motor ambulance to St Omer for a private burial in the military cemetery there.

John Brough's military career had been unusual. There were several parts of it Alan Brough did not know. His elder brother had been to Staff College, then served in the Cameroons on the staff of the commanding general in the eighteen-month-long campaign of 1914–16 against the Germans in their steamy West African colony. He had been mentioned in dispatches and promoted from major to temporary lieutenant-colonel. All that was on file. On John Brough's return from West Africa, where 'he had contracted fever', he had been shuffled uncomfortably round London seeking new employment. The Royal Engineers turned him down.

Brough at last formally transferred to the Royal Artillery – his nominal masters at the Admiralty seemed quite keen to let him go. Then, by some strange intervention, he had been inducted in late May 1916 into some shadowy branch of the recently formed

---

suffered self-inflicted wounds – including fatal ones – but the Treasury insisted that pension rights should not be automatic but at the War Secretary's discretion.

The estate duty relief of the Killed in War Act 1914 (amended by the Finance Act 1918 to embrace brothers and sisters of the dead) was, however, left unconsidered. Other ranks (generally) were not wealthy enough to have taxable estates – and officers were not meant to be cowards, deserters or suicides. The Brough case would seem to have been highly unusual if not unique.

'Machine Gun Corps'. He was supposed to command a battalion of its 'Motor Service'. He ended up commanding what was later to be called its 'fighting side'. They were tanks, the first in history.

At a highly secret experimental ground in East Anglia, he had demonstrated these strange new machines before the Secretary of State for War, the Chief of the Imperial General Staff and King George V. He had written a prototype manual of tactical doctrine. He had sought out wounded soldiers and German prisoners in London hospitals to inform his men just what was really going on in the Somme fighting – when General Headquarters in France would not reveal a thing. Then the time had come to take them into the line. But when John Brough's own commanding officer turned up in France he found his second in command had seemingly vanished. There had been, he was informed, 'certain difficulties.'

Alan Brough had this to say about what happened. His position was sensitive, he was still a serving officer in the third decade of his military career. Eight years after the events in question he told the War Office:

> On the termination of the Cameroon campaign [my brother] returned to England and was employed on special duty with the Tank Corps.* In September 1916 I happened to meet him at St Riquier in France where tank demonstrations were carried out. He looked thin and told me he was having a difficult task in connection with getting tanks out from England and up to the front line for their first appearance in the war.
>
> It is a matter of common knowledge that the employment of tanks during the Somme battles of Sept. 1916 was not a success in all respects and I gather that my brother was blamed for his share in the proceedings. It is not for me to question the justice of the case, but it is quite evident that he had worked very hard, and he took his lack of success very deeply to heart . . .

They had met again in July 1917 at Hesdin, not too far from the old Somme battlefield, a few days before the 61st Division's move north in preparation for the Flanders offensive. John had seemed 'terribly depressed' and had begged him to try and get him a job at GHQ. Then, on the evening of 29 July, Alan Brough received the

* Then known as Heavy Section Machine Gun Corps.

wire from Zegerscappel saying his brother had gone missing. He did not spell it out but the implication was clear. It was the events of September 1916 that had led his brother to kill himself. It was the blame attached to 'his share in the proceedings'.

In the autumn of 1924 the octogenarian Col. William Brough was increasingly frail. Still there was no redemption. The Estate Duty Office reviewed the matter once more and said no. The surviving son made his own appeal direct to the War Office. It was nothing to do with tax. It was a matter of honour. 'I regret having to bringing these painful facts to your notice,' he wrote. 'After perusing them . . . I hope the Army Council will agree that my brother's death was directly attributable to the war.' Somebody high up was prepared to do so.

The letter was batted around Whitehall in-trays. 'Have you any note that this officer's work was not considered satisfactory in 1916? There is a suggestion he was censored and this led to him going out of his mind,' one official enquired. 'This officer was in the Royal Marine Artillery until shortly before his death. We have no notes that his work was satisfactory or otherwise' – so the Adjutant-General's department scrawled its reply on the minute sheet. Anything to do with Lt-Col. Brough and subsequent events on the Somme was wrapped in the deepest obscurity.

But the ministry would be merciful, as the old colonel had implored in August 1917. The letter was considered and the 'painful facts' it outlined reprised by higher authority. The permanent under-secretary at the War Office informed the Estate Duty Office on 24 October: 'I am commanded by the Army Council to inform you that fresh evidence has now been produced in this case. It is now the consideration of the Council that the strain of military duty undoubtedly caused the mental condition that prompted this officer's suicide.'

Box (a) on Form W.3428 had been checked. There was honour in that.

The Whitehall officials and the little court of enquiry held on the Franco-Belgian border seven years before had missed the obvious. If anyone had made the connection, no one admitted it. It was something that happened the day before the colonel died. On 28 July 1917 the experimental force that Brough had briefly commanded had become 'The Tank Corps' by Royal Warrant. Notice had gone to the 61st Division and the rest of the armies in France. It was a reason to celebrate. John Brough collected his revolver, ordered his driver, got out of the car, walked on alone up the Chemin d'Eringhem, climbed into the undergrowth and put a bullet through his brain.

Alan Brough did not believe that his brother had gone mad. He thought all along that it went back to St Riquier and the 'tanks' in summer 1916. It was something to do with being blamed for what had gone wrong when they went into action afterwards. He was wrong. Lieutenant-Colonel (temporary) John Brough blamed himself for what had gone wrong before.

2

A mining village in north-east France might be said to be the birth-place of armoured warfare. It looks an unlikely proposition. There were no 'tanks' or armoured cars involved in the fighting to capture the village of Loos in September 1915. Behind the lines 'motor lorries' had toiled to bring forward a new and cumbersome secret weapon in heavy steel canisters; three armoured railway locomotives had been employed and a few tracked caterpillar tractors imported from America had been used to haul guns. Otherwise it was the epitome of the Great War stereotype of wire, machine guns and an asinine plan of attack. The battle fought by infantry, engineers and artillery (the cavalry never left their start lines) achieved little tactical or strategic purpose. It cost 43,000 British casualties.

In spite of the use of the new weapon, poison gas; in spite of scientific methodology in the artillery bombardment; in spite of an apparent sufficiency of shells – the offensive was a bloody failure. It was the first test of the men of the New Armies, those hundreds of thousands of optimistic patriots who had answered Field Marshal Lord Kitchener's call to arms on 7 August 1914. But a realization in the minds of certain British soldiers, politicians and technologists at least came out of the dismal affair – that there must be a better way of solving the problem.

This was the problem: how to evict the German invader from his barricaded trenches and push him back to where he had come from? The spike-helmeted armies which had poured into Belgium and north-east France twelve months before had failed in their com-manders' intention of routing the French in a great battle of manoeuvre. The tiny British Expeditionary Force under its Com-mander-in-Chief, Field Marshal Sir John French, had arrived across the Channel just in time to be pushed aside.

Trench lines which had begun as scratched-out rifle pits had rapidly ossified into a huge linear fortification, eventually stretching from the North Sea (it was called the 'German Ocean' in English language atlases of the period – that would change) to the Alps. Europe's late nineteenth-century birth-rate had delivered enough young men to hold parallel battle lines four hundred miles long. It had all come as a bit of a shock.

Britain's war had begun thirteen months earlier with divisions in the Cabinet, politicians summoned from country house weekends – and Parliament going into emergency session as Bank Holiday crowds milled outside. On Tuesday 4 August 1914 the 'cabinet war' spilled into the streets. Lord Kitchener of Khartoum, the nation's martial icon, was appointed Secretary of State for War (political head of the army), a minister in Herbert Asquith's Liberal government. Two days later he sought parliamentary approval to raise an army of half a million men; his stern, finger-pointing countenance was conjured by a graphic artist into the cover of the magazine *London Opinion* that appeared the same day. Someone at the War Office thought it might make a recruiting poster.

Telegrams flew and postbags bulged as offers of service were made and reserves were summoned to their stations. Recruiting offices were besieged. Long-retired professional soldiers and outright amateurs clamoured to get in on the fight, all gripped, as the Cambridge undergraduate Basil Liddell Hart recalled his own urgent motive for enlisting, by 'the general belief that the war would be over by Christmas'.

Like those in the path of some natural catastrophe, the outbreak of general war in Europe caught the King-Emperor's subjects wherever they found themselves.

Victor Huffam, a twenty-seven-year-old engineer born in Norwich, had just landed at Tilbury docks on a P&O steamer having spent an adventurous seven years in the gold fields of Australia as an agent of the Crossley motor company. His parents met him at the quayside. He had joined the volunteer 18th Australian Light Horse – with 'a troop of 450 men and one 1-pdr Pom Pom' to defend the sub-continent.

He was a trained soldier, the empire was at war. Trooper Huffam went to Australia House on the Strand to seek guidance and was told he was either to go home or join the British Army. He soon found himself along with thousands of others in Hyde Park clutching a suitcase as a private in the 'University and Public School Battalion 18th Royal Fusiliers'.

After six months of 'trench digging and route marches round Epsom in company with the flower of England's manhood – the War Office decided to take five hundred of us as officers', he wrote many years later.

In the spring of 1915 the former Private Huffam found himself a second lieutenant in the Norfolk Regiment, commanding a company of 'tough old sweats . . . some twice my age' at Felixstowe on the bleak east coast. In spring 1916 he would march them to the station and get on the train taking them to France. He discreetly got off 'at Ipswich', bearing different orders. Second Lieutenant Huffam would not be going to war as an infantryman.

Twenty-three-year-old Basil Henriques, privileged son of a cultured west London Sephardic family, clamoured for a commission in the Queen's Royal Regiment, the oldest in the English army, even though he had 'hated the OTC' at school and at Oxford he had found it little more than a 'pleasant form of recreation'. At Harrow membership of the Officer Training Corps 'had been nothing more than part of the school routine . . . with its ridiculous field days when no one knew what one was doing or why . . .'. His elder brother had been commissioned in the Queen's in 1912. Lieutenant Ronald Henriques was killed on the Marne on 14 September. The grand old regiment, for whatever reason, would not have him. The spindly Basil did not look like much of a soldier. His greatest achievement thus far had been founding the Oxford and St George's-in-the-East Jewish Lad's Club in Wapping (a girl's club would follow).

Eventually he was directed to the Dover depot of the Royal West Kents where 'large numbers of newly gazetted officers were quartered in barrack dormitories'. He had few martial skills, could not ride a horse, could not drive a car, not that that mattered much. There was a boy in the throng who could. They exchanged notes about it. He had 'pale blue eyes and an almost girlish complexion', was eighteen years old and not long out of Winchester. His name was George Macpherson and he came from Wolverhampton. George and Basil became the best of friends. Two years later they would go to war together on the Somme, but not as infantry officers. On

15 September 1916 they would both face the enemy for the first time.

Christopher D'Arcy Baker-Carr was a professional soldier to his fingertips, a veteran of South Africa. He had left the army in 1907 as a twenty-nine-year-old captain in the Rifle Brigade. But in August 1914 even his spell as an instructor at the Hythe School of Musketry in Kent could not find a him a job back in uniform. He was a bit too old. A 'brother rifleman' at the War Office suggested he try the Royal Automobile Club which had some strange scheme to send its members to the front. Baker-Carr could certainly drive but just then did not own a motor car.

It was true. In their fitful pre-war flirtation with the internal combustion engine, the War Office had contracted with the RAC to employ twenty-five 'owner driver' volunteers as chauffeurs and messengers in the case of an emergency. Private Baker-Carr soon found himself spiriting all sorts of brass hats out of harm's way as the Germans advanced, driving a powerful 'Mércèdes donated by an elderly patriot'.

There were others like him. Hugh Richard Arthur Grosvenor, the Second Duke of Westminster, rushed off to France on the outbreak of war to offer the services of himself, his chauffeur, Powell, and his Rolls-Royce to whomsoever would have him. Toby Rawlinson (brother of General Sir Henry Rawlinson, Commander of the Fourth Army) and the American racing driver Frederic Coleman bowled along French roads with urgent dispatches. The army did not expect them actually to fight.

Baker-Carr's career would prosper. The BEF established its first machine-gun school at Wisques in November 1914 under the newly promoted major. He would become the apostle of the weapon that would define the nature of the first phase of the war. He would command a brigade of the weapon that would define its second.

Albert Gerald Stern was immensely grand, slightly plump with thick wavy hair, a thirty-six-year-old Old Etonian member of a wealthy Jewish banking dynasty (he had converted to Christianity) who had advanced the family fortune running Stern Brothers operations in Frankfurt and on Wall Street. He had brokered a loan to the Sultan of Morocco. That turning day of 4 August saw him at an emergency meeting of financiers at the Bank of England worried lest the money should run out to pay Britain's workers. His two brothers were both part-time soldiers – officers in the Yeomanry (territorial cavalry). Stern was all for volunteering but had a broken ankle. He was rich, he owned a splendid Rolls-Royce. He must do something.

Some eager patriots found themselves far from their native land. Jules Crawford Silber was a businessman in New York City, in early middle age with an incipient heart condition. He had gone to South Africa as a young man, and served the British Army (he was a natural linguist) as an interpreter during the Boer War. In 1900 he had travelled with the thousands of Boer prisoners shipped from Cape Town to camps in Ceylon and the Punjab in British India (others were confined on Bermuda and St Helena). The experience had given him certain views.

Clutching certificates of good service, in August 1914 he approached the consulate in a heady rush of patriotism and offered his services. He was instructed to cross the Canadian border and make his way to England as best he could, there to seek war work. He duly did, and was appointed a postal censor in the rapidly growing bureau run by the domestic intelligence service MO5(g). He would conduct his strange war from a terraced house in Liverpool.

In the summer of 1916 he would read a letter from a British soldier's wife to her sister in Ireland which hinted at some unusual weapon being made ready at a 'camp' in Suffolk. Mr J. C. Silber was born in Breslau in Silesia (now Wroclaw in Poland). He was a spy.

A forty-two-year-old bachelor and career soldier found himself in London on the outbreak of war – John Brough, a colonel in the Royal Marine Artillery. His father had been a gunner, his younger brother Alan was an engineer, but he had gone to the Royal Naval College, Greenwich, where he had made a special study of fortifications. Three years commanding a company of cadets at Sandhurst had made him a curious army-navy crossover.

He had briefly been a War Office bureaucrat, thence an officer of the West African Frontier Force in Nigeria and commander of the force defending the Royal Navy's coaling station at Freetown, Sierra Leone. It was as obscure a posting as imaginable. In August 1914 he was in London to be summoned to the Colonial Office for an urgent meeting with Lt-Gen. Sir C. M. Dobell, commander of the expeditionary force which it was intended would capture Duala, capital of the

German colony of Kamerun. Brough would be GSO2 on his modest staff.

On the 31st he departed Liverpool aboard the steamer SS *Appam* fitted out as headquarters and hospital ship heading for West Africa. Twenty months of chasing two hundred or so Germans round swamp and jungle awaited him. He returned to wage a different kind of battle.

Ernest Dunlop Swinton was four years older than Brough, whom he knew vaguely at the club, the United Services on Pall Mall which, in the rush to war, would be the great employment entrepôt for retired officers jostling to get into the fight. Swinton was a Royal Engineer and still on the active list – not quite yet a 'dug-out' (a retired officer recalled to active duty). Notice of his place in this new war arrived by telegram at his Blackheath villa – he had been promoted temporary lieutenant-colonel and appointed deputy director of railways for the British Expeditionary Force. He mustered, so he recalled, 'india rubbers and pencils' for the battles ahead.

Born in 1868 the son of a judge in Bangalore, Swinton had made a mildly distinguished career as a professional soldier since being commissioned at the age of twenty. He had served in South Africa and been official British historian of the Russo-Japanese War. In 1913 he had been appointed second secretary of the Committee of Imperial Defence. Swinton was that unusual thing in the Edwardian army, a bit of an intellectual. In 1907 he had published his first novel, *The Defence of Duffer's Drift*, a curious story set in 'Dreamsdorp', a flyblown village in the Transvaal. The hypothetical Lt Backsight Forethought has fifty men and a mission to hold a dried-up river crossing – which he first undertakes fresh from officer training – totally unaware of the realities of combat. He loses humiliatingly at first, but is given six chances to refight the little battle.

At the end Lt Forethought prevails, thus delivering lots of tactical lessons for the modern, thoughtful, twentieth-century soldier. Regarded as a classic of small-unit warfare, it remains recommended reading at the US Army Command and General Staff College.

Swinton's literary talents would quickly rescue him from his railway siding. Fleet Street's eager corps of military and naval correspondents were banned from the front. A cabinet committee cobbled together stories. It included the input of the First Lord of the Admiralty (political head of the navy), Winston S. Churchill. There was anguish in Fleet Street, but, like the rest of the nation in its Hun-hating spasm, newspaper proprietors fell into compliant defence-of-the-realm sleep. The morale of the Home Front (the phrase had yet to be coined) mattered only to deliver its unending stream of volunteers.

But when a brave reporter described the retreat from Mons in terms of a rout, Kitchener decided something must be done.* He had vaguely known Swinton in South Africa. The colonel was sent to France as 'Official Observer at the General Headquarters of the British Expeditionary Force'. His yarns would be directly routed to the Secretary of War – released to newspapers and published under the anonymous byline 'Eyewitness'. Let the news be good.

Although of necessity anodyne, the lack of passion in Swinton's dispatches made them exemplars of a much later school of war reporting. They were not even first-hand accounts – Swinton confessed in his memoirs to preparing a bulletin each night from the reports of liaison officers coming back from the front to GHQ, then based after several upheavals in the little town of St Omer twenty miles inland from the coast. Stripped of jingoism they were remarkably propaganda free. The Germans, in spite of certain 'dastardly ruses', said Eyewitness, were 'a formidable enemy, well trained, long prepared, and brave . . . Their soldiers are carrying on the contest with skill and valour.'

Any armchair warrior with an inkling of military knowledge reading Swinton's anonymous reports would be rapidly disabused of the idea that it would all be over by Christmas. This war would be nasty, brutish and long. Kitchener had told his shocked Cabinet colleagues at the outset: 'We must be prepared to put armies of millions in the field and maintain them for several years.' What Eyewitness had to say (and Kitchener vetted the drafts) supported his entirely accurate prognosis.

At first the colonel's dispatches centred on how the invader was being checked, not entirely by selfless gallantry or supernatural inter-

---

* *The Times'* notorious 'Amiens dispatch' of 30 August in fact caused a leap in recruitment. Barred from the British and French fronts, American pressmen got to Belgium with the German Army, following the invader's wake and reporting freely on the trail of devastation.

vention, as other excitable accounts would have readers believe, but by the killing power of modern weaponry. A dispatch dated 23 October ostensibly from the Lys river declared: 'The [Germans] made five desperate assaults on our trenches, advancing in mass and singing "Die Wacht am Rhein" as they came on. Each assault was easily beaten back, our troops waiting until the enemy came to very close range before they opened fire with rifles and Maxims, causing terrible havoc in the solid masses . . . It was a holocaust.'

It worked both ways. Stopping the invader was only the beginning – if he could be stopped. He would have to be beaten back, pushed out of the territory that had been conquered. When the Germans had first begun to dig in on the line of the river Aisne in mid-September 1914, Field Marshal Sir John French had informed the King: 'I think [the Aisne fighting] to be very typical of what the battles in the future are most likely to resemble. Siege operations will enter largely into the tactical problem – the spade will be as great a necessity as the rifle.'

Everybody began to dig. French and British trenches might stop the invader claiming any more territory. German trenches, with their ever thickening belts of barbed wire and machine gun firing posts, might prevent the Allies claiming back what the invader had already won. Swinton's dispatches of autumn 1914 foreshadowed the titanic defences that were to come.

He reported from GHQ at the end of September what he had heard of events unfolding on the river Aisne: 'The [German] infantry are holding strong lines of trenches among and along the edge of the numerous woods which crown the slopes. These trenches are elaborately constructed and cleverly concealed. In many places there are wire entanglements and lengths of rabbit fencing . . .

'The fighting now consists mostly of shelling by the artillery of both sides . . .'

The colonel noted with wonderment the sound of music coming from gramophones in the German trenches. Their inhabitants were settling in with bourgeois home comforts. Two weeks later he reported on how the defences were thickening:

> The situation of the works in the German front line as a whole has been a matter of deliberate selection, for they have had the advantage of previous reconnaissance, being first in the field.

Behind the front they now have several lines prepared for
a step-by-step defence . . .

Obstacles of every kind abound, and at night each side can
hear the enemy driving pickets for entanglements . . . or working forward by sapping . . .

The German machine guns are mounted on low sledges, and
are inconspicuous and evidently easily moved . . .

In spite of its inconspicuousness, the weapon that would prove
the scourge of British and French infantry was making its bloody
debut. It could be easily moved; that too was significant. It would
hog the limelight front of stage until some means might be found
to boot if off. Just how to do it would become Colonel Swinton's
obsession.

3

It was famously argued by historians writing fifty years after the events that the Europe-wide cataclysm of August 1914 was mechanistically triggered by the railway timetables, which, especially for the Germans, 'eliminated the breathing space between mobilisation and war'. But it did not end there. In a forceful essay published in the *Tank Corps Journal* in April 1922, Lt-Col. J. F. C. Fuller, wartime tank staff officer and intellectual of mechanized warfare, would also blame the railways. They had caused not just the strategic dysfunctions of the rush to war but the years of bloody immobility that followed. He wrote:

> Before its outbreak . . . the effect of the strategic utility of railways on tactics was not generally considered. What do we see? We see the railways like great cataracts pouring millions of men . . . We then see a strange sight – millions of men facing each other – gathered in armies like bloated pumpkins hanging on their slender stems. Then from time to time, like obese monsters, we see these armies struggling forward – every yard they advance from their rail heads making their supply more difficult . . .
>
> While in civil life the railway had increased the power of movement many hundreds of times, on the battlefield it had reduced it to zero.

It was machine guns and wire that would form the barrier that these gigantic rail-succoured armies could not break. It would take another device, itself brought up close to the front on railway trucks, to do so. The American-born inventor Hiram Maxim had devised the world's first practical 'machine gun' in his workshop in Hatton Garden, London. It cleverly used the recoil force from each bullet fired to eject the spent cartridge and deliver the next one to the breech. In 1885 he demonstrated his prototype weapon to the British Army – which, after four years of trial, formally adopted it. The

Germans, Austrians and Russians quickly did the same. The French went on their own development path. Sir Hiram (he became a British citizen and was knighted in 1901) would spend his patent-gleaned fortune on a huge steam-powered flying machine.

According to Basil Liddell Hart, 'Hiram Maxim's name is more deeply engraved on the real history of the World War than any other man.' He died in the year of the Somme and was buried in Norwood cemetery, south London, under an enormous palm tree.

Putting the firepower of up to a hundred riflemen into a single firing post seemed to portend a revolution in war. Would it make Britain's small, professional army less or more effective? In colonial conflicts ('savage warfare' in the phrase of the time) bronze-barrelled Vickers-Maxim guns had set Matabeles, Pathans and Mahdists to flight. Against skirmishing Boer commandos, however, they had proved less effective.

German colonial troops employed belt-fed Maxim guns in the HeHe wars of 1891–8 in East Africa and in the 1904–5 suppression of the Herero revolt in South-West Africa. The US Navy used Colt machine guns in China and in the Philippines. The French used St Etienne and Hotchkiss strip-fed weapons in Morocco. The lighter, more wieldy Hotchkiss used gas bled from the breech rather than recoil on its operating cycle. When two technically equivalent armies employed them in the Russo-Japanese war of 1904–5 (Russian-made Maxims confronted French-built Hotchkiss machine guns in Japanese hands) the result was an impasse – trenches, wire and mountains of casualties.

The Vickers-Maxim employed by the British Army since the 1890s with its bronze water jacket was heavy but reliable. The Vickers Mk 1 of 1912 derived from it reduced the weight using pressed ribbed steel. The British Expeditionary Force went to war with two machine guns per infantry battalion or cavalry regiment, making just eight guns per brigade and fewer than four hundred in the entire army. They were still regarded with a certain suspicion. Some senior officers thought their use 'unsporting'. Christopher Baker-Carr wrote of the sentiment prevailing in 1914: 'What shall I do with the machine-guns today, sir?' would be the question frequently asked by the officer in charge of a field day. 'Take the damn things to a flank and hide them!' was the usual reply.

The armies of Imperial Germany also learned from colonial experience. Five independent machine-gun detachments were formed in the Prussian army in October 1901. The Bavarian and Saxon armies followed. Technical developments continued at the government arsenal at Spandau outside Berlin, resulting in the Maschinengewehr Model 1908, or MG '08.

By August 1914 more than twelve thousand MG '08s were in service. Not only had the Germans developed specialized tactics but their machine-gun crews had been carefully selected and trained as an internal elite. Each three-battalion infantry regiment had three machine-gun companies of six guns each.

The MG '08's *Schlitten* (sledge) mount was heavy and provided a very accurate shooting platform but was quick to fold and carry, capable by clever design of being dragged like a stretcher to forward positions. The weapon itself, cooled by seven pints of water with steam condensing in an external can, could fire at 500 rounds per minute, the ammunition fed through in woven cotton belts of 250 rounds each. Each gun, on paper at least, was allotted 12,000 rounds.

German tactics soon adapted to the needs of positional warfare. Instead of six guns firing directly to their front, interlocking fire zones were devised to create an enmeshing hail of bullets. The middle two guns fired forward, the guns on the left and right flanks provided enfilading fire. Further the 'step-by-step' defence described by Swinton now had an even stronger second line, itself composed of intricately wrought earthworks which would require a distinct and separate assault to penetrate.

By early December 1914, Eyewitness was informing newspaper readers: 'The enemy has practically ceased his efforts to break through the line by assaults . . . Subterranean life is the general rule in the neighbourhood of the firing line. Even those men not actually engaged in fighting live in underground quarters. Some of these quarters, called "funk holes" are quite elaborate and comfortable and contain many conveniences not found in the trenches on the firing line.'

The military leaders of Imperial Germany had embarked on a strategic defensive in the west from which they would only deviate three times in the course of the war – in a semi-experimental action at Ypres in April 1915 (where poison gas was used for the first time), at Verdun in 1916 and, climactically, in spring 1918.

Hold what had been won and seek decisions in Russia and the Balkans. Unable to push them out, the western allies must eventually make peace. When they did, Belgium and a prime slice of industrial north-eastern France would be incorporated into the Reich. Germany would be the master of Europe.

4

French and British commanders had been promising to push the invader back to his frontiers since the first weeks of war. But how and with what? The classic elements of warfare – fire, movement and morale – had been shorn of their second limb. There was no physical space for 'manoeuvre'. Pre-war British military manuals were full of prescriptions for turning flanks and encounter battles, but siege warfare was a postscript. That is not to say some very deep thought had not been applied to making the British Army fit to survive on the modern battlefield.

In the decade after the South African war, when almost all aspects of the British military system had been found wanting in a colonial campaign against 50,000 farmers, the Edwardian army had been transformed. It retained its fault lines of class and hunting-field sentiment but it had perforce to strive to be as technocratic as any of its continental equivalents (and indeed the Royal Navy) in the matter of weapons and mobility. First it had to reinvent itself from the top.

In 1904 the Committee of Imperial Defence was formed, a body of soldiers and civil servants which advised the Cabinet on strategic affairs with a small secretariat under the direct control of the Prime Minister. The War Office itself, the ministry of state with its origins in the late eighteenth century responsible for the British Army, was overhauled the same year on the radical lines proposed by the post-Boer War investigations of the committee chaired by Lord Esher.

The three principal recommendations were the establishment of an Army Council on the model of the Board of the Admiralty, the forming of a General Staff, and a division of departmental responsibilities inside the ministry (which comprised both civil servants and soldiers) on 'defined and logical principles'. A splendid domed building in Edwardian baroque style was raised on Whitehall to house the modern major-generals who dispensed with their braided frock coats to don golf attire-like uniforms featuring collar and khaki tie.

The navy (whose officers had long worn technocratic ties) had already built their modern citadel for the Dreadnought era, the 1898 Admiralty Extension, then trumped the shiny new War Office with its theatrical Admiralty Arch raised in 1910, metaphorically screening the way to Buckingham Palace.

In the spring of 1915 this imperious corner of London would become a cockpit of intrigue, muffled figures slipping as anonymously as they could up back stairs to discuss the most tremendous secret. Very little of their discussions would be committed to paper. No one must know they were meeting at all. The enemy was just across Whitehall – in the War Office.

The General Staff ('Imperial' from 1907), was a complete innovation in the national military tradition. New posts were established – Director of Military Operations, Director of Transport, Director of Training, Director of Artillery, Director of Fortifications and Works and 'Director of Staff Duties', a kind of head prefect responsible for executive appointments and ensuring doctrinal orthodoxy. The Directorate's second chief appointed in 1908 was an ambitious cavalryman, Maj.-Gen. Sir Douglas Haig, latterly Director of Training. For the first time in its history the army was provided with official manuals laying down staff responsibilities and approved procedures. In his two successive posts, Haig oversaw their compilation.

In 1909, after a ripple of German spy scares (agents were supposedly communicating via small ads in the *Daily Mail*), the Committee of Imperial Defence recommended the formation of a 'Special Intelligence Bureau' as the fifth branch of the War Office's Military Operations Directorate (MO5) to act as a counter.

The Edwardian army had also to adapt to the revolution in technology that flowed from nineteenth-century scientific discoveries. Steam power had long been familiar. The Royal Engineers had been operating traction engines ('steam sappers') for decades. In the Boer War a futuristic unit of 'Electrical Engineers' had operated everything from searchlights to armoured steam-hauled road trains. Artillerymen experimented with steam tractors to haul guns.

But it was the internal combustion engine – with its much more practical power-to-weight ratio and liquid fuel that might be poured in cans rather than shovelled in great loads of coal – that promised the earth. Set behind a propeller in a fragile machine of wood, bracing wire and doped linen, it even promised the sky. Louis Blériot's Channel-crossing exploit of 1909 invited the famous line in a *Daily Mail* editorial: 'Britain is no longer an island.' A fleet of dirigible airships was rising across the North Sea, Germany's answer to the technological bravado displayed by the Royal Navy's HMS *Dreadnought* launched in 1906.

A Mechanical Transport Committee had been established within the War Office since the turn of the century. There were two clear lines to pursue: 'motor lorries' to supplant horse-drawn wagons in the army's supply train, and tractors to pull heavy guns.* A new sort of soldier would be required to operate them. In 1903 the committee reported: 'It is essential that the men who drive the machines should have at all events a knowledge of the machinery. Shops should be built at Aldershot . . . used not only for repairs but as a school for instruction for Army Service Corps drivers . . .'

So should officers be gently persuaded to come off their horses. The same year motor cars were 'distributed to General Officers Commanding at various stations and reports called for'. The marques were truly splendid – Napiers, Lanchesters and Wolseleys. It was not expected that officers should conduct the motors themselves. That was for their chauffeurs.

British civil society was rapidly mechanizing. Petrol-powered lorries and delivery vans bore the trade and omnibuses the clerical class of the nation. In the capital, for example, under the managerial regime of Capt. Wilfrid Dumble, an Ontario-born ex-professional soldier who had served with the Electrical Engineers in South Africa, the aggressively monopolistic London General Omnibus Company was transformed. Over three years from 1908 it put into service almost two thousand B-Types to supplant the horse buses which had long mobilized the metropolis and filled its streets with dung.† The resentful horsemen called Dumble 'the tin soldier'.

---

* The BEF would go to war with 25,000 horses and a stated need for 120,000 more – and just over five hundred mostly civilian-impressed motor vehicles. By 1918 the figures were almost 400,000 horses and 22,000 motor vehicles.

† Horse buses would trundle on a little longer – 'still profitable because of contracting out of horses to the Regular and Territorial Army during the manoeuvre season'. Frank Searle, the LGOC's engineering director, recalled the pre-war days when demonstrating the new Daimler X-Type bus, the old guard of management ignored it completely,

By 1913 the company employed more than 4000 motor drivers, most of whom it had trained itself (only one in eight horse-bus drivers volunteered to retrain). There were those modernists in the army who saw the rapid mechanization of London's streets as a model to be emulated. Other senior soldiers bemoaned the sudden lack of horses – or the 'social difficulty', as a future member of the Tank Corps would dub the harmless enough creatures. Farriers, harness makers, blacksmiths and wheelwrights were going the way of gas mantle makers. Kensington mews were full of garagists. What would the army do if, heaven forbid, there should be a war?

The working class found economic advancement in the progression of the motor trade. An increasing number of gentlemen found possession of a motor car a social necessity. That is not to say Edwardian motorists could not find class nuances of their own to fight over.

In the winter of 1908–9 a little war was raging in Britain – between the patrician Royal Automobile Club (est. 1897) and the somewhat arriviste Automobile Association.

RAC members, with their palatial headquarters in Pall Mall, tended to employ chauffeurs. Members of the AA (founded 1905) cheerfully got behind the wheels of their motor cars themselves – to drive, Mr Toad-like, as fast and as furiously as possible. After multiple police court cases in which the AA found fancy legal defences, the Home Office wanted it shut down.

In January 1909 the AA's committee had a patriotic wheeze to make itself thoroughly respectable – a proposal to the War Office that their members should make available 'four or five hundred powerful motor cars for one day' to engage in an experimental military manoeuvre of the General Staff's devising. The RAC President, His Serene Highness Prince Francis of Teck, got wind of it and wrote a splenetic letter to the War Office protesting at the Government's apparent consideration of 'cooperating with an unofficial association made primarily to stultify the work of the police'.

---

fussing instead over the sudden arrival at the depot of a large number of 'four-footed friends' who had come back from army manoeuvres bruised and bandaged. In 1917 Searle would become the Engineering Officer of the Tank Corps. The last fare-earning London horse bus ran (from Peckham Rye to Honor Oak) the day after the British declaration of war.

The AA's proposal was passed to the Director of Staff Duties, Maj.-Gen. Sir Douglas Haig, who approved of the notion. HSH's protests were ignored. On the morning of 17 March 1909 almost 300 shiny motor cars with their ebullient dust-coated drivers assembled at Crystal Palace in south London to embark over one thousand men of the 1st Battalion the Scots Guards. Thirty civilian lorries lumbered behind carrying ammunition and rations.

The exercise's war-game scenario fitted the sneak invasion mania of the time – a 'hostile force [was] threatening a landing between Dungeness and Eastbourne' on the south coast. Three defending infantry battalions had already been rushed by rail from the capital to Hastings, but 'information is received that the Sevenoaks Tunnel has been blown up by agents of the enemy'. AA members came to the rescue.

There were breakdowns and plentiful confusions on the fifty-four-mile journey from London to the coast (with a half-hour break for lunch at Bromley) but the great motorized *chevauchée* was judged a success. It was noted in the War Office report that 'the machine gun section should always be in front with their guns' – and that chinstraps on service forage caps should be lengthened 'in order to prevent caps being blown off when travelling at high speed'.

The volunteer automobilists had acted 'splendidly'. It was noted by Maj.-Gen. Haig, however, that they might not act so gallantly under wartime conditions.

Sir Douglas's suspicion of civilians was very typical. On the outbreak of war Kitchener would assess the military usefulness of the Territorials, part-time volunteers, as 'zero'. The regular army was a closed tribe which, for all its administrative reforms, remained Wellingtonian in its social order. An RAMC captain would write: 'There are plenty of those who remember the battalion officer of 1914, a feudal creature singularly remote from the age of machines who spoke of sappers indulgently as mad, methodist or married . . .'

Officers needed a private income to supplement their wages, and had to observe an internal mummery of regimental tradition and to obey an arcane code of deportment when exposed to public gaze. They were expected to travel first class by rail, for example, where on station platforms they should 'not be seen laden with parcels'. The rank and file joined because they were unemployed or unemployable.

Those who aspired to a technical skill were described as 'tradesmen'.

The army's internal anthropology and regimental castes (some were distinctly more fashionable than others) lagged decades behind evolving civil society – of suburban tennis parties, socialistic agitation and suffragists, of readers of *The Aeroplane, The Autocar, Commercial Motor* and *The Motor Cycle*. That was the world from which the volunteer New Armies of 1915–16 would largely come. That was where the men of the Royal Flying Corps (formed from the Air Battalion of the Royal Engineers in 1912) were already coming from. It was a world the Royal Navy had long understood.

It was where, in the spring of 1916, the men of the Heavy Section Machine Gun Corps (and some of its officers) would be thankfully found.

5

Before the crisis of 1914 the doctrine makers of Europe's armies had all stressed the primacy in battle of infantry and cavalry. The place of the internal combustion engine on the battlefield – in providing second-line transport and powering airborne observation platforms – was of increasing interest. 'Armoured cars' had been built experimentally in Italy, Austria and Germany. Railways had received enormous attention as a means of mobilizing armies towards a decisive battle which, it was assumed, would be fought on traditional lines. Fixed frontier fortifications had been national obsessions since 1870 but it was assumed (more or less correctly) that advances in artillery had made them obsolete. The Romanians had built a strange system in the 1900s on the designs of a Prussian army engineer, the 'Sereth line' in Moldavia which featured moving armoured cupolas on railway tracks. They were described in the contemporary literature as 'mobile forts'. A self-propelled land fighting machine was at the mad inventor stage.

Commanders and most military planners considered that if an advance was stopped in one place success in the field elsewhere or a grand outflanking move would restore strategic mobility and let morale and leadership prevail. Only a few eccentrics had studied the more brutal business of how to attack an entrenched position.

The British Army's *Field Service Regulations* published in 1909, amended in 1912, saw land battles as either mobile operations or sieges of isolated fortresses. Horse-drawn field artillery was regarded as a subset of mobile war. Its role was to support the infantry assault. Guns firing shrapnel were simply a different kind of infantry firepower, used to deliver hundreds of small lead bullets at longer range than rifles. Under cover of such a neutralizing bombardment, the infantry would gradually advance to charging distance – the 'artillery fire an intense burst' – then rush forward with bayonets fixed. The enemy must surely surrender. That was the plan anyway.

The war-making manual did, however, contain prescriptions for attacking defenders in various types of cover. Howitzers lobbing shells high into the air could drop them into trenches. So-called 'percussion shrapnel' should be used against buildings, since the slight delay of the impact fuse meant the shells would burst inside. The manual's section on mobile warfare ignored the problem of obstacles. 'Barbed wire' was not mentioned.

Big guns were there to pound into submission any garrison still holding out after the grand advance. How to defeat a garrison entrenched in a solid line was a mystery. The answer must lie in artillery. In late September 1914 representatives from the War Office and GHQ in France established a 'Siege Committee'. It proposed the immediate acquisition of 140 heavy guns at a cost of three million pounds. Kitchener pushed it through against the wish of the Master General of the Ordnance, the member of the Army Council responsible for the procurement of munitions. Still the move could not be presented as a response to the developing trench impasse. The guns were for 'use against fortresses on the Rhine'.

The British Expeditionary Force's first attempt at a planned set-piece attack was on 14 December 1914 up the Messines Ridge fortified with a primitive trench line. The gunners did what they could but there was no coherent plan, no realization that wire and revetted earth needed more to subdue them than banging away with shrapnel.

Rope mattresses were provided which the infantry were, bizarrely, supposed to lay on the barbed wire and clamber their way across as best they could. It was a shambles. According to the *Official History*: 'With the German trenches and wire practically intact and the ground hopelessly deep in mud, the most determined troops could not advance.'

France was fighting to liberate its national territory. Britain, with its mighty navy, dominions, colonial empire and history of expeditionary warfare, had found its tiny army first expelled from Belgium then enmired in trenches. If there was as yet no way through, there might be a long way round.

As Kitchener put it to Sir John French in January 1915: 'I suppose we must recognise that the French Army cannot make a sufficient breakthrough of the German lines to bring about the retreat of the German forces from northern Belgium. If that is so, then the German lines in France may be looked on as a fortress that cannot be carried by assault and also cannot be completely invested . . .'

Since a peace dictated on the invader's terms was unthinkable, the alternative to attacking in France was to find somewhere else. But where? The First Sea Lord, Admiral Sir John Arbuthnot Fisher (recalled from retirement in October 1914 to replace the 'German liking' Prince Louis of Battenberg), developed a strange plan to force the approaches to the Baltic Sea and make dispositions to land an Anglo-Russian army on the enemy's northern shore that they might march on Berlin. Could such a move against the heartland of the enemy be made via neutral Holland or Denmark? Proposals for some sort of British expedition against Austria-Hungary, the weaker partner of the Central Powers, mounted from the Adriatic, were examined and rejected as being too dangerous.

As the Balkan spark of August 1914 had gone round the world, there was suddenly a proliferating collection of other 'fronts' in which the military strength of the British empire might be more efficiently employed. Colonial skirmishes, although they demanded attention, were meaningless to the real business of the war. Expeditionary forces were assembled to head off for German East and South-West Africa, Togoland and the Cameroons.

The Russian invasion of East Prussia in the first weeks of the conflict had stumbled to disaster – outfought and outmanoeuvred by the generalship of two obscure commanders who were to become the martial icons of Germany, Field Marshal Paul von Hindenburg and General Erich von Ludendorff. A Turkish invasion of Russia (Turkey had joined Germany's side in October 1914) had seen an army of 80,000 advance into the Caucasus in a doomed adventure from which only 12,000 returned from the snowbound mountain passes. But the new enemy straddling Europe and Asia might similarly advance on the Suez Canal, the oil fields of Persia, India even. It must be contained. The southern front was open, volatile, perilous – but charged with possibilities. What was more the Royal Navy could take part. Unlike Berlin or Vienna, the third enemy's capital, Constantinople, was by the sea.

An ambitious thirty-nine-year-old politician, Winston Spencer

Churchill, Liberal MP for Dundee and First Lord of the Admiralty since October 1911, restlessly turned the possibility over in his mind. A year before that he had been Home Secretary, overseeing a curious urban warfare operation in the East End of London, the so-called 'siege of Sidney Street' in which riflemen of the Scots Guards, Maxim machine guns and 18-pounder field guns had been employed to address the failure of the Metropolitan Police in evicting two anarchists armed with 9-mm automatic pistols from a barricaded boarding house in Stepney. This episode would have a curious resonance later. Personally directing the operations in a top hat, Churchill had been lambasted in the Tory press for the former Sudan and South Africa cavalry officer's pretensions still to be seen as a man of action.

The responsibilities of mobilizing the Royal Navy and directing its first clashes with its German opponent might have seemed grave enough, but Churchill's restless energy was at the same time directed to where the drama was really in play – Belgium and north-east France. As First Lord he was responsible for a miniature army and air force – the Royal Naval Division (consisting of Royal Marines plus three naval brigades hastily raised from volunteer reservists and middle-aged surplus stokers) – and the pilots, mechanics and fragile flying machines of the Royal Naval Air Service.

The ethos of the navy was technical, men servicing the floating machines in which they lived, moved and fought. That naval spirit of free-ranging, machine-based warfare had been briefly brought to bear on land. In late summer 1914 the northern flank on the Belgian coastline was still open. From the British point of view, its closure (or its exploitation) would be largely a naval responsibility.

Asked by Kitchener that naval airmen should act in the defence of Britain against Zeppelins, the pugnacious Churchill, ever eager to press forward, dispatched a squadron of the Royal Naval Air Service, based at Eastchurch on the Isle of Sheppey, to the French port of Dunkirk. Its role was to operate against enemy airships, both defensively and by attacking their bases across the frontier. Officers' own private touring cars arrived soon afterwards by sea, for this was how things were done, with a collection of impressed motor lorries and several London buses – with more to come.

The naval airmen in Dunkirk, commanded by the buccaneering

Commander Charles Samson, were as toffish as the officers of any cavalry regiment. Sub-Lieutenant the Earl of Annesley turned up with his chauffeured Austro-Daimler – along with four lords, three MPs and Hugh Richard Arthur Grosvenor, the Second Duke of Westminster.

The gentlemen automobilists of Mr Churchill's 'Dunkirk Circus' (a disparaging press description fanned by the jealous War Office) set to arming their vehicles with whatever weapons they could find. Felix Samson, the commander's brother, fitted his Mercedes with a machine gun. On 4 September there was a blazing fight with the advancing enemy on the road to Cassel until the Maxim's firing pin broke. Some form of protection was needed.

Boilerplate 'armour' was quickly fabricated by a Dunkirk ship-builder. It was not much of an answer. A request for purpose-made vehicles was sent to London – to the Director of the Admiralty Air Department. Commodore Murray Sueter was a brave new warrior of the machine age who had gone with enthusiasm from working on submarines and torpedoes to flying machines and motor vehicles. He had advised Capt. Robert Falcon Scott RN on employing aircraft and motors on his ill-fated Antarctic expedition of 1910–11; aeroplanes had been ruled out but a tracked sleigh powered by a Wolseley motor car engine was employed (and found disastrously wanting).

Sixty machine gun-armed 'fighting cars' were quickly commissioned on three makes of chassis – Rolls-Royce, Clement-Talbot and Wolseley, with armour protection for the engine and some for the driver – but otherwise they were essentially open boxes, useful enough bouncing along *pavé* roads but incapable of crossing a ditch or clambering over an obstacle. The Germans were finding an answer to the British cars: lift the cobbles, dig a ditch or topple a tree across the road. Horsemen could go round such obstacles. Sailors on pneumatic tyres could not.

The invader bypassed the great inland port of Antwerp in the lunge across Belgium; now, in September, the Germans turned north-westwards to envelop the city with a siege train of fortress-cracking howitzers. Its fall could portend disaster along the whole Channel coast – the capture of the BEF and the potential invasion of southern England. By the end of the month the investment of the city's outer forts had begun.

On the night of the 19th the Royal Marine Brigade, clad in blue serge tunics and peakless Brodrick caps, was landed at Dunkirk from where Samson's extemporized armoured force was still operating. The commander, Brig.-Gen. G. Aston, 'had instructions to give the impression that they were the advanced guard of a large British force'. In London plans were being made to progress the illusion. According to Churchill: 'I formed a small administration to handle the business in which Colonel Ollivant was the moving spirit.*

The colonel's wheeze was remarkable – make the bluejackets move around a bit. The First Lord, a stranger to omnibus travel, leapt at the idea. On the 21st Churchill signalled Aston: 'Am endeavouring to provide you with 100 motor omnibuses to ensure mobility.' According to Capt. Geoffrey Howard MP, in charge of the Royal Naval Division's transport, 'attempts to use local buses failed through lack of discipline'. They would come from somewhere closer to home.

Captain Wilfrid Dumble, Boer War veteran and mechanizer of the metropolis, had a splendid garageful of new Daimler-engined double-deckers belonging to the Metropolitan Electric Tramways Omnibus Company (an LGOC rival turned commercial ally). Dumble was commissioned as a temporary lieutenant-colonel of marines. Churchill demanded immediate action. The Admiralty cabled the commander at Dunkirk: 'Steps are being taken to provide motor vehicles capable of carrying 2000 marines with the necessary supplies and ammunitions, each vehicle to be a self contained unit carrying some 25 men. It is to be hoped that this force will be organized in a week's time and that it will be possible for it, aided by armed motor cars and aeroplanes to carry out minor raiding operations of considerable importance on the German flank and communications.'

At 8.00 a.m on 25 September Lt-Col. Dumble's buses, painted shiny royal blue and cream and still bearing their destination boards and raucous advertisements for Dewar's whisky and Iron Jelloids – were mustered on the Thames Embankment. That night they were embarked at Dover for Dunkirk aboard the steamers *Elswick Grange*

---

* Lieutenant-Colonel Alfred Henry Ollivant, an artilleryman seconded to the Admiralty in 1913. Churchill is full of his praises in his war memoirs. In August 1914 he became GSO1 of the Royal Naval Division on its hasty foundation. He would end the war as GSO1 of the Supreme War Council with an important role on the inter-allied tank committee.

and *Twickenham*. Their youthful drivers (the horse-bus generation had been pensioned off) had been enlisted on the way from the capital as marines at Chatham barracks. Some still wore their dust coats and carriage office badges. Some had borrowed sailor's hats perched on their heads. The mood was cheerful. It all seemed rather comic – in spite of the Churchillian plan for 'raiding operations'.

The First Lord himself departed London early on the morning of 3 October by special train to arrive in Antwerp that afternoon. He took a late luncheon at the Hôtel Ste Antoine before telegraphing the Prime Minister from a suburban town hall with a bombastic proposal that he should command the port's defence himself.

It was turned down: he was a cabinet minister and his primary business was the fleet. He was ordered home. Churchill grumpily departed the besieged city on the 5th by road with an armoured car escort. The day before, as the Germans came up to the city's eastern ramparts with their all-conquering siege guns, the marines and three just-landed naval brigades had been dispatched forward from Dunkirk to the city aboard an improvised armoured train.

Antwerp was on the brink of encirclement, its rail links westwards about to be cut. The brigades of marines and hastily armed sailors arrived in the city just in time to be ordered to withdraw. On 7 October Dumble's buses mustered at Dunkirk were sent to the rescue, travelling the ninety miles via Bruges with eleven of Samson's Wolseley armoured cars leading the way. At least two vehicles had been fitted at Dunkirk shipyard with armour plate. Several were outfitted as ambulances with medical equipment and 'nurses standing in the space normally occupied by the conductor'.

The bus column, commanded by a Royal Marine, the aptly named Maj. Charles Risk, with its armoured escort got to Antwerp on the morning of the 8th. An RAMC captain remembered his improvised ambulance still bearing its destination board for Hendon. They entered the city looking 'shipshape and warlike', according to Samson – 'spoiled by schoolchildren climbing onto the rear platforms'.

The bus stunt was a miniature replay of the famous evening of 5 September 1914, when 600 Paris taxis were suddenly emptied of their fares on the orders of Gen. Joseph Gallieni to transport a reinforcing French army corps sixty kilometres to the Marne. Except this cockney version was a retreat. Churchill's pugnacious ideas of busborne raiding came to nothing, but they would have a resonance in the story of the development of an armoured fighting vehicle that was yet to come.

Forty-five of Dumble's buses survived the Antwerp rescue. The colonel mustered them as best he could at Ostend where Samson's armoured cars were now temporarily corralled. A much more purposeful force of fighting vehicles was meanwhile being raised in London at considerable expense. But their mobility problems when faced with wire barricades and cratered roads was obvious. On Churchill's own account: 'On 29 September I urged Ollivant and Sueter to investigate the practicality of a trench-spanning car.'

Wilfrid Dumble was also acutely aware of the problem. He resolved to contact an old friend, Col. Rookes Evelyn Bell Crompton, a septuagenarian technological polymath who, in the twilight of a long career, had turned to the commercial opportunities presented by motor transport. Dumble had served under him in South Africa as Adjutant of the Electrical Engineers. Perhaps the esteemed inventor might have a solution.

6

Antwerp had fallen. The race to the sea was over, the trench line continuous from the Flanders coast to the Alps. The service of taxis and buses in moving bodies of troops in dramatic reinforcements or rescues was no longer required. The Royal Navy's miniature mechanized army remained mustered at Ostend and Dunkirk.

Kitchener would not have it. The Secretary for War insisted that they be turned over to the army. Operational control of Samson's depleted armoured car force was passed to the British Expeditionary Force GHQ on 11 November. But the weeks of flamboyant action by Samson's airmen and the Antwerp drama had shown what armed motor vehicles could do – and might yet do on the battlefield. The Admiralty was not going to give up. Its assigned role as defenders of the metropolis against Zeppelin attack provided a kind of excuse. In November 1914 the 'Royal Navy Armoured Car Division' was formally established with a fashionable West End recruiting office under Commander Frederick Boothby RN – and a depot at Wormwood Scrubs where the *Daily Mail* airship shed had been patriotically donated for warlike duties by the press baron, Lord Northcliffe.

This dusty strip of west London, which quickly grew to embrace the Clement-Talbot motor works in an elegant Edwardian red-brick building in nearby Barlby Road, became the first land mechanized armoured warfare proving ground in history. Commodore Sueter oversaw recruitment. For his ratings he went for the motor trade and the big cities, London, Liverpool, Glasgow – and Derby (from the workforce of Rolls-Royce), with chauffeurs, garage mechanics and 'French speakers' especially preferred, even if any warlike opportunity for their employment in France had evaporated. In the winter of 1914–15, 4000 candidates applied to join the division. Four hundred were accepted.

The army sought drivers for the Army Service Corps, fetchers and carriers who now slogged away behind the front line in impressed civilian motor lorries. The commodore had an advantage. The navy gave qualified men the minimum rank of petty officer mechanic and ten shillings per day for service in France. Army 'overseas lorry drivers' got only six.

For his officers Sueter went for rich, young owner-drivers. Flight Commander Thomas Gerard Hetherington, for example, the armoured car division's Transport Officer, who had unconventionally gone from Harrow School to an apprenticeship with an engineering firm, thence into a cavalry regiment. In 1911 he had taken up flying, been a pioneer of the Royal Engineers' air battalion and in 1912 obtained an Airship Pilot's Certificate.

And there was Albert Stern, his broken ankle healed, his banker's duties discharged. In his words, he 'wrote to the First Lord of the Admiralty, offering to provide and equip an armoured car with crew complete', for Samson's headline-grabbing force (in fact its strange little war was by now effectively over). An official replied: 'Mr Churchill asks me to say that in his opinion an Armoured Car would be of little use to this unit, and that it would be much better if you were to arrange an interview with Captain Sueter . . . and offer the services of the Car and yourself to the regular Armoured Car section which is being organised under Commander Boothby at Wormwood Scrubs.'

He did – but instead of dashing off to war, Stern ended up behind a desk in Barlby Road as a Royal Navy Volunteer Reserve Lieutenant as the lowly assistant to Thomas Hetherington.

In October 1914 a Scots-Canadian engineer called Robert Macfie arrived at Wormwood Scrubs; he was a friend of Hetherington and fellow pre-war flyer. Family farming concerns had made him familiar with American 'caterpillar' tractors, especially those made by the Holt company of Peoria, Illinois. In early November he submitted a report inspired by a *Daily Mail* photograph of an Austrian artillery tractor, which he recognized as a Holt, explaining the caterpillar principle and its utility for hauling guns.*

---

* The populist Northcliffe-owned *Daily Mail* pioneeringly led its news each day with a front page of photographs. The edition of 2 November featured an Austrian gun-hauling Holt moving through a Belgian town, imperfectly captioned as being a 'German transport motor – the wheels are constructed to enable it to travel over rough

A month later the forty-year-old RN Volunteer Reserve Lieutenant Walter Gordon Wilson joined the division. Before the war he had been a successful automotive engineer and devised the 'Wilson-Pilcher' motor car of 1904 with an advanced, pre-selector gearbox.

Purpose-designed machines were coming from the factories to equip the division. By the end of 1914 the definitive 'Admiralty pattern' armoured car with a fully enclosed body and machine gun in a revolving turret on a silkily exquisite Rolls-Royce Silver Ghost chassis had been built (the type would stay in service for decades to come). The force was now mustered in 'squadrons' with the cars supported by supply wagons, ambulances, a wireless vehicle and motorcycles. The navy once again took the lead in developing a novel, mechanized, land warfare system by commissioning a special sidecar mount for a Vickers-Maxim machine gun protected by an armoured shield. The bike itself was the beautifully engineered, and expensive, twin-cylinder Scott.

But there was no call for their services. Kitchener wrote to Churchill on 23 January 1915 in terms more disparaging of the landlocked sailors at Wormwood Scrubs who sought excitement, as he said, in 'armoured trains,* bus transport and armoured motor cars', than the utility of such mechanical devices themselves: 'I find these irregular formations are only a means to enable certain officers and gentlemen without military experience and training to get to the front and take part in the war . . . I think it is even more important, if they are to be kept on, that they should be a part of the army . . .'

That is what would happen, but only after Churchill's fall from political grace. Meanwhile the glossy fleet of armoured cars lay 'derelict' in their airship shed. Some went to Norfolk on tedious anti-invasion duties. Others would end up in Russia, Gallipoli, and pursuing the Grand Senussi and his Turkish-backed tribesmen across the Libyan

---

ground with ease' (it clearly has tracks and its pedestrian escort wears a KuK peaked cap).

The next day's coverage and the next after that featured British naval armoured cars bristling with weapons. Putting the two together was a simple leap of logic.

* An armoured train equipped with wireless and anti-aircraft guns commanded by a Capt. Littlejohn RN stayed active on the Belgian coast until February 1915. The biggest enthusiasts for armoured trains were the Austro-Hungarians.

desert. The buses were turned over to the army.* Some lorryborne artillery would find its way to the Western Front. Meanwhile, there was little else to do but experiment.

Churchill summed up the position at the end of 1914. 'After the fall of Antwerp, the trench lines reached the sea,' he would tell the Commission on Inventions five years later, explaining:

> Thus at the very moment when the new armoured car force was coming into effective existence at much expense and on a considerable scale, it was confronted with an obstacle and military situation which rendered its employment practically impossible . . .
>
> The conclusion was forced naturally and obviously on me and no doubt upon others that if the armoured car could no longer move *round* the enemy's trenches and operate against the open flank of his army, some method would have to be devised which would enable them to traverse and pass *over* the trenches themselves . . .

And just how was that to be achieved?

---

* Who had formed their own 'Auxiliary bus companies' in October 1914 with 400 commandeered LGOC B-Types with a depot at Grove Park in south-east London. In the years to come tank crews would sometimes be ferried around in buses while their machines were moved by rail.

7

The British Army's experiments with moving men and materiel had continued since the motorborne Battle of Hastings in January 1909. Similar outings to Brighton and the Thames estuary followed – and in the 1911 summer manoeuvres the first test was made of the 'subsidy scheme' in which civilian lorries were made available under contract (like the LGOC's horses) for military use.

The War Office stuck to horses for its 'first line' transport, the wagons and carts that would bring rations and ammunition up close to the front line. The infantry were expected to march. Iron-shod hoofs and metal-studded ammunition boots remained the arbiters of battlefield mobility.

Hauling heavy guns was the second strand of development. Experience with steam traction was long familiar but embracing the internal combustion engine was more problematic. The use of motor spirit (petrol) was banned because of its 'inflammability'. Only heavy oil or kerosene engines were approved.

The source of power, however, did not matter so much as the means of transmitting it to the ground. Proposals for mechanical devices that could clamber across broken terrain had been around for decades. The application of steam to agriculture had begun the process. The English inventor James Boydell patented an 'elephant's foot' traction engine in 1846 and his 'steam horse' eight years later with a system of hinged wooden flaps round the rear wheels in an arrangement dubbed the 'Endless Railway'. The principle was simple: disperse the weight of a vehicle over the largest possible footprint by reinventing the wheel. Over the next half-century many more bizarre attempts to do just that followed.

For example, in October 1902 a strange machine was tested by the British Army at Aldershot, the German-devised 'Keller', or 'road ring tractor' – with four small-diameter driving wheels rolling within large-diameter road rings which 'revolving as the machine moves form a continuous rail for the driving wheels to turn upon', The 'tractor travelled over very rough ground in a remarkable manner' but pulling a load of five tons the inner wheels just skidded uselessly. A 'Little Lion' steam engine did much better. After a negative report by Col. R. E. B. Crompton, consultant to the War Office, the Teutonic device was abandoned.

The same year a British engineer named Bramah Joseph Diplock patented a refined version of the elephant's foot concept with internal springing better to maintain ground contact. He called it the 'Pedrail'. In 1902 he proclaimed the virtues of the device in an obscure book, *A New System of Heavy Goods Transport on Common Roads*. It was reviewed in the *Royal United Services Institute Journal*. Since 1899 the Diplock company had retained as consulting engineer the ubiquitous R. E. B. Crompton.

In 1903 H. G. Wells's famous short story 'The Land Ironclads' was published in the December edition of *The Strand* magazine – famous not just because of its prescient description of an invading army in some conflict of the near future whose advance is checked by a defensive trench line, but because of the way that line is broken. The affair is observed by a war correspondent, who graphically reports how the defences are quite suddenly overcome by an 'array of fourteen to fifteen monsters . . . the size of an ironclad cruiser' propelled by 'feet like those of elephants or the feet of caterpillars hung as it were on the rims of wheels'. The accompanying illustration showed colonial infantry being menaced by smoke-belching machines in the distance – looking like elegantly streamlined railway locomotives of three decades later.

The monsters cross no-man's-land while it is still dark, using searchlights to find their way and blind the enemy infantry. When their work of breaching the defenders' trenches is done, the attackers' infantry flood through on bicycles advancing 'in open order but unmolested to complete the work of the machines'.

Considering their means of locomotion, the dashing war reporter of Wells's story is reminded of 'a meeting in Victoria Street, Westminster, in piping times of peace with a Mr Diplock – he called them "Pedrails." Fancy meeting them here.'

H. G. Wells had read the *RUSI Journal* article. From military-technical obscurity came a story which would go round the world.

'Endless railways', 'road rings' and 'pedrails' were variations on wheels. Proposals for 'crawlers' – vehicles advancing on an endless chain strung around running wheels – had also been around for some time but were technically much harder to achieve. Primitive linked tracks of cast iron simply disintegrated under load. Two American engineers built a steam crawler tractor in 1888 but their concern went bankrupt after a year. Alvin O. Lombard, of Waterville, Maine, had more success in devising a 'steam log hauler' with primitive but functioning tracks and front-skid steering to pull lumber in the woods of New England. A patent was granted in 1901. Several were exported to Russia.

In 1903, Benjamin Holt, founder of the Holt Manufacturing Co. of Stockton, California, paid Lombard $60,000 for a licence. A year later Holt began testing a modified version of the company's Junior steam traction engine equipped with a set of linked tracks faced with wood-block treads. Steering was effected via a cumbersome single front wheel. On one account, the Holt company publicist, Charles Clements, coined the term 'caterpillar' in early 1905 after watching the tracked Junior clamber across a field. In 1910 the company moved to Peoria, Illinois, to manufacture petrol-engined tractors for agriculture and construction industries. Shrewd Ben Holt trademarked the name. Rival designations were crushed into the ground. If it had tracks, it was a 'caterpillar'.

The British Richard Hornsby company based in Grantham, Lincolnshire, developed a track laying system patented in 1905. The Hornsby tractor significantly featured a track-steer clutch arrangement, one track disengaging, the other staying under power to turn. The tractor dubbed 'Caterpillar No. 1' appeared at the 1908 royal review at Aldershot, to be captured on moving film. A bioscope show at the London Empire proved a popular attraction with special screenings for military officers and foreign defence attachés.

General Sir Stanley von Donop, Director of Artillery, however, remained firmly in favour of draught horses. Without a government order Hornsby pulled out of crawlers. Their patent was acquired by the all-conquering Holt.

Nor had Mr Diplock's experiments with elephant's feet been crowned with commercial success. In 1908 he turned to a new concept, a chain-linked, single track running on wide 'sleepers', with excellent weight distribution but difficult to steer. The name for the device remained the same.

The Holt company had begun exporting round the world. In 1913 the Hungarian franchise agent Dr Leo Steiner offered the Caterpillar-Holt tractor as a heavy artillery hauler to the Prussian and Austro-Hungarian war offices. Berlin stuck to horses. But the Kuk Kriegs-ministerium placed orders for a number of caterpillars to make mobile its outsize Skoda 305-mm siege mortars, broken down into three components – gun, mount and portable foundation – hauled along in a road train. In August 1914 every Holt in the dual monarchy was commandeered for military service. Several were assigned to their German allies, towing artillery for the great assault in the West.

After witnessing the pounding of Antwerp's defences by such weapons for himself, Churchill had also realized the need for heavy firepower. That October he ordered for the Royal Marine Artillery twelve enormous 15-inch guns (shell-lobbing howitzers of the sort that had reduced the Belgian frontier fortresses) from the Coventry Ordnance Works (in fact based in Glasgow). Its manager since 1909, Reginald Bacon, a retired rear-admiral and innovative former director of naval ordnance (he had been a pioneer of submarine construc-tion), duly supervised the prototype's manufacture and would take it proudly to France himself in early spring 1915, having been granted a special commission as a colonel in the Royal Marines.

It would be followed by another eleven of the ten-ton monsters. The problems of moving them were clearly going to be immense. According to Churchill, 'Bacon's monster gun could be moved in sections by eight enormous caterpillar tractors, the pictures of these vehicles were extremely suggestive.' They were the same images as those which had inspired Lt Macfie at Wormwood Scrubs and his paper on the Holt caterpillar.

The admiral went first to the Daimler company who referred him to a relatively obscure manufacturer of agricultural machinery, William Foster & Co. of Wellington Foundry, Waterloo Street, Lin-coln, who manufactured a tractor called the 'Agrimotor', weighing fourteen tons powered by a 105hp Daimler sleeve-valve engine. In 1913 they had developed and briefly marketed a tracked machine called the 'Centipede', but it was a technical and commercial flop. The tracks were too fragile. If they got snagged in barbed wire the device ground to a halt. Bacon was impressed by the big-wheeled tractor. The Agrimotor was quite the thing to tow his guns.

By early December 1914 the first of the machines, finished in battleship-grey with 'OHMS' painted on the flanks of their enormous radiators, were ready for naval service. Admiral Bacon went to see them being shown off in a Lincoln park – and was treated to a demonstration of the tractor crossing a ditch via an extemporized wooden bridge devised by Foster's managing director, William Tritton. Colonel Dumble was also there as consultant to the Admiralty, bringing his old friend and motor transport expert R. E. B. Crompton.

Who actually had the idea is contentious. Bacon would claim it was him. Could not the tractor itself carry a bridging device that it could somehow pick up and reuse? Tritton thought that it might. He would make an engineering model for the attention of the Admiral's patron, Mr Churchill. The admiral added another twist: his bridge-laying device should at its front bear a giant electrically lit magic lantern 'bearing the image of a ferocious Chinese warrior . . . to have a nerve-racking effect on the men in the trenches'. Bacon said he 'put the proposition before Mr Churchill who was pleased with the idea'.

8

In France, meanwhile, the restless Ernest Dunlop Swinton was brooding on the conundrum of the entrenched machine gun. In late October 1914 he was summoned to London to expedite the patriotic offer by Lord Northcliffe to donate 10,000 morale-boosting copies of the *Daily Mail* each day to the troops in France. Swinton also arranged an air drop of propaganda leaflets, printed on Northcliffe's presses, on the German lines. This freelance operation was not officially smiled upon.

Instead he went to see his pre-war boss, Maurice Hankey (a Royal Marine colonel), who remained secretary of the Committee of Imperial Defence and enjoyed Whitehall-spanning influence. Swinton explained that he had been in correspondence with a mining engineer a few weeks before the outbreak of war, a Mr Hugh Marriot, then working in Antwerp, who had suggested the use of a machine 'that might be of use to the army and navy' – a 'caterpillar tractor capable of some remarkable cross country travelling.' It was made apparently by the Holt company of Peoria, Illinois. Perhaps it could be turned into some sort of fighting machine.

'Colonel Hankey was full of sympathy and quite agreed with what I put forward,' said Swinton.

> I left him on the understanding that I would do my best to press the matter at General Headquarters in France, while he did his best to press the matter here in London.
>
> The next day as arranged I met Col. Hankey and Captain T. G. Tulloch and we discussed the conversion of caterpillar tractors for the purpose of meeting machine-guns ... On the 21st October I saw Mr Asquith and one thing I did impress on him was the number of German machine-guns and the damage they were doing. It was the only thing I did impress upon him.

Thomas Tulloch was an old friend, former chief experimental officer at the Royal Arsenal, Woolwich, who had been involved with the Hornsby tractor trials. Now he was the director of an ammunition company. It had been taken over by a German concern. It gave him interesting connections.

In 1913 Tulloch had gone to Berlin on a sensitive mission for Messrs Vickers, to demand of the Deutsche Waffen company why they had ceased paying patent royalties on the Maxim principle for their production of machine guns. They would neither pay up nor explain why not. He was told it was a 'matter of state security'. In a twist worthy of a John Buchan novel, a shadowy figure in the Reich capital had told the visitor this was because the figure would reveal 'the vast number that had and were being manufactured for the Prussian army', so Tulloch would testify in 1919. Disinformation or not, he had shared this alarming insight before the outbreak of war with Ernest Swinton.

On 23 October Swinton returned to France back on duty as Eyewitness. For the next two months he was 'more and more impressed every day with the vital need for improvising or creating some machine . . .'. At the beginning of an inauspicious new year, Swinton returned to London to sort out the army's Director of Fortifications and Works, Gen. George Scott-Moncrieff. Like Swinton, the sixty-year-old general was a Royal Engineer with long service in India and an author among other things of evangelical Christian tracts and a pamphlet on sewage purification. He listened to the proposals with a certain bafflement but was 'sympathetic'.

Buoyed up by this apparent breakthrough, Swinton arranged an urgent meeting the next day with Captain Tulloch, over a discreet luncheon at the United Services Club. They would, it was planned, take their caterpillar proposal to Scott-Moncrieff that afternoon. Other ears were tuned to their discussion. According to Swinton: 'When we met [Brig.-]General Louis Jackson of the Royal Engineers . . . who informed us that that was his section of the work, and would be obliged if we left him to push it forward . . . I left the matter there.'

The War Office had seemingly put up shutters. Swinton went back to his journalistic duties in France, still badgering anyone who would listen in the manner, as he described himself, of a 'monomaniac', believing a direct statement from the front that offensives were impossible without new technical means would sway the argument. No such declaration was forthcoming.

But in London, Maurice Hankey had not forgotten his earlier discussions with the self-confessed obsessive, nor had he failed to act on them. On 28 December he produced a briefing paper for the War Council (the inner ring of the Cabinet formed in August 1914) pointing out, tellingly, that the Allies were not advancing, nor were they killing Germans any quicker than they were being killed themselves. It was time to consider, he wrote, whether the impasse might be broken by finding a distant flank to turn – in the Balkans, perhaps, or in Turkey, which had come into the war on the side of the Central Powers in October. It began with a clear statement of the problem:

> The remarkable deadlock which has occurred in the western theatre of war invites consideration whether some other outlet can be found for the effective employment of the great forces of which we shall be able to dispose in a few months time . . .
>
> There is no reason to suppose that the enemy's successive positions can be captured merely by weight of numbers. The Germans themselves have proved [that] to us . . . by the failure to penetrate our own weakly held and fortified positions . . .
>
> Such deadlocks are not a feature peculiar to the present war. They have been commonplace of wars in all ages . . . Two methods have usually been employed for circumventing an impasse of the kind. Either a special material has been provided for overcoming it, or an attack has been delivered elsewhere which has compelled the enemy to react.
>
> In the ancient wars all kinds of devices were adopted to attack the enemy's ramparts . . . battering rams, catapults, movable towers on wheels, the 'Testudo' (tortoise).
>
> Can modern science do nothing more?

He proposed:

> Numbers of large heavy rollers, themselves bullet-proof, propelled from behind by motor engines, geared very low the driving wheels fitted with *'caterpillar'* gear to grip the ground, the driver's seat armoured and with a Maxim gun fitted. The object of this device would be to roll down the barbed wire by sheer weight . . .
>
> Bullet proof shields of armour. Sir Edward Henry [Commissioner of the Metropolitan Police] had a most interesting

bullet-proof shield designed after the Sidney Street affair. The War Office however consider it too cumbersome for use in the field . . .

Hankey went on to suggest: 'Smoke balls, burning oil thrown into enemy trenches by spring catapults or pumping apparatus, and rocket fired grapnels to tug at barbed wire entanglements.'

He confessed in his memoirs to having read 'quaint prescriptions in old books' on the breaking of classic and medieval sieges. He tested catapults in the grounds behind 2 Whitehall Gardens – 'burned down his own garden hedge with a home-made flame thrower', and with the assistance of his neighbour devised an armoured shield mounted on a lawn roller. Suburbia was doing its bit.

The cerebral civil servant was not alone in grasping at bizarre solutions. In the winter of 1914–15 the War Office would be deluged with proposed sovereign remedies from patriotic inventors in Britain and its empire. A distinguished chronicler of tank development has listed some of them – a fleet of armoured lawn mowers with wire cutters powered by compressed air; portable bullet-proof infantry screens; a 'travelling armour-clad field fortification' with a two hundred-man crew; 'Lemon's wheel and rotating machine', designed to spin a giant explosive-laden flywheel before launching it at the enemy at 100 mph; the substitution of tobacco snuff in shrapnel shells . . .

Experiments would later be conducted in Scotland aiming to demolish trenches with powerful water jets (it worked – but the headwater of a mountain loch provided the necessary pressure). In his paper Hankey conceded that any or all of his own suggestions might be considered 'fantastic or absurd . . . This brings us therefore, to the consideration of the second method of surmounting an impasse, viz., the possibility of a diversion elsewhere . . .'

The paper discounted the Russian or Balkan fronts offering hope of the required 'diversion'. 'Weaving a web around Turkey' held promise. Meanwhile an overland attack on northern Germany launched through Denmark or Holland, though hopeful of success, looked diplomatically self-defeating.*

* When the Ministry of Munitions began to assemble its history of the evolution of the tank in late 1918, Hankey was reluctant for these aspects of the paper to be published. He was sensitive less to the proposed barging into neutral countries than to the link with the Dardanelles misadventure, still laden with political opprobrium.

Proposals for 'rollers' and 'caterpillars' to confound the Hun might well have seemed absurd and fantastical, to most members of the War Council at least. But not to the First Lord of the Admiralty. On 5 January 1915 Churchill sent his own memorandum to Asquith. It was informed throughout by Hankey's thinking, which had been inspired in turn by the informal, unminuted conversations the War Council's secretary had had the autumn before with Ernest Swinton.

'My dear Prime Minister,' wrote Churchill. 'I entirely agree with Col Hankey's remarks on the subject of special mechanical devices for taking trenches. It is extraordinary that the army in the field and the War Office should have allowed nearly three months of trench warfare to progress without addressing their minds to this special problem . . .'

He proposed fitting up 'a number of steam tractors with small armoured shelters in which men and machine-guns could be placed . . . Used at night they would not be affected by artillery fire. The *caterpillar* system would enable trenches to be crossed quite easily. 40 or so of these engines prepared secretly and brought into position at nightfall would advance quite certainly into the enemy's trenches smashing away the obstructions and sweeping the trenches with machine-gun fire . . .

'[Then the] infantry rush through and rally on them. They then attack the second line.'

The paper mentioned the use of smoke and 'other matters too secret to put on paper* . . . the most serious danger is that the Germans are acting on and preparing these surprises . . .'

The First Lord was not content to keep things on paper. Sueter recalled him pacing his room at the Admiralty growling: 'We must crush them in – it is the only way. We must do it. We will crush them. I am certain it can be done.' He was as good as his word. On his account delivered to the Commission on Inventions five years later Churchill then:

'Sent a minute to the Director of the Air Division [Sueter] instructing him to make certain experiments with steam rollers with a view to

---

* Poison gas – Churchill admitted this is what he meant in his 1919 testimony. The first use was by the Germans in April 1915 at Ypres. The British would soon respond in kind.

smashing by mere weight of the engine the trenches of the enemy
. . . and burying the people in them.'

'Was the experiment made?'

'Yes it was. I did not witness it myself, but it was made and it was
abortive . . .'

Indeed it was. Two municipal steamrollers were acquired, lashed
together with chains and guided into action by Lt Barry set against a
dummy trench dug out at Wormwood Scrubs. They broke apart three
times within yards of starting and when they did get going their
smooth wheels spun hopelessly as they flailed the soft London clay
for a grip. In desperation Sueter ordered a single roller to charge
headlong at the trench from the side but as soon as it met an incline
it stopped, its wheels digging out a hole in which it hopelessly
entrapped itself. The Air Department chief prepared a glum report
and the steamrollers returned to road-making duties.

Winning the war with steamrollers borrowed from the Metropolitan Borough of Acton did seem absurd. It was the search outlined in
the Hankey memorandum for a strategic way out of the trench
impasse that demanded attention. There were growing political
voices which argued that the whole position of the British Expeditionary Force in France had become untenable. No breakthrough
was possible. Britain's tiny but rapidly growing army should be
withdrawn and set against some weaker flank of the Central Powers.

There was intense opposition from the French and British commanders to the idea of a diversion elsewhere; they insisted that to
send men off on some politically inspired expedition to the east
would invite a renewed enemy attack on the western front, risk its
success and end up in an invasion of England. But the generals could
not just sit on their hands.

Sir John French informed the War Office on 3 January 1915: 'It
is of the utmost importance that we should strike at the earliest
possible moment.' Breaking through, he urged, was chiefly a question of larger supplies of ammunition. There could 'be no question
of making an attempt elsewhere,' he said, *until the impossibility of
breaking through is proved*. It was impossible. Hundreds of thousands
of Britons would die finding out.

Kitchener at first supported these soldierly views. But he must hold the ring at the highest strategic level. The Russian plea for help had to be answered. Russia was in deepening trouble. The Turkish adventure in the Caucasus had ended in disaster but a Russian move against Austria through the Carpathian mountains had been beaten back by a German-stiffened counter-attack. A German offensive in East Prussia had forced the lumbering invaders already defeated at Tannenberg and the Masurian Lakes back across their own frontier. It was rumoured in London that the Russians had just six weeks' supply of ammunition left (this was not to stop them start building in the new year a titanic armoured landship of their own*). A new German offensive in the spring might prove disastrous.

On 2 January 1915 Kitchener had conferred with Churchill – where could a naval-led 'demonstration' against the enemy in the east have most effect?

There was a place, Constantinople, capital of Germany's Islamic ally, against which the Royal Navy could bring its guns to bear by sailing a fleet of elderly battleships up the narrow waterway of the Dardanelles through which the Black Sea, via the Sea of Marmara, communicated with the Mediterranean.

The venerable artillery forts that lined the Dardanelles would be reduced by naval gunfire. Churchill proposed that it could be done, magically it seemed, by warships alone.

No troops need be withdrawn from France (Kitchener vetoed this anyway), just small landing parties of marines and sailors were required, plus minesweepers to clear the way. Troops already based in Egypt – British, Australian and New Zealanders – might be readied for dispatch to the Aegean should some sort of support landing be judged necessary later.

On 13 January the War Council was treated to a forceful demonstration of the project by the First Lord with maps and charts. A fleet of old battleships otherwise destined for the scrap yard would be used. Minesweepers would clear the way. It was resolved: a 'naval expedition would bombard and take the Gallipoli peninsula with

---

* In early 1915 an engineer called N. Lebedenko designed a huge tricycle with an armoured turret. Called the 'Nepotir', a model of it powered by a gramophone spring clambered across Tsar Nicholas II's desk impressively enough for a sum of 200,000 roubles to be advanced. A prototype was built and trialed near Moscow but the twelve-metre-high machine got bogged down in soft sand. It lay still stranded in the birch woods until 1923.

Constantinople as its objective'. How battleships would 'take' a peninsula, let alone a capital city, was afforded no further detail.

Admiral Fisher at first backed the warships-only plan. Then he suddenly declared it could not be done – not without ground troops. The old admiral's wobble was tremendous. In a dramatic day of sulks and threats of resignation, his persuasive political master won him round. The War Council approved the expedition. On 28 January the attempt to blow Germany's eastern ally out of the war by blasting battleships through to Constantinople was set in motion.

The generals in France – the killing-as-many-Germans-as-possible school of how to win the war – remained deeply sceptical. What was needed was a mass army and mass firepower – artillery to blast a way through and let warfare return to its 'natural' state of manoeuvre and morale. At the War Office in London, however, there was a glimmer of new technical thinking. Hankey's paper had been seen by both Kitchener and Churchill. It was the naval chief who had responded in his rumbustious 'caterpillar' letter to the Prime Minister on 5 January with its wounding comments about three months of War Office inaction.

Herbert Asquith duly passed it to Kitchener. The sternly professional soldier did act this time, sending the letter down the line of bureaucratic command to Gen. Scott-Moncrieff whose in-tray still contained the caterpillar-machine-gun-destroyer proposal personally delivered by Swinton the week before.

Thus a small 'informal' committee was set up at the War Office to see what might be done, with the Director of Artillery, Maj.-Gen. H. Guthrie-Smith and the assistant director of Transport, Col. H. C. L. Holden, recalled from the Reserve List, as members. Swinton was by now out of the way in France but Thomas Tulloch kept the flag flying.

They looked at Hankey's memorandum, the newly completed model of Admiral Bacon's bridging device (Churchill had sent it to Kitchener who had passed it to the War Office) and an ambitious memorandum from Thomas Tulloch called the 'Land Ship' which proposed the design under 'the guiding hand of an automotive engineer' of a completely new machine. He outlined something made out of conjoined Hornsby tractors armed with 'quick firers, 12 machine-guns and carrying 100 men'. It seemed preposterous.

The Master General of the Ordnance, Maj.-Gen. Sir Stanley von Donop, was especially sceptical. Too many cranks were already clogging up his overburdened office with outlandish proposals. A new mass army was already in the making. Their outfitting would be the responsibility of the Ordnance Department, which, like the commercial companies to which it perforce now had to subcontract, was already struggling to keep the BEF as it stood provided with military basics. What the army in the field needed were more guns and more shells.

The opinion of the committee and Col. Holden's in particular was that 'the war would be over before an entirely new machine could be made' – only an adaptation of an 'existing device' would do.

But there was an existing device, which indeed the army already knew something about. Shrewd Ben Holt had been courting the War Office in London, as well as their counterparts in Berlin, Vienna, indeed Paris, since before the outbreak of war. In late October 1914 a Holt had been demonstrated to British Army officers at the Royal Arsenal, Woolwich, and orders for two and then ten more had followed for use as gun tractors. In spring 1915 a bulk order would follow.

On 13 January 1915, two Holts were inspected at Aldershot camp as potential trench crossers. On 17 February one of them was tested in much secrecy over mocked-up obstacles dragging a caterpillar-tracked trailer laden with 5000 lb of sandbags round the Shoebury-ness Proof Establishment and Gunnery School on the Thames estuary. The machine broke through wire entanglements but strained and wallowed in a pit full of barbed wire. The test was judged an outright failure.

Work at Lincoln, meanwhile, on the 'Bacon Tractor', now an army concern, however marginal, as much as naval, had hardly begun – and would stall completely when its originator went off to the front in France with two of his just completed giant Royal Marine howitzers towed by Daimler-Foster tractors.*

As far as the War Office were concerned it would have to be a

---

* The device would be taken up again by the War Office in the early summer of 1915. Foster's completed bridge-layer was tested on 9 June over the range at Shoeburyness. Because it had to reverse to pick up its bridge, it could not cross a double line of trenches, got stuck and was hauled out by a Holt which itself 'crossed trenches at top speed'.

completely new machine. Asked by Scott-Moncrieff a week after the Holt trial whether he could suggest the name of any firm competent to design a suitable land cruiser, Col. Holden replied: 'I am afraid I cannot.'

He might have considered France. Schneider et Cie, the great artillery concern of Le Creusot in the Bourgogne, had been commissioned by the French War Ministry that same January to develop a heavy artillery tractor. The company sent its chief engineer, Eugène Brillié, who had designed motor buses for Paris and an armoured car for Spain, to Illinois to investigate the same Holt tractors the British War Office had just found so unsuitable as a trench crosser. On his return an enthusiastic M. Brillié convinced the management to start development not just of a gun tower but of a *'tracteur blindé et armé'* based on the Baby Holt chassis. Two were promptly ordered to be shipped across the Atlantic.

The British Army's interest in landships had expired in a Thames estuary bog. In a more opulent corner of London, however, wild visions of terrestrial fighting craft were already rising into the cigar-scented air.

9

The Churchill-inspired trench-crushing steamroller experiments had flopped but the First Lord had remained insistent on doing something. In their west London idleness, officers of the armoured car division had had time to indulge in all sorts of experimental urges. Churchill's enthusiasm for armoured shields had not abated. The division had made extensive tests of plate when engineering its cars. Now they were revived for a series of experiments which sought to advance the idea of the Metropolitan Police Commissioner for their employment against anarchists on the cobbled streets of London.

How to make the proposed shields move on the battlefields of Europe? On Sueter's account he saw a trade advertisement for an obscure company in Wyfold Road, Fulham, south-west London, which made a little horse-drawn truck for use in the colonies, mounted on a kind of continuous rolling road. It was called the 'Pedrail'. One was acquired.

It seemed to have remarkable powers of crossing broken ground, even if the system was very complicated. It was proposed by Sueter that a motorcycle engine might animate the device. It was in its modest way a 'caterpillar', of the sort that Hankey had mentioned and Churchill had expounded in his letter to the Prime Minister. Sueter thought a little further. He sketched a curious vehicle like a scaled-down submarine – mounted on pedrails. It look liked a ship on land.

Even with a great fleet assembling in the eastern Mediterranean, the First Lord of the Admiralty had time for other diversions. On 14 February he was at dinner in the opulent surroundings of the Duke of Westminster's London residence, Bourdon House in Davies Street, Mayfair. Also present at the table were Flt-Cdr Thomas Hetherington, the armoured car division's transport officer, his assistant Lt Albert Stern and Squadron Commander W. Briggs, its engineering officer. They were sailors but the talk was of dishing the Hun on land.

Over brandy and cigars Hetherington proposed something quite extraordinary – a gigantic gun platform on wheels which might roll not just over the enemy's trench lines but all the way to Germany. He had already been playing with the idea for months, beginning with a proposal to somehow make tactically mobile a Dreadnought-scale gun on a huge wheeled platform weighing a thousand tons. His superior, Sueter, had warily taken it up in January but Sir Percy Scott, the Admiralty's great gunnery expert, had turned it down on the grounds that: 'They would never allow such a thing in France.' The thing was filed away.

And maybe the authorities, whoever they were, might indeed have baulked at letting the bizarre machine loose anywhere on the European continent. In its final version the 'Revised Hetherington Proposal' was still eye-popping – a land battleship with a skeleton framework like a truncated Blackpool Tower mounted on two forty-foot-diameter wheels with a smaller 'stern' wheel behind.

Ground clearance would have been a tree-challenging seventeen feet, weight an estimated 300 tons. There were to be six four-inch guns in twin mounts, like the turrets on a destroyer, the stupendous device clanking towards the enemy at a hoped-for 8 mph – powered by electric motors charged by two submarine diesel engines. It might break not just through the enemy front – but roam deep in the rear, crashing through 'woods and towns, spanning rivers with ease . . . attacking railways' like some privateering frigate.

Churchill was highly animated by the whole business. After the dinner he 'went home determined that I would give imperative orders without delay to secure the carrying forward in one form or another of the project in which I had for so long believed . . .'.

Two days later, on the morning of 16 February, the First Lord was treated to a demonstration (Sueter claimed to have arranged it) on Horse Guards Parade in Whitehall of something seemingly much more practical: it was the Diplock colonial pattern truck running on a pedrail track – a kind of mobile builder's skip intended for employment in 'the Malay'. It was designed to be pulled by a mule but, even loaded with half a ton of bricks, it could be readily pushed into motion by a bow-tied cabinet minister in early middle age. For now the intention was still to use the pedrail to mobilize Churchill's pet armoured-shield project. The little cart proved a point. Running on its single 'sleeper' track, it bore its burden with apparent ease. Perhaps it could float across shell-churned ground and trenches just as readily.

Churchill pressed the land battleship idea eagerly on a startled Admiral Fisher, and urged Hetherington to place both his giant tricycle and the 'caterpillar' principle before the Director of Naval Construction, Mr Eustace Tennyson d'Eyncourt. The flight-commander did so in a paper dated 18 February – a proposal to build 'a new type of gun carrying war machine . . . a cross country armoured car of high offensive power'. It was the lunatic land battleship back again. Sir Percy Scott was horrified. The paper sat in the DNC's locked in-tray like an unexploded shell. Mr Churchill could hardly contain his excitement. He was about to win the war in one bold blaze of naval gunfire after all.

At 9.51 a.m. the next day, 19 February 1915, the great gamble in the eastern Mediterranean began, with a long-range seaborne bombardment of the outermost Turkish defences at the mouth of the Dardanelles. It was ineffective – the ships would have to move in closer. A storm blew up that night. The fleet would have to ride it out. It would last for five days. In frosty London, Churchill was gripped by a chill.

Winter colds, meanwhile, did not blunt the the First Lord's enthusiasm for progressing war on land by naval means, either by attacking Turkish coastal forts or German trenches hundreds of miles from the sea. On 20 February, a Saturday, Churchill convened a little conference in the Admiralty Extension. It would prove historic. In his words: 'I was ill at the time and it was held in my bedroom.' Present were Hetherington, d'Eyncourt, Colonel Dumble, and William Tritton of Messrs Fosters, agricultural machinery makers of Lincoln.

The First Lord, conducting the meeting from his bed, was persuasive. Mr d'Eyncourt complained of overwork but agreed to chair a small committee to progress the matter. The steering group, styling itself the 'Admiralty Landships Committee' (the title would be changed later in the year to DNC Committee for 'reasons of secrecy') met formally for the first time on the 22nd. Two advisers with knowledge of 'automotive engineering' were then invited into the circle.

One was the caterpillar enthusiast, Sub-Lt Robert Francis Macfie from the armoured car division. The second, on Col. Dumble's recommendation, was the seventy-five-year-old consulting engineer Col. R. E. B. Crompton, sage of land transport and all things mechanical.

The first item was Hetherington's land battleship. Sadly for military fantasists the gigantic tricycle was dropped. Members agreed their primary task was to decide between wheels or tracks – and the best way to do that was to build prototypes of both. A weight of twenty-five tons for the proposed device was deemed practical. Crompton listened to Macfie's exposition of the latest American caterpillar developments with interest. Dumble quit, departing for a lucrative post in Manchester with W. G. Armstrong, the armaments manufacturer. The 'Landship' had its godparents.

Meanwhile, the weather in the Aegean quietened. On 25 February the naval gunfire assault on the Turkish artillery forts guarding the Dardanelles was renewed. The defenders seemed to have run away. Minesweepers got six miles up the straits but found no mines – although light artillery had engaged them ineffectually from the shore. The British admiral commanding assured London that the Turkish capital would be under his guns within two weeks. There was elation at the Admiralty.

10

The Admiralty Landships Committee got down to work. Its chairman, Eustace Tennyson d'Eyncourt, was forty-six, the son of a magistrate who was a cousin of the Poet Laureate, Alfred, Lord Tennyson. Since becoming director of naval construction in 1912 he had single-mindedly pursued delivery of the greatest battle fleet in the world. The committee's patron, Churchill, was an egoist politician with a weakness for military adventure. Its consultant, R. E. B. Crompton, was a Yorkshire-born version of Thomas Edison. Most usefully so far for mankind perhaps, in 1898 Crompton's company had developed the world's first electric kettle. Hetherington was a dashing cavalry-man-turned-pilot. This mismatched alliance were going to make a fighting machine that would smash open the Western Front. That was the intention.

Crompton was a living monument to the heroic age of Victorian engineering. In 1856 by a curious domestic arrangement he had been placed at the age of eleven in the care of his 'mother's cousin', the captain of HMS *Dragon*. But the Royal Navy frigate was bound for the Crimea where Britain was at war with Russia. Young Crompton was made a midshipman en route and witnessed the siege of Sebastopol.

As an army officer in India a decade later the precocious Crompton had built a steam-driven road locomotive and been appointed 'Superintendent of the Government Steam Train' that plied the Grand Trunk Road from Rawalpindi to Peshawar. Electricity was his next great enthusiasm and foundation of a fortune. His 1887 generating station at Kensington Court was the first in London. He still lived alongside it in a steel-framed, red-brick mansion called Thriplands with an instrument-packed laboratory in its attic.

In 1900 he had been recalled to military service, promoted colonel and given command of a unit of Royal Engineers. In the new century of horseless carriages he had chaired the government Road Board and made a new fortune out of tar spraying. He had been Vice President of the Royal Automobile Club (where he still ferociously played racquets and devised the club's standard ball) and consultant on mechanical transport to the War Office.

Crompton was as shrewd a businessman as any Yorkshire coal owner. He agreed a salary of £130 a month and the appointment of an assistant, Mr Lucien Legros, past President of the Institute of Automobile Engineers, founder of the Iris motor company and expert on trams. Their payments, like all other DNC Committee expenditure, were buried in an existing navy budget line for 'auxiliary machinery'.

The two men represented the nation's highest expertise on mechanized movement by land. Now they were working for the Admiralty.

It was the War Office's fault; perhaps they thought the venerable engineer was too old or too cranky to employ themselves. They had no excuse for ignoring his talents. Through the autumn of 1914, Crompton had been pestering the army's Directorate of Transport with intended solutions to the problems of 'military traction', advocating the utility of his old friend Mr Diplock's pedrail system for moving stores. The War Office had reviewed the proposals politely – and done nothing.

He had next come up with what he called his 'trench straddling engine', borne not on tracks but on eight-foot-diameter wheels with a deck to carry fifty troops intended to clamber across no-man's-land and pause astride an enemy trench while its occupants dropped ferociously down through a trap door. Teams of infantrymen would, meanwhile, have to travel ahead of it like railway navvies with picks and shovels 'filling in shell holes'. It was wildly impractical, with no relation to the realities of the front. Getting information from the front line in France was to be one of the greatest difficulties the armour pioneers would face, and would remain so even when their machines were on the eve of going into battle for the first time.

The War Office remained indifferent. On behalf of his new naval patrons the elderly Crompton acted with astonishing energy, venturing himself to Lincoln to discuss the wheeled machine with Tritton, heading for the Bishop's Field in Fulham to see Mr Diplock's latest pedrail device and scouting out a manufacturer who might build the tracked machine of which he was now an ardent enthusiast. He lighted on the steam lorry manufacturers Messrs Fodens of Sandbach in Cheshire for the tracklayer. Foster & Co., still labouring with the Bacon automatic bridger, would get the wheeled device. Foster's managing director, William Tritton, had been sceptical of caterpillar devices since the pre-war failure of the company's own 'Centipede'.

Crompton would design the tracked vehicle himself, with the assistance of Lucien Legros and the erratic Bramah Diplock. He sketched out something like his original wheeled 'straddling engine' but mounted atop a tandem pair of fiendishly complex pedrail tracks. It was not a heavy gun platform so much as a storming device – a 'Trojan Horse' to take men through the wire and hail of machine-gun bullets and dump them in the opposing front line to finish the job with bayonets and hand grenades. It was a people carrier, a landing craft, not really a land warship at all. Churchill had no objections.

The generals in France were preparing, meanwhile, to obey Sir John French's new year dictum: 'It is of the utmost importance that we should strike at the earliest possible moment.' The commanders were keen, so were the men after a winter spent in freezing half-flooded trenches. But this time, unlike the fiasco with rope mattresses at Messines in December, the assault would be more scientific.

Barbed wire was the problem. Trials had been conducted at Shoeburyness using replica German defences to find the way to cut entanglements. Armoured compressed-air lawn mowers and giant exploding Catherine wheels were not on the agenda. It must be done by existing weapons. Could machine-gun fire do it? Were high-explosive shells more efficient than shrapnel? The experiments pointed to shrapnel as better – it cut the wire clean from the posts, whereas HE left it in churned up but still impassable entanglements.

The wire could be cut, but what no one knew was how much firepower would carve a path right through. And was wire cutting a more efficient use of scarce guns and shells than bombarding the trenches echeloned behind to kill or cow their inhabitants?

The War Office had also been exploring means of making infantry firepower more effective in an offensive. Any lingering suspicion of machine guns had evaporated. Mass orders had been placed for the belt-fed Vickers Mk 1 and in early 1915 the lighter, air-cooled

US-Belgian Lewis gun was put into licensed mass production by Birmingham Small Arms. Weighing thirty pounds it was just about man-portable (although it needed a second gunner to carry and load the drum magazine). A burly soldier could fire it from the shoulder or hip.

What to do with belt-fed machine guns? Could they do more than just sit and wait to be attacked? If they could be animated, made to move, Mr Maxim's invention might be made to undo the deadlock it had itself imposed. Admiral Bacon recalled a demonstration at Shoeburyness of a Maxim gun mounted on the back of a mule. It ended in predictable disaster.

Experiments began with 'indirect barrage fire' spraying bullets over the heads of advancing infantry and way behind the German trenches to disrupt rear areas in the manner of artillery. Brigadier Raymond Brutinel, senior machine gun officer of the Canadian Corps, took the lead, employing the technique to particular effect when Canadians would go into action with tanks for the first time. The defenders hated it. Lieutenant Ernst Jünger recalled their effect in his epic memoir *Storm of Steel*: 'The British made various attempts on our lives by means of high angled machine-guns . . . we were especially irritated by one . . . who sprayed his bullets at such an angle that they came down vertically, with acceleration produced by sheer gravity. There was absolutely no point in trying to duck behind walls.'

Tactical manuals were suddenly full of recommendations about how belt-fed machine guns could be pushed forward by soldiers on foot alongside the leading waves of an infantry attack. It was very difficult. Captain George Macintosh 'Boss' Lindsay, Boer War veteran and former instructor at the School of Musketry at Hythe saw that this might be better achieved by putting machine guns not on mules but on motorcycle sidecars. His enthusiasm was all-conquering. An Army Order put into effect in February 1915 approved the addition to each division of a 'motor machine gun battery', drawn from a new military formation to be known as the 'Motor Machine Gun Service'.* The Coventry offices of *The Motor Cycle* magazine, edited

---

* Batteries of the MMGS mustered eighteen cycle/sidecar combinations, carrying six Vickers machine guns with ammunition and spare equipment; eight motorcycles without sidecars; two or three wagons or cars; and a sidecar combination for the officer commanding.

by Mr Geoffrey Smith, were listed as the new service's recruiting office.

The opportunities for their employment in truly mobile operations remained limited, reflected by the fact that they were first mustered as part of the Royal Field Artillery. They used Vickers Mk 1 water-cooled machine guns mounted on Scott and Clyno combinations, their crews dashingly attired in soft caps, goggles, leather gaiters and gauntlets. A depot and training school were established amid the late Victorian splendour of the National Rifle Association of Great Britain's shooting club at Bisley, Surrey. A South Wales Borderer was in command, the forty-two-year-old Old Harrovian Lt-Col. Robert William Bradley – an amiable sort – a bit of a dug-out but open-minded and forward-looking. A contemporary would describe him a little later as 'a florid soldier with a mechanical turn of mind and much elderly smartness'. On matters of discipline, however, he was perhaps less sound. He was married to the daughter of the Bishop of Swansea.

Spring was coming, a renewed 'fighting season'. In Britain those hundreds of thousands of optimistic patriots who had answered Lord Kitchener's call to arms were undergoing basic training. Industry creaked and groaned in its effort to equip them. In north-east France the reinforced remnants of the original British Expeditionary Force prepared to attack again. General Sir Douglas Haig, commanding First Army, favoured an operation aimed at a slight German salient around the village of Neuve Chapelle twenty miles north-west of Lille, with the aim of capturing a piece of high ground that offered an observation point. The assault on a very narrow front began on 10 March after a so-called 'hurricane' bombardment. It was a euphemism for short – thirty-five minutes. But it was comparatively effective, far more so than the flop at Messines. The navy got into the fight but under army control. Admiral Bacon turned up with two of his monster marine howitzers and the Duke of Westminster lobbed shells into the German lines from the back of an armoured Seabrook lorry.

After a stunning advance in the first few hours, the assault 'clogged and stopped', in the words of the *Official History*. Broken communications (it was all meant to be done by telephone) delayed the advance of reserves and the Germans occupied a second line that the British could not break. In fact the wire cutting had mainly worked, but the supposedly all-conquering bombardment of an entrenched enemy had not. Enough defenders had survived to scramble out of dug-outs, man their machine guns and cut the plodding infantry down.

There were reasons to be hopeful. If communication on the battle-field could be improved and artillery techniques refined, the trench line must in the end be broken.

This was the logic that would drive the Allied efforts for the next two years. If the invaders' defensive crust could be pierced, great things were possible. If the railheads and junctions that succoured the linear fortress could be captured, the whole front would crumble or be rolled up from behind. If that was too strategically ambitious, there was the prospect of capturing 'high ground' from which the enemy rear could be observed and long-range gunfire directed. Break through the wall of extruded metal and revetted earth. It seemed simple. Cut the wire and smash the trenches. Artillery was the key to the door.

Artillery was the lock that was keeping the Anglo-French fleet out of the Dardanelles. After the shock of the opening bombard-ment, the defenders of the straits with their German advisers had found the will to resist. Field guns, man-handled from rock to rock, flayed the armada bobbing hesitatingly up the straits. The big ships might have been invulnerable but not the minesweepers crewed by civilian trawlermen who baulked at going further.

Still the fleet had not passed the Narrows, a canalized pinch point less than 2000 yards wide with artillery forts on either side. On 18 March the climactic moment came as the Narrows were reached. A French battleship blew up and three British battleships also struck mines – two of them went straight to the bottom. The fleet turned back.

It was an extraordinary confrontation. Massive, mobile armoured gun platforms had come up against echeloned land-based defences (masking the minefields in the waterway itself which did the real damage) and been thoroughly defeated.

In London Churchill argued forcibly for the assault to continue but this time Fisher had had enough, as had the admiral commanding on the spot, pacing the stateroom of his flagship HMS *Queen Elizabeth*, now anchored off the Greek island of Lemnos twenty miles from the mouth of the straits.

That was the end of the warship-only idea. The defences must be reduced by a land assault. Lord Kitchener informed the War Council that the army was willing and able to undertake the task. The first troops had already begun to arrive from Egypt on Lemnos.

The Admiralty was wreathed in gloom. There was a distraction two days later, on 20 March, when Churchill was presented with scale models of the two landships – Crompton's tracked machine and Tritton's big-wheeler.

The Lincoln proposal was for a semi-articulated vehicle with four fifteen-foot-diameter wheels, the powered section at the front with its driver in a little turret, towing a 'two wheeled armoured wagon after the design of a gun and limber' which might carry either a field gun or a 'storming party'. Articulation would separate the engine with its 'red hot pipes' from the petrol and ammunition, something Crompton saw as highly desirable. It was estimated the pedrail could be ready in fourteen weeks, the big-wheeler in twelve.

To drive production forward, at the beginning of April Albert Stern, the former banker and guest at the Duke of Westminster's dinner party in February, was informally appointed the Landship Committee's secretary, a role he would grasp with ever increasing (some would say overbearing) authority.

Churchill was prepared to bend the rules. Accounting procedures were ignored. On 26 March the First Lord signed off orders for twelve pedrails to be built by Fodens – and six wheeled landships to be built by Foster's at cost of material, labour and establishment to the manufacturer plus 10 per cent, an estimated £70,000. 'On account of secrecy this may be taken as full sanction,' he minuted.

'Did you invite the Board of Admiralty to share the responsibility?' he would be asked at the Inventions Commission.

'Not formally.'

'Did you inform the War Office?'

'No.'

'Did you inform the Treasury?'

'No. I thought it very essential to keep it absolutely secret.'

There were others with secrets to keep. The War Office censorship concerning conditions at the front applied to naval officers backed by an ambitious politician as much as to journalists. A landship design would stand or fall depending on what conditions were really like on the ground. In the last week of April, Crompton, Stern and Hetherington went to France on the First Lord's orders to find out what they could. No formal permission was sought or granted; they would have to pull it off by bluff. They had as much chance as a battleship getting to Constantinople.

The elderly engineer proudly donned his colonel's uniform with a Crimea ribbon, took luncheon with the Duke of Westminster at his rented villa at Dunkirk and proceeded with his naval colleagues in the direction of army General Headquarters, hopeful of a grandstand ticket to the front line at Neuve Chapelle.

'At GHQ at St Omer [we were] received by Major Hutchinson,' wrote Hetherington. 'Landships were a joke,' he was informed. The obstructive Major (later a lord) Hutchinson 'not only refused us permission, but gave us a lecture on *the folly of wasting public money in this way*. We therefore returned empty handed.'

Crompton would not be put off. He wrote imploringly to Gen. Sir Horace Smith-Dorrien, commander of Second Army, asking for help. 'I am an old colonel of the Electrical Engineers now employed by the Admiralty to prepare designs for trench attacking devices,' he revealed. The general could do nothing. Crompton was getting careless of the Churchillian secret, especially where it was most dangerous – with the army.

Frustrated on their farce-prone visit to the front, Crompton and his colleagues did what they usefully could by inspecting the roads that led towards the 'Forbidden Zone'. Not all of them were the straight, poplar-lined axes of Napoleonic centralism. Many were heavily embankmented, or twisted their way through brick-built villages. The numerous canal bridges were seen as a major problem for transiting landships that must surely demolish them with their weight.

A new proposal was advanced by the elderly colonel: the tracked device should bend in the middle, like his Indian 'road train' of four decades before, made up of two platforms on caterpillars with armour protection against small arms and carrying as many machine guns as practical.

'It is proposed that these vehicles should cross our front line,' he informed d'Eyncourt, 'by specially prepared arrangements, then wheel rapidly and sweep up alongside the enemy's entanglements and when sufficiently close . . . grenades to be thrown therein mechanically, for the final attack the attacking force [fifty-four men] can jump direct from the side aisles into the enemy's trenches.'

After the blighted promise of Neuve Chapelle, the British Expeditionary Force went on the offensive again on 9 May at Aubers Ridge and at Festubert two weeks later with supposedly trench-crushing bombardments aimed at a two-mile-long fortified line, followed by infantry 'storming parties'. Eleven thousand men fell at Aubers and achieved nothing. After a sliver of initial success, the attack at Festubert also floundered.

The French had embarked on spring offensives just as bravely in the Artois and been comprehensively slaughtered. There were not enough heavy guns, not enough shells. The infantry were flayed on uncut wire. The artillery's attention to technical detail had not been sufficient. As Hankey had minuted in December 1914, could not 'modern science do more?'.

11

The shortage of artillery ammunition had blown up into the great 'shell scandal'. In a remark leaked to *The Times*, Sir John French blamed 'the want of an unlimited supply of HE' for the failure at Aubers Ridge. The *Daily Mail* blamed 'Lord Kitchener's Tragic Blunder' for the paucity of firepower, embarking on a campaign to hound the Secretary of War from office. It backfired – copies of the newspaper were ceremonially burned in London streets.

The Dardanelles operation, wildly oversold by Churchill, was also descending into fiasco. Troops were landed on 25 April supposedly to clear a way for another attempt at a breakthrough by the fleet. It happened just as the Germans launched an attack in Flanders using poison gas, a reminder of the dangers of the real cockpit of war. On 15 May Admiral Fisher theatrically resigned and went into virtual hiding in Scotland, declaring: 'The Dardanelles will be our grave.' The Liberal government's authority crumbled.

The Conservative opposition lambasted Churchill as a battleship-squandering amateur who had defied the admirals' expert opinions with disastrous results. He had to go. In the newly formed national coalition government, Arthur Balfour took over political control of the navy. David Lloyd George became head of the new Ministry of Munitions. The new ministry set businessmen managers with their brisk American business methods alongside soldiers, a social experiment without parallel. It would have an 'Inventions Department' (open to suggestions from the public and soldiers in the field) and a Trench Warfare Department. GHQ in France set up its own experimental committee.

The higher reaches of the army, depicted almost invariably as horse-loving obscurantists, had in fact undergone their own kind of cultural revolution. Major C. H. Foulkes RE, founder and commander of the Special Brigade (poison gas), found that 'British officers of high rank tend to be almost *too* receptive to novel proposals, especially when they were based on anything mysterious . . .'

Something very mysterious was being cooked up in the Admiralty Extension.

On 26 May 1915 Churchill departed the Admiralty tainted by scandal and failure, to linger in government as Chancellor of the Duchy of Lancaster. His enthusiasm for warships on land remained undiminished.

The Landships Committee had mounting problems of its own. Construction of the Foden-built pedrail had been stalled by strikes. It did not matter too much as the concepts on Crompton's drawing board kept changing, first the single rigid pedrail of March then the double-headed bending version of a month later.

Crompton had had growing doubts about the stability of the pedrail system on a big machine. Its powers of manoeuvre were limited (it was supposed to be steered by moving the tandem tracks out of alignment on their central pivots). The eccentric Mr Diplock was getting more and more difficult to work with (Crompton complained of his fellow inventor's 'arrogance – nothing can be altered').

On 7 May, after Crompton had confessed to his deepening doubts about Mr Diplock, the ambitious order for eighteen prototype machines had been cut by Churchill to just two – one example of the Tritton big-wheeler now approaching a final wooden mock-up at Lincoln and a single articulated caterpillar machine. It would not be mounted on tandem pedrails but on parallel tracks of a completely different design to be obtained from the United States.*

Crompton urgently sent a former assistant named George Field, specially fixed up with a commission in the Royal Naval Volunteer Reserve, to America to report on the latest commercial track-layers. The Holt was ignored – surprisingly, as there was a growing pool of experience in the Army Service Corps using them as artillery tractors.

---

* No complete pedrail assembly and no chassis to Crompton's design was ever built for the navy, but a single prototype was eventually completed. Designs and models were taken over by the Trench Warfare Department which oversaw its completion by the Bath-based engineers Stothert and Pitt as a potential platform for a heavy flame thrower. Walter Wilson drove it at the factory where it made a 'nasty lurch'.

   Tested at last by the army in August 1916 at Porton Down, Wiltshire, it proved incapable of crossing trenches. Fitted with an unarmoured tram-like body it failed further tests on Salisbury Plain. Crompton referred to it as 'the fireship'.

A chronicler of the matter asserts that it was precisely because the army were involved with the Peoria company that Holt was kept out. Their London agents would surely tell their existing customers of the approach; the Admiralty must preserve its secret from the War Office. The secret, however, might seem to have been compromised already.

On his American trip Lt Field sounded out two other likely manufacturers. The first was the Killen-Strait company of Appleton, Wisconsin, who made a tricycle tractor, an example of which the navy had been experimenting with at Barlby Road since April when Crompton had arranged its acquisition via the company's London agent. The second was the Bullock Creeping Grip Tractor company of Chicago, Illinois, manufacturers of heavy crawlers for agriculture and civil engineering.

An example of the Bullock (like the Holt, a wheel and track combination) was also already in Britain, so Field messaged, apparently working on marsh reclamation at Greenhithe in Kent. It was quickly located and duly inspected by Crompton and members of the Admiralty Landships Committee, who were impressed enough to order two of the company's largest machines, the 'California Giant', to be shipped across the Atlantic as soon as possible. At the beginning of July the pedrail was formally abandoned.

On 16 May Maj. Hetherington went to Lincoln to inspect the mock up of Tritton's big-wheel machine. His report was gloomy. It was too big, too high, a lumbering target that a field gun could cripple with a single shot. It would be 'a constant menace to traffic in the event of a breakdown'. The caterpillar, the Landships Committee resolved, was the only practical way forward.

The two Bullock tractors ordered by Lt Field, meanwhile, had arrived in Britain aboard the White Star liner SS *Lapland*. As a first step to proving the concept of an articulated landship, they were linked together back to back, the tracks bunched in the middle and wheels at either end, joined by a flexible 'ankle' devised by Crompton.

Tests began at a field near Burton-on-Trent, Staffordshire, on 16 June 1915 overseen by a newly recruited member of the committee, Walter Gordon Wilson, another veteran of the armoured car division. The articulated Bullocks looked ingenious but the contraption got stuck whenever it tried to tackle a trench. The forward–reverse gearing was out of synch – as one tractor pulled the other pushed. The tracks were too short, the steering arrangements unworkable. But Crompton would not let go – two sets of specially extended Bullock tracks were ordered from the manufacturers. The big-wheeler, meanwhile, had been formally abandoned on 8 June. Tritton was summoned to Barlby Road to be told the bad news.* The bending trench-stormer was still just about alive as a concept, depending on the success or failure of the elongated tracks that would take two months to manufacture and come by rail and sea from Chicago. Landship development hung by a thread.

The Admiralty Committee was gripped by rows and dissension. The peppery Commander Frederick Boothby raged against d'Eyncourt's apparent slowness (d'Eyncourt evicted Boothby in response – he was exiled to a bleak airship station in Barrow-in-Furness). There was a bizarre sideshow when Lt Macfie went off on a design path of his own, employing the services of a litigious west London garage owner to create a caterpillar out of a commercial lorry.

Of the four Sea Lords, only one (Admiral Frederick Tudor-Tudor) now had any enthusiasm for going on. His colleagues wanted shot of the lot of them. The Fourth Sea Lord, Commodore Cecil Lambert, flayed the Barlby Road experimenters as 'damn idlers' whose caterpillar landships were 'idiotic and useless . . . no-one has asked for them and nobody wants them'.

Churchill held meetings of the persecuted sect at his private house, 21 Arlington Street in Mayfair. Arthur Balfour could find no official objection to his extramural activity.

The naval armoured car units, some of which had been sent futilely to the Dardanelles, others to Africa and the Middle East, were at last poached wholesale by the army – except for the recently raised No. 20 Squadron retained after a fight by Sueter as a training and experimental organization. It seemed a dead end.

---

* Tritton kept the idea going for a while with a proposal for an 'Electric Trencher'. It was a design for an outsize tricycle with fifteen-foot-diameter tractor wheels bearing an armoured hull containing an electric motor. Power was to be supplied through a cable paying out from a rear-mounted drum charged by a generator installed in the friendly trench lines. The device might carry troops and guns, or, unmanned, a monster explosive charge to be detonated once it had trundled its way towards the enemy front. It never left the drawing board.

12

Ernest Swinton, still acting as Eyewitness in France, had not abandoned his lonely campaign. Hovering around GHQ at St Omer he persuaded Maj. Ralph Glyn, a War Office liaison officer, to badger the generals in London. He buttonholed industrial chiefs on visits to France, pestered an old contact, Gen. the Earl of Cavan, with his 'juggernaut scheme' – and petitioned the army's Engineer-in-Chief, Maj.-Gen. G. H. Fowke, who turned out to be 'wholly unsympathetic'. From Glyn he heard a rumour that the navy were working on some sort of caterpillar weapon. The major promised he would find out more.

Ralph Glyn was an excellent investigator. He discovered details of the failed War Office experiment with the Holt tractor at Shoeburyness. Much more dramatically, he uncovered the fact that Churchill had at some point formed a technical committee to experiment on 'landships' for the navy. There had been some bizarre plan to make a machine described as a 'Crystal Palace on wheels' (Hetherington's land battleship) and now 'caterpillars' were on their way from America. Glyn had reported these and his other findings to the Director of Military Operations, the amiable Gen. Charles Caldwell, who in turn was now pressing his War Office colleagues to discover if there was any truth in 'what seemed like a fairy tale'. Glyn returned to France and told Swinton what he knew.

Swinton's pestering had already produced one important result. On 18 May the Master General of the Ordnance grumpily forwarded the War Office's thin file on its own experiments to the office of the Chief of the Imperial General Staff. Looking at the scant results and armed with Maj. Glyn's discoveries, Gen. Caldwell suggested to the CIGS that it might be 'desirable to obtain information on certain armoured tractors which he understood the Admiralty has in hand . . . certain parts of which are being obtained from the USA . . .'.

Tactful overtures were made. 'Consultation [by the War Office] with Mr D'Eyncourt was essential,' it was quaintly noted in the Ministry of Munitions postwar history of the affair, 'because of the analogy of the strain to which the machine might be exposed and that of a warship in stormy weather'. Actually it was because the army had not got anywhere.

The navy's smokescreen of secrecy was blowing away. On 30 May Admiral Frederick Tudor-Tudor gave whatever details he could of the 'orders then existing' to Scott-Moncrieff, explaining that the departed First Lord, Churchill, had sanctioned them: 'Because this was essentially a war of machines and machines and armour protection hardly seem to have been employed on shore as yet.' The first such machine, he indicated, would be ready in about six weeks.

On 1 June 1915, dimly aware of the existence of an Admiralty initiative, Swinton submitted a lengthy memorandum entitled 'Armoured Machine Gun Destroyers (General Description)' to GHQ in France. It spelled out his old obsession – how to meet entrenched machine guns on equal terms. One answer was to acquire enough artillery and high-explosive shells to blast a way through – as, indeed, was being attempted.

An alternative answer, he argued, was 'a caterpillar, petrol-engined tractor' protected sufficiently to be proof against the new German steel cored armour-piercing bullets that were being reported from the front.* It should be capable of crossing a four-foot ditch – and be armed with two machine guns and a 2-pounder gun. Swinton was aware of the difficulties of trying to fire guns from a lurching, bucking metal box, a dinghy in a storm more than a land battleship. He proposed that the crew should be accommodated in 'bosun's chairs' slung from the roof, with angular steps within trod by crew wearing 'rubber-soled shoes'.

Swinton proposed: 'Such machines should be built at home secretly and their existence not disclosed until they are ready. The destroyers should be brought up to the railheads the day before the attack and distributed at night along the front of action.' He stressed that wherever possible 'individual destroyers should be targeted at a

---

* 'SmK', *Spitzgeschoss mit Kern*, bullets fired from rifle or machine gun that could go through the armour plate employed by snipers. Also known as 'K' rounds.

specific, previously identified machine-gun – driving straight at it as supporting infantry moved up behind'. The biggest threat to the proposed machine was hostile artillery. Major-General Fowke, the Chief Engineer, saw the paper, minuting sharply: 'The writer should descend from the realms of imagination.'

On 9 June the army's last fitful experiments came to nothing with the failure of the Bacon bridge-layer in trials held at Shoeburyness. The pedrail flame-thrower, now the property of the Trench Warfare Department, was looking distinctly unpromising.

A marriage of convenience was looming. Churchill was man-oeuvring in the background meanwhile, suggesting to his successor as First Lord, Arthur Balfour, that the committees be conjoined with himself as chairman. It was not to be. On 15 June War Office representatives were at last appointed to the Admiralty Committee but there would be no formal position for the former First Lord.

D'Eyncourt remained chairman and Lt Albert Stern was now formally appointed secretary; he found grander accommodation for himself and an assistant, Petty Officer Percy Anderson of the armoured car division, in elegant surroundings at 83 Pall Mall, home of the Commercial Motor Users Association. The arrangement was, as he recalled: 'At my own expense – no Government department would provide any office for us.'

It turned out to be rather convenient. The War Office with its feuding fiefdoms could be kept at one remove while the landship enthusiasts got on with it. Stern would keep paying the rent himself for six months. General Sir George Scott-Moncrieff seemed positively relieved.

Churchill's profligate way with public money would not be repeated. The new First Lord, Arthur Balfour, approved navy funding for just one machine. There would be no orders for more until a practical prototype had been demonstrated. If it worked – if the army actually wanted it – production would become the responsibility of the Ministry of Munitions.

Swinton's paper of 1 June with certain technical refinements went to the BEF's experiments committee in France, 'the monkey tricks department', and its businesslike director, Major Henry Guest. The view from France was to the point – 'the object for which the caterpillar cruiser or armoured fort is required . . . is for employment

in considerable numbers in conjuction with . . . a general attack by
infantry against an extended front of a hostile position. The tactical
object is attack . . . the arm therefore should if possible include one
light low velocity gun plus two Lewis guns . . . two crew to handle
the gun and one man to handle each Lewis . . .

'Crew for propelling power (should be two) propelled by an
internal combustion engine being more silent and less noticeable than
is possible with steam . . . the caterpillar should be as low as possible
. . . weight should not exceed sixteen tons . . .'

It passed up the bureaucratic chain at GHQ to reach Field Marshal
Sir John French himself. He read it cursorily, forwarding his opinion
(drafted by Guest) to London on the 22nd. It was positive: 'There
appears to be considerable tactical value in this proposal which adapts
the peculiar qualifications of the caterpillar mode of traction to the
transport of a species of armoured turret . . . across uneven ground
. . . particularly if the production of these machines can be a surprise
to the enemy.'

The C-in-C approved. 'France' was in favour. Perhaps there really
was something in it. News of the strange proposal spread through
the upper reaches of the War Office through indiscreet correspondence and clubland gossip. General Bird, the Director of Staff Studies,
early in on the secret, described it as 'a kind of armoured Noah's
Ark on caterpillars'. Senior figures beyond the sonorous circle of
Scott-Moncrieff's committee sniffed the significance of what was
being proposed. Careers could be made on it.

It was clear some sort of grand handover was coming. Would the
naval experimenters see their work stifled by War Office torpor? On
30 June 1915 Stern arranged a live demonstration in London of work
in progress, designed so he said, 'to raise enthusiasm among the
army'. Booted and spurred staff officers arrived at Barlby Road to
witness armoured shields on pedrail tracks being pushed along by
sailors, a drive past by motorcycles and purring Rolls-Royce-turreted
armoured cars. Frederick Stokes, inventor of the eponymous trench
mortar ('with the tank the most important fighting invention of the
war', according to Admiral Bacon), cheerfully lobbed shells from his
crude stovepipe into the skies of Ladbroke Grove. They landed in a
perfect circle.

Star of the show was a display of the Killen-Strait tractor with

Flt Cdr Hetherington at the controls, who took the machine equipped with a (still highly secret) 'Pioneer' naval torpedo-net cutter smartly through bales of barbed wire. Canopied in stripy, scallop-fringed canvas, it looked like an ice-cream cart from Brighton pier.

The little tractor was then miraculously transformed into a much more formidable looking fighting machine when the body of an Austin armoured car was bolted on to it by the ingenious Lt Kenneth Symes.

But the real purpose of the caterpillar stunts at Wormwood Scrubs was political. Churchill and Lloyd George watched from the touchline, the former First Lord beaming with delight as the Killen-Strait went through the wire – 'like the reaping operations of a self binder' – selling the whole thing to his cabinet colleague. Keep the Admiralty in the driving seat – then let the Ministry of Munitions take things forward.

The Admiralty might still be in charge of development, but it was the army who were now deciding the path to take. Two days after the grand demonstration the War Office presented its own 'general desiderata' to the DNC Committee. It was basically Swinton's pre-scription as smiled upon by the C-in-C. The whole design emphasis was changed. The infantry-carrying trench-stormer was out. That the army had come to it was ironic. What the soldiers wanted was not some sort of armoured Antwerp bus crammed with infantry but a machine carrying the biggest weight of armament manned by the smallest crew practical. In that sense it really was a warship on land.

Crompton proved adaptable, coming back with yet another articulated machine – with two superfiring drum turrets on each segment armed with 75-mm guns like a miniature warship. He found a discreet address at No. 12 Drayson Mews, behind Kensington Church Street, to work on the 'highly secret project' as he described it. Foster's chief draughtsman, William Rigby, who had joined the company as an apprentice in 1903, was sent to Kensington to assist.

But Crompton's end was nearing. His approach was too painstaking, the obsession with a double landship too baroque. According to d'Eyncourt, writing a year later: 'His proposals gave no promise of producing any satisfactory . . . results. They were in fact in matter of detail wholly impracticable . . .'

On 22 July came a turning point. The Admiralty Committee met and resolved to commission a prototype landship on the lines the army desired.* Target weight was eighteen tons. Articulation was out; it would be a unitary machine carrying as heavy an armament as feasible, able to cross a trench four feet wide. Design and construction of the prototype would be the responsibility of William Foster & Co. with William Tritton as production engineer. Walter Wilson was to be the 'admiralty superintendent', the link to Whitehall.

After two weeks in limbo Crompton and Legros were dismissed. An official turned up at Drayson Mews to impound all plans and drawings. The elderly engineer would brood on his treatment for years to come. All that remained of his (indeed all the navy's) work were the pedrail plans and some pre-assemblies, now the property of the Trench Warfare Department plus the extended Bullock tracks still on their way by sea from America.

Ernest Swinton's term of duty as Eyewitness in France had come to an end. One man churning out reports from GHQ was not sufficient to the task of keeping Fleet Street in war news. He returned to London at the end of July, summoned by his old boss Maurice Hankey to discover that he had been appointed acting Secretary to the 'Dardanelles Committee' of the Cabinet (the Committee of Imperial Defence in new guise). It was 'an Open Sesame', in his words, a key to every secret door in Whitehall.

'It did not take long to discover the existence of something called the "Admiralty Landships Committee",' he wrote, 'directed by one Tennyson d'Eyncourt, to whom for further information I was advised to apply.' A few days later he met the committee's secretary. 'Stern bounced into my room, bubbling over with enthusiasm, and proceeded to explain what his committee was doing.' Swinton would not be invited to join the inner ring of the secret circle – just yet.

The design team in Lincoln of Tritton and Rigby (with visits from

---

* Thomas Hetherington, then air attaché at the British Embassy in Rome, animatedly told the Official Historian in October 1934 that it was incorrect to imply, as did the draft of the volume covering tank development, that 'Col. Swinton or any other army representative had handed to the Admiralty any specification for the machine'. All that had been supplied were 'specifications of the dimensions and types of trenches which would have to be crossed,' he insisted. Edmonds diplomatically amended the official line to read: 'The Admiralty Committee were given full details of what the Army required the machine to do.'

Wilson) established themselves at the White Hart Hotel on Bailgate with as much secrecy as they could. A little fire blazed each evening even in sultry August as the day's jottings were consigned to the flames. What soon emerged on their drawing board was an armoured box enclosing the Daimler engine and two-speed gearbox from the existing artillery tractor set on top of the tracks ordered by Crompton that were supposed to be arriving imminently from America. They got to Liverpool aboard the SS *Orduna* on 3 September. Eight days later the first metal for the hull was cut.

But Walter Wilson was already thinking of something different. His experience with the coupled Bullock tractors at Burton-on-Trent had not been encouraging. He had an idea for a machine with tracks running around the entire perimeter of a 'quasi-rhomboidal' frame, as he described it. It would have a sharply angled prow – ideal for climbing trench walls. The big track would have the footprint equivalent to an enormous wheel. It was a bold leap of faith: the tracks would have to be devised from scratch and where would the armament go? In a turret on the top? It was looking too high already.

An outline sketch was shown to d'Eyncourt at the end of August who noted: 'Proposal for next with equivalent of fifty foot wheel. All parts can be made in England. I think well of this. Wilson's idea.'

Tennyson d'Eyncourt authorized construction of a wooden mock-up, himself proposing that the armament be carried in side-mounted 'sponsons', a configuration long familiar to naval architects as the mounting for close-in armament against torpedo boats (the soldiers would describe them as 'bay windows'). He would design them himself. Production of the first machine on the American tracks should continue.

Ernest Swinton was about to stage his own little coup in London. On 26 August he saw the Prime Minister, to badger him on his pet subject once again. Asquith agreed: the Committee of Imperial Defence itself should sponsor an 'inter-departmental conference', which met two days later at 2 Whitehall Gardens, the CID secretariat, chaired by Scott-Moncrieff.

The conference's agenda spelled out the new direction. They were there to discuss 'land cruisers or armoured caterpillar motor cars for the use of the Army'. They were clearly not going to be commanded or crewed by sailors. Swinton was there wearing his Dardanelles

Committee hat – so was his excitable old friend Thomas Tulloch, who
gave a warning that if the enemy got there first with a fleet of 'land
vessels' the shock compared with the Germans' first use of poison
gas would appear 'infinitesimally small'. Countermeasures against
the very weapon they were making should be investigated, he urged.
Meanwhile, secrecy was all.

The meeting (it was dominated by soldiers with the rumbustious
Stern flying the flag for the navy) formally agreed that the Admiralty
was to continue development, taking instructions from the War
Office via the Director of Staff Duties, the influential military bureaucrat, the one-legged Gen. Wilkinson Bird.

At last GHQ in France supplied intelligence reports of the latest
German field works and trench systems – deepening, widening, hardening under concrete. There were reports of quick-firing guns in steel
cupolas. The specification would have to change. The caterpillar was
now required to cross a trench five feet wide and climb a four and a
half foot parapet.

The meeting made the first reference to the men who might have
to take them to war: 'Personnel would have to be trained almost as
trick drivers to get the best out of the cruisers,' the conference noted.
It was a prescient insight. The BEF's own experimental committee in
France was in on the secret. Its secretary, Maj. Henry Guest, forwarded
suggestions from bored soldiers seeking distractions from trench life.
A Maj. Glasfurd suggested a 'cyanide sprayer on pedrails'. A certain
Capt. J. Rose proposed mounting 'a big siren or buzzer' on a fighting
machine to 'shatter the nerves of all orders on arriving amongst the
enemy'. Admiral Bacon's Chinese warrior now had sound effects.

By early September the 'Number 1 Lincoln Machine' was almost
complete – an armoured box set atop the nine-foot Bullock tracks
with a pair of tail wheels for 'steering', Tritton's idea. A dummy
cylindrical turret was perched on top but carried no armament. The
prototype first crawled on its own power across the factory floor on
8 September.

Ernest Swinton got wind of it. 'The naval people are pressing on
with their first sample caterpillar,' he informed his confidant, Maj.
Guest, at GHQ on 10 September, 'but are not ready for trial yet,
though they have succeeded in making an animal that can climb
4' 6'' and turn on its own axis like a dog with a flea on its tail.'

He had evidently also heard something about the 'Wilson'. 'They have apparently got a modified machine,' he wrote, 'that can cross larger gaps and climb vertical faces of 5'. This is only in the stocks.'

By 14 September the Number 1 was ready for its first outdoor trial – in Foster's factory yard – where the tracks promptly became detached. Tritton tried various modifications and a further test was carried out at Burton Park, just outside the city, on 19 September, where a number of the firm's employees and their families turned up in their best clothes to see their creation in action.

Swinton was present, unofficially, borne to Lincoln in a somewhat suspicious Hetherington's car. D'Eyncourt and Stern were also there, animated, expectant – but they were to be disappointed. The tarpaulin-swaddled machine failed to climb a five-foot-vertical height. Every time it tried to straddle a trench, the American tracks sagged from their rollers and came off. Swinton thought the presence of the company's picnicking workers was a serious security breach.

'Luckily, from the point of view of secrecy, the machine failed to comply with the test to which it was put,' he would write in his memoirs, 'and in order to discount the revelation of what we were aiming at, it was arranged that a report would be put about that the whole idea was impractical and would be dropped.'

There was something else in store: a glimpse of the 'Wilson' rising in wooden mock-up in one of Foster's erecting sheds. It was extra-ordinary, nothing like the armoured box set on a Holt tractor that Swinton had first envisaged. How its tracks were meant to work was a mystery. He returned to London elated, consuming a 'joyous dinner' on the blacked-out train.

The Bullock tracks on the Number 1 Machine had proved useless. Tritton resolved to design a system from scratch. A combination of pressed steel plates riveted to heavy castings linked by steel pins worked much better. The castings were fitted with flanges, and – this was the clever bit – were configured to run in guide rails in the inner faces of the track frames, so that they could not droop away when suspended in thin air over a trench. In this arrangement the suspension could not be sprung, but no one was thinking of crew comforts. Would it work as a gun platform? That had yet to be discovered.

The flanged track was the breakthrough. On 22 September the Lincoln team sent a birth notice telegram from the 'proud parents' to Stern's modest secretariat at Pall Mall. The new track system worked. It meant they could be made much longer and configured to run round the perimeter of the entire vehicle, as Wilson wanted.

The Number 1 Machine was rebuilt, using the same engine, body and rear-wheel arrangement but with Tritton's flanged track system in a completely new underbody. The dummy turret was removed. The thing rumbled about the factory, crossed piles of logs, and the tracks stayed on. It was officially being styled 'Juggernaut'. The women workers at the Wellington Foundry in Waterloo Street were already calling the remade machine 'Little Willie' (named, according to local legend, after William Tritton. Another attribution is to the disparaging name rolled out in newspapers and propaganda sheets for the Kaiser's son, Crown Prince Wilhelm). Little Willie might now do everything that had originally been asked of it but that was no longer enough. The War Office had changed their specification yet again. The proposed landship must now lift itself over a parapet four foot six inches high and span a trench eight feet wide. The Wilson might do that and more.

Rather than bring Whitehall to see the Wilson, the dummy landship would come to London, transported by 'motor lorry' setting off from Lincoln in darkness on the evening of 28 September. The next morning officials from the Landships Committee, the Ministry of Munitions, GHQ's own experimental committee and the War Office met in Tennyson d'Eyncourt's office at the Admiralty. They were told that 'a landship [Little Willie] had already been constructed and tried'. The results had not been entirely satisfactory it was true but the track system was a success. There was, however, another machine which used the same motive principle in an entirely different design. They would be seeing that today.

Bowler-hatted civil servants and bemedalled military clambered into a little fleet of motor cars to be borne from Whitehall to the Trench Warfare Department's experimental station at Wembley Park, north-west of the capital, formerly a suburban pleasure ground promoted by the Metropolitan Railway. A corner had been taken over by 20 Squadron RNAS. A *coup de théâtre* orchestrated by Albert Stern awaited.

There – 'guarded by sentries and screened off in an enclosure such as might have sheltered . . . the fat lady at a fair,' as Swinton described the scene – was the extraordinary machine with dummy guns poking out of the side. It had a little nameplate announcing its new name – 'HMLS [this Majesty's Landship] Centipede'.

The conference reconvened in Whitehall after an agreeable lunch and swiftly decided to ditch the 'existing landship' and 'proceed with the design exhibited'. The Centipede had triumphed.

They recommended some technical tweaks. The armour at the front should be ten millimetres thick – 'capable of stopping the German reversed bullet fired from ten yards range'.* The crew would be eight, 'the exact distribution of their duties to be decided later', a top speed of 4 mph on the level to be aimed at, and armament two 57-mm naval 6-pounder cannon, plus Lewis machine guns.

Construction of a mild steel prototype proceeded rapidly. It would have the same Daimler engine and transmission as Little Willie. Just over nine weeks later it would be ready for testing.

* A standard 7.62-mm round but with the lead bullet reversed in the cartridge case. Mauser ammunition like this was found in captured trenches in February 1915. The British thought these might be 'dumdum' bullets (and therefore banned) and carried out various tests amid press outrage. It was decided they were intended to be used against sniper shields and the matter was dropped.

13

As His Majesty's Landship Centipede was being prepared for its Wembley debut, the greatest assembly of men and munitions thus far in British military history was being readied in north-west France for a great offensive. It would become known as the 'Battle of Loos'.

Allied commanders had met at the end of June 1915 and agreed that, in spite of the disasters of the spring, offensive efforts on the Western Front must continue. In manpower terms Great Britain was becoming not such an unequal partner to France. Within a few months the first of the New Armies would be ready for active service in the field.

It had been agreed. That autumn the French would attack on two fronts – around Reims in the Champagne and in the Artois region north of Arras. The British blow would be made in the coal-mining area around the town of Lens, chosen simply because it then formed the junction between the two nations' armies. The strategic intention was bold. Infantry would break open the defence line and the cavalry be 'pushed through', heralding a general offensive which would compel the Germans to 'retreat beyond the river Meuse and possibly end the war'.

On the axis of the proposed advance was the mining village of Loos with its steel-lattice winding towers, brick-built pit-head buildings, railway lines, crumbling slag heaps and huddled rows of miners' houses incorporated into the German front line. The British operational commander, Gen. Sir Douglas Haig, had misgivings at first. The terrain was comparatively open but punctuated by fortified villages, greatly favouring the defender.

A new weapon would clear a path for the attackers. It was called the 'accessory'; any mention of what it really was was forbidden. It was in fact chlorine gas manufactured by the Castner-Kellner Alkali Company of Runcorn, Cheshire, to be released from more than five thousand heavy canisters brought up by trucks, then hauled into the front-line trenches by 'special companies' of the Royal Engineers. It was up to the wind to carry it the essential bit further to the enemy. Gas might asphyxiate men in dugouts or cause them to flee, but of course it would do nothing to cut belts of barbed wire. The intense artillery bombardment preceding and following use of the 'accessory' was supposed to do that.

Six infantry divisions would mount the opening assault, with the Guards and two untried New Army divisions in reserve. The numerical superiority over the defenders seemed overwhelming, at some places seven to one. It would still not be enough.

Royal Flying Corps meteorologists had fretted for days. A breeze of at least 6 mph blowing generally north-west was required for the gas to move in the right direction. It had been tried over 'experimental' trenches two days before and seemed to work. Major Charles Foulkes, the Royal Engineer who had been plucked from relative obscurity to command the 'special brigade', recalled the night before the assault fretting in his little office attached to First Army's forward HQ in a château behind the lines: 'As the hours passed, General Butler, Sir Douglas Haig's chief of staff, looked in from time to time, inspected the map and rejoined the army commander to report on conditions.' An hour before dawn on Saturday 25 September, Gen. Haig observed the drift of an aide's cigarette smoke. He climbed a wooden observation tower and peered into the darkness towards the brooding objective. The leaves of poplar trees gently rustled in a stirring wind. At 05.40 a.m. he gave the order to release the 'accessory'. A light breeze was at their backs. It was judged sufficient.

At some points in the line there was no wind whatsoever. The special engineer companies were ordered to open the valves nevertheless, turning the cocks with clumsy spanners, chlorine passing from the tanks pressurized 'like soda siphons', via rubber tubes to iron pipes poking through the sandbagged parapet. It was described as 'rushing out in a yellowish white vapour, which developed into a greenish yellow cloud a few feet from the pipe'. The gas clung to the ground, eddying in gathering pools reeking of household bleach. Then it began to drift hesitantly across no-man's-land in the general direction of the enemy.

The artillery opened up, with shrapnel and high explosive. Forty minutes later the first waves of attacking infantry climbed out of their trenches and began to walk forward – in soft caps and smothering fabric gas masks. Where the gas had carried well, they prevailed. The village of Loos itself was taken after fierce fighting. A little to the north-east, around the village of Hulluch, a change in the wind blew the green cloud back into the British lines resulting in 2632 casualties, although only seven actually died.

By mid-afternoon the British were scrabbling to hold on to what they had captured. Where were the reserves? They were still slogging towards the front line on traffic-clogged roads in drenching rain. The decision to commit them (they were under the command of the C-in-C, Sir John French) was not made until mid-afternoon on the 25th.

The next morning they went into battle – in broad daylight, with no element of surprise, thankfully, perhaps, without the 'accessory' – and hardly any artillery support. The two New Army divisions walked towards the second defensive positions, according to one German description: 'Line after line, some of their officers even on horseback as if carrying out a field day drill.' The wire was intact – four feet high and in some places nineteen feet across. German machine-gunners kicked up the back sights of their water-cooled MG '08s, ammunition belts coiling – waiting for the first wave of advancing khaki-clad infantrymen to come within range.

Private W. Walker published this account of the 21st Division's assault on the German second line. Having moved through the shattered village of Loos late on the evening of 25 September:

> It was Sunday, if it mattered. The sun peeped brightly over the hill. Except for a general murmuring from the serried and prostrate ranks, there was scarcely a sound. In the early light an appalling scene lay before us. The ground was strewn with dead and dying men . . .
>
> At six o'clock, word came along that a general advance was to be attempted; already some had left the shelter of the roadway and were running over the open plateau.
>
> The shellfire was deafening enough, but the clatter that commenced with our further advance was abominable. It was as if the enemy were attacking with a fleet of motorcycles – it was the hellish machine guns. I saw no foe. Our chaps fell like grass under the mower, mostly shot in the guts . . .

Private Walker did not see the enemy but they saw him. The war diary of the 26th Infantry Regiment recounted: 'With barrels burning hot and swimming in oil, [the machine guns] traversed to and fro unceasingly . . . The effect was devastating. The enemy could be seen literally falling in hundreds, but they continued their march in good order and without interruption . . . doggedly onwards, some even reaching the wire entanglement in front of the reserve line, which their artillery had scarcely touched.'

It could not be done. Whatever the apparent advantage in manpower, however brave the attackers, however crushing the bombardment – even the offensive use of poison gas – the fiendish barricade of uncut wire and entrenched machine guns was impassible. The Germans called Loos *Der Leichenfeld*, the field of corpses. What he saw reminded another New Army volunteer, the nineteen-year-old Harry Fellows, of the flypaper in his mother's kitchen. Years afterwards he recalled approaching the second defensive line near Hulluch:

> The leading men would have been about 100 yards from the German wire, and I was about the same distance from my starting point, when all Hell was let loose. As if from some predetermined signal the enemy machine guns opened up with a murderous fire, both from the front and enfilading fire from some buildings which had been out of sight behind some trees. Men began to stumble and fall, then to go down like standing corn before a scythe . . .
>
> A squadron of tanks would have cleared that hill in no time, but we had no tanks. Some months later, during the Battles of the Somme, Winston Churchill put the whole problem in one phrase when he said it was: 'Bare chests versus machine guns.'

After the shambles of the second day, the Battle of Loos sputtered on for another miserable seventeen. In the end it had achieved nothing. It was the first experience of action by the New Armies and, although it showed their courage, it demonstrated both their lack of training and the mistakes and lack of flexibility of their professional commanders.

There had to be a scapegoat. The 'mishandling' of the reserves was widely commented upon. Who had hesitated to commit them? Sir John French, the C-in-C himself. He was removed, given a peerage and a home command and replaced – after much shameless backstairs manoeuvring – on 19 December 1915 by Gen. Sir Douglas Haig. Four days later Sir William 'Wully' Robertson, French's Chief of Staff, who had begun his long military career as a private soldier, was made Chief of the Imperial General Staff.

New men were in charge. A new weapon was in the making.

What lessons had been learned from the shambles at Loos? The 'accessory' was fickle. Artillery was not: the heavier the bombardment, the greater the chance of success. Brig.-Gen. Noël 'Curly' Birch, Haig's adviser on artillery matters, would become more and more influential. If the defence was arrayed in depth, so had the operational concept for the attack to be. Breaking the first line was not enough. If the conundrum of the echeloned defence could be mastered, the game was by no means over. Birch saw offensive battles ahead as a series of staged advances, step by step, each covered by an ever more elaborate fire plan. More guns were the answer, medium guns and heavy guns firing high explosive rather than shrapnel, guns with calibres ranging from six inches to battleship proportions, reaching deep into the rear. After such monstrous pounding the enemy must at last be so demoralized, so depleted of reserves, the crust, however deep, would break.

Another lesson had been learned. After the bloody apotheosis of the German machine guns at Loos there was a major reorganizational move within the British Army. After a forceful campaign by George 'Boss' Lindsay and the former musketry instructor-turned-chauffeur Christopher Baker-Carr, the 'Machine Gun Corps' was created by Royal Warrant on 14 October 1915 with a training centre at Grantham in Lincolnshire. From March 1916 it would have a depot at Camiers, just north of the BEF's ever growing base camp on the coast at Etaples. Each army brigade would now have a machine-gun company of four sections.* The heavy belt-fed Vickers were withdrawn from infantry battalions and replaced by the air-cooled, drum-magazine-fed Lewis.

---

* There were usually six men in a Vickers gun team. In his book *With a Machine Gun to Cambrai*, George Coppard explained how it worked. 'Number One was leader and fired the gun, while Number Two controlled the entry of ammunition belts into the feed-block. Number Three maintained a supply of ammo to Number Two, and Number Four to Six were reserves and carriers, but all the members of the team were fully trained in handling the gun.'

As well as the 'infantry machine-gun companies' the corps would consist of 'cavalry machine-gun squadrons' and 'motor machine gun batteries', which absorbed the old Motor Machine Gun Service with its training centre at Bisley. It was now designated the 'Machine Gun Corps (Motors)' with the amiable Col. Robert Bradley still in command. But the swashbuckling unit, darlings of the illustrated propaganda sheets like *War Pictorial*, could do little other than muster around Frensham Ponds looking purposeful for photographers. Trenches and wire made them as impotent as armoured cars had been rendered in late 1914.

The new Corps badge consisted of crossed Vickers barrels surmounted by a crown but officers reportedly clung to their old tribal adornments, 'so great was the lure of the regimental system'. Other ranks had no such choice. Private George Coppard swapped his Queen's Royal West Surrey Regiment insignia 'with some regrets but welcomed the new one', noting: 'We were no longer in a small unit subject to the dictates of every infantry officer and NCO. From then on as members of a specialised corps, we came under the orders of our own superiors. Carried down the scale this meant that a lance corporal in charge of a gun in action who became detached from his own superiors, would be the sole judge as to the best position for his gun, and when and where it should be fired.'

Tolerance of such small-unit independence was novel. The infantrymen of the New Armies were thought to be capable of little more than advancing in ordered lines, before closing on the enemy with the bayonet and Mills bomb (a grenade). The Machine Gun Corps could now enlist its own recruits, pick and choose instead of relying on drafts from the rejects of other regiments. It began to look on itself as some sort of elite, master of the device that was master of the battlefield. They had a swagger, a machine-oil-stained arrogance. According to Coppard: 'No military pomp attended its birth . . . It was not a famous regiment with glamour and whatnot, but a great fighting corps, born for war only and not for parades. From the moment of its formation it was kicking . . .'

From such men would come the Heavy Section of the Machine Gun Corps, 'Born for war only'. It could not have been a better description of the tanks.

14

In December 1915 Col. Winston Churchill (he had resigned from the government the month before) was on active service on the Western Front with the 2nd Battalion, Grenadier Guards, undergoing a month's training before himself taking command of an infantry battalion in the Ypres salient.

The tools of Whitehall warfare, the position paper and the mimeograph machine, still had attractions for the fallen political star. Brooding in a billet at Lawrence Farm, Ploegsteert, Churchill wrote a long paper called 'Variants of the Offensive', like Hankey and Swinton before him looking for a solution to the conundrum of echeloned defences. The shock of Loos had apparently inspired no revulsion against generalized slaughter. His opening remarks were as stark as anything Haig might later have to say about the necessity of the 'wearing out battle'. Churchill wrote: 'Any operation on the western front is justified if we at least take a life for a life ... We may also proceed on the assumption that our army is more numerous and on the whole more handy and keen than the enemy.'

But what was the point if the equation was not a life for a life? The defence still dominated. The New Armies, a million citizen volunteers, would expend themselves as futilely as the first of them in the field had done at Loos. Churchill's paper proposed technical solutions – including his old favourite, portable bullet-proof shields – and digging huge saps reaching towards the opposing trench lines. The longest section, however, dwelt on 'caterpillars', of which 'about seventy are now nearing completion in England', so he wrote. Their powers seemed remarkable: 'They are capable of traversing any ordinary obstacle, ditch breastwork or trench, they are capable of carrying two or three Maxims each and can be fitted with flame apparatus. Nothing but a direct hit from a field gun can stop them. On reaching the enemy's wire they turn to left or right and run down parallel sweeping his parapet with fire, crushing and cutting the barbed wire in lanes and in a slightly serpentine course.'

An attack by caterpillars would require 'frost, darkness and surprise ... above all surprise,' wrote Churchill. 'Until these machines are actually in France, it is not possible to measure the full limit of their powers, but it is believed that during the dark hours of a winter's night, not one but several successive lines of trenches could be taken by their agency.'

He added: 'None should be used until all can be used at once.' That line would reverberate for decade. A copy of Churchill's typewritten paper went to Sir John French, who just then had other things on his mind. He was about to be evicted from command of the British Armies in France.

Churchill's paper (like those of everyone else involved in the matter – and there were more and more of them) stressed surprise and secrecy. Something strange happened in London almost simultaneously. In a debate on the conduct of the war on 8 December 1915, Mr James Hogge, a Liberal MP, otherwise known for interventions on the kelp industry and the grievances of munitions workers, rose to his feet in the House of Commons to ask Harold Tennant, Undersecretary of State for War, 'Whether the Ministry of Munitions Inventions Department had yet reported to the War Office on the use of mobile forts propelled by caterpillar tractors for use in traversing ground honey-combed with trenches; and if so has he reported favourably on their utility.'

Mr Tennant replied that no such report had been received.

Hansard printed it. Swinton grew alarmed – wary that 'inventors who had hit upon a similar scheme might cause the Germans to be put on the scent of our operations'. Maurice Hankey warned off the press (parliamentary pages did not report the remarks) and the Speaker of the House to avoid any such references in future.

The Hon. Member for East Edinburgh seemed very well informed. He could have been referring to a crank proposal sent by a constituent to Armament Buildings (the Inventions Department received over 20,000 proposals for bizarre new weapons in the year following its creation in August 1915), but mobile trench-crossing forts propelled by caterpillar tractors was pretty close. The day before Mr Hogge's outburst the prototype Schneider artillery tractor on Holt-derived tracks had been demonstrated to the French army. The matter of 'leakages' would get much murkier.

On Christmas Eve 1915 the 'inter-departmental conference on caterpillar machine-gun destroyers or land cruisers' met again at the CID secretariat's offices in London to consider 'the question of the provision of these machines, their equipment, manning and cognate subjects'. The soldiers were now totally in the ascendant. Major-General Sir George Scott-Moncrieff was in the chair and Swinton acted as secretary. Stern represented the navy. The conference reviewed a paper from Swinton dated 17 December which looked especially at just who was going to operate the new machines.

'It will necessitate the enlistment and special training of special officers and men of technical qualification, each of whom will have to perform the duties of a mechanic, an expert motor driver, and a QF [quick-firing gun] and machine guns,' the colonel wrote. 'It will be no easy matter to obtain men of this class, and they will have to be formed into a corps of specialists much of the nature of the machine gunners of the German army.'

The conference concurred with Swinton's paper. 'As regards the class of officers and men, it is thought that both should have some mechanical knowledge and aptitude, and that they should be drawn from those now serving in any branch of the forces or from civil life', it was minuted. 'Each member of this body of men should be trained to perform every duty which he might be likely to be called up to carry out; and that since it cannot be formed into an independent corps, it should form a detachment of the existing Machine Gun Corps.' Swinton had previously suggested it should be an offspring of the Royal Engineers. It was not to be.

It was decided 'to recommend a preliminary approximate establishment at the rate of one officer and ten rank and file for every Land Cruiser to take the field, with 50 per cent in reserve.' The paper saw a potential requirement for fifty machines, 'should the Army Council after inspection of the final experimental Land Cruiser' decide in favour.

But what to call the new engine of war? 'Land Cruiser' gave the game away; besides, it was uncomfortably naval. So was 'Machine Gun Destroyer'. 'Noah's Ark' would not do at all. In a letter to General the Earl of Cavan telling him confidentially of the wondrous new device, Swinton had called it – the 'insect'. In one unfortunate pun he had referred to 'Armouredillos'.

'Slug' had its adherents, so did 'Juggernaut'. Neither seemed appropriate to morale-boosting military nomenclature. Swinton claimed in his memoirs that he had been instructed when drawing up his report to find some noncommittal word for the machine. In a discussion with his CID colleague, Lt-Col. W. Dally-Jones, they ran through possibilities – cistern, reservoir, water carrier, tank, receptacle: it was a big metal box after all. It was Albert Stern who got to it. Water carrier was no good, the initials you see. Smutty remarks would be inevitable. Water tank was better. 'Tank' was best of all. The Whitehall conference signed off its report with the words: 'Their provision should be the responsibility of a small executive committee, which for secrecy shall be called the Tank Supply Committee.'*

Fifty machines, a crew of ten each plus half as many again in reserve – the projected force would muster 750 men in total. It should be called, said the conference report: 'The Tank Detachment of the Machine Gun Corps.'

---

* In a postwar lecture tour of America John Charteris claimed the term originated in his intelligence department at GHQ where references to water tanks to drain the river Yser were switched to the new weapon. There is no documentary evidence for his claim.

15

As the committee met in London, Sir Douglas Haig was briskly taking over the levers of command at GHQ in France. There was a curious document in the departed Sir John French's confidential papers – some sort of strategic hocus-pocus from Col. Winston Churchill which talked of offensives being launched using 'caterpillars', a fleet of which had apparently already been constructed in England. In fact the prototype was only just complete and no production order had been given. Haig read it on Christmas Day 1915. (Churchill later claimed that he went to St Omer to give the document to the new C-in-C in person.)

The departed French – who had personally backed the machine-gun destroyer the summer before and had sent a representative to witness Centipede's debut at Wembley – had clearly not been minded to impart the secret to his loathed successor. Haig minuted in the margin: 'Is anything known about the caterpillar referred to in Para 4, page 3?'

Major Hugh Jamieson Elles, a thirty-six-year-old Royal Engineer, himself the son of a distinguished general, working as a staff officer on GHQ's operations branch, was ordered to find out. There was someone already in France who might help – the author of the paper himself. According to Churchill: 'I received instructions to go to one of the departments in St Omer and to explain matters to an officer whom I had not before met. I think it was a staff officer I have since learnt to know as General Elles. I was asked by him to explain what was the position on the manufacturing of these engines . . . he was sent over to England to obtain the very latest information for the army in the field.'

The intrepid Maj. Elles, armed with his GHQ *laissez-passer*, snooped round the jungles of Whitehall and made an excursion to Lincoln to find out what he could. He did very well. Within a week he personally delivered a pithy briefing paper, a photograph of Little Willie and a sketch of the prototype to Sir Douglas Haig in France.

'There are two producers of landships,' he wrote, 'Trench Warfare working alone and the Admiralty Landships Committee working with the War Office . . . in fact they work separately.'

He described the Trench Warfare Department's pedrail flame-thrower-carrier which 'would be ready in six weeks' – but clearly much more interesting was what the navy had been up to. 'The Admiralty has already built one ship [Little Willie] which was not accepted,' Maj. Elles reported. 'The second ship [Mother] will be ready for trial soon at Hatfield Park.' He had seen it himself, jacked up in the erecting shop at Wellington Foundry. 'A great many people have a finger in the pie,' he told Haig, 'and there had been a great deal of discussion and interest . . .'

Elles understood. This ingenious, primitive thing, still as yet a prototype, might work if employed as a weapon of shock and surprise before the enemy could find a counter – such as 'putting field guns in the front line,' as he noted. Secrecy, he told Haig, 'was essential'.

Of course it was. The device was meant to conquer machine guns, but its own vulnerability to some higher form of destructive countermeasure had been obvious to all from the beginning. It would become a guiding imperative as landships moved from fantasy to reality. They would have one chance. Once revealed to the enemy in battle, their utility would be over. A single leak from the factory or the recruitment depot and even that chance might be denied. Secrecy would be ramped up to the point of paranoia. As Stern noted: 'Everybody connected was sworn to secrecy. Anybody suspected of talking was threatened with internment under DORA. Ladies were sometimes found to have heard something about us and had to be visited and told it would cost thousands of lives if the secret reached the enemy. It was easy to stop all talk amongst those who knew of the start of our enterprise by informing them that our efforts had entirely failed and that we had lost our jobs, which they were only too ready to believe.'*

* Internal security was the responsibility of Military Operations Fifth Directorate (MO5), also known as the Special Intelligence Bureau, headed from April 1915 by Brig.-Gen. George Cockerill, a confidant of Swinton's and later Tory MP for Reigate. G Section of MO5 was directly responsible for counter-espionage, and its director was a former

Over Christmas and New Year the wooden Wilson had mutated into the mild steel prototype, animated by the same engine and drive train that had propelled Little Willie. Now it had Admiralty-supplied guns poking from the side sponsons that d'Eyncourt had devised. There are claims by contemporaries that it first moved under its own power as early as 3 December 1915, but its official debut was on 12 January 1916 when it successfully climbed over a series of obstacles in Foster's yard.

It was a 'tank' – the word had been coined – but enough naval tradition pertained to give it a personal name. For a little while, according to Swinton, it bore that of the wooden mock-up, HMLS Centipede. Then, out of someone's imagination, came a new coining. The super secret prototype was 'Mother'.

During the night of 19–20 January 1916, Mother was taken, sheathed in tarpaulins, to Burton Park, near Lincoln, where, the next morning, it again did all that was asked of it. A cameraman recorded the scene – grinning naval ratings, army officers in British Warms, a man on a white horse trailing behind, two ladies (unidentified) in big hats and fur tippets. One of the pictures featured Mother and a little white dog, a Staffordshire, belonging to Mr C. W. Pennel, the chairman of Foster's. He would feature in the orders given to the

---

Captain of the South Staffs, Vernon George Waldegrave Kell, and his deputy was an energetic Royal Engineer Major named Eric Holt-Wilson, who had drawn up the draft DORA regulations before the war.

It was a tight-knit group. When Kell left the Committee of Imperial Defence Historical Section in October 1909 to found the Home Section of the Secret Service Bureau (MO5(g) from April 1914, MI5(g) from January 1916), Swinton took his place. Swinton and Eric Holt-Wilson were good friends; both were sappers, and three of the stories in Swinton's 1915 book *The Great Tab Dope* (published under the pseudonym 'Ole Luk-Oie') were actually accounts of things that had happened to Holt-Wilson during the Boer War. Swinton's domestic security contacts were therefore exemplary.

After the Armistice, Cockerill publicly congratulated his staff for keeping what he described as the 'three great secrets of the war ... the evacuation of the Gallipoli peninsula, the construction of tanks, and the build-up before Cambrai'.

A special Ministry of Munitions Labour Intelligence department ('MMLI'; later renamed 'MPS2') was set up in February 1916 to monitor enemy-inspired sabotage, trade unionists and 'socialist' agitators – and screen aliens (mainly Belgian refugees) for work in war factories. Kell is known to have seconded a number of G-section agents to it. Swinton mentions personally going to Lincoln to investigate 'too much talk'. Stern in his memoirs mentions a spring 1916 scare about 'information leaking out from Birmingham, via twelve men and one woman who were working for a Swiss company at the Metropolitan Works who were closely watched. One of the men wished to return to Switzerland but was interned.'

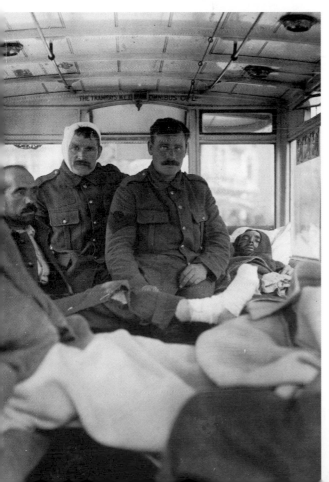

Above London buses of the Metropolitan Electric Tramways were sent across the Channel in October 1914 by the Admiralty in an attempt to save the Belgian port of Antwerp from capture. The First Lord, Winston Churchill, envisaged their being used to carry 'raiding parties' of marines to hit the enemy's flanks; instead, many of the Daimler-engined X-Types in their bright blue paint fell into German hands or were used (*left*) to evacuate wounded and weary naval infantry. The omnibus drama was a pioneering example of mechanised, mobile warfare. The first tanks would be called 'buses' by their crews.

US-made Holt caterpillar tractors were used by Austro-Hungarian artillerymen hauling siege mortars into Belgium in August 1914. A press picture inspired various individuals – including Churchill – with the idea that a tracked vehicle could solve the deepening 'riddle of the trenches'. The British War Office placed an urgent order for Holt gun-haulers, while the US Army would use them in Mexico (*above*).

Meanwhile the little extemporised force of naval armoured cars in Belgium had also been confounded by earth and wire. Here Rolls-Royce Admiralty-pattern armoured cars guard a Suffolk chemist from invasion in February 1915. Putting an armoured body on tracks was the next step. The Navy's 'landship' programme was born.

Landshipmen: Naval officers at the Barlby Road proving ground, West London, in summer 1915 take a break from the pioneering armoured warfare experiments, including (*far left*) Bertie Stern and (*far right*, in army uniform) the racing driver and aviator Thomas Hetherington, who had inspired Churchill over dinner with a proposal for a monstrous land battleship.

Experiments with an articulated machine using coupled tractors proved a dead-end. The venerable inventor, Col. R.E.B.Crompton (*right*, in army uniform, in this picture of late 1915), maintained that his concept was right all along and gave postwar testimony that the first 'tanks' that went into action in September 1916 were in fact an outright failure. The caterpillar enthusiasts meanwhile got on with it as best they could. Churchill (hidden by the barbed wire post) and David Lloyd George, Minister of Munitions, watch an American Killen-Strait tractor fitted with a torpedo wire-cutter showing off at Wormwood Scrubs, summer 1915.

Left William Tritton, the robust managing director of Fosters of Lincoln, poses with the Foster-Daimler tractor fitted with a bridge-laying device in early 1915. As a trench crosser it proved ineffective.

Much more practical was Walter Wilson's rhomboid-shaped machine with an all-round track (*below*), under inspection here by various officers and fur-muffled ladies in Burton Park, 20 January 1916.

Bottom Many of the work force who made the first tanks were female. Lincolnshire 'munitionettes' pose with a piratical flag at Fosters factory a little later in the war. Before the tank's first action there was much concern about 'leakages' and mysterious 'lady spies'.

Left By summer 1916 the first production tanks were ready for testing and training at Elveden in Suffolk, home of Earl Iveagh. Lt-Col. Ernest Swinton (pictured postwar) fought the Whitehall battle, while Lt-Col. John Brough (pictured here as a stalwart of the Army Staff College cricket team, Camberley, *c*.1907) prepared the unit for its combat debut in France. Dismissed on the eve of going into action on the Somme, Brough later shot himself.

No. **151**

PASS BEARER 2ᵈ Lt. J.G. Scott.

ELVEDEN EXPLOSIVES AREA.

Elveden was sealed off and villages around evacuated. It was codenamed the 'Explosives Area'(this pass, signed by Lt-Col. Brough, is preserved in the Swinton papers) and security was supposedly as tight as possible, although someone managed to take this picture (*below*) of D Company under the pines. Note the crossed Vickers cap badge of the Machine Gun Corps.

The ambitious Royal Engineer, Hugh Elles (pictured in early 1916), was General Sir Douglas Haig's tank expert at General HQ. When Lt-Col. Brough objected to the plans for the tanks' use, he was sacked. Elles raised no objections.

> Till the enemy know exactly what they hav[e] deal with they cannot arrange or prepare an antidot[e]
>
> We must therefore endeavour to keep them [a] mystery as long as possible.
>
> 13.   The really important question for decisio[n] therefore is how we can best do this.

Above The British C-in-C's plan was simple – 'throw them with determination into the fight regardless of cost', as this margin note in Haig's handwriting reveals.

Tanks went into action at dawn on 15 September 1916, but less than half of them got over the shelled battlefield to grapple with the enemy to any purpose. Lt Stuart Hastie's tank D.17 Dinnaken is pictured ditched outside Flers with infantry. A field telephonist sprawls on one of the tracks.

Nevertheless the action was hailed as a triumph by a primed Fleet Street. With strict photographic censorship in force, a multitude of bizarre artists' impressions appeared in magazines like *Punch*.

When Churchill was hailed in one newspaper as the 'Man who made the Tanks', Lord Northcliffe's *Daily Mail* countered with an attack on 'this self-advertising politician', praising instead 'Sir Douglas Haig and his brilliant staff'. Tank frenzy seized the nation.

The Somme 'experiment' over, new men arrived in late 1916 to propel the renamed Heavy Branch into further action. Hugh Elles (*third from left*) ran Tanks HQ at Bermicourt with a relaxed efficiency. His GSO1, 'Boney' Fuller (*far left*), took a brisker approach.

Above right Capt. 'Boots' Hotblack, the unit intelligence officer (shown here in a portrait by William Orpen), had a talent for snooping out the enemy's secrets. Meanwhile a major industrial complex called the 'Central Workshop' (*below*) sprang up in the Ternoise valley to tend the needs of the tanks. Much of the work would be done by Chinese labour.

first tank crews ever to go into battle. The dog's name is a mystery. Mother fired its 6-pounder guns. According to Stern: 'Major Hetherington fired the first shot. There was a misfire and while we were examining the breech the gun went off itself. No one knew where the shell [solid, armour-piercing and therefore not explosive] had gone. We feared the worst . . . Lincoln Cathedral was in danger, but after two hours spent with a spade the shell was found buried in the earth.'

Like the wooden mock-up, Mother would have to be demonstrated to its expectant sponsors. Wembley Park was too public.* Stern started looking for somewhere near London to which the bigwigs could travel with ease and where the great test could be conducted in secrecy. His eye alighted on a suitable place just north of the capital.

On the night of 25–26 January Mother made her ponderous way via the Great Northern Railway from Lincoln to Hatfield in Hertfordshire. The Fourth Marquis of Salisbury had patriotically provided his private golf course in Hatfield Park as a test range. The bunkers and greens had been transformed into a 'bogus field of battle', as Swinton described it, complete with shell craters and staged 'enemy trenches on the Loos pattern'. A stream was dammed to create a suitable bog.

The first 'private' run was on 29 January 1916 when the Foster's foreman tester Charles Maugham and the ratings of 20 Squadron RNAS took Mother round the frosty links for the benefit of the DNC Committee.

The first prototype had also been brought from Lincoln to Hatfield. According to Swinton, 'There were Mother and Little Willie, side by side, a gigantic canvas covered sow with a sucking pig alongside. On that day they became Little Willie and Big Willie.'

---

* Eyebrows had been raised when the Prime Minister and Lloyd George turned up at a flame-thrower demonstration at Wembley Park one evening in late September 1915. Mr Asquith brought Mrs Asquith – with their youngest son and a school friend. 'It was more appropriate to a fireworks party than a secret weapons trial,' according to one authority. 'Gen. Jackson was mortified. The equipment duly performed. This hiatus caused Mother tank's trials to be staged at Hatfield.' Nor could the ousted Churchill resist gossiping. Asquith wrote to Mrs Churchill: 'My dear Clementine . . . Please thank Winston for his letters . . . I have heard a great deal about the caterpillar, from those who have seen it . . . and we hope great things . . .'

Colonel Crompton, still sulking after his sacking, was charitably invited to attend the private view. He was not in the mood for levity. The 'slug', as he called Mother, was 'clearly too heavy to negotiate the canal bridges in France' (so he estimated by the simple empirical evidence of observing the crushed grass in her wake), the obsession which had inspired his doomed articulated machines. The dress rehearsal was a success. Mother's big day out came four days later. It would be codenamed Operation Puddleduck.

The morning of 2 February 1916 was bright and cold. Lord Kitchener arrived for his own private view. Mother's Daimler engine was cranked into life, the machine lurching round the mocked-up battlefield beneath Lord Salisbury's elms. Tritton recalled that he and the Secretary of State sat on a fallen tree – and that 'K' was unimpressed. He described it to the Foster's engineer as a 'pretty mechanical toy but without serious military value', a famous piece of phrase-making that has echoed ever since.*

Bertie Stern and Maurice Hankey gave Reginald McKenna (the Chancellor of the Exchequer) an agreeable lunch at the United Services Club before motoring smartly northwards in Stern's Rolls. More grandees were arriving – Lloyd George, Arthur Balfour – with the War Office chieftains close behind – Lt-Gen. Sir William 'Wully' Robertson, the newly appointed CIGS, his deputy, Gen. Robert 'Wigwam' Whigham, and Gen. Sir Stanley von Donop, Master General of the Ordnance, still sceptical, still grumbling.† But clever Ernest Swinton, the consummate office politician, had already warmed up opinion where it really mattered – 'France' – with the mission of Haig's emissary, a youngish sapper, clearly a coming man. 'Major Ellis [sic] has been home and seen everything there is to be seen at

---

* The 'Tank invention' claims that so incensed H. G. Wells in 1941 rumbled on for years after the end of the Great War. In 1925 a certain Capt. Bede Bentley demanded £300,000 from HMG, claiming he had been contracted to build an armoured, gun-armed B-Type bus by Lord Kitchener in 1914 but had been sworn to secrecy. He had thus 'invented the tank'. All the wartime caterpillar luminaries were hauled back to the High Court to give testimony that the claim was nonsense. Sir William Tritton testified that 'Lord Kitchener arrived [at Hatfield] at 10.00 a.m. and had an early trial all to himself . . . they both sat on a tree and discussed the matter. He remembered that Lord Kitchener made use of the phrase "it is a pretty mechanical toy" and he did not stay for the official trial.'

† He backed the wrong horse. Tainted by the 'shell scandal,' soon afterwards von Donop was sent off into obscurity to command the Humber garrison.

present and knows all about the present condition of the menageries,' Swinton told a confidant at GHQ on the eve of the Hatfield trial.

General R. H. K. Butler, Haig's Deputy Chief of General Staff,* had arrived from France to represent GHQ – along with two front-line infantry corps commanders, Brigadier-Generals Charles Corkran and A. J. Reddie – there to make operational judgements for the C-in-C. They would turn out to be the most important first-night critics of all. The members of the Tank Supply Committee, by now veterans of such performances, awaited the judgement of their distin-guished audience.

The afternoon performance began. In Swinton's words, 'it was a striking scene when the signal was given and a species of gigantic cubist steel slug slid out of its lair and proceeded to rear its grey bulk over the bright yellow clay of the enemy parapet . . .'

Robertson seemed impressed by the sight of Mother crossing a nine-foot trench. Arthur Balfour was taken for a ride, coming out of the entry hatch feet first before Mother took the widest trench. Commodore Murray Sueter found himself in trouble for saying out loud 'we should order three thousand at once'. 'Who is this damned naval man?' a testy brass hat had responded.

General Butler asked Stern quietly: 'How soon can we have them?'

Kitchener left the afternoon session halfway through with Robertson and Whigham, looking distinctly gloomy. Colonel Cromp-ton picked up the mood a week after the Hatfield trial when he gleefully recorded the latest Whitehall gossip in his diary: 'Kitchener objected to it as too great target and too slow.'

But Richard Butler gave the Official Historian a different version eighteen years after the event:

> On the night of the secret trial at Hatfield, Lord Kitchener took
> me to dine with him at St James's Palace. We discussed the
> whole problem of tanks. LK gave me the impression that very
> little would make him turn the whole thing down. He took the
> line that he [had to] be assured and convinced that we in France

---

* General Richard Harte Keatinge Butler, b. 1870, an Old Harrovian career soldier, friend and confidant of Haig's since the 1900s. In the post-French purge at the end of 1915, Haig had wanted to make him Chief of General Staff at GHQ but Butler was judged 'too young'. Butler was intensely protective of his chief. His 1935 *Times* obituary described him as 'a barrier to Army commanders in their intercourse with the C-in-C'.

really wanted anything of the kind, that the machine he had seen that day really met our requirements, that the cost in money and material [was worth it].

After two hours LK agreed definitely for manufacture to be proceeded with and wrote an order for six – and to tell the chief of the project.

It was moreover decided not to give out anything that would lead the enemy to think that the trial had been a success and rather imply the contrary.

In the matter of tanks disinformation was all.

On 8 February a third demonstration at Hatfield was arranged so that King George V could see what the fuss was about. Swinton accompanied him on the carborne journey from Buckingham Palace. The sovereign seemed buoyed up by the general euphoria, noting in his diary, 'I saw the Caterpillar which is an armoured motor with guns which goes over trenches and through wire and with which we hope to attack the Germans. I hope we shall have a 100 of them.' Swinton had clearly breathed in his ear as the royal Daimler headed for Hatfield. Kitchener thought six might suffice. One hundred was much more like it.

As d'Eyncourt told his former Admiralty chief Colonel W. S. Churchill, now Officer Commanding 6th Scots Fusiliers at Ploegs-teert, a week later:

> The King came a day or 2 ago and saw it and was greatly struck by its performance as was everyone else . . . wire entanglements it goes through like a rhinoceros through a field of corn.
>
> It carries two 6-pdr guns in sponsons (a naval touch).
>
> I enclose photo. In appearance, it looks like an antediluvian monster especially when it comes out of boggy ground which it traverses well and I hope it will scare the Boche. The wheels behind form a rudder for steering a course and also absorb the shock over banks, but are not absolutely necessary as it can steer and turn in its own length with the independent tracks.
>
> After losing the great advantage of your influence I had some difficulty in steering the scheme past the rocks of oppo-sition, and the shoals of apathy which are frequented by red herrings which cross the main line of progress at several intervals.
>
> The great thing now is to keep the whole matter secret and produce the machines all together as a great surprise. I have

already put the manufacture in hand under the aegis of the Minister of Munitions . . .

And d'Eyncourt had indeed done so. It had all happened with remarkable speed. Kitchener may have appeared dismissive but the key was Haig. The C-in-C in France was already alert to the potential of the machine revealed on Lord Salisbury's golf course. He seemed to know all about it. Major Hugh Elles's 'many fingers in the pie' report in January would have whetted his appetite for backstairs intrigue.

The day of the royal demonstration, Brig.-Gen. Reddie had reported approvingly to his chief, but he specially warned that the enemy might develop a counter *once the secret was revealed*. 'Even if 50% were knocked out I consider their employment justifiable,' he wrote. That figure would prove no deterrent. The C-in-C had told the War Office in a handwritten letter dated the next day: 'The officers who represented me at the trials lead me to the conclusion that these "Tanks" can be usefully employed in offensive operations by the force under my command. It is understood that thirty to forty would be available by May.

'I recommend that this number should be ordered at once . . . and would be glad to be informed what number might be supplied by the middle of July . . . secrecy is of the highest importance . . .'

In the words of an eminent biographer: 'Haig began, from that moment, to count them among the resources at his disposal for the great battle.' Three days later, after a meeting of the War Council, Lloyd George, the Minister of Munitions, had authorized the construction of 100 machines. It was the Army Council, after Haig's nod of approval, which gave the formal order. Kitchener, its nominal chairman, was barely consulted. Production was to be overseen by the provisional Tank Supply Committee under Stern's chairmanship, answerable to the Ministry. Contracts were drafted – to Foster's in Lincoln and to the industrially much more muscular Metropolitan Carriage, Wagon and Finance Co. of Wednesbury, Birmingham.

It was also agreed that d'Eyncourt would continue as chief technical adviser with a brief to continue development of new and improved armoured fighting machines. That night the Director of Naval Construction wrote his triumphant letter to Churchill. The shoals of apathy had been navigated. Tanks were being made – one hundred of them – a fleet in being.

Who would man them? Who would command the strange new arm – a cavalryman, a gunner, an engineer? It was not going to be a sailor. On 14 February the forty-six-year-old Ernest Swinton learned that it would be him. 'I happened to meet General Bird, Director of Staff Duties, in a corridor at the War Office,' he recalled. 'To my astonishment he informed me that the Army Council had selected me to raise and command the Tank Detachment . . . I was to be in charge of it at home, while in France it was to be under the local commanders.'

In his 'I recommend' letter of 9 February, Haig had not just been playing with abstract dates. A grand Allied conference had been held at Chantilly, outside Paris, in early December 1915 and agreed on a simultaneous general offensive in the summer of the year to come, when the Russians were 'stronger' and Britain's New Armies trained and equipped. The army already in France was bigger than anything the nation had ever put into the field before, but it was still not nearly big enough. At the end of January 1916 conscription was introduced.

There was a brief flurry of try-another-way-round sentiment in the War Cabinet, expeditions to the Balkans, to the Middle East – Balfour proposed sending a British field army to Russia – but after the Gallipoli fiasco (the blighted peninsula had finally been evacuated in the first week of January) the generals in France would not have it. The 'military Moloch' (Lloyd George's phrase) of the Western Front prevailed. The French C-in-C, General Joseph Joffre, and Haig met again to discuss how to evict the invader. On 14 February they agreed it should be a joint offensive mounted 'arm-in-arm' that summer astride the river Somme. Both men had intimations of a novel weapon that might in some degree contribute.*

Swinton got down to work. The Officer Commanding Tank Detachment set up in the cockpit of bureaucratic action, Whitehall,

---

* On 12 December 1915 the fifty-six-year-old artilleryman Col. Jean-Baptiste Eugène Estienne had presented GQG with a plan to form an armoured force equipped with tracked vehicles, *chars d'assaut*, based on the Schneider-Holt prototype that he had seen demonstrated the week before. The plan was approved and a production order for 400 machines made on 25 February 1916.

inhabiting Room 337 on the fifth floor of 'Armament Buildings', otherwise the Hotel Metropole commandeered as offices by the Ministry of Munitions. Letterheads and message forms were printed, with the telegraphic address 'TANKORGIZE'. 'Half a stenographer and an orderly room sergeant', as Swinton described his staff, would provide support for the bruising trial by memorandum and rubber stamp to come.

Lieutenant-Colonel Robert Bradley, commandant of the Motor Machine Gun Service Training Centre in genteel Bisley, would be his second in command. There was an immediate question. How were these novel fighting machines to be used in battle? Swinton very quickly produced a briefing document, 'Notes on the Employment of Tanks'. It was dated 16 February. A key section read:

> Impossibility of Repeated Employment: Since the chance of success of an attack by tanks lies almost entirely in its novelty and in the element of surprise, it is obvious that no repetition of it will have the same opportunity of succeeding as the first unexpected effort. It follows, therefore, that *these machines should not be used in driblets** (for instance, as they may be produced), but the fact of their existence should be kept as secret as possible until the whole are ready to be launched, together with the infantry assault in one great combined operation.

He foresaw an offensive being launched on a five-mile front with ninety vehicles in an extended line abreast, but made no provision for a reserve. Night operations were ruled out but an attack launched just before dawn was judged ideal. 'Strong bodies of bombers [hand grenades] would be required to attend the tanks and deal with deep dug-outs.'

'A tank will carry enough petrol for a sixty mile run [a great overestimate] and an advance of 12 miles is therefore well within its capabilities,' he wrote. 'Thus our troops might expect to get right through the German defensive zone in one operation and preparations to send forward reinforcements . . . should be made accordingly.'

The Western Front was still congealed by winter. The French army's Operations Branch busied themselves with preliminary planning for the great punch to come that summer on the Somme,

---

* Swinton's own emphasis.

discounting fractious intelligence reports of a German build-up oppo-site the complex of fortifications around Verdun on France's eastern frontier. But an offensive *was* coming – terrifying in its power and its strategic intent – which was not to break through the defence and return to a war of manoeuvre but to destroy the counter-attacking French armies in a set-piece battle of attrition, to 'bleed them to death' in the infamous words of the chief of staff, Erich von Falken-hayn. In the blighted spring to follow the German plan would show every sign of succeeding. The opening of the attack had been fixed for 12 February, delayed by snowstorms until the 21st. It began with a fearsome bombardment achieving complete tactical and strategic surprise.

French losses mounted in hecatombs of casualties. A 'relief' offen-sive would become ever more urgent – but its main weight would now have to be borne by the British – by the ever expanding New Army divisions scarcely yet trained as fighting soldiers. The question was when. 'The moment I mentioned August 15th,' Haig wrote in his diary, 'Joffre at once got very excited and shouted that the French Army would cease to exist by then.' The clock was ticking. It would be June–July. 'Tanks' might even be ready by then.

16

Tanks were being built – a hundred of them. Who might take them to war? Lieutenant-Colonel Robert Bradley's Bisley-based motorcyclist machine-gunners provided a nucleus of technically competent officers and men – 'of superior education having motor or mechanical engineering experience'. The naval armoured car veterans were just as competent and some had seen fighting – but there were not enough of them.

An establishment of at least 150 officers and a thousand other ranks would have to be raised and done so in secret. The mania for bluff and disinformation was unabated. No one must know just what it was they were volunteering for. At the end of February the name 'Tank Detachment' was judged to be too cryptic (recruits were bound to ask the obvious questions – what's a tank?). The shadowy outfit was now renamed 'Machine Gun Corps (Motors)'. The Adjutant-General's department was asked to 'select and warn personally, good fighting subalterns of resource and courage – conversant with motor cars or motor cycles'.

Swinton set out to find them for himself. Cadet battalions and home-based units were discreetly canvassed for suitable candidates. He went to Oxford and Cambridge to trawl for talent in the manner of a latter-day spymaster. The colonel resorted to the kind of mystery-cloaked derring-do more familiar from boys' adventure stories or inducements to join polar expeditions.

In the spring of 1916 Victor Huffam was a company commander of the 3rd Battalion the Norfolk Regiment resting at Felixstowe. But instead of returning with the grizzled veterans to the front line, he was 'summoned to the Adjutant's office', as he recalled, to be shown a cryptic printed announcement. It read:

WAR OFFICE
Strictly secret and confidential

Volunteers are required for an exceedingly dangerous and haz-
ardous duty of a secret nature. Officers who have decorations
for bravery and are experienced in the handling of men and
with an engineering background, should have their names submitted to this office and suitable officers will be required to
attend Wellington barracks at a date which will be specified
later.

Second Lieutenant Huffam was enticed. He was soon in London
– 'in company with three hundred other lieutenants, volunteers from
every unit in the British Isles to meet [Col.] Swinton . . . who warned
us we had volunteered for a very dangerous mission . . . then we
were told that only 28 were required, the others probably later.
I was one of the 28.' Swinton's methods seemed to work. On
another account: 'Of the subaltern officers probably seventy-five per
cent represented as good material as could be found anywhere – a
high proportion in view of the extraordinary and haphazard pro-
cesses by which the commissioned ranks of the New Armies were
filled.'

To find other ranks and NCOs, equally baroque measures were
adopted. *The Motor Cycle* magazine ran a weekly 'recruiting section'
calling for men who could drive 'light cars'. The editor, Mr Geoffrey
Smith, once again offered his Coventry offices at No. 19 Hertford
Street as a recruiting depot, personally touring the country to screen
a stream of eager applicants. The magazine printed the names of
those who had been successful throughout the spring and summer
– plus jolly items about the spruceness of the kitchens, sporting
opportunities ('several professional footballers have joined the
ranks') and the picturesqueness of their Surrey surroundings. A
watchful intelligence officer in Berlin might have been intrigued
by some of the weekly journal's pronouncements. For example, on
25 May 1916 it was announced: 'The Armoured Car Section of the
MGC is now popularly referred to in the camps as the "Hush-hush
section" . . . The Heavy Section, the recruits for which have passed
through the editor's hands for some weeks past, has now been gazetted. Lt-Col. R. W. Bradley, DSO, formerly commanding the Motor
Machine Gun Service has moved over . . .' It was all terribly amateur,

but it seemed to work. If the Germans had a subscription to *The Motor Cycle*, they failed to spot the significance of what was being brought together in its name.

The ratings of 20 Squadron RNAS, the transport and experimental establishment, might have seemed a likely source of recruits, – but when Swinton went to address them at Wembley Park not one volunteered. The colonel was not surprised. Navy pay as petty officer mechanic was three times higher. Sometimes a more direct approach worked. Private Phillip Page, a sapper, recalled many years later suddenly being mustered on the parade ground at the Royal Engineers' depot at Chatham. 'This officer, don't know who he was . . . red tabs all over . . . he came in and said "fall out all plumbers, fall out all gas fitters" . . . why they picked on us like that I don't know. Anyway I wasn't sorry.'

Preparations for the great offensive ground forward. In March, in a burdensome reshuffle of men and logistics, the British Army took over the French sector of front stretching twenty miles from Arras to Maricourt, just north of the river Somme that flowed west–east, and formed the new Fourth Army to man it. The rolling chalkland seemed, according to its commander, Gen. Sir Henry Rawlinson, 'capital country in which to undertake an offensive, once we get a sufficiency of artillery'.

He looked set to get it. In comparison with the shortages experienced the year before, the flow of guns and ammunition to France now seemed astonishing (in fact the biggest warlike store by bulk crossing the Channel and clogging up the railways was horse fodder – and would remain so until the end of the war).

The new 'instantaneous' Mk 106 artillery fuse promised much. By not burrowing into the soil before detonating it allowed howitzer-fired high explosive to be used to cut wire in addition to shrapnel. In fact it was more efficient at it and it did not produce craters – the blast went sideways rather than down and up. It was first tested successfully in March 1916.

But no miraculous fuses would have been series-manufactured by the time the offensive opened, and just a handful of Mark I tanks would have been constructed let alone their crews trained by the date now fixed as 1 July. Swinton and his little band of enthusiasts had sold the concept too well. The great offensive was coming. Like the half-trained men of the New Armies, everything must be staked on its success. The urgency of the French position demanded it.

Haig's interest in tanks was deepening. On 23 March he reviewed the report of his second personal representative at Hatfield, Brig.-Gen. Charles Corkran, commander of 3rd Guards Brigade. 'They can be looked on as a means of destroying enemy wire, emplacements, trenches etc and of killing as many men as possible,' he noted starkly. 'It seems appropriate that each one is commanded by an officer.'

The first written reference to the new engine of war in the C-in-C's diary came on 5 April, a proposal for 'making use of our new "tanks"' to capture a strip of high ground 'west of Serre' and use them as *'points d'appui* to hold it while it is being entrenched'.

On 7 April Haig told the VIII Corps commander, Lt-Gen. Sir A. Hunter-Weston, 'that I hope to use "tanks" and that we must be fully prepared to take advantage of the surprise and demoralizing effect which seem likely to produce [sic] the first time they are used'.

That same day he requested that a further fifty tanks be added to the initial order of a hundred. The War Office and Tank Supply Committee readily concurred. Two additional companies would have to be raised to man them, making a total of six, each comprising four sections of six tanks with one spare – 150 machines in total. Each company had a nominal strength of twenty-eight officers and 300 men.

There was also a major production engineering decision. Half the vehicles ordered would be completed armed with 6-pounder shell-firing guns. The others would be completed with redesigned side sponsons, each mounting a pair of water-cooled Vickers machine guns in line with Brig.-Gen. Corkran's laudatory view after Mother's Hatfield trial of a 'tank' as a device to 'kill as many men as possible'. At Loos, poison gas had not proved equal to the task of extermination.

The unit's name changed yet again. From the beginning of April it now announced itself as the 'Special Armoured Car Section, Motor Machine Gun Service'.* It was all most unmilitary. Who were they supposed to be under in matters of pay and discipline? A general official complained: 'Orders are given to the MMGS by

---

* A document of late March calls it the Machine Gun Corps 'S' Detachment. On 1 May it became the 'Heavy Section Machine Gun Corps', the name under which it would go to war four months later.

"tank" officers. Regimental funds for the former are used by the latter. Altogether it's entirely chaotic. London is full of officers reporting for duty with – I presume "tanks." We do not know who wants them, where to send them or what to tell them. Secrecy is alright but not when it goes to the point of making muddles and wasting time.'

By the middle of the month the Special Armoured Car Section had its six company commanders, Maj. C. M. Tippetts, Maj. T. R. McLellan, Maj. Allen Holford-Walker, an Argyll and Sutherland Highlander, who had been badly wounded and transferred to the Motor Machine Gun Service, Maj. Frank Summers, an RNAS veteran of Gallipoli, Maj. N. H. Nutt, also late of the RNAS, and Capt. W. F. R. Kyngdon, a gunner. To extinguish any lingering naval sentiment, Albert Stern and Walter Wilson were commissioned as majors in the Machine Guns Corps.

Swinton had War Office sanction to recruit a second immediate subordinate. 'In addition to the regular [officers] furnished by the MMGS, I succeeded with difficulty in securing one or two more,' he recalled in his memoirs, 'among them being Lt-Col John Brough of the Royal Marine Artillery . . . Brough was a staff college graduate which fact nearly prevented my getting him.'

It was a curious choice. Brough was forty-four, a graduate of both the Royal Naval College, Greenwich (where he had made a special study of fortification) and the august establishment at Camberley that trained senior British Army officers, plus a smattering of sailors. Since the Boer War it had been a driving force of the new professionalism. Brough was a stalwart of its cricket team. He had been gunnery officer on the battleships HMS *Nile*, *Ramillies* and *Dominion* and in 1903–07 a 'company commander of Gentlemen Cadets' at the Royal Military College, Sandhurst. This service hopping was unusual; in a collection of jealously warring tribes that especially marked the British Army, it was not a primrose path to promotion. Brough had briefly been a War Office bureaucrat, thence an officer in the deeply unfashionable West African Frontier Force. On 31 August 1914 he had departed Liverpool aboard the Smith Elder steamer SS *Appam* heading for the Cameroons in West Africa as GSO2 on the staff of Lt-Gen. Sir C. M. Dobell in command of the Colonial Office-sponsored expedition to conquer the German colony of 'Kamerun'.

After over a year of pursuing the enemy through steaming swamp and jungle, aided by a single Rolls-Royce armoured car, the campaign ended in February 1916 when the last German defenders crossed into Spanish Rio Muni with four machine guns and 6000 still loyal native troops. Brough had returned to London as a colonel, with a mention in dispatches, a DSO and a case of fever. He had never been anywhere near the Western Front. The Navy List notes him 'Lent to Army, Temp Lt-Col, 3 June 1916.'

Swinton told Butler cheerily a few days later, 'I propose sending over to you Lt-Col Brough. He was to have been a battalion commander but is now assisting me as a sort of staff officer . . . I am too tied up to come over myself but Brough is PSC, knows all that we are doing and is quite capable of getting your views on the different points on which we want information.' If Brough thought GHQ would be forthcoming on any scrap of military intelligence whatsoever, he was in for a rude awakening.

The clock was ticking. In mid-April Haig was in London to progress plans for the summer offensive. On the 14th he held a meeting at the War Office with Generals Butler and Whigham; tanks were on the agenda. Haig wrote in his diary that night: 'I next saw Colonel Swinton . . . regarding the "tanks." I was told that 150 would be provided by the 31st July. I said that was too late – 50 were urgently required for 1st June. Swinton is to see what can be done . . . I impressed on him the necessity of thinking over the system of leadership and control of a group of "tanks" with a view to manoeuvring into a position of readiness and during an action . . . After lunch I went out shopping with Doris.'*

In a letter to Butler at GHQ dated twelve days later Swinton promised to deliver seventy-five tanks plus crews by 1 August – 'strikes and acts of God permitting'. He had already told Maurice Hankey, however, of his concerns that 'France' might just take him at his word and throw whatever 'tanks' might be ready into the offensive that everyone knew was looming. As Swinton could have predicted, Hankey turned to Haig's boss, the CIGS, 'Wully' Robertson. The War Cabinet Secretary wrote:

* Lady Haig.

My dear General

I very rarely offer a suggestion on purely military questions ... I only depart from my rule in this case because my suggestion concerns matters with which I have lately been very closely connected.

Briefly my suggestion is that Sir Douglas Haig should be asked to do all in his power to avoid being committed to anything in the nature of a decisive infantry attack until the caterpillar machine gun destroyers are ready ... and to put all possible pressure on [Marshal] Joffre to do likewise.

A very large sum of money has been spent on them and a great number have been ordered ... if only a few weeks before they were ready, we had lost a very large number of infantry ... in an attack unproductive of material results, it would be most unfortunate. It might even happen that in the few weeks immediately preceding the arrival of the 'caterpillars' our army might have become so exhausted that no attack could be carried out for some weeks or months, by which time all prospect of their employment as a surprise would have been lost ...

But 'France' would admit no back-sliding. Hankey thought that 'this new weapon [with] the element of suprise, may just turn the scale', and so clearly did Haig.

His Chief of Staff, Gen. Sir Lancelot Kiggell, saw Swinton in London at the end of May to keep up the pressure. In a table drawn up afterwards listing resources available for the coming battle – men, guns, trench mortars, gas – Kiggell noted: ' "Tanks" 1st Aug. 150 ... of which only some may have been delivered in France, and only half the crew trained.'

The C-in-C was banging the drum. He wanted as many tanks as possible as soon as possible. Two confidants at GHQ, the Deputy Chief of General Staff Maj.-Gen. Richard Butler and Brig.-Gen. John 'Jock' Burnett-Stuart (who would prove wittily acerbic in the matter of tanks), were briefed to ensure the urgent attendance of Swinton's men on the battlefield. In London, Gen. Robert Whigham, the Deputy CIGS, and Gen. Wilkinson Bird, the Director of Staff Duties, were briefed to keep a close eye on the colonel and his deepening eccentricities.

Ernest Swinton was about to lose a powerful protector in London. On 5 June Kitchener boarded the cruiser HMS *Hampshire* en route for Russia. The warship struck a mine off the Orkneys and was lost with all hands. After a month of manoeuvring, Lloyd George became Secretary of State for War.

Volunteers for the Special Armoured Car Section kept arriving, led to the door of the mysterious outfit in Surrey by all sorts of arcane means. Lieutenant Henry Groves, for example, a machine-gun officer in the Scottish Rifles, had a 'friend who had just joined a hush-hush unit'. 'I wrote and asked him how I could apply. About a week later, a War Office letter arrived ordering me to report to . . . Bisley. I arrived on the 15 April. I was accepted after interview by Col Tippetts . . . [who told me] it was all secret, but that plenty of adventure was guaranteed.'

Basil Henriques described a preliminary interrogation with Swinton in London.

'Do you know anything about motor cars?'
'Absolutely nothing.'
'What machine-guns can you use?'
I mentioned one, having just returned from a course in musketry.
'That's the only one we don't use. Do you know the Lewis?
The reply was in the negative.

Henriques left the encounter 'more mystified than ever'. He too was directed towards Bisley where Maj. Allen Holford-Walker told him he 'would have to drive an armoured caterpillar which could go through and over anything and knock down trees'.

But there was no sight of any armoured caterpillars – not even of 'light cars'; indeed, there was no official explanation of what they were expected to do. All there was at first was square bashing. But soon there was training on Vickers machine guns conducted at the Siberia range, so-called because it was at the far eastern end of the Bisley site. Victor Huffam recalled encountering 'a sponson with machine-guns stuck on a sandy rifle range, a steel protrusion with room for two Vickers guns . . . We still hadn't seen a tank.'

It was all a bit of a joke. According to one account of the training at Bisley published soon after the war, 'It would be absurd to pretend that any of this was taken very seriously . . .'

Heavier ordnance was on its way. Two 6-pounder guns dis-mounted from Mother (which had been returned to Lincoln as a pilot engineering model) arrived in late March. Swinton reported at the time: 'We fired ninety-seven rounds in one day but six of these ricocheted almost at right angles into the Chobham Hills. Luckily no damage was done but the War Office has refused to allow us to continue firing at Bisley.'

A move soon afterwards to a new location, Bullhouse Farm, a few miles away, brought little extra room for live firing among the otherwise tranquil borders of Surrey and Hampshire. It would serve for now, at least until the first real live tanks arrived. Just when that would be was a matter for conjecture.

17

Ernest Thwaites was one of the last arrivals at Bullhouse Farm. He recalled embarking on the 'great adventure of my life', enlisting in early June 1916 as a private at the age of thirty-seven when he read the advertisements in *The Motor Cycle* 'recruiting for the Motor Machine Gun Corps'. He sought out the editor, Mr Smith, who steered him in the direction of Bisley. There was no mention of tanks, just a warning to beware of recruiting sergeants who would eagerly snap him up for the infantry. He avoided that all too common trap.

Arriving late in the evening, Thwaites was informed by an orderly that the 'MMGS was full-up' and sent to a strange sounding outfit based a little way away at Bullhouse Farm. He got there in darkness. 'I found the orderly room situated on an upper floor in the farmhouse . . . the NCO in charge treated me to finest flow of sanguinary language I ever found,' Thwaites recalled four years later. 'Did I think they worked all ***** night as well as all ***** day?'

He spent an uncomfortable night in a bed-bug-infested bunk before being enrolled next morning on the 'roster of F Coy HSMGC'. There followed plenty of drilling and rigorous training on the Vickers but no intimation as to why. The only recreation was the occasional boozy night-time visit to Woking (a lively establishment called the Croft figures in several memoirs), dodging the military police to get back to the camp at Bullhouse Farm.

Discipline was getting patchy. Confusion and resentment grew. Swinton had to tell them something – the officers, at least. On Sunday 28 May: 'We all met after luncheon in a small orchard outside the mess at Bull House,' he recalled. 'Everyone sat on the ground, pipe in mouth, under the cherry trees in full blossom. After a warning as to the secrecy of what I was about to say, I explained the whole scheme and object of the Tank and read them my printed memorandum.'

It was the colonel's essay of February, 'Notes on the Employment of Tanks', which spoke of a mass attack by ninety machines, of breaking right through the enemy front. For the months to come it would be the only guideline as to what they were expected to do. Much confusion would be the result.

'The stress I laid on the fact that the Heavy Section was being created to save the lives of the infantry,' Swinton continued, 'naturally aroused special interest among those who as infantry had already experienced the enemy machine guns.'

Real tanks were on their way from the factories. Something much bigger than the Siberia range was needed in which to experiment and train, somewhere remote from prying eyes, grumbling farmers and suburban pub gossip.

Major M. O'C. Tandy, a resourceful Royal Engineer, late of the Survey of India, was in England convalescing from wounds when he was recruited by Swinton to find somewhere suitable. The New Forest and Salisbury Plain were scouted out and judged not to be suitable. The mapping section of the War Office advised him to try the 'big shoot country of Norfolk and Suffolk', the arcadian pleasure ground of dukes and earls which for half a century past had hosted the grandest shooting parties in Europe.

In early April Swinton received a telegram from the major telling him that he had found the ideal place, fifteen square miles of arable heath and woodland – remote enough from prying eyes for the secret to be kept – given suitable precautions. It was sparsely populated, although 'there are a few inhabitants who will have to be removed'. A main-line railway ran close by, readily adaptable to the needs of moving ponderous secret weapons from the factories in Birmingham and Lincoln. It was also close enough to London to prevent its inhabitants from going completely native. According to Swinton, inviting a general to attend a demonstration later that summer: 'You can depart the United Services Club at 9:30 and motor up to the Area by lunchtime.'

Straddling the main road to Norwich, five miles south-west of the town of Thetford in Norfolk, was Elveden Hall, home of Lord Iveagh, the Anglo-Irish brewing magnate. He had acquired it at a bargain price in 1892 from the India Office, after its previous inhabitant, the Maharajah Duleep Singh, last king of the Punjab, had abjured his government pension and run off to St Petersburg to offer his services to the Tsar heading an invasion of British India by Imperial Russia in alliance with Irish-Americans.*

Lord Iveagh had subsequently extended the house, maintaining the oriental taste, inside at least, in a strange hotchpotch of Hindu ornament and Edwardian baroque. There were modern stables and motor houses, and half-timbered estate workers' almshouses in the nearby village, tenanted farms with barns and outbuildings, open heaths and concealing broadleaf woods†.

Swinton, on his account, went to the Lands Branch of the War Office, where a temporary official, Mr Jonas of the patrician estate agents, 'did the deal at remarkable speed'. Lord Iveagh was telephoned. 'He was not pleased but he accepted the situation with good grace. His view was that if anyone's shoot had to be spoilt, it might as well be his.'

The military moved in, armed with all the arbitrary powers of the Defence of the Realm (Lands Acquisition) Act 1916. The population was decanted, tenant farms evacuated, Elveden school shut down, old retainers evicted from their almshouses to make way for brisk lieutenants with typewriters and message pads. The long straight public road from Mildenhall to Thetford, 'the Turnpike', running through the estate, was shuttered at each end by two lines of guards – 'the first group challenged and if no result the second fired without warning'.

The whole perimeter was sealed with wire and dotted with guard posts manned by men of the Royal Defence Corps,‡ white-mustachioed veterans of Spion Kop and Omdurman billeted in outlying villages. Joseph Turner, an under gamekeeper at Elveden, remembered taking 'a jug of cocoa to them each morning. His older brother Arthur would later join the Heavy Section. Cavalry patrolled the forest paths. An inner ring guarded by regular soldiers known simply as the 'Area' was established.

Bernersfield Farm, south-west of the Hall, became both C Company headquarters and the Heavy Section's HQ. Canada Farm, a

---

* See this author's *The Maharajah's Box* (HarperCollins, 2000).

† The mass planting of conifers which characterize Elveden began in the early 1930s.

‡ A kind of Home Guard. They wore red arm bands emblazoned 'GR' and were known as 'Gorgeous Wrecks'.

quarter of a mile to its north, became D Company's HQ. A tented encampment sprouted around New Farm near the Bury St Edmunds–
Elveden road. Each camp, each company, was kept in its own state
of secretive isolation.

The Iveaghs stayed in the big house with a reduced staff, although,
according to Swinton, the earl was 'not informed of the purpose for
which his land had been seized'. His bafflement would deepen.

The stable block of Elveden Hall was adopted as the officers' mess
with a steward, former head butler at the Senior Army and Navy
Club, a man 'renowned for his cocktails'. A closely guarded depot
was established at Barnham station on the Great Eastern Railway's
Thetford–Bury St Edmunds line that clipped the eastern edge of the
estate where the little Army Service Corps detachment would indeed
be the first men in tanks. Driver Robert Parker recalled many years
later:

> At Barnham siding there were some tents . . . and a big shed.
> Lord Iveagh had started a tobacco-growing experiment and
> there was a big shed for tobacco drying and we used it as a
> mess.
>
> The people who'd been handling them for a few days before
> we got there, they taught us . . .
>
> We had a willy cover – a tank cover – strung on a long line
> between two trees and a six-foot barrack room table and two
> six-foot forms, that's where we lived . . . It was a hundred pound
> fine or six months' imprisonment if we disclosed what we were
> on . . .

The depot was supplanted in early July by a specially built spur
terminating near Culford Lodge Farm in the twin-tracked 'Government Siding' with a central loading ramp for whatever it was that
was coming in such secrecy.

A Royal Engineer officer, Capt. Giffard Le Quesne Martel, with
experience of front-line trench warfare arrived with a brief to re-
create an 'authentic' one-and-a-half-mile-wide slice of front line.
Three battalions of Pioneers (former Welsh miners with a propensity,
according to Swinton, 'for singing') laboured under his direction to
construct the replica – British support and front line – shell-pocked
'no-man's-land' with craters blown out with explosives – the enemy
first, support, second and third lines, complete with wire entanglements,

dugouts, even signs in German. The whole thing was carefully modelled, on the 'Loos pattern'.

Censorship was total, leave passes impossible to obtain. One telephone line, 'Thetford 37', connected the CO's office with the outside world. 'The Elveden Explosives Area', the cover name for the world's first tank proving range, would be for a time the most secret place in England.

Second Lieutenant Clough Williams-Ellis (the future distinguished architect), an early arrival, found himself in a camp 'more ringed about than was the palace of the Sleeping Beauty'. There were local rumours that a tunnel was being dug under the sea to Germany, so great were the evident movements of earth and sand. When an innocent aircraft flew overhead it was 'greeted with a hail of machine-gun bullets', although Royal Flying Corps officers from Thetford aerodrome seem to have been welcome guests at the mess.

More and more men were coming in each day as Bisley and Bullhouse farm were evacuated, trooping down the road the seven miles from Thetford Bridge station. Second Lieutenant Huffam recalled arriving at Canada Farm 'through a little white gate up a lane'. 'But as we marched in we were surprised to see cavalry, Indian units and elderly soldiers . . . at varying perimeters from the farmhouse and buildings. We were told there were three perimeters around us. Not only could we not get out, no one could get in, and that our future existence depended on one thing – absolute secrecy.'

Corporal Harold Sanders recalled the 'large number of visitors' at Canada Farm, 'to wit countless thousands of earwigs which stormed into our tents, clothes and kit bags'.

18

Still no mysterious 'armoured cars' had arrived. According to Williams-Ellis: 'The machines had long been expected. Almost daily someone in the camp had heard an unfamiliar engine throb. The wildest rumours were afoot. The car could climb trees! It could swim! It could jump like a flea!' Then the waiting was over.

At the very beginning of June the first tank rolled down the extemporized ramp at Barnham station. It was Mother, veteran of the Hatfield trial. For two and a half weeks the proto-tank, now reunited with her guns, reigned alone in her secret realm. Driving practice began on 7 June in the hands of C Company.

'The veil was completely lifted,' recalled Victor Huffam. 'We were told more tanks were coming, that we were to make ourselves proficient in tank handling so as to train others who would follow.'

On the 16th the first production machine arrived under heavy tarpaulins by rail to be 'driven across country to Bernersfield farm by a few officers and other ranks who been sent to Lincoln to train' – then promptly burst its radiator and seized a driveshaft. Swinton dismissed such incidents in a message to Butler as 'childish ailments'.

But the emissary from GHQ, now comfortably set up in the Savoy Hotel in London, wanted hard answers. When would Swinton be ready? Twenty-five tanks could be in France by the third week of July, he now considered – fifty by the first half of August, all one hundred and fifty machines by the beginning of September. The schedule had slipped since the promises of April but was still wildly ambitious.

More and more machines arrived each night to be unloaded in darkness at the government siding. The provisions for secrecy were elaborate. Messages in Cyrillic were painted on their sides (a Swinton wheeze) and cover stories floated – they were snowploughs for the Russian front, water tanks for Mesopotamia. The great secret was getting ever harder to keep. The toiling Welshmen blasting out the assault course were kept strictly away from any sight of the hush-hushes.

In his memoirs Swinton recalled a London 'actress who knew too much and had to be frightened into silence', and a lot of talk of 'women spies'.* A *'Fraulein Doktor'* was said to 'have tried to betray the secret to a German technical officer who would not listen to her warning and committed suicide in remorse at his mistake'. On his account, a mature lady at 'a luncheon party' had also questioned the colonel rather too closely. He wrote: 'I remembered that a certain young officer in the Heavy Section bore her name and made a shrewd guess at their relationship. Unless she promised to maintain silence I would order that individual's arrest by telephone and have him tried by court martial for treachery, the penalty for which was death.'

Pressure to stage some sort of live demonstration was mounting. On 16 June Swinton promised a 'very minor show' for the edification of General Butler, with whatever he might have available – up to five tanks – not necessarily fitted with their sponsons and armament. It was not just a matter of having enough machines, it was about the men who must clamber inside and make them work.

The first priority was to make the machines move and manoeuvre at all. 'Most of the officers and men were already engineers or mechanics, but they must be trained exactly in the strange machine they were to use . . . the monster which they had to render animate . . .' wrote Clough Williams-Ellis. 'Above all, crews must train together, be accustomed to work under their officer, each with his special work as brakeman, guardsman, driver or gunner, but each still part of an organic whole.' It would not be that straightforward. Vickers machine guns had instructors who knew their weapons blindfold. Who knew how to drive a tank – let alone teach anyone else how to do it?

Not everyone was a mechanical genius. Like Basil Henriques at

* By late 1914–15 the much-vaunted German naval spy network already in place in Britain had been rolled up by MO5's Section G and several of its agents executed in the Tower of London. A 'female spy' scare raged instead with several West End plays featuring treacherous *Kameradin*. Boatloads of German governesses were shipped home in 1915 via Holland. Herbert Asquith, the Prime Minister, would come under intense newspaper attack when he was alleged in December 1916 to have shielded his own children's tutor, the harmless Frau Anna Heinsius.

his first confessional interview with Swinton, Henry Groves admitted: 'My knowledge of the internal combustion engine was nil but in my crew of seven men I had a fully qualified electrician and two engineers so we were well away, my batman I remember was a barber by the name of Fertig and he often had me shaved before I woke up.'

Wilson, Tritton and Rigby had put together Mother in a matter of weeks. Armament, propulsion and protection had been engineered from a ragbag of what was available (apart from the tracks); providing tolerable conditions for the crew was a subsidiary concern. The petrol engine occupied the centre of the hull, exhausting through the roof. Ventilation was minimal. The unsprung ride over broken ground was bone-jarring. While being pummelled and vibrated, crew were broiled. The noise was deafening, the exposed petrol engine blisteringly hot.

The side gunners had little motorcycle seats on which to perch, but could not stand fully upright. The 6-pounder was aimed by swinging it by muscle power alone. The driver and commander had more room, afforded by a raised cupola fitted with opening flaps, but closed up for action they must peer through tiny vision slits back-faced with crude glass prisms.

An RAMC major drew up a report called 'Medical Aspects of Tanks' later in the war. It was a combination of toxicology report and trauma manual. Impetigo-like skin rashes were common, caused by exposure to 'inferior brands of petrol and oil used in training'. Oppressive fumes caused 'burning of the nose and throat and smarting of the eyes'. Carbon monoxide poisoning led to, in sequence, 'headache, giddiness, palpitation, vomiting, unconsciousness, collapse and convulsions'. Before passing out, crews suffered 'mental confusion'. After several hours' exposure to such conditions, according to the report's author:

> The men sit and stare in front of them and merely repeat orders without putting them into execution.
>
> There is drowsiness and irresistible desire to sleep. Two cases have occurred of defiance of discipline where superior officers have been attacked. In another, a man ran about shouting and cursing in an aimless manner.
>
> Unconsciousness is relatively frequent. In one tank during

a long approach march the driver became totally unconscious and was found holding his controls in a convulsive grip. He was succeeded by the second driver who after a time shared the same fate. Finally the tank commander took over until he had to be dragged from his post unconscious.

Captain Richard Haigh in his evocative memoir, *Life in a Tank*, published in New York soon after the Armistice, described his first encounter with a Mark I tank. It was in the autumn of 1916 when some crews were already combat veterans, but the mood of the former infantry officer and that of his fellow ingénus remains that of the summer pioneers:

> 'There it is,' cried Gould and started forward for a better look at the Willie. A look of pain flashed across the face of Rigden, the instructor . . . Don't call a tank *it*! . . . A tank is either he or she, there is no it.'
> 'What's the difference?'
> 'The female tank carries machine-guns only,' Rigden explained, 'the male carries light field guns as well as machine-guns. Don't ever that mistake again . . .'

The demonstration tank was a female – on which 'instruction proceeded rapidly'. The instructor opened 'a little door in the side of the hull' and invited the novices to enter for the first time:

> It was about as big as the door to a little old-fashioned brick oven built into a chimney beside a fireplace – Rigden's head disappeared and his body followed afterwards, swallowed up save for a hand waving to us and a muffled voice which said, 'come on in you fellows.' The rest of us scrambled in.
> When you enter a tank you go in by the side doors (there is an emergency exit – a hole in the roof – which is used by the wise ones). You wiggle your body in with more or less grace and then you stand up. Then, if it is the first time, you are usually profane. For once you have banged your head . . . you learn that it is impossible to stand up. Each one of us received baptism in this way . . .
> We looked round the little chamber with eager curiosity. Our first thought was that seven men and one officer could never work in such a place . . .
> When it came to going into action moving around inside would be impossible, there was not enough room to pass each

other. At the front are two stiff seats, one for the officer, one for the driver. Two narrow slits act as portholes. In front of the officer is a map board and gun mounting. Behind the engine, one on each side, are the secondary gears. Down the middle is the petrol engine, partly covered with a hood, and along either side a narrow passage ... There are four gun turrets, two on each side. There is also a place for a gun in the rear.

Along the steel walls are numberless ingenious little cupboards for stores and ammunition cases are stacked high. Every bit of space is utilized. Electric bulbs light the interior ... All action inside is directed by signals for when the tank moves the noise is such to drown a man's voice ...

Like a Trafalgar-era frigate, the job of half the crew was manoeuvring their vehicle, in part to bring the side-mounted guns to bear against a target. Another first-hand account described the flesh-and-blood drive train in action:

It was a hard job to turn ... it needed four of the crew to work the levers and they took their orders by signals. First the tank had to stop. A knock [by the commander] on the right side would attract the attention of the right guardsman. The driver would make a clenched fist, the signal to put the track into neutral.

Then repeat the signal to show it was done. The officer who controlled two brake levers, would pull on the right one, which held the right track. The driver would accelerate and the tank would slew round on the stationary right track while the left track went into motion. As soon as the tank had turned sufficiently, the procedure was reversed ...

In the first days of training, at least there was still enough of the funfair ride about the whole thing to keep men amused. As Capt. Haigh recalled:

One after the other we slide through the little door ... bolted behind the last to enter. Officer and driver slip into their respective seats. The gunners take their position. The driver opens the throttle a little and tickles the carburettor and the engine is started up. The driver races the engine to warm her up. The officer reaches out a hand and signals for first speed on each gear, the driver opens the throttle. Willie – moves! ...

Thirty tons of steel rolls along with its human freight. The driver rings a bell. He presses another button and signals ...

the right hand track into neutral. The tank swings round to the right. The right hand guardsman gets the signal 'first speed' and we are off again at a right angle to our former direction.

We are headed for gentle slope, as we approach the tank digs its nose into the base. She crawls up. The men in the rear tip back and enjoy it hugely.

If the hill is steep they will find themselves lying on their backs or standing on their heads. The tank is balancing at the top and we go over with an awful tumble forward. This is rare fun . . . Three or four weeks of this sort of thing and we are hardened to it at last.

Elveden was providing a home to a growing band of eccentrics. The society painter Solomon J. Solomon RA arrived in late May with a commission in the British Army as a lieutenant-colonel and a brief to disguise the rhomboid shape of the 'cubist slug', as revealed at Hatfield, through the art of camouflage. The idea, evidently, was Lancelot Kiggell's, who knew the painter's efforts as a *camofleur* in the BEF's 'Special Works Park' in France.

General Butler, now liaising daily with Swinton, was hugely suspicious of an artist on the loose. 'Solomon needs a firm hand,' he messaged on the 15th. 'He wants watching or he will run riot all over the place and start with suggestions as to their employment etc.'

Swinton replied: 'I have packed Solomon off up to Elveden Camp with tons of paint and miles of canvas. You are right about him. One has to keep the safety valve shut up tight.' The Royal Academician quickly got down to work in a barn at Bernersfield Farm, commandeering Mother when she was still the only tank at Elveden.

Basil Henriques recalled Solomon working for 'a good part of the day during which he painted her with as much care and trouble as if he were covering a canvas for the Royal Academy . . . The final effect was a kind of jolly landscape in green against a pink sunset sky.'

Gunner E. W. Thwaites, the thirty-seven-year-old who had enlisted as a gentleman ranker in the Motor Machine Gun Corps, recalled night-guard duty in the bosky Suffolk summer, watching over 'tanks parked on the edge of a wood – abounding in pheasants and rabbits'. There was a steady trade for the cooking pot.

Life for some within the secret area was not so agreeable, however. At the end of June a team of Army Service Corps drivers arrived under the command of the brisk Maj. Hugh Knothe, DSO, MC. Known as 711 (Motor Transport) Company, most of the drivers had previously been posted to the military port at Avonmouth, near Bristol, unloading, preparing and dispatching onwards Holt caterpillars from Illinois for the front in France. It was not revealed to them whether they were expected to remain toilers on rear-area roads or become front-line soldiers. According to Capt. H. P. G. Steedman, the unit's second in command: 'The first batch consisted of overseas lorry drivers . . . They were badly frightened at the sight of the tanks and pretended they knew little or nothing about internal combustion engines and were returned by Major Knothe as incompetent.'

The penal colony atmosphere of the secret area did not help. 'The men were ripe for mutiny,' wrote Capt. Steedman, 'they were refused leave, had poor and insufficient food . . . the site had become a quagmire.'

As with all soldiers when presented with a new piece of kit, the temptation to adapt and experiment was irresistible. The need for some sort of communication system was obvious. Swinton noted ambitiously that tank crews might penetrate 'far ahead of the infantry and be in a position to gather information of the utmost value'. Royal Engineer wireless operators were detached to Elveden and a three-mile range spark apparatus experimentally fitted in a tank. But while Morse transmissions might be sent, 'reception . . . was not possible owing to the noise and vibration when the engine was running'. That would not be the end of the story.

Sporadic experiments were made with signalling lamps flashing at overflying aircraft, and with 'reflecting glass spheres for the roofs for aeroplane spotting of tanks by our own aviators'. There were trials with telephone cables ('Fullerphones', a clever device that allowed a scrambled signal to be sent in Morse) unspooling from a tank's rear, buried in a six-inch groove cut in the earth by a ploughshare.

Tank-to-tank communication was tried with metal discs arrayed above the hull like railway signals, and by 'little flags' waved out of a hole in the roof. Kite balloons were tested, flown from vehicles' sterns to 'serve as a land-mark in the sky', by which, in Swinton's words, to 'steer a course and make signals above the smoke of battle' (by sending smaller hydrogen-filled balloons up the cable in the manner of a warship's signalling mast). Pigeons would prove marginally more reliable.* That or waving a shovel out of the escape hatch (a favoured means of communication that would be a constant until the end of the war), a sign to the infantry to 'dig in here'.

Swinton urged that consideration be given to some form of over-head protection should tanks find themselves in villages (he was clearly thinking of them going beyond the opposing trench lines) and be attacked by grenades from above. A kind of shed roof made of chicken wire was devised. The constant experiments, the tweaks demanded of the factories, the mad professor brainstorming, were driving Gen. Butler into a choleric frenzy.

Colonel Jean-Baptiste Estienne, the French advocate of *les chars d'assaut*, was treated to a secret glimpse of the Lincoln factory and the strange goings-on in Suffolk. At the end of June he watched a Mark I pushing over a tree, telling Swinton that his prototypes were not so powerful but more manoeuvrable – like 'rabbits'. He urged his host not to 'disclose their existence before the French were ready to put their own in the field', a view with which Swinton could only concur. Williams-Ellis reported on their Gallic visitor's preference for pale blue spats worn without socks.

For the true believers the fact the wonder weapons existed at all seemed miraculous enough. Tanks worked. They were mechanically robust – just about. They could span trenches and knock down trees. In spite of the noise and heat inside with the engine running – in spite of the unsprung suspension and the train-crash ride – they were habitable, it seemed, by ordinary soldiers. You did not have to be a midget to get inside. Basil Henriques, for example, was six foot three and could just about accommodate himself in the commander's position.

The engineering component of the trench-wire/machine-gun conundrum had seemingly been solved. But could they really survive on the battlefield? Although there had been extensive tests of armour plate, and much concern raised about the German SmK bullet, the tanks were too precious to blast a single one with a field gun or rake with .303 British bullets to see what happened. Their fate was obvi-ous. As Swinton recalled: 'No proof was needed that they themselves could be knocked out by shell fire.'

---

* The balloon apparatus was taken to France but found to be hopelessly impractical.

What were they supposed to do? Were they some giant manned shell that would deliver itself upon the enemy and self-immolate in a blaze of high explosive, or were they the 'gun' that could be fired several times over? Nobody knew. And how were these machines moving at 2 mph meant to work with their own infantry and artillery? There were no combat-seasoned troops at Elveden with whom to devise battle drills. They would have to be improvised at the front. All that the pioneers of the Heavy Section might do for now was confide their thoughts to paper.

Swinton had laboured over schemes for their tactical use from almost the earliest days. His February 1916 'Notes on the Employment of Tanks' – with mass (ninety machines) and surprise on their side – had been reviewed and apparently approved by Haig in April, but no meaningful dialogue with GHQ had continued. Swinton had had his paper printed, and revealed it to his officers at Bisley. It remained the tank men's lodestar as to what they were actually expected to do. But as Williams-Ellis noted, 'The paper was very short and very objective, and was more concerned with an analysis of the place of tanks in the orchestra of battle than with the difficulties presented by the individual score.'

In the summer tranquillity of Bernersfield Farm, Lt-Col. John Brough composed his own modest essay soon after Mother's arrival: 'Owing to the limited number of Tanks that will be available every endeavour should be made to evolve a simple form of tactics and any attempt at a complicated system of manoeuvre should be avoided and the handling of the individual tank on the battlefield should be reduced to its simplest elements.'

He had this to say on the growing 'driblets' issue, whether to use them piecemeal or in an armoured mass: 'The argument as to whether Tanks should be employed in one general line or by "driblets" appears to require no elaboration; in order to get the full value of the machine combined with the element of surprise it would appear to be unwise to disseminate the force and power of this weapon . . .'

That might have seemed sound enough. But he added this: 'It would appear not alone desirable but even necessary that the whole unit (Heavy Section) should be employed in the same zone of operation and should operate under its own commander, in accordance with its pre-arranged plan of attack.'

A fundamental divide was opening up. The enthusiasts, watching their little fleet manoeuvre round Lord Iveagh's monkey puzzles, might have visions of tanks rolling forward shoulder to shoulder, through and even triumphantly beyond the opposing front line. The view from France was different. For example, in early June the supply specialist, Maj. Knothe, suggested consideration be given to how to get ammunition and supplies up to potentially ever-deeper-ranging tanks on the move, perhaps by lorry. Brigadier-General 'Jock' Burnett-Stuart responded sternly from GHQ: 'These engines will be an adjunct to an offensive in trench warfare, and are not likely in action to get further from the startlines than three miles, supposing them to start from a point one mile behind our front trenches . . . They may return to safety after doing one trip or may be compelled to stay out in front . . . and ammunition must be man-handled up to them or taken out in hand carts.'

It could not have been made clearer. Tanks were an adjunct of the infantry. As to whether they should be used in 'driblets' (Swinton's phrase of February, picked up in Brough's tactical notes) or in one armoured mass – that was for commanders in the field to decide. But the fleet would certainly not have its own admiral. Brough's call for the Heavy Section to operate 'under its own commander' was presumptuous, impudent even. This officer might prove difficult.

The plans for the Big Push had been laid, meanwhile, tanks or no tanks. In under four weeks' time, almost one million men, British and French, would stand to at first light and clamber out of their trenches and begin to walk towards the enemy.

19

The strengths and weaknesses of the German position on the Somme were well known. The invader had occupied the area sixty miles north-east of Paris since the first months of fighting. Two defensive lines had been constructed, with dugouts excavated deep in the chalk and massive belts of wire. A third was being built.

General Rawlinson made a plan. In view of the ground and the number of troops and guns at his disposal, he foresaw a frontage of attack no wider than 20,000 yards with a depth of up to 5000 yards. It should be assaulted in two steps of roughly 2000 yards each, he proposed, one for the German first line, and then – after the field guns had been ponderously moved forward – the enemy second line might be pounded to cut the wire and methodically destroy machine-gun nests all over again. The bombardment would need to be in daylight for airborne observers visually to confirm its effects. Then the infantry would move in.

The concept was described as 'bite and hold'. The C-in-C concurred and for a few weeks Haig had talked about only advancing as far as the artillery could prepare the way. But, as had happened before, Haig's confidence rose as the offensive approached. Four days before the bombardment was due to start he demanded something bolder. The attack should go beyond the first enemy line at the first bound – through the second line – even as far as the opposing gun line – and on a front 25,000 yards wide. Even the firepower enthusiast Brig.-Gen. Noël 'Curly' Birch, Haig's artillery adviser, thought that this was going too far.

Through all the various plans, Haig treated initial success as certain and devoted his attention to planning the later stages of the battle – breakout and envelopment. Lieutenant-General Sir Hubert Gough's Reserve Army (to be renamed Fifth Army during the closing stages of the battle) was mustered to push through the gap and, it was planned, make a grand turning movement northwards.* Rawlinson, responsible for ensuring the initial success of the break-in, was less confident.

In the end the tactical plan was a mixture of the two. It comprised a punishing opening bombardment lasting a week, the explosion of huge mines dug in tunnels under strongpoints – followed by the massed assault of Fourth Army's infantry – walking behind a 'lifting barrage' designed to cow any survivors of the initial bombardment, progressively extending its range from one line of objectives to the next.

The fireplan at least was within the competence even of the novice artillerymen of the New Armies. But using individual initiative on the battlefield was judged not to be. The great mass of infantry, civilians less than a year ago, could only move to fixed orders. They must attack in waves plodding forward mechanically in parallel lines. Bomb throwing and bayonet fighting were practised intensively but training in tactical movement – for the most part – amounted to little more than drilling in extended order, with the progress of the barrage creeping 'forward' in front of them represented by men on horses waving flags.

The weight of high explosive would be unprecedented. It would destroy everything in its path. Gas would play only a minor role. But unlike Loos, this time the defences, so it was promised, would be crushed across their whole depth. The infantry would just have to make their way into the shambles and take the survivors prisoner.

A great deal of attention was given to wire cutting. As the Germans added greater depth in their defences, it became more important to cut distant wire, an even more difficult target. Midsummer grass sprouted tall in the rust-brown entanglements, making them hard to spot from aircraft, while the wire covering the German second line was effectively invisible from the British front lines. The artillerymen toiled over their range tables and fireplans. In mid-June, Haig and his staff decamped to 'Advanced GHQ' in the tree-shaded

---

* General John Charteris, Haig's intelligence chief, wrote to his wife on the eve of the attack: 'Darling – long before this letter reaches you the veil of secrecy will be off. We do not expect a great advance or any great place of arms to be captured. We are fighting principally to kill Germans.'

Château Valvion at Beauquesne, twelve miles east north-east of Albert.

That an attack was coming was obvious. The Big Push was the gossip of the leave trains. Where the British blow was intended to fall was also clear. Fourth Army's build-up was readily observable from the air. As the countdown shortened, the artillery's 'registration' fire, finding the range by trial and error, showed the defenders where the intended main targets were. There was no concerted effort at secrecy. The only surprise left to the Germans was the exact date and time of the attack.

The Somme bombardment began on 24 June. It was said you could hear the sound of the heavy guns in London. 'Although at Elveden we could not . . . the reverberations of that cannonade were ever present in our minds,' recalled Swinton. Two days later there was a conference at the War Office attended by Butler, Burnett-Stuart, Swinton, Brough and Bradley. Tanks would not be ready for the opening of the offensive, that had been clear since the late spring, but their time might yet come. Butler laid down the arrangements for their command and control with steely charm: 'The Officer Commanding Heavy Section will command the whole unit in the usual way but naturally cannot be responsible for the tactical handling of the unit as a whole or a part during operations . . . OCHS must always exercise central control and supervision of the whole under the General Staff GHQ and be responsible for all the arrangements up to the moment of the attack precisely as the OC, the Special Brigade, is responsible.'

Brough and Bradley offered no major objection; nor, evidently, did Swinton. No one had proposed that the 'special' troops who had opened the gas stopcocks at Loos should operate under their own commander as a single unit, no more so than should the artillery observers and their protecting scouts of the Royal Flying Corps.

Swinton wondered how central control could be applied if the role of Officer Commanding Heavy Section was to be purely administrative and advisory, but the prescription fitted his own February note: tanks were an auxiliary to the infantry and in operations should be under the same command.

The meeting agreed some detailed tactical points. Before the attack, tanks should be brought up at night guided along taped routes to their start point, thereafter to advance in one line strung out at intervals of 150 yards. They would precede the infantry who would only go forward once the tanks had reached the enemy front trenches. As to their tactical use: 'The Tanks should move forward so as to reach the German front line position by dawn followed up by our infantry which is to start forward from our line as soon as the Tanks reach the first line of the enemy; that in the further operations that will ensue by daylight, Tanks should precede the infantry from place to place as quickly as possible . . .'

The opposing second or third line should be the ultimate objective, to be gained by a continuous line of tanks across the whole front. Nothing was said about the number to be employed; that depended on how many Swinton could deliver.

20

At 7.30 a.m. British Summer Time* on 1 July whistles blew along a
front of almost eighteen miles and waves of British infantry began to
walk forward towards the enemy wire. Swinton wrote that evening
from Elveden to GHQ enclosing 'a trench map' of the training ground
in the Suffolk heaths. 'I am pleased the news from France is so good,'
he signed off brightly.

The real news from France was of the bloodiest day in the history
of the British Army. There was no breakthrough. The artillery, after a
week of pounding, had failed to subdue the opposing front line, let
alone scratch the second position. Just as at Loos, defending machine-
gunners (emerging this time from exceptionally deep shelters dug into
the chalk) manned their firing posts, ammunition belts snaking, water-
cooled Maschinengewehr 'O8s raking the hundred-yard blood-foamed
horizon of erupting chalk, strung wire and stumbling human forms.

There are plentiful accounts of what happened that morning. The
letters files of the Official Historian, canvassing the ex-officer class of
Britain and its empire for recollections of the first day on the Somme
almost twenty years later, are full of them. Some are pompous. A
few are angry. Most are austerely rueful. One tiny snapshot: 'Two
facts stand out: A Lewis gunner firing from the hip while on the
move . . . [mobile infantry firepower, a bold individual initiative] and
several officers who went over the top smoking Corona Cigars – they
were all either immediately killed or wounded.'

The disaster was so great that it was impossible to grasp its scale.
For a few days, British newspapers printed descriptions of the meth-
odical capture of the whole of the enemy's first system of defence.
Then came the casualty lists. Those were printed without comment.
Some of the truth began filtering into the press.

* An innovation of 1 May 1916.

The Big Push was turning into the Great Cock-up. GHQ would not admit it; how could they? The strategic reasons for the offensive meant the attempt would not stop after one day. It was the German machine guns that were to blame, as they had been ever since Eye-witness had been made aware of their baleful power on the river Aisne. On 6 July Swinton wrote to the War Office from Room 337: 'So far I have not seen any official information on the subject of the recent attack on the Somme, but from practically all the accounts given by newspaper correspondents the theory upon which the inception of the idea of an attack by tanks was based has been more than fully borne out.'

The Somme was clearly a shambles. Even corralled within Elveden's perimeter, the Heavy Section could sense it. But Swinton's urgings would be a double-edged sword. By promising the solution he surely knew the time would come when he would be expected to deliver. When that time came his behaviour was not to be entirely honourable.

On 9 July there was change of guard at Armament Buildings. Since Kitchener's loss at sea a month before, Lloyd George had been very coy about accepting Asquith's offer of the Secretaryship of War. At last he had done so and Edwin Samuel Montagu supplanted him as Minister of Munitions, the first Jewish-born cabinet member since Benjamin Disraeli.

There was a huge flap at Elveden the next day, but nothing to do with ministerial changes in London. Evidence of what happened is scanty. All that can be reconstructed is from a one-line entry in a diary discovered in extraordinary circumstances. It was abandoned by a crewman of the Heavy Section on the battlefield on the morning when the tanks would at last go into action, and retrieved by a Bavarian intelligence officer and translated into German. Discovered almost eighty years later in a Munich military archive it read: '10 July 1916: Search in whole camp for a spy, who it was said had crept in somehow. Without success.'

Swinton and Stern had a new concern. The production order for the first 150 machines was on target for completion. Should the highly skilled operations at Lincoln and Birmingham simply be broken up? Swinton had pointed to press hints on the true Somme casualty figures in his 6 July letter as a reason for making more.

There would also have to be a decision whether to continue with the Mark I or to switch to a more heavily armoured design already in draft by the tank supply committee.

Tanks might yet come to the rescue, but there were some in France who had yet to be convinced of their miraculous powers. Where were the damned things anyway? GHQ declined to agree to any new order until it had seen 'at least twenty tanks, fully equipped and manned, functioning in accordance with some definite tactical scheme', so the sceptical Lt-Gen. 'Jock' Burnett-Stuart informed the Director of Staff Duties on 10 July.

That was more difficult than it sounded. Any such 'tactical scheme' must match realities at the front. Getting anything definite out of GHQ, with its mania for secrecy, seemed impossible. If they were to help the infantry, if they were themselves to survive when their turn came, the men of the Heavy Section must know what they were really up against. Few of them had even an inkling. Brough had been plucked from the jungles of the Cameroons. Swinton was a desk warrior, some sort of writer in uniform. Bradley had commanded a unit of motor cyclists. Few of the company commanders were combat veterans, none of the junior officers had ever seen the face of battle; the NCOs and other ranks were just as green.

As Clough Williams-Ellis wrote: 'This was where the training of the first tank crews fell short . . . their teachers had a rather hazy mental picture of the actuality of battle. They did not squarely face the essential question upon whose answer all specific preparation depends, the question, that is, *what is it going to be like?*'

The means of finding out were ingenious. Captain Martel, the Royal Engineer who had supervised the blasting out of the assault course at Elveden, had gone back to the fighting. He informed Brough in a clandestinely routed dispatch from the Somme dated 18 July:

> After the last show here, I am more than ever convinced that your things would be of the greatest value. The Germans were all in deep dug-outs . . . and laughed at our bombardment.
>
> It would appear to be absolutely imperative the hush-hushes should be used without the preliminary heavy bombardment, especially as this did so little good.
>
> I do not think a hush-hush would be in danger once it crossed no man's land. I do not think they will have any difficulty in

finding the Germans' machine-guns and silencing them. It is very difficult to say whether the infantry should cross with the things or wait until they have reached the front line. If they do the former they may (as happened here) be mown down by the MGs and if they do the latter they will catch the German barrage. Personally I would rather risk the latter. Nine tenths of our casualties (and we had 6,000 in the division) were from machine-gun bullets.

In an extraordinary freelance intelligence mission, John Brough smuggled an officer out of No. 3 London General Hospital, Wandsworth,* in south-west London, and got him to Elveden aided by an RAMC major named Hyslop.

Captain R. L. Money, a Cameronian Highlander who had been wounded in the bloody fighting round Fricourt on 1 July, evidently gave intimate details of how enemy machine guns were handled, 'moving from shell-hole to shell-hole . . . bringing cross fire on every square inch of no man's land'. He produced a sketch of a machine gun on wheels found in a dugout.

A Bavarian officer who had led the defence of the fortified village was now a prisoner of war in England, Capt. Money had revealed, 'who had come over to this country in the SS *Asturias* and discussed the position of his guns with some of our own officers . . .'

Lieutenant-Colonel Brough signed off his statement dated 19 July 1916 defensively, as if he knew his intelligence-gathering adventure had been full of risk: 'Capt Money . . . was not informed of the armament of our unit; in fact he was given no details whatsoever, but he expressed the view that if we have any weapon which can deal effectively with German machine-guns the British infantry can get to Berlin . . .'

The only 'German machine-guns' at Elveden were made of wood. There were no facilities even for live firing of the male tank's own 6-pounder main armament let alone practice firing on the move. The air of unreality was tangible. Basil Henriques would describe the preparations in Suffolk as: 'One huge game . . . we used to look for trees to knock down and had one or two craters about a hundred feet width across which we would show off to the brass

* Established in 1914 on the site of the Royal Victoria Patriotic Asylum on Wandsworth Common, a gothic edifice built to house children orphaned by the Crimean War.

hats who came to look at us. We pictured ourselves slowly wending our way to Berlin over beautiful parkland such as we were now practising on.'

Henry Groves recalled fifty years after the event being ordered to act as 'infantry'. It was pretty basic stuff: 'I was in a building and was not allowed to look until a signal was given, I opened the top of the stable door and there thirty yards away was a colossal monster moving along at 3 mph with guns sticking out from all sides.'

GHQ still wanted their grand day out. The tank men were naturally eager to comply, and on the day they could even muster five more machines than had been demanded. It would prove more of a gladiatorial spectacle than any 'definite tactical scheme'. Nevertheless it was historic – the first demonstration of a mass, mechanized armoured force in history. It was scheduled for 21 July. Everyone, including the minister, wanted to be in on it.

'Robertson, Maurice [Maj.-Gen. Frederick Maurice, Director of Military Operations as the War Office], Brough and I spent the night of the 20th at Elveden Hall as guests of Lord Iveagh,' Swinton recalled, 'and there were in addition at dinner that evening Bradley and Mr Bland, Lord Iveagh's land agent.'

The group took a spartan dinner, and then assembled 'two figures in evening dress, five in khaki' (mess dress was consigned to mothballs for the duration) around the billiard table in the Oriental Saloon. Lord Iveagh was let in on the secret of what had been going on amidst his partridge coverts (he might have guessed by now).

A large-scale map of the Somme was spread over the green baize 'lit by the fierce glare poured downwards from the billiard table lamps in their green silk shades'. The dent in the German line was mockingly small.

'After three weeks, those present knew – to a greater or smaller degree – what the cost had so far been, whatever the estimate of the plan,' wrote Swinton. 'General Maurice then . . . proceeded to tell us of the coming renewal of the offensive and explain what the tanks were expected to do.'

Fourth Army had begun a renewed attack on 14 July in an attempt to exploit their scant first-day successes on the right of their front. New techniques had been tried, a daring but successful night assembly in no-man's-land, and a sudden intensification of the three-day preliminary bombardment in the five minutes before Zero Hour. The infantry went in just before dawn under a creeping barrage, capturing some 6000 yards of the German second position on the Longueval–Bazentin Ridge.

But as the mustachioed warriors gathered in the billiard room at Elveden Hall on the night of the 20th, this second set-piece attempt at a 'breakthrough' was sputtering out in bloody failure. Two crucial defensive positions, Delville Wood and High Wood, defied capture. The so-called wearing-out battle to gain 'a satisfactory base of departure' (Haig's expression) was beginning. When that had been achieved – when the Germans had been worn down to the tipping point – Fourth and Reserve Army would try again.

The next morning Lloyd George arrived at Elveden by special train. Robertson, the CIGS, who earlier that morning had cheerfully inspected Heavy Section HQ at Bernersfield Camp, took his place in the 'grandstand', a raised knoll of turf in the centre of the 'British' line, as close as was safe to the principal obstacle of a nine-foot-wide trench. 'Mr Lloyd George wore a hat of uncommon shape and a flowing cloak as he wore on his visits to France,' according to Swinton. The Union flag was broken from the jack staff and a signal rocket fired the moment the Secretary for War reached the grandstand. Swinton recalled the moment:

> The air quivered with the roar of exhausts as twenty-five tanks started from some way behind. The general idea was for the tanks to cross our front line, no man's land, the German front line and press on through the enemy zone to his artillery positions. They were to concentrate on searching and shelling or flattening out the enemy machine-guns made of wood.
>
> To test the [female tank's] defensive power there was to be sudden counter attack by the hostile infantry from a clump of farm buildings. The lack of artillery rendered the whole operation unnatural and uncanny, for loud as the tanks were the sound was no more than a vast humming sound . . .
>
> The 'Boche infantry' with broad red tapes round their caps rushed forward but could do nothing.
>
> At one o'clock the cease fire sounded. Mr Lloyd George expressed his great satisfaction and all the spectators were much impressed.

Lieutenant-Colonel Solomon recorded:

> Thursday July 21 – gala day – all the munitions people, home defence staff, Generals Butler, Haslam and others from France invited to a tank demonstration . . .
>
> By an odd chance the tank we were following had just missed a pheasant's nest well lined with eggs. Pointing it out to Brough I could not resist saying 'Hen roost.' 'Sh! sh!' said the horrified Brough, fearful Mr Lloyd George would hear . . .
>
> Sir William Robertson enquired if was possible to hide shadows, I told him much could be done in that direction . . .

Lloyd George recalled a tank transiting a partridge nest without crushing its occupants.

Swinton was jubilant. 'The essential fact of that morning's exercise – although not carried out under war conditions – was that it was possible at last to overcome the strongest defence devised since the introduction of firearms,' he wrote. 'For the designers and constructors of the new engine of war it was a day of triumph.'*

The delegation from GHQ had departed London by car that morning. Swinton's prescription of a three-hour journey from the United Services Club to Elveden had been ambitious. They had broken down at Epping. They missed both the main demonstration and lunch. General Butler thought they should have waited. He was furious.

Lieutenant-Colonel John Brough came out of the gala day with his pennants flying. On the 24th he was formally appointed second in command to Swinton. The CIGS himself recommended it be so. He would take the Heavy Section to France, ostensibly to be its commander in the field while Col. Swinton held the ring from Armament Buildings. The unit's other lieutenant-colonel, Robert Bradley, was appointed commander of Elveden and what remained of the training operations at Bisley and Bullhouse Farm.

---

* Swinton had wanted the 21 July demonstration recorded on cine film, both as an historical record and as an aid to training. The society surgeon turned pioneer film maker Dr Edmund Distin Maddick, who had been liaison officer for British film camera operations on the Western Front in 1915 (Swinton had encountered him as Eyewitness), was all set to do so when GHQ vetoed it – 'nervous that not enough precautions were being taken at home'. In spite of the flap over secrecy (presumably a result of the 10 July spy scare) there seem to have been cameras at Elveden as several group photographs of officers testify. The Royal Flying Corps detachment at Thetford took aerial photographs of the great demonstration, although these have proved impossible to find.

The test had been passed.* But Butler wanted tanks on the Somme, not still lumbering round Suffolk. The day after the grand demonstration, 22 July, 'It was agreed at a conference with representatives from GHQ that if possible one section of six tanks with a workshop should be on the sea by the end of the first week of August,' so Swinton recalled, 'the remainder of the tanks to follow in lots of twelve at weekly intervals. The tactical idea underlying this was the employment of six tanks at a time.'

Swinton 'disagreed entirely with the proposal', or so he said in his memoirs. Evidence of such a stand is hard to find. This was disastrous, a reversal of everything he and the true believers had been urging from the beginning. 'I was shocked that High Command seemed set on employing a few [tanks] as soon as they were ready and were not prepared to wait for the whole number,' said Swinton, 'throwing away the chance of achieving something really big.'

Their urgent presence was required at the front, so Butler declared, to 'raise the morale of the troops'.

Douglas Haig would later be lambasted by far more significant figures than Swinton for 'squandering surprise' – 'selling the secret for the battered ruins of a little hamlet on the Somme', for using the British wonder weapon in 'penny packets' in a gamble to snatch victory from the bloodbath on the road to Bapaume. It became the central charge in the gathering assault on the Commander-in-Chief's reputation that began after his death in 1928. It was primed by Basil Liddell Hart in his book *The Real War*, published in 1930, accelerated by Swinton in his own book, *Eyewitness*, published two years later, and blasted by Lloyd George in his 1933 *War Memoirs* (on which Liddell Hart acted as military consultant). Fuller came a little later to the feast in his own 1936 *Memoirs of an Unconventional Soldier*.

In the informed words of John Terraine, Haig's biographer, writing in the early 1960s: 'Haig's decision to use the small number of tanks that were available . . . [was the] decision that brought upon

---

* Major Allen Holford-Walker's brief report on the exercise, 'tactical handling of tanks in action', pointed out some shortcomings – 'although implicit instructions were issued to section commanders as to detailing tanks to definite duties . . . Little Willie Redoubt was hardly touched . . . three emplacements in the Citadel (North Stow Farm) were untouched while four were destroyed. When cars reached their objective, in two cases cars did not know the positions of their neighbours.'

him more particular criticism than any other.' For a much-criticized soldier – Loos, 1 July, Passchendaele – it must have been a pretty bad choice.

But Edward Swinton had led him here. The colonel had made his declarations and they were being called to account. What Swinton did now might be thought worthy of greater condemnation than that levelled at Haig. While promising more and more tanks, he tried to pull out.

21

The crawl of the caterpillars towards the Somme was moving with a momentum of its own. On 24 July Swinton himself placed the 'continuation' order for the production of a further fifty machines with Stern's committee. Robertson formally agreed the arrangement within twenty-four hours. But the CIGS also felt compelled to bring the grumblings of the 'people connected with the supply and construction of tanks' to Haig's attention in a letter dated the same day, 25 July. It had been copied to Lloyd George, who thought it more than appropriate that the Commander-in-Chief should know quite what was at stake, and formally comment on it in writing.

The phraseology in Robertson's communication must have been familiar; it had Swinton's fingerprints all over it.

'The use of tanks in small *driblets* will militate against their eventual value because' – there followed a long list of reasons to hold back, clearly drafted in a hurry by Swinton, Brough and Stern. Once the tanks had been revealed the Germans would surely find an antidote – 'putting quick firing guns and pom-poms taken from fortresses and warships into the front line'.

The paper pointed out that although 150 tanks of the present type would be available during September, 350 more could be ready for the field in January 'if an order is placed now'. Caterpillar-borne self-propelled artillery was said already to be under construction.*

The CIGS encapsulated the argument: 'That to await the employment of a large number of tanks in January as outlined, will do more to ensure final success on a large scale than to use them in detachments now and so discount the future full value of a new method of fighting which is at present in its infancy.' Both he and

* A 'gun carrier' had been designed in March 1916 by Walter Wilson. The WO Ordnance Board had turned it down, but Lloyd George signed it up for the Ministry of Munitions on 17 June.

the Secretary of State for War were, of course, in 'no position to dictate . . .' It was for the C-in-C to decide.

Haig replied: 'It is not my intention to employ tanks in small numbers unless and until I am convinced that the advantages to be gained by doing so are great enough to outweigh the disadvantages of making known to the enemy the existence of these new engines of war.'

The day before the C-in-C's reply, 26 July, a bearded figure arrived at the Barham siding by special train, under the cover of a 'Russian general'. It was King George V. Five machines rumbled over the assault course before he was welcomed aboard the tank of Maj. Holford-Walker. He suggested to his driver, Gnr Robert Tate, that His Majesty should be given a ride over a bumpy course. 'At a point no more than half-way round, the King got out, thanked the crew and returned on foot.'

'The Royal Party returned to London by train,' recalled Swinton, 'in which Brough and I had the honour of accompanying His Majesty who expressed his gratification at what he had seen.' It might seem likely that the two men used the opportunity to lobby discreetly about the inadvisability of 'driblets'. If they did so, the King did not confide it to his diary: 'Col. Swinton and Col. Brough met me and took me in a motor about six miles past Elveden to a place on Cadogan's property where he showed us six caterpillars which went over trenches, craters etc. and through woods knocking down trees. There are 150 ordered besides 50 more to carry larger guns. I think they will be a great success, they really are moving forts. Lovely day, very hot sun . . .'

Lord Iveagh had already had enough. The Court Circular for the 24th records him 'leaving Elveden for London'. He would return in November when German prisoners of war arrived to undo the Heavy Section's depredations and restore his partridge coverts.

Haig could not wait. Higher demands were pressing. On 29 July Robertson informed the C-in-C: 'The powers that be are beginning to get a little uneasy in regard to the situation. The casualties are mounting up and they were wondering whether we are likely to get a proper return for them . . . It is thought that the primary object, the relief of pressure on Verdun, has to some extent been achieved.' The Germans had reverted to a defensive in the second week of July.

The casualty figures were indeed 'mounting up', but they could and would be presented as practical military housekeeping intended to wear the enemy down before the 'advance' was triumphantly rejoined. The new form of warfare in which flesh and blood soldiers on both sides would be expended like shells was delicately called the 'wearing out battle'.

After the check of the set-piece attack of mid-July, Fourth Army would continue to bear the gruesome burden, spending the next two months on the Longueval–Bazentin Ridge rallying again and again in a series of bloody local attacks which were among the bitterest actions of the entire war. They were intended to 'straighten the line' to improve the infantry jumping off positions and artillery targeting for one last great offensive effort.

The defence of the ridge was ferocious, German losses immense. General Fritz von Below, commanding Second Army, demanded that 'the enemy should have to carve his way over heaps of corpses'. The policy of stubborn linear defence and relentless counter-attacks was subduing the German army in the kind of battle that Haig had already contracted to fight. His intelligence chief, Brig.-Gen. John Charteris, filed report after report that the enemy was on the brink of cracking. Summer would soon be turning to autumn. 'Breakthrough' was still possible. Tanks might just tip the balance.

But just as Swinton was telling everyone who would listen in London that to use them now would be a calamity, he could not resist propounding his own views on how they should be used. On 29 July a bizarre single-page document was routed to GHQ via the War Office headlined:

> Suggested notes for officers who may be in charge of operations in which male and females are employed.
> Both sexes will climb can traverse almost any ordinary obstacle likely to be met. They can knock down trees but there is considerable danger when they pass through close woods that their sponsons and guns will be wrenched off. It must be remembered that neither sex, especially the male, is suitable for isolated action and they must therefore in all circumstances be closely supported by infantry.
>
> Preparatory to action it is essential that routes to be traversed by these animals should be carefully reconnoitered by their keepers, their sense of direction being somewhat inaccurate.

General Wilkinson Bird forwarded it to GHQ, noting dryly: 'OC Heavy Section states that the notes are purposefully framed in veiled language in case a paper should get into the wrong hands. It appears to be open to question whether they would not rather excite curiosity rather than allay it in the form they are written.'

The colonel's reputation for eccentricity was deepening. Messages between Room 337 and Advanced GHQ would now break down in a shambles of half-truths and broken promises. On 3 August Stern dropped a clunking spanner into the proceedings. He calmly informed Lloyd George there would be no spare parts available until the end of the order; that was how production had been scheduled. 'In my opinion the sending out of partially equipped machines as now suggested is courting disaster,' he added. Stern and d'Eyncourt went personally to see Robertson, the CIGS, to tell him the same thing. Col. Estienne and M. Jean-Louis Bréton, the Sous-Secrétaire des Inventions, arrived urgently in London to plead for restraint until the French too might be ready. Edwin Montagu gave them a brittle but sympathetic hearing.

Into this maelstrom blundered Lt-Col. John Brough, 'sent to GHQ at the beginning of August to ascertain the tactics it was proposed to employ as regard tanks. Unfortunately his visit was fruitless, for no ideas apparently existed on the subject', as an account written four years after the events by one who came a little later to the tank story put it. He had no real authority. There was the question of his position in relation to Lt-Col. Bradley, who was, in the words of one of the pioneers who would very soon come to share Brough's anguish, 'the co-ordinating officer. I call him this because he was not in command of the two companies that first went to France. He was appointed purely as a liaison officer between the companies who were independent accounting units and the formations to which these companies were attached . . . everyone wanted to have a finger in the pie and if possible [get] kudos out of the tanks. It was an impossible position for any except a man of the strongest character . . .' Bradley was not that man.

The former marine artilleryman wandering about the Somme rear area was in an impossible position. His own boss, Swinton, was telling the Secretary of State for War that the force Brough was supposed to imminently propel into action was not ready. To use it in the manner being prescribed, in 'driblets', would compound the catastrophe.

Was that what he, a temporary lieutenant-colonel, late of a triumph over a handful of Germans in the Cameroons, was meant to tell the Commander-in-Chief? Men who proved 'sticky' did not prosper in France. Divisional commanders who had seemed reluctant to press home an attack were regularly sent home. Haig had declared dispassionately enough that he had 'sacked over a hundred brigadiers'. After a few days of this agony Brough returned to brief his superior. A message to Swinton from GHQ dated 6 August said simply: 'Col Brough proceeds London tomorrow Monday returning [to France] Wednesday. He will meet you at U[nited] S[ervices] Club 6.00pm. He is in full possession of the facts.'

John Brough presented the 'facts' as they had been given to him. GHQ would use the tanks in a manner of their own choosing however few or as many as were available. Further argument seemed futile. Swinton excused himself in his memoirs: 'My duty was to carry out orders; and as the decision had been taken, I perhaps wrongly made no further protests.'

The lack of spares suddenly looked a positive advantage.

When the colonel at last told GHQ about the problem, Gen. 'Jock' Burnett-Stuart responded tartly from GHQ on 8 August, 'The whole organisation of this show at home has been on fancy rather than practical lines.'

Richard Butler had lost all patience. On the 11th, Haig was informed of difficulties with 'accessories for tanks'. 'This is disappointing,' he wrote in his diary, 'as I have been looking forward to decisive results from the use of these "Tanks" at an early date.' Terse coded signals from 'Chief' came direct to 'TANKORGIZE' signed off by Lt-Col. Kenneth 'Kitten' Wigram, the ambitious GSO1 at GHQ (and brother of Sir Clive Wigram, Assistant Private Secretary to the King).

The timetable was revised again. With an overwhelming effort, the factories working day and night, two companies, C and D, might be across the Channel in the last week of August – fifty tanks to be dispatched in four waves with spares following. The men and machines of A and B Companies might be ready to move by mid-September. E and F were nowhere near a condition to be mobilized. Swinton was obliged, meanwhile, to have a note of important decisions counter-initialled by Butler or Kiggell. Swinton came close to being accused of deliberately lying. The naughty schoolboy antics would have to end.

John Brough returned to the Somme and busied himself organizing somewhere the Heavy Section might set itself down before, as now seemed inevitable, it must go into battle, whatever condition it was in. There was a suitable area in the sprawling suburb of hutted encampments and commandeered villages that tended the British position on the Somme. The immediate task was to set up a forward staging area, find billets and make arrangements for realistic battlefield training, if that was possible.

The fields and villages around the old town of St Riquier east of Abbeville were commandeered as a training area, an Elveden-sur-Somme. The villages of Yvrench and Yvrencheux were taken over as billets, with a nearby railhead at Conteville where the tanks were to be detrained. A bicycle-mounted police force of thirty NCOs drawn from 'garrison troops' on the lines of communication was drafted to guard them.

The secrecy paranoia that had surrounded the hush-hushes in Suffolk obtained in France. Lieutenant-Colonel Walter Kirke, deputy intelligence chief at GHQ, was in charge of security. In a memo of 5 August he spelled out the arrangements: 'Two members of the Sûreté under an Intelligence Corps officer will make a very careful examination of the inhabitants of the area . . . Any person about who there is reasonable doubt will be evacuated south of the Somme.'

Kirke further insisted there should be extra vigilance by the French postal censor, and 'additional surveillance of letters of troops training with the Heavy Section'.

Moving the machines on flat-cars of the Etat railway (otherwise used for carrying lengths of railway track) up from Le Havre in secret was going to be difficult enough. Judging by the to and fro of messages, 'Kitten' Wigram clearly found the complexities of loading gauges and railway tunnels all highly vexatious. 'In order to give the railway authorities in France the benefit of our experience, I sent out to GHQ an officer who had been attached to much such work, being in peacetime an official of the Indian Railways,' wrote Swinton. 'On the subject on which he was an expert he could not obtain a hearing.' The unfortunate Lt A. C. Bussell, a former Royal Engineer recalled to duty who had known Swinton in India, did what he could in conditions of extraordinary difficulty. It was just about enough.

22

The men of the Heavy Section knew nothing of the exquisite deliberations between Whitehall and Advanced GHQ that would decide their fate. But all of them could sense the time approaching for the great unpicking from the sandy heaths of Suffolk and the journey to France.

The strictures on leave were loosening. Lieutenant Victor Huffam recalled supervised outings in the back of a Leyland lorry to Bury St Edmunds where 'we could dine at the Angel and the Suffolk Hotel for the NCOs'. Gunner Ernest Thwaites recalled: 'We worked hard all day with the occasional route march, but being so far from a town rather spoiled our spare time, unless one possessed a motor bicycle for a run into Thetford.

'Those of us who were not so lucky had to make the best of camp where the YMCA provided a large marquee and our section was installed in a canteen of our own, in a motor garage just out of camp. A small committee of us ran it with a piano hired from Bury . . .'

Henry Groves remembered: 'Many of the officers and men had cars and motorbikes, and after a day's work were away all over the countryside with all the locals trying to find out what was in the Area.' The secret still held.

Training continued at a pace, men and machines cruising around looking for imaginary machine-gun emplacements. Still there had been no practice in firing the 6-pounders on the move. A suitable range was not available until late July (the War Office had not issued the necessary safety certificate) when at last butts were set up around North Stow Farm in the middle of the Area. The proper gun mountings did not arrive until the first week of August. No consideration to equip crews with first aid measures other than field dressings was considered until the first were already on their way to France. It would seem charmingly amateurish if it was not so serious. Each day on the Somme the infantry were dying in their thousands.

Swinton produced a little tactical guide, childlike in its simplicity, called 'Tank Tips'. It was more Scouting for Boys than Biffing the Boche:

'Remember your orders

Shoot quick.

Shoot low. A miss which throws dust in the enemy's eyes is better than one that whistles in his ear.

Shoot cunning . . .'

According to Basil Henriques, the spirit of improvization had certain moral advantages. 'There was always healthy competition and this carried us right out to France,' he wrote. 'Besides that, tank commanders had the very great advantage of training their crews themselves . . . we knew our men thoroughly. If anything went wrong . . . they used to look upon it not as a bore but as a pleasure to put it right.'

Things were going wrong. The condition of the tanks after weeks of lumbering round the Area looked as if none of them would be shipped to France, whatever GHQ might demand. Major Hugh Knothe, the Army Service Corps commander, thought the rash of broken tracks and worn-out drive trains would take two months to put right. Stern drafted in forty volunteers from the Birmingham factory to tune and fettle the weary machines. They were billeted by the Thetford police and fed from a Great Eastern Railway buffet car on the Government Siding. It took ten days to get the Elveden fleet back to a state where they might be considered battleworthy.

On the early evening of 13 August, a Sunday, Swinton was back at Elveden, to repeat the contemplative, pipe-smoke-wreathed muster he had staged with his officers five months before at Bullhouse Farm. 'The whole of C Company, some thirty officers and 250 other ranks, gathered under the pine trees on a slight rise behind the centre of the British Line,' he recalled. His headmasterly address said nothing of his own battles with the War Office, but was concerned more with what the men of the Heavy Section might face on the other side of the Channel – the presiding mystery – the *Front*. He reminded them again of the plight of the infantry.

They shuffled, they grinned, they cheered patriotically. A group photograph was taken. It was all a bit like school.

As dusk fell the next day the bruising work began at the Government

Siding to load the first thirteen machines on to a train of flat-trucks. The drivers and mechanics of No. 711 Company laboured for that night and for the next under the glare of sputtering acetylene lamps. The job was done, the tracks south-westward to the port of embarkation cleared. GHQ was messaged with the news.

A little after dawn on 16 August the first 'heavy train' with its humpbacked, tarpaulin-swaddled load clanked its way on to the Great Eastern Railway mainline under the command of a single officer, accompanied by the complement of Army Service Corps drivers who would manoeuvre them off the flat-cars at Avonmouth docks outside Bristol and into the holds of waiting ships.

Their crews would travel separately. Ernest Thwaites recalled seeing 'lorry loads of men in full kit leaving camp in the early hours of the morning' (accompanied by 'a terrible row and noise as they were leaving', according to another account). They were C Company heading for Thetford Bridge station – and the train for Liverpool Street.

In the coded movement orders, the detachment of personnel was called 'Alpaca', the tanks 'Armadillos', the mobile workshop that would follow later was codenamed 'Antelope'. The Heavy Section was going to war.

PART TWO

Never Mind the Heat

'There were no tank tactics when I joined, the only tactic was to get into your tank and drive towards the enemy. The infantry with any luck would follow you . . .'

Col. Norman Dillon,
Heavy Branch Machine Gun Corps veteran

23

The day the first tank train left Elveden, 16 August, Haig sent the commanders of Fourth and Reserve Armies the first formal notice of the planned offensive in which 'Heavy Section armoured cars' would play some part, fifty or sixty of which were 'expected to arrive from England during the next few weeks'.

The commander of this still-mysterious unit would have no operational independence. The line was the same as Butler had spelled out at the War Office conference on 26 June. 'His position in relation to the Heavy Section will be analogous to that of the OC Special Brigade [poison gas] in relation to the Special Battalions . . .'

Included with the notice was an eight-page typewritten paper reproduced in blue ink on a mimeograph machine called 'Preliminary Notes on the Tactical Employment of Tanks (Provisional)'. A photograph was attached – a two by four print of Mother snapped at the Hatfield trial complete with little white dog.

It bore no signature but its drafters at GHQ were obviously familiar with Swinton's February memorandum and the papers that had followed. In a preliminary paragraph it described, although it went on to condemn as 'difficult', the idea of using tanks 'in large numbers in line at intervals of 100 yards'. It stated:

> The tank is a novel engine of war and untried. Its use will require careful study and preparation on each separate occasion. Special care must be taken that the tanks do not fall into enemy hands . . .
>
> Each tank attack will be a definite operation against a limited objective allotted to a selected number of tanks and a selected body of infantry, all under one commander. In certain cases a pair of tanks supported by a platoon might suffice . . .

A section of six tanks was suggested as 'suitable distribution' for each infantry division. Their vulnerability to shellfire was emphasized, to be countered by 'surprise . . . rapid movement and in getting to close quarters. It must emerge from cover (either material cover or the cover of smoke or darkness) and it must return to cover or find other concealment or safety when its task is done. Also it must have the infantry with it.'

As only small numbers would be available they 'should be used to overcome strong points that threatened to hold up the infantry advance, and should operate in pairs against previously identified objectives'.

Captain Money, the wounded Cameronian smuggled by John Brough into Elveden in early July, had explained that such 'objectives' were illusory – the Germans moved their guns from 'shell hole to shell hole'. Indeed, six weeks of shelling had reduced the first two defensive systems in the German line to a series of barely connected craters. That did not mean they were any less dangerous when manned by determined machine-gunners. It made them more so. The fighting for the village of Guillemont, raging as the notes were being circulated, was showing how difficult it was to subdue such a position with artillery alone.

'Pairs of tanks' spread across the whole assault frontage, chasing the enemy from crater to crater. That was GHQ's grand plan.* The true believers had lost the great driblet battle. They had lost it right at the very start.

On 19 August Swinton himself paid 'a hurried visit' to Advanced GHQ at the Château Valvion. 'Sir Douglas Haig saw me and pointed out on the map the sector where he proposed to throw in the tanks. He did not enter into any discussion . . .'

But nor did Swinton, even after having read the GHQ-drafted tactical plan. It was broadly what he himself had proposed after all. The colonel had urged in his February paper that tanks 'should be under infantry command, as their role is that of auxiliary . . .'. He just wanted more of them. He wanted them used together. He wanted more time.

Haig informed Robertson three days later: 'I am counting

---

* Explaining the failure of the Somme barrage Haig's artillery adviser, Brig.-Gen. Noël 'Curly' Birch, told the Official Historian twenty years later: 'There were miles and miles of wire and no instantaneous fuzes, and poor Haig – as he was always inclined to do – spread his guns.' Now the C-in-C could do nothing else but spread his tanks.

on getting at least 50 tanks available. If I get them, I hope and think they will add very greatly to the prospect of success. If I do not get as many as I hope, I shall use what I have got . . . as I cannot wait any longer for them, and it would be folly not to use every means at my disposal in what is likely to be our crowning effort for the year.'

On 25 August, GHQ issued an outline of the operational plan for the climactic offensive. It aimed to establish a defensive flank on the high ground north of the Albert–Bapaume road which bisected the battlefield and to press the main assault south of it, with the object of securing the enemy's last line of prepared defences between the villages of Morval and Le Sars – opening the way, of course, for the cavalry corps of five divisions to pass through into open country. In the grand vision the mass of horsemen were to capture Bapaume, cut the railways and roll up the enemy's front northwards.

The attack front of almost eight miles ran in a shallow curve running west from Thiepval, the heavily fortified hinge of the defences, dipping down to Combles in the east. The attack would be launched broadly northwards out of the strip of shattered woods and villages already pulverized in eight weeks of fighting. It was called the 'devastated zone'.

In overall concept the 'crowning effort' was the same as that which had floundered on 1 July – but on a narrower front – with a shorter preliminary bombardment but greater concentration of guns. 'The general objective is the same as hitherto,' minuted Haig, 'destruction of the enemy's field forces, ditto our plan, namely to break the enemy's front, advance on Bapaume.' How 'tanks' were to be fitted into the fireplan had yet to be resolved. The C-in-C called on the army commanders to submit formal proposals.

'The presence of the fifty "tanks" raises entirely new, but at the same time problematical possibilities,' wrote Rawlinson. 'Should they prove successful we might lose . . . a valuable opportunity by confining our operations only to the capture of system "a" [Combles, High Wood, Martinpuich].

'On the other hand we may be expecting too much of the "tanks" and be tempted to undertake an operation which is beyond our power and which might cause very heavy losses to the tanks themselves and to the infantry engaged in their support,' said the Fourth

Army commander. 'However if the attack failed the secret of the tanks would be given away once and for all . . .'

His proposed solution was a variation on bite and hold, a staged advance over three successive nights – tanks operating by 'moonlight' – and withdrawing in the dark like a thief in the night. 'The mysterious appearance . . . and withdrawal under cover without leaving any sign of what they are . . . would most certainly have a great moral effect,' he wrote. 'Till the enemy knows exactly what they have to deal with they cannot arrange or prepare an antidote. We must therefore endeavour to keep them a mystery as long as possible . . .'

Haig could only concur, but was clearly prepared to employ the tanks with the recklessness of a man looking for a last chance. 'I agree,' he scribbled in the margin of Rawlinson's plan, adding: 'But when we use them they will be thrown *with determination* into the fight regardless of cost!'

He insisted, therefore, on a plan that would deliver 'exploitation of success in the first few hours'. He suggested a much more muscular operation, with 'tanks to be used boldly' and 'success pressed to demoralize enemy and try to capture his guns . . . Operation of tanks at night in an unknown country beyond our lines is unlikely to give good results,' he wrote.

Rawlinson fell in line. While attacking along his entire front, the main effort would be aimed at capturing three villages – Gueudecourt, Lesboeufs and Morval, roughly three miles behind the main defence system. They would be seized 'before noon', leaving eight hours of daylight for the cavalry 'to exploit the success'. Tanks would be employed tactically as per GHQ's existing instructions.

'Gen. Rawlinson was disposed to make as little alteration as possible in the accepted method of bombardment and attack, for he did not expect too much of the tanks,' noted the Official Historian. The response of Gen. Hubert Gough commanding Reserve Army contained no detailed proposals for the use of heavy armoured cars. He preferred to wait until he knew 'more of their capabilities'.

As Haig and his army commanders debated the utility or otherwise of the new weapon (none of them had yet seen a tank) the first machines and their crews were arriving in France. The leading component of 'Alpaca', the advance party of C Company commanded by Maj. Allen Holford-Walker, had stepped ashore at Le Havre on

17 August. Their tanks had followed from Avonmouth on the night of 20–21st, delayed by a U-boat scare, to be unloaded at a remote part of the docks and manoeuvred gingerly by their ASC drivers on to the groaning flat-cars of the Etat railway. The sponsons were unbolted, travelling separately from the hulls to meet the loading gauge, everything hidden by heavy tarpaulins. C Company's second twelve tanks followed two days later.

The reaction to their arrival was not universally enthusiastic. 'The first lot have arrived . . . and have been coaxed onto the trucks so we will see what happens to the railway . . .' Gen. Burnett-Stuart informed Whigham at the War Office on the 24th. 'These beasts are troublesome and I fear rather helpless units – Swinton does not appear to function on very practical lines.'

The tanks of D Company, commanded by Maj. Frank Summers, were coming behind them, in three trainloads which left Elveden on the nights of 26–27 August and 1 September followed by a trainload of spares. Like C Company who had preceded them, the crews travelled via the Great Eastern Railway from Thetford Bridge to Liverpool Street Station, marching (one account states travelling via the 'tube') across London to Waterloo where their 'leather helmets aroused much curiosity among the public'. The train for Southampton awaited them, and berths on the troopship that would bear them to France.

C Company's first twelve machines began their slow, clanking journey from the docks at Le Havre towards the Somme on the 22nd, moving via Rouen and Abbeville to the old town of St Riquier (codenamed 'Cheam' in the movement orders) in the north-west corner of the *département* of the Somme. They arrived on the 24th. Their crews were already there, having journeyed 'packed up like sardines' in the infamous *24 Hommes 8 Chevaux* trucks of the Nord Railway. The journey was comfortless.

Gunner F. S. Cutting of A Company who made the same transit on 13–14 September remembered: 'No fires allowed and food short. The next two solid days I spent penned up in this awful box, nearly frozen at midnight. The train never exceeded 6 miles per hour, it stopped at a siding when it was dusk and started again at 9am. No wash or shave since Thetford.'

The personnel of D Company came the same way, the men of

1 and 2 sections clambering out at St Riquier on the morning of 1 September – hungry, sleepless, dirty – to cook breakfast by the tracks in the station yard. The officers sought out estaminets in the town for bread and omelettes, before moving on again to the forward railhead at Conteville. The second half company would get there on the 6th.

Half the Elveden tanks and their crews were now in the forward area. Ten more were coming direct from the factories to act as a reserve. The twenty-five tanks of Maj. C. M. Tippetts's A Company plus eight spares and a mobile workshop would take another two weeks to get to France, with B Company coming behind them. With his schoolboy humour Swinton would codename their movements 'Lobster' and 'Turbot'.

The arrangements for their command remained chaotic. On 24 August Burnett-Stuart informed a confidant at the War Office, 'We have had to wire again today for the HQ to be sent out as there is no machinery for command . . .'. Three days later instructions were given for 'one officer [Capt. W. F. R. Kyngdon] and two other ranks to report to Col Brough at GHQ'. At last Brough got a car, a Sunbeam, and set up his tiny headquarters with the baffled Capt. Kyngdon and two orderlies at the Château Yvrench – 'Tanks HQ' – as it was grandly entitled. An urgent request was sent to connect it to the military telephone system. It was all a bit pointless.

The days in midsummer Suffolk may have seemed dream-like. Now in France the men of the Heavy Section were supposed to train with infantry under something like battlefield conditions. On the afternoon of the 26th, Haig, his Chief of Staff Lt-Gen. Sir Lancelot Kiggell, plus Generals Gough and Rawlinson watched five tanks from C Company, the very first to have arrived in France, stage a mock attack on a small wood, Le Bois Grambus, near Yvrench. A battalion of the Middlesex Regiment lumbered behind looking as purposeful as they could in the circumstances. Their bemused commander had only received the order for their employment the night before. It was secrecy – again. It was considered that infantry who had seen the tanks might be captured and interrogated or spread gossip. Sometimes there were thousands of troops, sometimes none. Live training was descending into farce. One officer described the first days in France as 'a comically complete nightmare'.

Sir Henry Rawlinson noted in his diary: 'Saw a tank at St Riquier. Interesting show. Less visible and less noisy than I expected. They will be most useful at night. Doubtful if possible to use by day in line.' Haig was also impressed by his first sight of tanks nosing their way into Le Bois Grambus. 'One entered a wood ... and easily walked over fair sized trees,' he confided to his diary that night. 'Altogether the demonstration was quite encouraging, but we require to clear our ideas as to the tactical use of these machines.' It was a little late for that.

Rawlinson wrote to Sir Clive Wigram, the King's Assistant Private Secretary: 'We are puzzling our heads as how to make the best use of them. They are not going to take the British army straight to Berlin, but if properly used and skilfully handled ... they may be very useful in taking trenches and strong points. Some people are rather too optimistic as to what these weapons will accomplish ...'

And who might these people have been? It was not Swinton, who was back at Beauquesne on 29 August, the day Rawlinson drafted his letter. This time he was accompanied by Bradley. John Brough for some reason seemed to have vanished. 'The official atmosphere was not very helpful,' Swinton recalled. 'In many quarters there was an air of amused tolerance or contemptuous scepticism ... In some a tendency to place too much reliance on the influence of a few tanks to make up for the recent disappointment of the offensive. They are in the ascendant.'

He remembered being 'taken aside by a senior officer [it was 'Jock' Burnett-Stuart] who besought me to exert my influence to prevent the whole plan of operations being allowed to depend on ... these untried machines, I endeavoured to do so, but those in control were in no mood to pay attention to me or indeed anyone from home.'

The mystery of Brough's disappearance was solved. '[He] must have shown his feelings rather plainly,' wrote Swinton, 'for I was pained and astonished to be told he was not *persona grata* at GHQ and that his replacement by another officer was desired. The reason given was that he was "difficult".

'He probably was. He certainly had reason to be. He rightly pointed out that but little was known as yet of the power of the tanks, and that there had been insufficient time to train their crews properly.

He deprecated the employment of a small number of machines and urged the necessity for a first effort on as large a scale as possible . . .'

Poor Brough. He had been fighting GHQ and the appalling 'driblets' plan to the end. He had lost. There had been some sort of confrontation at Fourth Army HQ; its substance is not recorded in the otherwise copious surviving documentation of 'Alpaca's' fitful journey to the battlefield. Rawlinson wrote in his journal: '3 September: I spent the morning at St Riquier looking at the "Tanks". I was not pleased with them and it does not seem to me that anyone is taking them in hand and teaching them. Brough their CO is no sort of good – I made a fuss and complained to Tavish* and Butler at GHQ when I got back.' His fate was sealed.

Swinton had played a higher political game in London but that too had failed. His second in command paid the price. Swinton absolved himself in his memoirs, stating: 'That [Brough's] views were unacceptable at GHQ, was, however, no justification for changing the commander of a brand-new force two weeks before it went into action for the first time. It was in addition, an injustice to a very capable officer.' Swinton claimed he got a promise that Brough would be employed in France in the future. It did not exactly help.

Who would take over? From the tone of contemporary documents, for a day or two Swinton clearly thought it would be him. But Swinton was 'forty-eight and looked it', in the words of an anonymous obituarist – 'Haig always preferred younger men'. For now at least it would be the 'florid' Lt-Col. Robert Bradley who would take command. Haig and Butler were already sizing up a successor. But let the motorcycling Old Harrovian flap around on the sidelines as the plan for the first tank attack was put together. If it went wrong, he could take the blame.

---

* Major-General Sir John 'Tavish' Davidson, a senior figure on the staff at GHQ where, in the words of one historian, 'he tried (and usually failed) to counter the over optimism and strategic grandiosity of his Chief [Haig] . . .'

24

John Brough had evidently put up another 'black'. The men of the Heavy Section arriving in their trainloads at Conteville had quickly found themselves obliged to perform as some sort of 'circus act'. Brough had objected.

They were being treated as a 'new kind of toy', Swinton was 'horrified' to discover on a visit to the training area later on the day of his 29 August meeting with Haig. After their first outing at Le Bois Grambus three days earlier, gossip had indeed spread. They had become, in one description, the 'star variety turn of the Western Front'. Everyone wanted to see them.

The twenty-two-year-old Prince of Wales, a Grenadier Guards subaltern on the staff of XIV Corps, was one such. He wrote to his father, King George V:

> On Friday [1 September] I motored to a place called Yvrencheux W. of Amiens with Gen. [Lt-Gen. Sir Thomas] Morland to watch the trials of ½ dozen of these 'land submarines' of which you have heard about I expect. We watched them assault some trenches with infantry. The scheme is they should be launched against the Huns behind the 1st wave and go right on to the 2nd objective in front of the 2nd wave of infantry. I enclose a rough sketch of these land submarines or 'Tanks' as they are called for secrecy. The Huns have no doubt got accurate drawings of them and have by now produced a superior article!! Personally I think they are nice toys and worth trying; but not to be in any way relied on for success for I don't think they will be a success.
>
> Gen. Putty & a whole crowd of staff officers were also at these trials and we lunched together afterwards . . .

The heir to the throne's charmingly A. A. Milneish letter contained competent drawings and accurate technical specifications of the 'land submarines', as he called them (a curious coining – he described other points from the battlefield to his former naval officer father in similar nautical terms), and a plan of how they were going to attack the 'ennemy'. But the young man seemed dismissive of their chances. And it was all meant to be awfully secret. It seems odd therefore that he should tell 'Papa' that the Huns not only knew all this but must have acted on their knowledge already. It was a reflection perhaps of how persistent the popular notions still were of highly placed 'secret enemies of the empire', or the 'hidden hand' on which all setbacks might be conveniently blamed.

A thirty-eight-year-old Captain of the Ox and Bucks Light Infantry, John Frederick Charles Fuller, was another who wanted to see the tanks. Newly arrived on the Somme, he ventured to Yvrench to see the fabled beasts for himself. He was reminded of 'Epsom Downs on a Derby morning. There were scores and scores of cars there and hundreds and hundreds of spectators both English and French. Everyone was talking and chatting, when slowly came into sight the first tank I ever saw. Not a monster, but a very graceful machine, with beautiful lines, lozenge-shaped, but with two clumsy looking wheels behind it.'

Le tout Somme was arriving by the carload to see the 'antics of the tanks' — tree-demolishing performances and elephantine pirouettes that had no tactical or training value but which were, meanwhile, exhausting crews and breaking machines. Repair facilities and spare parts supply were as yet non-existent. A tank with a broken track had to be abandoned at Conteville and cannibalized for spares. Major Holford-Walker had to send a 'man back to England' to bring out fifteen sets of spanners that he had telegrammed his wife to obtain from a tool shop.

There were some attempts at practical training. Basil Henriques recalled sporadic instruction with different sorts of gas masks and 'unexpectedly issued' pigeons. But between time, as he wrote, 'we were for ever showing off, not to the men with whom we were to fight, but to the "brass-hats" from HQ, who found us a highly amusing diversion.'

Haig visited St Riquier again on Sunday 3 September (the day John Brough got the black spot), this time bringing General Joffre, who 'seemed much impressed . . . He ran about on his little feet till he poured with perspiration,' as the C-in-C recorded in his diary that night. The Prince of Wales witnessed the Heavy Section's evolutions.

So did a young infantry subaltern of the King's Royal Rifle Corps, 2/Lt Anthony Eden. He saw a tank crush a machine-gun cart, a particularly unpopular piece of equipment, to the cheers of the infantry. Lord Northcliffe turned up at GHQ with the faithful *Times* foreign editor Henry Wickham Steed and was soon eagerly 'inspecting something called tanks which Sir Douglas Haig had strongly recommended us to see . . . He had given us no hint of what the tanks might be. Sir Julian Byng [the Canadian Corps commander] merely smiled a weird smile . . .'

The press baron 'squeezed in by the manhole on the top . . . but stuck midway and had to be pulled from inside . . . getting out was even harder'. Clive Bigham, MO5's liaison officer in Paris with the Bureau Central Interallié, the leaky Anglo-French-Russian intelligence clearing house and common censorship overseer, came for a look. Edwin Montagu, the Munitions Minister, arrived at GHQ, and seemingly just like every other visitor from London urged the C-in-C to hold the tanks back until more might arrive from England. Haig noted simply: 'Mr Montagu came to see me . . . he seems capable and agreeable. He is to return later, when he is less busy (he is apparently a Jew).'

Later that day, 7 September, it was Herbert Asquith's turn, accompanied by Maurice Hankey on a visit to the front. Hankey recalled: 'We drove on to see the caterpillars of which we found around sixty-two, painted in grotesque colours. While we were there a German aeroplane flying at a great height came overhead and the whole of the tanks took cover under trees etc or were covered in tarpaulins painted to look like haystacks.'

It was all very impressive but the Downing Street mission was there for a purpose. Dining at GHQ that night, Hankey later claimed that he 'pressed restraint on the two principal staff officers' (presumably Butler and Wigram) and urged them to 'keep the tanks for an offensive over less weary ground'. The Prime Minister, he said, urged the same point of view upon Haig, 'with equal lack of success'.* The tanks were in the field. They would be committed to the battle.

* It was Winston Churchill who by his own account brought about this last-minute high-level intervention to overturn, as he put it, the 'proposal to expose this tremendous secret on such a petty scale . . .' He then 'sought an interview with Mr Asquith of whom I was then a very definite opponent' to make the point, so he told the official historian in 1926 (sending him proofs of the second volume of his own *The World Crisis* for comment). 'The Prime Minister listened so patiently to my appeal that I thought I had

Haig wrote to his wife with an uncharitable story about Asquith's intake of brandy that night. He was 'unsteady on his legs as he retired to sleep'. It was all very amusing. The Prime Minister went to Fricourt the next morning and drove out to see his son Raymond. The Grenadier Guards lieutenant had ridden cross country to meet his father at some blighted crossroads. Father and son seemed overjoyed to see each other.

The tank crews did not seem to mind the attention. But grease-smudged and curiously outfitted in motley overalls and their leather 'anti-bruise' helmets, they were already beginning to excite the disapproval of a certain caste of officer who expected 'the smartness and precision of a military tournament turn'.

As they emerged from their machines grinning at the end of their circus stunts, the Heavy Section's individual approach to discipline was becoming ever more apparent. Loyalties built within the confines of a metal box, useful on the battlefield, might prove troublesome off it. However, in an uncharacteristic lapse in War Office starchiness, at Yvrench something remarkable happened – the 'hush-hushes' were given names.

Who sanctioned the move is unrecorded, as is exactly why. It was at the company commander's discretion and later in the war the practice of 'naming' tanks was unsportingly suppressed. But in summer 1916 there were precedents. Artillerymen gave their big guns names, so did fighter pilots and armoured-car crews of the Royal Naval Air Service.

The army's Motor Machine Gun Service painted the names of girlfriends ('Gert', 'Daisy', 'Queenie') on the fuel tanks of their motor-cycles. Perhaps it was a nod to the 'landships' naval origins. There was a ready excuse to get out the paintbrushes. Colonel Solomon's Fauvist daubs applied at Elveden had, meanwhile, proved too testing for GHQ. The Heavy Section were ordered to paint over his 'pink sunsets' in sterner blobs of brown and grey.

Names were applied on the bows of the tanks as on warships – tokens variously of military ferociousness, suburban whimsy and lovers' keepsakes. It was the individual tank commander's preroga-

---

succeeded in convincing him.' Any proposal from Mr Churchill would be guaranteed to make GHQ do the opposite.

tive, as long as they kept to the alphabet and chose nothing too vulgar. D Company went for 'Die Hard' and 'Dracula', 'Delphine', 'Daphne' and 'Dolly'. C Company emptied the drinks cabinet – 'Champagne', 'Chartreuse', 'Chablis', 'Crème de Menthe' and 'Cordon Rouge'. Lieutenant Stuart Hastie in a horrid Scots pun called his machine numbered D. 17 'Dinnaken'. Second Lieutenant William Sampson inevitably dubbed his tank 'Delilah'.

The lack of real training was a serious matter. Clough Williams-Ellis would write of the days at Yvrench: 'Most of the men and many of the officers had not been to France before. [There was] no staff of instructors, stages were too short and the conditions for battle practice quite unlike that which prevailed on the Somme. But it had to suffice – the tanks were wanted at once.'

According to Basil Henriques: 'We had no training with the infantry, even at home, and the infantry with whom we were to fight had never heard of us until they actually saw us in battle. We had never driven in England with our flaps closed, so that we had never used the periscope and we had only driven with a clear view on perfectly level ground.'

Haig's call for 'clear ideas as to the tactical use of these machines' was being progressed, meanwhile, within the confines of Advanced GHQ and Fourth Army headquarters at Querrieu. The practical realities of going to war in experimental machines crewed by combat novices were scarcely considered.

Major Allen Holford-Walker recalled a terse meeting with Rawlinson at his forward HQ. The Fourth Army commander wanted to know 'whether his men were trained'. They were 'not fit to fight immediately,' he replied, because, 'I had not one man or officer who had seen a shelled area.'

Brigadier-General Sir John Gathorne-Hardy, XIV Corps' Chief of Staff, was even brusquer, asking no questions, merely passing over a map marked with prescribed tank routes – 'fixed with no reconnaissance by any officer who knew anything about a tank'. The company commander would find himself with nothing to command, orders being issued directly to junior officers responsible for two or three tanks. Almost twenty years later, in his correspondence with the Official Historian, Holford-Walker would describe the results as 'literally disastrous'.

Frank Summers' mood was even bleaker. According to D Company's adjutant, recalling events forty years later: 'Headquarters was a box van and Summers monopolised that for office and sleeping. I just dossed down where I could – more often than not under the horns of a tank . . . When Summers was in one of his moods – no one dare go near the box van . . . Yes, he was difficult at times – impossible to be charitable – I think he was a sick man.'*

The opening of the offensive was less than two weeks away. Brough was packing his valise at Yvrench, Bradley was sheepishly preparing to take over 'command in the field', whatever that was. Swinton was back in London brooding in Room 337 of Armament Buildings, girding himself, whether the tanks triumphed or failed, for the inevitable political battles to come. Heavy Section HQ in France was emasculated.

At Fourth Army's preliminary planning conference on 31 August, no one from the Heavy Section was invited to contribute. The meeting agreed unsurprisingly that the tanks would be used as per GHQ's dictum of mid-August – in sub-sections of two or three, adjuncts to the infantry against strong points – dispersed more or less along the whole attack frontage. There was the question of the use of artillery after the opening bombardment. The creeping barrage of 1 July that was supposed to suppress machine guns as the infantry plodded forward had not succeeded. That of 15 September would be more intense, moving at a third of the pace, fifty yards per minute, three rounds of shrapnel per 18-pounder gun. Were the tanks supposed simply to crawl behind it?

Sixteen tanks were allocated to XIV Corps on the right, ten to the Guards Division, and the remainder divided between the 6th and 56th divisions. Eighteen tanks were allotted to XV Corps and eight to III Corps which formed the left wing of the Fourth Army. The other six were given to the Reserve Army which allotted them to the Canadian Corps on its right wing.

On 4 September Lt-Col. John Brough left for England, another 'dud' officer posted home to drift around the United Services Club. He had never got near the brutal realities of the Somme. At least he was still alive.

---

* Summers had just lost his only son, a midshipman aboard the battlecruiser HMS *Indefatigable*, sunk at Jultand.

25

As the men of the Heavy Section moved ever nearer the front, the landscape of the devastated zone began to reveal itself. As Fourth Army's preliminary orders recognized, 'Tank officers are without exception strange to the ground and to the conditions of the battle.' What they found was banal and quite horrible all at once.

The Somme was like a 'decaying suburb', in John Buchan's famous phrase describing the four-mile-deep, twenty-mile-long strip of tortured earth, brick and smashed trees after three months of fighting (the novelist-turned-official chronicler was writing in October 1916). The battlefield was 'pockmarked with shell holes, littered with cartridge clips, equipment and fragments of wire and every kind of tin can. Over all hangs the curious, bitter, unwholesome smell of burning.'

On the horizon was a reminder of what had been – and where the Fourth Army might even yet find its point of breakthrough. 'Look east beyond our front line and the smoke puffs,' wrote Buchan, 'across the Warlencourt and Gueudecourt ridges and on the skyline there appear unbroken woods and here and there a church spire . . .'.

The Heavy Section officer Clough Williams-Ellis described the scene at night: 'At some point or other in our line, far away, a star shell could always be seen sailing up from behind a rise of ground . . . giving some fringe of shattered wood or ruined sugar factory a fleeting silhouette against its cold white light . . .'

The north-eastern horizon might have been as distant as the mountains of the moon. It was not the chalky uplands of Gueude-court that concerned the men in tanks. It was the stinking mire at their feet. They were called 'crumps', rimmed craters blown out by burrowing high-explosive shells, garnished by human and horse flesh, their gaping mouths made seemingly bottomless by the long shadows of late summer evenings. As Hugh Elles noted, it was all 'Very different from that which Swinton and their designers had in their minds, they had something in the nature of the Battle of Loos, smooth ground intersected at intervals by shell craters large or small. The Somme ground when dry was like aerated soft sand and when wet a quagmire, conditions which simply appalled the tank officers to whom I showed them.'

Would tanks be able to move at all in this moonscape already pocked and churned by the impact of two million shells? It was due to be smashed up again by almost another million more.

On 4 September at Fricourt Farm, one of the few points captured in the opening days of the offensive, having been pulverized by British shelling, Hugh Elles conducted a very practical if belated test. Tanks took five minutes to traverse just 100 yards of cratered ground. A Fourth Army conference considered the report the next day. General Rawlinson noted: 'The difficulty of course is to get them going fast enough in front of the infantry, if the infantry overtake them they will not be much use . . . In regard to Flers [the fortified village in the centre of the attack front] I suppose the best plan is to put them down the main street, a group down the middle and a group round either side. It is downhill into Flers and we ought to get a better speed out of them . . .'

He was taking a more direct interest in their tactical handling. Tanks might move in 'diamond four formation against strong points,' Rawlinson suggested, 'with the usual artillery barrage maintained between the groups'. So the tanks would grope their way down 'lanes' 100 yards wide, as the creeping barrage (moving more slowly and more intensely than ever before) erupted either side of them. But if the tanks did not work, or failed to get into action, the infantry must still advance without the cover of a barrage. This would cause bitter anguish when it was put to the test.

There was the matter of High Wood to consider, the flyblown, corpse-strewn, shattered stand of trees on rising ground in the centre of the III Corps area that had resisted capture since July. The opposing trench lines carved into its southern edge were too close for artillery to be employed, it was considered (no one seemed to have suggested simply evacuating the British-held positions). Could not tanks act as a substitute? The 5 September conference considered the possibility.

The Corps commander, Lt-Gen. Sir William 'Putty' Pulteney, thought that they could, as 'they would have cover all the way' (he seemed to mean provided by trees in leaf – even though the wood had been blown to bits) 'and could go quickly'. The faintly ridiculous Bradley stayed silent. Brough had been sent home in disgrace the day before. It was down to the ambitious Royal Engineer, the hardworking Hugh Elles, to represent the views of the tank men, but he seems to have calamitously bungled it.

In the judgement of two prominent modern historians of the Somme: 'It was desperately necessary that Pulteney's views be corrected. Colonel Elles, a tank expert at GHQ [he knew as much anyone – which was very little] attempted to do this . . . but he dissipated his whole message by telling Pulteney that tanks could not get through Trônes Wood, a position that had fallen two months previously. Yet more remarkably, he did not mention High Wood at all. The end result of this dialogue of the deaf was that Rawlinson . . . left the decision to Pulteney. The results would be quite disastrous.'

The divisional commander, Lt-Gen. Sir Charles Barter, also proved 'sticky'. A move round the flanks might be more productive, so he suggested. Rawlinson stayed aloof. Elles had made a fool of himself. Bradley expressed no opinion. Barter was overruled. Pulteney's views prevailed. The tanks, however many of them might be available, would precede the infantry into the wood.

Work by the Quartermaster General's department on a tactical staging area forward of Yvrench had begun at GHQ's instructions in the third week of August, adapting a point on the railway that ran from Fricourt to Bray-sur-Somme where it made a horseshoe-shaped bend known to the French as the Fer à Cheval and to the British as 'the Loop'. There had once been a village there. Now it was just a 'shattered pile of bricks'.

Half of C Company's tanks departed Conteville on 3–4 September, the rest set out the next morning. D Company followed on the 6th, also in two detachments. The exhausting work of removing sponsons, loading machines on flat-cars, detraining, refitting sponsons and fettling machines began all over again, even before the bruising task of loading ammunition ('bombing up', as British tank crews would come to call it) was begun. In Suffolk the men and machines of A and B Companies were getting ready for their own voyage to France.* Even at the Loop there was renewed attention from curious brass hats. H. Perry Robinson, *The Times*'s intrepid war correspondent,† was allowed a censored glimpse (when the lid came off it would result in a bravado piece of journalistic self-aggrandizement). On 10 September there was an enormous gathering of senior staff from Fourth and Reserve Armies. The surreal August Bank Holiday atmosphere continued. Williams-Ellis quoted one tank commander: 'It rather reminded me of Hampstead Heath. When we got there we found that the infantry brigades had been notified that the tanks were to perform daily from 9 to 10 and from 2 to 3 and every officer within a large radius and an enormous number of the staff came to inspect us. We were an object of interest to everyone.'

There was basic housekeeping to be done, the problems of which, according to Basil Henriques, 'became acute – stowing two gas helmets, one pair of goggles, service cap, anti-bruise helmet, field dressing, first aid dressing, revolver, haversack, iron rations. There are eight people in a tank and as soon as they get in they naturally take off all these things which lie about on the floor . . .'

Personal effects jostled with 'Sixteen loaves, thirty tins of food, cheese, sugar, tea, milk, one spare drum of engine oil and one of gear oil, two small drums of grease, three water cans and two boxes of revolver ammunition, four spare Vickers barrels, one spare Vickers gun, a spare barrel for the Hotchkiss and two wire-cutters and three signal flags.'

Lieutenant Victor Huffam added 'half a cow' to his strange mani-

---

* A Company would arrive at Le Havre on 14 September, the men of B Company three weeks later. F stayed in England. Eight tanks of E Battalion (as it would be retitled) would be sent to Palestine in early 1917 to fight the Turks – where it was found they could operate in the sands of Gaza 'as long as their tracks were not greased'. It was a brave but futile diversion.

† The strictures on a war correspondent in 1916 were described thus: '[His] licence to correspond is issued from the War Office by the Army Council, and is forfeitable on conviction by court-martial, or if in the opinion of the Commander-in-Chief in the field, his return to obscurity is desirable in the national interest. He may not employ any means of communication other than the postal and telegraph service . . . nor may he write in cypher, code or foreign languages. The use of balloons, aeroplanes, motor cars and motor bicycles is also prohibited, but he may possess one horse, which must not be white or light grey. The correspondent and his servant must dress inconspicuously, and are not allowed to carry arms, except against an uncivilised enemy. So far, the Huns have not been placed in that category.' *War Budget*, 16 November 1916.

fest, and Williams-Ellis further accounted for: 'Two carrier pigeons, 33,000 rounds of small arms ammo, a signalling lamp and one telephone trailing a 100 yard wire from the tank's stern.' A bottle of turps was provided, a crucial piece of kit for battlefield communications. Huffam recalled: 'While loading that afternoon we had yet another visitor, who having got into D.9 by a small door 2ft by 2ft, bumped his head on the low steel roof, let fly some real oaths. On turning to see who it was and having sworn in reply, I was a little taken aback to see the Prince of Wales . . . He sat on the engine platform as we loaded . . .'

Fifty tanks had so far been sent from Elveden with ten more arriving directly from the factories as a reserve. Two weeks of transit and the cavorting at Yvrench had worn them down. The number of serviceable machines was now forty-nine. A and B Companies were still working up in Suffolk. The clock was ticking.

On the 11th Bradley was summoned to a conference as Fourth Army moved to its forward HQ at a château near the village of Heilly, where he seems to have contributed very little. The former commandant of a training school for motorcyclists did not have enough 'weight of metal' in Liddell Hart's phrase, to argue with the red-tabbed gods, even if he had wanted to. Allen Holford-Walker's judgement (given to, but certainly not published by, the Official Historian) was especially damning. 'Bradley knew absolutely nothing about tanks . . . [at the conference] he said it was possible for tanks to drive on a compass bearing . . .'

It was indeed possible, but the tanks themselves, big chunks of steel, were magnetized. Any such bearing was going to be unreliable. The moonscape they must cross meanwhile made driving in a straight line more than problematic. According to Holford-Walker, 'this statement of [Bradley's] resulted in a direct order to an officer to proceed on a bearing of forty-two degrees. He attempted to do so . . . and as a result got completely bewildered. I expostulated as soon as I heard but I was told by the Division in question to mind my own business.' The still embittered company commander had another target for retrospective blame – Hugh Elles. It was the test drive the ambitious Royal Engineer had arranged at Fricourt evidently on 5 September following Brough's removal, where the 'ground was a billiard table compared with the terrain around Guillemont, Ginchy and Thiepval.

I quote this tank trial because I consider that it was at the bottom of a great deal of the trouble that we had on 15 September, it gave an erroneous idea of what the tank could do . . .'

Fourth Army's own 'Instructions for the Employment of Tanks' were issued at the gathering on the 11th, a reprise of GHQ's doctrinal paper of a month before, for corps and divisional commanders to tinker with to suit their own circumstances.

The voices in London urging restraint had gone quiet. Those who had been given the grand tour, seen the great secret, seemed mesmerised by it. That it was the loathed Churchill and now evidently the French who seemed infirm of purpose just made GHQ more determined to throw in whatever was to hand. As the Prince of Wales excitedly told his father, writing on the evening of the 11th: 'I attended a conference held by Lord Cavan at Guards DIV HQ this morning which was attended by all DIV commanders; I gather that there is to be a huge and final attack next Friday (15th, Sept.) when the "Tanks" will be used.'

Herbert Asquith, the Prime Minister, had returned to London from his emotion-laden journey to the front the week before, evidently buoyed up by what he had seen. The meeting with his son, the C-in-C's brandy and the sight of the caterpillars had instilled a new confidence in the competence of GHQ. The civilian authority – the 'frocks' – might have nominal control over the strategic direction of the war, but when it came to the conduct of operations the 'brass-hats' had the power. But perhaps not yet over the use of a novel weapon. The War Cabinet that met in Downing Street at 11.30 on the morning of the 12th was therefore not about to abort the renewed offensive (the artillery bombardment had already begun, four hours earlier) but it might still decide the fate of the Heavy Section. Or could it?

Edwin Montagu, the Minister of Munitions, opened the discussion on the 'Western Front', advancing the hold-the-tanks-back argument by relaying information from M. Thomas, his counterpart in Paris, that the French had ordered the construction of '800 caterpillars' and that he was strenuously urging that 'we should not put ours into the field until they were ready'. (Someone in the magic circle was clearly furiously leaking to the French.)

Asquith was chastened. The Prime Minister thought this 'an

extraordinary request'. Montagu replied with some subtly advanced secret intelligence:

'There are rumours the Germans are making something of the same kind,' he said. 'It would be serious for both us and the French when once these machines had been used they lost their value as a surprise . . . If only fifty out of a thousand should be used, the surprise of the balance is finished . . .'

For a moment Asquith seemed to swing his way. 'They [the caterpillars] are purely an experiment,' he said. 'Their only chance lies in surprise . . .'

He described what he had himself observed with Hankey on the Somme the week before, and gave his colleagues a respectably accurate technical account of the new weapon's capabilities. 'I have seen them packed together,' he told Lord Curzon; 'they have been coloured after the cubists' style in an ingenious manner – so as to make them invisible . . . experiments have been made with aeroplanes flying above them and they could not be distinguished . . .'

But someone in London had got to him. Asquith next read out Swinton's typeset 'Notes on Employment', specifically drawing his Cabinet colleagues' attention to paragraph eleven, which stressed the 'impossibility of repeated employment'. There was one chance and one chance only. They could all agree on that. But Swinton, Brough, Churchill, M. Thomas in Paris – who were they in the face of the titan at the Château Valvion?

'Sir Douglas has not yet made up his mind how and when to use them,' Asquith said across the cabinet table (in fact he had – it would be in three days time!). 'He has twenty-five and is very sanguine as to their value . . . so is Sir Lancelot Kiggell.' Sir Edward Grey, the foreign secretary, said quietly: 'It seems best the decision be left to the man on the spot.' Asquith had run out of puff. So had everyone else round the table. There was no Churchill in the room to make a noise (although he was metaphorically banging on the door).

Field-Marshal 'Wully' Robertson, uniformed, hugely mustachioed, the brooding martial presence (but no Kitchener) in a room of frock-coated civilians, said precisely nothing. That was it. The tanks would be committed.

At a renewed Fourth Army conference on the afternoon of the 13th, intimate proposals for the employment of tanks were presented, down to the last strong point. This time Robert Bradley did contribute something, and it was rather strange. When the Cavalry Corps commander, Lt-Gen. Sir Charles 'Black-Jack' Kavanagh, asked whether 'following the breakthrough' tanks might not move forward with his horsemen to more distant objectives, Bradley said they could cover sixty miles on the petrol carried, depending on the nature of the ground and other circumstances. It was a bizarre exaggeration.

That night the tanks began to move, under their own power from the Loop under heavy rain along a road crammed with infantry and ammunition wagons, the four miles or so to their Corps assembly areas. C Company's HQ was at 'Le Briquetterie', a ruined brick-works near Trônes Wood, and D Company's at 'Green Dump', mid-way on the shell-pocked road between Longueval and Bazentin-le-Grand. The six tanks allotted to Reserve Army were corralled outside the ruins of Albert. According to Williams-Ellis: 'They found themselves in a strange world. Endless lines of transport crawled over incredibly bad roads bordered by stumps of trees and by a sordid and tragic litter of dead men and horses, rags, tin cans and rotting equipment.'

To the infantry preparing to go forward to their jumping-off positions, the new engines of war were just as alien. Few of them had heard of 'tanks' before, let alone seen one. Were they frightening – or were they funny?

Stephen Foot, an infantry officer who would later join the Tank Corps, thought they were hilarious. Watching D Company's machines arrive at Green Dump he remembered: 'One wanted to laugh . . . standing still they were funny, moving along they were a scream.'

Lieutenant Geoffrey Malins, the cinematographer who was there to make the official film record of the battle, could not take his eyes off the first tank he saw, 'waddling, ambling, jolting, rolling . . . doing everything in turn . . . Presently it stopped, the humming ceased. The spell was broken. We looked at one another and then we laughed. How we laughed! Officers and men were doubled up with mirth.'

But the funfair mood was fading. The sound of tank-inspired laughter was joined by the boom of artillery. The British bombardment had opened half an hour after dawn on 12 September – 1258 guns and howitzers pounding the whole German defensive system across its depth and deep into the rear as far as Bapaume. Road junctions were drenched with gas shells.

The day before battle, 14 September, was spent laid up in hastily corralled positions close to the British gun line under whatever shelter might be found, snatching sleep, brewing tea, 'cleaning and greasing'.

The gunners were on their third day of labour, the passage of their shells filling the air with solemn moans and shrill whistling. The sound did not seem to travel anywhere, with neither start point nor destination – that was the surprise. The shudders of the bombardment enwrapped the battlefield novices of the Heavy Section. Sleep was fitful.

Everywhere along the line, dispersed in their sections of six tanks or fewer, crews tinkered with engines, tightened tracks and checked weapons. Corporal H. Sanders extemporized a meal of 'meat and onions', cooked up in the lid of a biscuit tin over a wood fire. His 'skipper', Mr Huffam, declined to eat it.

In the last hours of daylight, tank commanders fretted over trench maps and aerial photographs handed to them by brisk divisional officers. The overhead shots of their intended routes were 'clear when seen from the air but completely indistinguishable when one was on the ground', according to Hugh Elles. They must proceed to such and such a point, moving in accordance with the artillery timetable, using clock and compass, then engage such and such a strong point.

They had not been trained for anything like this. According to one young tank commander: 'I and my crew did not have a tank of our own the whole time we were in England . . . our tank went wrong the day it arrived . . . Again we had no reconnaissance or map reading . . . no practice or lectures on the compass . . . we had had no signalling and no practice in considering orders.'

Division's mimeographed instructions were an alphabet soup of map references and timetables. The *Official History* commented: 'Having received his instructions, the tank commander was to prepare his own map showing the distinctive features of his route, his compass bearing from point to point and the time that he must arrive at each. It is to be feared that in many cases young and inexperienced commanders found themselves overburdened with directions which had to be memorized as there were not enough copies to go round.'*

Someone tried to simplify things. In the Tank Museum at Boving-ton is a fascinating document – 'handwritten notes for tank com-manders', crudely run off in purple ink from a 'Banda' mimeograph machine at a company assembly area probably a few hours before the attack. Considering what was waiting for the young men who read it, its cheery practicality makes it truly heroic:

> Tell your men all about everything you know or think you know yourself and make them interested in the whole operation.
>> Learn exactly what you have to do and teach your whole crew.
>
> Don't drive too close along a communication trench.
>
> Stop your engine when possible to save petrol.
>
> You can take all the petrol cans you can get hold of or carry to fill up at every possible point. You can always throw this overboard if necessary.
>
> In action. Keep a good look out all round. Be at the right place at the right time. Drive as straight as possible, fast if necessary, but be late rather than smash up.
>
> If counterattacked, rush in among the enemy firing every available gun.
>
> Under no circumstances must your tank fall into enemy hands.
>
> If in danger of capture loose off your ammunition, pour out petrol and set on fire.
>
> If in danger of capture pour petrol on all orders and papers and set fire to them. Only take with you what is absolutely necessary, e.g. your map, sketch of route and time table.
>
> Prisoners must be left with the infantry.
>
> Don't bunch.
>
> Pigeons are not to be used except in the most dire necessity.

Around 7.00 p.m., as darkness began to fall, Daimler engines were again cranked into life (it took four men to swing the outsize handle) for the final move one or two miles to the 'points of deployment'

---

* According to the machine-gun expert Christopher Baker-Carr, who was with the Heavy Section on the eve of battle: 'Even the spoken jargon of war required explanation to a young tank commander already over-awed at finding himself in conversation with a major-general. It is amusing to think how within a year the same young officer was to lay down the law before division and brigade commanders, but before this came about, much blood was to be soaked into the earth.'

behind the British front-line trenches. Several vehicles failed to start outright or stopped dead with breakdowns. A wallowing tank going nose down meant the gravity feed from the fuel tanks, so ominously flanking the commander and driver, was shut off. The carburettor had to be hand-primed by pouring petrol from a can. A tank jammed at an angle, straining to extricate itself, would lose engine lubrication as the oil sloshed in the crank case beyond reach of the return pump. Crankshaft bearings disintegrated. Sprocket wheels were prone to break up after running twenty miles.

Several machines were swallowed whole by the earth when they ran over and collapsed a dugout. According to Williams-Ellis, one driver baulked when he found he had to 'go down a sunken road full of the bodies of dead Boches'.

Lieutenant Basil Henriques left his holding position in 'Chimpanzee Valley' at dusk on the evening of the 14th, nosing forward at 2 mph. He got out of his tank in the darkness, 'to go ahead on foot to see what sort of ground we would have to cover. It was a clear night and we got our first view of what looked like impossible ground . . . hardly a yard was not a shell crater. What on earth had been the use of all that training in the meadows of Elveden?'

At midnight Henriques reached a position a thousand yards behind the British first line in XIV Corps' sector facing a defensive position known as the Quadrilateral, then 'switched off the engine to allow it to cool down'. In the shuffle forward from Chimpanzee Valley his friend 2/Lt George Macpherson's tank broke down once, restarted, then expired completely. Then the tank of Capt. 'Archie' Holford-Walker, the brother of the C Company commander, broke its tail still short of the British first line. 'He came back and reported that he was out of action and that I was to go on alone,' recalled Henriques. In the grinding progress he realized he had consumed half the fuel. Sixteen gallons of petrol were scrounged in the darkness.

Orders would change and change again as the hours ticked away into the night. They came from division, brigade, battalion, even in some cases company – the latest intimate instructions given 'orally' – to be scribbled on already irrelevant trench maps by the light of a sputtering candle in a dugout as tank and infantry officer together made of it what they could.

One by one the tanks were dropping out, beaten by breakdowns and the tortured terrain. Out of forty-nine that had departed the Loop, around thirty were left in Fourth Army's Area, and the six allotted to Reserve Army heading for their corps assembly area a little east of Albert.

Some crews, it might seem, just did not fancy it at all. Writing of the events of 15 September two years later, the officer who had found such reluctance among the Army Service Corps drivers at Elveden to climb inside a tank in the first place had a different target to blame. Captain Steedman thought it worthy of reporting that:

> The Machine Gun Corps as a unit were over officered and under disciplined . . . Many failed to go into action in circumstances in which an inquiry would be interesting.
>
> Several were lost on account of incompetent [sic] caused by the substitution of one of the MGC for an ASC driver. Engines seized in the most strange way: Oil was found to have been completely drained. Reports would come back that such and such a tank was hopelessly bogged. An ASC party would go out and have no difficulty in moving it . . .

Breakdowns, ditching and a degree of human intervention had now reduced the force to thirty-two. Second Lieutenant Arthur Arnold commanding D.16 Dracula got to the start line. He recalled the final move-up:

> It was only three miles or so from Green Dump to my particular spot and I have always been puzzled as to why it took nine hours . . . for we seemed to be travelling the whole time and made no deliberate stops. But it was a case of bottom gear all the time – a speed of a thousand yards an hour . . . [and it was] necessary at times for one of the crew to get out and scout a way round a particularly bad patch . . .
>
> As the dawn began to show the going was now simply one succession of shell craters. The rate of progress was now desperately slow and I suppose the last thousand yards took two hours to cover . . .

The British first line – and no-man's-land – lay beyond. Then there were the Germans.

26

Basil Henriques had found his extra petrol. The engine of C.22 was cranked into life. The crew scrambled aboard through the female tank's tiny doors beneath the machine-gun sponsons. The burst of a star shell flash-lit the lumpy porridge bowl ahead of them then faded to inky black. An infantryman with little lanterns on his back led the way into a lane marked on each side with luminous tape. A last check of watch and compass. No sign of Macpherson or 'Archie' Holford-Walker's tanks, still stuck in Chimpanzee Valley. They were alone. The engine was warming now, the metal box a fug of fumes and human sweat. Henriques banged the hull for both gearsmen to engage – first speed – a blip on the throttle. At 4.00 a.m., C.22 began rolling:

> Squashing dead Germans as we went. We could not steer properly and I kept on losing the tape. At five I was about 500 yards behind the [British] First Line. I again stopped as we were rather too early. There was to be a barrage of artillery fire through which a space was to be left for me to go . . .
>
> I reached another English trench but was not allowed to stop for fear of drawing fire upon the infantry so I withdrew 20 yards and waited five minutes, but nothing happened and I decided to go forward.

The morning dawned cool with an eddying mist and a slight ground haze. The sun rose at 5.40. Strewn out along a front of almost ten miles between Pozières on the left and Combles on the right, thirty-two surviving tanks were in cumbersome motion, following their luminous-taped routes to their start points, facing into the hundred-yard-wide zones that the artillery fireplan was supposed to keep open.

If the infantry at first sight had found the tanks 'funny', their presence was not so amusing now. 'It was her slowness that scared us as much as anything, the way she shook her wicked old head and stopped to cough,' a wounded London Territorial told Beach Thomas of the *Daily Mail* afterwards.

Tanks were supposed go into action with their hatches closed – navigation in the half-light effected by squinting through vision slits faced by those crude glass prisms – orders to the brake and gearsmen given by shouts, bangs and hand signals as the engine clattered, pigeons cooed, gunners swore and the drive train grumbled.

It was already going wrong. A preliminary move had begun in the darkness just after 5.00 a.m. with three tanks in XV Corps area supposed to clear a forward enemy trench system called Hop Alley, between Delville Wood and the village of Ginchy, before the main offensive opened at Zero-Hour eighty minutes later. One tank's engine stopped (D.5 Dolphin), another ditched. The single tank which managed to station itself correctly was D.1, number one tank of D Company commanded by Capt. Harold Mortimore. Gunner Albert Smith recalled: 'White tapes had been laid down to Hop Alley, at one period one of our crew got out and guided the driver with red and green lights showing from a belt he had round him . . . At zero we moved off . . . I think we all had the wind up but we were a good crew and collected. We were getting along nicely, all guns manned when there was a crash and we stopped dead.'

D.1 had begun rolling at 5.15 a.m. British Summer Time, five minutes late, blasting its way into Hop Alley, followed fifteen minutes later by two rifle companies of the 6th King's Own Yorkshire Light Infantry. The infantry outran the tank – into a second defensive position known as Ale Alley, to be caught by enfilading machine-gun fire. All the officers were killed. The shell which then struck D.1 was probably British.

'Sgt Davies [the starboard gunner] was shell-shocked', so Gnr Smith's account continued. 'We put out the flags [to indicate] that we had broken down, the infantry were then passing and we could not help them. We got Davies out and the RAMC took him away, we had been hit by a shell in the starboard sprocket. We stood by the tank waiting for orders but we got none . . .'

The eastern sky was lightening. Zero-Hour for the main assault came at 6.20 a.m. BST. Whistles blew, and infantry scrambled out of their trenches to begin the plod across no-man's-land in the wake of the barrage of shells which at zero plus six began to creep ahead of them at fifty yards a minute. But this time, in the special supposedly 'shell-free' lanes at least, they were preceded (in some cases followed) by tanks. The Heavy Section were meant to have left their own start lines in the precisely choreographed plan twenty minutes earlier. Some had done just that. Others had not started at all.

A little more than thirty had managed to get into action, around 250 officers and men of the Heavy Section on whose success or failure, according to the *Official History*, 'the Fourth Army plan of attack had been gambled'.

On the extreme far right of the Fourth Army front, the XIV Corps area, one tank (C.16, commanded by 2/Lt Eric Purdy) got far enough from its start line to a position facing the fortified village of Combles, before being hit by a British 18-pounder shell. Purdy survived to be awarded the Military Cross and later become a member of the concert party of C Battalion Heavy Branch, 'the Willies'.

Of two tanks operating to C.16's left, one commanded by Lt Sir John Dashwood broke a track, the other cruised around the edge of Bouleaux Wood. Its commander, 2/Lt Francis Arnold, 'who had never seen a shot fired in wrath in his life', went further than his orders prescribed, intent on 'attacking Germany all on his own . . . shooting at every living thing he saw', according to his company commander. It was in vain. The infantry were way behind. C.14 ditched in a shell hole, the tracks spinning uselessly. They got out to dig but came under grenade and sniper attack. Corporal Gerald Pattison picked up a stick grenade which landed at his feet. It exploded in his hands. Gunner T. H. Bernard shot dead a Bavarian with two shots from his pistol. They scrambled back into the 'car'. Arnold sent a message by pigeon to divisional HQ describing their plight.

The female tank was jammed at an angle, unable to use her starboard Vickers guns. Gunner Bernard 'potted away' with his revolver 'through the loopholes of the conning tower'. After six hours of this ordeal 'it was decided to abandon the car and we made for a short trench . . . which had been made by connecting a few shell holes,' Bernard recalled in a diary entry made a few weeks afterwards. Six of the original crew would survive.

The 6th Division, the next in the line from the right, was intended to capture the village of Morval, having overcome the Quadrilateral with the aid of three tanks. As Basil Henriques' account explained, two machines had already broken down on the run-in from Chimpanzee Valley. What happened next remains contentious. According to the *Official History*: 'The machine [not identified] passed through . . . at about 5.50am and by mistake opened fire on the waiting troops. This was stopped by the gallant action of Captain A. J. G. Crosse, 9/Norfolk, who approached the tank under heavy fire and pointed out its true direction. The machine was afterwards seen to turn northward firing as it did so.'

It was in fact Basil Henriques in C.22, accused in various subsequent accounts of shooting up men of the Norfolk Regiment from behind and causing 'heavy casualties', believing them to be the garrison of the German front line rather than the assault troops waiting to attack it. A letter to the Official Historian from a Maj. A. Weyman described Capt. Crosse banging on the side of the tank to make it stop firing. 'As far as I know the tank caused no casualties but it undoubtedly upset them a good deal and they were furious with it. It was many months before the 16th Infantry Brigade wished to have anything to do with tanks . . . not until the Cambrai show,' the former infantry officer wrote in 1934.

The infantry duly followed in Henriques' wake towards the Quadrilateral in two assaults launched fifteen minutes apart. They got hung up in uncut wire under machine-gun fire from the flanks. British artillery 'shorts' began to fall on them. It was the customary disaster – the presence of a 'tank' just made it worse. The survivors took 'shelter in shell holes and stayed there', the *Official History* states dispassionately. 'The tank, with German bullets through its sponsons and petrol running low, had already returned.'

This was ghastly, an especially tragic debut of man and machine among a million tragedies. Henriques did not mention it either in his contemporaneous account or that written in the late 1930s, admitting only that his supposedly premature arrival was thought responsible for bringing down a German bombardment. But he hints at a deeper anguish: 'The physical, mental and nervous exhaustion after my first experience of warfare . . . still haunts me and fills me with horror,' he wrote.

Another authority who forensically examined this incident almost eighty years later produced a different verdict. The Norfolks were not even in the front line trenches at the time Henriques passed through them; they were still on the track up. It seemed as probable that a gunner in C.22 fired off a test burst on the run-in, alerting the Germans to the noise and exhaust sparks of something moving in the British line. The bombardment did the damage, Henriques got the blame.

The attack of the Guards Division out of Ginchy towards the village of Lesboeufs had been allotted ten tanks. Their efforts dissolved into chaos from the very start – breakdowns and ditching left four vehicles in two pairs on the flanks, all of which strayed off course, ditched or turned back for lack of petrol. When the tanks stopped so did the infantry.

James Attenborough, once an infantry officer now a solicitor, told the Official Historian in a letter of 1934:

> The men . . . were very excited at the idea of a tank and went merrily at first until the tank got straddled and refused to move. The Germans were momentarily too staggered at the sight of the tank to make much resistance but as soon as it stopped [the defence] very much stiffened.
> The fellow in charge of the tank got out and asked my second in command what he should do – and he told him to go back and fire off all his saa which he did. I don't remember the tank being hit.

The Guardsmen were flayed by machine-gun fire in a grim series of futilely brave assaults. 'Officers and men fell fast,' in the words of the *Official History*; 'for a moment there was check, then the Coldstream rushed forward . . . By 7.15 am the 2nd Guards Brigade, woefully reduced in numbers and with a few officers left, had reached a part at least of its first objective.' The tanks had seemingly disappeared.

In XV Corps' sector straddling Delville Wood in Fourth Army's centre, fourteen out of the eighteen tanks of D Company allotted to the assault on the fortified village of Flers were runners on the day. The preliminary move on Hop Alley had already gone wrong in the darkness. D.3, commanded by 2/Lt Harold Head, managed to start on the right going forward with the infantry of the 14th Division following. Lieutenant Charles Storey's D.4 ditched inside the wood. From a rise in the ground he could see the spires of Bapaume. The lieutenant would survive for another attempt to open the way to the fabled objective ten days later. In the same sector D.5 Dolphin, commanded by 2/Lt Arthur Blowers, had at last got his engine going. Dolphin crashed forward, heading northwards out of Delville Wood. A young infantryman* who was there recalled many years later: 'We in the ranks had never heard of tanks . . . We were told that there was some sort of secret weapon but we didn't know what the devil these things were. I was in the top left-hand corner of the area and we saw this thing go up in the right-hand corner of Delville towards Flers . . . then three or four more . . .'

Any training, any clue even as to how they were supposed to work with 'tanks' was non-existent. 'Whether officers – whether our subalterns had been told anything, I don't know. There was no suggestion as to how these things might give you cover. The ones that were ditched, I got as far away from as possible because you got a lot of bullets coming off them . . .'

The four tanks allotted to the New Zealand Division on the left of the Corps sector were slow in starting but caught up with the infantry. The first to arrive at its objective, D.10 (2/Lt H. Darby) was hit by a shell, shattering its vision prisms. The next two, D.11 Die Hard (Lt Herbert Pearsall) and D.12 (Capt. Graeme Nixon), got as far as the western outskirts of Flers. Pearsall would keep his tank up forward all day and the following night. A fourth tank, D.8, hooked round on the left flank when its prisms were shattered and it wallowed to a stop, effectively blinded.

In the centre of XV Corps sector, seven out of ten managed to start, setting out with the infantry of the 41st Division. Two ditched before even reaching the start line, two more, Lt Victor Huffam's D.9 and D.14 commanded by 2/Lt Gordon Court, became stuck in an abandoned support trench just a few hundred yards into no-man's-land.

In a postwar reminiscence for the *Tank Corps Journal*, an anonymous infantryman recalled the road running up to to Flers:

> There was only one approach to where the infantry lay . . . at
> the turn the road was protected from the north by a steep

---

* Private Arnold Ridley, a twenty-year-old private of the Somerset Light Infantry. More than five decades later he would find national celebrity playing Pte Godfrey in BBC TV's *Dad's Army*.

mound for a short distance. Anyone or anything going up or down from the line halted at this protected spot; the former for a last breather before plunging into the unknown, the latter for a spasm of profane ejaculation of gratitude for having reached so far. An advanced dressing station had been established and the wounded lay about the road, some on stretchers and some not. When zero hour came some infantry reached a line of ditches . . . one thing seemed certain and that was that our attack had been held up.

So far the only tanks we had seen were two overturned monsters lying deserted in the mud. We lay among our wounded waiting to make another attempt when joy of joys, that melodious low hum of a tank engine could be heard approaching up the Flers road.

Why it was not put out of action on a road in which the Hun could hit a penny piece on nine shots out of ten, we never knew. The fact remains that this noble warrior advanced up the road and disappeared among the ruins. I did not see it again.

If the purpose of sending up this isolated tank was to enable us to reach our objective it was fruitless, on the other hand if this noble creature ventured through almost certain perdition in the hope of stimulating our drooping spirits – it scored a certain amount of success . . .

The eighteen-year-old RFC pilot Lt Cecil Lewis and his observer saw the tanks' fitful progress towards their objectives from their BE2c artillery spotter:

We found the whole front seemingly covered with a layer of dirty cotton-wool . . . shellbursts. Across this were lanes, drawn as it might be by a child's fingers in dirty snow. Here no shells were falling. Through these lanes lumbered the tanks. By 6.20 they had reached the front line and the barrage began to roll back as they advanced, the infantry with them. We could see them sitting across the trenches and enfilading the enemy . . .

Some took fire, some suffered direct hits; but later many were still to be seen, refuelling in Flers, the red petrol tins visible on the brown backs.

It was hardly 'many' that had got to the objective. Only three machines, D.6, commanded by 2/Lt Reginald Legge, 2/Lt Arthur Arnold's D.16 – and D.17 commanded by 2/Lt Stuart Henderson Hastie, had managed to go forward in the centre. On the orders given the evening before, Hastie was to go for the main street running northwards around which the oblong-shaped village clustered, Legge in D.6 to break out to the east when his machine reached Switch Trench, flanking the shell-cratered road running north-west into Flers. Arthur Arnold in D.16 was to drive around to the west.

D.16 was far enough west of Flers to be in among the New Zealanders. Arthur Arnold recalled mounting his forward Hotchkiss machine gun as they crossed the first-line trenches which had been 'shelled out of existence' and broke into the support line: 'A row of German heads appeared above the parapet . . . at point blank range I drew a bead and pressed the trigger. It did not fire!'

The gun had been disabled by a shell splinter, but the side mounted Vickers came into action, annihilating the defenders.

Stuart Hastie's Army Service Corps driver, Pte Charles Wescomb, struggled to keep D.17 from ditching. With its damaged tail wheels now dragging uselessly behind, steering had to be effected by track braking – 'running the bearings on the engine's big ends'. At Switch Trench, 2/Lt Legge, still leading, broke away eastwards as ordered. Hastie and his crew were on their own, heading up the straight road for the barricaded village, its southern end now erupting in explosions.

27

Thus far it was their own mechanical frailty, 'crumps' and stray British shells that had depleted the attackers. It would be German machine guns and field artillery that would now test the tanks' vulnerability. Their steel insides sparkled with blue flashes as machine guns raked their flanks, spraying superheated streams of molten metal into faces and eyes.* Vision prisms shattered under rifle fire. In some places, defenders clambered on to the backs of machines to poke pistol barrels and bayonets through loopholes or hurled grenades at the diminutive conning towers. When a field gun found the range, directed by telephone from an observation balloon, the result was usually fatal.

After the troubled crossing of his own front line, Basil Henriques in C.22 had a charmed passage across the first hundred yards or so of no-man's-land, running with his visor flaps open. The defenders of the Quadrilateral had no idea what they were facing (even if they had been issued with armour-piercing SmK bullets, they were told they were for 'use against aircraft'). A German officer recorded his men laughing at the mud-coloured blob moving imperceptibly towards them. Then muzzle flash from machine guns crackled from its sides. The defenders did not run. They fired back with everything they had. Henriques closed down his flaps. They were groping around already half-blind. He recorded:

> Then a smash against my flap at the front caused splinters to come in and the blood to pour down my face. Another minute and my driver got the same. Then our prism glass broke to pieces, then another smash, I think it must have been a bomb right in my face. The next one wounded my driver so badly we had to stop. By this time I could see nothing at all. My gunners

* The phenomenon known as 'splash'.

were on the floor I couldn't make out why. As the infantry
were approaching and it was impossible to guide the car . . .
I decided that to save the car from being captured I had better
withdraw.

Streaming blood from splinters in the face, Henriques reported to
Brigade HQ, where he found a grinning 2/Lt George Macpherson,
his great friend, alongside whom he had endured an interview with
Swinton in London three months before. They had been in the same
infantry regiment together, trained at Elveden together, were in the
same section of the same company. Macpherson's tank – the one
that had broken down the night before on the crawl from Chimpanzee Valley, leaving Henriques to attack the Quadrilateral alone – was
back in the fight. Around 12.30 p.m., 'with a smile he got back into
his tank,' recalled Henriques, 'and went off to follow the infantry. It
was the last I saw of him . . .'

On the south-western approach to Flers, two small bands of
British infantry from the 41st Division had reached the wire covering
Flea Trench blocking the way into the village, with all but two of
their officers dead in the process.

At around 8.10 a.m., five minutes after the barrage lifted, Stuart
Hastie and the crew of D.17 caught up with them.

A Royal Flying Corps observer saw a tank break through the
barricade, pause for a few minutes across the trench shooting up its
defenders. He reported by wireless.* Then the tank moved forward
again, manoeuvring round intact buildings heading for what remained of La Place, the village square with its cattle drinking pond.
Khaki-clad figures seemed to be pressing close behind it. It was D.17.
The message book of Fourth Army HQ reads: '9.00 am XV Corps
Artillery Air Observer reports he has seen three tanks entering Flers
at 8.40 am and think our troops have taken second objective. 10.03
am Aeroplane reports received by telephone from III Corps state our
troops in line from South of Flers . . . Also Tanks seen in main street
of Flers followed by large numbers of our troops . . .'

Around 300 infantrymen of the 122nd Brigade had got into the
village with Hastie's tank, staying close up, hugging its rear for some

---

* When an account of the action was later revealed to the press, a newspaper sub-editor
would famously embellish the message as: 'A tank is walking up the high street of Flers
with the British Army cheering behind.'

kind of protection, but the defenders of the village were still fighting. As Gnr A. H. R. 'Roy' Reiffer, No. 2 on D.17's starboard 6-pounder, recalled: 'We were fired on by German machine-guns . . . the impact of their bullets was making the inside of the armour plate white hot . . . flakes coming off and if you happened to be near enough you could have been blinded by them. Gunner Sugden on the port side was wounded that way.'

Second Lieutenant J. Wilfrid Stadden of 12/East Surrey Regiment was one of the very few infantry officers who had got as far as Flers who was still standing. Years later he recalled a tank commander who 'shouted at me from the port side of tank D.17 for directions to the fourth objective . . .'. It was Hastie. The tank proceeded up the main street and disappeared.

British shells were now landing in the centre of the village.

According to Roy Reiffer: 'We were within fifty yards of the crossroads when we were stopped by a runner who told us that we were in our own barrage and had orders to retire . . . the infantry had met stiff opposition and the second objective had been abandoned. Mr Hastie turned us about and I think all of us . . . heaved a sigh of relief . . . So we were told to go back . . .' Hastie himself recalled:

> The engine was beginning to knock very badly . . . we made our way up the main street during which time my gunners had shots at various people who were underneath the eaves in some cases or in windows of some of the cottages. We turned right where the main road turned right . . . went on for a couple of hundred yards . . . we had to make up our minds what to do because the engine was in such a shocking condition. I had a look round (so far as it was possible to do that in the middle of a village being shelled – at that time by both sides) but could see no signs of the British Army coming up behind me [the account delivered in 1963 was tinged with irony] so I slewed the tank round and made my way back . . . to the beginning of the village.

Arthur Arnold in D.16, approaching Flers from the western side, recorded a strangely tranquil scene:

> I saw a tank preceding me up the road into Flers [it was D.17].
> I sent off a pigeon with a message notifying the situation to
> Corps HQ. It was now about 8.00 am – things were quiet except

for spasmodic shelling and it was a lovely morning [an observation balloon took interest and the shelling seemed to come in their direction].

I withdrew Dracula behind the shelter of a belt of trees. There we made tea and had breakfast; filled up with petrol from the reserve which we carried in a box on the stern wheels . . . We went over with fire extinguishers to see if we could help with a tank that was on fire [D.12, commanded by Capt. D. Nixon, operating with the New Zealanders on the left of XV Corps], but it was raging furiously, the ammunition going off inside like squibs . . .

With tanks apparently setting the defenders of Flers to flight, the way had seemed open to the further objective – Gueudecourt. 'You could see the clock in the church steeple', an old tanker remembered. But the infantry were exhausted and leaderless, the Webley-waving exhortations of their youthful subalterns silenced. As Wilfrid Stadden recorded many years later: 'Two officers only reached the protecting wire belt and my colleague, Lt Chesters, died there while exhorting his men to charge the last lap towards the Germans . . . I crawled under the wire, largely on my back pulling it over me, and thus presented a very small target.' Nor were more senior officers simply watching it all through binoculars. Three lieutenant-colonels had been killed in the opening assault on the village.

Second Lieutenant Wilfrid Stadden recalled wandering alone, a long way forward of Flers 'in seemingly unoccupied country'. His account given in 1963 to Haig's biographer, John Terraine, is dreamlike. The sight of enemy infantry coming forward in open order for an evident counter-attack caused him to scurry back to the village, where he found '28 of my men, a machine-gun subaltern and an orderly room sergeant' still alive. This was no deep penetration, no armoured spearhead. For the infantry it had been the habitual massacre. The tanks had seemingly vanished. Wilfrid Stadden ruefully recalled: 'I personally don't believe anybody was frightened of them [tanks], nor indeed interested in them – they were too thin on the ground. It would have been different if they had been field kitchens . . .'

When the barrage lifted, at 10.50 a.m. according to the timetable to drop shells on the approaches to Gueudecourt, the surviving infantry did not move, clinging instead to the captured trenches at the southern end of Flers. But some of the tanks did go on. Reginald Legge in D.6 swung past Flers to get as far as the approaches to Gueudecourt, with its barricading Gird Trench, before being hit by a field gun. The petrol tank exploded.

Seven crew got through the hatches; Legge was the final man out. 'He was last seen standing by the tank', according to the company war diary. Legge and two crew were cut down in the open by machine guns. One burned inside. One was captured. Three crew got back. Reginald Charles Legge was hastily buried on the battlefield near his ruined tank. His will found on his body by the Germans reached his family in London via the Red Cross.

Arthur Blower's tank, D.5 Dolphin, the late-starting tank from XIV Corps' sector, also got as far as just south of Gueudecourt, cruising around waiting in vain for the infantry to arrive. It was in danger of capture. Its commander turned round and started to go back – and was struck by a shell. Six of the crew survived. It was the furthest run of any tank on the day. Arthur Blowers would get the Military Cross, his second in command Cpl Edward Foden and ASC driver Pte G. H. Thomas the Military Medal. Gnr Leslie Robert Gutsell was killed. His body was recovered from the wreck and buried on 30 September, but the grave was subsequently lost. His name and unit (Machine Gun Corps (Motors)) are recorded on the monument to the missing of the Somme at Thiepval.

Stuart Hastie and his crew also made it back, but not in D.17. After being ordered to turn round in the centre of Flers, Hastie had found a sizeable group of infantrymen, apparently officerless, digging in at the south-western fringe of the village in expectation of a counter-attack. D.17 clanked back 'down the road on which we had come that morning', until the engine at last coughed and banged to a dead stop.

According to Gnr Reiffer, the sudden silence as the engine gave out alerted the crew to the 'hellish' German barrage dropping 7.7-cm shells around them. The tank was hit. Hastie was already outside, sprinting for a tank (D.3) about a hundred yards away, better protected from the shelling by a fold in the ground which might offer a chance of rescue. Corporal Shelson ordered abandon tank, seven men scrambling though the barrage to reach the comparative safety of 2/Lt Harold Head's D.3, itself immobilized and abandoned. They waited 'until nightfall'. In the darkness they picked their way back to the British front line.

D.17 Dinnaken, the conqueror of Flers, lay derelict on its eastern approach.

After their insouciant pause for breakfast, 2/Lt Arthur Arnold and the crew of D.16 Dracula had come out of their hiding place and 'cruised about for a while in front of the village', engaging a German counter-attack with its Vickers machine guns. Arnold had 'collected a bullet through my knee while outside'. He was pulled back into the tank by his gunner. A field gun had found his range, and with British infantry clinging on to the village now having been reinforced, Arnold 'judged it was time to get back', so he recalled almost fifty years later. The crew had also picked up a badly wounded New Zealand officer. Pursued by shells, Dracula 'proceeded on a toilsome way back ... to our headquarters at Green Dump'. The company commander produced a tumblerful of whisky, which 'induced a nice muzzy feeling which took the jolts out of a ... ride in an ambulance car'.

Eight tanks had been allotted to III Corps on the left of Fourth Army's assault frontage. Four were to be used against the fortified village of Martinpuich, of which two tanks apiece were slated to the 50th (Northumbrian) and 15th (Scottish) Divisions for the attack preceded by an intense artillery bombardment. D.25, commanded by 2/Lt Edward Colle, reached the objective under continuous shellfire, setting a large group of the Bavarian defenders to flight.

Of the two machines with the Scottish Division, D.23, commanded by Capt. George W. Mann, broke a track on the run-in, D.20 (2/Lt H. Harold Drader) lumbered forward through gaping shell holes at crawling pace, as British 'shorts' came dangerously close. The first objective, Bottom Trench, had already been abandoned. At Tangle Trench the defenders surrendered without bringing their machine guns from the dugouts. Low on fuel, Drader turned round to refuel and rearm. Captain Mann took D.20 back into action later in the day.

Major H. Armitage, an artillery officer with 15 Division, came into the village not long after Drader's tank. The defenders had already departed. He found a communication trench 'littered with rifles with fixed bayonets, belts, discarded steel helmets, but no dead. There was

every sign of a *sauve qui peut*. I put it down to the effect of the tanks
... We set up in a topping little dug-out which looked just like home,
with nice chairs and a leather settee.'

By nightfall the village's defences were effectively subdued – the
bombardment had been especially effective, the 'surprise' of the tanks
an excuse to surrender. At Martinpuich the bulk of the infantry were
spared the kind of mauling the 41st Division received at Flers. D.20,
its commander 2/Lt Harry Drader, his second in command Cpl Rowe
and a black French farm cat mascot featured in a re-creation of the
action for the film *Battle of the Ancre* made by the official cinematographer Geoffrey Malins.*

The remaining four of III Corps' machines were intended to support 47th (2nd London) Division's attack on the remains of High
Wood. Because the opposing trench lines were so close the defenders
in the first German line at least could not be subject to the usual
artillery pounding. The divisional commander, Maj.-Gen. Sir Charles
Barter, listened to the Heavy Section's qualms about operating in the
shattered tangle of stumps and shell holes, and brought them to the
attention of his superior. But the Corps commander, Lt-Gen. Sir
William Pulteney, insisted.

The infantry, London-recruited Territorials, left their trenches at
Zero-Hour – 6.20 a.m. The four tanks which were starters were meant
to have gone forward almost half an hour earlier, indeed by then to
be at the German first position in a line carved east–west inside the
wood, doing what the artillery bombardment was meant to do by
smashing up the defences. Only one machine had got near it.

Lieutenant Frederick Robinson and the crew of D.22 had got into
the southern end of the wood, blundered about looking for open

---

* Malins had filmed the preparations for, and a brave chunk of the actuality of, the
great infantry assault of 1 July. The resulting hour-long, five-reel film, *Battle of the Somme*,
released in Britain on 22 August, was a huge popular success. The royal family had a
private showing. Sir Hiram and Lady Maxim enjoyed the performance, according to *The
Times* – just a few days before the machine-gun entrepreneur's death. A special screening
(preceded by a Charlie Chaplin short) was staged at Fourth Army headquarters at
Querrieu on the eve of the 15 September offensive, according to an approving entry in
Gen. Henry Rawlinson's journal. So great was the film's popularity that Malins and his
collaborator, John MacDowell, returned to the Somme in September just in time to film
the tanks preparing for and going into action – with another and much bigger bite at it
in early October. The result, *The Battle of the Ancre and the Advance of the Tanks*, was
released to general excitement in January 1917. The tanks could do no wrong.

ground and then broke back into its own lines – to fire on men of
the 6 Battalion London Regiment waiting to go forward. A second
tank, D.21 (Lt Alex Sharp), wallowed into a shell hole and shed a
track still short of the British front line.

C.23 (commanded by 2/Lt Andrew Henderson 'on loan' from C
Company) ditched in a British front-line trench having gone just fifty
yards from its start point. Its commander sent off a pigeon with a
message that he was 'hopelessly stuck'. The crew stayed glued to
their guns doing what they could.

Second Lieutenant William Sampson in D.13 Delilah, a female,
lurched into the wood just after 6.00 a.m. Private P. A. Bloomfield,
the driver, struggled to prevent the machine impaling its thinly
armoured belly on shards of tree stump. They actually reached the
German front-line trench, but far from fleeing before the lumbering
monster, according to an account given in a letter to his sister by Gnr
William Divall: 'Two or three Huns are brave enough to creep on the
back of the tank from behind . . . we open a small trap door and
shoot them with a revolver . . .'

The defence of the wood was ferocious. According to the *Official
History*: 'It was reported that a German infantryman had crept up
to the tank, opened a loop-hole and shot one of the crew in the
leg.'

Delilah pushed some fifty yards further towards a German support
trench before the engine died. Sampson ordered abandon tank as
field guns found the range, a shell passing through the hull without exploding. An RFC observer reported the stalled machine was
'obviously captured'. It was not – but it might as well have been.

Then the fuel tanks ignited. Sampson and his battered crew began
to pick their way back out of the tree stumps, stumbling into the
German trench they had crossed so dramatically half an hour earlier.
Its occupants surrendered to the little pistol-armed party, just as men
of the Civil Service Rifles arrived to hustle them to comparative
safety.

High Wood was captured in the space of that day by the infantry
of the 141st Brigade attacking round its flanks at enormous cost. But
the use of tanks in the wood had been a fiasco. The battered Lon-
doners in retrospect blamed their suffering on the presence of the
Heavy Section for 'warning the enemy of our infantry attack [who

then] had to advance without covering artillery fire . . . for fear of damaging our tanks'.

It had been the same on the road to Flers. Denied the 'protection' of the creeping barrage in the tank lanes, infantry stumbling along behind had been flayed by machine guns. The tanks had either not been there at all or failed to do the extermination job as effectively as shrapnel. There was something else. A tank was a magnet for the defender's artillery. The infantry were learning. Be near a tank and the enemy's guns would soon find you.

It was Pulteney who had insisted on using tanks in the wood, but blame was placed on the divisional commander, Maj.-Gen. Sir Charles Barter, who was dismissed within a week for 'wanton waste of men'. He demanded an enquiry. It was not to be granted. The High Wood business was a little too sensitive for that.

On the far left of the line facing the village of Courcelette, the Canadian Corps of Reserve Army had six tanks allotted, intending to use them in two groups against the fortified sugar-beet factory blocking the road into the village. As they moved from their assembly area on the night of the 14th through the ruins of Pozières, German artillery strafed the road. Trench raids hit the Canadian lines through the night. Prisoners taken the next day stated that the mysterious sound of engines had alerted the defenders to something unusual about to fall on them.

One tank broke down on the start line, three more bogged down in captured trenches. Single survivors from each group ploughed on – C.5 Crème de Menthe (Capt. Arthur McCulloch Inglis, the section commander) and C.6 Cordon Rouge (2/Lt John Allan).

A ditched tank was not a ticket out of the battle. Lieutenant A. J. C. Wheeler in C.1 Champagne reached his deployment point for the attack on Courcelette at 2.30 a.m. He reported:

> A runner explained that this was the nearest point to our front line trench to which the tank could advance without being visible to the enemy. We left the starting point at 6.20 . . . at 7.00 am car bellied, tracks running round without moving tank.
>
> All members of the crew started digging out operations at once continuing up to 11.00 am being helped by three Canadians attached to the tanks. By 10.45 the shelling (enemy) had become so heavy that after one more effort at digging out, I

ordered the crew to cease work, bringing crew back to Park near Pozières ... one member of the crew [ASC driver Pte Horace Brotherwood] was struck by a shell from direct hit [it severed his jugular artery] about 10.55 am and died two minutes later.

C.2 Cognac broke a stub axle, lost its steering tail and was jammed in a communications trench in the opening crawl across no-man's-land. 'We shored the side up with timber and managed to get the tank on the ground . . . under heavy shell fire,' so its commander, Lt Frank Bleumel reported. 'We eventually had to cease work at 8:00pm owing to the [German] shelling caused by our infantry moving up. We removed our gunlocks, fastened up the tank and brought the crew back.'

After losing his way on the run-in, Capt. Inglis in Crème de Menthe got to the approaches to the sugar-beet factory just after 7.00 a.m. – behind the infantry. A Canadian private recalled:

Away to my left rear, a huge gray object reared itself into view, and slowly, very slowly, it crawled along like a gigantic toad, feeling its way across the shell stricken field. It was a tank, the 'Crème de Menthe,' the latest invention of destruction . . . I watched it coming towards our direction. How painfully slow it travelled . . .

Suddenly men from the ground looked up, rose as if from the dead, and running from the flanks to behind it, followed in . . . The last I saw of it, it was wending its way to the sugar refinery. It crossed Fritz's trenches, a few yards from me, with hardly a jolt.

Lieutenant Allan and his crew in C.6 Cordon Rouge reached the objective more or less simultaneously with Inglis in C.5, in time to cruise round to the rear and flail the defenders holding out in the red-brick ruins with its Vickers guns, while Crème de Menthe blasted away with its 6-pounders from the front . . .

What was left of the garrison, barricaded in the factory cellars, came out with their hands up. The surviving tanks limped back towards Albert, C.6 shedding a track on the way. The route to Courcelette was open. It was captured by reinforcing Canadian infantry that night.

Tanks had gone into action. Casualties among Fourth Army's infantry battalions remained gruesome, half the men and 80 per cent of the officers. Tank crew casualties, in the words of Clough Williams-Ellis, 'were insignificant'. Corporal G. L. Viner wrote to his wife, conscious of the censor:

> Dearest – it is no use saying anything about what we have done because it would only be crossed out, so take the paper account (if there is one) and imagine our car as one of those in action. I fancy we did good work too. Some of the men I knew well will never return, one, Corporal Pattison, I knew well.
>
> Several of our own heavies have been blown to atoms, they rained Jack Johnsons on us all the way back but we were lucky that our car was marked all over from with bullets and shrapnel . . .
>
> I am glad Billie likes his school and the boys like him, tell him I have been in a real battle and have fired a real-quick-firer at some real Germans and also brought some badly wounded Tommys back with us . . .

Lieutenant-Colonel Walter Kirke wrote to his wife from GHQ on the night of the 15th. He used a curious code: 'Darling . . . Capt Steedman's motors have been a great success, although a large proportion would not move when it came to the point . . .'*

Henry Rawlinson ruefully wrote in his diary: 'A great battle. We nearly did a big thing.'

Around twenty tanks remained. A handful of machines had made it back intact from the battlefield to Green Dump and the Brickworks, but most were saved from destruction by breakdowns and ditchings in no-man's-land or before crossing the British front line. Salvage parties laboured all day and all night in noisome mud with pick and shovel.

Who was dead, who had survived? Who had last seen whom? It only became clearer when tankless crews trickled in overnight from dressing stations and from front-line trenches to where the infantry had borne them. Gunner T. H. Bernard, for example, who, after beating off grenade attacks for hours, had escaped the stricken C.14 late on the afternoon of the 15th. He had found himself in a shell

---

* Capt. H. P. G. Steedman was in charge of the ASC detachment at Elveden. A curious letter of January 1916, written on Ministry of Munitions paper, to Mrs Kirke thanks her for an introduction to Gen. Scott-Moncrieff. This sharing of confidences might imply that Steedman was an MO5 plant in Suffolk.

hole with remnants of an infantry battalion waiting for dark. 'A chap was shot while crawling over my knees,' he recalled in a diary entry written in a base hospital four weeks later. He had scrambled and ducked his way to the British line, to be directed to a valley where 'two of our tanks were waiting'. Next morning he got to the Brickworks and reported to the adjutant.

'The OC sent for me and congratulated me on coming through.' Mr Arnold was also alive, so he discovered that evening, as was the driver, Pte Heath. Of the gunners, he would discover later, one was blinded in the left eye, one had shell shock, one was on his way back to England from a base hospital, one had been killed by a sniper in the scramble from the wood.

Basil Henriques lurched back from the shambles of the Quadrilateral in C.22 to be pulled bloodied from his machine, then decanted rapidly from a dressing station to a hospital train heading for Rouen, across the Channel to an eye hospital in London. He said later of the journey that the further he travelled he 'became more and more haunted that he was fleeing from the battlefield as a coward'. He went to see Swinton, 'begging to be sent back to my tank that afternoon'. The colonel told him that his friend George Macpherson was dead. No one was quite sure what happened.

'The fine and likeable young fellow', in the words of one of his crew, 'had never been on an actual battlefield before.' He had crossed the line at around midday with another tank following the same route as Henriques towards the Quadrilateral, to be shot up by machine guns firing SmK armour-piercing bullets. The crew survived. His loyal gunner said many years later: 'I regret to say however that Lt Macpherson going back to HQ to report was killed by enemy shell fire.'

It seems not to have been quite like that. In his second account of the action written in book form a quarter of a century later, Henriques said: 'Of my company one officer went mad and shot his engine to make it go faster, another shot himself because he thought he had failed to do as well as he ought, two others including myself, had what I suppose can be called a nervous breakdown.'

The only complaint by an infantry officer canvassed by the Official Historian for his comments on a draft account of the events of the day was: 'That it understated the horrors of the 15th for the infantry in front of the Quadrilateral and the appalling demands made upon the young tank officers facing the unknown. I remember one committing suicide in the afternoon.'

C Company only lost one officer killed on 15 September – George Macpherson. It seems he was taken wounded from his tank and brought to No. 34 casualty clearing station, at a place called 'Grovetown'. He rose from his bunk, retrieved his sidearm, went outside the tent and shot himself. He was twenty years old. The company war diary says 'Lt Macpherson died of wounds'. That is what his family were told.

Everyone had a view, everyone had a story. There was the matter of the pigeons.

An anonymous source in touch with Basil Liddell Hart compiling his book *The Tanks* forty years after the events of September 1916 informed him:

> It was the intention that at appropriate times a tank commander should write a message of tactical use to his superiors. He should fold it correctly, place it in the very small container, clean his hands with the turps provided, remove a pigeon from the basket using the correct hold, attach container to the pigeon's leg, change hold to the correct one for releasing, open port, avoid bumping the poor bird's head, release pigeon and then get on with the battle . . . the pigeon would fly to the grounds of a château somewhere.
>
> It didn't happen that way very often. The pigeons were pretty sick at being bumped about and breathing engine fumes. Tank commanders hands were covered in oil in spite of cleaning with turpentine – if the bottle hadn't broken – and pigeons cannot fly with oily wings. On being released they usually sat somnolently somewhere on the tank refusing to be shooed away. If dislodged by a direct hit from a lump of mud they would perch somewhere else nearby.

There was the story of a corps commander receiving an unsigned message from a tank reading 'can't bear to keep this poor bird any longer it looks so unhappy'. The tale may well be true. A. B. Cunningham, who ran the pigeon loft (a converted London omnibus painted white, unsportingly shelled by German artillery), gave the Official Historian his most significant recollection of the historic day:

During this the first appearance of tanks, when there was so much else to occupy their minds, it may be worth recording that the personnel liberated their pigeons if for various reasons the tanks had to be abandoned.

A German intelligence officer reported: 'A big grey box . . . operating in the neighbourhood of Combles on the 15th. It was attacked with hand grenades. One of these exploded, presumably in the vicinity of the petrol tank. Flame and heavy smoke rose up and at the same moment the machine gun stopped. A flap was opened and a carrier pigeon flew out.'

It was the crew of 2/Lt Francis Arnold's C.14 fighting for their lives at Bouleaux Wood. The pigeon got through.

There had been jubilation at Fourth Army's HQ at the first news from Flers (received not by pigeon but by telephone from XV Corps HQ). But it was clear by late morning that the advance was hopelessly stalled. Heavy German shelling was now falling on Flers. The third defensive line centred on Gueudecourt was being reinforced and was still out reach of British field artillery. At 4.00 p.m. Fourth Army informed Advanced GHQ that most of the tanks were out of action. At 6.25 p.m. Rawlinson called the battle off. The horses of the five cavalry divisions held in their lines close up to the front impassively munched their oats. There had been no great ride to Bapaume. The path even as far as Gueudecourt was still barred. As Basil Henriques wrote: 'If we only had a little more sleep and little less showing off, what a marvellous story this Somme battle might have been. As it was this precious secret was out, and our own infantry hated us . . .'

The mood at Advanced GHQ late on the morning of 15 September was cheerful. As the first computations were made of objectives seized and at what cost there were some reasons for optimism. The first German line had been breached on a front of 9000 yards and at Flers 4000 yards of the second line were in British hands.* High

---

* The six square miles gained on Friday 15 September represented about twice the area of ground won on 1 July for roughly half the number of casualties – 30,000. But as a proportion of the force engaged, roughly half of the attacking battalions were dead, wounded, missing or prisoners. The figure was not much less than that suffered on the calamitous opening day.

Wood, which had defied capture for two months, would be taken that day, but not by tanks.

A dispatch on the actions of the morning was telegraphed to London by GHQ and released by the Press Bureau* at 12.50 p.m. It mentioned the employment for the first time of 'a new type of heavy armoured car that has proved of considerable utility'. Before retiring at the Château Valvion the C-in-C confided to his diary: 'Some of the tanks have done marvels.'

Some had. Where more than one machine had managed to operate together – at the sugar-beet factory, at Flers – there had been some sort of success. High Wood, the assault on the Quadrilaterial and the Guards attack out of Ginchy had been a shambles. Almost a third of the Heavy Section had failed through breakdown and ditching to get into action at all. Of the thirty-two that had, eighteen machines, less than one hundred and fifty men, had actually engaged the enemy to any purpose. And they were supposed to win the war. Tomorrow they would try again.

---

* A civilian operation in Whitehall under the scrutiny of MI5(g).

28

Victor Huffam in D.9 had ditched early on the morning of the 15th, to be dug out by a Chinese labour battalion later in the day. 'We commanders were ordered to proceed that night to Flers as the second objective Gueudecourt was to be attacked,' he recalled, 'six tanks and 50,000 men to take part. On 16 September four other tanks, D.2, D.4, D.7 and D.19 which had got stuck on the opening day were also ordered to Flers . . .

'At dawn I reported to an Australian colonel. My reception was rude; I was told to take my bloody stink box away out of it, they were being badly shelled.'

The infantry were learning. The fairy godmothers of the day before had turned into ugly sisters, inviting a storm of enemy shell-fire whenever they appeared. The infantry attack on Gueude-court had been cancelled, so the brusque Australian colonel told Huffam, but D Company's CO, Maj. Frank Summers, arrived to announce the tank assault on the village would proceed. The shambles of ditchings and breakdowns on the first day had been repeated. Out of a hoped-for five, there were only two tanks left to make the attempt.

'On a lovely morning in September, D.14 [commanded by the South African-born 2/Lt Gordon Frederick Court] and D.9 started up,' recalled Huffam. 'As D.9 entered Flers, piles of dead British and Germans were in our path, attempts to clear a passage had to be abandoned, shelling was too intense . . . eventually we left . . .'

They had no choice. German field-gunners had found the range and were plastering the two tanks. Huffam's driver was blinded by splinters from the smashed vision prism. Huffam opened the flaps to find himself astride an enemy trench, full of defenders – flayed by the starboard pair of Vickers machine guns. His account continued:

On moving off, we watched D.14; it appeared to stop and immediately exploded. I went to the port side gunners to see why their guns were silent . . . both gunners [L/Cpls Andrews and Chapple] were dead . . . we were all in bad shape when we were hit by a larger shell, there was an explosion, then fire, and I came round to find myself lying on top of my corporal [H. Sanders], his shins were sticking out in the air. I had already been issued with morphia tablets and I quietened him with these. We were close in enemy lines and my corporal in agony and all others damaged and shell-shocked . . .

'I was trapped in the wreckage,' recalled Cpl Sanders, 'but managed to reach the small escape hatch in the rear . . . and throw myself on the ground; and there I found Mr Huffam and some of the crew in a shell hole. I managed to crawl over to them.'

They were in mortal jeopardy, another blood-spattered gaggle among thousands in a shell hole expecting to die. Huffam was still conscious, his corporal insensate. He shackled his belt to the more seriously injured man and began to drag him away from the ruin of their tank. 'Men of the Durham Light Infantry had seen our plight and brought us in,' Huffam recalled. Both the tank commander and the corporal survived.

What of D.14 and its crew, 2/Lt Gordon Court's tank that Victor Huffam had seen through his vision slit erupting in a fireball? 'While in hospital in Oxford I received a visit from Mrs Court, Court's mother,' he recalled. 'He and his crew of D.14 were posted as missing, believed killed and I had to tell her that her son was truly missing.' The crew of D.14 had been blown to bits.

29

It had been pretty much a shambles. But the true believers and the sceptics could both claim they had been proven right. The paucity of training, the unseemly rush to action, the tactical naivety of spreading tanks across the front – all could be blamed by the enthusiasts for the thin results.

The doubters saw tanks proven only as a morale-booster for the lumpen infantry, as long as they could still pull off a trick or two. The Germans for now kept their counsel. And the tank men themselves – what did they think? As Clough Williams-Ellis wrote:

> Half-choked with engine fumes, boxed up for many hours in the intolerable clamour and shaking of their machines ... worse, having wrestled for hours under heavy shelling with a broken-down tank, they were inclined to consider the exasperations of the battle rather than its success. It is curious to note the difference in tone between the accounts of those who saw the tanks dispassionately from without ... and those who weltered within – between those who saw what the tanks did and those whose view of the achievement was coloured by a knowledge of what might have been.

In the moment, the greatest enthusiast of all turned out to be Haig himself.

Swinton had been summoned to France a day too late to see 'his babies' '* baptism of fire. He picked up the mood soon after landing at Boulogne on the evening of the 15th – 'it was in the air, rumours of a great success'. The colonel drove first to Montreuil, the echoing, almost empty GHQ where 'Jock' Burnett-Stuart was one of the few senior officers still in residence. He was distinctly gloomy about what the tanks might or might not have achieved that morning.

---

* A phrase he would use extensively in a series of self-serving newspaper articles in the 1930s.

At the Château Valvion the mood was much brighter – it was handshakes all round and plaudits for the 'grandest success we had had'. GHQ's arbiter of fashion, John Charteris, breezily told Maj.-Gen. G. M. Macdonough, Director of Military Intelligence in London, 'the tanks were a great success – although they were limited by numerous mechanical breakdowns – some were struck by direct hits from field guns, I think they only hit them by sheer fluke after they had got stuck in the mud'.

Albert Stern arrived from London to confer with Swinton. A 'senior officer' (probably Butler) told them the chief was 'too busy' to see them, but later on the evening of the 16th Haig himself suddenly appeared 'outside General Butler's mess'.

He was beaming, 'cordial', full of praise. Haig told Swinton, 'Although tanks had not achieved all that had been hoped for – they had saved lives and justified their existence; that he wanted five times as many; that he wished the existing arrangement to go on; that I should go home and continue to command, raise and train the force, and Stern should carry on with supply.' Stern's account was the same. Haig told him: 'Wherever the tanks advanced we took our objectives, and wherever they did not advance we failed . . . we thank you.'

The C-in-C's diary entry written the night of the meeting bubbles with enthusiasm for getting hundreds of shell-proof 'super-tanks' that Stern was now promising. 'They are of an improved design of a heavier nature – 68 tons', so Haig wrote; 'General Butler goes to England . . . to press my views.' They were enthusiastic.

The ambitious Richard Harte Keating Butler was indeed packing for a trip to London, but in order to effect a higher agenda. For now it was very confidential. It had to be. Just as Haig was pouring praise on those who had raised and equipped the Heavy Section, Butler was intending to get rid of them. John Brough had already been defenestrated. Bradley would be next, Swinton and Stern were already in his sights.

The bloodletting began almost immediately. The next day, the 17th, Swinton picked his way through the shambolic rear area to Bray-sur-Somme where Lt-Col. Bradley and his vestigial HQ Tanks had decamped. He found his second in command 'in a state of great perturbation . . . from him I learned something of our casualties'.

Swinton returned to the château to be told that Bradley would also be one of those on the boat home. 'It was thought desirable that command of the Heavy Section in France should be held by an officer . . . who was familiar with the nature of the fighting, the existing organization and methods, etc., etc,' Swinton recalled in his memoirs. 'After what had happened to Brough I was not surprised . . .' He blamed an 'exclusive clique' for the move.

Albert Stern went to the Loop to see what was left and found a collection of 'new tanks and battered tanks'. Most of the crews, blackened, exhausted, elated, were very much alive. Burnett-Stuart had predicted 50 per cent casualties. It was a kind of miracle so many had survived. If Stern had ever felt that tanks were on a one-way mission – why bother with spare parts? – he was wrong.

The irony was that Butler's gathering purge was initiated not because the tanks had failed, but because they were perceived, by Haig at least, to have been a success. Not everyone thought so. The next morning, a Sunday, Swinton headed for Reserve Army HQ. General Hubert Gough was elsewhere; his views expressed later would not be enthusiastic. On to Fourth Army at Heilly where Henry Rawlinson was taciturn on the matter of tanks.

The ubiquitous Admiral Bacon was at Advanced GHQ when he was asked by Haig for his opinion. He had been to see surviving machines and question crews at the Loop that morning, and encountered a great deal of grumbling about 'steering and ventilation'. He advised the C-in-C that they should all be sent home while spreading a report that 'they had been an outright failure'.

'It seemed a pity to dribble them into action in small numbers,' he noted. Trying again with a three hundred-strong fleet of improved machines was a different matter. Bacon said in his memoirs that he discussed such a prospect with Haig who agreed with him. They discussed a project to man a hundred tanks with sailors. The admiral and the general would get down to some very secret discussions on a different and even more ambitious armoured warfare plan soon afterwards.

The Asquiths were weekending at their country house in Oxfordshire. From her diary notes for 17 September, Margot Asquith recalled her husband's return from the Somme a few days before. The sight of his son had been tremendously uplifting, the promise of the caterpillars irresistible. Things seemed to be going splendidly:

> [He] looked well and approved of what he had seen of the
> improvement in our organisation there – the tanks and the
> troops as well as the guns. Our offensive is going extremely
> well . . .
>
> I was called to the telephone . . . to be told that Raymond
> was shot on the 15th. Haig writes full of sympathy but no
> details. I went back into the sitting room. 'Raymond's dead'* I
> said to the servant. 'Tell the Prime Minister to come and speak
> to me . . .'

The place to enact urgent tank business was now Whitehall.
Swinton, Butler and Stern departed Beauquesne by staff car on the
morning of Monday 19 September, heading first for Paris.

They arrived in time for lunch at the War Ministry, where they
met the newly promoted Gen. Jean-Baptiste Estienne, the French
caterpillar enthusiast who in late June had been let into the secret
of Elveden. At the army's proving ground at Trou d'Enfer fort, near
Marly-le-Roi, they saw the prototype Schneider *char d'assaut* and the
St Chamond *char de rupture* – 'steel boxes placed on copies of the Holt
track' in Stern's stark but accurate description, a fleet of which their
hosts promised would be ready in the new year. There was a distinct
coldness, however, from M. Jean-Louis Bréton, the Sous-Secrétaire
des Inventions who, according to Stern, expressed his sorrow at 'the
heart-breaking precipitation of the English in prematurely using their
machines before we were in a condition to deliver the enemy the
decisive blow'.

There was a cheerful dinner, toasts to gallant allies and the
onward march of the tanks, then a fast, late-night drive to Boulogne
where a destroyer was in steam waiting to bear them across the
Channel. They embarked at two in the morning and were at Folkestone within an hour, where Stern's chauffeured Rolls-Royce was
waiting.

In the south London suburbs they picked up the first editions of
the morning papers. The news was out: 'His Majesty's Land Navy' –

---

* Asquith's eldest son by his first marriage, serving as a lieutenant with 3 Bn Grenadier
Guards, had been critically wounded in the attack launched out of Ginchy early on the
morning of the 15th in which the tanks' performance had proved so lamentable. He
died later in the day.

'Huns Cry Unfair' – 'New Forts on Wheels Make Huns Run Like Rabbits'. The tanks were a sensation.

'The Man Who Made the Tanks', proclaimed the *Daily Sketch*, with a front-page photograph of a grinning, Astrakhan-collared Winston Churchill posing as the armoured impresario. That was not quite what was wanted at the War Office. 'His Majesty's Land Ships: Some Facts', countered the *Daily Mail*: 'The usual attempt is being made on behalf of an advertising politician to grab the credit for these new weapons . . . The practical application is due to Colonel Swinton, the Eye-Witness of the early days round Ypres. Its development is largely the result of a patriotic businessman, Mr Stern. Its successful application at dawn on Friday morning is one of the many proofs of Sir Douglas Haig's quickness in seizing on new methods . . .'

That was much more like it. *The Times* printed an editorial oleaginous in its praise of Haig. The *Mail*'s proprietor Lord Northcliffe, who the C-in-C had cleverly squeezed into a tank at Yvrench before the battle, told the Australian journalist Keith Murdoch* that same day: 'The war is going splendidly. We have thrown up a military genius in Haig who is blasting his way into Germany by the only possible means.'

Butler and Stern, after a spruce-up at their clubs, headed for the War Office; Swinton went blearily homewards to Blackheath. General Robert Whigham chaired the meeting at which a sleepless but ebullient Butler conveyed his chief's dramatic demand for no fewer than a thousand machines to be delivered by 1 March 1917.

One hundred more Mark Is were to be completed to keep the factories in Lincoln and Birmingham working, and 'a supplementary order for 1,000 more of a modified type' would be put in hand. The French were understood to be producing 800 of their own 'smaller and handier' types.

All that was required was for the Army Council to place the order formally. The conference reconvened the next day to consider the

---

* Murdoch in October 1915, after an incident-filled visit to ANZAC Cove, had, with the collaboration of *Telegraph*-man Elles Ashmead-Bartlett, managed to dodge the censorship and expose the alleged military incompetence of the commanders and the appalling conditions endured by the troops at Gallipoli by addressing an impassioned 8000-word 'letter' to the Prime Minister of Australia. Northcliffe took him up, printing the revelations in the *Sunday Times*. Keith Murdoch was knighted in 1933 two years after the birth of his son Keith Rupert, founder of the News Corporation.

question of who was going to man them. This time Swinton was present, as were the doomed Bradley and poor John Brough, summoned to Whitehall for an uncomfortable performance. Butler was in total command, putting forward a paper recommending 'the expansion of the Heavy Section (Tanks) Machine Gun Corps'. According to Swinton, 'my superior glibly roughed out on his blotting paper a war establishment desired by the C-in-C down to the last batman.'

Butler proposed establishing five 'tank brigades', one for each of the British armies in France, each consisting of 144 vehicles with seventy-two spares. Forming a distinct 'corps' on the lines of the RFC with 'wings' and 'squadrons' was suggested.

A thousand tanks, twelve thousand men: this was heavy metal, a new power in the land. The days of the eccentric visionaries and military amateurs plucked from obscurity were over. New men were needed. Who would command it in the field? It would not be Bradley.

Butler and Haig had already found their man – Col. Hugh Elles, the Royal Engineer, who had undertaken the C-in-C's own little espionage mission in February 1916 to get what he could out of Churchill and visit Lincoln to discover the truth about the 'caterpillars'. Swinton went to Windsor on 21 September to give the King a (coolly downbeat) report on the Heavy Section's achievements. He should have been watching his back in London. Butler sent Elles a discreet letter the next day:

> Since you have been away I have arranged for an extensive reorganization of the Heavy Section . . . It will be organized approximately on the lines of the RFC . . . in wings and brigades, and the three companies that are now in France [A Company had arrived at Yvrench the week before] will be considered to be the first wing of the First Brigade . . .
>
> It will be commanded by Bradley (for the present at any rate) but we shall require an HQ in France and an HQ at home, more or less the counterparts of Trenchard and Henderson [the RFC commanders in London and in France] but on a smaller scale.
>
> You will be appointed forthwith in command of the Heavy Armoured Car Corps in France or whatever the name will be, and we will select a General to take command of the whole Corps at home. I will tell you, for your own information, that

Swinton will not be remaining in the organization, but keep
this to yourself for the present.

The new organization is . . . to put roughly a thousand tanks
into the field . . . I have arranged for a joint conference between
the English and French engineers [which will] design the super
tank . . .

'Manufacture will be independent of the ordnance and (for the
present) will be under Stern,' so the general conspiratorially added.
Swinton was doomed but did not know it yet. The 'patriotic businessman' Albert Stern also seemed to be on the way out. He would
survive – for now.

It is an old story and yet a very modern one. Those who innovate
find their creation taken over as soon as it is perceived to be a success.
But the debut of the tank was more serious perhaps than the launch
of a newspaper. The jealousies and back-stabbing that surrounded
the Heavy Section in autumn 1916 would shame the most ruthless
corporate warrior of any era. There were differing opinions on who
was the intriguer-in-chief.

Captain Giffard Le Quesne Martel (the sapper who had informed the Elveden ingénus of combat realities on the Somme in
July 1916) would tell Basil Liddell Hart in 1948: 'Swinton was probably correct in his belief that R. H. K. Butler was a prime factor in
his removal from command . . . He and 'Kitten' Wigram were both
rather lukewarm about the tanks, but at the same time they had
their own plans for taking over charge of them. It is probable they
had someone in mind, perhaps one of themselves . . . Not Elles, he
was chosen by Haig and his selection caused considerable annoyance
as he was so junior.'* Martel would join the tanks in October 1916
and become an important figure in their turbulent interwar history.

But Allen Holford-Walker, the commander of C Company on
15 September, seethed with a deeper indignation. He clung on to it
for years. Writing from Kenya he told the Official Historian in 1934,
'Neither Col. Bradley or Martel ever came near me in those first

* Major Elles's ambitions were heightened perhaps by being overlooked for promotion
as the plans for the Somme offensive were being laid at GHQ. As John Charteris informed
his wife on 4 June: 'Poor Hugh Elles has only got a DSO out of the last gazette. I hoped
he would have got at least a Lieutenant-Colonelcy. He deserved it. A DSO does not help
him much and it means he will not get a brevet for some time now . . .'

shows, possibly they were too busy consolidating their positions among the job-snatchers.' He scribbled an angry postscript:

> As you probably know, Brough, who was a great friend of mine, was not au fait with the nabobs at GHQ and was very unfairly treated indeed. I was in the 'B' Mess at Querrieu, 4th Army HQ, before the Somme and Elles was even then digging his feet further and further in – and from remarks I heard there I was very sure that it was only a matter of weeks before the tank people were shelved and replaced. Out of five company commanders only two were left at the end of the initial battles. Summers and self, and Uzielli* openly said in the HQ mess the sooner the original tank personnel Bolos were fired the better. After the way we were mishandled on the Somme and having worked like hell, I got very bitter hearing these remarks.

While the generals (and ambitious majors) intrigued between the Somme and Whitehall, the Heavy Section was still fighting for its life. Fewer than twenty working tanks remained in the field, a gallant band now split up between Reserve Army for a planned assault on Thiepval Ridge and Fourth Army for a last try against Gueudecourt. Five fresh infantry divisions were brought into the line, and four tattered divisions pulled out. The assault, which would effectively be the last throw of any significance on the Somme, was mounted on 25 September.

One tank, a female commanded by 2/Lt Charles Storey, breached the now notorious Gird Trench blocking the way to Gueudecourt, sweeping it with its Vickers machine guns, aided by a low-flying aircraft. This time there was a mass surrender and a mile of trench was captured with minimal casualties to the attackers. Storey's tank clanked on towards its objective and promptly ran out of petrol. The shattered village was at last captured by infantry the following day.

General Hubert Gough's Reserve Army had eight tanks for the assault on Thiepval Ridge launched on the 26th. Two were knocked out in the opening moves and the other six all ditched, but one kept going long enough to engage defending machine guns in the ruins of Thiepval château before getting stuck in a trench.

There was confusion in Whitehall, meanwhile, when Butler

---

* Captain Theodore Uzielli, appointed quartermaster of the Heavy Section in November 1916. 'Bolos' refers to Bolsheviks, i.e. troublemakers.

contested just what had been decided at the elated morning meeting on the 20th; was it a thousand more of the tanks of the type that were still fighting in France or the 'super-tank', a completely new design incorporating the ideas which they had discussed with Gen. Estienne in Paris? Butler sent Whigham a note from GHQ dated the 26th, querying the minutes of the meeting. It would take a day to reach London.

But Whigham had already formally notified the Ministry of Munitions that morning that the War Council 'concurs in a further order for 1,000 additional "Tanks" being placed in continuation of existing orders'. Of what sort was not specified. That message too was sent on the 26th, but had merely to pass from Whitehall to Armament Buildings. Stern got it that afternoon.

Then Butler's letter arrived the next morning. What sort of tank had just been ordered? The Army Council met urgently (without the Secretary for War in the chair) to try and find out. It was all rather embarrassing. No coherent reports of the Heavy Section's effectiveness in battle had been received since Butler's overnight, Haig-inspired Channel dash in a whirl of triumphant newspaper headlines. The production of tanks at the rate of three a day should be adhered to, the council decided. 'Accordingly the proposed order for one thousand should be held up pending further investigation as to the utility of those now employed.' Meanwhile, Stern and most of the Tank Supply Committee were back in Paris, at the Marly-le-Roi tank range, for them to see what the French were up to. The two sides conversed best, apparently, in technical German.

Whigham deferred to Haig as final arbiter. In a note to Butler sent on the night of the 27th he asked that the C-in-C should clarify and formally state his requirements. There was no hint in the breezy message that the chief would change his mind on the raising of a great armoured force.

'I can think of nothing better than "Tank Corps" for the name,' Whigham wrote. 'That soubriquet has certainly come to stay, and "tankodrome" seems quite suitable for tank camps and training grounds.' He added something much more conspiratorial. 'The thorny problem of Swinton's dismissal has to be handled carefully,' so he told his confidant at GHQ. He signed off jauntily: 'The war goes splendidly with you – More power to you! Yours ever . . .'

Lloyd George waded in requesting a formal statement from the Commander-in-Chief about whether the action at Thiepval, reports of which had just reached London, had caused any change of mind. With no 'clarification' coming from Haig or anyone else, it was announced by the Army Council on 30 September that the great tank order was cancelled.

Stern got back from Paris to be told the news. He was aghast. So was Lloyd George; he was the damned minister and he had not been informed. 'Wully' Robertson, the CIGS, a man of 'glum omnipotence' as the War Secretary described him, was given a dressing down. Stern kept very quiet for now. The 'men of business' running the industrial war effort were becoming a target of special derision by the men in riding boots. The Christian-convert Jewish banker Albert Stern was moving to the top of the list. Soothing noises were made. It had all been a misunderstanding. More time was needed (it had not been granted when the Heavy Section had been decanted from Suffolk and pitched into battle). On 2 October Haig replied to the request for clarification: 'This new engine has proved itself to possess qualities which warrant further provision on a large scale . . . Meanwhile I have the honour to recommend that the principle of the expansion of the existing Heavy Section of the Machine Gun Corps be accepted . . .'

He would present proposals for design improvements in due course, based on reports from subordinates on experience gained, no one could argue with that. It was not the rave review of the opening night when Butler had rushed to London to demand a thousand 'super-tanks', but neither was it a stinker.

General Henry Rawlinson asked his own commanders for their views on the tanks' utility in the efforts of 15 September. The results were broadly favourable. The commander of the 41st Division thought they were 'very useful' in breaking down the wire at Flers. The GOC of the Guards Division thought they had been 'of little assistance' (and he was right). Lieutenant-General Sir William 'Putty' Pulteney, who had presided over the fiasco in High Wood, thought they had done 'excellent work'. But he had a special grumble. He thought there was 'Much room for improvement in the morale of the crews. Much weeding out has already been carried out particularly among the ASC drivers, who appear to have lost their heads in many cases early in the fight.'

Rawlinson compiled his own leaden post-battle appreciation. The events in High Wood were hardly mentioned. 'The tank was not at present sufficiently reliable to justify any departure from normal tactical methods,' he concluded. After the postage-stamp-sized triumph at Guedecourt he wrote to a lady confidante: 'The "Tanks" are the weirdest looking things you ever saw. They did their job very fairly well but now they are no longer a surprise they will not be so useful.' On 5 October a memo appeared over the signature of Lancelot Kiggell, the Chief of the General Staff, announcing that in their 'present state of development tanks were to be regarded as entirely accessory to the ordinary method of the attack and their employment must not interfere with the combined action of infantry and artillery.'

The C-in-C did not bend from his views of 2 October. He still wanted a thousand tanks. On the 6th Tennyson d'Eyncourt sent Lloyd George and Robertson a memo claiming that the Germans 'from the moment they first saw them have started making tanks – probably more powerful. If we don't keep ahead in numbers and power of type they will beat us in what is at present our own game.' It was Haig's view that mattered. Eight days later the order was reinstated.

Butler had won. The men who had raised the Heavy Section, trained it and taken it to France, were all on their way out. Lieutenant-Colonel Bradley packed his bags. On 29 September Hugh Elles took over at Heavy Section headquarters now set up in 'one small hut in the square of the village of Beauquesne', conveniently close to the Château Valvion to be under Advanced GHQ's thumb. He was now, however, the possessor of a 'charter' assuring a kind of quasi-independence. It read: '[Tanks] HQ in France is to command the Heavy Section MGC in the field, to be responsible for the advanced training and for the tactical employment of the corps under the command of the C-in-C.'

Ernest Swinton paid a last mournful visit to the Somme on 4 October, where an officer took him aside to tell him 'in a certain circle the whisper had gone round Swinton must go'. He recrossed the Channel accompanied by an apparently embarrassed Hugh Elles. From Folkestone he telephoned Hankey at his desk in London who told him it was true. He'd been sacked. Elles, shamefaced, confessed on the station platform that he 'knew what was brewing but had no hand in it'. He would not tell the colonel who was responsible. Swinton could have guessed. In an interview at the War Office, the gruff 'Wully' Robertson explained that he was not considered the man to carry out the big expansion. Whigham said simply that '"France" was being difficult . . . Carry on until relieved.' In his memoirs Swinton says he extracted a promise from the deputy CIGS that John Brough 'should be sent back [to the front] with no bad mark against his name'.

Swinton told the Official Historian in a private letter years later: 'My intrusion was resented from the beginning by most of GHQ, especially the "cavalry spirit".' A few weeks later Robert Whigham fell off his horse at Marble Arch while taking a morning canter in Hyde Park. He would be out of action for months.

The men of the Heavy Section fighting on the Somme scarcely saw the face of the enemy. There are few accounts of 'Fritz' in first hand recollections of the events of 15 September. Like Arthur Arnold, who glimpsed a row of German heads through his vision slit before his Hotchkiss jammed, or Basil Henriques, with his driver blinded and his periscope smashed in the assault on the Quadrilateral, enclosed in their metal worlds they might as well have been driving submarines.

Only in cases like Sampson's crew in High Wood, who found themselves in a trench full of surrendering Bavarians, or in C.14's fight at Bouleaux Wood, where crews evacuated a stricken tank to continue the fight with pistols, did they see the flesh and blood enemy close up. Where there was a local surrender it was the job of the infantry (eagerly seized upon) to hustle prisoners back to the British line. There is a curious account in the Tank Museum archives of a senior German officer being brought back to Pozières from the sugar-beet factory at Courcelette inside a British tank. The press took the story up. It seems to be apocryphal.

The Heavy Section's task was brutal – to grind Jerry (the 'Boche' to the officers) into the dirt. The glamour that attached to the fighter pilots of the Royal Flying Corps did not transfer to the mud-wallowers. But there were some who clearly adored what they did. Even being blown up. A tank commander who fought on the Somme later in the autumn confided in a letter to his mother:

> One of the officers who was in the stunt you read about is in hospital here, he is suffering from shell shock and collapse, after his car had a pretty thin time of it. Tail blown away etc . . . I saw him and he was very enthusiastic about it all. Don't believe all that drivel the *Daily Mail* have been writing about the heroic courage required to take a tank into action. If you have ever seen a Willie and handled one you would never rest until you

had taken one into action. It is more pleasure than anything else.*

If the tank men felt for their opponents' fate, like the artillerymen who laboured at the same task of trench extermination from three miles distant they expressed scant feelings in their letters and memoirs. But what Fritz felt about the tanks was very important. If the defenders could stand their ground, the enterprise in armour was meaningless.

It was the newspaper correspondents who were admitted to the rear area two days later who wove stories about Huns melting away before the fire-spitting monsters. Usefully for history, however, they gathered the statements of prisoners. The *Daily Mail*'s William Beach Thomas† recorded: 'One German officer I met said it was "an impertinence" to use them, and some of the German soldiers regarded them with some sort of superstitious terror for the first few minutes, till daylight disclosed their true nature . . .'

That seems a highly accurate account. One German officer thought he was being assaulted by some sort of agricultural threshing machine. At Bottom Trench at Martinpuich the garrison fled before a tank even got near them. But overall the Germans had engaged the 'terrifying monsters' as if they were any other target – shooting for the vision slits, lobbing grenades, clobbering them with field guns. The defenders stood their ground. It was the weight of the infantry assault (encouraged by tanks) that in places was irresistible. A Bavarian company commander on the northern defence line of Flers reported later: 'I succeeded in holding out until mid-day . . . the enemy made a mass attack from the west and rear . . . the attack from the left was led by a tank which, armed with small cannons, came from the flank and fired along our whole position with devastating effect. The attack itself was carried with hand grenades and bayonets . . . it was quite impossible to hold out any longer.'

But at certain points where armour-piercing bullets had been issued it almost looked as if Fritz *knew* the tanks were coming.

* The letter's author would die in his tank at Arras six months later.

† Parodied in the *Wipers Times* as 'Mr Teech Bomas', who wrote of his trip in a tank: 'How could one fear anything in the belly of a perambulating peripatetic progolody-mythourodus? . . . with a triumphant snort we went through Bapaume pushing over the church in a playful moment before steering a course home . . .'

The true believers – Swinton, Churchill, Tulloch – had warned all along that using tanks in battle was a once-only opportunity. They were Haig's cheerleaders in the sense that they kept the faith in a war-winning 'breakthrough'; the tear in the line would just be brought about by novel means. But once the secret was out, the Germans must surely find a sovereign remedy. Or, as Thomas Tulloch had warned in 1915, build a countervailing fleet of tanks themselves.

It did not work out anything like that. But a mainspring of Haig and Butler's justification for using the tanks so precipitately was that the secret was going to leak anyway. Butler told the Official Historian in 1934 as the post-mortem push against the reputation of the boss he had so closely guarded in life was gathering: 'The C-in-C has been much criticised for not waiting until he had more tanks, enough to put Swinton and the politicians' plans for a massed attack into action . . . If he [Haig] had not urged that he had wanted them for the *next* attack, production would have been delayed even further. The longer the delay . . . the Boche would most certainly have got to know.'

The relevant volume of the *Official History* itself, published in 1938, deferred to the retired general's view: 'If instead of employing a limited number of tanks in autumn 1916, several hundred had arrived in France to train with the infantry during the winter, the secret could hardly have been kept until the spring,' it stated. There followed a simple-looking line: 'To what extent the nature and capabilities of the tank would have become known to the enemy in the meantime is of course impossible to say.'

In his book *Eyewitness* published six years earlier, Swinton had set up the great 'premature disclosure' argument that would engage clubbable old soldiers over whisky and soda for decades. Haig was a damn fool. Haig had no choice. Swinton's 'vast and sprawling memoir' came out in a blaze of publicity in 1932 eagerly fanned by the author, depicted as 'the man who had to fight the War Office harder than he fought the Germans'.

'Various reasons have been put forward for the decision [to use the tanks],' Swinton wrote. 'One is that the secret could not have been kept much longer, that even before the 15th September the Germans had some inkling of the surprise in store . . . A second reason is that there had been a leakage at home . . .'

He mentioned vague stories of 'a discovery in the censorship of a person who had seen the tanks sending details to correspondents in neutral countries', and that a similar betrayal had been revealed in letters from the armies in France. 'I heard nothing of such leakages, except in cases I have cited,' he said.

The colonel was referring to his and Bertie Stern's ungallant but seemingly necessary adventures with London actresses, officers' mothers, 'women spies' and the mysterious '*Fräulein Doktor*'. He conceded in his account that prisoners captured on the day had told of a warning given on the 14th, and that on one sector of the attack front 'special bullets' had been issued 'for use against aircraft . . .'

'But even if the enemy did get wind of something it was the very last moment. It was a surprise,' the colonel insisted. There had been that reference in the Commons nine months earlier to 'moving forts on caterpillars' by the Scottish MP James Hogge. If they were reading Hansard for December 1915 in Berlin nobody seemed to notice.

But there are references to such a 'leakage' in the published works of Lt-Gen. John Charteris, Haig's intelligence chief, a figure very roughly handled by both contemporaries and historians. In his biography *Earl Haig* published in 1929, he made this curious statement:

> It has been argued by Mr W. Churchill and others that the [tanks] were still only few in number. Within a limited period a vastly greater strength might have been accumulated – these considerations were all taken into account when Haig decided to throw them into the battle. His intelligence service had already information that showed that the Germans were even now alive to the existence of some new implement of war . . . It could only be a matter of time before the German intelligence service would obtain complete information and be able to evolve an adequate protection . . .
>
> There was a leakage at home. A demonstration of the tanks had been given in England at which very large numbers of unofficial spectators, including members of the House of Commons, had been present. Letters taken by the censorship had shown that full information was being sent by one at least of the spectators to neutral countries, whence it would inevitably reach Germany. Censorship of letters from the armies in France revealed a similar danger.

Charteris's second book *At GHQ*, published in 1931, is in the form of a contemporaneous journal, giving extended accounts of day-to-day goings-on at the BEF's headquarters and the thoughts of both the author and his chief – 'D H'. Charteris admits in his preface that 'where records were incomplete I have amplified them by my recollections . . . in the main the book is as written at the time . . .'.

The entry for 4 May 1916 describes the author's dealings with the press in preserving secrecy, praising the 'loyalty of the correspondents and the tact of the censors'.

'The Secret Service takes more time and takes more thought,' he added, but he 'could not talk about that'. 'The press censorship is automatic . . . only [matters concerning] discipline and espionage come to me.'

One such 'espionage' case had come to him via mail interception. Charteris found the affair 'amusing'. A letter signed with 'a fancy name' had been intercepted, evidently by the French civil censorship (the responsibility of the Sûreté), disclosing important information to a young lady in Paris, so Charteris stated, with its subject appended as a footnote. The information was 'about the tanks'.

The letters were opened and resealed before reaching the point of delivery. Their origin was much harder to discover as they came from different places. The British were alerted through the BCI, the Bureau Central Interallié. 'It took some time before the writer was traced and sent home,' said Charteris. 'His amorous missives were signed off "ton Richard, coeur de Lion" and he was an elderly amorist too!'

There were very few people in France in early May 1916 who knew anything about tanks. Lieutenant-Colonel Kirke had started his super-censorship operation in the training area in mid-August as the first tanks were arriving. There *was* a florid gentleman who knew a great deal about them and who *did* have a mistress in Paris. He was sent home – but that was in November 1917. His name was Lt-Col. Robert Bradley.

31

What did the Germans really know? The construction of a fleet of tanks in England and the recruiting and training of their crews was one of the greatest secrets of the war.

In the transit of 'Alpaca' across southern England, in the journey of men in 'curious leather helmets' on the London underground, on the seaborne passage of the 'Armadillos' from the Severn to the Le Havre docks – on to St Riquier via Rouen and Abbeville, in the training era and at the Loop where thousands saw their 'antics' – many had seen their passing but the secret had been kept. As the tanks moved to their final assembly areas the Royal Flying Corps maintained a barrier to keep out prying airborne camera lenses, although a German balloon observer reported 'large armoured cars' moving behind the British front on the 14th.

That there were local tactical warnings the day before is clear. A primary document from the British side, III Corps' typewritten post-battle assessment, contains this remarkable account taken from a group of German officer prisoners captured on the 15th: 'They said they had been "warned" on the eve of the attack that "land cruisers" were going to be used against their front. One of the officers himself with his forward observation officer had seen one through a telescope on the 14th a long way behind our line and reported the fact.'

Otto Scholtz, a company commander in a Westphalian regiment who had been at the Courcelette sugar-beet factory, recalled: 'We had heard rumours of a new allied weapon and our intelligence sent us notes on the vehicle which they believed was being built in certain French factories. The rumours said it was a sort of armoured car and we had been given supplies of armour piercing bullets of the type usually used for shooting at sniper's loopholes in pillboxes.'

He was right. At certain points in the line, German riflemen and machine-gun crews had been issued with the SmK armour-piercing ammunition, the development of which had vexed Swinton and the Tank Supply Committee so much. They had drilled holes in the side of D.22 and forced the unfortunate Basil Henriques and George Macpherson to retire from their doomed attacks on the Quadrilateral.

Leutnant Scholtz, interviewed by a British author when he was a civilian messenger working for the British Army of the Rhine in the early 1960s, was remembering events after fifty years. But another prisoner in the III Corps bag in September 1916 had something much more interesting to say just hours after the action itself. According to the Corps intelligence summary: 'About six weeks ago an account of the Land Cruiser had been given over the telephone in a sort of summary of special occurrences circulated to units from HQ. These they read out to the men on parade. In it it was stated that these land cruisers were armoured 5 to 6 cm thick and they had attacked trenches on a certain part of the front. Infantry were powerless against them . . .'

No tank in France had been in other than mock action before 15 September, yet the warning had seemingly come at the beginning of August. 'This may be a German agent's account of experiments made in England,' the interrogation report suggested dispassionately. It was a direct suggestion that there had been a spy at Elveden.

John Charteris clearly read the III Corps summary. His recon-structed diary entry chose to mention the incident, but not the timing of the warning. Instead he emphasized the notion that somehow the Germans had fallen for a cunning ruse: 'Friday 20 September: The fighting power of the enemy seems definitely decreasing . . . a good deal is no doubt due to the tanks, but not all. The Germans increased the moral effect of the tanks by warning notices which they had issued to troops. They knew that something was coming but not enough to foresee absolutely their effect . . . their nerves were strained with anticipation of some very new powerful instrument of war, the full effects of which they could not know . . .'

If Haig's loyal intelligence chief thought some sort of timely leak had *increased* the tanks' battlefield efficacy, what was the point of all that hush-hush secrecy? It had restricted training in England and France and shackled tactical planning. If straining the enemy's nerves was the only intention, the Heavy Section might just as well have gone to war in a fleet of cardboard cutouts.

That was the view of John Charteris, apostle of 'morale' and the wearing-out battle. But it would have a powerful resonance later when the battle for Haig's reputation was joined. That is why the Official Historian, Brig.-Gen. Edmonds, was so equivocal on the 'impossibility' of 'knowing to what extent the nature and capabilities of the tank would have become known to the enemy', should the tanks have been held back. Edmonds was being semantically careful. Knowing the 'nature and capabilities' of the fabulously secret weapon was one thing. The fact that it existed at all was another.

It seems clear from sources both primary and secondary that German military intelligence did have an intimation that some sort of armoured trench-crossing vehicle was being prepared in England. Details of just what it was, where, when and how it was to be used were much later in coming.

The evidence of the defenders' technical surprise is in the fact that first assessments of the British machines (variously *Motor-Panzerfahrzeug, Panzerauto, Panzerkraftwagen, Panzerautoähnlicher* – the Germans were scrambling for an umbrella noun) came from the battlefield itself. These first reports were extraordinary in themselves. They were based on accounts of what individuals had seen and a snatched photograph of 2/Lt Francis Arnold's vehicle C.14 on the fringe of Bouleaux Wood taken by a reckless infantryman who had crawled up to the ditched tank with a camera. No complete machine had yet been captured.

The most complete information came from the interrogation of a Heavy Section prisoner captured on the morning of the 15th. His captors were Bavarian. The Bavarian army's archives survived the Second World War. Those of the Prussian army in Berlin were destroyed by Allied bombing. An eighty-year-old record discovered in Munich by the tank historian Trevor Pidgeon described the interrogation by Hauptmann und Nachrichtenoffizier Weber of Sixth Army of an unnamed man of the Motor Machine Gun Corps, taken prisoner early on 16 September while wandering with burns to the head on the road north of Flers. He was interrogated in a rear area first on 18 September and on three subsequent days.

The prisoner had evidently spoken freely. He was not attached to any division or similar unit. He described to Haupt. Weber the training for two months 'in Norfolk in England' for the newly invented motor vehicles and his transit by rail to a place behind the front where the machines had been unloaded from the trucks on the afternoon of 13 September. He was a 'mechanic' who occasionally had instructions on the use of the Hotchkiss guns and had been taught how to drive the vehicle. There were 'three more such units' in Norfolk, he revealed, where 'the vehicle is constructed'.

He had gone into action at 5.30 a.m. British time heading in the direction of Flers with a second machine. Machine-guns bullets bounced off the armour plating. They had stopped a short time in the village then drove on further, to Ligny-Thilloy, where a direct hit exploded the petrol. The second tank was also hit.

The prisoner tallied the crew members and their roles. He himself had been wounded in the head and managed to get out of the burning tank but could give no information on the fate of the rest of the crew. He described the vehicle, which Haupt. Weber recorded as an 'egg-shaped steel housing that moves on tracks, steered by a wheel at the rear.' His report for Sixth Army HQ continued: 'It creeps forward over open country. The speed is believed to be at the most four English miles an hour, over broken ground one English mile per hour. The vehicle has two 6-pounder guns at the side in the form of swallows' nests. It carries 250 shells and food for three days. Entrance is through doors at the side . . . There is electric lighting inside. At the front there is a periscope for the officer in command plus a number of prisms so the crew can see out.'

The prisoner described the agonizingly slow transit from the start line to the outskirts of Flers. According to Haupt. Weber: 'Noise – the generation of heat were very great . . . it was frightful. He was happy to have escaped this death journey with his life and cannot understand why the officer allowed them to go so far forward. When the vehicle passed to the east of the village he wondered what was going on. Whatever was happening was known only to the officer who did not tell anyone else . . . In the opinion of the prisoner the vehicle is a completely failed invention . . .'

The prisoner would say that. Haupt. Weber reserved judgement for now. In an admirable feat of historical reconstruction, the retired diplomat turned author Trevor Pidgeon, who had found the interrogation transcript researching his extraordinary book *The Tanks at Flers*, worked out who he was – Gnr Herbert Clears, who escaped the destruction of Reginald Legge's tank, D.6. He was the only Heavy Section prisoner who survived his wounds longer than a few hours; anyone else left on the battlefield was already dead. Gunner Clears survived the war as a prisoner of war and came home. His medal record card says simply 'PoW 15 9 16–11 11 18'.

From Herbert Clears' description, Haupt. Weber prepared a reasonably accurate drawing of a tracked, egg-like device with a single wheel trailing behind and a little periscope sticking out of the top. As more first-hand reports came in, infantry prisoners were interrogated and other evidence collated (a written operational order had by now been found in Francis Arnold's abandoned C.14), the tactical intention of the enemy became clearer. The tanks were supposed to attack in groups of six, overrun strong points, get through the defenders and shoot them up from the rear. But only in isolated cases had more than 'one or two tanks managed to come forward over the English lines', so Weber reported.

Why had the English not used more of them together? Because so many had broken down or ditched in the shell holes of the attackers' own making. 'Whether this weapon will be successful to the extent the enemy perceives we will wait and see . . .' Haupt. Weber confided on 28 September.

Trevor Pidgeon found something else in the Munich archive – the typescript translation into German of 'a diary' retrieved from the battlefield. From its contents it seemed not to have been taken off a dead body but was somehow lost by a crew member of 2/Lt Eric Purdy's tank, C.16, whose owner had in fact survived. Taking such a record into harm's way was a punishable offence. The culprit was unidentified and his transgression only came out after eight decades.

It gave fascinating details of its author arriving at a camp near 'Stetford'; of the arrival of the first tank with the *Spitzname* 'Big Willie'; of a French general's appearance; of the grand demonstration of 21 July; of visits by Lloyd George and the King (he claimed Asquith was there) – all providing a feast of information for any intelligence officer, if rather belatedly. It described the Channel crossing of the tank crews escorted by 'five torpedo boats'. It described a mass exercise at Yvrench with 15,000 infantry and how 'hundreds' of officers had come to see them at the Loop.

Hauptmann Weber's reports went up the command chain. On

2 October the Supreme Army Command (Oberste Heeresleitung –
OHL) was informed that since 15 September armoured British motor
vehicles had been appearing on the Somme front. A full description
could not be relayed, the report continued, since none had so far
been captured. Nor could a true estimate of their potential be given,
but it was feared that with improving construction these machines
might become a respectable form of warfare. They were very slow,
apparently invulnerable to machine-gun fire, but not to field artillery.

Within a week a general description was sent to Abteilung IIIB,
the *Nachrichtendienst*, or intelligence service, of the General Staff at
the War Ministry in Berlin. A preliminary drawing showed a curious
oval-shaped machine with a small wheeled appendage surmounted
by a nautical-looking ventilator. It was animated by a *Kettenband*
system – a 'creeper chain'. On 23 October OHL forwarded more
detailed drawings and descriptions, adding, significantly, that the
French were developing a similar fighting machine. 'Without overestimating the effectiveness of these devices, it would be appropriate
for German industry to do the same,' said the report.

There was no place yet for *Panzerkraftwagen* in the high command's plans. The strategic defensive would continue. Steel would
be used to reinforce concrete blockhouses and bomb shelters, not yet
to build a fleet of tanks. But the two martial titans recalled from the
east, Field Marshal Paul von Hindenburg and First Quarter Master
General Erich von Ludendorff, who supplanted General Erich von
Falkenhayn at the top of the German General Staff, had distinct
views on how the defence might be better conducted. Ludendorff
wrote of the Somme in his memoirs: 'Our infantry without doubt
fought too doggedly clinging too resolutely to the mere holding of
ground . . .' Colonel Fritz von Lossberg, First Army's new chief of
staff, would emerge as the presiding genius of the 'defence in depth'.

Planning began in the early autumn on the construction of a
colossal new defensive position, the *Siegfried Stellung*, on a shorter
line and on commanding ground with the lessons learned on the
Somme, built into its concrete-studded carapace and gaping trenches.
That would include how to stop tanks. The great secret was out. In
Berlin they were scrabbling to learn all they could. All they had right
now was the transcript of the interrogation of Gnr Herbert Clears.

Oberst Walther Nicolai, head of the *Nachrichtendienst*, described the tank prisoner incident in his book *Geheime Mächte*, published in English translation in 1924. He described him as a 'sergeant' who had worked in the 'tank factories'. He also indicated just why the prisoner gave so much information: 'He had escaped . . . from a tank when it had exploded. For days he trembled and shook . . . and in this frame of mind he gave . . . details so complete that a model of the tank could have been constructed from them.* The Intelligence Service doubted the whole story until facts were ascertained which broke down our unbelief.'

Facts were indeed ascertained. Whether Oberst Nicolai was referring to more reports from the battlefield or something that had reached his department quite separately is opaque. A more junior intelligence officer confessed in 1929: 'Information about this apparently fragile weapon emerged – but our officers were not technically literate enough to realize their significance. An engineer in a neutral country forwarded details of the construction of a tank – but it turned out to be a forgery . . .'

If there was a spy in Suffolk, he or she was very unobservant. Any account of experiments in England would surely describe what it was that was being tested. No engineering drawing, it seemed, had been leaked from the factories. No gallant tank officer had been seduced by a female spy. Nobody had been snatched from a Suffolk beach by submarine. There was no Marconi wireless apparatus concealed behind an ancient fireplace (a favourite spy mania yarn of the time). There had, however, been a thumping leak from England.

---

* In such a shell-shocked state, according to the colonel, 'French and Belgians were loquacious' under interrogation. But experience of heavy artillery fire usually 'caused an Englishman to be completely obdurate . . . The English officer was a model of silence, though sometimes English non-coms and men of long service excelled him.'

Gassed men were often very talkative. Alternatively, kindly treatment in a dressing station would induce men to talk. British experience was the same: 'We found that prisoners were much more inclined to be communicative immediately after capture . . . if treated with kindness and given a cigarette.'

32

In August 1914 a German-born bachelor in early middle age found himself in New York. He approached the German consulate and offered his services to the Fatherland. His name was Julius Crawford Silber; he had left Breslau, in Silesia, as a young man for South Africa. He was recruited as an interpreter in the war of 1900 and became a mail censor for the British Army, eventually travelling with Boer prisoners to a detention camp in India.

He travelled without passport to England via Canada and quickly found employment with His Majesty's Government, in spite of the alien mania gripping the country. Herr Silber was in a uniquely useful position – working in the Office of Postal Censorship, an offshoot of MI5(g) and, ironically, its most effective arm for detecting spies. He duly opened and read thousands of letters looking for information that might aid the enemy.

But Silber *was* the enemy. His first role was in London monitoring the letters home of POWs. In 1916 he transferred to the regional office in Liverpool where he watched the US, South American and Irish mails,* He lived in a modest terraced house at No. 5 Amberley Street, Toxteth. His work continued undisturbed as his Section G colleagues lifted sundry suspects including a number of Belgian and Dutch women posing as circus performers and music-hall artistes – the network put together in Antwerp by Elsbeth Schragmuller, the '*Fräulein Doktor*' who had so excited Ernest Swinton. She was 'a buxom good-looking creature', according to a semi-official postwar account. With lady spies rumbled†, by 1916 the preferred

* Watch on the Irish mail began with the first attempt to introduce conscription in early spring 1916 and rumblings of a German-backed nationalist rising. The Liverpool operation employed 170 men and more than 1200 young female 'censorettes'.

† Writers of popular fiction (and Sunday newspaper journalists) got on to the great sex-and-tank-secret-betrayal story remarkably quickly. A French patriotic thriller novel published in 1917 called *Les Tanks à la Bataille de la Somme* had three German agents, in the thrall of the beautiful 'Fraulein Anna K . . .' of Amsterdam, ordered to join the

German cover for agents in England was evidently 'American journalist'.

Silber was never caught. He transmitted his information via neutral Scandinavia in letters stamped 'passed by the censor'. In 1919 his (British) wartime chief sent him a message of thanks for his service. He retired to a cottage in Somerset and burned his papers. In 1924, still passportless, via a day trip to Ostend he got to Berlin which he found 'impoverished and broken'.

In 1931 he found a publisher in Breslau for his memoirs, *Die anderen Waffen*, larded with 'Germany shall rise again' nationalist sentiment. It was published in English soon afterwards as *Invisible Weapons*, to general consternation. It had a foreword by Maj.-Gen. Lord Edward Gleichen, Director of the Intelligence Bureau at the Department of Information (1917–18), asserting that a J. C. Silber had indeed been employed as a postal censor. The book contained this passage:

> It was in the summer of 1916 that I first heard of a novel weapon, which later came as a terrible surprise to our forces . . .
>
> A letter was submitted to me written by a woman to her sister in Ireland. She wrote with great relief that after months of uncertainly she had found out where her husband was, an NCO in the Royal Engineers. He had managed to let her know by means of a previously arranged code that he was at a training camp the existence of which had been kept a close secret. He was employed testing 'tanks' and there was no chance of him getting any leave at present. The examiner very properly held up the letter since it clearly disclosed a grave breach of military law, even though the man had communicated only with his

---

British army and, in the guise of 'Hampshire fusiliers', at all costs penetrate 'the hangar of the tanks'. There is a copy in the Tank Museum, Bovington.

Awaiting execution after her February 1917 arrest and trial for espionage, the Dutch-Javanese exotic dancer Mata Hari was described in the *New York World* as 'having learned vaguely of tanks early in 1916 . . . that the tanks were being constructed in England and would be shipped to France via certain ports'. Not only on this account did she travel to a certain 'English industrial city' in an (unsuccessful) attempt to see the secret machines for herself – she 'arrived at a certain French port almost simultaneously with the first consignment of tanks shipped over from England'. The story got even better. 'Soon Mata-Hari returned to Paris', it was reported. 'She was seen . . . with an English officer who wore on the lapel of his collar an insignia denoting his branch of service, a little twisted brass dragon. Months later, when more of these badges were seen on British officers passing through Paris, it became known that the dragon was the official insignia denoting service with the tanks.' The beautiful spy had a jewel-encrusted version, it was further reported, which she promised to wear to her date with the firing squad.

wife. Strictly speaking we should have sent the letter to the military authorities where the man was stationed . . . we knew of course the name of the offender. The laws were very stringent in such matters.

Silber was coy about whether or not the 'authorities' were informed. His account continued: 'I was not interested in having the man punished for his letter had aroused my curiosity. Why was this building of tanks kept so secret? Tank simply means a container for liquids. Was this something connected to gas warfare?'

Silber said he had lunch with a major at his bridge club who thought the whole thing absurd. The post office spy decided: 'to go and visit the NCO's wife, not very far from Liverpool. She lived with her mother and two children in a very modest cottage and was very distressed when she realised she had really endangered her husband. She answered my few questions readily; told me the name of the camp and something about caterpillars. She obviously did not know anything more . . . This word was at least a slight hint.'

After more bridge club discussion with his expert friends, this time on artillery towing, Silber 'came to the conclusion that these "tanks" must be some sort of armoured car mounted on caterpillar wheels and armed with a number of guns, which were probably intended to be used in quantities at the front'.

'My first report on tanks [was] completed and sent off to Germany in the usual manner,' he wrote . . . 'A few months later in the autumn of 1916, a number of tanks were sent to France and used for the first time in the fighting around Thiepval.'

Silber's vague timings put the leak from Elveden picked up second-hand in a letter to Ireland sometime in early to mid-July. That is when there was some sort of fruitless spy hunt at Elveden, the one described as happening on 10 July in the diary of a tank crew member recovered from the battlefield and translated by Haupt. Weber.

If this was the result of Silber's boss in Liverpool informing MO5(g), it would be the responsibility of the Military Police to arrest the hapless 'Royal Engineer NCO'. But the search was made by men of the Heavy Section themselves – *Ohne Erfolg*, as Haupt. Weber translated the entry from the captured diary – 'without result'.

There is another explanation for the big flap. With no information from the Somme front after the disaster of the first day, extraordinary measures were resorted to. John Brough's smuggling of the wounded Cameronian from a hospital in Wandsworth could well have been the trigger for the 10 July scare. He wrote nine days later, 'Capt Money . . . was not informed of the armament of our unit; in fact he was given no details whatsoever.'

Swinton insisted there was no leak right up to the eve of battle. He repeated garbled versions of Charteris and Julius Silber's accounts (made in book form in 1929 and 1931, the year before his own book was published) before dismissing them outright. The *Official History* backed him: 'The examination of prisoners and captured documents showed that the surprise was complete,' said its editor, Brig.-Gen. J. E Edmonds, an old friend of Swinton's and himself a founding figure of Edwardian military intelligence. A German historian concluded in 2006: 'IIIb was unable to obtain any "hard" intelligence about the tank. Their first employment on the Somme on 15 September 1916 came as a complete surprise.'

Edmonds's statement directly contradicted the III Corps' own intelligence summary with its tale of 'experiments in England' and warnings being given to 'troops on parade' six weeks before the attack of 15 September.

But perhaps someone in Berlin had been given cause to take a closer look. On the night of 2–3 September two German army Zeppelins, L32 and L16, flew over Elveden Hall and Barham siding just as the last trainload of tank spares for 'Alpaca' was being loaded under the sputtering glare of acetylene lamps. The German army airships harmlessly dropped some incendiaries on the fringes of the estate causing light damage at Six Mile Bottom. (Swinton used it as an excuse for further delay.) One of them 'circled like an owl' before heading back at high altitude across the North Sea to its base. In his memoirs the colonel insisted they were looking for Thetford aerodrome.

On the account revealed in 1931 by Herr Julius Silber, the bland, balding, treacherous mail-opener of Amberley Street, Toxteth, sniffing the secrets of parted lovers, the *Nachrichtendienst* received notice of the Elveden caterpillars sometime in late July. Oberst Walther Nicolai*

* Nicolai played with nationalist politics post-1919, opened a private detective agency in Berlin and later became an intelligence adviser to the Turks. Soviet intelligence (clearly the Russians had long memories) arrested him in Nordhausen in 1945. He died in prison in Moscow in 1947.

was dissembling. His department got the Liverpool report – and did not believe it. It was the interrogation by Haupt. Weber of Gnr Herbert Clears, the trembling and shell-shocked prisoner, that were the 'facts that were ascertained'.

General Richard Butler justified his chief's rushing into action of the Heavy Section because the secret must surely leak. Haig was right. It already had.

33

The secret was out. In London it had happened in slow motion. The official dispatch from GHQ released by the Press Bureau at lunchtime on the actions on the early morning of 15 September 1916 mentioned the employment for the first time of 'a new type of heavy armoured car'. The London evening papers carried brief stop-press items. The late-to-stone *Globe* managed to print a speculative front-page piece asking 'What kind of cars are these that can give successful results over terrain such as the Somme battlefield – an area which must be as full of holes as a colander?'

What sort of cars indeed? They were 'tanks'. There had been that dry stuff in the first few days about who was behind it all – the 'self-advertising' Churchill or the perspicacious Haig? What news editors wanted to lift Home Front gloom were sensational reports of the all-British wonder weapon that had set the Hun to flight. They were not long in coming.

Newspaper correspondents had been admitted to the front – or, rather, to a carefully corralled château near GHQ – since May 1915. After months of reporting the 'calm heroism of our gallant men' and similar platitudes, the advent of the tank let rip a tide of superheated prose. The infantry and everyone else were forgotten, the tank men were supermen, even if one early report claimed they were manned by 'airmen who had lost their nerve'. On the 19th the embargo came off, filling the presses with the stuff that met Butler, Swinton and Stern when they made their dramatic drive to London for the War Office meeting.

If excitable correspondents could not get to the front, they could get in to London hospitals, where whole wards seemed to be filled with guffawing Tommies, brought back in hospital trains from the Somme, laughing off their wounds – and all of them ready to fill a newspaper yarn (the presses were waiting) with patriotic quotes real or invented: '"They are the caterpillar boys", a nurse explained, "the lads who polished off the Huns after tanks or caterpillar-like armoured cars had almost scared them to death",' so one desperate wordsmith reported. 'A lance-corporal told me it was like a panto-mime . . . No wonder someone called them the Hushes. I think they ought to go into action with someone inside the caterpillar playing the cornet:

'"Hush! Hush! Hush!

'"Here comes the Bogey-Man . . ."'

The men of the Heavy Section loathed it. They knew exactly what the tanks had done, which was not much. The press stories – 'ignorant flapdoodle composed by correspondents who never left their comfortable château' – made them laughing stocks. At the front 'they became the subject of more chaff than even the London Scottish'* – which was saying something apparently. The British public did not care. They wanted heroes.

For the first weeks no photograph or technically accurate artist's impression of a tank was permitted to be published. But the trench humour of the infantry, even through the filter of censorship, could still convey the 'monstrous absurdity' of the strange device and its oily crew. Every kind of zoomorphic metaphor was employed. The machines were 'saurians', 'toads', 'kangaroos', 'pachyderms', 'ichthyosaurs' – 'hedgehogs'. The men inside were 'Trojans', 'Jonahs', 'Little Picts'.

Machine guns had been crushed like 'wasps' nests'. Trenches were 'floated over', stands of trees 'smashed like twigs' (and that was the reporting of High Wood) – the Huns crushed as the infantry cheered the tanks on to Flers and beyond in gales of laughter. It was all nonsense. But what did get through the censor was a clear implication that on the day it was the infantry who had done the business. The *Daily Mail*'s William Beach Thomas wrote: 'The enemy ill-distinguished the guise of these iron monsters, which in truth amused our men rather than encouraged them. They were a jest, cheering hearts, possibly faithful creatures, but no rival to the bay-onet . . . The courage of the men who took this virgin journey in the

---

* The London Scottish had been the first Territorial Division to go to France in 1914 – the press pumped them up for months afterwards.

Trojan motor-cars was rewarded. The "tanks" did not make the success of the day, but they did good service . . .'

The British public, meanwhile, could still only speculate as to what the moonlit apparitions of September were really like. Journals such as *Punch* and the *Illustrated London News* printed graphic fantasies. Tank men were celebrities, alive or dead. For example the *Woking News and Mail* recorded on 6 October: 'Mr and Mrs Brotherwood of 1 Elm View Villas, Goldsworth Road, Woking have received news of the death, in action in France, of their son Pte H. Brotherwood of the Heavy Section Machine Gun Corps [the driver of C.1 Champagne killed trying to dig the tank out at Courcelette]. It is understood that Pte Brotherwood has been engaged with the famous tanks.'

On 22 November the *Daily Mirror* was the first to break the picture embargo, printing a front-page photograph of a real Mark I tank – it was C.5 Crème de Menthe that had crashed into the sugar-beet factory on the Canadian sector at Courcelette. 'HUSH HUSH – A TANK GOES GALUMPHANT INTO ACTION ON THE WESTERN FRONT' ran the headline above an excitable story. Publication was massaged by the Canadian-born MP Max Aitken (created Lord Beaverbrook and Minister of Information in 1918) in return for the paper paying five thousand pounds to war charities. C.5 looked completely alien with one tail wheel missing and its bizarre camouflage scheme, but its cannon armament and caterpillar-propelled purpose were clear. Neutral and German newspapers picked it up later.

A plethora of photographs and rousing artist's impressions quickly followed. Patriotic songwriters embraced the theme – 'we're the tanks that broke the ranks out in Picardy' – as did manufacturers of earthenware teapots and piggy banks. Selfridges offered an 'exclusive' clockwork tank and impresarios of musical theatre eschewed the tango for the latest thing: 'Come and do the Tanko / I'll teach you the Tanko / Life is nothing but a blank-oh / Till you've learned it / It's quite easy when you once begin / It will teach the Kaiser and Co. / [That] we know how to win / When they see us dance it right into Berlin . . .' sang Miss Regine Hory and the chorus girls of the Palace Theatre in Mr Alfred Dutt's hit review for Christmas 1916, *Vanity Fair*.

The ciné film *The Battle of the Ancre and the Advance of the Tanks* premiered at the Scala Theatre in London on 15 January 1917. 'See the "Tanks" in action as our brave soldiers saw them as they first went forward against the enemy,' proclaimed the breathless publicity; 'see the crews getting ready for the fray; watch them creeping from their hiding places and follow them . . . as they crush down the German entanglements . . . It is a wonderful film of a wonderful subject, a film to which you can take your wife and your children.' The film reached its tinkling piano climax as His Majesty's Landship 'Dodo' loomed on to the screen, with the caption: 'The men of the tanks . . . are they downhearted?' Dodo's commander, Lt Hugh Swears,* and his grinning crew seemed not to be. It went into over a hundred theatres. There were queues round the block.

The public and the politicians had been sold. The fêted survivors of the Heavy Section cringed under 'one unbearable round of facile jest' courtesy of the rest of the army. The red-tabbed dullards had been transformed into brilliant innovators. Poets raged at the folly of it. Nothing, it seemed, could stop the tanks now.

Hungry for new twists, newspapers had demanded to know who had 'invented' the wonder machines. In answer to a parliamentary question on 12 October, Lloyd George mentioned d'Eyncourt, Hankey, Stern, Churchill and Swinton. Tritton and Wilson were ignored.† Later that month Stern's department was recast as the futuristic sounding 'Mechanical Warfare Supply Department' – as a separate directorate within the Ministry of Munitions and moved from Pall Mall to a government-requisitioned building at 17 Cockspur Street, off Trafalgar Square. It was pointed out that 3000 skilled men would be required to build them.

Nevertheless Albert Stern proposed that his expanding tank empire could do even more. On 1 November Robertson told Haig: 'This man Stern who has something to do with the production of tanks has been telling Lloyd George that he can put in hand yet another 1,000 tanks for you.' Right now a thousand was enough.‡

---

* 'Dodo' was the pet name of his younger sister. Swears would be killed in action on 11 April 1917.

† William Tritton was furious. He telegrammed the Admiralty from Lincoln theatening to 'now make all facts known my own way'. The Director of Naval Construction made every effort to calm him down.

‡ In fact the thousandth tank would not be completed until early September 1917.

A conference at the War Office on 23 November (Haig was there in person) concluded: 'Tanks are required in as large a number as possible.' And if the battlefield lessons of the Somme could not be incorporated in time, 'almost any design now is likely to be better than no tanks'.

There was another spur to action. Since 1916 MO5 had been producing a digest of information on enemy intentions and capabilities for discreet Whitehall circulation, based on pooled reports from the Bureau Central Interallié, in Paris. The typewritten mimeographed document featured a section on 'Mechanical Transport'. It began to get very interesting. 'They have begun to construct in Germany armoured motor cars known as land cruisers carrying up to 45 men,' so a report from the Russian capital, Petrograd, stated in late October. A week later a report from Copenhagen declared more or less the same thing. In December 'a reliable agent of the Italian Military intelligence stated that the Germans were in possession of particulars [of] British tanks and are considering machines of larger and more powerful type.' The Italian report continued: 'From October [1916] they have begun to construct in Germany armoured motor cars . . . egg shaped in form . . . The motors are made by the Benz company and the gears worked by hydraulic apparatus . . . the steering control is in the rear.' The Germans, it seemed, were building tanks.

The Somme fighting, meanwhile, was fizzling out in wintry mud. There were some armoured sallies in late October on the Flers–Gueudecourt sector, ending in the capture of a few hundred yards of waterlogged trenches. Tanks from A Company went into action south of the river Ancre on 13–14 November, one achieving a considerable local success when 400 defenders of a position it attacked with its 6-pounders put up the white flag. The battlefield was a morass. Tanks were useless. On 19 November the muddied survivors crawled out of the battle zone under their own power, heading for the railheads by which they had come.

It was over. The tank force in France had been spent, but the lives of the Heavy Section had not been expended in anything like the same proportion as the infantry of the New Armies and their young officers. The tank men had been as brave as any of them. Nevertheless, they had failed.

In the judgement of the *Official History*: 'The Fourth Army plan of attack gambled on the success of the tanks ... It is no matter for surprise that the tanks which went into action on the 15th September should have proved unequal to their heavy responsibilities.'

Out of the sombre ashes of the Somme the 'dear old tanks' provided a cheery glow for the Home Front, if not for those in France who had seen how little they had actually achieved. But there was hope. It was not what they had done. It was what they might yet do.

PART THREE

Never Mind
the Noise

'The battle waits for the rain to stop . . .'
Lt-Col. Hugh Elles,
OC Tank Corps, August 1917

34

A thousand tanks, fifteen thousand men. The organizational plan thrashed out in the War Office by Butler and Whigham on 20–21 September 1916 had to be made a reality.

It was conscription now; the inexperienced, trusting British Army of summer 1916, its innocence expended on the Somme, was being supplanted by an experienced, cynical one. Overwhelmingly it was still an infantry force. The 'technical branches' needed skilled men. So did war factories, however many head-scarved women toiled in the shell-filling plants. The story of the Heavy Section (formally renamed 'Branch' on 18 November) would be of a struggle for manpower as much as a struggle to survive on an ever more hostile battlefield.

Elles was told by the War Office in late October that any idea of a quasi-independent corps was off. There would be no 'wings' or 'squadrons'. But the four battered companies now in France (the personnel of B had been sent in October to fill losses under the codename 'Turbot') would be expanded threefold into twelve battalions of three companies each, the officers and men coming from 'voluntary transfers from units now serving in France'. The days of Swinton's eager 'mechanical gentlemen' and motorcycling corporals were over. Likely sources, according to an internal memorandum, included 'Bantam battalions,* the Royal Naval Division and the Army Service Corps – and Category B.1 men throughout the armies'. Five more battalions would be raised in England from scratch. Recruits should show: 'Good muscular development, a high standard of intelligence and good eyesight are essential but short stature and such defects as flat-feet and varicose veins should not of themselves be a bar to selection. Mechanical knowledge or aptitude is desirable but not essential.'

To begin with it was relatively easy. There was no more need

* Men of between five feet and five foot three inches in height.

for secrecy; after the newspaper sensationalizing, the tanks seemed almost romantic. Anything was better than the trenches. The Adjutant-General's department circulated an army-wide notice inviting 'officers and men to volunteer for service'. When canvassed for transfers, line regiments were always eager to decant their malcontents to the Machine Gun Corps or trench mortar platoons. Here was a new receptacle for the odds and sods. The Adjutant-General's department seemed grateful, meanwhile, to have somewhere it might post officers who had proved 'difficult'. Some blundered in by accident.

Second Lieutenant Daniel Hickey had been caught up in the fervour of autumn 1914. He was an undergraduate at London University studying Spanish (he had been born in Argentina). He could drive a car and wanted to do something with 'motors'. His father, with all the enhanced patriotism of an expatriate, insisted 'my son shall shoulder a rifle'. He found himself in the Suffolk Regiment doing not very much. In autumn 1916 he was at the machine-gun school at Grantham, Lincolnshire, when: 'I saw outside a newspaper shop a poster with an illustration of a tank.' Much would follow.

A thirty-four-year-old infantry officer, Capt. Clement Attlee, veteran of Gallipoli (evacuated with dysentery), wounded in Mesopotamia (in the buttocks – by a British shell), had been hospitalized home then passed fit for light duties. He was rescued from command of a catering depot in the Midlands by his old battalion commander at Gallipoli, Col. H. K. Woods, now commander of the fledgling I Battalion. Attlee arrived at Wool, in Dorset, in December 1916, still an officer in the South Lancashires, attached to Heavy Branch. It was a desk job. He would stay at it through 1917, making several 'instructional' visits to the front. Thirty years later (When in Downing Street), Attlee would inform his 'interim biographer' that 'He liked some of the other officers one of whom gave his profession as editor of a newspaper, master of two packs of fox hounds and doctor of divinity at the University of Oxford – but he did not take a liking to the great influx of officers from horse regiments. The place was full of cavalrymen, he complained.'*

---

* There were some doubts about the future Prime Minister's performance. According to a junior officer of I Battalion writing many years later: 'The Company Commander, a Royal Marine on loan to the Corps called Major Poe, thought Attlee was a damn fool. My pleas were in vain and Capt. Attlee was jettisoned.'

There was a scramble to get in. According to one of the Heavy Branch, 'we were overwhelmed with applications . . . in consequence we found ourselves in the happy position of being able to pick and choose'. That did not exclude an unusual type of character in both the leaders and the led. It seemed an advantage.

There were enduring cultural conflicts. Was the Heavy Branch a technocratic force of machine-age warriors or one as hidebound by military conservatism as any other unit? In reality it was both. Lucien Legros, who had been Col. Crompton's cup-bearer in the pursuit of the doomed bending tank, had perceptive views. He told an industrial conference in October 1916: 'This is an engineers' war . . . yet the mechanical engineer is not a recognised factor in the army . . . men of high mechanical ability and qualifications are officered by men with only ordinary military knowledge and mere administrative capacity.'

That remained in part true of the Heavy Branch and certainly of the higher command who would commit them to battle. The actions on the Somme, however much they were larded up by excitable newspaper correspondents, had changed no minds at GHQ or in Whitehall on how to employ tanks. Tennyson d'Eyncourt at the Admiralty wrote a futuristic memo for the new Prime Minister early in the new year claiming that tanks might 'not be just an adjunct but would take the place of infantry . . . Had we [had] large numbers at the Somme, and used them on suitable ground, there is no doubt we should have had a much greater outcome.' Just so, but the military was in no mood to hear that sort of thing. The function of 'Tanks HQ' would be administrative, technical and advisory. Never would Lt-Col. Hugh Elles's organization have real control over men and machines in the field.

Even the advanced tank headquarters which might be established in the months to come, according to circumstance, would be administrative centres. Tactical advice might be offered, but Elles and his growing band of believers would not make decisions on the higher conduct of operations. Their role would be to persuade. In the battles to come, tanks would be under the command of the higher infantry formations to which they were subordinated, just as they had been on 15 September 1916.

The 'fighting organization', the force in the field that Brough and

Bradley had so briefly commanded, would stay in the cockpit of war with what had been salvaged from the autumn fighting, waiting until the new force being raised in England was ready. Elles had escaped GHQ's thrall at Beauquesne in October and set up shop at a small village called Bermicourt, a mile north of the Arras–Hesdin road in a dilapidated château. It would rapidly spread, in that greedy military way, into the fields and villages of the surrounding Ternoise valley, through which a sleepy railway picked its way eastwards (it still does). Several Tank memoirists pause nostalgically amid its hollows in Pierremont, Eclimeux – and Humières for example – a village of 'medieval quiet,' or in Blangy where a subaltern found himself billeted 'in a fine house with sheets' whereas 'the men slept in a cowshed.'

A company commander found his men 'luxuriating at Auchy-les-Hesdin, the most desirable village in the . . . area. It was full of good billets and estaminets – and here was an officers' tea-room where the law of the APM did not run.' The men seemed suprisingly well presented, clean shaven, clothes deloused. He thought it was 'due to the presence of a cotton mill which employed a number of girls with large admiring eyes . . .'

By mid-1917 Elles's organization was 'a small state' with a colonial empire of satellite workshops, driving schools and gunnery ranges strewn across north-eastern France from the Somme to the Channel. Staff would come by a variety of routes. A small number were already tank veterans, some were outright opportunists, some were rehabilitated 'dug-outs'. All seemed tinged with a certain eccentricity. It was Richard Butler who put the core of them together. He was also looking for a Swinton replacement, to 'command at home', someone safe, someone reliable. Haig stayed aloof. 'Owing to somewhat strenuous times I have not had the chance of discussing this with the Chief,' so Butler told Whigham in London.

Captain [Frederick] Elliot Hotblack, the reconnaissance officer, was already a tank veteran, a former brewer, described as 'brooding, unsociable . . . and fanatical about the war'. 'Boots' Hotblack had worked in intelligence at GHQ then joined the Heavy Section. He had won the DSO for guiding a tank to its objective by walking in front of it through a snowstorm at Beaumont Hamel in November 1916 (an incident heroically depicted in *The Graphic* magazine), one of the very last tank engagements on the Somme. He could speak

German. His penchant was snooping – 'reconnoitering all over the front in india-rubber soles'.

On the operations side was Capt. Giffard Le Quesne 'Slosher' Martel, the fighting sapper of Elveden fame. He was 'a man of desperate bravery . . . with a deep hoarse laugh', and a champion boxer – hence the nickname. His idea of fun at the front apparently was 'to get into a shelled area and dodge about to avoid the bursts'. But 'Slosher' was not a mindless bruiser. In November 1916 he produced a futuristic paper called 'A Tank Army' which foresaw fleets of armoured vehicles battling each other for mastery of the Continent.

Captain Theodore Uzielli, the quartermaster, would turn out to be the universal provider who 'never left the Tank Corps in want'. The table at Bermicourt was better than most. He was 'small, dark, suave and clever . . . disregarding no nuance of good living and comfort'. A less charitable description was 'King of the Grocers'.

Major Frank Searle was the engineering officer, late of the London General Omnibus Company (LGOC). After a row with the old guard he had gone to work for the Daimler company (its bus-building operation had become a subsidiary of the Birmingham Small Arms Co.) and thus fallen within the Ministry of Munitions' orbit. Searle had been sent to New York on a procurement mission and evidently been enraptured by the city, bringing back a collection of ragtime phonograph recordings which he played endlessly in the mess, apparently re-creating a romantic encounter in Manhattan. He was a snappy dresser, affecting, according to one contemporary description, 'a civilian-cut khaki jacket and lion-tamer's boots'.

More busmen came with him: John Brockbank, who had been in the pre-war 'special reserve' of the Army Service Corps, and George Rackham, former chief draughtsman, who had helped Searle design the famous B-Type for the streets of London, and the hard-swearing Capt. G. A. Green, another LGOC manager who had also worked in New York. He was fiercely loyal to Searle in what would turn out to be endless rows with Uzielli. It was all rather ironic. Loyalties formed in the Dollis Hill bus garage would prove as enduring as those of the smartest cavalry regiment.

A heavy-repair workshop was set up under Brockbank's command at Erin-sur-Ternoise, two miles up the road from Bermicourt with an ever-expanding railhead. Lieutenant Stephen Foot, the infantry officer whose first glimpse of the tanks in September 1916 had convulsed him with laughter, had joined the Heavy Branch that autumn. He moved into snowbound Erin as Brockbank's adjutant, bartering with local mayors for draught horses and timber. It began with a couple of broken-down sawmills and a village smithy taken over from a M. Delaby of Blangy-sur-Ternoise. It might have seemed biblical if the purpose of it all had not been so warlike. By January a basic technical and repair operation was running. A 'Bessoneau' hangar was blagged from the Royal Flying Corps. It would grow from a clutch of barns and Nissen huts to become a small industrial town. It was a realm that traditionalist officers would enter with reluctance, a place of Wellsian Morlochs. For visiting political dignitaries, however, the 'Central Workshop' would become the must-see attraction of the Western Front.

One odd character turned up at Bermicourt a little later – the fifty-three-year-old Capt. the Hon. Edward Evan Charteris, a long-ago lieutenant of the Coldstreams. He was terribly well connected, the sixth son of the tenth Earl of Wemyss, a golfer and a King's Counsel specializing in the Parliamentary Bar. In 1915 he had acted for the London County Council to draft legislation to control 'massage parlours' which had sprouted around the capital's railway termini. The Old Etonian's Mayfair apartment at 96A Mount Street was much more salubrious. A friend and patron of Augustus John and John Singer Sargent,* he had been recalled to military duty in 1916 and had worked for a while with Swinton. A year later he arrived in France to take up what he called 'a sort of nondescript post as historian of the Tank Corps' (Hugh Elles had asked for such a record to be kept). In 1920 Charteris produced not an operational summary but the extraordinary *HQ Tanks*, an account of life at Bermicourt, twenty copies privately printed, bound in leather, with its principal personae identified only in code. The library of the Tank Museum at Bovington has one – plus the handwritten key to their real identities.

This most unmilitary account has been mined before by military historians as a portrait of his brother officers as they strut and fret, but its waspish insights, a mix of homoerotic hero worship and Lady Bracknell, are too good not to revisit.

* Whom Charteris would persuade to paint the men and machines of the Tank Corps at the front.

Charteris found Uzielli, for example, on first meeting, 'a well-appointed little man, Greek I imagine in origin with much of the ingratiating technique of the Oriental'. Elles was a 'paladin of the war . . . admirably good looking, reasonably vain of appearance but quite modest as to his attainments'. Of Maj. Searle it was reported: 'Engineers said he was no engineer. Businessmen said he knew no business, soldiers said he had no idea of discipline. In spite of this the mechanical side of tanks seemed to develop under his hands. Huge workshops sprang up, remarkable feats of construction and repair were performed and the complaints about the mechanical efficiency of the tanks grew steadily less and less.'

The most daring (and, it would turn out, far-reaching) appointment of all was that of the GSO2 (GSO1 from April 1917), Maj. John Frederick Charles Fuller, the thirty-eight-year-old infantry officer who had had his first encounter with a tank watching the antics of C Company at Yvrench before they went into action on the Somme.

Born in 1878, the son of an Anglican parson and a French mother, educated at Malvern and Sandhurst (neither of which he liked), Fuller was commissioned in the Oxfordshire Light Infantry at the age of twenty. He served in South Africa and India, where mysticism (oriental and otherwise) took hold of him. In 1906 he had married Margarethe Karnatz, a Polish lady known as 'Sonia' whose interests seem to have been as eccentric as his.

In 1907 he wrote a strange pamphlet, *The Star in the West*, praising the magician and occultist Aleister Crowley, later to be dubbed 'the wickedest man in England'. They fell out in 1911 over a sensational libel case. As an adjutant of a Territorial regiment since 1903, Fuller had also made a small name for himself extolling what seemed to be ever crankier ideas in military journals. He had spent most of 1915 as a staff officer in Tunbridge Wells working on plans to evacuate Kentish sheep to the safety of Wiltshire in the event of a German invasion.* He had gone to France as a staff officer with VII Corps, part of Third Army, not engaged directly on the Somme but nevertheless in a position to observe 'its absurdities'.

---

* Other invasion contingencies of the period were equally extraordinary. Girls' schools were to be evacuated on the grounds that 'they had parents' to go to, but girls' orphanages were to be left in the path of the invader. All alcoholic liquor in public houses and hotels was somehow to be spirited to safety.

It affected him greatly, but not necessarily on an emotional level. It was the sheer stupidity of the infantry tactics that enraged him. Intellectually arrogant, he would come to sit in the 'brain barn' at Bermicourt devising wheezes just to show the old guard how clever he was.

Uzielli had recommended Fuller's appointment to the Heavy Branch. Arriving at Bermicourt 'about tea time' on a freezing, late December day he met Elles for the first time in his wood stove-heated room at the château, who told him with a certain manly gruffness: 'This show badly wants pulling together, it's all so new that one hardly knows which way to turn.'

Charteris summed Fuller up succinctly: 'A small man with a bald head and a sharp face and a nose of Napoleonic cast, his general appearance, stature and feature earning him the title of "Boney" . . . He stood out at once as a totally unconventional soldier, prolific in ideas, fluent in expression, at daggers drawn with received opinion . . . In the mess, his attacks on the red-tabbed hierarchy were viewed in the spirit of a rat hunt.'

The merry band at Bermicourt knew who the rats were. The 'nabobs' at GHQ would come in for Bermicourt's much-commented-upon sardonic chuckle as Haig's staff waxed and waned in their enthusiasm for tanks according to the chief's moods. Albert Stern in London, 'an officer with no military knowledge' in Elles's description, would rank among the dunderheads as new tanks failed to materialize. The 'home organization', the new recruitment depot and training school in south-west England and the Tank Directorate at the War Office (established in spring 1917), would come in for their own share of derision.

Elveden had served its secret purpose. In October 1916 a sprawling site in Dorset was approved as a new training ground, 1300 acres of heathland around the parishes of Bovington and Wool that had been acquired by the War Office at the outset of the Boer War. Since 1914 it had been a recruit camp housing on any one day 12,000 men who, when in possession of a leave pass, soon discovered whatever war-coarsened distractions the nearby fleshpots of Poole, Weymouth and genteel Bournemouth had to offer. Men of the Heavy Branch would be following.

But at first secrecy was as strict and leave as hard to get as it had been at Elveden. Tanks were hard to disguise. According to Capt. Douglas Browne: 'The inhabitants of Wool were annoyed rather than mystified by the melodramatic precautions attending the arrival of every trainload of tanks . . .' They were constrained to draw their curtains and sit in their back parlours as the mechanical Godivas went by.

The new flesh-and-blood arrivals faced a much stricter regime than the pioneers enjoyed during the loucher days under Robert Bradley in Suffolk. The history of 8 Tank Battalion records:

> Lt-Col. the Hon. Claude Willoughby was entrusted with the formation of the new unit at its inception [in December 1916 as the 4th Battalion Heavy Branch MGC]. An ex-Guardsman, he brought to his work high ideals of discipline and military achievement and each arriving Officer and man was quickly impressed with the responsibility which the wearing of the King's uniform imposed upon him . . . he was early made to feel that he was no longer merely an individual but a member of an intricate organisation that demanded of him obedience, smartness – and above all team-work.

First it was the turn of the junior officers, 'many of them arriving straight from cadet school'. They soon found themselves 'doing their first parade on the square under the RSM and were not released from this duty until the Colonel was satisfied with the smartness of their drill and the correctness of their word of command.'

Daniel Hickey found himself being shouted at by a Coldstreamer RSM who 'instilled all the latest drill from Chelsea Barracks'. Colonel Willoughby admired the eventual punctiliousness of the subaltern's own shouted commands and intimated that if he carried on like this 'he would gain promotion'.

Sergeants and corporals were, according to the battalion history, 'similarly examined and instructed, while for the men, drill was the order of the day. The battalion commander set himself from the first to instil into his command as much as possible of the spirit of the famous regiment in which he himself had been trained.' The type of recruit was the same ideal that Swinton had been after: a trained soldier with a knack for machinery. 'A very large percentage of the personnel owed their original choice of unit to an interest in motoring of one kind or another and the number of motor cyclists in the battalion was considerable,' said the battalion history. 'At this late stage of the war however it was impossible to hold in any way strictly to these standards and all kinds and conditions of men formed the raw material of the new unit . . .' A junior officer newly arrived at Wool expressed it more laconically: 'Apparently infantry battalion commanders had been circulated and asked to recommend their most intelligent men, particularly those with some mechanical knowledge . . . Such a request produced the inevitable results and we found that the new drafts consisted not infrequently of agricultural labourers and men with interesting crime sheets.'

Pounding the parade ground in Dorset, Lt-Col. Willoughby might have tried to make his disparate flock think and behave like Guardsmen. When they got to France, their new instructor (although himself no less keen on discipline) would strive to do the opposite.

Just as in Suffolk, the start in Dorset was an epic of improvisation. The first workshop was housed in a canvas aircraft hangar. Live 6-pounder- and machine-gun firing was carried out to the north of the camp until complaints from the locals led to a move to the coast at Lulworth. The workshop companies were found from the Army Service Corps depot at Grove Park in south-east London. There was also the urgent question of a commander for the 'home side'.

Ernest Swinton had been sacked without too much fuss (he went back to the Committee of Imperial Defence).* Butler and Whigham seemed keen on a rather grand figure, Brig.-Gen. W. Thwaites, a Royal Horse Artillery brigade commander who was quite ignorant of tanks. Whigham thought him an 'excellent man'. It was not to be Thwaites (he would end up head of Military Intelligence.) On 20 October, the fifty-two-year-old Brig.-Gen. Frederick Gore-Anley, DSO, veteran of the Sudan, South Africa and the Marne, was appointed in Swinton's place, and Lt-Col. E. B. Matthew-Lannowe,

---

* Swinton moved shrewdly meanwhile to secure his reputation in various corners of influence. On 17 October he sent Buckingham Palace a frank summary of the operations on the Somme. 'It may interest you to know that the Heavy Section, or otherwise 'the Tanks', is now going to be expanded into a very large arm of the service and I am shortly ceasing to be in charge of it and returned to store at the Committee of Imperial defence!' he informed the King via his private secretary. The next day he treated Eric Holt-Wilson to his 'first ride inside a "tank" over obstacles', presumably at Elveden. The King replied encouragingly, hopeful that 'experience gained during the last month in these weapons will enable you to turn out a really efficient and effective machine'. That task, however, would not fall to Swinton.

DSO, was appointed his deputy (later dubbed 'Potsdam' by Charteris by dint of his Teutonic command methods). Their joint knowledge of mechanized warfare was nil.

A week later the move to Dorset of what was left of the operations in Suffolk began. Lord Iveagh thought it time to return to Elveden Hall, now that German prisoners of war had been sent to his battered estate to clean up the mess just in time for the end of the pheasant season.

Frederick Gore-Anley was no Ernest Swinton. His primary motive, according to one authority, was 'to have a quiet life and avoid antagonising his superiors'. Fuller described him as 'a pleasant little man; the problem was in inverse ratio to his size. He may have been a good infantry brigadier but he knew nothing about tanks. On one occasion I heard him say, "Little Anley is like a small china pot, floating among a lot of big iron ones; little Anley is not going to get cracked".'

He was not out to win friends among his subordinates. On his first visit to the troops (at the time still in Suffolk), in the words of one who was there: 'He gave an encouraging tone to the proceedings by declaring quite openly that he knew the moment he arrived that he had come to put some discipline into the corps – that he took no interest whatsoever in the tanks – and that he did not want to see them.' His first lecture, according to the training centre war diary, was on the tactical lessons of the retreat from Mons. He was replaced at Wool by Brig.-Gen. W. J. T. Glasgow, a competent enough former Quartermaster General. His opening deposition to the assembled troops was on the subject of 'Discipline'. Everyone could see where all this was going. From the beginning the Heavy Section had been thought 'scruffy'. It was time to sort that out.

Gore-Anley went to London as 'Administrative Commander Heavy Branch' with a swanky HQ at British Columbia House, No. 1 Regent Street, supposedly to perform the old Swinton role of liaising with the War Office and with Stern's operation. John Brough was installed as the lonely 'staff officer of tanks',* whose 'office will be the central bureau, so to speak, where all the information from the

---

* He seems to have lived above the shop. The home address on John Brough's will is Carlton Chambers, 8 Regent Street.

different departments of tanks will be joined up'. It was a pious hope. He would not last long, and nor would his boss. Rows between Tanks HQ in France, Gore-Anley and the Mechanised Warfare Supply Department started immediately but Bertie Stern still enjoyed a direct line to the Secretary of War, used whenever the military proved obstructive.* Anley tried, and failed, to shut it down. Hugh Elles was also stirring the pot. He complained of the Ministry of Munitions' tardiness in a letter to Wigram: 'Dear Kitten . . . we want facts and dates not hot air . . . d'Eyncourt of course is very reliable.'

Little by little, new-built tanks were arriving in Dorset, clanking along the tracks of the London and South-Western Railway to be offloaded at Wool station and driven into the camp. For now the men who would be trained to take them to war came from the same sources that Swinton had tapped. Among them was the first wave of conscripts. In the last months of 1916, according to the war diary of F Battalion:

> The new personnel began to arrive . . . The men who were transferred from the Training Centre were from the Motor Machine Gun Corps, and were formed into A Company.
>
> B and C Companies were formed almost entirely from men called up in groups, under the Derby Scheme [a system of voluntary registration for national service that preceded conscription].
>
> During the last weeks of November the men arrived in great numbers, fresh from their civilian occupation. Each day large numbers were marched up from Wool Station, and passed before the Medical Officers, those who were passed fit being taken in hand by the Quartermaster's Department, and the rejected were sent back to their homes . . . those men selected were very keen to get into the tanks, and to take part in the most up to date method of fighting.

It was not just young proto-conscripts who were keen to be 'up to date'. Transfer to the Heavy Branch was open to front-line soldiers, keen to fight but just as keen to survive. Captain Richard Haigh, who had been on the Somme as a junior officer with the Berkshire

---

* Albert Stern also enjoyed a personal friendship with Frances Stevenson, Lloyd George's secretary and mistress. After the war she considered marriage to the banker. In 1922 Stern married Miss Helen Orr-Lewis; they had two sons.

Regiment, spelled out his own reasons very soon after the end of the war:

> A man of course is ready to die for [his country]. But he does not think about it. He lights a cigarette and tries to be nonchalant for he knows that his men are watching him and it is his duty to keep up a front for their sake . . . but there is nothing heroic about going over the top.
>
> This then was our possible second reason for preferring to attack inside bulletproof steel; not that death is less likely in a tank, but there seems to be a more sporting chance with a shell than with a bullet. The enemy infantryman looks along his sight and he has you for a certainty, but the gunner cannot be so accurate. Above all the new monster has our imaginations in thrall. Here was novelty and wonderful developments.

Second Lieutenant G. E. V. Thompson had enlisted in the London Regiment on the outbreak of war. He was eighteen, a clerk in an accountant's office. He survived Second Ypres, and missed the subaltern-culling of July on the Somme by dint of a throat infection which had put him in hospital. He saw his first tank in late September 1916, wrecked in the charnel house of High Wood. As he recalled: 'I was in charge of the burying party . . . I used the tank as an office where I could muster my lists out of the rain.'

Round came the circular calling for volunteers. The mass burials went on in the wood, day after day, a padre intoning 'overlong' services under 'light shelling'. The tank (William Sampson's D.13 Delilah) became a grim kind of refuge. Thompson, chastened by the horror in the trees, thought the Heavy Branch might just be the way to get through. He was accepted. His career in the Tank Corps would be full of incident. He lived long enough to write a memoir 'for his grandchildren'. It resides in the Imperial War Museum's department of documents.

Captain William Watson was gloomily commanding a company of the XI Corps Cyclist Battalion near Béthune in autumn 1916. He too thought there might be a better way of soldiering:

> To us in our damp and melancholy retreat came rumours of tanks . . . We learned from an officer, who had met the quarter-master of a battalion that had been on the Somme, the approximate shape and appearance of tanks. We pictured them and

wondered what a cyclist battalion could do against them. Apparently the tanks had not been a great success on the Somme, but we imagined potentialities. They were coloured with the romance that had long ago departed from the war. An application was made for volunteers . . .

Watson would be a tank company commander at Arras, in Flanders and at Cambrai and write one of the most insightful and honest histories of the tanks and the 'weary men' inside them, published soon after the end of the war.

The tank men in Dorset, after the Anley-inflicted regime of square-bashing, would go to France the same way the Elveden pioneers had done, but this time with bands playing them down the road from Bovington. The villages turned out in the early spring sunshine to see them board the train at Wool station for Southampton docks and the crossing to Le Havre. The primitive days at Yvrench, without spares, without proper training, without a clue as to what they were actually supposed to do, were gone. This time a basically competent instructional and engineering operation would be put in place, with a specialist staff to try and make it all work. The problem was getting hold of enough tanks. The Heavy Branch had learned some lessons. As to their employment in battle, GHQ had learned nothing and forgotten everything.

The small band of staff officers was in place at Bermicourt; now 'fighting' commanders began to arrive. The newly formed 1st Tank Battalion (mustering C and D Companies, the veterans of 15 September) went to Lt-Col. Christopher Baker-Carr who had gone to war an age ago in a borrowed Mercedes as a general's chauffeur. The 2nd Battalion went to Lt-Col. A. Courage ('a little grizzled officer with a porcelain chin, his own having been shot away in the Mons retreat') and in April the 3rd Battalion was raised, commanded by Lt-Col. J. Hardress-Lloyd, like Courage a former cavalryman although his claimed patrician origins were rather mysterious. According to Fuller he started the war as 'stowaway . . . but kept a good table and a fine stable'. The Heavy Branch could still be grand.

The futuristic unit attracted a ragbag of volunteers to fill its subordinate staff commands. Their pre-war skills were diverse. There was a music-hall proprietor, a Dumfries baker, the heavy-drinking former mayor of Hythe, a circus trapeze artist. The 1st Battalion padre was a rural parson. According to Baker-Carr: 'My adjutant came from a box factory in Wallasey, my equipment officer was the best known bee-keeper in Wales, my reconnaissance officer was a London lawyer, my engineer officer from the Hillman Car Company of Birmingham, my Medical Officer from the South Pole where he had been for the past two years with Shackleton.'

Junior officers, the youthful subalterns who would command the tanks in action, their section commanders who would ride in or walk beside them into action – and company commanders who would sit in forward dugouts fretting over their fate – began to drift in. They came from England, and they came from the line in France. Some were combat veterans, a handful were 'old tankers' from the Somme. According to the nineteen-year-old 2/Lt Wilfred Bion they were a 'patchy' lot. 'There were some good ones, others were largely men who had seen a good deal of fighting and gone into the tanks to avoid it . . . when the tanks got into action their low morale let them down and they were gradually weeded out . . .'

Most of them had been infantrymen. William Watson, for example, the bicycle company commander (that was regarded as suitably mechanical), had sent in his application for transfer in December 1916. On the 28th 'he was ordered by wire to Bermicourt', accompanied by his servant. After a brisk interview with Elles he was appointed commander of 11 Company, D Battalion.

That was the officers. Then there were the men. On his first day after arriving, Maj. Fuller got a shock. He took an early morning drive round the Heavy Branch area and its outlying villages where the men were billeted alongside the locals. Pigs grunted as bleary figures in khaki emerged from tumbledown cottages. 'Boney' Fuller drew his own stark conclusion. He wrote in his memoirs: 'I had never seen such a band of brigands in my life.'

Perhaps it was the living conditions. They were not conducive to razor-creased smartness.* William Watson set up home at Blangy in the freezing Abbé Ste Berthe, a hospice for consumptives with patients and caring nuns still in residence, plus a combative Mother Superior. The mess was in the abbey's ancient hall, fitfully warmed

---

* In 1919 the *Tank Corps Journal* invited suggestions for postwar uses for tanks. One submission was 'trouser press'.

by a huge log fire and on all accounts rather jolly. The circumstances seized men in odd ways. The officers of one section all shaved their moustaches off, another cropped his hair to a fuzz. Other ranks got on with life as best they could.

The motor cycle dispatch rider Driver F. S. Cutting described his new billet in the village of Humières, of which he uncertainly took occupation on 6 January 1917:

> A pigsty! Len Pipler built three ship bunks to sleep in, one on top of the other. A ten gallon oil drum made a fireplace which smoked. On the wall were placed photos of our dear friends and the St Saviour's almanac. We had our meals in the farmer's kitchen who was over sixty and was a fireman on the railways. The farm was carried by his wife and daughter. We drew our rations . . . we three DRs did the cooking.
>
> Reg [Pte R. Combes] had his 21st birthday here. His Dad sent him an iced cake. I was the cook – roast fowl, beef, sprouts and Yorkshire pud. Custard, figs and chunks.

Who were this raggle-taggle army? These were not the raw, drilled drafts from England he might have expected. Fuller was informed that recruitment had been open to the whole BEF. For men in the trenches a desire to be 'up to date' might not be the presiding motive for seeking a transfer. The Heavy Branch was a haven, Fuller concluded, for 'every disgruntled and impossible soldier in the field': 'There were cavalrymen, infantrymen and gunners; ASC men, sappers and actually a sailor, though how he found his way to Bermicourt I cannot say. There were men in trousers, men in puttees, men in trench boots and men in kilts. There was every kind of cap badge and deficiency in cap badges; the men looked exactly what they were – the down and outs of bawling Sergeants and unfriendly Corporals.'

Hugh Elles would explain after the war that the men he had commanded were a 'citizen force' with a tiny percentage of its eventual 20,000-strong ranks having started as professional soldiers. Its officers were city clerks and junior solicitors, its engineers had been bus garage managers. The caste system of the old army was irrelevant. As the 'esprit de tank' developed it was based on the personality of battalion and brigade commanders – and, indeed, on Elles's own (a word portraitist in the 1920s would dub him rather unfortunately 'Il

Duce'). But for all its piratical pretensions (an unofficial skull and crossbones badge had come into use) the corps would not develop as some black-uniformed elite. Elles stressed, as Swinton had done under the pine trees at Elveden, that 'they were there to save the lives of the infantry' – who were 'not lucky enough to have an inch or two of armour plating between themselves and the enemy's bullets'.

They came from anywhere and everywhere. Captain R. P. Butler, a Canadian sapper, for example was charged with forming a salvage company in late 1916 and went looking for personnel. 'Generally a unit was ordered to send us a certain number of men and they naturally sent us those they did not want,' he recalled some years after the war. 'Some who came were very good, others were of little use. We asked for some fitters and they arrived in due course, but we found that they were gas fitters – experts in fitting up chandeliers but completely ignorant of internal combustion engines.'

The little unit (the salvage companies would expand dramatically in size and importance) spent the winter of 1916–17 on the Somme battlefield, striving to recover 6-pounder guns from derelict tanks. The few ex-Royal Engineers Butler managed to get hold of came from the 'special section' – gas – 'purveyors of frightfulness' in his own words, 'who dealt with flame throwers, poison gas and such things, but in fact knew nothing of engineering of any sort'. He got some Australians 'who had been mechanics in civil life . . . all were excellent fellows and good workers', before GHQ reclaimed them as infantry just before third Ypres. Their life expectancy had shortened.

It was Fuller's self-set task to turn the band of brigands into something more soldierly. Spring was coming, a new 'fighting season'. Time was pressing. At the end of 1916 the white-mustachioed 'Papa' Joffre was elevated to Marshal of France and replaced as commander-in-chief by the pugnacious cavalryman-turned-artillery technician Gen. Robert Nivelle. He promised to evict the invader in a climactic offensive in the Champagne. Haig urged an offensive in Flanders against an enemy 'weakened by the Somme' to aid the French. The recurring vision of a breakthrough beckoned, with the railway junction of Roulers as the objective – that and a strategic imperative to push the enemy off the coast and capture the submarine bases at Ostend and Zeebrugge.

But the Germans moved first by enacting operation 'Alberich', the withdrawal beginning on 23 February to the heavily fortified defensive position – the *Siegfried Stellung*. The British Army crept into the ransacked, booby-trapped devastation. 'Pursuit of the retiring Germans might have been possible,' recorded Evan Charteris, 'but during the first week of March there was not in France one single tank fit for action.' There were plenty of stories of the Hun's frightfulness. The Heavy Branch officer Richard Haigh despaired at the discovery in one village that every cat – 'black ones, tabbies and little kittens' (bred by the Germans themselves as ratters) – had been systematically beheaded.

At Bermicourt it was personal hygiene that demanded attention. Fuller told Uzielli: 'The [men] must be bathed and scrubbed and cleaned up, and not until then can I set to work. Soap is our start point . . .'

Bathhouses and a laundry were set up at Blangy with 'one forewoman, twenty washerwomen, ten women ironers and four women menders' recruited from the local villages. 'Four and fifty men were able to bathe each day of the week except Sunday, thus every eighth day the turn of a battalion to bathe came round,' according to a Heavy Branch record. Mobile canteens and cinemas were established. Each battalion would have its coloured shoulder strap, and a corps badge was devised to bring order to the existing jumble of military heraldry.* A chocolate-coloured one-piece overall became official issue, replacing the ragbag of boiler suits that had been worn before. Officers procured their own tailored versions of this otherwise shapeless garment – 'the effect of wearing them is to cause one to slouch'.†

---

* Various designs were canvassed, among them a gauntlet, a rhinoceros and a side plan of a rhomboid Mark I, which was eventually adopted. Swinton claimed he originated it. It was not universally popular. According to the anonymous diarist of 5th Brigade writing in summer 1918: 'It is difficult to convey the disgust which it received when it was introduced and the dislike with which it it still regarded. Both officers and men will wear the badge of any other regiment to which they may belong rather than the corps badge . . . a mounted knight in full armour, an Assyrian chariot, a charging rhinoceros would seem preferable . . .'

† Hardress-Lloyd issued orders for the 1st Tank Brigade on 19 March: 'Fighting kit for tank crews has been decided upon as follows: trousers and puttees, cardigan waistcoat, ankle boots with all nails and steel plates removed from soles and heels, steel helmet, brown dungaree boiler suit (officers and NCOs must wear badges of rank on shoulders or sleeves), leather waist belt, revolver in holster, revolver in ammunition pouch, box respirator.'

After cleanliness came fitness. Fuller set about hardening his men with football, team games and more. There were daily runs up a hill to inspect the nearby battlefield of Agincourt. 'The heavyweight boxing champion of England was lent to the Heavy Branch, an NCO attached for a week to each battalion in turn to stimulate an interest in offensive [someone substituted 'combative' on the original type-written Tank Corps record] sports.' 'Slosher' Martel was always look-ing for a fight.

At last there was some training on the weapons and machines themselves, conducted with the battered remnants of the tanks that had withdrawn from the Somme on a 'tankodrome' of freezing mud. Fuller, like Swinton and Brough before him, had his own ideas on how to proceed. His first 'Notes on Training' stated: 'Every exercise and movement should, if possible, be reduced to a precise drill.' That seemed to fit when the instructing staff were themselves nearly all tank novices.

Dummy tanks were constructed out of wood and canvas, manoeuvred like pantomime horses. Some days it was so cold that the tank engines froze. Instructors imparted their knowledge as they might. The former infantry subaltern 2/Lt Harold Davies gave lectures on the Lewis gun. Lieutenant 'Fanny' Field, who had come from the artillery, explained the workings of the 6-pounder. Lieutenant Eric Money, late of the Cyclist Corps, gave instruction on basic mechanics. Indoor lessons on the Lewis gun were always popular, apparently, conducted in an estaminet where *café au rhum* was readily available.

Then there was morale. Fuller composed uplifting lectures delivered by candlelight in Blangy's schoolhouse – little tabernacle of the machine-war cult. The officers would prove more resistant to indoctrination, so Fuller confessed. They had to be de-educated and remade. Fuller got the required results because these were 'temporary soldiers'. Their minds had not been 'permanently spoilt' by regimental mummery.

Fuller was not a military commander. As 'GSO1' he was an ideas man to Elles, who himself could only advise higher commanders on any plan of attack. But like Swinton in the spring of 1916, that did not prevent him producing tactical ideas of his own on how the new arm should be employed in battle.

His first major essay on armoured warfare was written in February

1917, the dull-sounding 'Tank Training Note number 16'. It was judged so loopy by one military historian that he doubted Fuller had ever actually set foot in a tank. 'Tanks had nothing to fear from shrapnel, shell splinters or bullets,' he stated, and 'could navigate practically over any ground and through all entanglements.' It was an ambitious judgement but, as Fuller stressed, the absurdity of a front 500 miles long but only five miles deep was crying out for rupture across its depth – into the second and third lines – which the infantry and artillery together had never been able to do.

His paper took complex positions on 'internal flanks' and the utility of the creeping barrage. It did not argue yet for dispensing with bombardment, only that it should be shorter – forty-eight hours maximum. Artillery should deal with the first line, tanks should breach the second. The 'weapon of exploitation' was still cavalry. But the horsemen should cooperate in some mysterious manner with tanks, which had proved themselves thus far incapable of keeping up even with the foot-slogging pace of the infantry. Fuller restated the heretical Heavy Section doctrine that had seen John Brough sent home in disgrace, that tanks should be used in mass, 'in echelon and with strong reserves'. GHQ ordered his paper withdrawn.

35

More and more men of the Heavy Branch were arriving in the drafts from England, but not the thousand-strong fleet of 'super-tanks' that Haig had imperiously demanded the September before. The Anglo-French machine had never materialized. The French had built their own, for use in the coming offensive that Gen. Robert Nivelle, hero of the Verdun counter-offensive and the recapture of Fort Douaumont, was promising would win the war in two days. On 6 January 1917 Haig announced he could not assist Nivelle unless his pet project for an attack in Flanders was sanctioned. He was overruled, and in February Lloyd George* agreed at a meeting with Nivelle at Boulogne to put the BEF under French command in the hopes of avoiding another costly British offensive or paying the political price of removing the god-like C-in-C. Haig threatened to resign. He was soothed into staying by a personal letter from the King.

On 25 January 1917 the War Cabinet, headed by the new Prime Minister, met to discuss what seemed like a ray of hope – tanks – and especially to address the growing divide between what the minutes of the meeting described as 'the view of the General Staff that tanks should exclusively be used as an adjunct to infantry' and the 'view of the designers', that they should somehow 'operate on the flank of the attack moving over areas which had not been pitted with shell fire and did not draw fire upon our own infantry'.

The Downing Street meeting reached no conclusion on the correct way to employ tanks. It did agree to sponsor a further conference inviting interested parties from France. GHQ grew restive. Lancelot Kiggell replied on the C-in-C's behalf. 'On the face of it the idea is somewhat peculiar and it would appear likely to be more useful if

---

* Lloyd George had succeeded Asquith as Prime Minister on 7 December. Edwin Montagu, an Asquith loyalist, resigned as Minister of Munitions, succeeded by Christopher Addison. Lord Derby became Secretary of State for War.

the manufacturers got on with construction and left tactics to the soldiers.'

There was dramatic new secret information from Petrograd to consider, meanwhile. In mid-February 1917 Russian intelligence was reporting: 'Germany is building a large number of tanks, the highest serial number seen is 120. Armament will consist of 22-mm QF guns and machine guns.' There was more in the report: 'Defence against tanks – the most effective is considered to be long-range fire with armour-piercing shells. Concentration of artillery on stretches of road, continuous machine-gun fire and deep pits are also used.'

The promised second conference took place in London on 4 March. It was Ministry of Munitions-inspired but the military were in the ascendant. Generals Kiggell and Butler came from GHQ, Elles from Bermicourt and Robert Whigham, who had recovered from his unfortunate accident in Hyde Park. General Estienne, the French armoured-warfare prophet, had duly been invited. He proposed something very novel, a surprise attack *without* previous artillery bombardment to break the opposing trench line, then using 'light tanks' (the French were working on a machine-gun-armed, two-man *faible tonnage* skirmisher) in the manner of cavalry to go through the breach. Albert Stern was very excited by the idea.* That the Germans were apparently working on a tank fleet was not on the agenda.

Butler and Whigham were sceptical but not entirely so. Of course everyone could agree that tanks at this stage of their development were a supporting arm only. But the occasion might arise when large numbers were available – and the ground was suitable – where a large-scale surprise attack might work. Elles said nothing. Fuller was not present. It would need a revolution in the gunner's art (it was coming) to make such a surprise attack possible. Meanwhile, discussions of that nature were meaningless without tanks. There should have been 400 Mark IVs by now. Just a handful had been completed.

---

* A lighter British tank was in the making. William Tritton had visited the Somme after the Heavy Section's debut and was sounded out on the prospect of building a lighter, faster machine. This would lead to the Tritton Chaser, later dubbed the 'Whippet' and more formally the 'Medium Mark A'. 'The only engines available were omnibus engines,' he later told the Official Historian; 'by using two per tank I made some sort of compromise.'

A prototype mock-up was complete by February 1917. Hugh Elles came to inspect it at Lincoln but it would be another year before production vehicles were ready.

Production in Lincoln and Birmingham had been stalled by Tanks HQ's own indecision in saying just what they wanted, and more so by shortages of manpower and raw material, the issue which would dominate the story of the tanks for many months to come. In the early spring of 1917 the Heavy Branch could muster a few rehabilitated Mark Is and marginally improved Mark IIs (they had transverse metal bars called 'spuds' on their tracks to improve grip and the steering tail was dispensed with) and some forty or so Mark III 'training tanks' that had been built with mild steel plate just to keep the production lines in business. They had no protection in the face of the SmK bullet. Brigadier-General Gore-Anley tested the battle-worthiness of the machines at Bovington by poking their flanks with a chisel. It seemed adequate. They would be sent to France.

It seems scandalous in retrospect. The Russian agent (seemingly high in OHL counsels) had already forwarded details of stiffening anti-tank measures. GHQ had forwarded its own report in February, derived from an 'officer prisoner', that 'special guns for use exclusively against tanks are to be used about ten yards behind the front line'. A few weeks later there were more revelations from Petrograd in the intelligence digest for the Ministry of Munitions. 'Special anti-tank batteries [will be employed] in advanced positions whose crews are in dugouts close at hand. Six of these guns are allotted to a corps sector of two divisions i.e. (on Western Front) about six kilometres.' And they were sending toy tanks to France with eighteen-year-olds inside them.

Stern foresaw a catastrophe. The Mark IIIs that were on their way to the front were unarmoured, built solely for clambering around the training ranges in Dorset. To use them in battle would compound the near disaster of September 1916. On 12 March he told Dr Christopher Addison, the new Minister of Munitions: 'Their failure will undoubtedly ruin the confidence of the troops in the future of mechanical warfare. For the sake of sixty machines, the whole future of thousands of tanks will be unjustifiably prejudiced.'

Keeping the existing force going was difficult enough. On 24 March, Frank Searle, the engineering officer, told Elles starkly:

> So far as tanks are concerned this summer's offensive is going to see one of the worst failures and scandals of the war, unless certain spares in sufficient quantities are forthcoming . . .

[because] of spares required we have only been able to maintain an average of twenty-five tanks in service out of 125 in France. Sixty of this number were certainly left on the Somme, but many of these could have been brought in had spares been available . . . it would be a crime to manufacture and send to this country machines which there is no possibility of maintaining.

It was this force, as feeble and unprepared in many ways as that which had been blooded on the Somme, that would be committed to an attack around Arras to 'draw in German reserves' as Nivelle embarked on his attack on the Chemin des Dames to the south. The invaders' strategic withdrawal had already grossly disrupted both planned offensives' usefulness.

The first Mark IV machines reached Dorset on 2 April, three months later than planned. The first batch of nineteen reached Le Havre docks on the night of the 17th–18th. By then the force of ill-armoured machines sent out from Bovington and the few cannibalized Mark Is scraped together by Elles had already gone into action.

The British bombardment heralding the Arras offensive began on 20 March; the infantry assault was planned for 9 April, Easter Monday, on a fourteen-mile front. The sixty tanks available would once again be spread along the front in the 'driblets' that had broken the heart of the Heavy Branch on the Somme. Just as then, consultation was minimal. Major William Watson commanding 11 Company was summoned to a staff conference on the 4th in a ruined château at Bihucourt. 'It consisted of an awe-inspiring collection of generals seated round a table in a stuffy room full of maps,' he wrote. 'The details of the attack had apparently been settled before I arrived . . .'

In taut, emotive prose, Maj. Watson described watching his company moving up to the front:

On the night of the 5th April, as soon as it was dusk, my tanks moved forward. One by one they slid smoothly past me in the darkness, each like a patient animal, led by an officer, who flashed directions with an electric lamp. The stench of petrol in the air, a gentle cracking as they found their way through the wire, the sweet purr of the engine changing to a roar when they climbed easily on to the road – and then, as they followed the white tape into the night, the noise of their engines died away, and I could hear only the sinister flap flap of the tracks, and see only points of light on the hillside . . .

Major Watson went forward, to be with a section of 11 Company moving into their final assembly position as the equinoctial hours ticked away to Zero-Hour:

> Stand with me at night and listen. There is a little mist, and the dawn will soon break. Listen carefully, and you will hear a queer rhythmical noise and the distant song of an engine. The measured flap of the tracks grows louder, and, if you did not know, you would think an aeroplane was droning overhead. Then in the half light comes a tired officer reading a map, and behind him another, signalling at intervals to a grey mass gliding smoothly like a snake.
>
> And so they pass, one by one, with the rattle of tracks and the roar of their exhaust, each mass crammed with weary men, hot and filthy and choking with the fumes. Nothing is more inexorable than the slow glide of a tank and the rhythm of her tracks. Remember that nothing on earth has ever caused more deadly fear at the terrible hour of dawn than those grey sliding masses crammed with weary men.

Late on the night of the 8th the tanks of C Battalion began their crawl up the line, transiting a swampy valley near the village of Achicourt, south of Arras. A tank commander quoted by Clough Williams-Ellis described what happened:

> We had got word of trouble near the railway cutting . . . where some half a dozen tanks were wallowing in a bog of black mud, tanks that should by now be miles ahead and getting onto their battle positions for the attack at dawn . . .
>
> The crews sweating and filthy were staggering about and trying to help their machines out by digging away at the soil under their bellies and by thrusting planks and brush under their tracks. Now and then an engine would be started up and some half submerged tank would lift its bulk up and out in unsteady floundering fashion little by little in wrenching jerks as the engine raced and the clutch was released . . .

All this was under artillery fire. Achicourt was smoking and glowing, but it was the noise of the British guns that Williams-Ellis's correspondent remembered. 'The great thing is to go about with an open mouth. It equalised the pressure on your ear-drums. I am acquiring a permanent droop of the lower jaw.'

The opening infantry attack went well; it was far more effective than the debacle on the first day of the Somme. North of Arras the Canadian Corps, part of the First Army, seized a section of Vimy Ridge in a carefully rehearsed and skilfully executed assault in the space of three hours. In the centre, the Third Army advanced three and a half miles, the biggest gain since trench warfare had begun. This time Mk 106 artillery fuses cut the wire without cratering the ground. Phosgene gas rained on the defenders' gun line. The creeping barrage cowed the front-line machine-gunners. But the Germans had their new defence tactics. The second line held. Thirty-six surviving tanks did what they could.

A youthful officer of 12 Company of D Battalion was moving up on the night of 9 April to mount an attack out of Neuville St Vaast at dawn the next day:

> Zero was [set for] 5.50am and from midnight everyone had that depressed let's get it over feeling which banished sleep. At last only five minutes to go and all the engines were gently ticking over . . .
>
> The [infantry] went over the top . . . but the [tank] company was fated not to catch up . . . we reached Hunland, the shelled area which the night's rain had turned into a sponge, quite unable to bear 30 tons or so. Before the Boche second line was reached every commander was outside, picking a way for his tank, but even that method was no use and halfway to the Lens road every single tank had bellied and remained so despite two to three hours spade work by the crews . . . There was nothing to do but wait for orders which Major Watson brought personally during the afternoon when the crew were withdrawn to camp.
>
> Casualties fortunately were small, the cars were dug out the next day by means of large working parties . . .

11 Company was moving up on the night of the 9th from a quarry four miles behind the front line for an attack to be made with the Australian 4th Division, planned to go in at first light on 10 April against the fortified village of Bullecourt. A snowstorm blotted out the dimly lit path. Machines were milling about in darkness still two miles behind the start line with just an hour to go. The infantry were

already deployed in the open and taking casualties. The attack had to be put back for twenty-four hours. Major Watson recalled: 'Our tanks lay hidden against the bank at the side of the road shrouded in their tarpaulins. My men were busily engaged in making them ready. One engine was turning over very slowly. It was bitterly cold and snow still lay on the downs.'

He gathered his officers in Brigade HQ in the village of Noreuil, established in the cellar of a ruined brewery, to tell them of the postponement. 'All my officers were assembled in the darkness, I could not see their faces. They might have been ghosts. I heard only rustles and murmurs, I explained briefly what had happened . . . the night passed . . . while my tanks were crawling forward over the snow . . .'

The tanks parked up in the Noreuil valley to try again before dawn on the 11th. Watson waited for news in the cellar in a 'fug of pipe and cigarette smoke' as his little staff nervously sharpened pencils, checked telephone lines and stared at blank action report forms. Gunfire boomed and rumbled above them. It was still snowing. He wrote:

> Few reports arrive during the first forty minutes of battle. Everybody is too busy fighting. Usually the first news comes from the wounded . . . Brigade HQ as a rule are an hour behind the battle . . . At last the reports began to dribble in . . . There have been casualties before the German wire was reached . . . Fighting in the Hindenburg trenches but few tanks to be seen . . .
>
> One [tank] company want a protective barrage put down in front of them but from another message it seems probable that there are Australians out in front. The brigadier must decide.
>
> There is little news . . . 'no tanks have been seen,' a tank 'helped clear up a machine gun post,' 'a tank is burning . . .'
>
> At last one of my commanders bursts in. He is grimy, red eyed and shaken, 'Practically all the tanks have been knocked out.'

The *History of the 123rd Grenadier Regiment* gives a glimpse of what happened from the German side:

> On 11 April 1917 near Arras, the CO of the 3rd MG Company, Leutnant der Reserve Schnabel, waited for a British tank to come within 150 metres of his gun and then fired 1,200 rounds

of armour piercing ammunition against the [male] tank's side. The tank was disabled within 50 metres of our front line. The tank was set on fire from at least three shots striking the engine and the resulting fire set off the ammunition inside. Seventy-seven rounds were later counted that had gone through both sides of the machine.

Richard Haigh, Watson's second in command, told the story of the assault on Bullecourt on 11 April set in the same, smoke-filled cellar in Noreuil. His account of a floundering attack has the power of any fictionalized drama. Published in New York eighteen months after the events, the author, like the official war diarists, thought it wise to suppress real names. A pseudonymous tank commander, Lt 'McKnutt', has just returned to the Company HQ, his vehicle having ditched:

> 'Any news of the other buses?' he asked. The buzzers [telephone operators] shook their heads warily. McKnutt rushed up to a couple of men who were being carried to a dressing station.
>
> 'Do you fellows know how the tanks made out?'
>
> One of them had seen two of the machines on the other side of the German line, he said. Then on the top of the hill against the skyline, they saw a little group of three or four men. James (the driver) recognised them.
>
> 'Why there's Sergeant Browning and Mr Borwick, sir. What's happened to their tank?'
>
> 'What do you think happened?' [said Lt Borwick]. 'A trench mortar got us full in one of our tracks, and the beastly thing broke. So we all tumbled out and left her there.'
>
> 'Didn't you go on with the infantry?'
>
> 'No. They had reached their objective by that time . . . so we saved the tank guns. Then we strolled back and here we are.'
>
> 'But where's the rest of your crew?'
>
> Borwick said quietly that Jameson and Corporal Fiske got knocked out coming back. He lit a cigarette and puffed at it. There was silence for a moment.
>
> 'Bad luck . . . have you got their pay books?'
>
> 'No. I forgot them,' Borwick answered.
>
> But his sergeant handed over the little brown books which were the only tangible remains of two men who had gone into action that morning . . . they had been used as pocket books and held a few odd letters which the men had received a few days before . . .

Relatives were always grateful for those.

Watson put together what had happened for his post-battle report. It made harrowing reading. Of the tanks that had gone forward in the centre:

> [Capt. 'Fanny'] Field's section of three tanks were stopped by the determined and accurate fire of forward field guns before they entered the German trenches. The tanks were silhouetted against the snow, and the enemy gunners did not miss. The first tank was hit in the track before it was well under way. The tank was evacuated, and in the dawning light it was hit again before the track could be repaired.
>
> [2/Lt Eric] Money's tank reached the German wire. His men must have 'missed the gears'. For less than a minute the tank was motionless, then she burst into flames. A shell had exploded the petrol tanks, which in the old Mark I were placed forward on either side of the officer's and driver's seats. A sergeant and two men escaped. Money, best of good fellows, must have been killed instantaneously by the shell.
>
> [2/Lt Arthur] Bernstein's tank was within reach of the German trenches when a shell hit the cab, decapitated the driver, and exploded in the body of the tank. The corporal was wounded in the arm, and Bernstein was stunned and temporarily blinded. The tank was filled with fumes. As the crew were crawling out, a second shell hit the tank on the roof. The men under the wounded corporal began stolidly to salvage the tank's equipment, while Bernstein, scarcely knowing where he was, staggered back to the embankment. He was packed off to a dressing station, and an orderly was sent to recall the crew and found them still working stubbornly under direct fire.

Two tanks had been seen to go forward 'beyond the Hindenburg Line' followed by Australian infantry – as far, it seemed, as a village called Hendecourt. They did not return. Second Lieutenant Harold Davies was thought to have pulled off some great coup before being cut off by a counter-attack. The infantry were pinned down in no-man's-land or in the first line of captured trenches, until their surviving officers ordered every man for himself. Most of them were killed by enfilading machine guns as they tried to escape. The apparent tank exploit, meanwhile, was glowingly mentioned in Haigh's dispatch and trumpeted in the press. The digger infantry spat with rage.

But months later, Harold Davies's fiancée received a letter from a prisoner of war in Germany. It was from a crew member of the vanished tank: 'We were in an attack in the morning of 11 April, when our tank was put out of action, Mr Davies was badly wounded and I and my comrades did all we could for him. Acting on his orders we tried to get back to our own positions to bring assistance but we were cut off and taken prisoner. I am very sorry to tell you that unless he had proper treatment I am afraid it will go hard for him.'

The true facts of the overall disaster were put together later. In the centre section, a mortar shell hit 2/Lt McIlwaine's tank track shortly after starting and the crew evacuated before it received a direct hit. Of the left section, Lt H. Richard's engine cut out and the crew evacuated while their commander went looking for his section leader for instructions. Stopped by military police, some of the crew refused to go back to the tank as they now had 'no one in command'.

Lieutenant Eric Money got stuck in the third belt of wire and took four mortar hits. Armour-piercing bullets ignited the petrol. Money, his driver and two more crew burned alive. Private Benjamin Bown, aged twenty-two, got out of the blazing tank only to be cut down by machine guns by the side of his tank.

Watson's company lost fifty-one out of 103 officers and men killed, wounded and missing. The snowbound battlefield was littered with smouldering machines, hit by shells and riddled with SmK bullets. The infantry of the 4th Division had been massacred. The Australians lost 2250 out of 3000 officers and men.

The balls-up in the blizzard the night before enraged the Australians, that and the feeling that some crews had seemed to abandon their vehicles so lightly. Their commanders wrote damning reports: 'The organisation seemed to be so bad and no one appeared to be in direct command of the show' . . . 'personal safety and comfort seemed the [tank crews'] sole ambition'. One Australian company commander said he had: 'Never seen a more windy lot of officers . . . it was not the tanks' fault but the chicken hearts who manned them.'

A sanitized report of the action was produced, the names of individuals withheld from war diaries and official histories 'for fear of reprisals'. An Australian politician would claim after the war that some crews had deliberately put sand in their petrol to sabotage their engines.

There remained the exploit at Hendecourt. What had happened to the two tanks that had disappeared? It took years and the interrogation of German witnesses to discover the truth. One commanded by Lt Harold Clarkson had been struck by a direct hit, killing the entire crew. Davies's tank had been shot up with AP bullets, igniting the fuel. A sergeant and three crewmen got out, their clothing on fire, dragging the terribly wounded Davies with them. They were taken prisoner. They never saw Davies again. Tank 799 was the first British machine to be captured and held on to by the Germans. It was taken to Charleroi substantially intact. Technical experts probed inside the blackened metal.

The offensive launched out of Arras with such promise was juddering to a halt. In the boggy ground south of the river Scarpe, where the infantry gained ground but supply lines across the shell churned battlefield broke down, the Germans reinforced, bringing up more artillery. The gains in the north were extended on 12 April, but in the centre the front was stuck.

Nivelle's promised war-winning 'punch' was launched on 16 April along a fifty-mile front from Soissons to Reims. In the first twenty-four hours the French suffered 40,000 casualties, a parallel disaster to that suffered on the Somme by the British on the first day. One hundred and thirty-eight Schneider and St Chamond tanks were lost on the first day in a shambles at Berry-au-Bac. Those tanks which did not ditch (the Schneider on its Baby Holt track proved fatally nose-heavy) were blown to bits by field-gun fire. The field commander of the *artillerie d'assaut*, Commandant Louis Bossut, went into action himself. His vehicle was one of the first to be hit. His body was not found for two days. It was buried near the battlefield. The clumsy St Chamond *char de rupture*, with its 75-mm gun poking out of the front – the whole thing wobbling on Holt tracks – proved even more vulnerable and almost impossible to escape from once set on fire. Almost 180 crew were killed, wounded or missing, many of them burned to death. A solemn memorial was raised on the site in 1922. Nivelle went on with the offensive. The catastrophe was compounded.

Had the BEF been operating on its own, the 'diversionary' Battle of Arras might have been broken off, but it had to be prolonged because of the state of the French. Conditions degenerated into fighting like that in the later stages of the Somme. To the north, the second phase began on 23 April, when, after ferocious fighting, a mile was added to the British gains all along the front.

It was not over yet. Haig ordered the offensive renewed on 2–3 May, with another attempt on Bullecourt. Following the debacle of April, the British Fifth Army set about properly planning and training for it. With the Australians' 4th Division shot to pieces, the task fell to their 2nd Division. The plan of attack was similar to that that which failed previously – the Australians would assault the eastern side of Bullecourt and the 62nd (West Riding) Division attack the village itself. The Heavy Branch would accompany the Yorkshiremen. The Australians refused to have anything to do with tanks.

The result was 'for its scale the bloodiest of trench killing matches and on balance [the] most unprofitable' on the Western Front in the entire war, 'a ghastly example tactically of what to avoid', in Liddell Hart's description. One tank commander got disorientated in the pre-dawn light, forcing the accompanying infantry to retreat. The Germans were waiting, confident after the shambles of 11 April. Shoot the English *Panzerauto* with machine-gun bullets and they seemed to blow up with ease. According to the D Battalion account:

> Six tanks moved forward with the infantry, two operating north of Bullecourt, two frontally and two south. The remaining two were to follow 45 minutes later and go through and exploit . . .
>
> The Germans were undoubtedly expecting us and no man's land was filled with gas. All six tanks reached the Boche front line. The two northern ones, both females commanded by Lts Chick and Conney, moved up and down machine-gunning heavily.
>
> The infantry, badly gassed, were unable to penetrate the wire in any numbers in support. Then the armour-piercing bullets began to take their count . . .
>
> The two southern tanks met with little better success. Lt McColl was temporarily blinded . . . and as far as is known, drove into a trap consisting of a deep pit specially dug . . . We had fondly imagined disappearing into the blue. The casualties among the men were heavy and of the tank commanders seven out of eight were wounded. One tank had thirty holes from AP bullets . . .

William Watson went through the same grim routine of waiting for news at headquarters as the survivors of his company tried again:

The first messages began to arrive at 5:30 am. All the tanks had started on time. There was an interval . . . then the first real news dribbled in . . .

With that tremulous excitement that mothers and fathers and wives of the crews would have seized and smoothed out these flimsy scraps of pink paper – so did we. 'Tank in flames at . . .' 'That might be Jimmy's tank.' 'No it must be David's.' Pray God the airman had made a mistake. Report after report came in and gradually we began to build up a picture of the battle . . .

The division attacking Bullecourt could not get on. Furious messages came back from Maj. ROC Ward. His tanks were out in front but the infantry could not follow.

One of his officers commonly known as 'Daddy' was sent back in Ward's car. Daddy was dirty, unshorn and covered with gore from two or three wounds. He was offered breakfast of whisky and soda and having consumed both told us how he had found himself in front of the infantry, how the majority of his crew had been wounded by armour-piercing bullets.

Armour-piercing bullets, tank traps, flooded ditches: it would seem the defenders had the measure of the Heavy Branch. The intelligence report from Petrograd had predicted it all – now 'special anti-tank batteries with their crews in dugouts close at hand' might be expected. Faith in the usefulness of tanks was wavering at GHQ and in Whitehall, but not quite yet at Bermicourt. Haig himself still seemed optimistic. His new offensive was in the making, to the north in Flanders. French operational control had been lifted. Large numbers of new Mark IV tanks would be ready – and ever more men passing through training in England and France.

But it would not be steel-cored bullets that would defeat them. It would be the mud.

36

The post-battle reports from the first attack on Bullecourt had scarcely been drafted when, on 13 April, the commander-in-chief asked for an increase of the Heavy Branch establishment to eighteen battalions. It was effectively doubled, requiring 900 more officers and 8500 extra men. On the 24th Haig and the ubiquitous Richard Butler met Stern in Paris where the need for as many tanks as possible was reiterated. Why were they taking so long? Haig wanted to know who the doubters at the War Office were. Stern replied it was the Adjutant-General's department which continued to scoop up skilled production workers as infantrymen. Haig took it up with the CIGS, noting: 'The recent battle around Arras confirms my view, that a large number of reliable tanks should be put into the field as soon as possible . . . I also hold that tanks will greatly contribute to economy in men, because not only can a few men accomplish in a tank, without loss, far more than a greater number of men can do without a tank; but that the employment of tanks has been found to greatly reduce the number of casualties among the infantry.'

The C-in-C's concern for husbanding infantrymen's lives may seem to have struck a new, humane note. The fighting at Arras had continued on a reduced scale until the end of May, when the British had lost 150,000 men and the Germans well over 100,000 – the daily loss rate of more than 4000 men between 9 April and 17 May was higher than the Somme at its worst. Even with conscription the manpower resources of the British empire were not inexhaustible. A skilled 'mechanist' could not be building a tank in Birmingham and fighting from it at the same time.

Nor were France's manpower resources infinite. On 4 May 1917 Nivelle's second attempt on the Chemin des Dames ridge collapsed with huge casualties. A renewed attempt with tanks was a disaster. Out of sixteen St Chamonds engaged, only one managed to cross a trench. The veteran 21st Division refused to go into battle. One regiment left its cantonment shouting '*A Paris!*' then hid in a wood for three days. Mutiny rippled through half the army.

General Philippe Pétain, who on 17 May had replaced the discredited Nivelle as commander-in-chief, moved swiftly to snuff it out with executions of 'ringleaders' and a ruthless censorship to blind the enemy as to the true state of morale. It was said that only two reliable divisions stood between the front line and Paris. The Germans did not stir.*

In response to Haig's 'economy in men' letter, Lord Derby, Secretary for War, convened an interdepartmental meeting on 1 May to shake things up. The C-in-C wanted more tanks – what was the Ministry of Munitions doing about it? The War Office acted on its own. Gore-Anley was ousted, banished to a command in Egypt and replaced in London by Maj.-Gen. Sir John Capper, a Royal Engineer with apparently modernist leanings. In 1907 he had piloted the army's first airship, *Nulli Secundus,* over the capital. Capper was made head of a new 'War Office Tank Committee' supposedly to correlate battle experience with design and production. No one from the fighting side in France was asked for an opinion. In spite of his pioneering credentials, in the eyes of Tanks HQ he was a bit of a plodder. The waspish Evan Charteris would dub him 'the Stone Age'.

After a bleak period shuffling paper in London, then instructing the machine-gun course at wintry Grantham, John Brough had already gone back to the front as GSO2 of a second-line infantry division. Bradley was now in charge of some seaside rest camp. Swinton was long out of it. For any ambitious officer, getting command of 'tanks' seemed like being passed the black spot. Hugh Elles, meanwhile, was gazetted brigadier-general. Perhaps he would last longer.

The demanded 'expansion' of the tank force was not that easy. It was put forward for approval by the Army Council on 12 June; there would be ten weeks' delay as the impact on other arms was assessed. On 9 August 1917 Haig would be told that men required for the new 'Tank Corps' could only come from the infantry. The manpower pot was emptying. The obstructionists at GHQ in France were gaining the

---

* It looked like a success for French censorship but recent research points to a reluctance by the German high command to embark suddenly on an opportunist offensive.

upper hand. It was Brig.-Gen. 'Kitten' Wigram (who Martel suspected after the Somme of wanting to take charge of the fledgling arm himself) who was now doubter in chief. As Fuller described him: 'He seemed to be possessed by a horror of all the newer arms, trench mortars, machine guns, gas, tanks etc. "You must not ask for anything more [he would sigh]. What of the poor infantry? Everything we can give them must go to them . . ." Wigram excelled at blowing blue pencil dust into the military machine and in consequence nearly brought our part of it to a standstill.'

The 'fighting side' withdrew to the Ternoise valley to lick its wounds after the battles of April and May. William Watson thankfully set up home in Humières, in a 'double Armstrong hut under some great elms at the edge of a big grass field. Most of the officers and men were billeted in the cottages and barns – with little shady gardens and luscious grass with a few lazy cows . . .' he recalled. 'The château was still occupied by the countess and her three daughters.' He was also glad to be able to take a bath at the lunatic asylum at Bailleul which was 'open to officers twice a week'. There were new diversions and a new geography to explore. A driving school was set up over a sprawling complex of old German trenches between the villages of Wailly, Blairville and Ficheux in a French-held sector a little way south of Arras.

A gunnery school was established on the coast at Merlimont-plage near Etaples, with its 'sand dunes and gimcrack villas', once the seaside summer homes of aspirant Parisians. Sentry posts were set up in bathing huts and a 6-pounder gun, retrieved from a Somme-veteran Mark I, installed outside the commandant's office. It was fired each day at noon.

Tank Corps reminiscences tend to pause nostalgically amid the blowing dunes. 'Bathing parties were arranged each day under an officer, and the whole Company would sometimes be in the water together.' One exhausted tank officer, mustard-gas-blown, amazed still to be alive, wrote to his wife of his arrival 'At a little shacky place in the sand hills but miles of lovely shore to slack about on . . . You remember B? he was snooping about on some job and had a wife over at the next place, Berk [sic], which was on French ground.'

In charge at Merlimont was the great survivor, Lt-Col. Robert

Bradley. His 'wife' at Bercques, however, was not the respectable daughter of a Welsh bishop.

Wailly village had been comprehensively wrecked by the Germans in their great retirement. The tanks made the trek there overland under their own power, a curious sight. According to Watson: 'Each officer at this period carried a wire bed on the roof, with a chair and perhaps a table.'*

The place held certain charms, in spite of its 'fearsome' trenches in which trainee drivers regularly got stuck and the hazards of bored crewmen firing flares and tossing live German grenades, of which there still seemed to be an abundance in the abandoned dugouts. William Watson was delighted to see, after three months without encountering a civilian, 'old people returning to their village, it is always the old who are the first to return'. Copses were in leaf and fruit trees were in blossom; oats for long-departed horses sprouted in the barns. 'There was rhubarb in the gardens and the birds were singing.'

There were a few veterans of Flers-Courcelette around at Wailly to tell old soldiers' tales. To the new drafts, the Somme seemed like ancient history: 'Of the men who were in that fight . . . the lyrical ones told how they had found their sides dripping with the molten lead of German bullets . . . The more truthful confessed how they lost direction or their tail wheels broke . . .' Old-stagers were routed through Bovington to tell their stories in more formal circumstances.

There were rest tours to Merlimont for sea-bathing and cricket on the beach. There were concert parties and pierrot shows. There was football, and for the officers rubbers of bridge (played incessantly on rail movements), pontoon and an obscure game called 'Slippery Sam'. According to 2/Lt G. E. V. Thompson: 'Church parades I am sorry to say were never very popular.' For him, as for everyone else, 'leave in England was the greatest reward . . . it used to come round every three to four months, seven days only – the great thing was to see as many shows as possible – musicals for preference . . .'.

Lieutenant Thompson named his tank 'Baby Mine' after an American romantic comedy playing in London. But there were some who could not wait for leave or the prayed-for 'Blighty One' – the

---

* A later order effected as the war was coming to an end forbade the transport of pianos on tanks.

non-fatal wound that would put them on the Red Cross train home. Lieutenant Thompson found out a lot about wangles. Swallowing soap was briefly popular with the men, until a foaming mouth on sick parade invited a dose of No. 9, the universal purgative. Claiming deafness was an officers' trick, until wary MOs discovered mean-spirited ways of rumbling them (bursting paper bags as they exited the room, apparently). Nor were the tank men immune from SIWs. According to Thompson: 'Self-inflicted wounds were much more successful. A man cleaning his rifle or an officer his revolver would put a bullet through his foot and claim it was accidental. Sometimes however the angle of entry did not tally with the story and punishment not England resulted.'

There were other distractions at Wailly – a 'tank' cross-country race and overnight outings to the Hôtel du Commerce in Arras. On 4 July King George V came to visit the 2nd Brigade tankodrome at a place called 'Clapham Junction'. The accompanying war correspondents found another excuse to drool about 'Leviathans' and 'Behemoths'. 'His Majesty saw the tanks operating and he himself with the Prince of Wales went in a tank called the Faugh-a-Ballaugh', according to the Court Circular. 'The King saw a tank commanded by Mr Hasler negotiate with success a large concrete dug out with a sheer drop on one side of about twenty-five feet.'* Second Lieutenant Thompson was there. According to his account, 'the King spoke in such a guttural voice he might as well have been the Kaiser'.

The King and Queen of the Belgians arrived to express their thanks for the liberation of Messines, and make the now obligatory test drive. King Albert insisted on boarding an unprepared tank and emerged with his uniform covered in oil and his fingers burned when he touched the engine cover. Queen Elisabeth fared better in a machine specially fitted out with a red carpet and comfortable chair. It was all a bit of a stunt. 'Frequent demonstrations were given to Army and Corps commanders', according to F Battalion's diary, 'illustrating the action of tanks in assisting infantry in attacking a trench system . . . After these demonstrations staff officers would be given rides in the tanks – good drops and jumps being carefully selec-

---

* The manoeuvre rendered five of the crew insensate. Second Lieutenant Hasler would be killed in action a month later.

ted.' One tank turned over and drenched a general in boiling water from its radiator. Turning over a tank was meant to be impossible.

On 28 July the Heavy Branch became the Tank Corps by Royal Warrant. Notice was posted that morning as an Army Order across the British Expeditionary Force. It gave details of new pay rates: 'Tank mechanists', classed as privates first class, got 2s 8d per day, privates second class 2s 2d. Their 'trades' included 'wheelers', 'painters (camouflage)', 'drivers', 'electricians', 'fitters and turners', 'coppersmiths', 'draughtsmen' and 'boilermakers'. Second lieutenants got 9s 6d per day, lieutenant colonels 15s. There was also the matter of 'swank'. The new corps was keen to show off its separateness from the poor bloody infantry. Watson recalled certain resentments at Blangy when a new draft arrived from Bovington: 'Their uniforms were new, they saluted smartly, wearing on their sleeves the badge representing a tank for which we had waited so long. Here were four battalions of veteran volunteers given the privilege of watching these immaculate recruits, of whom many were conscripts, swaggering with their tank badges . . .'

There were more practical considerations as the new Mark IVs arrived. Their armour was proof against SmK bullets, and the petrol tank was now mounted outside the hull at the rear, feeding the engine through an 'Auto-vac' vacuum pump.* Driving and steering were more practical (although still a five-man affair). The talented engineering officer Maj. Philip Johnson began experiments with an 'unditching beam' mounted on rails above the hull which could be swung round under a stranded vehicle as a means of getting out of trouble. On the 'females' the belt-fed Vickers guns had been replaced by drum-fed, air-cooled Lewis guns, by no means regarded universally as an improvement.

Much more secret were experiments made for the so-called 'Hush operation', a scheme cooked up by Haig and Admiral Bacon in the spring. As part of the forthcoming push in Flanders it was proposed that a force be landed from the sea on the German flank. It would include tanks. This was very novel stuff, cited by those who question the standard portrait of Haig as an outright military conservative. A

---

* The space where the petrol tank had been in the front cab of the Mark I was now occupied by the notorious 'officers' locker' containing rum, whisky and, it would seem on several accounts, quantities of champagne.

volunteer detachment was formed commanded by Maj. the Hon. J. Bingham and sent to an 'isolation' camp near Dunkirk to train.

Frank Searle at the Central Workshop worked on detail modifications and a special detachable ramp to get tanks up and over the sea wall of the projected landing zone near Ostend. Three 600-foot-long barges were commissioned in British shipyards to carry them (the blueprints show stowage provision for an enormous quantity of bicycles) and were towed across the Channel to Dunkirk from where the actual mission was to be mounted. The planning was very detailed. Captain Elliot Hotblack, with typical thoroughness, found the Belgian constructor of the Ostend sea wall and with his advice a mock-up was constructed at Merlimont. It was intended to bring the landing pontoon into action lashed between two heavy-gun-armed monitors. An infantry corps was moved up to make a linking thrust along the coast. The problem of German super-heavy coastal artillery was given special consideration in the bombardment plan.

Fuller was deeply sceptical. Secrecy was irrelevant, he thought, as such an operation was 'already the talk of the leave trains and London drawing rooms'. In his opinion the scheme was 'crack-brained – a kind of mechanical Gallipoli affair'. But Searle's wall-climbing tanks did seem to work. A demonstration of the 'conjuring trick' (Fuller's phrase) took place in July 1917 in front of Haig, Kiggell, Rawlinson and Capper. But how were the tanks supposed to advance inland? Fuller was also concerned about the effects of 'seaweed' as the heavy machines slithered up towards the esplanade. When the mock-up of the Ostend sea wall was constructed at Merlimont it was seen that the tanks were indeed able to mount it with ease, seaweed or no seaweed. For a while the Hush operation dominated everything. 'This infernal Bingham business is turning my hair grey,' Elles complained. The special detachment would stay on the coast waiting for its moment once the great offensive in Flanders had thrust forward and it was time to take the defenders in the flank from the sea. It would be a long wait.

Meanwhile, visitors continued to come to Bermicourt and its outstations. George Bernard Shaw arrived dressed in tweed plus-fours and trench-boots (and talked exclusively about himself), and the tub-thumping politician Horatio Bottomley. The celebrated Irish painter William Orpen came to paint Elles's portrait and drink the

Heavy Branch's whisky.* Churchill turned up to growl loudly, according to Hotblack, about Haig's folly in letting loose this immature instrument on the Somme. An escaped German prisoner, 'a great bullet-headed ruffian', was found inside a newly arrived tank. He had evidently slipped aboard the 'heavy train' moving up from Le Havre and stowed away.

Serbians, Russians and Belgians came to see, as did Italians, Swedes and Chinese. A tour of the furnace-lit workshops had become the equivalent of an outing to the Earl's Court motor show, according to Evan Charteris, until the tank men got fed up with the constant intrusions and started denying their visitors lunch.

'On state days a pompous assembly of high placed generals in Rolls-Royces would gather to witness tanks go through their paces,' he wrote. 'One notable day saw a great concourse of the ruling class when tanks performed prodigies of mobility, doing things that in their wildest dreams the red tabbed officials had never deemed to be possible.'

Two American officers (the USA had entered the war on 5 April) came to see the show and began behaving in a furtive manner about some secret plan involving the use of tanks and low-flying aircraft. They were 'Hell-bent on victory', according to Charteris. The secret document was later discovered abandoned in an Arras restaurant.

Charteris recorded the visit of a 'Princess'† accompanied by her elderly lady-in-waiting and the Director of Medical Services at GHQ, a pompous doctor evidently fond of off-colour jokes. The Princess kept commenting – in German – how big everything was – '*Gott, wie kolossal es ist*' – which, according to Charteris, 'made for a momentary awkwardness'.

---

* The painter was as impassioned a portraitist in words as he was in paint. Of Elles he said 'a great chap – full of go . . . Hotblack was mild and gentle, full of charm, one could hardly imagine he had all those DSOs and wound stripes – Hotblack, who liked to go for a walk and sit down and read poetry. He said it took his mind off devising plans to kill people better than anything else . . .

'Then there was the colonel of the tanks [Fuller] – Napoleon they called him. A great brain he had. Before the war he knew his Chelsea well and the Café Royal and all the set who went there.

'I regret that one night when I was staying at HQ Tanks I got Blotto,' confessed Orpen. 'It wasn't altogether my fault, people were so hospitable . . .'

† The sixty-eight-year-old HRH the Princess Louise, Duchess of Argyll, Queen Victoria's sixth child.

In his seaside fastness at Merlimont, meanwhile, the gunnery school commandant Lt-Col. Bradley, 'one of the aborigines of the Tank Corps', found his own distractions amid the boom of the 6-pounders and the 'Hush' preparations. The 'florid soldier' was reportedly:

> Greatly attached to an opera singer who lived at Bercques about eight miles away, and it was a constant grievance that the authorities denied him the use of a motor car. He would toil over most days to the singer, driving a very inefficient bicycle over the sands and return late for dinner . . . always with the same excuse [a puncture].
>
> His small staff usually gave him some sympathetic response but he was surrounded by an undercurrent of titter which contributed to his final downfall.
>
> He . . . looked on the war as an intrusion on the scheme of life he had formed for middle age. Bercques was a godsend and as long as the singer was there he seemed to recognise that Providence was doing what it could to alleviate the situation. But even Bercques had its season and towards the end of October [1917] the singer migrated to Paris. [His] demands for Paris leave became rather frequent . . .

GHQ disapproved and Bradley was sent home to lecture at Wool. One by one the 'aborigines' were on their way out. In London it was Albert Stern's head that was being demanded. There were too many delays, too many excuses, his activities beyond War Office control increasingly vexatious. Relations with Capper, Director of Tanks, were icy. It was a ghost of landships past that would provide the catalyst. Colonel Winston Churchill had returned from the front to front-line politics. D'Eyncourt suggested he go off to the USA to buy steel and push the Americans towards the creation of a tank army. Christopher Addison offered him control of the entire tank programme. Instead Churchill replaced Addison as Minister of Munitions on 17 July 1917. Lord Derby threatened to resign as Secretary of State for War at this reckless appointment of a discredited adventurer. But at least, as far as the generals were concerned, the architect of Antwerp and Gallipoli had no direct say on the conduct of the war. Sir Philip Sassoon, Haig's private secretary, told Lord Northcliffe, 'It would be disastrous if Churchill were to come back to power at this juncture with his wild-cat schemes and *fatal* record.' As a way of building bridges to the War Office, Churchill would join them in the campaign against Stern. The 'patriotic businessman' had a new fight on his hands.

The Flanders offensive opened in slow motion. It began in early June at Messines in an operation designed to 'straighten the line' of the Ypres salient in the methodical manner pursued on the Somme. This time it was a tactical and technical surprise – with the detonation of nineteen enormous mines under Messines Ridge on a ten-mile front. Sixty-two brand new Mark IVs of the 2nd Tank Brigade were employed over ground that was cratered but dry. They met little resistance and twenty-five reached their planned objectives on the opening day. According to the Tank Corps' own statistics, only nineteen tanks rendered any assistance to the infantry. One successfully led an assault on the village of Wytschaete. 'Supply tanks' (reworked old vehicles carrying ammunition and spares) were used for the first time.

At the end of the Messines affair forty-eight tanks had ditched but only eleven had been knocked out by gunfire. Steel-cored rifle bullets (the Germans now issued a clip of five to each infantryman) bounced off the Mark IVs' hides. Things looked propitious for the much bigger blow to come. More than 230 tanks with fresh, eager crews were in transit from the training area northwards to the salient. It was all rather jolly. There were letters home to write. Death was all around, but young men could not yet quite believe it was stalking them. Dispositions must be made nevertheless. According to Daniel Hickey: 'Before the move to Ypres six of my fellow officers gave me addresses of relatives or sweethearts. Four of these fellows had a fiancée or a wife. I rather envied them.'

The summer weather stayed fine and dry. F Battalion's diary recorded:

On 6 July the whole Battalion moved to La Lovie, on the Poperinghe–Crombeke Road ... In a short time, battalion life was going on again in full swing. Spare tarpaulins thrown over saplings lashed to two trees made good messes both for officers and other ranks, and although the wood resembled a gipsy encampment, yet it was surprising how comfortable one became under canvas in La Lovie Wood.

There would be an early morning parade and inspection
unless conditions made it impossible . . . breakfast at 8 am under
mess bivouacs . . . The band at this time flourished exceedingly,
playing its selections each evening.

There was the usual flap over secrecy. Captain D. G. Browne
recalled being in Poperinghe just before the battle – 'full of squalid
shops and extortionate shopkeepers . . . the restaurants packed
with garrulous officers . . . as for the depressed creatures in the farms
near the line it was generally taken for granted they were spies . . .
the usual stories flowed of lamps flashing by night and cattle manoeuvring suspiciously by day.' As far as tanks were concerned there
was not much to give away.

General Gough commanding Fifth Army viewed the offensive as
an artillery–infantry conflict in which tanks would have to take their
chances. Secrecy and surprise were hardly paramount. There would
be no 'artillery lanes', no willingness to deny infantry the fitful
advantage of the creeping barrage.

The artillery bombardment began on the 16th. The shelling supposed to blast the defenders out of their built-up earthworks and
concrete blockhouses (the water table was too high to dig trenches)
churned up the barbed wire. But day by day it was also comprehensively wrecking the already grossly depleted drainage system of the
Flanders plain. The enemy would be fighting from shell holes. That
had not hampered him before. The weather was fine. Then, as July
turned into August, it began to rain.

In his typically detailed planning 'Boots' Hotblack, the Tank
Corps' intelligence officer, had sought out Belgian Ponts et Chaussées
department records and questioned local civilians on the direction of
flow of the man-made '*beeks*' which were supposed to drain the
marching polders. Seemingly open terrain described on tactical maps
as 'pasture' was, he discovered, 'reclaimed land that was liable to
flood and too wet for cultivation'. Elles's tanks were supposed to
move across it. Royal Flying Corps photographs disclosed shell holes
like inkwells brimming with black water. From such sources Hotblack
laboured to produce 'swamp maps' updated day by day which
showed the flooding spreading, as the bombardment did its work,
into a 'long oozing moat of mud stretching from the north of the
Polygone de Zonnebeke through St Julien northwards past Langem-

arck', as it was described. The results were modelled in brown and blue Plasticine. Hotblack's kindergarten productions were dismissed. GHQ saw no reason to change the plan of attack.

At 3.20 on the early morning of 31 July the tanks began to move slowly to their start lines, three brigades, more than one hundred and thirty machines with eighty more in reserve. They were supposed to reach the defenders' third line. If they were stalled there, there would then be a two-day pause to bring forward artillery to blast open the path to the Passchendaele ridge two miles beyond that. Cavalry would pass through the breach and charge in the direction of Roulers. That was the plan. At dawn the first wave began to go forward. One by one they sank under their own weight into the mire. Worm casts of mud came squirming in through every port and pinhole, 'like sausage meat of fantastic shapes and sizes'. Then the defending field guns got to work.

Second Lieutenant Popplewell in G.3 slithered to a halt on the road to St Julien Farm: 'I put my unditching gear on but was unable to move so set to work with shovels . . . after working for fifty minutes under very heavy shell fire, the tank was struck by a shell which burst five yards in front, wounding one of my crew and severely shaking three of the others including myself. I managed to get my crew into a shell hole nearby thoroughly exhausted.'

On the afternoon of the 31st it began to rain. By evening it was unrelenting. The churned-up ground was already a morass. Seventy-seven tanks were swallowed up on that first day, their crews evacuating through the top hatches like distressed submariners. Tracks revolved uselessly. Trying to dig them out only made them sink faster. Second Lieutenant Wilfred Bion described an attempt to move forward on the Wieltje–St Jean road:

> The ground was so bad and so badly shelled that one gun was below the level of the earth. The tank was on a slope and couldn't right itself so we went out like that. At last she became permanently stuck. We fixed the unditching beam, but this only shifted the tank a few inches at a time [when] it got right underneath. We travelled literally one foot to each revolution of the tracks . . . the steering brakes broke and the transmission broke. As a direct hit was merely a question of seconds, we abandoned the tank . . .

To use the unditching beam was asking for trouble. Crews had to
get out and climb on top of the tank to bring it into action.* Snipers
and machine guns picked them off. Stuck in the mud they were
even more vulnerable. Eighteen floundering tanks were destroyed
by shellfire near Hooge as they tried to engage a strong point called
'Clapham Junction'. Salvage officers (an increasingly important Tank
Corps calling) did what they could. Being detailed to bring back a
stranded machine was a mission the tank men quickly came to dread.

Wilfred Bion's account explained why. An intelligence officer
interrogated him the next morning. He and six other survivors were
ordered to retrieve one of the abandoned tanks from the section.
With them was 'a boy called Foster'. As Bion told the story in his
reconstructed diary the mission in the darkness has the quality of a
surreal nightmare cum public school romp – asking directions of a
machine-gunner cowering in a shell hole who answered in 'unintelligible gibberish', an officer suddenly appearing who seemed to make
some sense. 'Great Scot, is that you, Bion? . . . I recognised him as
an Old Stortfordian. Poor fellow . . . he was killed just a few weeks
afterwards.'

The tank was out of reach, the enemy shelling intensified and the
eighteen-year-old Foster (a pseudonym, like most of the names in
Bion's 1919 narrative) had had enough. 'He simply fell down on the
road and struggled and kept shouting "keep them off, keep them
off . . ."'

Bion (who later became a psychoanalyst) looks repeatedly in his
account at how sentient humans beings continue to operate when
everything around them is dissolving into violent chaos. He presents
himself as an incompetent soldier and hopeless tank commander, yet
rails at the venality and stupidity of others around him. He admits
his own limitations and (not so) irrational fears – especially of stumbling in the darkness and being crushed into the mud by his own
tank as he leads it from the outside. This prospect features in several
tank memoirs. It seemed to hold a particular terror, as great as that
of burning.

Still it rained. On the third day of the Flanders offensive, Fuller,

---

* In a later design it could be operated from a special armoured turret at the rear of the
hull.

after floundering around trying to get near the front, reported to Elles at La Lovie. 'How are things going?' his commander asked cheerily enough. All Fuller need say was 'look at me'. He was plastered from head to foot in mud.

Fuller knew then 'that the battle was at an end as far as tanks were concerned', or so he stated in his memoirs. But neither Elles nor he had any real control. Their anguish was tangible. They had been 'astonished' at the initial suggestion that they were to operate in the fens of Flanders – but the weather in July had been good. Messines had been a sort of success. Wrapped in their messianic mission hatched in Fuller's 'brain barn' – so eager to show the old guard what they could do – they had signed up to this self-made catastrophe.

Evan Charteris offered a kind of excuse when he wrote three years afterwards: 'It was only by a "joy ride" that one became aware of the real misery and muck. Our minor discomforts and small dangers were very negligible and life was healthy and agreeable – passed in a kind of middle distance between the dangers of the front line and the remote superiority of GHQ.'

Well, now they were at the front line. That night of 2 August, when the mud-caked Fuller had wandered round Tanks HQ like a golem, his commander did break ranks and challenge that remote superiority by 'suggesting' to Fifth Army that his force be kept for another attempt – to be made 'under more favourable conditions and on more favourable ground'. Fuller thought there might be such a place. Elles's suggestion was turned down. Tanks would go on fighting. They would either aid the infantry in the sought-for breaking of the line through which the horsemen would charge in the direction of Roulers, or the tank would bring its own 'economy of men' to the brutal equation of the wearing-out battle. John Charteris's glib assessment of enemy losses and state of morale were fed to the C-in-C just as before. According to Fuller, these 'effervescent calculations were received by his chief with as much confidence and faith as they were met by disdain and derision on the front line'.

This weather was freakish, unprecedented; it must improve.*

Fuller recalled meeting a squadron of cavalry on the Hazebrouck

* The late summer weather in Flanders was indeed unusually wet. Some on Haig's staff put it down to the passage of shells through the lower atmosphere. Crown Prince Rupprecht, commander of the German Sixth Army, called it 'our greatest ally'.

road. Wearily asking an officer just what he thought he was expected to do, he was told there was 'a ridge of hard sand' over which the gallant troopers were capable of advancing, so GHQ had informed them. The cavalry officer sought the fabled spit in vain. Fuller and Elles bounced back to Lovie Wood and its leaky tents in their staff car. They concluded that GHQ 'must be stark staring mad'.

It kept on raining. For four days the battle was broken off. On the 10th the weather temporarily improved. The few tanks that managed to go forward did what they could. One machine, F.41 Fray Bentos, went a way ahead of the infantry, ditched, then for three days held out as a kind of pillbox (the British side also engaged the stranded tank with artillery, assuming the enemy must have captured it) until all its crew were dead or wounded.

On the 16th there was a fleeting bright spot when a composite battalion commanded by Capt. Douglas Browne, aided by reconnaissance officer Capt. Clough Williams-Ellis, advanced up an intact section of the St Julien road (without a preliminary artillery bombardment this time and with smoke laid beyond the objective, screening it from counter-artillery fire) to capture two formidable double-storey concrete blockhouses called the Cockcroft and the Maison d'Hibou. They set the garrisons to flight and sustained twenty-nine casualties. The success-starved press fell on the story. According to Browne, 'even Mr Beach Thomas of the *Daily Mail* . . . felt impelled to leave the seclusion of the Ternoise Valley and gather copy among the tents at Lovie'.

Intact stretches of road were rare in Flanders and getting rarer by the day. Tanks could not operate off them. If one in the file got hit, the rest were sitting targets. It was as frustrating as it was terrifying; sometimes it was beyond endurance. In one fragmented snapshot: 'One commander arrived at Hill Top Farm – just behind our original front line – a raving lunatic. He was not normal again for many years.' Daniel Hickey, struggling forward on some insane mission towards the end of the campaign, encountered the by now infamous 'tank graveyard' at 'Clapham Junction' (where so many tanks had been knocked out on the first day). The front line was now a few hundred yards ahead. Captain Clement Robertson had been killed a few days before leading his section on foot down the same route, poking the mush with his stick. He had got the VC for it.

Major Philip Hamond, the mercurial, blond-haired, blue-eyed

'Viking' commanding 18 Company, was trying to get eight tanks from F Battalion forward on the night of 21 August. He described the perils of operating on the notorious 'road' to St Julien:

There was an abyss of mud and water on each side . . . if any tank broke down and was knocked out during the approach march, every one behind needs must wait on the road until daylight and then be shot like a garden thrush; too easy . . .

The holes in the pavé were filled with broken rifles, kit and corpses, the whole overlaid with stinking slime.

We could only crawl along and the Boche kept putting over small shells but all burst in the ditches either side except two or three which actually burst on the road between the tanks. When we got level with Rat Farm which was to be my advanced HQ . . . I turned round and spoke to 'Dad' Hill in the leading tank, and just as I did so there was a violent explosion and sheet of flame right under his offside track by my legs.

It blew me way off the road but I got up and came back to 'Dad.' I told him to come very slowly ahead as there was the horrible probability that his track was broken and if we could catch up the ends of the track on top of the tank we might still be able to mend it and save the situation. With my heart in my mouth I watched his track coming gently and steadily along and thank God it had suffered no damage. I saw that we had run over a box of rifle grenades and they had all gone up with a bang.

An engineer officer was sent forward to try and unblock a tangle of stricken machines on the fatal spit through the bog. It was night. The scene was lit by flames, flaring and guttering from burning vehicles fuelled by petrol and flesh. It was, he said, like being 'at the centre of a giant primus stove'. Clough Williams-Ellis recorded the anonymous officer's experience soon after the war:

As I neared the derelict tanks the scene became truly appalling, wounded men lay drowned in the mud, others were stumbling and falling through exhaustion, others crawled and rested themselves up against the dead to raise themselves a little above the slush. On reaching the tanks I found . . . men had crawled to them for what shelter they could afford. The nearest tank was a female. Her sponson doors were open; out of these protruded four pairs of legs . . . men had sought refuge in this machine, the dead and dying lay in a jumbled heap inside . . .

Some could not take it. In a telling letter to a friend (identified only by the initials 'WA') written from Blairville in October, Philip Hamond described the kind of incident which was not recorded in the postwar battalion histories. The men of his company were supposed to be greasing tracks and filling Lewis-gun drums before moving up the road again. Two commanders, 'H' and 'R', seemed to be missing:

> All the fighting crews who ought to have been fresh and rested had to set to and get this work done on time. A gunner from R's crew appeared out of the darkness and with actual tears told me that the two officers had been hiding in a trench about 300 yards away all day and that they would not allow the men to go over to the tanks. I went with him to try and find these two, but could not find them, as I proposed to shoot them myself on the spot. These cowardly bastards were well on the way to getting us all scuppered . . .
>
> I never seem to be let down by an NCO or a man but I am sick of some of the bloody rubbish we get as officers nowadays.
>
> How I longed to kill them but I left written instructions . . . to put them under arrest and see they were tried for their lives* if I ever came back . . .

Hamond's assault ended in predictable disaster. Half his crew were killed. On the shambolic road back, the survivors encountered Gen. Gough himself who 'inspected my few survivors all of us with filthy bandages somewhere about us except old Bindley who was drunk . . .'. The general told Hamond 'to make them rest and keep them sober as you can, if they break out now they will be worse in a week's time'. A ticket to Merlimont resulted.†

There was anguish in London. The overall casualty figures were baleful enough; to throw away tanks in a mire seemed especially careless. On 22 August Tennyson d'Eyncourt wrote to the C-in-C to

---

* There were two capital courts martial in the wartime Tank Corps, both for desertion and both in Flanders – Cpl (acting Sgt) H. King in August and Pte A. Morgan in November 1917, commuted respectively to five and fifteen years of penal servitude.

† For a while only the front line was real for Hamond. 'I *like* living here I *hate* strangers,' he told his friend. 'The sight of a red hat is as a red rag to a bull.' Of the fate of the 'cowardly bastards', he wrote: 'Hardress-Lloyd [OC 3rd Tank Brigade] came to see me to make me withdraw charges against R and H after the show the company had put up . . . I reluctantly agreed if he dealt with the matter personally. I never saw either of them again. I think [the fact] their crews were ready to murder will arrange it . . .'

point out in the politest terms that perhaps tanks might be better used on 'ground . . . for which they had been designed . . . preferably rather hilly country where the wet drains off . . . possibly without much artillery preparation'. It was a perceptive statement. Haig replied: 'The choice of front . . . must be made with regard to many considerations . . . [Tanks'] true powers are still more or less a matter of conjecture.' He recognized the conditions were 'unfavourable', of course, but had decided 'on the whole, it is advisable to make use of them'.

But as Fuller had stated right at the outset, it was effectively over as far as tanks were concerned almost as soon as it had begun. On 7 September Elles formally requested GHQ to withdraw five out of eight tank battalions. They would eventually concede four. The battle would grind on until November, the Tank Corps playing an ever more insignificant part in a series of small-scale sieges in places where the mud allowed them to move at all.

Lieutenant Horace Leslie Birks of 11 Company, for example, set off with eight tanks on the morning of 8 October in the direction of Poelcappelle, picking their way in file along the precarious strip of pavé, when the defender's barrage began to erupt around them. A shell hit in a flash of smoke and flame. He gave this account to Basil Liddell Hart thirty years later:

The fire was on the starboard side of the tank and the driver with great coolness switched off and put it out with his pyrenes. The direct hit had been occasioned by a shell which came in through the starboard side . . . and hit the engine . . . there was nothing in sight and all we could do was to evacuate the tank into the nearest shell hole. One gunner had practically lost his leg, he subsequently died, three others were badly wounded . . . the last tank appeared in sight some twenty yards behind us commanded by 'Rosy' Stephens. We crawled back dragging our wounded with us and explained to him that the road was hopelessly blocked and to leave it courted instantaneous bogging. The driver . . . managed to turn his tank on the narrow road swinging inches at a time . . . every tank which had started was stopped apart from Hugh Skinner's . . . and Stephens'.

We did our best to bypass the chaos, but the morass was too much. A very brave advance stretcher party took off the man without a leg. We eventually found a dressing station to drop the rest of the wounded but were halted by MPs who said it was for stretcher cases only. For the first time we were able to deal satisfactorily with an enemy face to face.

Still it rained. Elles told Capper on 12 October, 'The weather is perfectly ghastly, there must have been two inches of rain since yesterday. I am told that even the Poelcappelle road which is our last avenue of approach has gone to pieces.'

Some of the defenders had also reached their limits. A captured German officer told his interrogators: 'There were tanks so my company surrendered – I also.' But the number of tanks left was down to a handful. William Watson recalled:

> When the line had advanced a little, Cooper and I went forward to recce the road to Poelcappelle and see our derelicts. Two of the tanks had been hit. A third was sinking into the mud. In the last was a heap of evil smelling corpses – either men who had been gassed and crawled back into the tank to die or more likely men who had taken shelter and had been gassed where they sat . . . A shell came screaming over and plumped dully into the mud without exploding. A decayed German pack, a battered tin of bully and a broken rifle lay at our feet.
>
> We crept away hastily, the dead never stirred.

'In the third battle of Ypres the reputation of the Tank Corps was almost destroyed,' wrote Watson. 'We . . . must have left behind two or three hundred derelict tanks sinking by degrees into the mud . . .'

The Tank Corps had become an embarrassment long before the sodden failure in Flanders had spluttered to an end. By the middle of August, Gen. Hubert Gough had been openly dismissive of their 'pinpricks of success'. 'The moral effect of their appearance on the Germans is diminishing rapidly,' he minuted, 'except in the case of very young soldiers.' The enemy by now seemed indifferent to their presence. The mood at GHQ changed from day to day, from one fleeting success to the next morning's perceived disaster. According to Evan Charteris, 'no matter how much they proved themselves, it was beyond the imagination of GHQ to lay down a policy . . . Either the tanks were good or they were bad, either they saved lives or they were costly in manpower.' '"I hear the tanks are going to be abolished" was a common refrain in well-informed London circles,' according to Williams-Ellis.

The day after the glimmer of success at the Cockcroft, for example, Bermicourt's war diary laid out what happened with ironic starkness: '20.8.17: General Capper goes to GHQ and is informed that tank expansion is to be stopped because every endeavour has to be made to obtain reinforcements for the present battle.'

The diary's author meant infantry reinforcements. Replacements would have been a better word. The infantry was bleeding away. The Flanders offensive continued, mud or not. There had been a grim little conference at GHQ on 21 August, which Elles attended, to address the growing manpower crisis. His force should be 'combed out for its fittest men', he was told, for them to be sent to the trenches. Numbers could be made up by drafting men from the 'venereal class' and from lines of communication troops. If all 'dental work was to be suppressed during the winter' then several thousand more men would be found. The army was decaying.

The sour mood was reflected in London. The press found little to say (other than the usual overblown heroics) about the real fate of the tanks at Third Ypres, but the glum truth was palpable. Who was to blame? Albert Stern, who had managed to alienate everybody, hung on by his fingernails. He had either delivered machines which had 'lumbered up to the front and proved useless' or he had not delivered enough. There was another row with Churchill in early September when the Minister of Munitions asked how many tanks there were at the front. 'I do not know – they will not let me know what are destroyed. I suppose they think it is not my business,' Stern replied (and he was right in his view of GHQ's attitude). Churchill told Lloyd George it was time for Stern to go.

A Whitehall meeting on 29 September was especially fractious. Generals Butler and Whigham were there, so were Capper and Elles. In another example of exquisite vacillation, expansion in the Tank Corps' manpower had been postponed but not in tank production. Seven hundred heavy and six hundred medium types (a new, faster machine designed by William Tritton) were wanted by 1 March 1918; Stern could offer less than half of that. The Mark IV was still inadequate; where was the promised machine with its new Wilson-designed gear train that effectively needed only one man to drive? Stern could only bluster. Hugh Elles delivered the *coup de grâce* with a memorandum to the War Office on 7 October 1917 stating: 'The ideas and suggestions both of designers at home and of the practical users in France are in the hands of an individual [Stern] who has seen one battlefield for the space of three hours. A very serious lack of confidence exists . . .'

He wrote in the margin of his paper: 'Desiderata – get rid of Stern.'

Churchill gave the man who had written to the Admiralty three years before offering the use of his Rolls-Royce a tremendous dressing down. Stern replied that he had been 'fighting the forces of reaction' since the cancellation of the thousand-tank order soon after the Somme. He directly accused his minister of playing personal politics but not of enacting good public policy. Churchill was incensed. Lloyd George could not save his old protégé. The banker-turned-tank-maker was smartly moved out of the Mechanical Warfare Supply Department, to be replaced by an admiral.

Bertie Stern was down but not entirely out. He swiftly became the British commissioner on the 'inter-allied tank bureau' established in June 1917 as a political move to rope in the Americans. In November it was recast as the 'Overseas and Allied Mechanical Warfare Department' at the Ministry of Munitions. Stern ruthlessly embraced it as a vehicle for renewed empire-building. He already envisaged an 'inter-allied tank army' being unleashed on the entrenched invader in the year 1919.

The production programme for the Mark IV had been progressed competently enough in the circumstances. Scores of them might now be sinking in the Flanders mire, but there were hundreds more coming from the factories, at Wool and arriving by rail at Erin. New drafts of eager young officers and less eager conscripts (but not yet of the 'venereal class') were undergoing training in Dorset or were mooching around the newly established reinforcement depot at Le Tréport on the Normandy coast. On 6 October the order cancelling expansion was itself cancelled, and two days later a new 'tank Committee' was formed on which the fighting side in France was at last represented.* King George V became Colonel-in-Chief. The Tank Corps had not lost all its glitter.

---

* It was supposed to meet once a fortnight alternatively between France and England. On it were the Director of the Tank Department at the WO (Capper), the OC Tank Corps in France (Elles), the DNC (d'Eyncourt) and the Director of the MWSD (Admiral Sir Archibald Gordon Moore, Stern's replacement).

On 6 November Canadian infantry reached the ruins of the village of Passchendaele, four miles from the start line of 31 July and after a quarter of a million British casualties. No tanks were involved in the last act in Flanders as hardly any were left in the field. Elles had already pulled out what machines he had been allowed. To the men in the field the real enemy was clear. 'What brought a sense of togetherness more than anything was the frightful way in which Haig behaved, doing anything he could to break us up,' the reconnaissance officer Lt Norman Dillon would recall many years later. 'We didn't peg it down on Haig and GHQ for a while and the pig-headed people who were running it, but there was very strong feeling among all the tank units, we'd made a world beater and it was being frittered away.'

The Tank Corps was still intact. They might do something yet. This time their own commanders would have a less than marginal say in how and where it might be newly employed. It would not be in a swamp.

37

The Germans in the fastness of the Siegfried Line and the deep-layered positions in Flanders* had little imperative to consider an offensive tank force of their own. Russia had been beaten by traditional enough mobile operations. The strategic defensive in the west would continue. Survivors of the Somme commented ruefully on the *Materialenschlacht*, the sheer weight of shells that the English had rained upon them. In response, in late 1916 a huge industrial initiative was proclaimed – the 'Hindenburg programme', to quadruple artillery and machine-gun production and double the size of the air force.

Submarines (the offensive weapon of opportunity on which the defeat of Britain had been gambled and which might yet blunt the effect of American intervention) were a production priority – but not tanks. As Ludendorff wrote after the war: 'We had no tanks to provide company for our infantry. Tanks were merely a weapon of attack and our attacks were successful without them.' And it might seem in the winter of 1916–17 that detailed improvements in defence would defeat the English wonder weapon.

On the tenth day of the new year, instructions for artillery anti-tank measures were sent to every German army commander. 'Close range batteries' of six 7.7-cm guns were to be formed and placed a kilometre behind the first line covering axes of approach. Fifty thousand armour-piercing shells were ordered. Issue of the SmK bullet was generalized.

Since Haupt. Weber's first dramatic reports from the Somme, however – and Oberst Nicolai's admission that the secret had already been filed away and forgotten in Berlin – there were some at OHL who thought the best response to the British innovation would be

---

* The *'Flandern Stellurg'* – just as formidable but incorporating more above-ground concrete because of the high water table.

another tank. The Prussian War Ministry (which was also the Imperial War Ministry) at first responded to these proposals with a rapidity that Col. Ernest Swinton would have found dazzling.

A month after the Heavy Section's debut, talks were held between the German army's Motor Transport Inspection Service (*Verkehrstech-nische Prüfungs-Kommission*, or VPK) and the motor industry, heavy truck builders in particular. The War Ministry drew up a desired specification largely based on Haupt. Weber's intelligence reports, including the interrogation of Gnr Herbert Clears.

Some sort of presiding engineering genius was clearly required, and a German equivalent of Mother's progenitor, Walter Wilson, quickly emerged. His name was Joseph Vollmer, a designer of military lorries who had won the Kaiser Wilhelm II prize for such activities. The new project to build both a tracked armoured fighting vehicle and a cross-country load carrier on a common chassis was code named 'A7V' – after the seventh directorate of the War Ministry, responsible for army transport.

The Germans would go through the same roller, big wheel, ele-phant's foot versus track agonies that the Landships Committee had endured, but they got to a 'caterpillar' much more quickly. Joseph Vollmer remembered his old colleague Dr Steiner, the pre-war Holt agent in Austria, and his American machines used as artillery tractors. An Austrian army Holt was dispatched to Berlin in late November 1916 to be put through its paces on the Tempelhofer Feld clambering across sandy ramparts and dummy shell holes. It was assumed that the track system could simply be copied but that proved difficult. The Holt company's central European agents (America was not yet at war at this point) willingly supplied technical assistance, although physical components were denied by the Allied blockade. British intelligence seemingly made no attempt to stop them.*

---

* Mr J. G. Bakker, Vice President of the Holt Manufacturing Co., told the *New York Times* after the news broke of the Heavy Section's debut on the Somme that 'we had sold about a thousand [caterpillars] to the British government for towing guns . . . we did not have anything to do with armouring or arming them', but he thought the Somme machines were his, transformed in some secret way into 'tanks'.

'Germany had some of these tractors before the war,' continued Mr Bakker, 'and although I do not understand just how it occurred . . . I believe she may have got others since then. We have sent some to France and to Russia . . .' The newspaper looked forward in a neutral-spectator sort of way to the titanic clash of 'charging squadrons of "tanks" in the European war', something it saw as inevitable.

By the end of the year a design was ready, a girder lorry-type frame on three pairs of Holt-derived roller trucks on each side surrounded by a continuous steel link track – with two 100hp Daimler engines in the middle. On to this would be bolted a symmetrical steel box with a raised commander's position in the centre, main armament at the front and machine gun positions all round. By January 1917 a complete chassis and wooden mock-up body were ready for inspection.

It was clumsy looking and its trench-crossing ability was poor but for want of anything better ten experimental models were ordered. Formation of two 'tank' units – *Sturm Panzerkraftwagen Abteilungen* (armoured assault detachments) – was authorized, to be raised from the infantry. They actually began trials with another vehicle, an armoured version of a commercial lorry on which primitive tracks replaced the four wheels, the so-called 'Bremer-Wagen'. At a demonstration at Mainzer Sand before Hindenburg and Ludendorff on 11 March the machine proved barely capable of moving off the road. This was not the British 'rhomboid' device they had seen in intelligence reports and that had seemed so clever in crossing trenches. Ludendorff lost interest. The little mechanized infantry unit was disbanded.

Joseph Vollmer tried to please by producing a design called the 'A7V-U' that looked like a shameless copy of the 'Wilson', with all-round track and cannon armament in side sponsons. A single prototype was ordered to be ready by 1 September 1917.

Just as in the story of Britain's landships there were several engagingly cranky diversions. A giant device was proposed – the 'Kolossal-Wagen', a tracked land battleship on which Thomas Hetherington and Winston Churchill would have smiled. A big-wheel roller was commissioned, and a curious boat-shaped vehicle called the Orion-Wagen propelled by pedrail-style 'feet'. Both were actually built.

They were tested at Mainzer Sand on 14 May against the now complete prototype A7V with its wooden mock-up body. The roller and the Orion machine were rejected; construction of ten A7Vs was approved. That June the prototype vehicle (unlike Mother, no *Spitzname* was given) was demonstrated before a collection of generals crossing wire and dummy trenches at the Daimler company's proving ground in a Berlin suburb. Only the Marquis of Salisbury was missing to make it a simulacrum of the Hatfield trial. Kaiser Wilhelm II turned up to see the machine but unlike his cousin, King George V, did not take a tank ride.

Swinton had shamelessly massaged royal favour in his project, but imperial patronage seemed to achieve nothing in Berlin. General Erich von Ludendorff as yet had little interest in offensive warfare. There was no Churchillian figure politically pushing landships beyond sight of the Treasury. Lieutenant-Colonel Max Bauer, head of Section O-II (munitions procurement) would only guarantee second-priority steel allocation. After the first flush of excitement it all seemed to stall.

Anyway, the German army seemed to have the measure of the 'tanks'. The French Schneiders and St Chamonds had self-immolated in April, and what had the English achieved at Arras? A captured tank was in their hands (Harold Clarkson's bullet-riddled T.799 taken at Hendecourt). It seemed pathetically vulnerable. In August 1917 the improved Mark IVs would go forward in Flanders and drown in a bog of the enemy's own making. If British commanders behaved like this there was nothing to fear.

Production of A7Vs continued at a trickle at the Daimler plant at Berlin-Marienfelde, with the familiar fight over allocation of steel and skilled manpower. Construction of five giant K-Wagens was commenced that summer with no real clue how to use these monstrous engines of attack. The chief of the responsible department, Colonel Meyer, was no Ernest Swinton, or even a John Brough, and produced no tactical ideas as to how his machines might be used in battle.

In August it was agreed that the *Sturm Panzerkraftwagen Abteilungen* should be revived, two of them with five tanks each plus cars and lorries, five officers and 109 NCOs and men per section. They were mustered as part of the rear area motor transport branch, hardly a mailed fist. By the end of October the first A7V was ready. More were following. Their crews for now were former bus men and brewery dray drivers. Their brief moment on the battlefield would come.

Ernest Swinton and Thomas Tulloch had been inspired by an American Holt tractor, the British War Office had more or less begun their fighting caterpillar experiments with one, so had Eugène Brillié at Le Creusot and Joseph Vollmer in Berlin. The results were mixed.

It might have been assumed that when an American Military Mission arrived in Paris in May 1917 the resources of the US motor industry would produce a tracked fighting machine like a genie from a bottle. It was the opposite: America's tiny but rapidly expanding army would have to get its combat equipment from France and Britain. That would include tanks.

Tanks had already played big in the US press (fanned by British propaganda efforts). The mission sought as much information as possible. Their brief initial report was favourable. The US C-in-C, Gen. John J. Pershing, set up a tank board to find out more, hence the semi-comic appearance at Bermicourt of the 'Hell-bent' American officers, Majors Frank Parker and James A. Drain.

The board reported on 1 September 1917. The British anguish in the Flanders morass could be put aside as an aberration. The board concluded that the tank 'was destined to become an important element in this war' and that a fleet of 2000 light and 200 heavy tanks be procured – the French two-man Renault FT-17 and the projected British Mark VI thirty-tonner being the best available to equip the American Expeditionary Force.

Discussion went on through the autumn in Paris, London and Washington on co-production proposals. It was complicated stuff, British tanks with American engines, for example, being assembled in France. Major Drain was made representative of the Inter-Allied Tank Commission – Albert Stern's counterpart. The major noted that Americans would make good tank crews because they 'are a strong race and of good character'. He recommended that personnel with 'a high standard of fighting quality' be selected 'from the ranks of these good men'. A 'Combat Tank Service' order of battle was drafted in outline, requiring almost 15,000 personnel.

A thirty-two-year-old cavalry captain, George Smith Patton Jr, bored with a headquarters staff job in France, applied to join. He wrote to his wife Beatrice in San Gabriel, California, telling her 'not to worry . . . people [in tanks] are pretty safe . . . and it would be a long time yet before we have any'. He was right in that respect.

In his formal letter of application sent to the office of Gen. Pershing himself, Patton stressed his mechanical skills, his 'aggressive spirit' and the fact that he was 'the only American who had ever made an attack in a motor vehicle'. It had happened in Mexico in

May 1916 when Patton had shot up the *ranchero* of the rebellious Pancho Villa's chief lieutenant from a machine-gun armed automobile. He could also, he claimed, 'speak and read French better than ninety-five per cent of American officers ... I have always gotten on well with Frenchmen.'

Then he withdrew his transfer request. Perhaps it was rumours of what had happened to the British Tank Corps in Flanders. Instead he sought command of an infantry battalion.

A week later Patton changed his mind again. He accepted an offer to become head of the AEF's 'Light Tank School', eventually to be established at Bourg, in the east of France, five miles south of Langres on the road to Dijon. For all his boasting Capt. Patton knew little about the workings of motor vehicles, let alone tanks. On 19 November he arrived at the French training school at Champlieu in the forest of Compiègne. He drove a little Renault, noting its 'comfort' and ease of handling. It bucked and reared 'like a horse' (which pleased the former cavalryman) and could 'bulldoze small trees'. He was still not sure he had made the right decision, but throwing in his lot with tanks 'aperes [sic] to be the way to high command if I make a go of it', he wrote to his wife in San Gabriel.

The next day something happened that changed the way George S. Patton Jr, and almost everyone else, would think about 'tanks'.

PART FOUR

Think of Your Pals in the Infantry

+++ THE ARMY IS FIGHTING FOR ITS LIFE AND WE ARE
STANDING BY TO PUT NEW WEAPONS IN THEIR
HANDS THE VERY INSTANT THEY TURN TO US Stop LET
THERE BE NO MISUNDERSTANDING THEREFORE BUT
ONLY CONFIDENCE AND FULL STEAM AHEAD
(sgd) CHURCHILL +++

telegram from Minister of Munitions, March 1918

38

Success has many parents. The claimants to be the progenitor of the operation launched by the British Third Army in November 1917 are numerous. It would end in gloomy failure, but on the number of those who bagged the idea as their own (and the claims of lesser players pressed by revisionist academics), the 'Battle of Cambrai', as it came to be known, was a thumping triumph.

The name of the famous battle, famous as the first, mass-mechanized armoured attack in military history, is a misnomer. Cambrai, the cathedral city fifteen miles north-east of the old Somme battlefield, might have been the intended objective, but it was never actually attained. In fact in the final plan of attack it was not even to be entered, just 'surrounded and isolated' by cavalry. In the end they never got near it. In his first report Hugh Elles called it the 'Battle of Albert'.

On the fourth day of the Flanders misadventure, 3 August 1917, Elles had 'suggested' that his force be pulled out and conserved for using 'somewhere more suitable'. The offensive had continued and the reputation of the Tank Corps had almost 'drowned with it in a morass', in the bitter words of one who was there. Artillery and tanks did not work as combined weapons, infantry and tanks just about still did. But tactical surprise seemed impossible to achieve. The guns gave it all away.

Like the invention of the tank itself, the credit for the genesis of the Cambrai operation has been much disputed. Some claim it came from a relatively junior divisional artillery commander, Brig.-Gen. Henry Hugh Tudor, who was filling in for his superior on leave when he took the opportunity to gain the ear of the newly appointed Third Army chief, the fifty-five-year-old Gen. the Hon. Sir Julian Byng, latterly commander of the Canadian Corps. He had been known since Eton as 'Bungo'.

Brigadier-General Tudor was an advocate of 'map shooting' and 'silent registration' – judging the range through precise surveying and the novel technique of sound ranging, aided by careful ballistic appraisal of shell batches, barrel wear and basic meteorology. The Mk 106 fuse had changed much already. The new arts of artillery would change much more.

Ernest Swinton felt a proprietary glow when, at the end of it all, Hugh Elles sent him a telegram: 'All ranks salute you. Your show.' There are claims made for Gen. Estienne who had bruited such an operation without the artillery overture in London in the spring of 1917. Winston Churchill, in a letter to the Official Historian written in January 1938, made his own claim to be the putative father: 'The misuse by Sir Douglas Haig of the tanks in the bogs of Passchendaele and his final adoption of a proper tank attack at Cambrai . . . how this was wrung from GHQ I do not know, but the tank attack at Cambrai followed almost exactly the lines outlined by me more than two years before in my ["Variants of the Offensive"] memorandum . . .'

He suggested that he and Gen. Edmonds (the Official Historian) 'might have lunch one day and talk the matter over'.

Most accounts trace intellectual ownership to 'Boney' Fuller, the plan cooked up in the 'brain barn' for what was originally going to be a 'tank raid' rather than an attempt at a strategic breakthrough. Haig himself had ordered preliminary examination of a potential attack to be made in the 'quiet' sector in front of Cambrai, now the rail junction anchor of the Siegfried position between Lens and St Quentin (the sizeable town at the meeting point of the French and British-held fronts), even while the Battle of Arras was at its height. The task fell to the staff of III Corps commanded by Lt-Gen. Sir William Pulteney of High Wood fame. They developed a plan for an assault on a feature called Flesquières Ridge in the Third Army sector, command of which had just been taken over by Byng. Flanders, meanwhile, was soaking up all attention.

But not 'Boney' Fuller's. Brooding at Bermicourt he had already produced a paper called 'Projected Bases for the Tactical Employment of Tanks in 1918', which in diplomatic enough language emphasized that tanks could only move over ground that would at least bear their weight. It went to GHQ for consideration. According to Fuller's memoirs, Lancelot Kiggell dismissed it.

The day after he stumbled into Elles's HQ covered in Flanders mud, Fuller came up with a new 'Project for the Capture of St Quentin by a Coup de Main'. It opened combatively with the statement: 'From a tank point of view the Third Battle of Ypres may be considered dead.' The project's self-declared aim was to 'restore British prestige and strike a theatrical blow against Germany before the winter . . .'.

He discussed it first with Elles who said GHQ would not wear it, especially as it seemed to require cooperation with the French. Fuller claimed famously that he then stared at the map on the wall, leapt up and put his finger on a particular point in the line. It was just south of Cambrai. 'Why not here?' he said. There was a major railway junction. The ground was relatively flat and well drained with waterways on each side making a limited effort on a narrow front less open to flank attack. He drafted a short paper.

Elles took it personally to GHQ and a copy went to Third Army HQ in the hands of Col. J. Hardress-Lloyd commanding the 3rd Tank Brigade. Byng already had the III Corps Flesquières outline and showed himself open to the idea that 'tanks' might be interwoven – however low their reputation stood – in the plan of attack. The proposal went to Haig who was taciturn. Kiggell saw it as a diversion from 'business elsewhere' – Flanders. Elles himself was keen on a 'raid' on Lille in September, so he told the Official Historian.

Fuller pushed his own ideas further, producing a paper on 8 August called 'Tank Raids'. The Cambrai operation should be no more than a grand demonstration to scoop up prisoners and guns, an eight-hour excursion – 'advance – hit – retire'. The tank force acting as a 'travelling circus' might be mustered, he thought, at different points in the front to do the same trick several times over. The hit-and-run tactics of Confederate cavalry leaders were invoked. It would be a theatrical gesture certainly, it might save the reputation of the Tank Corps, but what might it practically achieve? Fuller expressed the limitations of his Cambrai plan in a 1921 article in the *Tank Corps Training Journal*: 'Strategically it was unsuited to tanks, for the canals rendered most difficult any widening of the battle front; tactically it was all but perfect, for it was a veritable tank race course.' Ideal for a raid, but not for a breakthrough. Fuller, however, would make few complaints as the thing got bigger and bigger.

He sent copies of the paper to figures in London, including

Churchill. He claimed Tennyson d'Eyncourt's plaintive 'hilly country' letter to Haig was a result. Lloyd George got to see it.

The innovative artilleryman H. H. Tudor's quite separate proposition had also progressed – another bit of showing off – with a proposal to use his new 'unheralded registration' techniques to hit the Siegfried defences with a 'bolt from the blue'. The bombardment would come down at Zero without warning. His plan incorporated tanks, which, covered by smoke, would do the job of cutting the wire which had previously required weeks of industrial-scale effort by toiling gunners. Then the infantry would go forward. The Tudor plan went up the command chain from 9th Division via IV Corps (Lt-Gen. Sir C. L. Woollcombe) and reached Byng's HQ on 23 August – with a modest recommendation from Woollcombe that 'a tank officer should come and reconnoitre'.

It was Elles himself who did so. Thus it was that the commander of the Tank Corps' fighting side was summoned to an army HQ decked with every obscurantist prop to discuss the next big thing – an attack by his gallant caterpillars without the high-explosive overture. There would be no cratering. The ground would be firm.

Hugh Elles poked about the Third Army front 'incognito'. The enemy seemed indifferent enough. The IV Corps sector was quiet, almost luxuriously so, the downland splashed green and tawny brown by two years of unharvested crops. Woods and copses were in high-summer leaf. The churned chalk and already rusting wire belts of the Siegfried position bisected the landscape, a man-made anthill kicked sideways. Beyond that, it was known from aerial snooping, yet another line was in the making, 'Siegfried II'. But on this side was something nature and man together had made – the great wood of Havrincourt with its crisscrossing rides and stands of ash, oak and blackthorn. You could hide an army in there.

For now Hugh Elles kept everything to himself. Even Fuller did not know what he was up to. The tanks withdrawn from Flanders (GHQ had acceded to the 7 September request) were having the mud picked out of them at Erin. Separate proposals for a tank operation at St Quentin and north at Lens (in the area of the old Loos battlefield) were examined and discarded. It 'degenerated into a plot to take Lens by the Canadians and two tank battalions. A futile project which never materialised', according to Elles.

One officer, Brig. Ernest 'Napper' Tandy, a specialist in manpower at GHQ – clearly still chastened by the losses in Flanders and having to 'ensure a continuous trickle of freshened up divisions' – heard rumours in late September of a big new operation being planned. He told the Official Historian in a letter almost thirty years later:

> I was called one afternoon to the Chief's château. I found him alone with General Byng. His opening gambit was 'you know Bungo don't you.' He then quietly announced that he intended to attack with Third Army with tanks in early November (I think).
>
> I remember my quandary as I had to tell him that none of those [divisions] he had selected . . . would be fit to go into the attack by the date named, as they would not have had the minimum time necessary to absorb their reinforcements without which they would not be battle worthy. I thought he would eat me . . .
>
> I was horrified at the Chief talking of an operation on this scale just a few weeks ahead . . . it was a fool's paradise.

Around 15 October the secretive Elles discreetly told Fuller and Frank Searle what was brewing – an extensive tank operation to be mounted on Third Army's front. A week later the rest of the Tank staff were let in on the secret. The date of the assault would be 20 November; the place would be Cambrai.

It was considered a quiet sector by the Germans, a 'sanatorium' where battle-weary divisions from Flanders might be posted to recover some of their nerve. Intelligence began to put together an order of battle for the opposing 'Caudry group' (named for the town behind the lines where its HQ was sited) commanded by Lt-Gen. Freiherr von Watter. The 20th Landwehr Division was deployed either side of the Cambrai–Bapaume road, the 54th Jäger and 183rd divisions held a front of eight kilometres between Havrincourt and La Vacquerie, the 9th Reserve Division adjoined to the south. Second-line units, nothing especially formidable.

The whole plan had taken shape under Byng's patronage. Tanks HQ could not have sold it on their own. In an undated (but contemporaneous) handwritten note in Fuller's papers, Hugh Elles stated his own view of its origin: 'Actually Sir J. Byng had been turning it over in his mind and sent for me in September. The plan was Sir

J. Byng's and the choice of place his too.* He also proposed the
scheme of attack without bombardment.'

Thus it progressed quickly from 'raid' to a combined-arms offensive with cavalry sweeping forward once the line was ruptured. There
was novelty in the horse-based planning: saddle-borne engineers
would carry demolition charges to blow up railways, intelligence
officers were to go through with them, and fan out behind enemy
lines equipped with homing pigeons. After three years of pawing the
ground at last it looked to be the cavalry's great chance.

That would have helped get Haig's attention but was not the sole
reason why the C-in-C approved. He expressed himself in late
October 'determined to carry out the operation', according to Byng's
recollections, but the general himself was confused as to why. The
Third Army commander originally understood it to be a 'diversionary'
contribution to the slogging match in Flanders, but that was stalling
in mud and exhaustion anyway. Lancelot Kiggell expressed it afterwards thus: 'The Chief's main reason, I think, was that he hoped to
shake up the Boche to prevent more Germans being sent in against
the Italians.' He further told Liddell Hart a quarter of a century later:
'Unfortunately the French C-in-C had to be told, always a grave
danger to secrecy. Byng's original idea was to exploit eastwards and
try and get Cambrai and I fear he hankered after that all through . . .'

Haig himself expressed the curious view that the enemy might
regroup behind his fortress line and suddenly break out to attack the
French, which would lead them to cry for British forces to come to
the rescue under their command. That was a special abomination.
An Austro-German attack had routed the Italians at Caporetto and
red flags flew in Petrograd. The invader squatted sullenly in his
impregnable defences. The audit of the expiring year was disappointing. Something must be done.

Julian Byng outlined the plan to his corps commanders at Third
Army HQ at Albert on 26 October. The offensive would be in three
stages, the first to break through the German line (five miles deep)
between the Canal du Nord and the Canal de l'Escaut, using tanks
and infantry. Stage two would push through the cavalry to capture
Cambrai with its railway junction and the wooded Bourlon Ridge

* Fuller scribbled 'No!' in the margin.

and seize crossings over the river Sensée ten miles to the north. The third stage was a general advance northwards taking the German line from the flank and rear. There was no talk yet of winning the war.

The whole of the Tank Corps in France would be employed. A total of nineteen infantry divisions (the main assault being the burden of III and IV Corps) would be committed, of which three would be held in reserve (V Corps) to reinforce success or resist counter-attack. Almost 300 aircraft were mustered under Third Army control, four squadrons of which were specially trained and equipped for low-level ground attack.

Bourlon Ridge, with its village and crowning square mile of dense ash and oak, was considered more important a gain than Cambrai itself. It was that old favourite, a high place on which artillery observers might perch, their telescopic view reaching even as far as Valenciennes. The venture was codenamed 'Operation GY'. Fancy names were the preserve of a later war.

Even those who drafted the plan thought the provision of reserves was thin. Haig himself declared in his 'Cambrai dispatch' (issued in January 1918), 'Eventually I decided that despite the various limiting factors, I could muster enough force to make a first success sufficiently sure to justify undertaking the attack, but the degree to which this success could be followed up must depend on circumstances . . . Unless opposition could be beaten down quickly no great results could be looked for.' He promised Byng (who promised everyone else) that unless the results of the first forty-eight hours were decisive, the operation would be abandoned.

As in tank actions past the matrix of the assault plan was set by army, corps and divisional commanders into which the Tank Corps were expected to fit their own still mysterious imperatives. 'Driblets' were no longer an issue; almost 500 machines would go into action on a front of only six miles, more than ten times as many as had ventured even halfway forward on the Somme on a wider front. Still, they would be spread across the whole of it, one machine to approximately every 100 yards, this time luxuriously echeloned in two waves.

Fuller and his planning staff were at least allowed more tactical input than they had been at Arras and Ypres. Before the grand plan was finalized, a basic battle routine was drafted. The tanks themselves should advance in threes, one out in front, two staged behind on each flank – in so-called 'unicorn formation' – with a company of infantry walking in file behind them. A precise choreography of first and second trench-line crossing was devised and would be rehearsed over and over again (Fuller claimed it was based on a battle drill devised in antiquity by King Cyrus of Persia in his wars against the Medes).

Each infantry company had four platoons. The two leading ones would act as 'trench cleaners'. The rear two were 'trench stops', expected to seal off the French, deal with prisoners, and keep the path forward open. When the tanks reached the first-line trench they were expected to enact a clockwork-like drill, enfilading it from the front, going over and enfilading it with either 6-pounder or machine-gun fire from the rear. The support trench behind was then to be dealt with in the same way. Instructions were issued by Third Army on 30 October.

After Arras the Germans had dug deeper, wider trenches to thwart their armoured tormentors. The solution – 'fascines' – was found by the ingenious Maj. Philip Johnson and produced at the Erin Central Workshop under the direction of Frank Searle. Fascines were bundles of brushwood bound by chains under compression, each weighing almost two tons, 'an abomination to manhandle . . . fifteen to twenty Chinamen being required to push each fascine though the mud at Erin'. The bruising work of manufacturing more than four hundred was begun on 24 October. Tanks were used in pairs like log-hauling elephants to pull the chains tight around the four-foot-diameter bundles, which were designed to be dropped into the defender's excavations as a crude but effective bridge. Massive ammunition and fuel-carrying sledges were constructed. New tanks from the factories were fettled and tuned, and 127 mud-choked machines salvaged from Flanders brought back to something like fighting condition.

The work was done by the 51st Chinese Labour Company. Indentured civilians brought all the way round the world via Canada, the 'jabbering chinks' (one of the milder contemporary descriptions) first arrived in the Ternoise valley in July 1917. Corralled in their own camps with their strange caste of Mandarin-speaking, ex-missionary officers, a labourer contracted to work for two francs a day; his family could expect one hundred US dollars in case of death. Lieutenant E. F. Churchill, the Royal Engineer signals specialist with 1st Tank Brigade, recorded (among much else) this memoir of them:

> The Chinese Labour Battalion which was near us and whose officers had become rather friendly invited our mess to a display by the Chinese troops. This was rather a special favour as they were very chary of letting the foreign devils see the show. It was a most extraordinary performance. During the whole time two or three people kept up a long wailing sound to the accompaniment of a kind of violin but nobody seemed to take much notice of them. They had races on stilts, chasing a pig and one man of very fine physique gave a display with a sword.

'Our Chinamen are an unknown quantity,' Elles told Capper soon after their arrival. In the preparations for Cambrai they were toiling brutes. It would be different thereafter, but without their sheer muscle power the tanks would not have moved into battle at all.

Was it still to be a tank raid or was this really a full-blown offensive? In his memoirs Fuller recalled a Third Army conference on the morning of 8 November when 'the two Corps commanders [Pulteney and Woollcombe] seemed out of their depth and the main subject under discussion was the cavalry . . .'. Lancelot Kiggell was also there, 'who sat pensively silent wrapped in the deepest gloom'.

Fuller was seemingly having another go at GHQ, contempt for which splenetically bubbles beneath the surface of his memoirs. In fact five corps commanders were at the meeting, plus Lt-Gen. Sir Charles Kavanagh, the cavalry commander whom Robert Bradley had bamboozled with his tanks-can-go-sixty-miles outburst on the eve of the Somme attack.

No similar declaration was made this time. No one proposed, other than in some private Bermicourt fantasy, that tanks should drive deeper than the canal line (although the furthest objectives were to be reached having left the infantry behind). It was the cavalry who must go forward to any green fields beyond. Their HQ was at Fins, five miles behind the front and twelve from the key objective of the canal bridge at Masnières which tanks must take on the first day for the horsemen to cross.

In the unfolding planning for Operation GY the cavalry imperative was taking over. For enthusiasts the prospect was glittering. On 17 November Third Army issued orders that stressed: 'If . . . we are successful in overrunning the enemy's line of defence, a unique opportunity for the cavalry action becomes possible. This action may have a most far reaching effect, not only on the local situation, but also on the course of the war.'

The ordinary 'fighting tanks' would crush the wire for the infantry, but thirty-two special 'wire pulling' tanks equipped with grapnels and cables devised at Erin would be allocated to clear three sixty-yard-wide lanes for the horsemen. Dismounted troopers with special equipment would follow in their wake. It was reckoned the lane clearing would take just twenty minutes. The 'WP' detachment would be led by Capt. Stuart Hastie, Dinnaken's commander at Flers, one of the few Heavy Section 'aborigines' still in the line.

Three lines were drawn on the map: the first, in red dots, snaked behind the British front trenches, '1,000 yards from the enemy outposts', showing the tank's jumping-off positions at Zero, considered the nearest point they might get to before their engine noise alerted the listeners in their forward burrows pushed out into no-man's-land. Second was the 'Blue Line', covering the front defence system into which the fortified villages of Havrincourt and Ribecourt had been incorporated.

Third was the 'Brown Line', drawn along the far side of the Siegfried support system which included Flesquières Ridge. On the left of the attack front the wooded heights of Bourlon lay beyond that. So, on the right, did the bridges over the Canal de l'Escaut at the villages of Masnières and Marcoing. Flesquières village was in the middle, the key axis of advance for 1 Cavalry Division.

A first wave of machines, two-thirds of the striking force, was intended to advance along the whole six-mile front to capture the Blue Line. The second wave, following sixty minutes later, would pass through and on to the Brown Line, joined by those that had rallied from the first objective. Thereafter tanks were to 'exploit' forward without waiting for infantry to capture Bourlon and the canal crossings. There would be a mechanical reserve of six tanks per battalion of thirty-six machines to plug holes caused by breakdowns. There was no strategic reserve other than one company allotted to an infantry unit to be used a little later on the opening day.* Virtually the whole of the front-line Tank Corps would be committed from Zero-Hour.† The *Official History* expressed the plan in the succinct words of an unnamed tank commander: 'We go straight in and sit on the Germans until the cavalry come.'

There would be no preliminary bombardment. But more than a thousand guns assembled under the artillery plan would let loose deep on the defenders' rear positions and lay down smoke and high explosive on the forward ones, 'nowhere nearer than 500 yards from the line of advancing tanks'. The artillery itself was then supposed to move boldly forward to aid the 'later stages of the advance' – draught horses pulling field and heavy guns through the remaining wire which the tanks had not crushed, which would be cut if necessary 'by hand'.

Training in infantry–tank cooperation began at Wailly and around the old Loop area in the first week of November. Five divisions would be rotated over ten days. Everyone was suspicious at first. A tank veteran of Flanders recalled the 'usual rush of young officers for the back seats at a Brigade conference', but he emerged little the wiser: 'As far as I can remember it was chiefly concerned with what a chance we were going to get . . . after losing two tanks in the Ypres salient I was a little sceptical as to whether our view of a first-class show coincided with that of our optimistic brigadier.'

The Tank Corps did its best to show the doubters they could do more than ditch in the first trench or blow up after a few rifle hits. Haig came to see for himself. This was all a long way from the circus stunts at Yvrench. The methodical drill of releasing fascines, crossing trenches and infantry accompanying was rehearsed over and over again. It looked pretty slick. But Fuller's training 'Notes' were no more than that. Corps, divisional, even brigade commanders could make of them what they liked. It was that most gentlemanly British army precept, the 'delegation of command'.

---

* In direct opposition to Tank HQ's original proposal of late October: 'A strong reserve should be kept in hand to turn the accident of battle in our favour. If continuity of action is aimed at, tank units should be formed in sufficient depth to enable the leading echelon to be withdrawn and refitted so that it may be ready to return into action a little before the last echelon is exhausted.'

† On the day 476 machines were operational. The number broke down as: 378 fighting tanks; 54 supply tanks; 32 wire pullers; 2 bridgers (allotted to the cavalry); 9 wireless; 1 telephone cable (under Third Army control).

A IV Corps instruction, for example, quite sensibly suggested that if a tank broke down infantry must 'swerve from its own line of advance' to keep clear of the now sitting target. One commander, Maj.-Gen. George Montague Harper, had been peppery about the whole thing from the beginning. Presented with the draft of Operation GY, he described it as 'a fantastic and most unmilitary scheme'.

The snowy-haired 'Uncle' Harper, commanding the 51st (Highland) Division,* had his own ideas. His view of tanks was coloured by Arras and Ypres. They were magnets for enemy fire, their real utility highly questionable. Rather than being careless of his men's lives, his intervention was designed to husband them. The postwar view of Christopher Baker-Carr, commanding 1st Tank Brigade, would be excoriating: 'He had laid down a system . . . which was, essentially, based on disbelief,' he wrote. 'If it all went well with the tanks, "my little fellers", as he affectionately called his division, could take advantage of the situation; if however things fared badly, then his men would not be implicated in any disaster . . .' Fuller joined the postwar literary onslaught on Harper. Revisionist historians have striven to rescue something of his reputation.

In Harper's revised plan the first wave of tanks would be split into two, so-called 'wire cutters' moving off first and 'fighting tanks' second. The enfilading pirouette of the trench line of Fuller's devising was dispensed with. The infantry, rather than advance in 'worms' in file behind, would advance in ragged 'waves' (less vulnerable to machine-gun fire from the flank, according to Harper), ordered to come no closer than a 100 yards of the machines in front. The divisional commander had the last say. That is how the training would be done, that is how on the day the integrated assault of men and machines would be configured. According to one tank subaltern allotted to Harper's division: 'Liaison with the Highlanders consisted of simple tactical exercises by day and the most colossal binges by

---

* A Scottish Territorial division that had been through the mill since its arrival in France in early May 1915. It had fought without much distinction at Festubert and was considered to be untrained and with low morale. When Maj.-Gen. Harper arrived in September 1915 they self-deprecatingly called themselves 'Harper's Duds', from their divisional sign – HD. By 1917 its fighting reputation was higher. It had fought in Flanders, and gone into action with tanks on 31 July with some success.

nights. In the circumstances it was not possible to do more than practise very simple evolutions with the infantry.'

Several memoirs linger amid the 'hilarious nights of elbow lifting' with the unquenchable Scotsmen. Come the day, there would be no hangover cure.

Whatever the differences over tactics, everyone could agree that, with no preliminary bombardment, shock and surprise were all. This time secrecy really was an imperative. According to the *Official History*: 'The most elaborate precautions were taken. Even senior staff in the Operations Section of GHQ were kept in ignorance . . . Third Army arranged for many false rumours to be spread in Amiens and similar resorts. Tank officers visiting the front did so in disguise.'

And they did just that. Fuller gumshoed around in a muffling Burberry wearing, on his account, 'blue-tinted glasses'. False beards were considered but discarded according to the architect-turned-reconnaissance officer Clough Williams-Ellis. General Byng snooped around dressed as a Canadian private. Invitations to congenial messes were spurned in case too much whisky might be taken. Elliot Hotblack would routinely disappear from Albert for nocturnal visits to the front, feeling the ground, sniffing out the defence's weak points. Documents were prepared on special numbered typewriters. Tanks were referred to as 'Ospreys'.* Advanced HQ in Albert was known as the 'tank training office'. A 6th Division order read: 'All unofficial discussion and surmises regarding the nature of the operations by all ranks are strictly forbidden. This applies particularly to discussions by officers in messes, clubs and other similar places. Operations are not to be discussed however inconvenient this may be in the presence of orderlies, servants or clerks.'

The game might be won or lost in the assembly and final move up. Fuller toiled over rail movement schedules. The detailed work on provisions for camouflage, lying-up points and routes to the thousand-yard line was immense. Havrincourt Wood was a godsend. Even in late November the blackthorn was in masking leaf. The Germans would get a warning, but it did not come from a lucky aerial photograph.

Z-Day would be 20 November. From the 16th, tanks and their crews were brought in from Wailly, the Loop and the other training

---

* This codeword had been also been used in Flanders.

grounds in the rear area to be assembled at the 'Plateau' railway sidings near Bray-sur-Somme, then shuffled forward by night along fingers of railway track into the forward area to rumble off the flat-wagons for the last time. It took thirty-six trains to do it.*

Gunner Reginald Beall recalled his journey, the other ranks crammed uncomfortably into one of the ubiquitous Nord railway boxcars. The officers got a third-class carriage, hitched to the tank train itself. In one of the innumerable stop-starts, a passenger train was halted on the other line. 'The troops made for it like a brigade of ants,' Gnr Beall remembered, stripping it of its horsehair-stuffed seat cushions to provide a little eve-of-battle comfort. One ended up inside his tank.

William Watson arrived at the Plateau, evocatively describing the scene of worker-ant activity in his memoir, *A Company of Tanks*: 'A major in the Tank Corps felt insignificant among the multitudinous rails, the slow dark trains, the sudden lights . . . the lorries that bumped through the night . . . Quiet railwaymen, mostly American, went steadily about their business . . . I found a hut with a fire in it and an American who gave me hot coffee and some wonderful sandwiches made of sausage and lettuce . . .'

The detrained tanks crawled forward under their own power in bottom gear to the allotted assembly areas scattered through stands of trees and ruined farms. D Company 'tracked' from the railhead at Ytres at dead slow into the gloom of Havrincourt Wood. It took four hours and glugged down petrol. They were covered with camouflage nets and brushwood. In some places barns were simply collapsed on top of them. Fuel and ammunition were stockpiled forward, plus vast quantities of horse fodder. The cavalry plan was as detailed as that of the Tank Corps, almost down to the last oat. Cooking fires were forbidden, even in daylight. So was smoking (on penalty of being shot, according to the MGC corporal George Coppard). Track-cut ruts were back-filled by fatigue parties. Divisional artillery was discreetly gathered by night (the heavy stuff towed by Holt tractors) in Havrin-court Wood behind enormous brushwood screens. Fortuitous low cloud kept hostile observation aircraft on the ground.

---

* Elderly Victorian locomotives were shipped out to pull them. They were given suitable new names – 'Mons', 'French'. One was called 'Haig'; it was still working on British Railways in the 1950s.

The secret still held. There was a scare when a German trench raid in the early hours of the 18th snatched an NCO and five men of the 36th (Ulster) Division. There were two more trench raids and more prisoners taken on the 19th. The news of their capture reached Tanks HQ in Albert later that day. This was very bad. According to Williams-Ellis: 'We were uncertain how much these men knew, and how much information they would give under examination . . . if they gave away the gist of our plans the enemy would have twenty-four hours to bring up reserves. There was, however, nothing to be done except to await the event.' Which is what they did.

That night a muted rehearsal was held by infantry and tank commanders to ensure that men and machines would be in the right places. Tapes were laid to points 200 yards behind the British front line, with the most forward German outposts 800 yards beyond that. Elles prepared his famous brown, red and green battle flag* from the only colours left in a French draper's shop's depleted stock of silk.

Two junior officers were given the strange task of crawling into no-man's-land late on the night of the 18th to see 'if we could hear our tanks moving'. They ended up 'laughing uncontrollably'. One of them recalled: 'Instead of the rumble of engines, what we could hear was the most superb flow of foul language. The steel bodies of the tanks gave a bell-like resonance to a man's voice and across the 2,000 yards came: 'Lock your diff you ******* fool', 'Mind that ******* tree' etc. What the enemy made of it all I never knew.'

The 19th was spent laying up, greasing, filling Lewis magazines. Still not all the tanks were in the line. Horace Birks remembered his section being 'ordered out of the wood in indecent daylight to make room for hundreds of guns pouring in. As dusk deepened all you could hear was the jingle of harness and the snorting of gun teams.' Late in the afternoon individual tank commanders were briefed for the first time on 'the scheme of operations' and given maps and aerial photographs showing their objectives. Crews still did not know where they were going, even where they were. Older hands managed a reasonable guess. For the majority of them, the drafts from England certainly, this was their first experience of going into battle. To

* 'Through mud and blood to the green fields beyond.' The phrase was Elles's coining but the flag seems to have been originally created on the eve of the Flanders campaign in summer 1917.

twenty-year-old subalterns, the few veterans from the Somme and Arras seemed like old men.

Hugh Elles enjoyed a modest eve-of-battle supper in their rat-infested little mess over 'a couple of bottles of champagne' with Uzielli, Fuller and Evan Charteris. The general made a last-minute decision (too late, according to Baker-Carr, for his superiors to find out and overrule it). His famous 'Special Order No. 6' was drafted that evening. The handwritten original in pencil on flimsy duplicating paper is in a modest file in the National Archives. 'Tomorrow the Tank Corps will have the chance for which it has been waiting for many months, to operate on good going in the van of the battle . . .' he declared. It ended with a surprise. 'I propose leading the attack of the Centre Division.' He summoned his driver to take him to the front.

Fuller had proposed doing something 'theatrical' in his earliest sketch of the proposed operation. Hugh Elles would give him his money's worth.

'Boney', the hyperactive brain box, had nothing to do on the actual day. As the minutes ticked away to midnight, in his own words he 'retired to bed'.

39

Midnight passed. There were six hours to go. The 'Ospreys' began to make their last dispositions. Shuttered torches and the glowing ends of Woodbines (a dispensation for officers only) guided the way into each position marked by a stencilled flag. Track rollers were greased, Lewis guns checked, extra two-gallon tins of motor spirit loaded. Myriad little dramas were enacted in the darkness. Captain J. K. 'Jake' Wilson, a section commander with I Battalion, recorded:

> When filling with petrol before the battle, a driver came up to me and said one tin contained water. 'The petrol had been "flogged".'
> 'How do you know?' I asked him.
> 'The tin sounds funny.'
> He emptied it to just a few drops which he tasted with his finger. It was water. We had to get hold of some rubber tube and the whole petrol tank was rapidly siphoned empty.

Lieutenant Norman Dillon, company reconnaissance officer with E Battalion, was intimately concerned with getting the tanks into their planned position. 'It was a fair distance to do in the dark – three miles,' he would subsequently recall, 'but we did my usual trick of laying tape from the front line to the back, dodging round things we wanted to avoid ... We started the tanks moving up – with a shrouded torch. I got caught up in some barbed wire, the leading tank bearing down on me. It couldn't stop, I could not get hold of it. I shone my torch into the driver's visor; he stopped with a volley of oaths. I got free.'

Frank Heap and his already weary crew manoeuvred Deborah into her jumping-off position on the north-east fringe of the masking wood. Men began to realize just how new this all was. In many parts of the line, the shrouding trench, the horizon of earth and sandbags, was gone. 'It was the queerest sensation,' recalled George Coppard, 'packed with a vast crowd of warriors out in the open after living like rabbits in burrows . . . nothing disturbed us as we lay on the ground dozing.' The blackness of Havrincourt murmured with thousands of men, whispering, snoring, cursing. Highlanders muttered guttural oaths, gagging for a forbidden smoke.

Major Robert 'Roc' (R. O. C.) Ward, 12 Company's rugby-playing commander, briefed his officers. In accordance with divisional instructions the 'wire pullers' would be off first at 6.20 a.m. The main body – 11 Company – would start rolling four minutes later. 12 Company would move off at 6.50 to pass through and join up with the survivors of the first wave at the rallying position. The infantry of 153 Brigade* would be walking behind in lateral lines as Gen. Harper had decreed. Their objective was a fortified village in the Hindenburg support position. Intelligence reports placed field guns at the east and western ends of Flesquières, but the bombardment and an RFC ground-attack mission shortly before first light† should deal with them. E Battalion's tanks would be operating on their right.

The bespectacled, gangly Heap peered at his map (the Flesquières batteries were marked in red) and told his sergeant the good news. D.51 Deborah would be in the second wave.

There was tea, Oxo, Horlicks, mock turtle soup, every kind of soluble patent foodstuff known to English grocery. The official eve-of-battle victualling provisions, however, seem to have been highly developed. According to a post-battle description:

> The four section cooks proceeded up to the line with their sections. Two camp kettles and one hot food container were taken up by each section. Rations for the next day [hardtack and bully beef] were put up by the crews in sandbags. The Company HQ cook remained at Headquarters . . . all fresh meat was cooked the day of issue and sent up to the crews cold. Before action each section cook made tea, filling the hot food containers. This was taken up on the approach march and issued at the starting point. Rum was also issued at the same time . . .

There is evidence of less-structured catering arrangements, of sausages being cooked inside a tank on 'a primus stove behind the

* The 1/5th Gordon Highlanders and 1/6th Black Watch.

† Sunrise was at 7.27 a.m. BST. The RFC mission was timed for 7.00 a.m.

engine'. There are lots of reminiscences about the rum. One youthful tank commander commented soon afterwards: 'It is really astonishing how much whisky the British Army carries into battle.' On archaeological evidence from the battlefield, large quantities of brown sauce seem to have been carried into action.

Fuller's memoirs reprint the account of a Tank Corps officer on a late-night carborne journey to F Battalion's assembly area near Gouzeaucourt. It was not just for a final briefing, it would seem, but to deliver an SRD earthenware flagon to a particular tank in the front line. The band of three young officers in their Vauxhall are late and have a long way to go.

The usual rear-area perils of lumpen infantrymen, ASC columns, German shelling and military policemen are encountered in the darkness on the way. The description of the mission – blundering into huts full of snoring Tommies (impossible to wake), found 'sleeping amid the remnants of cake and smudges of butter' – has a literary power more affecting than the flash-bang of going into action.* Fuller's correspondent recalled encountering Highland infantry moving up the road to Gouzeaucourt: 'They moved at a pace just on the active side of standing still. None of them spoke, and their silence, the weight and slowness of their tread . . . [was such] that one felt as if one were hailing men who were no longer of this world.'

Fuller at his own time of writing confessed that rereading the eve-of-battle account still gave him a 'mysterious thrill'.

With three hours to go – barring a few breakdowns and vehicles bellying on tree stumps – almost all the tanks were in the line. Engines were switched off. The metal boxes cooled rapidly. Frost bloomed over steel plate inside and out, making it stinging to the touch. The infantry shivered in their assembly trenches and out in the open, too cold to sleep, everyone longing for a forbidden cigarette. In some places blankets were issued. Machine guns kept up a sputter-sputter. Conversations were in whispers. For those who were still awake, the amount of boozing seemed prodigious.

Fuller's correspondent made his rendezvous and handed over the rum. Up close to the line he wrote, 'one could hear tanks moving,

---

* Infantrymen's accounts of tanks – 'fire-spitting monsters' etc – are monotonously similar. George Coppard offers one of the best vernacular accounts: 'Here's an old bitch', or 'There goes a bloody great bull'.

purring very mildly on their second speed ... and one could see pin-points of light, no bigger than fireflies, issuing from their port holes. Some of the men were trying to sleep on tarpaulins.'

At around 5.00 a.m. the enemy line came alarmingly to life with machine-gun and rifle fire. Then it faded to silence. A false alarm. 'One could hear low voices in the clearing station close by,' recorded Fuller's correspondent. He heard 'a man whistling "Tipperary" in the distance. A change was coming in the sky ... The tension was extreme.'

Philip Hamond had found three German army ration containers like 'huge tin thermos flasks' and 'strapped them to the back of the tanks ... one filled with tea, the next with stew and so on', so he told his wife in an incident-filled letter. 'At 2:00 am I went off to see the infantry CO and when the whisky was done I then went to see the blokes and have a mug or two of rum. Everyone was in jolly good trim and all too ready to light up when the whistle blew.'

More than 400 machines were strung out in their hides, formed up in a rough line abreast along a front of almost eight miles. Starting handles were swung in a rippling mechanical chorus. Drivers opened the throttles to get the engines warm – then back to tickover. Outside, the noise of the sleeve-valve Daimlers was a mumbled purr. Inside it was deafening. 'Company commanders visited their tanks and wished everybody good luck and assured them it would be a walkover ...'

Around 6.10 the first-wave tanks began to move. A few hundred yards ahead of them the infantry were making their final preparations.

'The darkness had paled,' Fuller's correspondent wrote. In the dawn in the great girdle of autumnal woods 'partridges were calling to one another'.

Major D. N. Wimberley, a staff officer of the 51st Division, wrote: 'The last half hour before zero of the Cambrai battle, I shall never forget. It was perfectly quiet and the approaching November dawn had a sharp snap of cold ... The men lay about the parapet of the trench sipping tea, cracking quiet jokes. We officers sat in a bunch. One thought was uppermost – would it be a walkover as intelligence had predicted, or had this ghastly stillness a more significant reason?'

There was ground mist; a light wind blew from the south-west. The Tank Corps had already begun their slow roll forward, picking up the infantry as they clambered out of their trenches or left the shelter of the trees to fall in behind them. Gunner R. Beall of A Battalion on the extreme right, moving at a crawl out of Dessart Wood, recalled those last ten minutes:

> We moved off with the dawn over some real felt-like land that might have been a park, so beautiful was the turf and countryside. Then we came to a halt at what proved to be our second line trenches. The sight was breathtaking.
>
> The sandbags looked as precision laid as a brick wall. No sign whatsoever of any disarrangement by any shells or bullets. It just blended into nature. Yet it didn't. That fellow sitting on the fire step with his eyes open wasn't moving. He was dead! How? It was all so quiet.
>
> 'Puff!' Fancy that! Just a single burst of shrapnel about fifty yards to the right . . .

The stillness still held, the seconds ticking away. 'Boney' Fuller was in Albert, alert, animated, but miles from the action. His planning job was done. 'A little before six I was up,' he wrote. 'It was still dark and misty, when about a quarter of an hour later I left the hut and went over to the GS office. As I neared the toppling Virgin, I looked at my watch – it was 6.18. I paused for what seemed a long time though it was only two minutes and then at length I heard a faint rumbling . . . it was the opening barrage – the battle had begun.'

Second Lieutenant Wilfred Bion was in the line, his engine idling. 'I thought it would be tempting Providence to stop it and hope to start it again.' On his account: 'My watch hand crept on to zero and there were three individual bursts from our artillery. Then at once a moaning in the air. The enemy's trench system was picked out along its length by our barrage, unregistered yet bursting, at most, twelve feet above ground level in a precision I have never seen equalled. I could have cheered as I saw the white puffs shot through with white sparks picking out the pattern in the pearly light.'

The whole mass of artillery opened up. A two-mile-long curtain of thermite smoke bloomed along Flesquières Ridge. The phosphorescence lingered for minutes before fading to deepest black.

The tanks were nosing forward now, their progress almost sedate. Philip Hamond started to laugh, 'and I laughed and laughed until I couldn't bear it'. It must have been the rum, he confessed in a letter to his wife. Behind them plodded the infantry. Some paused to light cigarettes. Some had their rifles slung. It was a walk in the park.

The tanks reached the wire belt, so thick you could 'hardly poke a broomhandle into it'. Gunner Beall recalled going through. His CO thought it time to be matey: 'It screeched against the hull, it lifted up the tracks even, again with a sound I can only compare to the buckets of a dredger. Snapping and scraping, snapping and grating, it eventually fizzled out and we had got through . . . the officer was letting himself go: "Mind no flirting with the girls when we get to Cambrai . . ."'

Alarm flares from the outpost line scissored the sky. Defenders scrambled from their dugouts in the first and support line to bring the MG '80s into action. The British fireplan's 'jumping barrage' rained shells on both in succession. The 2 mph progress of the tanks flattened the triple-wire belt, as one excitable account described it, like 'beds of nettles'.

The Official Historian used *Boy's Own* prose to describe the effect on the enemy: 'Stunned by the devastating precision of this sudden storm of fire, the defenders were confronted with a new terror, the clattering onset of the tanks plunging through the gloom.' Heinz Guderian was equally charged up in his account given in his famous 1937 prescription for armoured forces, *Achtung Panzer!*:

> The artillery barrage . . . and all our troops took cover in the dugouts, leaving only sentries outside. On past experience several hours should now elapse before the enemy infantry attacked, and the German artillery fired no more than a feeble barrage ahead of our outpost line . . . suddenly indistinct black forms could be discerned. They were spitting fire and under their weight the strong and deep obstacle line was cracking like matchwood. Alarm! . . . the troops rushed to their machine guns; it was all in vain! The tanks appeared not one at time but in whole lines kilometres in length!

Captain Daniel Hickey left his sponson door open during the break-in, the better to stay close to the infantry: 'A side glance through the doorway gave me a sudden shock,' he wrote. 'There was a British soldier lying face downward, dead, his inert body twisted. It already seemed slightly swollen.' Second Lieutenant Hardy got out of his machine to check a German in their path who seemed to be shamming dead. He shot him through the heart with his revolver. Hickey noticed the man was 'quite elderly, his neck wrinkled and weather beaten'. 'Roc' Ward led Deborah and the second-wave tanks of D Battalion across the start line on foot. Within a few minutes he fell dead, 'struck by a stray bullet'.

Excited reports flowed into the corps HQs of 'tanks going on', 'the enemy running away'. An RFC pilot recalled seeing British infantry 'trudging forwards with cigarettes alight', and the 'expressions of amazement on the upturned faces of German troops' at La Vacquerie, the fortified farm in III Corps' centre.

They were through the outpost line and into the first ('fire') trench. The unicorn formation worked like a dose of No. 9. So did the fascines. According to Hickey: 'A red flag stuck in the parapet of the trench ahead of us showed where the leading tank had dropped its fascine. We ran up to it and approached slowly to make quite certain of dropping on it, and crossed over. It was an enormous trench, and there was one horrid moment when the tail dropped on the fascine when it seemed to be touch and go if we could get over.'

Lieutenant J. B. Hassall had volunteered for the Heavy Branch after the press trumpeting of Flers. Posted to H Battalion at Boving-ton, he had found himself being barked at by Col. Willoughby's drill sergeants, then had a miserable time in the Ypres salient. His recollections of Cambrai were happier, in spite of a drama-filled cross-ing of the German front line: 'The fascine bumped down. Sgt Cadogan [the driver] then very carefully let the tank down onto it . . . [but] we ourselves became stuck . . . Cadogan was a very good mechanic and said I will race the engine and put in the clutch and jerk the whole thing. It shuddered again . . . one track bit onto the fascine and out we crawled. I clapped him on the shoulder and said good chap . . .'

Then the infantry fell on the defenders with bayonets and Mills bombs (to be used, according to divisional orders, 'only when surren-der was refused' – a directive that did not seem to mean much). Evan Charteris recalled a 'wrathful' Tank Corps commander seeing 'numbers of Germans being shot by our men after they had given sufficient indication of their inability to resist any further'.

John Brockbank, the busman-turned-tank engineer, saw a 'Tommy drive a pick through the head of a German as he emerged from a dug-out', and when he had criticized this as a rather cold-blooded proceeding, the Tommy said: 'This morning when I was taking in a prisoner he made a bolt for it, and I've had enough of that sort of thing.'

'There was, in fact; great bitterness of feeling that day,' wrote Charteris. The ferocity was generalized. The tanks led the way but it was the infantry who did most of the killing. Major Wimberley wrote: 'One dugout I remember well, as at the entrance we found three dead bayoneted Germans in their stocking feet – who were but partly clad, they could not have known of the attack until the first Jocks were on top of them.'

But it was the tanks that proved the 'bloody frightener'. One German account described the experience of an artillery officer searching for his battery near Fontaine. An infantry captain stumbling back from the fighting momentarily blames him and his like for the catastrophe: 'Pig of a gunner! Where are the guns? . . . [the officer quietens and begins to shake] Sturmwagen! . . . it is terrible. We cannot do anything. The front is broken.'

As he had promised at the eve-of-battle supper in Albert, Hugh Elles went into action personally. It might have seemed an odd decision, a fit of bravado. Evan Charteris clearly thought it slightly vulgar. But the general had not much else to do. There was no armoured reserve to commit – he could not direct the battle once it had begun (the wireless tanks with primitive spark apparatus were entirely experimental) even if he had been allowed to. Tanks were deaf and almost blind. They could just about send shutter-lamp messages to each other. Otherwise it was down to runners and flags. Once it had started, it was all in the written orders. Either the tanks broke the defence in the course of one day or they did not. After that it was up to the cavalry.

Major Gerald W. Huntbach, commanding A Company, H Battalion, recalled what happened when 'a lithe figure with pipe aglow' appeared in the assembly position just before dawn. It was Elles. '"This is the centre of our line, I'm going over in this tank," he said. He tapped Hilda's off side sponson. I swung the door open and informed [2/Lt T. H. de B.] Leach of his distinguished passenger.'

Elles's 'flag tank' set off at Zero-Hour in line abreast with the rest of H Battalion in the general direction of Ribecourt, with its little standard fluttering. One account described Elles with his head poking out of the top hatch smoking his pipe. Hilda got stuck in a trench (to be pulled out later). 'The General got out and was back at Albert in time for lunch.' It was all terribly gallant.

Elles had time to send Swinton in London his 'your show' telegram from Third Army headquarters, just as Maurice Hankey was getting the first news at Whitehall Gardens from the War Office. He excitedly summoned Swinton by telephone to tell him of the 'fantastic gains'.

Ribecourt was taken by 8.00 a.m. without the loss of a single tank to enemy fire. There had been little shelling and the place was more or less intact, low-built houses of stone and red brick. A train chuffed urgently from its little station in the direction of Cambrai. At one point 'tanks were in a queue waiting to enter'. When they got into the village, according to Maj. Huntbach, there was an orgy of looting.

Sixty tanks of G, D and E battalions (ten had failed to start as a result of mechanical problems) were past Havrincourt by 9.00 a.m. The whole of the Blue Line was effectively taken within two hours, the second echelon of tanks and foot soldiers passing through to the next objective as the artillery barrage 'jumped' forward as per plan. By 11.00 a.m. the Siegfried support position had been overrun and tank crews were nosing into the rearward 'battle zone'.

The Mark IV's comforts had improved little over the debutantes of 1916. The bucking, lurching progress over trenches was just the same, the fume-chamber atmosphere inside just as noxious, the heat and noise no less punishing. One commander recorded his crew all spontaneously vomiting as they took their first draughts of fresh air after hours of 'foul confinement'. When the moment was right even on the battlefield the whole crew, less the driver, might get out and walk alongside, 'a common custom if things were quiet and the atmosphere inside became unbearable.'

Individual commanders improvised as they went, stopping to pick up tankless strays, getting out to guide a driver out of trouble, helping wounded out of stricken vehicles. Sometimes tank-crew wounded were dumped for infantry to pick up. Sometimes wounded infantry were taken on board, or tankless unwounded crewmen scooped up so that they might continue the fight. Metal doors swung open time and again as tank men slithered in and out of their machines as the

lot of them ambled forward at walking pace. On occasion, it might
seem, they did it for the fun of it. Gerald Huntbach in Harvester told
the story of an enormous black Newfoundland dog suddenly bounding
out of the support line. Naturally enough it was taken aboard. Its brass
collar announced it to be the mascot of a German artillery regiment.
Harvester was unsportingly hit by a shell. The dog survived.

Daniel Hickey explained: 'A section commander's job was to be
where he could be of most use to the infantry, while still keeping
control of his tanks . . . At Cambrai I went into action in Hadrian but
there were times when I walked outside.'

How to keep control? There were shutter lamps and disc signals.
Sometimes they worked, more often they did not. The battlefield was
wreathed in mist until mid-morning. 'At noon a pale sun appeared.'
On one occasion a tank commander tried to attract another's attention (its top-mounted wood-bundle fascine was on fire) by shooting
at its side with the Lewis gun. He succeeded. Waving, banging on
the hull, gesticulating like a bandleader – by such means were the
three-tank formations orchestrated across the battlefield. One section
commander was seen 'for some reason riding on the top of the tank.
He was hit in the shoulder almost at once, and grasping his arm he
rolled down the back of the tank and disappeared inside.'

As the assault drove deeper, outside became a more dangerous
place to be. Captain Hickey's section had just assaulted a farmhouse
the other side of Ribecourt: 'The tanks now separated to clear the
neighbourhood. About 11 o'clock I gave the return signal. I walked
outside Hadrian and was surprised to see Havoc's commander
escorting a bunch of prisoners at the point of his revolver [he had
chased them on foot into a dugout]. Single bullets swished past me
and I noticed that each time Havoc's commander and his prize made
a simultaneous genuflection.'

Second Lieutenant G. Dudley Hardy, Hadrian's youthful commander, told the story of their progress in the stark language of an
action report. Hadrian was in the second echelon – heading for the
Brown Line – and the break-out for the canal at Marcoing:

7:15   Crossed own front line.
7:25   Crossed Plush trench.
7:34   Crossed Hindenburg Line without difficulty behind
       Hermit.

8:08   Crossed support line behind Helen. Both crossings were accomplished on fascines dropped by other Ospreys.

8:15   Crossed Mole trench.

9:30   Fired first shot on outskirts of Ribecourt. Sent pigeon message.

9:40   Crossed Blue Line.

9:43   Fascine broke loose and fell.

9:55   Crossed railway. Sent signal: 'Assume battle formation.'

10:00   Reached objective. No opposition. Other Ospreys were going forward.

10:15   Opened fire with 6-pdrs on farm. After six rounds one German officer and about twenty other ranks ran out.

10:35   Reached the outskirts of Marcoing. No enemy resistance. Sent signal returned to rallying point.

10:45   Sent second pigeon message.

12:30   Returned to rallying point, camouflaged and greased up.

Hardy's report ended with some overall complaints. The engine oil was too thin, the Auto-vac carburettor constantly playing up, the Lewis guns jammed with the heat, 'and the fact that the deflector bags would not take up the empties quick enough'. Such grumbles seem universal.

The 29th Division, the last infantry formation outside the reserve yet to be committed, left the British lines at 10.15 a.m. to the sound of bugles, heading for the right flank with a company of tanks preceding. According to the *Official History*: 'Not a single battalion was kept in reserve, but organised opposition was not expected, the operation being regarded as in the nature of a pursuit.' Every single machine, excluding the few initial breakdowns topped up by the mechanical reserve, was now in the fight.

Graincourt on the left was secured by mid-afternoon at a cost of twenty ditched or broken-down tanks and twelve lost to German field guns. The Tank Corps' losses in personnel were astonishingly light. The wire-pulling detachment laboured behind them to clear lanes for the cavalry. On the extreme right, lateral communications trenches on the Bonavis Ridge were being occupied and hurriedly reconfigured as a flank guard.

On III Corps' centre, the drive to the furthest objectives had already begun – towards the villages of Marcoing and Les Rues Vertes– Masnières with their crossing points of the canal which followed the looping valley of the Schelde, more a stream than a river. The weary infantry were left behind by tanks that had rallied and refuelled from their supply sledges. At Marcoing they captured the small railway bridge before German pioneers could destroy it with a demolition charge. One of the few wireless tanks was able to transmit the news. Still the defenders melted away rather than stand and fight. The Machine Gun Corps corporal George Coppard was laboriously bringing his two Vickers guns up behind them: 'As we moved forward [towards the canal] the ground sloped slightly down; in the distance nearly a mile away I could see several tanks rolling forward steadily. There did not seem to be any organised defence . . . Some changed direction to meet isolated resistance, mostly from machine guns. One or two had come to a standstill, probably with engine trouble . . . it seemed to me that the German infantry had either fled at the apparition of the tanks or had pulled out deliberately . . .'

A tank commander who got as far as the canal recalled getting out 'to light cigarettes and in the fading light could just see the outlines of Cambrai. A fully armed German with some sort of wound to his hand jumped out of the long grass, he kept saying malevolently "Blessé: Tank" and spitting.'

Second Lieutenant G. E. V. Thompson got to the canal at Marcoing in Baby Mine. He was 'standing outside the tank having a smoke' when 'A detachment of cavalry came along led by a Major. He wanted to know why we had stopped. I was able to offer no information as the country forward was all wooded. With this negative information he led his detachment across the bridge. Almost immediately we heard machine gun fire and back came the cavalry and they galloped back the way they had come. That was the last we saw of them. So much for the breakthrough . . .'

Major Philip Hamond was rumbling up the road to Les Rues Vertes when a 'heavy thump' announced the demolition of the steel girder bridge taking the road over the St Quentin Canal into Masnières. Hamond got out of his machine, borrowed a rifle and went with his sergeant ('Roberts, a ship's fireman from Mussel-burgh') into Les Rues Vertes on the southern side of the waterway – to find 'Slosher' Martel already there. Masnières lay just the other side. The pugnacious engineer was of the opinion that infantry could still scramble over it. According to Hamond: 'Then a most ludicrous thing happened: there was great deal of clattering, galloping and shouting and a lot of our medieval horse soldiers came charging along the street; I yelled at them that the bridge had gone but they took no notice of me and went right up to it. One MG would have wiped out the lot, and they turned about and with a very pious air trotted back the way they had come.'

More tanks arrived. Hamond confessed in his letter that he was now swigging whisky from an infantryman's water bottle. A tank began to cross with infantry clinging to it. The southern end began to buckle. Both bridge and thirty-ton Mark IV fell into the water.* A cloud of steam erupted. There followed a curious episode famous in Tank Corps legend in which the crew of F.22 Flying Fox II evacuated through the top hatch during which the commander's wig came off and floated down the stream.

Hamond's 'medieval horse soldiers' were an advance patrol of the great mass of horsemen, five divisions, two of which were coming up uncertainly behind, picking their way through the sundered wire in columns which stretched back as as far as Villers-Plouich and Gouzeaucourt. A squadron of 7/Dragoon Guards got into Marcoing around 2.00 p.m. and crossed the St Quentin Canal on the little road bridge. At Les Rues Vertes, B Squadron of the Fort Garry Horse got across the water barrier into Masnières via a wooden footbridge pointed out by local inhabitants.

There was a new sight – people coming forward. They were clearly not soldiers but men, women, some with babies in perambulators, some driving small flocks of animals. A wide-eyed little girl in a woolly hat was snatched up by a grinning Tommy. Someone managed to take a photograph. Aimée Gaillarde of Masnières would be famous. Hamond was smothered in kisses from older girls and disagreeably whiskery old men. 'I returned in triumph with two cows, a bantam cock and two rabbits,' he informed his wife. 'I ate the cock – I don't know what happened to the rabbits.' The battalion would hold on to the cows for months to come. They were good milkers.

'Several hundred civilians and seventeen cows have been recovered

---

* According to a forgiving William Watson, the intention was deliberately to 'put the tank in the canal so that another might drive over it'.

from the captured villages,' wrote a staff officer that night.* His diary
entry recorded what he knew:

> The Boche do not seem to have had time to blow up the bridges
> . . . the cavalry are through the gap but as far as I can gather
> they do not seem to be acting with quite enough vigour. The
> Army Commander has apparently had to hustle Genl. Kava-
> nagh over the telephone but this is just gossip.†
>
> Flesquières has rather held up the centre of the advance . . .
> Intelligence say the Germans cannot possibly get more than one
> division to Cambrai tomorrow so there is an excellent chance
> of our getting there . . .
>
> There are rumours everywhere, that two battalions in
> VI Corps took their objectives with four casualties between
> them, that a tank captured an entire [heavy gun] battery . . .
> that Pétain has been lurking somewhere about . . . also the
> C-in-C.

Haig, in fact, had spent the morning at Advanced GHQ at Bavin-
court, twenty-seven miles to the north, near Arras. In the afternoon
he went to Third Army at Albert. Its commander, Julian Byng, had
little practically to do; the battle was in the hands of the corps commanders now. The C-in-C's diary entry that night would be as im-
passive as a holiday postcard: 'Operations were very successful and
our casualties remarkably small. The attack was launched at 6:20am.
There was no artillery bombardment previous to this hour but the
infantry were covered by a number of Tanks which cut lanes through
the wire . . . The 51st Division was checked in front of Flesquières . . .'

In the IV Corps sector on the far left of the attack front the bridge
carrying the road to Cambrai over the flanking Canal du Nord had
been demolished long before tanks could get there. Then the capture
of Graincourt seemed to open the way to the most critical objective
of the day – Bourlon. But the troops were exhausted, the tanks had

---

* The refugees were taken to Péronne. General Byng would receive a letter, published
later as part of routine orders, from MM Mauruy, Delacourt, Lefèbre and Machet as the
heads of their families in the name of the inhabitants of Masnières thanking the British
Army for their 'deliverance from the hands of the barbarian'.

† The Cavalry Corps commander. According to the *Official History*: 'A number of the
senior [cavalry] officers remembered how vulnerable were bodies of horse to machine-
guns and with some reason were more fearful of wire than ever they were in the hunting
field.'

been running for six hours, their fuel and ammunition exhausted. *There was no reserve*. The 1st Cavalry Division, supposed to clatter into the wood with sword and lance, had not even left its start line (it was intended to go forward in the centre then wheel to the north-east towards Bourlon). Fontaine, a suburban outpost of Cambrai at the base of the Bourlon heights, was taken by four tanks and small parties of Highland infantry.

Then, at around 11.15 a.m., 1st Tank Brigade HQ received a message with the first information derived from interrogated prisoners. Corps intelligence had alarming news: 'Warning of our attack was conveyed to the Germans as a result of a raid by them. It is therefore possible that opposition may be encountered . . .'

Opposition – real opposition – was already being encountered and its tenaciousness had been directly inspired by a warning. In the centre before Flesquières it was having immediate results. The rambling village was marked by a brick-built château and a sugar-beet factory on the northern outskirts – loopholed, wired and bulwarked with concrete. As far as the British were concerned it was on the reverse slope of a lateral ridge; indeed, that was why German engineers had incorporated it into the rear battle zone. There were still some civilian inhabitants, some of whom had been compelled to labour in building its defences. The village and the ridge had been pounded in the opening artillery bombardment and shot up by low-flying RFC pilots early in the morning. But neither the shelling nor the airmen had substantially damaged the three batteries of Model '06 7.7-cm field guns plus several howitzers whose assigned role was to support five miles of front between Havrincourt and La Vacquerie to the south. The defensive scheme was exactly as the Petrograd report of the spring had described: guns in pits with alert crews close by. Except the defenders had had months to hone their skills.

D Battalion and two companies of E Battalion were coming straight for them. The village's garrison, elements of the 84th Infantry Regiment commanded by a Maj. Hofmeister, was part of the 54th Division, under the overall command of a Lieutenant-General Freiherr von Watter. His brother had encountered the English *Sturmwagen* on the Somme. A sibling exchange of information had alerted them both to danger ahead. Von Watter had devised crash drills to get guns rapidly into position to engage tanks over open sights. The division's gunners had flayed the feeble French *artillerie d'assaut* at their inauspicious debut at Berry-au-Bac six months before.

According to a German account published in 1937, von Watter's gunners were able to hit a moving target at 500 metres with the first round and a target at a 1000 metres in three. The guns were kept in reinforced pits burrowed under houses on the reverse slope, ready to be manhandled into firing position should an attack come over the ridge.

It was coincidentally a trench raid by the 54th Division which had snatched the sergeant and five Irish soldiers from the outpost line before Havrincourt early on the morning of the 18th. They had been decanted to Caudry where their interrogation had produced results.* At midday on Sunday the 18th, the 54th Division was alerted to the possibility of an attack around Cambrai. An eavesdropping operation on the Arras sector had also picked up a snatch of revealing telephone conversation which was sent to 2nd Army Headquarters.† The new intelligence reached Caudry Gruppe HQ late on the evening of 19th, with an intimation that an enemy attack on Havrincourt could be expected imminently, 'possibly with tanks'. The alert went out across the front. Hauptmann Richard Flashar, commander of No. 5 fighter squadron on a fogbound aerodrome five miles to the south-east, got a clear enough warning late that night:

> At 11.00pm the telephone near my bed rang. In the neighbourhood west of Cambrai the British were expected to make a big attack the following morning; the flight was to stand to and be ready to take to the air from 7.00am under orders from Army HQ.
>
> How frequently had such alarming reports reached us . . . Cambrai was a quiet part of the front. Heavy artillery fire the following morning wakened me from my sleep . . . the tele-

---

* Byng commented a year afterwards, 'luckily they were rather stupid and I doubt if they could have told the enemy anything'. General Percy Hobart's *History of Cambrai*, compiled in the early 1930s, states 'one [unnamed] prisoner said that he had seen a camouflaged tank in Metz-en-Couture and another that he had seen two in Havrincourt Wood'.

† Via an earth-grounded field telephone line 'which can be heard for voice up to 600 yards and buzzer up to 1,000 yards' according to a 1916 intelligence report by Walter Kirke; 'the danger is now understood and the remedy known,' he wrote, 'but . . . our troops are too confiding in this respect'.

phone keeps going – tanks at the front, airmen over the trenches! We must keep calm.

The 54th Division received the warning and had acted on it. Through the night of 19–20 November they had scrambled to bolster their defences. Flesquières' garrison had been reinforced by another field-gun battery which had come straight off the train from the eastern front. Emergency ammunition scales had been issued. In the centre of III Corps' attack front there were now three field-gun batteries, at least two of which were manned by crews trained to face tanks. They were sited at the eastern and western ends and in the centre of the village, their positions masked by the reverse slope.

At 6.20 the ridge had been hit by smoke and high explosive. Then the shells moved on, the smoke cloud dispersed. It was clear to the defenders what was coming next.

The 51st (Highland) Division with the first-wave tanks went forward at 6.20 a.m., machines and infantry configured in Harper's revised tactical scheme. To begin with it was easy going. The outpost line had been abandoned. On the first line 'old men with beards and immature youths' came out of their trenches almost without firing a shot. By Zero plus 135 minutes the leading tanks were in a position called the Grand Ravin, hardly a grand canyon but a 'large field drain nowhere more than six or seven feet wide' running laterally on the axis of advance. This was the way the 1st Cavalry Division was to come before wheeling northwards in its planned flanking move towards Bourlon. On the left flank of the ravine the infantry of 6th Division had actually outrun their tanks. The Highlanders, in contrast, walking forward in their 'waves', had been left behind. The tanks were early. The barrage was not timed to lift forward for another hour.

A halt ensued in the ravine to sort everything out. The infantry caught up and set to siting machine guns and dispersing defensive detachments. Tank crews switched off their engines and scrambled thankfully out of their vehicles to smoke or urinate and do other things that soldiers do. 'Élan was discarded, that irresistible urge to venture further was lost,' wrote a tank commander who saw it for himself.

One account states: 'Looting . . . slowed the infantry up seriously

. . . I met a sergeant of the Argylls who had collected eighteen watches and twenty-four gold rings by the time he had got to the Grand Ravine. The tanks too indulged in a fair amount of looting . . . and a very brisk trade was done in Mauser pistols, Zeiss field glasses and breakfasts . . .' (wristwatches were reportedly being knocked out that night at fifty centimes apiece).

One tank commander who had gone off for a scout round returned to find his tank empty, apart from the driver, one Cpl Hoggard. Expected back shortly, his crew 'trickled back in ones and twos laden with the most amazing collection of loot I have ever seen,' he recalled; 'a particularly tough little Scots Lance-Corporal came back with a frying pan of sausages . . .'.

The 51st Division's advance was renewed at 8.55. The infantry were gathered in from their section posts. The looting went on – cigars, soda water, schnapps, greatcoats, violins. It all took time. The tanks were nosing ahead, some themselves laden with booty. The Highlanders came behind, plodding as if they were following Somme-like in the wake of a creeping artillery barrage. They were falling behind. In some places defending machine-gunners held their fire until the tanks had passed, then opened up on the flesh and blood waves (an intelligence officer who examined the battlefield after-wards, however, could only find three small heaps of machine-gun cartridge cases). The 'gaps' in the wire became indistinguishable. The tanks were through the support system – but not the infantry.

The headquarters of Maj. Hofmeister, the German officer in com-mand of the defence of Flesquières, were located in a blockhouse in the support line east and in front of the village. After the midnight warning he brought forward two infantry battalions, the first under the command of one Hauptmann Willie. What he saw in the first light of day was alarming. English 'tanks' seemed to be crossing the wire and trenches of the first line with ease. He urgently requested reinforcements. Then news arrived that the battalion on their flank in the support line had been overrun. Hauptmann Willie telephoned the regimental HQ: 'The battalion has been cut off. No trace of counter-attack can be seen. But we hear clearly the shouting and orders being given by the British . . . All documents are being destroyed. Now a tank is rolling over the top of the battalion mess, which is separated from our dugout by a wooden wall . . . British infantry are attacking the trenches to our right, passing barely twenty yards away . . . Our position is desperate . . .'

The unfortunate Willie and his men were soon captured in the overall rout. But behind the support line, in the village itself, two battalions of the 27th Reserve Infantry Regiment under the command of a Maj. Krebs had been moved up from the rear area. They reached the village at around 8.00 a.m. Together Krebs and Maj. Hofmeister put together a plan of defence against the tanks that had seemingly floated with such ease over the forward battle zone. The 2nd Company, 108 Field Artillery Regiment, was ordered to get its guns into the open and aim them towards the top of the ridge from 'where the attack would come'. The move took place, according to German sources, 'Between 9:30am and 10:00, while the British 51st Division was taking an hour's rest, and at a time when the British artillery barrage had lifted to attack targets further behind.'

Minutes later, just after 10.00 a.m., the lead tanks of D and E Battalions arrived at the foot of the slope. In bottom gear they began to climb. The infantry were far behind,* the barrage far ahead. One by one the tanks crested Flesquières Ridge. A commander recalled:

'It was apparent that the tanks on the immediate right were running into trouble as first one and then another stopped, two more burst into flames and the crew of yet another could be seen evacuating in a hurry. It was not possible to see what was doing the damage, nor did anyone want to find out, particularly – in fact self-preservation inclined one to be steadily left-handed . . .'

Tank D.51 Deborah was one of the last to get to the bottom of the ridge. Frank Heap, the mild-looking businessman's son from Blackpool, squinted through the vision pinhole. Tanks were burning. Muzzle flashes bloomed from the village, a long and seemingly intact wall of low brick buildings 300 yards ahead. Bullets and shell fragments pinged on the tank's hide, blue light crackling inside as they struck. The machine stank of cordite, burning paint, petrol and sweat. They got over the ridge more or less intact. Heap ordered a shallow turn, heading for what looked like a barricaded entrance strung with bales of uncut wire at the north-eastern end of the village on the

---

* At least 150–200 yards behind as the tanks started going up the hill, so Elles told the Official Historian, adding: 'I know, I saw them.'

road towards Cautaing, a position marked on the trench map as Cemetery Alley. Where were the infantry?

The war diary of E Battalion, operating on D Battalion's right, described the shambles on the ridge in a commander's report:

> Tanks were all over the place, some with noses up, some afire, but all motionless. At the time we hardly realised what had happened, however we spotted the offending trench packed with Huns and their fire seemed concentrated on our tank . . . about twenty yards into the wire we received a direct hit which . . . wounded everyone except the driver and myself but left the engine still running. I ordered my driver to reverse out of the wire. We reached the fringe when the engine petered out . . . the carburettor was pierced by a splinter. There was nothing to do but evacuate, which we did one by one, carrying the wounded back . . .

Captain 'Jake' Wilson, whose petrol had been mysteriously 'flogged' on the eve of battle, had to abandon his tank during the break-in when the engine at last 'conked out with water in the jets'. He boarded another vehicle in the section, commanded by Lt George Parsons, and crossed the Hindenburg Line forward positions with comparative ease. They were trying to work round to the east of Flesquières:

> Climbing the slight slope to the ridge beyond was a piece of cake, but . . . when we showed our noses over the top . . . we got two direct hits in as many minutes, the first smashed the left track causing us to swing to the right to receive a broadside from the second. We had a drill for 'evacuating tank' if hit, which we put into action successfully, leaving only the driver and myself to receive the second one from which I escaped, but the driver, a young Scotsman, regrettably perished.

Wilson was badly wounded in the face. He got into a shell hole, did what he could with a field dressing, swigged rum from his water bottle and passed out. He woke up in hospital. George Parsons survived to go into action again the next day.

A defender of Flesquières, an artilleryman, left this stark account: 'The first tank arrived . . . we fire . . . A column of smoke and fire came out of the monster. Two of our men ran towards the tank and reported that everybody in there was half-cremated . . .'

Six tanks from D Battalion were knocked out in the space of ten minutes. Several simply ran out of petrol, then were hit. Two more Mark IVs blew up as they tried to drive round the western flank. On one account: 'They lay there . . . in a crescent, some with enormous holes blown in their sides and fronts. One or two were a shapeless mass of metal.' Captain Browne recorded the means of summary execution: 'A shell came through the cab, took off the driver's head and flung it on the knees [of the section commander] at the brakes, killed or wounded the two right-hand gunners and passed out at the stern without exploding.'

Heap and his crew were still in the fight. They clanked on, through a barricade, into the main street. His medal citation impassively relates what happened:

> Awarded MC. In Cambrai operations near Flesquières on 20 November 1917, he fought his tank with great gallantry and skill, leading the infantry on to five objectives. He proceeded through the village and engaged a battery of enemy field guns from which his tank received five direct hits, killing four of his crew. Although then behind German lines he collected the remainder . . . and conducted them in good order back to our own lines in spite of heavy machine gun and sniper's fire.

The history of D Battalion records: 'Only one tank succeeded in going through the village and this tank was knocked out at the eastern edge immediately it emerged from the shelter of the houses.' Another tank got as far as the château. Its commander recalled: 'It was tremendously satisfactory after seeing two years of nothing but ruins to shoot at those wide glass windows . . .'

'Uncle' Harper got the blame for the disaster* – from the tank

---

* Harper died in a car crash, aged fifty-seven, in 1922. In fact, in his immediate postwar report Baker-Carr described infantry–tank cooperation on the way to Flesquières as 'satisfactory' and the operation of the wire crushers ahead of the main body as 'excellent'. Much later analysis of the debacle on the ridge ascribes the bulk of the blame to individual tank commanders, one historian concluding thus: 'On the right a section of six tanks of E Battalion went ahead in a formation prescribed neither by Fuller nor Harper. For reasons never explained it went up in line ahead. As it breasted the curve of the slope each tank was silhouetted against the sky. The German field battery to the east of the village destroyed them one by one at 500 yards' range before they could enter the wire. In no way could the infantry have averted this disaster although the tanks themselves might, for, had they been in line abreast some of their 6-pounders might have destroyed the battery at such short range.'

men at least. Criticized in gentlemanly enough tones in immediate postwar accounts, he was excoriated in later published memoirs by Baker-Carr and by Fuller, who never deviated from his line that tanks could not operate without infantry. Harper's blunder was to detach one from the other. What had happened to the 51st Division? Just 'four or five machine guns' (a tank man's disparaging verdict, but he was under armour) had held them up when they renewed the advance after the fatal distractions in the Grand Ravin.

When the survivors, detachments of Black Watch, Argylls and the Gordons, got to the village the wire was intact and the tanks supposed to have crushed it lay smashed on the ridge. The unsubdued château at the south-eastern end was spitting machine-gun fire. A break-in was impossible. General Harper, whose HQ at Metz was seven miles away, held back from committing his small reserve which was meant to pass through Flesquières later that day.

William Watson followed his tank company on foot to find Highlanders in the Grand Ravin 'all smoking cigars.' He got further forward to hear of the hold-up at Flesquières and a rumour that one of his section commanders had been killed. The scene when he got to the outskirts of the village spoke of some greater catastrophe – the brick ramparts 'surrounded by derelict tanks like a boar at bay with dead hounds'.

Years later Horace Birks recalled his trek over the same route: 'We went up to Flesquières – there we prowled up and down, the infantry had been left behind. I think they were as astonished as everybody. It was the forty minute halt that did it . . . I was getting short of petrol. I'd been hit by splash in the back. I had six crew injured. So I started to go back. I ran into the CO, the first I'd seen of him for some time and Col. Kyngdon told me to go back to Trescault – and that was the end of Cambrai for me.'

Seven tanks that had rallied back at the Grand Ravin were ordered to make another attempt on the ridge from the east late that afternoon. Six of them managed to do so and actually drove through the village as darkness gathered. The defenders this time simply took shelter in their dugouts. By the time the infantry arrived the tanks had gone. Communications broke down. 'Pigeons were half trained and felt the effects of the weather,' commented the *Official History* feebly on this episode; 'it was afterwards reported that insufficient use was made of the wireless'.

The short November day was fading. The Germans evacuated Flesquières that night. Their position was untenable – the tide of the British advance had swept round its flanks at Havrincourt and Nine Wood. The village was entered the next morning by Scottish troops who buried dead tank crews in shallow graves where they found them (they were later retrieved and taken to pre-allotted burial sites).

Four charred bodies were splayed round a wrecked female tank on its own halfway down the main street. It was D.51 Deborah. They were buried in the garden of the Guidez family's modest house on the main street near the *Calvaire*. The hulk of Deborah herself would later be moved to the far end of the village before being buried.

Of the thirty-nine tanks of the 1st Tank Brigade destroyed by enemy action most were in or on the approaches to Flesquières. Crews stumbled back on foot to the Grand Ravin, dragging their wounded with them. One survivor estimated that 60 per cent of a particular company were casualties, a third of whom had burned to death. He gave thanks that some of them might have been already dead when the petrol tank ignited.

The cavalry had shown up at the Grand Ravin. The message had been passed at 11.35 to 1st Cavalry Division headquarters that 'Flesquières had been captured'. Now it would seem the way was blocked. The situation on the ridge was 'in doubt'. A Scottish soldier remembered glancing back to his own front line departed a few hours before to see what seemed to be thousands of horsemen wheeling in a khaki-clad mass. A detachment came clattering up under cover of the railway embankment. 'The officer asked a lot of questions, before they all turned about and merely rode back the way they had come.'

Daylight was fading. The horsemen's chance was expiring with it.

At Marcoing the detachment that 2/Lt Thompson had seen clatter into the village had indeed got across the canal only to be caught in the flank by machine guns. They had very smartly turned round. Breaking out of Masnières, the little force of Canadian cavalry that had crossed via the footbridge had got into the German gun line which they attacked 'at the gallop'. They then found themselves cut off and surrounded. Their commander was killed.

Lieutenant H. Strachan took over. There was nothing they could do. In his words, he ordered 'abandon horses . . . all the animals except five being wounded'. It was pretty unsentimental. 'The horses were stampeded in order to attract the attention of the machine guns.' The survivors filtered back to the canal in darkness with a number of prisoners persuaded at sword point to come with them.

There were Tank Corps prisoners. *The Times* would tell a morale-boosting story picked up in Amsterdam from a Cologne newspaper of a 'British tank sergeant who had just been captured, brought in a small motor-car to a country place to be examined. Children stand round the cottage into which he has disappeared. When the prisoner reappeared, young and old pressed bonbons, chocolate, bread and cold meat into his hands . . . His complexion, the look in his eyes and his bearing revealed a healthy youth, whose nerves had withstood, wholly unimpaired, the furious day.'

By 4.00 p.m. 'one of the most astonishing battles in all history had been won,' so Fuller wrote in 1920, 'and as far as the Tank Corps was concerned was tactically finished, for no reserves existing, it was not possible to do more than rally the very weary crews, select the fittest and patch up composite companies to contest an attack on the morrow'.

But the news filtering back far into the rear area was optimistic. Civilian refugees were being brought through the lines, something practically unheard of before. Huge columns of prisoners trudged towards the cages. Something astonishing had indeed happened. That night 'Albert was *en fête*,' recorded Evan Charteris. 'French and British flags made a feeble attempt at display. Children at the school were told what had happened and sang the Marseillaise and God Save the King . . .'. The jubilation would flash across the Channel the next day.

There were indications too, however, that something had already gone badly wrong on the ridge. That it must have an unusual cause suited the tank true-believers and would come to suit both GHQ and some latter German myth makers. A curious legend sprang up – of a 'lone gunner' who had single-handedly destroyed sixteen tanks at Flesquières before himself being killed. It was the talk of the Tank Corps survivors that night and would be picked over for years to come. Haig mentions it at length in his diary entry for 22 November, gleaned, he says, from the report of an 'eyewitness':* 'On the appearance of the first Tank all the personnel of a German battery (which was in a kind of chalk pit) fled. One officer, however, was able to collect a few men and with them worked a gun and from his concealed position knocked out Tank after Tank to the number of eight or nine. The officer was then killed.'

The C-in-C further massaged the myth with his 'Cambrai Dispatch' of February 1918 which cited: 'The great bravery of this officer [which had] aroused the admiration of all ranks.'† There were disparate stories of a 'tall German officer wearing an Iron Cross' found dead by his gun by the château wall, and of how a Tank Corps officer had silenced the crew with a dismounted Lewis gun.

Weimar-era historians did not make much of the defence of Flesquières. But those who came after did.‡ The gunner now had a name. An account in a German military journal of 1937 named him as 'Unteroffizier [2/Lt] Theodor Kruger' of the 108th Field Artillery Regiment. The Bürgermeister of Cologne erected a statue of Kruger trampling a stylized St George and the dragon a year later amid Nazi pomp.

The heroic NCO fitted National Socialist ideology. The German commanders in their postwar memoirs blamed 'the tanks' for defeat in the field. But the English *Sturmwagen* could be stopped by brave German soldiers. Flesquières proved it. It was not the tanks that had humbled the German army. It was the traitors at home.

---

* It was a Capt. Geoffrey Dugdale, intelligence officer with 60th Brigade, who wrote in a postwar memoir: 'After lunch I went for a tour of inspection with Whittingham [his batman]. The first thing we came to was a German field battery, every gun out of action with the exception of one. By this was lying a single German officer quite dead, in front of him were five tanks . . . a brave man.'

† This did not go down at all well with the Tank Corps. According to Christopher Baker-Carr, 'we all regarded [it] as a direct commendation to others to go and do likewise'. Haig seemed deeply affected by the affair, and the question mark it raised over tanks' vulnerability to a determined defence. 'Our experience has shown that [means of] defeating tank attacks has already been found,' he told Robertson on 23 November.

‡ 'Hotblack, our military attaché in Berlin for four years, made exhaustive enquiries about this supposed incident and was never able to substantiate any of it,' according to Hugh Elles, writing in 1944. 'I met the [German] official historian in Potsdam in February 1939 and he was unable to throw any light at all.' The legend was perpetuated into the Second World War and beyond. In 1940 the artist Franz Radziwill painted a depiction of the tank versus field-gun duel at Cambrai for the officers' mess of the Wehrmacht antitank school at Lubeck, and the image was repeated on a carpet for Hitler's Reichschancellery. Both disappeared at the end of the war. The Bundeswehr's Unteroffizier Krüger barracks in Kusel (Rhineland) were thus named in 1966.

40

It had all been a bit of a triumph. The bulge on the map was astonishing. The enemy wire 'had been dragged about like old curtains'. More than 100 guns and 8000 prisoners had been taken. Major D. N. Wimberley described them: 'A miserable looking lot, but so were we, either dirty, consumptive and small or grossly fat, some of them very young, most of them middle-aged with cartoonist's spectacles. They were a Landsturm division of "duds," poor devils.'

That, in a sense, was the problem. John Charteris, Haig's intelligence chief, had assured him on the eve of battle that the enemy had no reserves before Byng's army. The defenders were Landwehr and reserve divisions, or men brought to the 'Flanders sanatorium' to recuperate amidst the *gemütlich* comforts of the Siegfried position after the shell-hole horrors of the north. The whole huge gamble – for that is what it was – had to obtain a decisive result before the defensive line coagulated as the defenders' reserves were brought in. They would not be fat, bespectacled duds.

Third Army's own infantry reserve was minimal. Its three divisions had had no training for operations with tanks. Indeed, there were no tanks yet uncommitted. In his Haig-bashing book, *The Real War*, published in 1930, Basil Liddell Hart told the story with relish of the French general Franchet d'Espérey visiting the Albert HQ to enquire how the battle was faring. '"And where are your reserves?" he asked. "Mon Général, we have none." The French commander exclaimed, "Mon Dieu," turned on his heels and fled.'

German reinforcements were moved rapidly by rail from the flanks, from the trench garrisons facing Arras and St Quentin – that move could be predicted. But tougher, battle-hardened troops were on their way, whole divisions of them. That had apparently not been foreseen. Many years later Gen. Sir James Marshall-Cornwall, who in November 1917 had been a thirty-year-old intelligence officer at

GHQ, told Haig's biographer that 'he became aware *before* the battle that the Germans were moving three divisions to the area, showing they had wind of it'. He identified them – straight off the train. They had come from Russia. Very soon they could be in the line. Charteris said it was a bluff. It was not to be mentioned again.

'There is no doubt that when Haig made the fatal decision to press the attack on Bourlon after 21 November,' wrote John Terraine, 'the reason was the belief that the Germans were weak and that victory was in easy reach. It was this that caused him to allow the battle to take a course which was not only quite contrary to his original intention, but also nearly produced a disaster . . .'

Which is what happened. There was another reason for going on. After a year of gloom, after the year of Passchendaele, the coup of 20 November seemed to redress everything. John Charteris wrote in his diary on the 21st, 'We held up all the press messages yesterday so as to keep the Germans in the dark . . . Today's operations are vital. If we get Bourlon and the wood we are well placed.'

The embargo was lifted on the second day. The official dispatch from GHQ timed at 12.15 a.m. on the 21st was released by the Press Bureau in time for the evenings. Chief-subs exploded in an orgy of exultant headlines as they laid out the next morning's front pages. That afternoon the bells of Southwark Cathedral started to ring out unheralded.

Perhaps it was the bishop's fault, perhaps it was an excitable journalist, but soon after the release of the dispatch *The Times* religious correspondent conveyed the news to the Bishop of London, at that moment presiding over the Diocesan Conference at Church House, Westminster. The assembly immediately rose to sing the national anthem. The archdeacon of St Paul's and the Bishop of London proposed a general pealing, 'spreading throughout the country'. Lord Derby, Secretary of State for War, thought it better to wait until 'more details of prisoners and guns taken' were at hand.

The Thursday morning headlines were exultant: 'Splendid News From Haig', said the *Sketch*; 'Haig's New Blow' (*The Times*); 'Thousands in Pursuit – Tanks Shock to Huns', said the *Daily Telegraph*. All this and bells booming with joy. It was the sound of victory. Only the very tactically astute would have noticed with any foreboding the curt line in the official dispatch that mentioned 'fierce fighting around Flesquières'.

There were scenes in London like those of August 1914. Plaudits poured in for the C-in-C. Sir Julian Byng became a laurel-garlanded hero. His weary troops were the 'Byng-Boys,'* and Hugh Elles a rollicking 'admiral' who had invoked Horatio Nelson in an eve-of-battle message: 'England expects every tank to do its damnedest.' He most certainly had not done so and he squirmed with embarrassment every time it was mentioned (the phrase would pursue him all his life – he called it 'a vulgar and impertinent travesty'). The 1000-yard trundle in Hilda was fabulous of course. It is what everyone remembered. According to Horace Birks: 'Elles made his reputation by going into action personally at Cambrai. He was the father figure, God the father – and Fuller was God the son. He had a great sense of humour, very quiet – and like all sappers queer in some ways. His hat, for example: he usually had a couple of fishing flies in it. Later on he got lazy . . .'

The rugged general's wife and young daughters, Gill and Claude, featured in the Christmas edition of *The Tatler*. His likeness appeared in an advertisement for shaving cream.

The cavalry had achieved nothing, but how could the battle stop now?

On the second day a renewed attempt to gain a wider infantry bridgehead at Masnières was beaten back with heavy losses. A crazy attempt to drive six lorries loaded with fuel and ammunition through to Marcoing by road got as far as Ribecourt. On the left flank, IV Corps tried again to take Fontaine with tanks of the 2nd Brigade. Captain Hickey and his section came up from the south in Hadrian from an assembly point at the Flesquières beetroot factory, 'zig-zagging' across the broad valley to see the objective 'set serenely on a slight rise . . . with its peaceful roofs and spire silhouetted against the evening sky'. Then the Auto-vac fuel pump failed. The tank came to a dead stop. 'Automatically I tightened my tin hat and adjusted my metal mask.'† The second driver fixed the fuel supply. Hadrian started moving again.

---

* *The Bing Boys are Here* was the musical comedy hit of 1916. Gen. Sir Julian Byng's Canadian Corps had already gathered the popular title.

† The anti-'splash chain-mail' veil issued to all tank crews since the Somme, meant to protect eyes and face. Hickey also asked his parents to send a patent sorbo rubber helmet liner, available from Harrods.

The tanks went into Fontaine-Notre-Dame as darkness fell on the 21st with the infantry straggling far behind. The village seemed empty. H Battalion's surviving vehicles were almost out of ammunition, low on fuel and with engines running hot 'because of thin oil' (afterwards everyone blamed the grade of Mobiloil issued as not up to it).

The commander of Hermosa had seen some sort of light in the otherwise dark main street. Lieutenant George Keay got out of the tank and entered a house with his corporal to be embraced and kissed by its civilian inhabitants, two jubilant Frenchmen. An old lady pressed money from her purse into their hands. They accepted coffee. The infantry at last arrived and set up some sort of defence. The tanks withdrew on a gruelling four-hour journey back to their rallying point. A mile to the south, in open ground around the village of Cantaing, improvised cooperation between tanks and cavalry proved disastrous whenever Mr Maxim's invention made its appearance.

News of Fontaine's precarious capture reached Third Army HQ at 7.15 p.m. The Germans must be reinforcing, that was a given. The cavalry route across the canal was blocked. The three divisions of V Corps held in reserve were still uncommitted. The decision hung in the air. Go on for Bourlon or shut the offensive down?

On the morning of the 22nd, the C-in-C, accompanied by Richard Butler and Maj.-Gen. R. L. Mullens, commander of the 1st Cavalry Division, rode out towards Flesquières to see the terrain for himself. Tanks still smouldered on the ridge.

As they cantered across the downs, German reinforcements brought in by train from the Arras front were fighting their way back into Fontaine 'regardless of loss'. The tanks had withdrawn as per orders. The depleted Highlanders were evicted by 2.30 p.m. That afternoon Haig took tea with Julian Byng at Albert, and reviewed IV Corps plans still in the making to keep pushing up the Cambrai road, retake Fontaine in a renewed tank-led move from the south, and finally capture Bourlon. The reserve would be committed. The affair at the canal crossings seemed over. III Corps' already stalled offensive on the right was shut down. Cavalry chargers munched oats back at their lines.

There was an unusual act of bravery that morning. Unteroffizier Fritz Leu, a (judging by his photograph) somewhat portly, mustachioed army transport driver, crept aboard an abandoned tank, F.13

Falcon. He got it going in spite of 'hearing English voices nearby'. Aided by Leut. Muller he drove it lurching off the battlefield and all the way to the marketplace of Cambrai. At least one British tank reached the fabled city.

In his immensely readable history published a year after the armistice, Williams-Ellis quoted a 'letter home from a former tank officer' describing a late-night divisional conference in some miraculously surviving salon in the otherwise ruinous Havrincourt château. General John Ponsonby, commanding 40 Division (one of the three held in reserve), looked grave: 'There were a round dozen of us at the conference, a muddy rather blear-eyed party, some in tin hats and trench coats, revolver girt – some in honorific red and gold – all with slung gas masks ... One felt uneasily conscious of forming a part of a *Graphic* picture entitled "Advanced Headquarters," or "Planning the Battle."'

Elles was part of the dramatic tableau, and so was Baker-Carr commanding 1st Tank Brigade. They pored over maps by the light of 'two guttering candles stuck into German beer bottles'. The plan of attack was agreed – the tank officer took enormous rolled-up maps to Brigade HQ established in an underground working in the Siegfried support position complete with electricity generating station, where 'a gilt clock still kept German time'. The maps were of Bourlon Wood. They would not do the Tank Corps much good.

On the 23rd, tanks from B, C and H Battalions went back in force into Fontaine. Street-fighting knocked out two-thirds of them in short order. Some managed to withdraw, one disappeared completely. Tank Corps prisoners were taken. The suburb, just two miles from Cambrai itself, seemed impassable. According to a German account, 'light anti-aircraft guns on motor lorries put five tanks out of action'.

Thirty-nine tanks attached to 40 Division (which had no previous tank cooperation training) went northwards on the same desperate morning into the rising ground of Bourlon Wood with the village itself beyond. The fighting raged until darkness. The defenders were pushed into the northern edge of the trees and the village, but artillery-led counter-attacks increased in power and tempo. Tanks blundered about in the shattered stands of trees.

George Parsons had survived the wreck of his tank on the morn-

ing of the 20th and got back to Havrincourt Wood on foot. The MO
had judged him fit to continue. The next morning he was ordered to
take over a 'good clean tank with a good crew', whose commander,
a Canadian, had been killed. In I.28 Indomitable he drove 'direct and
fast' to the new assembly area east of Flesquières where he observed
'fourteen or so tanks . . . lined up on the skyline shattered, and a lot
of corpses mostly ours'. There were orders issued that late afternoon
to attack Fontaine once again, now a place of ill repute for tanks.
When the mission was switched to Bourlon, Parsons was 'relieved'.
Early on the 23rd they set out, 'eight tanks in Indian file'; Parsons
was fifth, swinging off the Cambrai road up the little track into the
wood.

Two senior infantry officers, both 'white as a sheet', came stumbling in their direction – a third had just had his head taken off by a
shell. Men in armour and men on foot must fight as they found
themselves. There was no grand plan this time, no exquisite map and
compass predestination. The file of tanks drove on. George Parsons
recalled: 'Near the top everyone stopped. We just sat there being
mildly shelled. I don't know why but there were no orders, nobody
knew anything. I decided I wasn't going to be trapped like that. I
swung left, climbed out of the sunken road, went about two hundred
feet and faced the enemy. I drove to the top of the ridge and there
was Bourlon village. I saw nobody and only a little smoke in the
morning haze.'

He got into 'a high gear' and went forward with the Lewis guns
firing dead ahead. The borrowed tank fell into a hole. The engine
stopped. They all got out 'in single turn' through the side doors.
Parsons scrambled out of the fatal wood and headed off on foot in
the general direction of Flesquières, whence he had started. He survived to write his letter of reminiscences to 'Jake' Wilson fifty years
later. He signed off with diffident cheerfulness: 'Perhaps I'll go over
to Cambrai one of these days, rent a bicycle and have a look.'

The newspaper frenzy still raged in London. On Sunday night the
Press Bureau issued the text of the Commander-in-Chief's Special
Order of the Day: 'The capture of the important Bourlon position
yesterday crowns a most successful operation and opens the way to
a further exploitation . . .'

Early on the morning of the 27th the last of the reserves were committed – the Guards Division which attacked Fontaine with twelve tanks – and the 62nd Division which, with twenty survivors of 3rd Tank Brigade, went back into the wood. John Charteris reported: 'No change in the enemy on Cambrai battlefront since yesterday. His troops are very thin except for Bourlon.'

It had begun to snow. 'There was, of course, no opportunity for reconnaissance or even to see the ground in daylight, and no chance [for infantry commanders] to come to any understanding with the tanks with which to cooperate,' so the *Official History* comments. The fighting for Fontaine was in houses, in the railway station, in cellars. Grenades rained down from attics. Snipers were in roof gables, battle-skilled now in going for loopholes, vision slits and seams in the plating. Tanks waved their side-mounted Lewis guns like helpless penguins. Stick grenades were bundled four at a time in sandbags 'always going for the tracks'. Walter Wilson's barricade-climbing rhomboid was not made for this. Fuller's 'Training Notes' had not covered fighting in villages. (Swinton had foreseen tanks getting involved in street-fighting back at Elveden and rigged up his some-what risible wire-netting shed roof. Fuller blamed himself afterwards for not planning for it.) Captain Daniel Hickey told a story of the defenders of Fontaine physically clinging to the Lewis guns to deflect their aim, hammering on the side demanding the crew surrender. One of his section's commanders thought they were doped with Benzedrine. Truck-mounted anti-aircraft guns ('K-Flak') firing on a flat trajectory proved just as dangerous as they had done the day before. Hauptmann Hoehner and Leut. Zoren shot up seven tanks of B Company, one blew up, three escaped but the engines seized. Three got back to Marcoing.

The German official communiqué stated: 'The enemy expended his forces in many fruitless assaults . . . Before Fontaine alone thirty tanks are lying shot to pieces, which gives a picture of the forces employed by the enemy . . .' Army photographers prowled the battle-field afterwards to make a detailed record of *Die Tankschlacht bei Cambrai* for good operational reasons. The images of incinerated tank crews sprawled round the doors of their steel crematoria were too gruesome for publication.

The renewed fight for Bourlon village turned into the same fatal street-fighting, the defenders getting close in with grenades bundled

Tanks HQ became a 'must-see' attraction of the Western Front for visiting dignitaries. King George V and Queen Mary visited in summer 1917.

A month later, the tanks were sent to Flanders – to 'drown in a morass'.

Lt Daniel Hickey (*left*) wrote tellingly of the ghastliness of it all in a book published after the war; he told the story of how the South African-born Capt. Clement Robertson (*above*) won a posthumous VC picking his way with an ashplant stick through the mud in front of his section of tanks.

British tanks had meanwhile fallen intact into German hands. Daubed with iron crosses, they would later be turned back on their original owners.

After the Flanders fiasco, there came a second chance in November 1917 – a mass attack over unshelled ground in the direction of the French town of Cambrai. Log bundles called fascines would be used for trench crossing.

At first the plan went brilliantly, as tanks led infantry through the defences into intact villages beyond. Shown here: captured German machine gunners.

The highlanders of the 51st Division (seen here in Flesquières on the morning of 21 November) proved ferocious in combat, but their commander had interfered fatally with the tactical plan.

When communications broke down, pigeons were blamed for being 'young and untrained'.

Opposite Hugh Elles's gesture leading the Cambrai attack in person reaped a harvest of patriotic praise, and secured his wife and daughters a page in *The Tatler* and this strange depiction (by the young cartoonist David Langdon) (*top*) of the armoured commander in an advertisement for shaving foam. The Nelsonian quote was a Fleet Street invention; Elles hated it. Nevertheless the spirit of the Tank Corps was by now indomitable, as expressed in this Christmas card (*right*). The hardest test, the great retreat of March 1918, was yet to come.

Preparatory to the attack before Cambrai, the Commander of the Tank Corps signalled his Captains, "England expects every Tank this day to do its damnedest!"

THE GREATEST SPECTACLE
THE WORLD HAS EVER SEEN
FOR THE GREATEST NEED
THE WORLD HAS EVER KNOWN

BRITISH TANK "BRITANNIA" IN ACTION

GRAND CENTRAL PALACE

HERO LAND

NOV. 24TH TO DEC. 12TH

ADMISSION 50¢

Top Tanks made good propaganda, exploited to the full by the British once America was in the war. In November 1917 the 'Hero Land' pageant opened in Manhattan and the Mk IV Britannia clanked down Broadway.

A cavalryman, Capt George S. Patton (*above*), set up the US Light Tank School in France; he liked the little Renault because it 'bucked and reared like a horse'.

The Tank Corps commander in France, Col. Samuel D. Rockenbach (*right*), meanwhile was more an administrator than a combat soldier.

The British tank force's apotheosis came east of Amiens on 8 August 1918 when almost five hundred new Mk V's and faster-moving Whippets outfought and outmanoeuvred the German defenders. After that the Germans never stopped retreating, although they put up stiff resistance against tanks. Here, Mk V's equipped with trench-crossing cribs prepare to storm the Siegfried (Hindenburg) position, September 1918. Traditionalists loathed the Tank Corps' apparent lack of discipline: note the officers' pipes and crew members' hands-in-pocket casualness. By now Winston Churchill was back in government as Minister of Munitions (here (*right*) inspecting Mk V's, autumn 1918), pressing for ever more tanks against continued War Office indifference.

The Germans produced only a handful of the cumbersome A7V Sturmpanzer-wagen in time for the offensive of March 1918. Heavily armed, with a crew of eighteen, they had a propensity to topple over. Captured British machines were more effective.

In November 1998 a unique relic of the Great War was discovered and brought to light – tank D.51 Deborah, buried beneath a spinach plot just outside the French village of Flesquières where her young commander, 2/Lt Frank Heap (*left*), had survived the dramatic action of 20 November 1917.

A battlefield clearance team, commanded by Col. Theodore Wenger (*above*), evidently interred the hulk after the war rather than blow it up (*left*). Her discovery by the Cambrai hotelier Philippe Gorczynski was a worldwide news event.

Below After her raising to the surface, men of the Royal Tank Regiment moved her reverently to a cathedral-like barn in the little village.

together, enough to blow off a track. 'Tanks and infantry found it a network of formidable defences little damaged by shell fire,' said the *Official History*. 'Progress was blocked by strong barricades. Of the fifteen tanks engaged, five came back.'

Any pretence of continued offensive operations was abandoned by GHQ that afternoon because, as it was stated bluntly, 'Third Army's means were exhausted.' Orders were given to defensively wire the perimeter of what might still be usefully held – in Bourlon – along the Flesquières Ridge and the Masnières bridgehead. All surviving tanks were to withdraw to the rear to lick their wounds in Havrincourt Wood. Those from 1st and 3rd Brigades that could still move on their own power should get to the railway spurs to be pulled out by train. Hugh Elles came to see them off. The seventy or so surviving tanks of 2 Brigade would follow when the tracks were clear. That was the plan. The Cambrai adventure was over.

41

The Cambrai adventure was indeed over, but not for the Germans. The build-up of reinforcements was continuous, eighteen divisions facing nine. At dawn on 30 November they fell on the thinly defended salient with a surprise and with a novelty in technique that matched that shown by Third Army ten days earlier. *Stosstruppen* (stormtroops) using infiltration tactics honed in Russia broke out of a position known as the Banteux ravine – through Masnières – and along the southern flank, expanding into 'a broad torrent which submerged the villages of Gonnelieu and Villers-Guislain, swept over gun positions and headquarters and surged forward as far as Gouzeaucourt'. Fuller recalled being in his office when the 'telephone rang with the news that the Germans were advancing on Gouzeaucourt Wood; was this a joke or an actual fact?'.

Low-flying ground-attack aircraft (with armoured engines and cockpits) hit the defenders scrabbling desperately to get out. Eight thousand British troops put their hands up in the space of twenty-four hours. There were scenes of 'disorder and panic'. William Watson recorded the scene at the crossroads on the morning of the 30th, where an APM, 'a huge man with mad blue eyes', cursed at the jam of vehicles and shambling men, urging them back into the fight. 'No possible fighting man passed beyond Metz,' recorded Watson; 'my own servant, who had lost me in the crowd, was arrested as a straggler.' The northern flank was pounded with high explosive and drenched with phosgene – but not yet assaulted. According to Ernst Jünger: 'The woods of Bourlon, which were not even under direct attack as they were too heavily defended, simply vanished in a chartreuse fog of gas.'

On the night of the 4th–5th Bourlon Wood was glumly evacuated, the villages of Anneux and Cantaing to the south set ablaze, and a tenuous defence line set up on Flesquières Ridge. Weary troops brought down from Flanders replaced wearier troops in the shrinking salient. The enemy tide was lapping at the points where the tanks had assembled just over ten days before, where 'machines were mostly in pieces, fitting new parts etc. Any that could be got going were hastily put together and sent off piecemeal into the fight irrespective of units . . .' George Parsons recalled the desperation of it all:

> I got another tank, a derelict really, but it moved. I think it was warped, it had a gradual swing to the left. Every 100 yards or so I had to stop and straighten direction. I don't even know who was in the tank, I just drove towards Gouzeaucourt . . . my next memory was seeing the Guards Division counterattacking, maybe I was ordered or not. I just swung behind them. I don't remember the tank firing a shot but it may have, by this time I was an automaton. Eventually we were relieved and on foot I guess I got back to the railhead and so on to Bray-sur-Somme. My recollections are nil. It didn't seem to matter much.

Captain Hickey and the survivors of H Battalion went into Gauche Wood, a little south of Gouzeaucourt, on the morning of the 30th in company with nineteen tanks, using no plan other than 'sheer weight of metal'. He wrote: 'As the tanks started to return we went to the rallying point at Revelon Farm. There I saw one of the crew of a tank which had been blown to pieces. He had lost his reason and was running about covered with oil and bits of flesh clinging to his clothes . . .'

Hermosa, Lt Keay's tank, had survived the street-fighting at Fontaine to go into action again. She made her last fight east of Gouzeaucourt when a field gun found the range. The tank blew up and within seconds was a 'roaring furnace'. Her entire crew burned to ash.

The salient the tanks and infantry had won was now a dangerous liability. On the morning of the 3rd a general retirement was ordered to a defensive line in the old Siegfried support position (Flesquières stayed in British hands). Bourlon Wood was evacuated. Derelict tanks were to be blown up where they stood, it was ordered. Survivors of the 2nd Tank Brigade hobbled out of the line as best they could. Philip Hamond recalled: 'One tank had a chunk of shell clean through the water jacket, cylinder pistons and all, how the hell they had crept home covered with boiling water I don't know. Anyway we cut out a complete cylinder, big end, con-rod and all and she ran well on five but the oil squirted over everything . . . they simply poured more in from a drum to keep her from seizing . . . we eventually crawled into Metz . . .'

The major had a moment of minor triumph, the discovery of a consignment of abandoned Armstrong huts still in their packing crates at the railhead. Their elderly guardian had no further use for them – it 'served their owners right for running away'. Hamond had found his shelter for the winter.

Rumours of some huge disaster in the field swept London. Warned that Lloyd George was 'on the warpath', Sir Douglas Haig replied that if he had lost the Prime Minister's confidence he must go 'in the interests of the cause'. 'The attack upon DH is in full-swing,' Brig.-Gen. Charteris told his wife. 'All our information is that LG, Curzon and Churchill are out to down him, and will try to do so by attacking him through his staff.' (They did; Charteris himself was on the way out, so was Lancelot Kiggell. Richard Butler got a Corps command.)

In a politically astute move the C-in-C himself ordered the army's own enquiry into the fiasco of the Cambrai counter-attack – with a 'jury' of generals who would meet at Hesdin in January 1918. They substantially blamed the junior officers and troops for the fiasco. One red-tabbed inquisitor noted: 'The lower ranks seem to be completely at the mercy of quartermaster's rumours brought up to them by the ration carrying parties. It is not therefore to be wondered that the public at home are misinformed, not merely by the newspapers and members of parliament, but by 400,000 officers and men who have proceeded backwards and forwards over the past two months. The most prolific propagators are the wounded. Moreover they get home before the telegrams . . .'

It was the fault of the pigeons* – 'they were young and untrained, useless in fact'. Machine-gunners had shown a 'lack of discipline'. Support troops had panicked and run when they met walking wounded stumbling back from the bombardment. Correspondents

---

* But perhaps it was their overfond masters' fault. According to Norman Dillon: 'One very kindly tank commander fed his pigeon on bits of seed cake moistened with whisky and when he tried to send a pigeon off through a revolver port it just sat there. The driver started the track running but it was no good; no amount of poking would shift it. It would not leave the source of its nectar.'

had filled 'the columns of their newspapers with a torrent of rubbish'.

'The battle of Cambrai has by now come to be regarded as a German success instead of a British victory, and I cannot help thinking that we soldiers, with our extreme reticence and horror of all forms of publicity, may be somewhat to blame for the result,' despaired Maj.-Gen. Ivor Maxse, Director of Training.

The report was kept secret but rumours of its blame-the-troops findings began to leak. There was growing anger. The C-in-C's godlike status started to wobble in previously loyal sections of the press. Northcliffe began a campaign aimed against Robertson and called for 'the punishment of those culpable for Cambrai' (warning Haig privately through his secretary that the campaign could flash over against him).

Mr James Hogge MP (who had almost given the caterpillar game away in December 1915) asked sarcastically: 'Will the Right Hon. Gentleman take steps to prevent the truth being told by soldiers who return on leave from Cambrai?' Another MP declared more directly of Haig himself: 'I appeal to the Government to see whether they cannot get a man with less bombast, less press puffings, but more brains and more ability to represent our magnificent Army.'

There were sulphurous rumours of wholesale purges of the military and counter-plots against the civil state. More of the C-in-C's loyalists were culled at GHQ. The *Mail*'s target 'Wully' Robertson was prised out of the War Office in February 1918 to be replaced as CIGS by Field Marshal Sir Henry Wilson. Lord Alfred Milner would replace Lord Derby as Secretary for War. Haig survived. So did the Tank Corps. For now.

42

The Tank Corps hibernated at the Plateau railway sidings near Bray-sur-Somme. Everyone ached for leave. Philip Hamond wrote to his wife: 'My darling – I'm coming home first chance I can. We're all right out of the war for a few weeks anyhow and my Armstrong hut is very desirable, warm and dry.' He was luckier than some.

It was a bitter winter, the Seine turned to ice in the heart of Paris and, further afield, snow fell in Florida. In his seasonal message the Kaiser ordered his troops to go 'Forward with God to fresh deeds and Victory'. His cousin, King George V, expressed his unshakeable belief in the same thing. The Western Front congealed in frozen squalor. RAMC doctors had already reported the first cases of a mysterious pulmonary infection at the sprawling base camp on the coast at Etaples. MOs called it 'Pyrexia of Unknown Origin'. The Germans called it 'Flanders fever'.

William Watson found himself at Méaulte – busy, as he said, trying to organise the refitting of 'a job lot of fifty old tanks, starting their engines frequently to avoid the effects of frost and in making ourselves thoroughly comfortable'. He fell ill with 'trench fever' and was hospitalized with 'a succession of unlucky but cheerful flying men' at a place called Dermancourt. He clearly recovered quickly – confessing that he 'and a convalescent APM' would prowl the newly arrived hospital trains – looking for nurses. Both decided they 'preferred our own'.

Captain Daniel Hickey ended up at Bray-sur-Somme in a snow-bound camp which had been a casualty clearing station in the summer of 1916, a place of flapping corrugated iron, dried bloodstains and ghosts. The former nurses' quarters were marginally more comfortable. Everyone was lousy. A sponge down of their grimy clothes with petrol had to do. There was no coal, stoves were kept going with wood from derelict dugouts and from railway sleepers.

Albert was 'an hour's walk away – Amiens twenty miles by car'. There were some attempts at festive jollity. Those tanks still in working order were frozen solid. They were not going anywhere anyway.

Drafts from England continued to arrive in France after the four months of training in Dorset. The diary of Gunner R. G. Forward of L (12) Battalion gives an intimate glimpse of what awaited them. 'Jan 4 1918: Southampton – Le Havre, film show at the YMCA. Sun 6th church parade. Mon. revolver inspection, lecture on "Belgium." Tuesday. Snow fight and football. Weds 9th. Route march, lecture on sex relationships.* Fri 11th To Méaulte. Bath parade.' It was all pretty comfortless.

Wilfred Bion was holed up with the remnants of B Battalion also at Méaulte, at the tankodrome south of Albert, trying to survive in a hut with blown snow an inch deep on the floor. He described Christmas Day 1917 in his reconstructed journal. Festivities started early:

> The men were given unlimited food and beer. No attempt was made to organize or do anything decently. By 10am **** the second in command of the company was carried to bed dead drunk, **** [a section commander] was hopelessly maudlin and collapsed a little later. Men were just shouting about and lying drunk round the camp. No one interfered. [The] battalion encamped near us were even worse. It took them a week to get sober.
>
> The whole day was spent in an orgy of eating and drinking and beastliness generally. Quainton and I were about tired of it by 6pm and left camp to walk out in the dark and the snow . . . we came to a YMCA hut and found a service going on . . . no attempt was made to sing carols or Christmas hymns – that would have been more than we could stand. Thus ended our first Christmas in France. Had everyone gone mad?

Fuller's Christmas at Bermicourt was a little more decorous although he managed to be miserable. He remembered especially 'the Cambrai Christmas card [featuring a festive Mark IV] . . . a children's party, Father Christmas and a dreadful film which was supposed to amuse the children; it consisted of an interminable series of English cathedrals'.

---

* A brisk address on venereal disease. One Tank Corps memoir describes an attempt at post-infection medication (by a captain) using Jeyes Fluid.

That the enemy was girding for a great offensive was obvious. The counterstroke at Cambrai launched out of the Banteux ravine on 30 November held menacing portents of new tactics and new manpower switched from Russia. Just how tanks were meant to fight defensively was by no means obvious. Rumours swept the Tank Corps – that they were to be scrapped altogether, that they were to be handed over to the Americans, that the enemy had built their own fleet of caterpillar fighting machines. In that the tank men were right, although it was hardly yet a fleet.

Since the Somme there had been voices at OHL arguing that Germany should build its own fleet of *Sturmwagen*. Germans were meant to be good at engineering, after all. Then the British sent their machines into the swamps of Flanders – it 'seemed the act of imbeciles'. Cambrai was different. OHL sent its opinion to Berlin on the third day of Operation GY – 'fighting in Second Army zone has again shown the actual and moral effect of tanks'. On 11 December the high command in the field declared that it placed 'the highest value on tanks for the Western Front. They are required as soon as possible and in the greatest numbers possible.' Hauptmann Fritz Leu's adventure in F.13 Falcon, meanwhile, had been repeated with a salvage operation to bring in repairable machines from the battlefield, not just to see how they might be countered but with the prospect of turning them against their former owners. There were scores of them, hauled off to a special workshop in a former factory in a suburb of Charleroi unromantically known as the 'Bavarian Army Vehicle Park'.

Kaiser Wilhelm himself went to inspect a captured Mark IV, at Bad Kreuznach on 19 December, and was photographed with his spike-helmeted retinue smirking like big-game hunters with a dead bison. The tank was taken by train to Berlin and driven to the zoo, attracting a large crowd on the way.

On 12 January 1918 the first *Sturm Panzerkraftwagen Abteilung*, five box-shaped A7Vs built by Daimler in Berlin, arrived by rail with their crews at the huge training ground at Bazeilles, near Sedan, where the new infiltration tactics demonstrated in the Cambrai counter-attack were developed and being taught to infantry divisions more used simply to squatting in trenches. A tank range was carved out.

At Bermicourt, meanwhile, the Tank Corps staff toiled away, absorbing the lessons of November 1917, and not just the obvious one of forcing an armoured breakthrough without any real idea what to do if it succeeded. There were detailed suggestions on how to do it better. The need for 'relief crews' was emphasized – when tanks came back intact and serviceable to the rallying points. 'After action the men have been unable to attend to the care of machines before resting', it was noted. First-aid provision was judged entirely inadequate: 'A collapsible stretcher is needed in all tanks. On one occasion in the Cambrai battle a wounded NCO was carried on the engine cover for a distance of four miles. It was impossible to carry the man more than a few yards at a time and in consequence he died on the journey.'

Another post-Cambrai report recommended: 'The biscuit portion of the iron ration should be changed within the week prior to action and put in a padlocked box made from a petrol tin. Steps must be taken by the section commanders to ensure that the cook should know the way to the rallying place where he should prepare tea for the crews. The greatest essential of all after action is the provision of a bath and a clean change of underclothing.'

That was not going to win the war. If there was hope it was in the west. Among those caught up in the Cambrai counter-attack debacle was a tiny unit of Americans, the 11th US Engineer Company, former railwaymen from New York, come to see how 'tanks' were so deftly switched round northern France. George S. Patton, commander of the AEF's fledgling tank-training school at Bourg, got a view from the top when he and Col. Frank Parker met Fuller at a somnolent Tanks HQ at Albert on the day the German counter-offensive broke. 'This battle of Cambrai shows what they can do,' Patton informed his wife in San Gabriel. 'I have a very long report to make out on them as no one knows anything about the subject but me.'

That may have been true as far as the US Tank Service was concerned. His report noted perceptively, 'Had the heavy British tanks been followed by an equal number of light tanks to exploit their success, better results could have been expected.' Others were drawing the same conclusions.

Patton went on to Paris, to the Renault factory at Billancourt to see the little two-man FT-17 on which the French army had now largely set its armoured ambitions. Patton wrote a long technical report and a Swinton-like blueprint for a US armoured force. The light tank had a dual personality; it was at once 'a heavily armoured infantry soldier' with 'greater destructive and resistant powers'. That was, of course, essential in terms of breaking the enemy's trench line; after that it could then 'assume the role of pursuit cavalry . . . and ride the enemy to death'.

Heavy tanks like those used at Cambrai were clearly useful in the initial break-in. Patton's paper turned to the kind of men an American Tank Corps would need – 'those with experience of automobiles, motorcycles, foundry hands, plumbers . . .'.

On 22 December 1917 another cavalry officer (serving dully as quartermaster in charge of port operations at St Nazaire) learned he would be 'chief of the Tank Corps, AEF' – Col. Samuel D. Rockenbach. Patton was chastened. He told his wife Beatrice: 'Now I feel hopeless and almost beaten but I will make a go of it or bust, Rockenbach or no.'

In early January, Patton and Rockenbach made a grand tour of their allies' tank operations, visiting Generals Estienne at Champlieu, in the forest of Compiègne, and Elles at Bermicourt, who did not have much to show them except the battered survivors from Cambrai. There was, however, much to discuss. The French seemed hot-bloodedly warlike and eager for action. On 16 January Fuller went to Champlieu in company with Elliot Hotblack. His estimate of their ally's potential was more jaundiced:

> I found their heavy tank a kind of kitchen range on tracks – unblushingly useless and their small Renault machines were nothing more than cleverly made mountings for battalion machine-guns. The general [Estienne] did not impress me although I found him an amusing little dud. The whole atmosphere was refreshing and depressing, it was nothing but cannon and women and women and cannon. Everyone wanted to fill his tank with seventy-fives and his billet with chorus girls.

The very first US tankers got to Bourg that same month – eleven officers of the Coast Artillery, all commissioned from the enlisted ranks. Still there were no tanks. All George Patton could do was fret over discipline, addressing new arrivals in the language of the football coach and bawling out sloppy reserve officers who kept their hands in their pockets. Corporal Earl T. Carrol, arriving at Bourg, was told: 'Well you goddamsonofabiches. Do you think the marines are tough? Well just wait till I get through with you. Being tough will save lives.'

Like Fuller at Bermicourt back in January 1917, the professional soldier Patton despaired at the citizen misfits that he had to get into shape. He ordered hair kept short so that the officers and men of the Bourg tank school should 'look like soldiers not poets'. Gasoline was to be freely used in the removal of grease spots from uniforms.

Patton confided in his wife: 'Unless I get some tanks soon I will go crazy for I have done nothing of any use since November and it is getting on my nerves.' More and more men arrived at the light tank training school, volunteers from within the AEF already in France. On 1 April Patton was promoted 'Major of Cavalry'.

Without tanks ('about as exciting as a dance without girls') Patton and his men were forced to make do with plywood mock-ups, just as the Heavy Branch had done before the Battle of Arras, with a turret armed with a Hotchkiss machine gun, the contraption mounted on a rocking device. The tiny corps also went through something called 'machine foot drills', imaginary tank sections being manoeuvred by men waving flags or operating klaxons. At last ten real live Renaults arrived on 23 March 1918. Drivers found it a bruising experience, the commander in the little turret instructed to transmit steering commands by kicking them in the shoulders. The signal to go was a kick in the back, to stop a kick in the head. Controls were car-like in simplicity, with steering effected by pulling right or left brake levers.

Just as on the British model there would be an armoured organization at home and at the front – the Tank Corps, United States (commanded from an office in Washington by Col. Ira C. Welborn, an infantry officer who had won the Medal of Honor in the Philippines), and the Tank Corps, American Expeditionary Force, Rockenbach's command. At Fort Meade, Maryland, then later at Camp Colt pitched on the Gettysburg battlefield, another eager pioneer was busy raising and training the US Army's first heavy tank battalion. His name was Capt. Dwight D. Eisenhower.

'Tanks' offered a seemingly glamorous way of going to war in a way that Europe had long forgotten. A magazine article asked, 'Who are the right men for the tanks?' They were heroes all, evidently: 'Men who will fight bravely and intelligently where other men would give up . . . men who smile with their eyes when you talk danger, a man whose women-folk believe in his fighting qualities. If he has a good record in sports, big game hunting or anything else that requires backbone and stamina, better still.'

The brave volunteers at Camp Colt seemed to require something else. Residents of Chambersburg complained of men 'parading drunkenly, cursing vocally and accosting ladies'. The War Department ordered all saloons within five miles of the camp placed off limits. The first tank, a Renault FT-17, did not arrive in Pennsylvania until early June.

Fuller had chosen the portentous motto 'Fear Naught' as part of his 'esprit de tank'. The US equivalent was 'Treat 'em Rough'. It worked – recruiting centres in the big cities were deluged. In April 1918 a young newspaper reporter, Ernest Hemingway, described the day a hard-charging officer of the Tank Corps, AEF, arrived in Kansas City to bang the drum.

> 'We want fighters for the tank service,' said Lieut. Frank E. Cooter, special tank officer at the army recruiting station, Twelfth Street and Grand Avenue, yesterday. 'Real men that want to see action. No mollycoddles need apply.'
>
> 'Have you ever had any gas engine experience?'
>
> 'Well, you might call it that,' replied William A. Whitman, 914 East Ninth Street. 'I've driven a Blitzen-Benz at the Los Angeles speedways for the last four years . . .'
>
> 'But have you had any military experience?' asked Lieutenant Cooter.
>
> 'Well, not regular military. I held a lieutenant's commission in the Nicaraguan army in the war against Honduras in 1909 . . . I had a commission in a couple of Central American revolutions, too . . .'
>
> Lieutenant Cooter shoved a blank toward him. 'Sign on the dotted line, man,' he said. 'You're too good to be true!'

Lieutenant Cooter got more than a hundred recruits. Ernest Swinton would have recognized the types: 'Besides the regular quota of mechanics, barbers, motor car salesmen, bartenders and college students who applied yesterday, Maynard Bush, 38 years old, instructor in journalism at Polytechnic Junior College, made out an application.'

Candidates were required to take a suitability test, including an examination on gasoline engines. One such, 1/Lt Newell P. Weed from New Jersey, recalled later: 'I did not know a magneto from a carburetor – but passed having read a pamphlet issued by some oil company.' (Weed was later awarded the Distinguished Service Cross for 'extraordinary heroism' in action near the Fôret d'Argonne in September 1918.)

They would be heading first for Pennsylvania and basic training, then they would cross the Atlantic, heading for Wool station in rural Dorset and the charms of Bovington camp. There would be upsets before any one of them got anywhere near a German.

43

The storm about to break on the Western Front was tangible. At a GHQ conference held at Montreuil in early December, Gen. Richard Butler had already laid out the situation – the employment of the British Army in 1918 was to be defensive. The role it had taken in 1917 was therefore to be reversed. The Tank Corps would conform to this policy.

The machines left in the Cambrai battle zone and the bravery of their scratch crews had demonstrated in their extemporized rally before Gouzeaucourt on 30 November that they could still be useful. But if tanks could not be made to fit the wider defensive imperative, if the Tank Corps just sat about in their expensive machines while the trench garrison grew ever thinner, the planned 'expansion' seemed irrelevant.

In the meantime where were new crews to come from? The manpower pot was empty. 'From munition workers, from the USA, the Navy or the colonies,' so Fuller recalled being told. An infantry division could be broken up, so Sir William Furse, the Master General of the Ordnance, proposed, even going so far as to suggest scrapping the cavalry and putting them in tanks. That did not go down well.

Churchill was at the 4 December meeting, impatient, mocking – with a wildly modernist agenda for more aircraft, trench mortars, mechanized transport, gas – and tanks as the way to win the war. GHQ wanted men in trenches. That was the view that prevailed. 'It would be a mistake,' the conference concluded, 'to exploit the Tank to the prejudice of rifle and manpower . . . and end in exalting the servant above the arm it exists to assist and serve.' According to Fuller: 'Throughout the discussion Churchill as Minister of Munitions maintained a sardonic smile contemptuous of the brain power of the professional soldier.'

Churchill had not lost his taste for gigantism. He put forward a plan inspired by Tennyson d'Eyncourt to build a fleet of enormous 'reservoirs' (a Churchillian pun) weighing 300 tons armed with four 18 pounder guns, which might be shipped across the Channel on special barges. Elles and Capper were briefly in favour but not Butler. The Tank Committee discreetly ignored the scheme.

Such stuff was nonsense, of course. In the winter of 1917–18 nothing really mattered but holding the line. Faced with a resurgent enemy the War Cabinet was set on completing the clear-out at GHQ, getting a political grip on manpower, diverting troops to Italy, taking over more lines of front from the French, unifying the Allied command – and waiting for the Americans. The C-in-C abhorred such precepts – apart from the arrival of the US Army in the field. The BEF set to doing what they could to copy the enemy's in-depth defensive principles (with some blundering misinterpretations). Labour battalions toiled on new earthworks. Concrete pillboxes were hastily constructed in imitation of the German model. Fatigue parties cursed at having to dig 'extra-wide' ditches lest the enemy lurch forward in something resembling tanks (the warnings from Russia were being acted upon). Haig actually seemed eager that the enemy should attack 'with the almost certainty of thoroughly losing'. Tanks did not fit. They took days to shuffle round by rail – to meet an enemy which could choose the time and place of attack. The artillery–infantry storm of 30 November had shown what they might be up against while the tank men themselves fully expected to be facing something new – tanks. According to Williams-Ellis: 'Sheets of the intelligence summary . . . were full of little items of a perfectly new sort . . . "tanks of some kind are certainly being made at Krupps" . . . There was not a hut in a single camp where wonderful new ideas for [tank versus tank] tactics and manoeuvres with which to annihilate the new enemy were not daily elaborated. We did not know that the bitterness and anxiety of a long retreat lay before us . . .'

British tanks would indeed encounter German tanks, but not quite yet. 'Boots' Hotblack, the Corps' politically astute intelligence officer, had been busy posting dramatic yarns gleaned from 'deserters' about a coming storm of *Panzerkraftwagen*. Such reports had been trickling into Whitehall for over a year. Now they became a weapon in the Tank Corps' own struggle for survival.

Fuller had turned up in London in mid-December flagrantly to lobby, at a clandestine meeting with Lord Northcliffe (who seemed to have information before the act about the purges at GHQ) and with Churchill at Armaments Buildings. The minister excitedly paced the room, sipping alternatively from jugs of 'Bovril and Vermouth' laid on a sideboard. Huge fleets of rival land ironclads manoeuvring for the mastery of Europe: this was better than his days at the Admiralty. Churchill 'expressed his disgust at the little enthusiasm shown at GHQ for tanks . . . and we left not much helped.' There was another conspiratorial meeting a little later, again in London, but this time in the louche surroundings of Evan Charteris's Mayfair flat. This time Churchill brought Arthur Balfour (the Foreign Secretary) with him, whom Fuller thought 'a fool' (no one was clever as Boney, at least he thought so). The munitions minister promised, so Fuller recorded in his journal, to 'force the military's hand by swamping France with tanks'.

The sniping between Albert Stern and the War Office, even in his semi-detached position as go-between to the French and the Americans, had meanwhile become a fusillade. Robert Whigham wanted Stern 'out of uniform' as quickly as possible, out of the whole business. Stern's urgings that the opportunity to create an Allied tank army was slipping away fitted Churchill's increasingly messianic mechanical agenda. He could hardly stay away from Bermicourt, visiting twice in February to listen again to the tank men's disparaging of the dullards beyond their gates. Lloyd George promised Stern that he would call a meeting of the War Cabinet, scheduled for 8 March. Again Fuller lobbied shamelessly, sending Churchill (who was not a War Cabinet member) a memorandum stating: 'GHQ is inert and will lay down no policy . . . the present tank organization is monstrous.' It concluded dramatically (and inaccurately), 'we are now faced with a race for tank supremacy'.

The minister got the point. He circulated his own paper larded with intelligence suggesting the Germans were building tanks in quantity. He included an estimate by Admiral Sir Archibald Moore, Stern's replacement as Director of the Mechanised Warfare Department, that if the enemy had begun preparations of engineering drawings on 1 January they would have completed construction of 440 machines by 1 August. Churchill again expounded his vision of a tank armada: 'The resources are available, the time is available, the result is certain; nothing is lacking except the will . . . We have instead only carried out a series of costly experiments each of which has shown us the chance we have lost . . .' It was a reasonable summary of the Tank Corps' history since the very beginning.

Now they faced another kind of test. How could they work in defence? Elles argued they should be kept together as a 'sword behind the shield'. Fuller was all for using them en masse in pre-emptive raids. General Sir Hubert Gough proposed digging them into the ground as pillboxes. GHQ came up with something called 'savage rabbits'. It was the idea, evidently, of Gen. Ivor Maxse, Director of Training, who proposed they be strung out along the whole defence line from Lens to Péronne, concealed in pits or farm buildings, to pop out and ferociously harry the enemy as he passed. The tank men thought it suicidal. One youthful commander recalled: 'We were sent to Lens to await the German attack in the woods of the Lovette ridge and practise the savage rabbit stunt in craters and ruins. We were to let the advancing enemy sweep past us and then to emerge from our lairs to harry them in flank and rear until we were blotted out.'

The manpower crisis forced a big decision. Hugh Elles himself explained the move made in January 1918 in an article in the *Tank Corps Training Journal* soon after the war: 'The sources of supply of so-called technical personnel were completely dry. The situation forced on us a very hardy experiment. Tank battalions consisted of three fighting and one workshop company. [These] companies were removed, battalions left with one engineer officer apiece and one mechanist staff sergeant per company.' Clough Williams-Ellis explained further: 'No damaged part was ever to be repaired in the field, mechanical efficiency was to be maintained by the broken bit of mechanism being immediately replaced by a complete new part. Reconditioning would be done in the central workshop – which had expanded to a second site at Teneur two miles from Erin.' Tank crews henceforth should know simply how to take out the broken bit and put in the new one. Major W. R. Powell-Chandler, engineering officer at the Plateau, deplored the new arrangement: 'Tanks from Cambrai were in a shocking condition. The battalion had just arrived out from England and most of the men had only just seen a tank and were quite ignorant of the work that had to be done; to make matters worse our workshops sections were taken away . . .'

But Hugh Elles was relieved. His men need no longer be mechanics who could fight. They could just be soldiers. As he wrote: 'It was possible to train and fight battalions hastily raised and consisting of precisely the same material as infantry or artillery – officered by lawyers, stockbrokers and architects, manned by farmers, butchers and clerks . . .'

If he could get enough of them.

The Yanks in Tanks were on their way, if terribly slowly. It had been recommended in February 1918 at the War Department in Washington that fifty officers and one hundred NCOs be sent to England to be trained on heavy tanks. By the end of that month enough men had been recruited to organize a three-company battalion, and the kernel of a second. They were mustered first as Engineers, then assigned directly to the new 'Tank Service'. Two weeks later the men of the 1st Battalion left Camp Meade on their way to New York harbour and luxurious berths aboard the White Star liner *Olympic*, heading first for Brest, then for Southampton. They arrived on 8 April. There was trouble almost from the moment they got ashore. According to Cpl David A. Pyle of A Company: 'A Scottish sergeant major came strutting down the platform with his colourful kilt and swagger stick under his arm. When our men saw him they began to direct remarks such as "she's going to sleep with me tonight . . . [a fight ensues]". About a dozen men broke ranks and the last I saw of him he was running off the end of the platform into the streets of Southampton with several officers trying to restore order and get the company back into line.'

They marched from Wareham station into Bovington camp without any more punch-ups. Schoolchildren waved flags of the Allied nations. On arrival two things in particular evidently caught their attention – the presence of females from the Women's Army Auxiliary Corps and the lousy quality of the straw-filled bedding.

British Army instructors set to work: physical jerks, brain-numbing drill, the grim regimen that the Tank Corps had endured at least since Bradley's departure. Gum chewing was forbidden. Patton in France had declared of his own men that 'working with machines has a very disastrous effect on discipline. It seems to run out of men as the oil soaks into them.'

'We have got the first US officers at Wool,' Capper wrote to Elles;

'most of them I am sorry to say have little if any knowledge of an officer's duties.'

It was British Army food that brought the men to the brink of mutiny. The diet of slum (a kind of porridge), tea, cheese, bread and occasionally 'a great luxury, jam',* failed to satisfy appetites more used to corn-fed beef. British Army mutton was a special abomination. There were raids on the cookhouse and on nearby farms, and breakouts to the Home and Colonial Stores in Wareham. The pickings were thin.

Mindless drill gave way to practical instruction on Tank Corps lines – on the Lewis gun, the 6-pounder, camouflage, the correct handling of pigeons. The first driving on real tanks began, on rehabilitated Mark IVs which still required the human drive train to operate the gears. Then it was 'battle' training, lurching over the ranges with their mocked-up trenches and blazing away on live firing runs at Lulworth. The Americans were all over the place. Their hosts despaired. Corporal Pyle recalled: 'They called us Uncle Sam's Rag Time Army, which pretty well represents my very own view.' The commanding officer of the unit (now designated 301st Tank Battalion), Lt-Col. Henry E. Mitchell, by all accounts was not quite up to it.

There were rest and recreation outings to London and to Bournemouth, where a musical play was staged at the Palace Theatre. Corporal David Pyle took up with 'saucy little Margarete Watkins, daughter of the manager of Lloyds Bank in Wareham'. A great Anglo-American tradition had begun.

The promised Mark VIII tank powered by a detuned Liberty aircraft engine had yet to materialize; there was agreement in late June to supply the Mark V,† but only enough to equip the 301st Battalion (two more were forming) – Haig shrewdly insisting that once in France the Americans should be put under the operational control of the British Expeditionary Force.

On 21 March the German offensive in the west opened along

---

* According to British Tank Corps subaltern G. E. V. Thompson, strawberry jam was quite palatable, but when it was realized that it was only issued on the eve of an offensive it became much less popular.

† With a clever gearbox of Walter Wilson's devising it only required one man to drive. The Mark V was also marginally faster; ventilation, however, was poor.

seventy miles of front with an artillery bombardment of unprecedented subtlety and power. D Battalion's war diary reads simply:
'21.3.18 The enemy attacked this morning. The order Man Battle
Stations was received at 5:30am.'

Along the fronts of British Fifth Army (Gough) and Third Army
(Byng), out of fog and smoke came *Stosstruppen*, fast-moving units of
highly motivated infantry armed with grenades and in some cases
with light automatic weapons. They swept through the trench lines,
bypassing strong points, moving with a stunning rapidity.

That afternoon of the 21st a place called Le Pontchu Redoubt,
south of St Quentin, was attacked by four ponderous A7V *Sturmwagen* emblazoned with skull and crossbones. Six officers and 150
men of the London Regiment surrendered. In a simultaneous action
north-west of the town, five tanks salvaged from Cambrai plastered
with iron crosses plunged into the defenders' outpost line. Hauptmann Fritz Leu drove one of them – but managed to get lost – and
the rest of the captured tanks could barely keep up with the storm
troops.

The Tank Corps in defence seemed impotent – 'the enemy often
swerved away on seeing them, the Mk IV was not fast enough to
catch up'. The savage rabbits proved less than ferocious. More than
120 machines (and a proportion of the crews) would be lost. Those
held in reserve some ten miles behind the front would have a better
survival rate.

On 24 March the withdrawal from the Flesquières salient broke
down in a shambles. Third Army began to waver. Fifth Army began to
retreat. The certainties of positional war, of Fuller's bloated pumpkin
armies hanging on their railway stems, were crumbling. On the 26th,
in a crisis meeting at Doullens, Haig and Sir Henry Wilson (who had
replaced Robertson as CIGS) agreed willingly enough that the French
General Ferdinand Foch should coordinate the Allied struggle to hold
the line. Tanks HQ was evacuated briefly to a place called Hamen-
court (and set up, inevitably, in a château) near Doullens.

Lieutenant Thompson was on the Third Army Front:

> We had started a game of football when we were ordered to
> man our tanks and move forward. Soon we met small parties
> of infantry on the retreat. From the rallying point we received
> orders to drive down the left flank . . . into the valley into which

large numbers of enemy were advancing. We had no idea if the infantry would follow, the only orders were that there were stacks of Boche and we were to get into them. My tank took a direct hit but was still running. Picked up many survivors of knocked-out tanks . . . we got back to our start point bursting at the seams. Only four tanks got back. Scratch crews were assembled to drive any tanks capable of being moved back to the rear . . .

Thompson spent ten days 'fighting' on foot, which meant mostly retreating, scrounging food from farms, sleeping in the open. Then, as he said, 'all Tank Corps personnel were ordered out of the line to report to the command area at Querrieu south of Amiens'.

On 21 March Daniel Hickey was in Vélu Wood, east of Bapaume, still with his section, veterans of the fight for Fontaine four months before. Several of their vehicles had also survived. Hong Kong went forth to meet the enemy and 'came back looking like burnished pewter' from machine-gun strikes. They glimpsed enemy cavalry in the distance. Infantry milled about without their weapons. This was a rout.

On a trek by road, tank crews always walked outside when they could – no packs, no rifles, maybe a revolver at the hip, ambling along with hands in pockets. It was a badge of honour. The columns shuffling westwards now all looked the same. 'The British army were a group of men wandering back on their own,' wrote Hickey. Tanks were not built for this sort of thing. Fuel consumption was half a mile per gallon. There were no supply dumps, no preordained 'rallying points'. One by one their engines were coughing to a stop as the fuel ran out. The thing was, the point which runs through every memoir of the period was to *save the guns*.

Hickey ordered the Lewis guns removed from Hadrian, and the veteran bus set alight. Two tanks remained. Crossing the old Somme battlefield, the horror of it undiminished by almost two years of decay and oxidization, he encountered Col. Willoughby, the martinet Coldstreamer from Wool. He expected the war to be over within four days.

Fuel was almost exhausted, so was food and water. A crate of Bass was thankfully found in the engine compartment of one tank. At Courcelette, scene of Crème de Menthe's triumph an age before at the sugar-beet factory, Hickey ordered the last machines to be set on fire. Now they were all walking, slouching back to a behind-the-lines tankodrome where some 'old crocks' were being fixed up to make a last stand.

Boney Fuller marvelled at the enemy offensive tactics and at the same time despaired at GHQ's and lowlier British commanders' floundering attempts to find a counter. 'Some of the stories we now hear are really ludicrous,' he wrote in his diary. 'In order to protect his chateau against imaginary German armoured cars, Genl. Harper, commanding the IV Corps, ordered up 8 tanks . . . such panic is disgraceful. This was the noted "dud" who through his ludicrous training and formations upset the battle of Cambrai at Flesquières.' There was the story of three terror-struck staff officers fleeing the training ground at Wailly in a staff car, with their landlady sitting on one of the officers' knees. At Colincamps three 'steam ploughs' had caused 3,000 men to panic and run, 'thinking them to be German tanks'.

On 12 April Wilfred Bion at Méaulte, south of Albert, was told what was coming next by the boss himself:

> At 8am as we stood on parade, a large staff car rolled up and Gen. Elles got out. He made no inspection but a short speech. The situation in the north he said was very serious. The enemy had broken through and not been stopped. The Tank Corps had been called on again and this time as infantry – there were not enough tanks ready and no scope for them if there were. Our job was to hold out in isolated posts and stay there even if the enemy got through . . . Then they were to open fire . . . we had no rifles. What we were going into we didn't know and didn't care – we hadn't any b**** tanks anyway thank Heaven.

Up and down the line, tank crews found themselves mustered as Lewis-gun teams, carted around in lorries waiting to be bussed to the latest point of the enemy's advance. The Tank Corps were an embarrassment, sitting about in the remaining machines – those which had not yet been simply left on the side of the road. Four were abandoned on the wrong side of a girder bridge when they proved too wide to cross in the general retreat.

'Boots' Hotblack blamed the higher commanders for the humili-ation. They had 'set far too low a standard of what is required from the fighting units. They were on occasion delighted with small shows in which tanks did their bare duty . . . there are several young tank commanders who are now running down the infantry boasting their deeds.'

The shipment of new machines to France was suspended. Ammunition and fodder for horses had higher priority. And what was the point of sending tanks across the Channel when it really looked as if the enemy might pin the BEF against the sea? Two and a half thousand men, after their four months of tank training at Wool, were told they were going into the line as infantry. It looked as if the whole Tank Corps would be following. Fuller blamed that 'mental eunuch' Brig.-Gen. 'Kitten' Wigram for the move, noting in his diary on 14 April: 'Elles went to GHQ to argue the pros and cons of reduction. Unfortunately he is too familiar with Wigram to command any respect.'

Churchill arrived to boost morale with a visit renewed to Bermicourt on 29 April bearing news of plans for an 'inter-allied tank factory'. But with the Germans still attacking, still seemingly unstoppable, that military–political vision might have seemed as fantastical as the plan Fuller suddenly produced – to go on the offensive with a mechanized army 12,000 tanks strong on a front of 100 miles. The promised advent of the 'Medium D chaser' tank, a design by Philip Johnson with a speed of 25 mph and a range of 200 miles, was its fountspring.* The author himself called the plan a 'military novelette'.

The Tank Corps' own metropolis was in the line of advance. In early 1918 the Central Workshop had begun a move two miles away to a village called Teneur. Erin had become the 'Central Stores'. Thousands of French refugees streamed through the whole area seeking shelter as engineers rigged the forges and machine shops for demolition. Captain Hickey was trusted with the tank defence of St Pol with a battered Mark IV: 'I was to block the road and use it as a fort.' Tank crews were formed as Lewis-gun teams. Most of the tanks had already been dispersed. No one really knew who was alive and who was dead. Elles told Capper, 'our loss in personnel so far as I can gather [has been small], allowing for the usual return of people

---

* Six were built after the war. Fuller's proposal is generally known as 'Plan 1919'.

accounted as being lost forever who are probably only wandering about the roads'.

But the thrust line of the German advance still ran miles to the south – poking menacingly towards the rail centre of Amiens, pivot of the whole British defence in the centre. On 24 April a large-scale assault was made on the village of Villers-Bretonneux just a few miles east of the city. Fourteen A7V tanks in three groups went in with the infantry at 7.00 a.m. concealed by thick fog.

The ponderous machine needed a crew of no fewer than eighteen to operate the vehicle and its armament, orders being given by a system of flashing lights, while more men would habitually cram on board. Three tanks of I Gruppe rumbled into the village, but two turned back to try and join up with their infantry. Tank 526 drove the length of the village, its commander, Oberleut. Skopnik, apparently thinking that British scrambling to get out were German assault troops trying to get in. He turned round and drove all the way back. The other two machines, Wagen 527 *Lotti* and Wagen 560 *Alter Fritz*, had rallied and were taking a wholesale surrender at the eastern end of the village. Some defenders still held out in the brick factory. Unteroffizier Ernst Volckheim, commanding Wagen 560, recorded his account of the strange battle twenty years later: 'There are plenty of targets. The effect is devastating. It is ghastly . . . yet we are proud of our quick success as it helps our own infantry advance. We attack again, Vietze's tank joins us from the opposite direction and the English are caught in our cross fire . . . instead of seeking cover the enemy runs into the open and tries desperately to escape. I order cease fire, but the machine gunners are slow to stop . . .'

In Fontaine-Notre-Dame the Tank Corps had found out how dangerous it was fighting in even a modest main street. The Germans had developed a simple technique for taking barricaded buildings – shoot up the front while a storming party got out of the side of the tank and clobbered the defenders with grenades. By 11.00 a.m. Villers-Bretonneux was in German hands.

Leutnant Theunissen in Wagen 506 *Mephisto* took the surrender of a large number of British infantry to the south of the village before the vehicle came to a dead halt with blocked fuel injectors. *Mephisto* got going again but promptly got stuck in a shell hole. Her crew abandoned tank. The derelict machine (blown up later in the day by

German engineers with a demolition charge) was salvaged later by Australian infantry. One tank, *Elfriede*, tipped over in a modest sand-pit (the Holt-derived tracks were pretty useless) and its commander, Leut. Stein, died trying to defend it with his pistol. The hapless *Elfriede* ended up as a trophy in the Place de la Concorde in Paris.

Unteroffizier Wilhelm Biltz in Wagen 561 *Nixe* got off three hours late, delayed by a mechanical failure. Tank Corps counterparts would have understood, even though the British-Daimler engine was different to the twin Daimlers of the A7V. The fog had lifted by the time Leut. Biltz, having missed his bearings, lumbered into the village of Cachy two miles south of Villers-Bretonneux on the morning of the 24th. A little bit of history was in the making.

With stragglers bringing in reports to 54th Division of German 'tanks' having broken through, three British Mark IVs had been sent forward. Second Lieutenant Francis Mitchell in Tank No. 1 of A Company, 1 Battalion (tank names had unsportingly been abolished in early 1918 but unofficially continued to be used), and his section commander, Capt. J. C. Brown, had already seen *Nixe* coming up the road. Unteroffizier Biltz saw the rhomboid shapes and ordered immediate reverse. Mitchell's gunners could not land a hit while pitching over broken ground. He ordered stop. *Nixe*, meanwhile, opened up on the accompanying Lewis-armed females with its main armament – armour-piercing 37-mm, quite deadly. According to Mitchell's own account: 'I saw to my astonishment that the two female tanks were slowly limping away to the rear. They had both been hit by shells almost immediately on their arrival and had great holes in their sides. As their Lewis guns were useless against the heavy armour-plate of the enemy . . . they had nothing to do but withdraw.'

Mitchell's right-hand gunner, Sgt J. R. Mackenzie, managed to land a shot on *Nixe*'s starboard front, killing the gunner, Kanonier Reiske, and mortally wounding Schütze Janz and Gefreiter Gutzat. *Nixe* slowly spun to the right – two more British shells hit her flank. Unteroffizier Biltz ordered abandon tank. *Nixe* sat motionless on the field, its two Daimler engines still running. With the scene of battle suddenly quiet, the depleted crew got back inside and travelled another two kilometres before the engine gave up.

Mitchell claimed to have engaged several more A7Vs before an infantry-fired mortar blew a hole in the track. He survived to publish a book, with lots of triumphant whizz-bang but more contemplative in its description of the artillery-delivered gas attack which hit the section's lying-up place in a wood before the main act had even begun. He went into action with a crew of just four – the rest were gagging, blue-faced, blistered – and those who were able to get into their tank and make it work at all had eyes red-rimmed and suppurating from mustard gas.

The first tank–tank encounter in military history, Mitchell versus Biltz, merged into a wider action when seven Medium A Whippets of X Company, C Battalion, commanded by Capt. Thomas R. Price (who seems to have directed the operation clattering along on a horse), arrived in time to flay with their machine guns an infantry regiment which had just arrived from Russia with no experience of the Western Front and none of tanks. There was mass panic – a massacre. The British *Official History* told it like this: 'A message dropped from an aeroplane gave the information that two enemy battalions were resting in a hollow in front of Cachy, and that they might be taken unawares if tanks could get there quickly. The tanks moved without delay and came on the two battalions of the 77th Reserve Division and at once charged in line southwards causing, it was estimated, at least four hundred casualties.'

According to Francis Mitchell: 'Three of the seven came back, their tracks dripping with blood; the other four were left out there in front, and their crews could not hope to be made prisoners after such slaughter. One broke down not far from Cachy, and I saw a man in overalls get out, and, with a machine gun under his arm, run to another Whippet, which stopped to pick him up.'

German sources dispute the scale of the mechanized reaping, preferring to concentrate on the exploits of Leut. Friedrich-Wilhelm Bitter, commander of Wagen 525 *Siegfried*, and Unteroffizier Albert Müller in 504 *Schnuck*, who engaged the Whippets aided by a field-gun battery. A German source says: 'Soon four Whippets had been knocked out and the commander of machine A.256, 2/Lt [Harry] Dale was killed and the remainder scattered . . . The *Siegfried* held the field . . . The success of the A7Vs cannot be denied. I and II Gruppe had accomplished their missions and only III Gruppe had not reached its objective' – and that seemingly was the infantry's fault for not catching up. The German tank commander, Haupt. Friedrich Bornsch-legel, declared in an order of the day: 'The first major action has brought complete success . . . the behaviour of the tank crews deserves special recognition as do the daring commanders Bitter and Biltz who led the very first tank-versus-tank action. Unfortunately we have to mourn the loss of one brave officer and nine stalwart NCOs and troopers . . . They gave their lifeblood for the fatherland . . .'

It was all very heroic but militarily meaningless. The village was quickly recaptured in a slick Australian counter-attack (*Mephisto* would end up as a war trophy in Brisbane). Everyone got pretty excited, however, except, it would seem, the German high command. Elles personally went looking for a German tank with Col. G. A. Green (they were unsuccessful) and both of them nearly got killed in the process. He told Capper on the 26th: 'This tank v tank affair is of very great interest – and has moved GHQ to action I think in the importation of the Mark V' (the supply of new tanks to France was turned on again after the stop order of the month before). There was an evocative echo of 15 September 1916. 'We have no guarantee,' wrote Elles, 'that the German will not repeat his mistake of using them in driblets. [We are facing] a formidable threat.'

Hotblack circulated a report based on the questioning of a tank prisoner, a mechanic who had been captured after wandering around no-man's-land for four days. It had the poignancy of Haupt. Weber's interrogation of Gnr Herbert Clears almost two years before. They could almost have been the same:

> The manufacture of these tanks was begun in spring 1917 at Daimlers near Berlin and one hundred machines were promised. Daimler had let them down and various models had been unsatisfactory. Prisoner referred to proceedings as a swindle. He was wounded on a mission to find lubricating oil. He said that while at Charleroi, Hindenburg had inspected the tanks. One became ditched on trial. Hindenburg openly said that he did not think they would be much use . . .
>
> Drivers and mechanics are volunteers from motor transport and the gunners and machine gunners are from the artillery and infantry. Double pay and double rations have been promised. The infantry had upset his engine oil . . . he did not think much of them as tank men.

The German tanks were too few and too feeble to make a difference. The Kolossal-Wagen was never completed, nor was a projected fleet of 500 light tanks designed by Joseph Vollmer ever even started. Handfuls of A7Vs and captured British machines would be expended as the German offensives one by one ran into the ground – in Flanders, on the Chemin des Dames and at last on the Marne. A last climactic effort to drive the British back to the Channel with a renewed attack in Flanders (Operation Hagen) was aborted. On 15 July came the Germans' last throw when twenty A7Vs led an assault east of Reims. It collapsed at the outset; an equivalent attempt to the west of the city stalled on the second day. A great French counterstroke began on 18 July with the battlefield debut of the Renault FT-17, four hundred of them attacking around Soissons. The Germans began to fall back. They would not stop until the war was over.

The Tank Corps had bent, hundreds of machines had been lost, but it had not been completely swept away in the great retreat of March and April. The line had held before any storm troops got to the Ternoise valley. The supply operation from England (with its GHQ-imposed interruption) and the Central Workshop continued to function. By mid-May the tank force was up to almost six hundred with Mark Vs now arriving in France at the rate of fifty a week. On 4 July at Le Hamel, a village north of Villers-Bretonneux, an exceptionally well-executed operation launched by the Australian Corps used sixty 'fighting' and twelve supply tanks to full effect. Of the tank crews, thirteen were wounded and none killed. All but two machines got to the objective, one hit by a German field guns one by British. In the eyes of the Australians the ghosts of Bullecourt were effectively laid. It was a 'brilliant little battle' which rehabilitated the tarnished tanks in the eyes of GHQ. On 18 June the cut in establishment was cancelled.

From the beginning the Tank Corps had enjoyed a kind of aloofness, even if their employment in battle had always been under the thumb of GHQ. The feud between Elles and Stern over adequate supplies of machine and spares, with the hapless Capper holding the ring, had ground on. Higher opinion on the utility, even the continued existence, of the 'new arm' swung wildly according to results on the battlefield. Flanders was a fiasco, Cambrai a hung election.

The crisis of the German spring offensive put the argument on hold. As late as 10 June, Haig's CGS could tell Capper, 'General Staff could not lay down its performance requirements as the role of the tank is not yet firmly fixed.' It was a little late for that.

Haig himself had never quite lost faith. His view was simple – 'Tanks must join the Army.' Tanks were still the darlings of the press, the symbol of final victory. Tank Week* had raised £13 million in war bonds. The Germans had flatteringly built their own version. What mattered was truly making them servants of the infantry. Haig's pre-war instincts as Director of Training came to the fore. A manual was required; a book of instructions for tank warfare, it would be compiled internally. When Hugh Elles went to GHQ in June 1918 to check on progress he found, according to Fuller, the new manual's draughtsman working off notes supplied by Lt-Gen. Richard Butler, whose 'suggestions were what one might expect from an intensely stupid man'. Fuller was horrified to discover how much influence the 'wooden-headed' Butler still had at GHQ, in spite of nominally being in operational command of a corps. The 'dunderhead D.H.' still sought the opinions of his favourite sycophant, he tartly noted in his diary.

Fuller's hauteur did him little personal harm. In a move to snuff out the corps' residual independence, Capper's directorate at the War Office was shut down. A small branch (SD7) in the Staff Duties branch was set up to look after tank affairs. It was safer having Fuller inside the tent than out. He left France in late July to take its Whitehall chair. The GHQ-inspired manual that appeared in August – 'Tanks and their Employment with Other Arms' – was not quite the disaster that the prima donna of Bermicourt had predicted. In the words of a historian of British armoured doctrine: 'When looked at without prejudice and certainly in comparison with Fuller's wild fantasy about the Medium D, this document appears the literary embodiment of sanity and commonsense.'

---

* An ingenious scheme launched in March 1918. A Mark IV, Nelson, was established in Trafalgar Square in the middle of London. Investors were invited to return to their homes or places of work accompanied by a Tank Corps soldier plus pigeon in a wicker basket. A cheque would be duly written attached to the pigeon which would convey it to the tank. The idea spread – Virginia Woolf recorded in her diary (5 April 1918) her suburban encounter with a tank at which the whole of Richmond was 'worshipping . . . like the hum of bees around some first blossom'.

A proof was in the making. Before the city of Amiens the British Fourth Army* prepared for an attack between the rivers Ancre and Avre with the French 1st Army to the south. General Sir Henry Rawlinson had the Canadian Corps and the Australian Corps, the most formidable fighting troops in the line – ten dominion divisions, four British, one American and three cavalry divisions, over 450,000 men. As at Cambrai, the whole available strength of the Tank Corps was concentrated (it was Fuller who persuaded Rawlinson to go for broke, perhaps his most important contribution to the conduct of the war), nine heavy battalions (326 machines, mostly Mark Vs) and two light (ninety-six Medium A Whippets).

This time Gen. Richard Butler, Edward Swinton's nemesis, had a field command, in charge of III Corps operating on the north side of the Somme. It had comparatively few tanks and got stuck. Putting the Whippets under the cavalry commander proved a mistake. Nevertheless the events of 8 August, when this great array of armour came out of the pre-dawn fog, redressed both the lost promise of Cambrai and the traumas of March and April. The German defences were extemporized, manned by second-line troops. First the creeping barrage, then the tanks fell on them. It was a traditional battle of the Great War in the sense that it was about static fronts, breaking an obstacle line – taking prisoners and guns before stopping for the day – and yet there were episodes when it looked to be moving at the pace of armoured warfare of a different generation.

The action at Amiens, for example, of Capt. Smeddle of 15 Battalion, who got through the wire to find himself engaging a railway train. Henry Smeddle from Bristol had enlisted in the ASC in June 1915 and transferred as a lowly lance-corporal to be commissioned into the Tank Corps on the eve of Third Ypres. He was a trained engineer, a public schoolboy; his military career prospered in the new arm. On 8 August he was commanding a section of three spanking new Mark V* tanks.† The technique was the same as at Cambrai: hiding up, making a discreet reconnaissance, taping lines of approach,

---

* Gough had been sacked after Fifth Army's retreat. Henry Rawlinson commanded the renamed Fourth Army.

† The Mark V(star) or V* was longer than the standard machine and could carry an infantry section. Ventilation was appalling.

an attack at first light. He recalled: 'There was to be no smoking or flashing of electric torches and no shouting, whistling or unnecessary noise during the march. Only tank commanders would be allowed to smoke, the glow of their cigarettes was to be the method by which they would guide their tanks whilst walking in front without undue attention.'

Henry Smeddle's tank moved off at Zero plus ten minutes, through the British front line from where the infantry had already jumped off before dawn. The first signs of battle were walking wounded and prisoners coming in the other direction. Smeddle dismounted, a runner took a bullet in the stomach, next an official film cameraman popped up. Quite suddenly they were out and into the open, moving into the enemy rear area at a pace which tank commanders of a different war would find halfway respectable.

> The enemy were evidently quite unaware of the rapidity of our advance for just as we were opposite Harbionnières we saw an ammunition train steaming into the station as if nothing was the matter. It was immediately shelled by all the 6-pdr guns of the approaching tanks. One tank must have struck a powder van for suddenly the whole train burst into one sheet of flame . . .
>
> It was followed by another one, a passenger train rushing up fresh troops. This was running on another track and ran right into our lines where it was captured . . .

Lieutenant C. B. Arnold had joined a 'pals' battalion of the King's (Liverpool) Regiment and been wounded on the Somme, then transferred to the Heavy Branch where his two brothers were already serving. On the night of 7–8 August 1918 he was waiting to take the light tank Musical Box of the 6th Tank Battalion forward from its lying-up point at Zero (4.20 a.m.) It would be a famous outing. 'He was ordered to support the cavalry – but he lost the cavalry,' Fuller reported with relish. In Lt Arnold's words, written after his return from prisoner-of-war camp in 1919:

> I found myself to be the leading machine, owing to the others having become ditched etc. To my immediate front I could see more Mk V tanks being followed very closely by Australian infantry.
>
> Two tanks on my right front were knocked out. I saw clouds of smoke coming out and the crews evacuate. The infantry

following the heavy machines were suffering casualties from this battery. I turned half left and ran diagonally across the front at a distance of about 800 yards. Both my guns were able to fire on the battery, in spite of which they got off about eight rounds without damage but sufficiently close to be audible inside the cab and I could see the flash of each gun as it fired.

Musical Box got behind and shot up the artillery position from there: 'The Germans, some thirty in number, abandoned their guns and tried to get away. Gunner Ribbans and I accounted for the whole lot,' recalled Arnold. Musical Box's adventures were just beginning. A patrol of cavalry was rescued from enfilading machine-gunners who fled into a cornfield at the tank's appearance.

Tanks had more staying power than horses. Arnold drove on into open country, through a valley crammed with 'Hun hutments', to see in the distance 'a train on fire being towed by an engine'. A column of horse transport and motor lorries was shot up, then fuel leaking from cans lashed to the tank's top began to slosh about. 'I was shouting to driver Carney to turn about . . . when two heavy concussions closely followed one another and the cab burst into flames. [Driver] Carney and [Gunner] Ribbans got to the door and collapsed. I was almost overcome but managed to get the door open and fell out onto the ground, and was able to drag out the other two men. We were all on fire. In this rush Carney was shot in the stomach and killed.'

Lieutenant Arnold got badly beaten up by his captors but survived.

The scenes of panic and insubordination along the defenders' front were like those which had swept the French army on the eve of the mutinies of spring 1917. By the end of the day, Rawlinson's army had advanced four miles and, according to German accounts, all but wiped out the line divisions opposite it. 'August 8,' wrote Ludendorff famously, 'was the black day of the German army in the history of this war.' It was the 'climax', according to Fuller; 'after that it was minor tactics.'

There would be no more doubts.* Captain Daniel Hickey wit-

* Even if, as the Official Historian declared in print in 1947 (to the fury of Fuller and Liddell Hart), 'The tanks were mechanically imperfect and slow . . . a very large number were soon knocked out. Materially they achieved little . . .'

nessed the exalted glow of approval himself: 'On Friday 16 August the tanks that were engaged in the battle were inspected by Sir Douglas Haig. The inspection took place in the actual battlefield. This was the first time the tanks had been complimented by a personal visit of the C-in-C after an action. I thought he looked very old and worried.'

In four days of fighting, Amiens cost the Tank Corps almost three-quarters of its machines – from all causes.* By 10 August the numbers engaged had dropped by four-fifths – and operations were 75 per cent unsuccessful – by the Tank Corps' own estimate. The rumps of five tank battalions supporting the Canadian Corps' attack in the Roye–Hally area on the 8th suffered 50 per cent casualties and achieved nothing. Wilfred Bion saw the aftermath on the Roye–Amiens road: 'One company had been proceeding in a line . . . all were knocked out. The shortage of men made it impossible to bury the dead, and for days these tanks remained where they were within easy sight of the road – a fearful sight for every soldier who marched up the main road into action. Everyone was convinced that the tanks were simply death traps.'

The Mark V had been largely successful but the Mark V*, with its provisions for carrying infantry and machine-gun sections inside the armoured hull, was not. The fumes left them gagging. The tank men for the most part were used to it. In the Amiens operations trying to operate light tanks and horsemen together proved disastrous. The first sniff of a machine gun and the cavalry withdrew. But it was improving German anti-tank tactics and weapons that were really doing the damage. The extraordinary Mauser T-Gewehr M1918 'elephant gun', firing a 13-mm armour-piercing bullet from a kind of upscaled infantry rifle, proved able to drill through British tank armour but required an exceptional soldier to fire it (the recoil regularly smashed the user's collarbone). The 7.7-cm field gun was still

---

* The *Official History*'s figures show that of the 414 tanks that were 'starters' on the first day of the battle, only six were starters on the fifth. But this apparently huge loss rate masks those machines that were available but ineffective on the day because of minor breakdowns or crews with heat-exhaustion. Contemporary research shows that only about 120 tanks were knocked out in the course of the Amiens operations as a direct result of enemy action. Tanks in fact proved remarkably durable and between 8 August and the Armistice over 800 armoured fighting vehicles were put back into the front line after having been salvaged and repaired.

the tanks' most dangerous opponent. Where the enemy stood and fought, they were as vulnerable as ever.

In June the storm-troop company commander Ernst Jünger found a clutch of them at Achiet-le-Grand on the old Somme battlefield west of Bapaume, a field classroom to teach his men the arts of tank hunting:

> In the vicinity of the embankment, looking like stranded hulls, were many shot-up tanks . . . I would have my company cluster round them to study methods of combating them, their tactics and their weak points.
>
> They carried names and emblems and designs* that were variously ironic, menacing or lucky; there was the clover leaf and the pig (for luck), and the white death's head. One was distinguished by a gallows with a noose dangling from it; that one was called 'Judge Jeffries'. All of them were in a bad way . . . I felt keen sympathy for the men in those fiery furnaces.

Henry Smeddle and his battered section were engaged on 23 August in an action launched out of the village of Courcelles towards the Albert–Arras railway. The day was sweltering, the interior of his tank, Odette, especially intolerable. In his manuscript journal Smeddle described a contretemps in Adinfer Wood, when a tank knocked over a tree, and the efforts of the company commander to regain order: 'He knew nothing about tanks or how to handle them so no one paid much attention.' Smeddle's own subordinates were an equally mixed bunch. 'Mr Payton,' for example, 'an effeminate little man who used to carry round a miserable little dog, a cross between a toy Pom and a poodle which he called Dolly . . . he had

---

* Like the naming of tanks, such signs and symbols had a purpose both as battlefield identifiers and as morale boosters. They seemed to blossom at random. According to Frank Mitchell: 'The neatest idea was that which was later adopted by 16 Company . . . represented by a hand of cards, and each section had a suit allotted to it and each tank a number. Thus F.1 had the ace of hearts painted on each side of the nose. In No. 9 Section each tank crew commander dipped his hand in red paint, and pressed it against the nose of the bus, thus christening it with the sign of the blood-stained hand.' When the Germans started using captured (*Beute*) vehicles, the front flanks of British tanks were painted in red-and-white stripes.

There were more exotic embellishments. According to an account by the former Tank Corps Private J. Laddy: 'The name of [our] tank was Delicia and the corporal in the tank wrote [to] Madame Delicia. She was a French dancer and she sent us a signed photograph and we put it on the front of the tank . . .'

no interest in the mechanical welfare of his machine but had a very good crew which was fortunate for him.'

After 'the usual straining and grunting at the starting handles' the section set off. Smeddle chose to walk outside (the steering levers were too hot to hold) but got tangled up in wire. Then an anti-tank rifle opened up:

[2/Lt] Bell's tank had not proceeded very far before a bullet struck the right-hand sponson severely wounding the gunner. He immediately jumped out and nothing was ever seen of him afterwards. Several more bullets struck the tank and two more gunners were hit. The anti-tank rifle was spotted by the man who had taken the 6-pdr gunner's place. He immediately layed the gun and fired, blowing the rifleman and all his gear to smithereens. [Another rifle opens up with AP rounds which] penetrated the cast-iron cylinder of the water jacket pouring out boiling hot steam.

Another pierced the front of the cab and wounded the Hotchkiss gunners. There were now only three effective men in the crew; the engine would be too hot to run, so Bell started to return. Armour-piercing bullets still struck and penetrated the tank but so far the driver had escaped. After about 150 yards the engine seized up . . . [They encounter Payton's tank, Olivia] He very sheepishly said the bally thing got ditched just after zero in that deep ditch near the starting point and was not able to get it out until an hour ago when it was too late so he went straight to the rallying point. Bill winked . . .

Wilfred Bion was engaged on 22 August in an attack on the old tankodrome at Méaulte, the scene of his ghastly Christmas the year before. It ended with all his section's tanks (except his own) knocked out. The crews survived. Bion turned round to go back. What happened next was especially harrowing:

As we trundled along we were hailed by numbers of [infantry] wounded who called to be carried back. The position was difficult. Tanks were expressly forbidden to take back wounded if limbs were broken. In a previous action they had been ordered, on coming out of action, to carry back all they could. The result was tragedy. At the end of half an hour's ride every wounded man that had been plucked up with broken bones was found to be dead. Now all the wounded men here were men with broken bones. The shelling had smashed legs or arms in every case. We were forced to refuse these people our help. I repeated the stale formula – 'full-up but will send a stretcher bearer,' and we went on cursed by men who had never before known one soldier refuse another soldier his help.

Any shell hole in France might be a cockpit of life-and-death drama; so might the enclosed world of a tank. Arthur Jenkin told a story in his book *A Tank Driver's Experiences*, published in 1922. The events took place in the late summer of 1918, during an attack which 'after ten minutes going the enemy was in full flight . . . I heard groaning. Looking back I saw one of the gunners lying full length on the floor with blood running fast from his nose.' Machine-gun bullets were beating against the hull; two of the crew started to vomit uncontrollably, 'mingling with the whining of the gunner who lay stretched along the blood and oil-saturated floor'.

'The whining of the sick man increased like the howling of a dog by night; his groans were piteous, his nerves seemed to have become entirely unstrung and it was beginning to affect the morale of the others. The crisis came; he appeared to be either dying or going insane. Then the officer ordered two men to put him outside. The tank was stopped and he was laid upon the grass in no man's land . . .'

Jenkin did not record the abandoned crewman's fate. He had put the others at risk and was pushed from the lifeboat. The subaltern who made the decision would have been no more than twenty.

44

Tanks had had little place in beating off the German offensive. After Amiens, what place would they have in pursuing a retreating enemy? The tanks could still only lumber after them at little more than walking pace. The true-believers might have visions of deep-flanking drives and continuous operations pressed by day and night, but the problem was not just the machines (Mark Vs were not expected to run much further than 100 miles); it was the endurance of the crew. The RAMC report *Medical Aspects of Tanks* had commented on cases of mania followed by unconsciousness after a few hours' confinement. You need not be a physician to know it. A report from 5th Tank Brigade on 5 September noted: 'When a tank is in good condition with a new engine, favourable weather, not exposed to hostile shelling or very severe fighting the crew may be counted on for twelve hours in action. The average time is however about eight hours – but very hot weather, hard fighting and engines requiring overhaul considerably lessen this . . . in the action of 23 August some crews were physically ill after two hours . . .' The early Mark Vs were miserably ventilated. It was reckoned a crew needed thirty-six hours' recuperation to be fit to fight again. Any idea of a dashing pursuit was fantasy. Still there were not enough of them. After yet another row about production promises not being met Admiral Moore was sidelined and a new Controller, Mechanised Warfare Department appointed, an industrialist-turned-Ministry of Munitions apparatchik called James Maclean.

Tank crews might still have a respectable chance of survival – up to now it was better than the infantry – but from late summer the Germans would knock out tanks faster than the British could build them. The shoulder-fired 'elephant gun,' and a new purpose-made anti-tank gun were put in the line. An outsize machine gun firing

armour-piercing bullets was promised.* Tank Corps casualties pro-
portionate to other arms climbed dramatically in the last months.
The Central Workshop could not keep pace with repairs. British tank
production, strung out among twelve firms between the Midlands
and the Clyde with myriad sub-contractors, was struggling to keep
up. Strikes (fanned, it would seem, by the employment of women
workers rather than by Bolshevik agitation) stalled production. Now
the factories must strain to equip the Americans.

On 23 August 1918 the 301st (Tank) Battalion sailed for France
with their Birmingham-built Mark Vs. Dorset girls may have been
sorry to see them go, but the British authorities were relieved to have
the US tank men firmly under their thumb in France. Christopher
Baker-Carr had the 301st attached to the 1st Tank Brigade for
training. It was all a bit of a shock:

> The commander was almost embarrassing in his protestations
> of inexperience in military matters . . . He told me he knew
> that, from our point of view, the discipline of his unit was terribly
> bad. I assured him I would do everything in my power to assist.
>
> The first thing was to hold a little ceremonial parade and
> give the men a short address. The battalion was drawn up on
> three sides of a hollow square.
>
> As I drew near, the second in command called the parade
> to attention. Every man in the ranks took a final whiff of his
> fag, threw it on the ground and expectorated generously. He
> then adjusted his cap and stood more or less to attention.
>
> It was difficult to repress a smile as I gravely took the salute
> . . . I walked slowly down the ranks stopping now and then to
> ask questions . . . One man had his cap over his left ear, one
> over his right, another the back of his head. One wore puttees,
> another canvas gaiters. Hardly ten men out of the four hundred
> on parade were dressed identically . . .

Like those British tank men who had gone before, the Americans
soon discovered that the dugouts of the Wailly training area were

---

* The so-called TuF (*Tanks und Flieger*) MG, firing the same 13-mm round as the
'elephant gun'. Its front-line advent was strongly rumoured but only six had been built
by the end of the war. One survives in a Russian tank museum. Fuller, unsurprisingly,
dismissed the power of anti-tank measures. 'German infantry were afraid' of the M1918,
he claimed. 'It is doubtful if one per cent of the A/T rifles captured in our tank attacks
had ever been fired.' Minefields (improvised out of artillery shells) he judged to be
equally ineffective.

still stuffed with old munitions. A machine gun was somehow brought into action. Some rifle grenades were lobbed at some hapless British officer who turned out to be one of 'Uncle' Harper's staff. Henceforth he referred to all Americans as 'barbarians'.

Several officers and NCOs were sent to the front line to gain some battle experience with a Canadian unit. Two American sergeants were killed by shellfire while advancing with British tanks in a night attack on 1 September near Wancourt.

Six days later the 301st, commanded by Maj. Ralph I. Sasse, moved by rail and road with its newly issued Mark Vs to a shell-blasted town ten miles south-east of Cambrai – to camp disconsolately in rat-infested dugouts vacated by New Zealand troops. British operational control remained absolute. On 29 September American tankers rolled forward against the Hindenburg Line with the British Fourth Army, which had itself managed to muster 181 tanks for this climactic operation. Three Mark Vs from the 301st's A Company were struck by shells before reaching their start line. The rest ran into an old British minefield: two tanks blew up, two broke down. Smoke supposed to aid the advance blew backwards and the survivors blundered around helplessly.

Fuller saw the aftermath, the ground:

> literally covered with American dead, all clean killed by machine-gun fire . . . burial parties were collecting them in long rows. From what I could learn the attack of the 27th American Division had been shockingly planned, prepared and executed. The infantry advanced 1500 yards behind their artillery barrage, which was placed 300 yards *behind* the German position. The result was slaughter and the 301st American Tank Battalion never having been warned of a minefield laid by the Fifth Army in February, floundered into it and was blown to pieces. Of the thirty-four tanks which took part in this massacre, only ten rallied. The whole episode was a fiasco and a disgrace.

C Company went forward ahead of its supporting (American) infantry. Of the few machines that got near the first objective, most ditched in shell holes. A brave but useless wireless tank was abandoned as Maj. Sasse resorted to trying to rally the survivors by shouting. Most of the tank men still alive were fighting hand to hand in trenches and shell holes. One machine commanded by 2/Lt Dunning got near its objective at Le Catelet when, surrounded by enemy, way head of any supporting infantry, its commander ordered the driver, Sgt Rosenhagen, to turn round. Then a plunging shell hit them smack on the roof. A dazed Sgt Rosenhagen thought he knew how he survived:

> It was the motor casing that saved us; we heard a big plop inside and we caught fire . . . I climbed through Lt Dunning's seat, the only way I could get out, and came along the motor over the 6-pounder, over the transmission; then I saw the lower door open on the right side and I slid out. Lt Dunning got his face burned getting through and out of the tank. I was lucky, as I kept my head buried in my arms and only lost some excess hair off my head . . .
>
> Lt Dunning and I were in the same shell hole, not very big. Our tank was burning and blowing up all afternoon with smoke belching out. I think the Germans figured we never got out of the tank.

A medal citation told a story repeated wherever tanks went into action in the last months of the war. The German army might be slouching eastwards but machine- and anti-tank gunners fought until their pursuers closed with bayonets:

> The Distinguished Service Cross is presented to Frank J. Williams, Jr, Sergeant, US Army, 301st Battalion, Tank Corps, AEF for extraordinary heroism in action near Ronssoy, France, 29 September, 1918. Sergeant Williams' tank received a direct hit, killing or wounding the entire crew. Although severely wounded, Sergeant Williams assisted his tank commander, who was temporarily blinded, to a position of shelter in a near-by trench. He then returned to his tank and under heavy fire continued to operate a 6-pounder against the enemy until driven out by armour-piercing shells. When it became sufficiently dark, he aided his tank commander to a first-aid station . . .

Lieutenant-Colonel George S. Patton, meanwhile, was under nobody's thumb. In the first week of September 1918 he was concerned with moving the 304th Tank Brigade by rail from Bourg to its operational area for a planned offensive against the German-held St Mihiel salient south-east of Verdun. The operation was to be conducted by the US First Army, the first independently commanded, large-scale action by US forces of the war. Patton would attack with two battalions of the 304th – now equipped with 144 two-man Renault FT-17s delivered just two weeks before – supported by the French with over 400 more tanks, heavy and light. Unlike Cambrai, there would be a four-hour preliminary artillery bombardment.

At dawn on 12 September US tank men fired up their engines and began to move forward. At first the going was good. Then it started to rain. Shell holes filled with water. Tanks slithered and wallowed, scrabbling for traction. The Renault was not an ideal trench crosser.

The enemy, mercifully perhaps for the unseasoned Americans, had largely withdrawn from the salient two days before, warned of the offensive (unlike the British in November 1917, secrecy was a shambles). Having lurched over empty trenches for twenty-four hours, Patton characteristically ordered a 'cavalry-styled' attack outside the town of Jonville. 'During the running battle the tankers killed or put into flight at least a dozen machine-gun crews and captured four 7.7-cm cannon,' according to the US *Official History*. Some die-hard Germans put up a fight, knocking out three tanks. At its end, water-filled shell holes, mechanical breakdowns and simply running out of petrol left the St Mihiel battlefield strewn with abandoned Renaults.

The Americans went into action again in the wooded valleys of the Argonne forest two weeks later in brigade strength – more than 300 machines. This time the Germans stood and fought. By midday on 26 September two-thirds of the tanks were out of action. At its end 367 French and 70 American tanks were lost on the Argonne–Champagne front, more than half of them due to mechanical failure. Crew casualties were about 50 per cent. Patton was wounded in the leg. America's first war in tanks was over.

The last hundred days cost the British Army over a quarter of a million casualties. The Tank Corps lost 561 officers and 2627 men killed, wounded and taken prisoner between 8 August and 20 October, around 40 per cent of those engaged. For the first time the loss rate was higher than that of the infantry, an indication of how hard the retreating enemy was still fighting and how they were concentrating on their lumbering armoured pursuers. Ernst Jünger saw the tenacity shown by both sides at a place called Favreuil in

September 1918: 'Four tanks crawled over a ridge, as though pulled along on a string,' he wrote. 'In a matter of minutes, the artillery had smashed them to the ground. One broke in half, like a child's toy car.' Drafts kept coming via Le Tréport from England, plus bumptious subalterns and place-seeking majors. The old hands were unimpressed: 'No sooner had the battalions been brought again to something like full strength by drafts of conscripted miners, strikers and professional footballers who might in time have been knocked into shape,' wrote Capt. Browne testily, 'than all these arrivals were released again . . . Bermicourt began to look like a poppy field for red hats.'

The last German action was at a place called Iwuy on 11 October when six A7Vs tried to hold up a British advance. A little east of Cambrai, ironically it had been an objective for the British cavalry in Operation GY. *Siegfried* (commanded by Leut. Wagner) and *Wotan* (Leut. Goldmann) went out in Wagnerian twilight. On the 20th the vehicle park at Charleroi was ordered to be evacuated and the surviving tanks began loading on trains heading east.

Just forty British machines were available for the Selle river crossing on the same day. On 4 November the last 'large' tank operation was launched – thirty-seven tanks on a huge front from the river Oise to Valenciennes. The next day eight Whippets of the 6th Tank Battalion saw fitful action north of the Forêt de Mormal. 'On the 5th November 1918 all I could put in the field was one composite company made up from an original 18 battalions!' so Elles wrote.

William Watson wrote of 'being billeted in a filthy village on the edge of the old rotting trench system, [and hearing] faint, incredible rumours that the end of the war was near. It was as if the offensive had failed completely and we are thrust back to '16. It was astonishing to us that the *émeutes*, the existence of which is now common knowledge, were not more numerous. The men were no longer soldiers, they were civilians impatient of control and eager to get home.'

It was over. The last days of the war were enacted without tanks. Hugh Elles's final war dispatch had an echo of the old underdog battle for acceptance: 'Since the opening of our offensive on August 8th, tanks have been employed on every battlefield . . . The whole scheme of the attack [at Amiens] was dependent upon tanks, and ever since that date on numberless occasions the success of our infantry has been powerfully assisted by their timely arrival.'

Tank men waited for demobilization. There was near mutiny at Le Havre and arrests of 'strikers' at the Central Workshop in December at the slowness of it all. Only when the Germans had surrendered 'their artillery and their fleet' would the Tank Corps be stood down. Those metal rhomboids were quaint things, hauled back to London, Paris and New York as ornaments for municipal parks and public squares. One would sit outside the British Museum for years. Another went to Hatfield House as a token of its patrician owner's role in the genesis of armoured warfare.* In 1918–19 British tanks went off to Dublin (to fight Sinn Feiners), to Liverpool (to break a dock strike), to Upper Silesia (to police a plebiscite) and to Russia (to bash the Bolsheviks). They cruised around Cologne with the British occupying army.

In February 1919 a Tank Association 'hut' was set up on Horse Guards Parade. Bertie Stern and Mrs H. J. Elles beamed at a little crowd. 'The comradeship of the Corps will continue when the Tanks are forgotten – when war is forgotten,' said Stern. The first priority was to find them peacetime employment. But the child-of-conflict unit did not disappear, and nor was war forgotten. Hugely reduced in numbers, the unit still attracted forward-looking professional soldiers (including some perceptive cavalrymen) who were not yet weary of fighting. Socially it adapted: the wartime motorcyclists had long left Bovington when a pack of hare-hunting Basset hounds ('fourteen couples') were presented by Lord Tredegar in 1920. Others sought the corps' very lack of flashiness. When his assumed identity as a humble aircraftman was discovered by the press in 1923, T. E. Lawrence quit the Royal Air Force for the even deeper obscurity of being No. 7875698 Pte Thomas Edward Shaw ('very clean, intelligent, hardworking and conscientious. A very reliable man'), Tank Corps.

In 1920 Congress ordered the US Tank Service disbanded. George S. Patton went back to the cavalry.

In the days after the armistice most of the German tanks ended up on a racecourse outside Wiesbaden. Hauptmann Bornschlegel made a last speech. The tank men's soldier's council gave him 'a

* Where it remained until 1970. The only surviving Mark I and the world's oldest surviving combat tank went to Bovington, where it was rehabilitated and repainted to depict C.19 'Clan Leslie', Archie Holford-Walker's machine on 15 September 1916.

vote of confidence', then headed for their homes. A trainload of Cambrai-veteran Mark IVs was abandoned in the Ardennes. Some captured machines were used by the right-wing Freikorps in street battles in Berlin and Leipzig. In March 1919 made-in-Birmingham *Hanni* rumbled menacingly around the Alexanderplatz, commanded by Leut. Theuneissen of *Mephisto* fame. The Allied control commission eventually claimed them.

The Royal Commission on Awards to Inventors reached its judgement on tanks in November 1919. Ernest Swinton presented his own case, claiming credit as far as the British Army was concerned. He got £1000. 'One thousand pounds – for winning the war,' he complained to Maurice Hankey. 'I am pleased with the result,' he told James Edmonds, 'and being of a vindictive nature not the less pleased because it is a slap in the face for DH, Wully Robertson, Whigham, Butler and all of a certain clique and gang . . . so far so good.' Eustace Tennyson d'Eyncourt, Director of Naval Construction, claimed £100,000. He got £1000. Swinton wrote to him with mutual loser's solidarity: 'Ha-ha! we can clap each other on the back . . . after all we have helped to save some lives in spite of certain people.' R. E. B. Crompton and Lucien Legros also claimed £100,000. They split £1550. Crompton argued that the Mark I 'was an entire failure which left tanks derelict on the Somme with defective track rollers'. The Australian corporal Lancelot de Mole, whose proposal to the War Office in 1912 had been ignored, was offered £40 expenses. He ended up with just under £1000.

William Tritton and Walter Wilson jointly claimed £100,000. They got £15,000 between them, the highest amount awarded.

In 1919–20 the landscape of northern France was again full of men, toiling to recover and rebury the dead and stitch the most obvious wounds of the toxic wastelands in which they had fallen. Much of the work on the British side was done by the Chinese Labour Corps. Hundreds of thousands of men remained missing. Myriad tons of ordnance were sinking into the ground. But 'tanks' were big things. The Germans themselves in winter 1917–18 had scoured the fields in front of Cambrai for machines that might be repaired and sent back into battle, but after two years scores of hulks still littered the landscape.

The British battlefield commission arrived after the Armistice of 11 November 1918 to blow them up and cart away the scrap. D.51

somehow survived. Flesquières had stayed in British hands until the great retreat of March 1918. The tank had evidently been dragged down the village street and half-buried by the Germans in an existing crater (Mme Bouleux had said she remembered Russian POWs doing the work) and used as a dugout in the defensive operations of September 1918 when the village was once again a battlefield. That explained the strange jumble of rubbish inside – Scotch whisky, English corned-beef tins, German grenades.

More research at Bovington uncovered the file of a Col. Theodore Wenger, a Tank Corps salvage officer, in charge of a battlefield clearance team around Cambrai in 1919. There was a photograph of Deborah, the number '51' clearly visible on the petrol tank – and the damage was the same. It was Wenger who completed the burial in the pit, or rather Chinese labourers did. The colonel seemed reluctant to blow the tank up as it was not out in the fields but still in what remained of the now inhabited village. A photograph was taken before the interment. That absolutely confirmed her identity. Deborah began her long sleep.

In spite of its press-puffed fame, in spite of its achievements, the Tank Corps was always a marginal affair. Even at its autumn 1918 apogee its ranks represented just 1 per cent of the British Army in the field – as Fuller pointed out – not even the equivalent of an infantry division. In terms of manpower the artillery was twenty-five times the size.

In 1919 the transport expert Lt-Col. Alan Brough was dispatched to Grozny in the Caucasus to run railways for the anti-Bolshevik forces in the doomed military intervention (which included forty tanks) backed by Winston Churchill (Secretary of State for War from December 1918). The Tank Corps went into action at Tsaritsin* in Mark Vs. More tank crew would die of typhus than from enemy action. Brough's disagreeable experience ended with having

---

* Later Stalingrad. Officially they were there to train Russian crews, but 'volunteers' saw fit to do some actual fighting. There were two further armoured interventions in Russia. A detachment of three Mark Vs was landed in the Baltic in October 1919 and got as far as Gatchina, twenty miles from Petrograd. Six tanks (nine officers and sixty men) were landed at Archangel in the far north. On the British evacuation, they were abandoned to the care of the White Russians, who towed them out on barges then sank them in the River Dvina as the Bolsheviks closed in on the Arctic port.

hurriedly to extricate British forces and the surviving tanks from the Crimea as Leon Trotsky's Red Army closed in on them.

In 1924 the matter of the late Lt-Col. John Brough came up again with the increasing frailty of the father. The correspondence was batted between the tax inspector, the War Office and the family solicitors until in October the Revenue was informed: 'I am commanded by the Army Council to inform you that fresh evidence has now been produced in this case. It is now the consideration of the Council that the strain of military duty undoubtedly caused the mental condition that prompted this officer's suicide.'

The council's chairman was the former miner Stephen Walsh MP, Secretary for War in Ramsay MacDonald's short-lived Labour administration. The undersecretary was Maj. Clement Attlee, late of the Tank Corps and future Labour Prime Minister. Walsh had been a member of the 1920 parliamentary commission on shell shock. He had lost his own son in 1918. The council's most senior military member was Gen. Robert Whigham.

The case is not mentioned in the council's formal minutes for the period. It seems likely that the 'fresh evidence' was simply Alan Brough's letter. The business of the tanks on the Somme in September 1916 was too messy to reopen. Attlee was in a position to have known the truth. The family got their asked-for redemption. It was in the nature of a pardon. Old Colonel William Brough died in 1929. The Commonwealth War Graves citation reads: 'Lt-Col J Brough, Royal Artillery GSO 61st Div, aged 43, son of Col William Richard Charles Brough (late Royal Artillery) and Annie Maria Brough, of Antelope Hotel, Dorchester – [buried at] at Longuenesse (St Omer) Souvenir Cemetery plot IV. C. 80.'

He is 'remembered with honour'.

AFTERWORD

The libel row of 1941 between H. G. Wells and Ernest Swinton had begun with the novelist's outrage that a British 'native invention has been turned by the Germans into the means to inflict one disaster after another upon us'. It was a paradox painfully obvious to everyone. The inadequacy of British tanks after the debacle in France of May 1940, undergunned, underpowered (but not necessarily under-armoured), would be dubbed the 'Great Tank Scandal'.

How could it be that not just the technical lead in armoured warfare, but the novel doctrinal thinking from which it sprang had not only been thrown away but seemingly handed to the Germans? Scapegoats were sought at the time and the matter has been comprehensively picked over by historians ever since.

Some laid the blame on Winston Churchill as Secretary of State for War and his financially stringent 'Ten Year Rule' of August 1919 to the effect that the armed forces should draft their estimates for weapons and force levels 'on the assumption that the British Empire would not be engaged in any great war during the next ten years'. It seemed logical enough (even if Churchill was at the same time sending British tanks to fight the Bolsheviks). He would repeat the assertion in 1928 as a Chancellor of the Exchequer looking for tax cuts. Until the rise of Hitler the prospect of a general war against an equivalent enemy anywhere in the world seemed remote. That did not preclude thinking about it.

In the early postwar years a new caste of military professionals was making the loudest noise. Fuller won the 1920 RUSI Gold Medal for a wildly radical essay which concluded 'the tank can replace infantry and cavalry'. Swinton was one of the judges. The former infantry officer-turned-journalist Basil Liddell Hart was chosen by the War Office to write a new infantry training manual. Fuller and Liddell Hart agreed that modern armies must strive for mobility

403

through mechanization, and it is Liddell Hart who is generally regarded as taking Fuller's 1918 ideas for armoured thrusts to break up a defensive front – into the philosophy of the 'expanding torrent' which would spread paralysis up through higher commands all the way to the enemy's capital. According to his own memoirs: 'The publication of Fuller's essay had been my first acquaintance with his views and vision. It led me to send him what I had recently been writing about the new tactics and that was the start of our close association and long friendship.'

Theory was well and good, but heavy tanks seemed increasingly irrelevant as army life went back to imperial policing and regimental soldiering. The public mood was forgetful of war. There were those like Maj.-Gen. Louis Jackson, the wartime Trench Warfare specialist at the Ministry of Munitions, who saw the tank as a 'freak', an offspring solely of 'circumstances not likely to recur'. Earl Haig made a famously obscurantist speech, gleefully quoted in Liddell Hart's memoirs: 'Some enthusiasts today talk about the probability of the horse becoming extinct and prophesy that the aeroplane, the tank and the motorcar will supersede the horse in future war . . . I am all for using aeroplanes and tanks, but they are only accessories . . . and I feel sure as time goes on you will find just as much use for the horse – the well-bred horse – as you have ever done in the past.'

The Tank Corps' own 'enthusiasts' were led by the wartime machine-gun protagonist Lt-Col. George 'Boss' Lindsay, its Chief Instructor (Inspector from 1926), who brought Maj. Charles Broad in to run the gunnery school, and Maj. Frederick 'Tim' Pile, another artilleryman, who later became Director of Mechanization at the War Office. Major P. C. S. 'Patrick' Hobart joined from the Royal Engineers. George Lindsay commanded three armoured-car companies of the Tank Corps in Iraq in 1921 (they were taken over later by the RAF) and, bowling across the desert, began developing ideas of an entirely mechanized force.

In Liddell Hart's words, 'these four men were all postwar recruits to the armoured cause. They all became generals, and would almost certainly have risen higher still if they had not become identified with a cause and a concept that was regarded as heretical and deviationist'.

It was all so different to begin with. In 1923 the Tank Corps became 'Royal', a definite seal of approval. Field Marshal Sir George

Milne, newly appointed CIGS in 1926, chose Fuller as his 'military assistant'. Liddell Hart became an unofficial adviser. All seemed set fair for tanks to prosper. The traditionalists railed against the upstarts who wanted everything for themselves and cuts for everyone else. The enthusiasts, meanwhile, argued among themselves, advocating every permutation of armour, infantry and artillery. The French chose to hide behind concrete. Russian tank ideas flared brilliantly (until Stalin's purges physically snuffed out the innovators); the Americans were almost totally quiescent.

For a while Britain really did lead the world. The Milne regime sponsored the futuristic demonstration staged by George Lindsay on 13 November 1926 at Camberley featuring every kind and type of mechanized vehicle, including the Vickers-built 'Independent' tank, a multi-turreted thirty-tonner. Fuller, after a posting to India, returned in October 1927 to find himself in charge of the '7th Infantry Brigade', in fact the kernel of an experimental mechanized force. The rhomboid trench crushers had all gone. The prototype force combined turreted Vickers Medium Mark Is, a motorized infantry battalion riding in half-tracks and six-wheel trucks, a flotilla of 'tank-ettes', mobile engineers and tractor-towed artillery. It was a brilliant innovation. There was a catch; Fuller's divisional commander was 'Jock' Burnett-Stuart, sceptic-in-chief of 1916. His views on tanks had changed, but not entirely. After much internal grumpiness, Fuller resigned. He was replaced by an infantryman, Brig. R. J. Collins. Liddell Hart made noises in the press (he was now military correspondent of the *Daily Telegraph*) which were taken up in Parliament. That year he published his theory 'Strategy of Indirect Approach', the blueprint for, as it was described, 'armoured forces racing on ahead of the main army'.

For two years the Experimental Mechanized Force (formally named on 1 May 1927) showed off what it could do – a miniature 'all-tank army' – exciting great press and international interest. The RAF joined the proceedings on several occasions. Other arms were losing out and began to complain. It was decreed; in the next two years of experiment tanks were to be diffused into mechanized brigades to support the infantry.

In 1931 the tank units were brought back together as a single force with Charles Broad in command. There was a flurry of brave experiment (such as the use of wireless to bring 180 vehicles under one command) against a background of deepening financial and political crisis. A 'qualitative' disarmament conference at Geneva bruited the abolition of heavy tanks. Such sentiments faded with Adolf Hitler's advent to power as German Chancellor in January 1933.

That year Milne was replaced as CIGS by Sir Archibald Montgomery-Massingberd, former Chief of Staff of Fourth Army on the Somme. One of his first proposals was to provide horses for RTC officers so that in the hunting field they might learn 'quickness of decision'. Broad departed, so did Pile. In 1934 Sir Hugh Elles was appointed Master General of the Ordnance. His views on armoured forces turned out to be as constrained as Sir Archibald's. There would be no big war in Europe for many years, declared the CIGS. Elles expressed the same sentiment, but if there should be the role of tanks would be the same as in 1917–18 – battering rams for the infantry. Further, they would have to bear monstrous armour to resist new anti-tank weapons.

It was a popular sentiment. The Germans, it was reported, had a secret new 'ultra-bullet'. In the midst of taking soundings on the draft of the *Official History* dealing with the advent of the tanks in September 1916, Brig.-Gen. James Edmonds told Liddell Hart in a portentous letter: 'Any tank that shows its nose will in my opinion be knocked out at once . . . the wars that you and Fuller imagine are past.'

The old gang were still in touch, ready as ever to be incensed by the latest judgement by the younger generation on GHQ's wartime competence or lack of it. 'Liddell Hart is a national danger,' wrote Robert Whigham to James Edmonds after some mildly critical news-paper commentary. The death of Earl Haig in January 1928 had opened the floodgates. Brig.-Gen. John Charteris's biography pub-lished a year after the 'chief' had been buried at Dryburgh Abbey in the Scotish Borders (marked by a plain Imperial War Graves Com-mission headstone) strived to shield his late master from the suddenly unleashed tide of post-mortem deprecation. His account of the tanks' debut and Haig's rush to action was underwritten by stories of 'leaks' by careless Members of Parliament and mysterious letters to neutral countries. His apparently more insightful *At GHQ* followed in 1931 but its value as documentary history was also to be doubted. James

Edmonds told Liddell Hart: 'It is whispered among the initiated that it is a fake . . . in some cases he reverses what is in the contemporary record.'

The story in that account of the 'elderly amorist' revealing the secret of the tanks in May 1916 to his Parisian mistress was a thumping example of fakery. The breezy letters home to the intelligence chief's wife contain lots of prurient gossip but no mention of caterpillar pillow-talk. The secret was already out, so Charteris directly implied; Haig was entirely right to use the tanks when he did. 'It could only be a matter of time before the German intelligence service would obtain complete information and be able to evolve an adequate protection,' he wrote.

Why all the fuss about the 'premature disclosure of this immature instrument', as Liddell Hart called the events of 15 September 1916 in *The Real War*, the book which made Haig-bashing intellectually respectable?

All this might not have mattered, except that the debate about the past was directly informing the debate about the strategic present. The official historian James Edmonds, for example, in his treatment of the events surrounding the disastrous opening of the Somme offensive (covered in the volume of the *Official History* published in January 1932) was prepared to be critical enough to trigger the formation of a special War Office committee to investigate. Lt-Gen. Walter Kirke, the security specialist who had long ago fussed over potential leaks of the tank secret from Elveden and Yvrench, was its president. It concluded among other things: 'The commander who selects the offensive and fails to surprise his opponent has lost the main advantage which the offensive confers.' The tanks were a surprise – or were they?

The Kirke report was suppressed by the new CIGS, Field-Marshal Sir Archibald Montgomery-Massingberd. Edmonds, the man in Liddell Hart's phrase 'responsible for drawing the right conclusions from the past for the Army's future', meanwhile fell back into bland hagiography as the official histories ground on. A 1943 newspaper interview described him toiling away in the National Library of Wales, starting each day at his Aberystwyth home with a routine of dumb-bells and pouring a jug of cold water over his head.

'He used to say that he could not tell the truth frankly . . . but hoped that it would be evident to those who could read between the lines,' according to Liddell Hart. General Edmonds's correspondence files, preserved at the UK National Archives, are filled with incident and anguish expressed by those survivors for whom passion about the past was far from spent. Especially about tanks.

In 1933 Montgomery-Massingberd, for all his reputation as a military conservative, decided to establish the 1st Tank Brigade as a permanent formation. The Le Corbusier-bespectacled Patrick Hobart, at the time the most radical of the RTC's modernists, would command it. In September 1934 it was included in the so-called 'Mobile Force', including a brigade of lorry- and half-trackborne infantry commanded by George Lindsay, and sent into mock battle against a traditional infantry-horsed cavalry force (equipped with some armoured cars) over a swathe of the Cotswolds and Wiltshire. The affair was flagrantly rigged by Burnett-Stuart who had already outraged tank men by mockingly thrashing a river with rod and line while they attempted to cross. The Mobile Force was humiliatingly trapped by a hastily laid minefield. Hobart called it a 'frame up'. George Lindsay felt grossly humiliated. He was posted to India. Fuller raged at the folly of it all in a newspaper article in the *Daily Express*.

The German armour enthusiast Heinz Guderian, Chief of Staff to the Inspectorate of Motorized Troops, ordered every scrap of information on the British manoeuvres to be gathered and translated. The treaty-restrained Reichswehr had begun secret experiments in Russia in 1928. When Hitler first saw a prototype armed tractor on the army ordnance testing ground in 1935, in outline it was derived from a British light tank that the Soviet army had been testing. The Führer famously told Guderian, 'That's what I want, that's what I need to have.' That year the German army formed its first tank battalion. Guderian read everything that Fuller and Liddell Hart might put out, but whatever either of them, or indeed H. G. Wells, might later have to say on the matter, the idea of lightning war was not entirely made in England.

By 1939 the German army would have six armoured divisions and an air force trained to support them. The British Army would have two. And whose fault was that? It was the long history of financial restraint, some said; it was the disarmament moves of 1932 which had blighted medium-tank development; it was deference too long to the cavalry; it was a failure to understand Hitler's intentions and get serious about rearmament until it was far too late. In 1936 eight British cavalry regiments began trading their horses for light tanks and armoured cars. To begin with it was a voluntary experiment. Mr Duff Cooper, the Secretary for War who had just published an approving biography of Haig, asked the horsemen for forbearance 'in their great sacrifice'. The rest of the cavalry would reluctantly follow until war with Germany was imminent.

In April 1939, Leslie Hore-Belisha, the new Secretary of State for War, made an announcement which stunned military traditionalists. A Royal Armoured Corps (RAC) was to be established embracing the RTC (to be renamed the Royal Tank Regiment), which was in the process of post-Munich-crisis expansion to eight regular and seven territorial battalions – eighteen already mechanized cavalry regiments and eight yeomanry regiments then in the process of saying goodbye to saddle soap and sabres. The stink boxes had won after all. All recruits to armoured units were to be put into a common pool with a central depot and training school – Bovington.

Cavalry officers and those of the RTR, meanwhile, would be listed separately. They would keep their regimental distinctions and their social exclusivity. Veterans of the suddenly defunct Royal Tank Corps were not so sure that their child-of-war patrimony was not being swamped by a bunch of toffs.

The British lead in armoured doctrine and method was eclipsed from the early 1930s onwards as personalities changed at the top of the army and rivals caught up. Of the key individuals who pressed for change to go further and faster, Fuller self-immolated in 1927 and George Lindsay wrote himself out after the humiliation of the Mobile Force 'farce' of 1934. Personalities rose, flared and burned out. Machines and those responsible for their design and procurement took longer to show their strengths and weaknesses.

Deficiencies in the quantity and quality of British tanks would become painfully obvious in the test of battle when it came round again in the spring of 1940. Where did blame lie for that? It was a long story. Almost all tank construction had been cancelled with the Armistice. The War Office took back responsibility for future design and development in March 1919 from the Ministry of Munitions; the General Staff would decide requirements and the Master General of the Ordnance would progress design and manufacture. The innovative Col. Philip Johnson was, however, given responsibility for experiments with a testing ground in Dollis Hill. Only four Medium Ds (the weapon that was going to swarm all over the Germans in 1919) were eventually built and in 1923 Johnson's operation was shut down. The armaments firm Messrs Vickers had a commercial design – the Medium Mk 1 – which seemed much more affordable.

The new Mechanization Directorate established by the War Office in October 1927 under the nominal control of the Master General of the Ordnance was responsible for every aspect of army mobility, from tanks to motorcycles. Development by the Vickers company of a radically modern vehicle, the sixteen-ton A6, was progressed by the department's assistant director, Frederick Pile.

In 1932 a new Director took over – Maj.-Gen. Alan Brough.

It might be thought somewhat ironic. John Brough's brother had become Britain's head of tank development and production. For two years he and Elles worked together. It was a seemingly disastrous combination. Just as the innovators in the field were getting their head, the money box was emptying. Brough's first move was to cancel the sixteen-tonner. Tanks would have to be built henceforth with commercial truck engines. In Liddell Hart's words, 'during the next four years little was achieved ... the inertia and shortsightedness of the mechanization board at Woolwich Arsenal contributed largely to this state of stagnation. A variety of experimental models were designed and tried and all proved unsatisfactory.'

Hugh Elles would prove just as clay-footed. Liddell Hart sat next to him at the Savoy for the annual Cambrai dinner (Churchill was guest of honour) on 20 November 1935. The conversation was uninspiring. 'Others at the dinner were vehement in their criticism of him for letting down the Corps,' he wrote. He described it thus in an aide-memoire:

> Montgomery-Massingberd made a speech which was received politely but with palpable chilliness. Hugh Elles amazed me with his inability to recognise that the conditions of warfare were changed – 'it's the man with the bayonet you want' he insisted, prodding me in the waistcoat ... he put the whole blame of lack of modern equipment on the treasury and the politicians ...

Each time I talk with him the more I have come to fear that he is merely a handsome and pleasant façade . . . and this, I find, is confirmed by those who were on his staff in the Tank Corps during the war . . .

The dashing hero clanking into action in Hilda had become a stick-in-the-mud, obsessed with slow-moving 'infantry' tanks capable, absurdly it might seem in retrospect, of resisting all known anti-tank devices.

Alan Brough hung on for four years as part of the stodgy regime. On his departure in 1936, 'Slosher' Martel (who had pursued an eccentric independent career advocating one-man 'tankettes') was brought into the War Office to be in immediate charge of all tank development. He went haring off to Russia to see Red Army tanks charging around at 30 mph, something he strived, against all sorts of opposition, to emulate successfully in a British-built machine. That the British Army of 1939–40 should have had any fast-paced 'cruiser' tanks at all was largely due to his belated and energetic efforts. Elles's legacy was the disastrous Infantry Tank Mk I, a barely mobile pillbox powered by a Ford V8 truck engine armed with a single machine gun, most of which ended up abandoned at Dunkirk. The War Office had codenamed its development programme 'Matilda'.*

Alan Brough's obituary in the *Journal of the Royal Engineers* was brief, compiled, it was said, 'from certain papers he had left behind'. 'His four years as director of mechanization was a most unhappy period as he could not get any decisions as to requirements either for tanks or wheeled vehicles', it said, 'and had considerable difficulty over the development of any kind of anti-tank gun . . . His work was interrupted by illness in 1935. In June 1936 he was very glad to retire.'

A colleague who remembered him as a young sapper officer in India, pushing a railway line through some dusty mountain range, preferred to recall his exploits as a hunter – and his principle that 'dangerous, wounded big game must always be followed up and mercifully dispatched'.

Alan Brough died aged eighty in 1956. He never married. General Sir Hugh Elles wrote a novel (under the pseudonym Adam Hughes).

---

* 'Mighty in battle' in old German. I am grateful to David Fletcher for this information. Other less authoritative sources ascribe the name to a newspaper comic duck popular at the time and the name of Hugh Elles's mistress.

In 1940 he became Civil Defence commissioner for Bristol. He died in 1945, having married three times. Sir Richard Butler retired from the army 'because there was nothing left for him to do' and died in April 1936. Sir Ernest Dunlop Swinton became a Colonel Commandant of the Royal Tank Corps and remained Chichele Professor of the History of War at the University of Oxford. where 'his humour was appreciated in the All Souls common room though he left no deep mark on the teaching', according to Liddell Hart, who failed in various attempts to winkle him out of his professorship and supplant him with himself. He was invited to Nazi Germany on several occasions where he was hailed as 'father of the tank'. His daughter was fatally struck by a US Army lorry while riding her bicycle in the Woodstock Road, Oxford, in March 1944. He died in 1951.

General James Edmonds reported in a letter to Swinton a few years later a meeting in clubland in London where 'boy admirals' and 'youthful brigadiers' of a more recent war hogged the bar at the Senior. Who of this bright new generation wanted to know about 'caterpillars' and the Somme? The Western Front was 'of another world'. The old guard, meanwhile, seemed past caring. 'Hankey was in . . . looking exactly the same . . .' so Edmonds wrote, 'and Alan Brough, much decayed and drinking again. Fuller was too deaf to converse with . . . When in London I went to Tussaud's wax works, I looked for Haig's effigy, could find none and, on inquiring, was informed it has been removed to make room for others . . .'

In 1939 the originators of Big Willie – Swinton, Sir Albert Stern, Sir William Tritton, Walter Wilson and Tennyson d'Eyncourt – were bizarrely reunited in a committee sponsored from the sidelines by Churchill. They produced a huge rhomboid tank (with a turret) called 'TOG-1' ('the old guard') designed to break a trench stalemate. Events overtook it.

'Boney' Fuller became an ardent member of the British Union of Fascists, and in 1934 military adviser to its leader, Sir Oswald Mosley. He was left untouched in the wave of arrests of June 1940, so it is suspected on Churchill's intervention. In 1942 the Beaverbrook press demanded his recall to the War Office to sort out the 'tank scandal' as British fighting machines were still proving so ineffective. He was not recalled and the nation's tanks did not get much better, although the two are not necessarily related. Fuller died in 1966.

In summer 2006 the family of Allen Holford-Walker donated his wartime papers to the National Army Museum. They contained a typewritten copy document from around 1934 addressed to 'Dear Bo' (presumably 'Boney' Fuller) explaining that this was his response to the 'verbiage' sent to him by the Official Historian – the draft history of the Battle of Flers-Courcelette and the events preceding. As well as flaying the likes of Gen. Gathorne-Hardy and 'infantry formation commanders' in general for their incompetence, Holford-Walker had something very direct to say about one officer:

> The scrambling for appointment on Tanks staff was the most ungentlemanly thing I have ever seen, and I am afraid that in the opinion of all the tank officers of that date the worst offender was General Elles . . .

And as for Robert Bradley, the feeble 'co-ordinating officer', his appointment was a 'definite embarrassment as far as my company was concerned because he knew absolutely nothing about a tank. [Thus it was] impossible for this officer to act as a buffer between the companies and a higher formation. This and the machinations were directly responsible for the death of a very gallant officer (Colonel Brough) . . .'

So Bradley was a fool and Gen. Hugh Elles – the hero of Cambrai – was a bit of a bounder. To the men who had blundered into action with no coherent plan of attack in September 1916 that was the case at least. No wonder Elles went crashing into the Hindenburg Line fourteen months later flying his brave flag from Hilda. It was indeed a 'very gallant show'. But his high command-defying recklessness was not just about raising the spirits of the Tank Corps. It was about John Brough. It was about the man who shot himself in a Flanders ditch.

That same summer of 2006 there came a strange twist in the story of the latter-day tank pioneers. The security service (MI5) released through the National Archives certain personal files on those it suspected of less than complete loyalty to the state almost seventy years earlier. Fuller's file was retained. That on Sir Basil Liddell Hart was opened to the public. It revealed feuds and infighting which went back to the debut of the tank. It was Brig.-Gen. James Edmonds who shopped him: 'My dear Kell' (Vernon Kell, veteran spy hunter from the MO5 days), he wrote in October 1939 on Historical Section

(Military Branch) official letterhead, 'I hear that Capt B H Liddell Hart is going round making defeatist propaganda. I saw the DCIGS and he suggested that I should let you know so an eye can be kept on him.' It was – throughout the war. His phone was tapped and his mail opened. Liddell Hart's original indiscretions were to make a series of newspaper pronouncements advising against continental entanglements, and from 1939 expressing doubt on Britain's ability to win a renewed war of attrition. His burning interest in tanks had waned long before. Now it was anti-aircraft defence.

An official wrote in 1944, it is 'unlikely that he no longer thinks an Allied victory impossible . . . except for his friendship with Fuller he does not crop up among those who would certainly cultivate him if he were known to them to be of their Fascist way of thinking'. The monitoring of the military writer went on after the end of Hitler's war (he was interviewing enemy commanders for his revelatory postwar book *The Other Side of the Hill*; perhaps he was a closet neo-Nazi, so it was somewhat strangely suspected). From the late 1940s Liddell Hart was also compiling information for his two-volume history, *The Tanks*. MI5 showed no interest in that.

Attached to the compendious file is a mail intercept of 18 June 1938, a postcard from Fuller to another BUF member: 'Liddell Hart is both a Jew and an ass – when will he learn from history?' he wrote. The matter in hand was not revealed. 'Boney' was always bursting with indignation. That is what made him such a useful campaigner in 1917–18 in the armoured cause. In 1940 it made him a potential traitor. He scarcely ever ventured inside a tank, but all along John Frederick Charles Fuller was perhaps the biggest brigand of them all.

And the tank men themselves? Every story was different. In early 2007 the advertised sale of some medals on an internet auction site triggered an especially poignant piece of filial remembrance. The decorations were those of Acting/Capt. Arthur Blowers, the twenty-five-year-old commander of D.5 Dolphin who got further than any-one else on 15 September 1916 and won the Military Cross in the process. The sale caused his son, Roger (born in 1940, the youngest of seven; Blowers himself was the thirteenth of fourteen Suffolk-born children), to contribute a fascinating family confessional to an on-line Great War forum:

He won his MC, I believe, for returning to his burning tank to rescue the driver. He told me that he sat in the tank that day, firing his Webley revolver at German infantry . . . he said, 'I fired over a hundred rounds . . . none of the targets was more than about 10 yards away, so I didn't miss many!'

He sustained head injuries . . . During treatment he was given morphine to which he became addicted and he told the story of having a vision of death standing at the end of his bed, saying 'I am coming for you!'

He spent some time . . . living in a tent, in the orchard of his father's farm, weaning himself off the morphine/heroin, by replacing it with large amounts of beer! He was eventually able to get off the alcohol, too, and made an apparently complete recovery, confounding the medics who'd given him 6 months to live.

Blowers became a schoolmaster and pillar of the local Conservative association. He evidently sought continued excitement in motorcycling. 'He was a selfish man,' wrote his son, 'but had considerable charm, which enabled him to get away with a lot. His family didn't forget that he had suffered a lot early in his life.' Arthur Blowers died in 1980.

At the time of the Munich crisis in 1938, with children trying on gas masks and MI5 tapping phones, a popular publisher had a kind of success with *Twenty Years On*, an illustrated 'part-work' history of the Great War (edited by the hyperactive Ernest Dunlop Swinton) which invited reminiscences from old soldiers. A 'former tank officer' gave some fascinating insights, some of which have been used in this narrative. He was aged twenty when he did all these brave things, but felt it appropriate to write about his current condition as a middle-aged man with another German war coming.

There is a meeting of tank veterans in some country pub. Bores and fantasists (and there were plenty of those) are forgiven – talk about the 'war' unites them all. They could go on for hours. Young people do not seem to want to know. 'Good old Fritz' is roundly toasted. At least he might understand what it was really like. The anonymous author has this to say: 'We who fought are corrupt with the old custom of the war and we cannot comfort ourselves with much besides. But who can blame us if we still nourish that old blind life within the brain – that the sound of a motor cycle is still fraught with expectancy of orders for action, or that our hearts are touched by the half-forgotten refrain of Tipperary coming from a passing charabanc . . .'

ACKNOWLEDGEMENTS

A work like this is a journey in time and space, and I must thank those enthusiasts for this story, amateur and professional, who have helped me physically and metaphorically along it. They include Philippe Gorczysnki and Jean-Luc Gibot, David Fletcher, Dr Nicholas Hiley, Kate O'Brien, Emma Golding, Margaret Brooks, Claire Knight, Richard Davies and the staff of the Special Collections, Brotherton Library, University of Leeds, Simon Moody and Alastair Massie of the National Army Museum, Dr A. R. Morton of the Royal Military Academy, Sandhurst, Chris Hobson, Head of Library Services, Joint Services Command and Staff College. Trevor Pidgeon kindly allowed me to quote some material from his book, *The Tanks at Flers*.

I must as always thank the staff of the British Library (St Pancras and Colindale) and the National Archives, Kew, for faultless service and help at every step, the staff of the London Transport Museum, the National Maritime Museum, the Imperial War Museum, the Tank Museum and the Intelligence Corps Museum, Chicksands, Bedfordshire.

I am grateful to The Penguin Group for permission to quote from *Storm of Steel* by Ernst Jünger (2003 translation by Michael Hoffman), Messrs Hutchinson for permssion to quote from Ernest Swinton's *Eyewitness* and Routledge for Lionel Loewe's *Lewis Basil Henriques: A Portrait*. Extracts from Wilfrid Bion's *War Memoirs 1917–1919* are reproduced by permission of Paterson Marsh Ltd on behalf of the Estate of W. R. Bion. Quotes from Clough and Amabel Williams-Ellis *The Tanks* are reproduced by permission of The Second Portmeirion Foundation, who inform me: 'Unfortunately, in 1953 a fire at Sir Clough Williams-Ellis's house destroyed all records of this era of his life.' Thanks to those numerous publishers who have dutifully pursued their records in response to requests for rights clearance in works quoted. Where every effort has been made to find appropriate copyright holders, some have proved impossible to locate or have not replied.

For permission to quote from the original papers and memoirs on which this work has drawn, I am grateful to the Trustees of the Churchill Archives Centre, The Tank Museum, the Trustees of the Liddell Hart Centre for Military Archives, the Imperial War Museum Department of Documents and Department of Sound and the Liddle Collection, Leeds for the appropriate permissions. Special gratitude is due to the Rev. Frances Forward, Mr E. W. Powell-Chandler, Maj. N. C. Wimberley, Catherine Hall, Mike Thompson and Dr J. E. Hodgkin not only for granting permission to publish but also for sharing further personal anecdotes and family reminiscences. Extracts from the diary of General Lord Rawlinson of Trent are reproduced by permission of the Rawlinson family. Correspondence and extracts from the diaries of King George V and the letters from the Somme of the Prince of Wales to his father held in the Royal Archives are reproduced with the gracious permission of Her Majesty The Queen.

The usual monomania has been inflicted on colleagues and friends as the aphids of the last investigation were supplanted by the caterpillars of this one. Thanks are due to those who stayed the course, including Vivienne Schuster, Stephanie Thwaites, Kate Fassett, Richard Johnson, Richard Collins, David Monaghan, Ronnie Payne and Peter Millar. Mrs Clare Campbell put up with it all with elegant grace, and Joseph, thanks to a visit to Deborah in her barn, knows what it's like to be inside a Mark IV.

To those men of the Tank Corps and its predecessors, to their relatives and descendants, to all those who remember them – I am grateful. Fear Naught.

A NOTE ON SOURCES

What the young men of the Heavy Section Machine Gun Corps really said to each other on going into battle for the first time is more or less beyond recall. Above the clatter of their Daimler sleeve-valve engines one imagines they mostly swore. The inside of a tank was not a place for philosophic discourse. An account by a youthful commander walking among his section in some damp corner of France just before dawn describes the human-made noises coming from within their armoured hides as they manoeuvre into line – loud shouting, whistling or metallic banging. There is none such from one tank about to go into action; the commander apparently is attempting to get things moving exclusively by hand signals. Shouting turns out best.

This book is neither an attempt to be an 'oral history' told entirely from contemporaneous letters and diaries (or from the twilight recorded memories of the very old), nor a military history in the classic sense of setting out which unit did what to whom by whose orders and where. But it is informed throughout by voices speaking directly of the matter in hand – and they talk across time through all sorts of ways.

The story of how 'tanks' came to be built in the first place is exhaustively documented in the National Archives of the United Kingdom – in Admiralty, War Office, Ministry of Munitions, Cabinet and Treasury files, especially perhaps because a postwar cash premium for whomsoever was deemed to have invented the tank invited millions of words of testimony in a set-piece legal process. Those involved were hard pressed to shut up at all. Especially Winston S. Churchill.

So 'tanks' were made and men had to be found to take them to war. Again the official documentation is tremendous – the travails of Ernest Swinton, Albert Stern, Richard Butler et al., the War Office – and GHQ in France – recorded in bulging bundles of letters, memoranda and telegrams preserved in the National Archives. Records in the Liddell Hart Centre for Military Archives at King's College London and in the Churchill Archive, Churchill College, Cambridge bring extra courses to the feast.

Then tanks went into combat. War diaries say what they do – which is not very much: 'Tank D.22 advanced on Ale Trench and did much slaughter . . .' etc. Similar accounts of the infantry they attempted to accompany into battle are also depressingly uniform. Some of the tank battalion histories compiled in 1918–19 (in the WO 95 series at the National Archives), however, can be much more discursive, almost lyrical. Take this from the 9th Battalion history (WO 95/107), for example, describing summer 1917 in Dorset, where there was 'plentiful fishing on the Trent and bathing at Lulworth Cove. This part of the world abounded with farms where one could get most excellent teas . . . Mr Debenham who owned the manor house at Morton very kindly placed several tennis courts at the disposal of the officers of the battalion . . .' How agreeable. Then they went to the Ypres salient.

The multi-volume *Official History* published between 1924 and 1948 falls in with the Hun-crushing mood of the war diaries (a terrific read and primary source, nevertheless). I am grateful to the new owners of the Telegraph Group for, following their 2005 takeover, ordering the newspaper's entire Great War archive of books and cuttings to be dumped in a rubbish skip outside Canary Wharf – to be salvaged by this former employee following an urgent call by a distraught librarian. The *Telegraph*'s well-thumbed *Histories* (including the 1914–15 crop inherited from the old *Morning Post*), now safely on my own shelves, have been constant waypoints through the mud and blood to the indices and source notes beyond.

What was it like to be one of the first men in tanks? A rash of I-was-there memoirs published soon after the end of the war (almost all by youthful officers) tell their stories modestly and poignantly. The 1919 history *The Tank Corps* by Clough Williams-Ellis (the architect of Portmeirion) is itself a wonderful anthology of recorded experience, his contributors released by the peace from the strictures of censorship. William Watson's *A Company of Tanks* (1922) ranks as a classic of war reportage, on the edge of great literature. There are several more tank memoirs almost as good. Add the sequence of true-life yarns (largely anonymous) published in *The Tank Corps Journal* throughout the early twenties and the close-to-the-event storytelling gets remarkably rich. It was the lieutenants and dashing captains, however, who tended to get the publishing contracts.

That gap was closed to some extent by the diligence of a generation of researchers who in the sixties and seventies sought to record the experiences of Great War veterans before they had all gone. And not just the officers. Headphones on (at the Liddle Archive in Leeds or at the IWM department of sound in south London), one can listen to the old and the bold tell their tales as cuckoo clocks strike the hour in suburban living rooms and soliticous wives or daughters bring tea. Old soldiers' memories can be pin-sharp at one moment – then dissolve in an instant. In the matter of tanks the officers tend to be roguish, the other ranks somewhat homogeneous in their recollections of 'metal monsters'. The same tends to be true of the written accounts collected by the Tank Museum in Bovington, Dorset. Posh subalterns, rude mechanicals. All are quite splendid nevertheless.

There is also the mood of more recent times to consider, and how they might affect the portrayal of events. For example, in a letter of 1970 preserved in the archives of the Intelligence Corps Museum in Bedfordshire, Maj.-Gen. Elliot Hotblack – by then the last survivor of the 1916–18 Tanks HQ – described the man from the BBC who had come to interview him for the *Horizon* programme as clearly being a 'communist': 'He seemed more interested in denigrating authority than anything I might have to say,' wrote the former Tanks Corps reconnaissance officer and military attaché to Nazi Berlin ('The Man who knows all Hitler's Secrets' as Fleet Street dubbed him in 1939–40) who had been intimately involved in the planning for the Battle of Cambrai. The veteran Hotblack felt no obligation to comment disapprovingly or otherwise on the American entanglement in Vietnam, as his interrogator demanded. The anti-war decade of the sixties, if that is what it was, ran parallel with the 'rediscovery' of the Great War fifty years on. It was not a coincidence. Invited to condemn the stupidity of the 'general staff' (and Haig in particular) as they reminisce, these gallant old men will willingly do so – especially in regard to the higher direction of the Tanks Corps and its predecessors. They will condemn 'war', any war, as utterly hateful. But they seem reluctant to participate in a wider sublimation that the eviction of the Germans from France and Belgium was in some way 'meaningless slaughter'. The young men in tanks were at the heart of that enterprise and proud of it. In fact, as they are keen to impart to the historical record, without them it might not have been possible at all.

More reliable as sources perhaps are memories recorded nearer in time to the events in question – especially those in the Cabinet Office files held at the National Archives – the result of the Official Historian and his colleagues canvassing the ex-officer class of thirties Britain and its empire for their reconstructed battlefield narratives and for comments on his draft judgements on the late war and its higher direction. Their views are informed and they are passionate. They can be self-serving and pompous at one instant, heart-breaking in their poignant insight the next. They act as useful counterweight to the monstrous egotism expressed in the postwar works of tank-credit-claimers like Churchill, Swinton and J. F. C. Fuller (hugely readable nevertheless). Some of these humbler correspondents were far too accusing of their erstwhile masters ever to have seen their words made public at the time or recorded as part of the 'official' narrative, as they themselves perfectly well understood at the time. Their views were registered nevertheless. The glimpses they give of the 'machinations' around the birth of the Tank Corps and its debut in war are at the heart of this story.

Thank goodness also for the rich seam of contemporaneous letters, diaries and ephemera in the Tank Museum, Bovington, in the Imperial War Museum department of documents, in the National Army Museum (the Holford-Walker deposit), the National Maritime Museum (Tennyson d'Eyncourt papers), the Royal Archives, the Churchill Archives Centre and the Liddell Hart Centre for Military Archives in London (the Stern, Swinton, Charteris and Fuller deposits especially), to whose curatorial staff I am glowingly grateful. Captain Sir Basil's career-long correspondence has been drawn on, plus the copious background research to his *The Tanks: The History of the Royal Tank Regiment and its Predecessors* – ten years in the making and full of incidents and aperçus that did not make the official regimental history published almost half a century ago.

I am grateful too for the existence of several modern published works without which navigating the turbulent history of tanks and the Tank Corps would have been much more difficult, especially J. P. Harris's *Men, Ideas and Tanks*, John Glanfield's *Devil's Chariots*, my friend Philippe Gorczynski's *Following the Tanks* (with Jean-Luc Gibot) and the extraordinary, self-published *The Tanks at Flers* by the retired FCO diplomat (and national service tankman) Trevor Pidgeon, a bravura piece of forensic historical investigation. David Fletcher's works have been lodestars, and the informed message traffic on Landships and the Great War Forum (1914–18.invisionzone.com) proved hugely engaging. A select bibliography follows of more published sources which have proved especially useful, or from which material has been quoted in this work.

Secondary Sources

SELECT BIBLIOGRAPHY

Andrew, Christopher, *Secret Service: The Making of the British Intelligence Community* (London: Heinemann, 1985)

Anon. (Charteris, Capt. the Hon. E. E.), *HQ Tanks 1917–18* (privately printed, 1920)

Bacon, Admiral Sir Reginald, *From 1900 Onwards* (London: Hutchinson, 1940)

Baker-Carr, Brig.-Gen. Christopher, *From Chauffeur to Brigadier* (London: Ernest Benn, 1930)

Barker, T. C., with Michael Robbins, *A History of London Transport*, vol. 2 *The Twentieth Century to 1970* (London: George Allen and Unwin, 1974)

Bigham, Charles, Viscount Mersey, *A Picture of Life, 1872–1940* (London: John Murray, 1941)

Bion, Wilfred (ed. Francesca Bion), *War Diaries* (London: Karnac, 1997)

Blake, Robert (ed.), *The Private Papers of Douglas Haig, 1914–1919* (London: Eyre & Spottiswoode, 1952)

Blumenson, Martin, *The Patton Papers* (Boston: Houghton Mifflin, 1972–4)

Bond, Brian (ed.), *The First World War and British Military History* (Oxford: Clarendon, 1991)

Brown, Malcolm, *The Imperial War Museum Book of 1918* (London: Sidgwick & Jackson, 1998)

Browne, Capt. D. G., *The Tank in Action* (London: W. Blackwood, 1920)

Charteris, Brig.-Gen. John, *Field-Marshal Earl Haig* (London: Cassell, 1929)

—— *At GHQ* (London: Cassell, 1931)

Childs, David J., *A Peripheral Weapon? The Production and Employment of British Tanks in the First World War* (Westport, Conn.: Greenwood) 1991

Churchill, W. S., *The World Crisis*, 4 vols (London: Thornton Butterworth, 1923–7)

Cockerill, Sir George Kynaston, *What Fools We Were* (London: Hutchinson, 1944)

Cooper, Bryan, *The Ironclads of Cambrai* (London: Souvenir Press, 1967)

Coppard, George, *With a Machine Gun to Cambrai: The Tale of a Young Tommy in Kitchener's Army, 1914–1918* (London: HMSO, 1969)

Crompton, R. E. B., *Reminiscences* (London: Constable, 1928)

Danchev, Alex, *Alchemist of War: The Life of Basil Liddell Hart* (London: Weidenfeld & Nicolson, 1998)

Deighton, Len, *Blitzkrieg: From the Rise of Hitler to the Fall of Dunkirk* (London: Cape, 1979)

Dugdale, Capt. Geoffrey, *Langemarck and Cambrai: A War Narrative, 1914–18* (Shrewsbury, 1932)

Edmonds, Brig.-Gen. J. E., *History of the Great War, Based on Official Documents. Military Operations France and Belgium, 1914–18* (London: Macmillan, 1922, etc)

Fletcher, David, *Tanks and Trenches: First-hand Accounts of Tank Warfare in the First World War* (Stroud: Sutton, 1994)

—— *The British Tanks, 1915–19* (Marlborough: Crowood, 2001)

—— *British Mark I Tank 1916* (Oxford: Osprey, 2004)

Foley, Cedric, *The Boilerplate War* (London: Muller, 1963)

Foot, Stephen, *Three Lives* (London: Heinemann, 1934)

Foster, William & Co., *The Tank, Its Birth & Development* (Lincoln, 1920)

Fuller, J. F. C., *Tanks in the Great War, 1914–1918* (London: John Murray, 1920)

—— *Memoirs of an Unconventional Soldier* (London: Nicholson & Watson, 1936)

Glanfield, John, *Devil's Chariots: The Birth and Secret Battles of the First Tanks* (Stroud: Sutton, 2001)

Gorczynski, Philippe, and J. L. Gibot, *Following the Tanks* (Cambrai: privately printed, 2000)

Guderian, Gen. Heinz (trans. Christopher Duffy), *Achtung-Panzer!* (London: Arms and Armour Press, 1992)

Haigh, Capt. Richard, *Life in a Tank* (London: Hodder & Stoughton, 1918)

Hankey, Lord, *The Supreme Command 1914–18*, 2 vols (London: Allen & Unwin, 1961)

Harris, J. P., *Men, Ideas and Tanks: British Military Thought and Armoured Forces, 1903–1939* (Manchester: Manchester University Press, 1995)

Henriques, Basil, *Indiscretions of a Warden* (London: Methuen, 1937)

Hickey, Daniel, *Rolling into Action: Memoirs of a Tank Corps Section Commander* (London: Hutchinson, 1936)

Hobart, Brig. P. C. S., *Cambrai: The Complete Narrative* (parts 1–3), reprinted in *Stand To!*, the Journal of the Western Front Association, issues 54–56, January, April, September 1999.

Holmes, Richard, *Tommy: The British Soldier on the Western Front* (London: HarperCollins, 2004).

Hundleby, Max, with Rainer Strasheim, *The German A7V Tank and the Captured British Mk IV Tanks of World War I* (Yeovil: Haynes, 1990)

Jenkin, A., *A Tank Driver's Experiences* (London: Elliot Stock, 1922)

Jenkins, Roy, *Mr Attlee: An Interim Biography* (London: Heinemann, 1948)

Jünger, Ernst (trans. Michael Hofmann), *Storm of Steel* (London: Allen Lane, 2003)

Lewis, Cecil, *Sagittarius Rising* (London: Peter Davis, 1936)

Liddell Hart, Sir Basil, *The Real War, 1914–1918* (London: Faber & Faber, 1930)

—— *The Tanks. The History of the Royal Tank Regiment and its Predecessors Heavy Branch Machine-Gun Corps, Tank Corps and Royal Tank Corps, 1914–1945*, vol. 1 (London: Cassell, 1959)

—— *The Memoirs of Captain Liddell Hart*, 2 vols (London: Cassell, 1965)

Lloyd George, David, *War Memoirs*, 5 vols (London: Nicholson & Watson, 1933–6)

Loewe, Lionel, *Lewis Basil Henriques: A Portrait* (based on his diaries, letters and speeches as collated by his widow, Rose Henriques) (London: Routledge & Kegan Paul, 1976)

Mallory, Keith, with Arvid Ottar, *Architecture of Aggression* (London: Architectural Press, 1973)

Miles, Captain Wilfred, *Military Operations, France and Belgium, 1916*, vol. 2 (London: Macmillan, 1938)

—— *History of the Great War, Based on Official Documents. Military Operations, France and Belgium, 1917: The Battle of Cambrai* (London: HMSO, 1949)

Mitchell, Francis, *Tank Warfare: The Story of Tanks in the Great War* (London: Nelson, 1933)

Moorehead, Alan, *Gallipoli* (London: Hamish Hamilton, 1956)

Nicolai, Col. Walther, *Geheime Mächte – The German Secret Service* (London: S. Paul & Co., 1924)

Occleshaw, Michael, *Armour against Fate: British Military Intelligence in the First World War* (London: Columbus, 1989)

Pidgeon, Trevor, *The Tanks at Flers: An Account of the First Use of Tanks in War at the Battle of Flers-Courcelette, the Somme, 15th September 1916* (Cobham: Fairmile, 1995)

Prior, Robin, with Trevor Wilson, *Command on the Western Front: The Military Career of Sir Henry Rawlinson 1914–18* (Oxford: Blackwell, 1992)

—— *The Somme* (London: Yale University Press, 2005)

Samson, Charles Rumney, *My Flights and Fights* (London: Ernest Benn, 1930)

Sheffield, Gary, with John Bourne, *Douglas Haig: War Diaries and Letters, 1914–1918* (London: Weidenfeld & Nicolson, 2005)

Silber, Julius, *The Invisible Weapons* (London: Hutchinson, 1932)

Steed, Henry Wickham, *Through Thirty Years, 1892–1922* (London: Heinemann: 1924)

Stern, Sir Albert G., *Tanks, 1914–1918: The Log-Book of a Pioneer* (London: Hodder & Stoughton, 1919)

Sueter, Rear-Admiral Sir Murray, *The Evolution of the Tank: A Record of the Royal Naval Air Service Caterpillar Experiments* (London: Hutchinson, 1937)

Swinton, Sir Ernest Dunlop, *Eyewitness's Narrative of the War from the Marne to Neuve Chapelle, September 1914–March 1915* (London: Edward Arnold, 1915)

—— *Eyewitness: Being personal reminiscences of certain phases of the Great War, including the genesis of the tank* (London: Hodder & Stoughton, 1932)

—— (ed.), *Twenty Years After – The Battlefields of 1914–18: Then and Now*, 2 vols plus supplement (London: Newnes, 1936–8)

Terraine, John, *Douglas Haig: The Educated Soldier* (London: Hutchinson: 1963)

Travers, Timothy, *How the War Was Won: Command and Technology in the British Army on the Western Front* (London: Routledge, 1992)

Turner, Edward, *Memories of a Gamekeeper's Son* (Holbrook: Malthouse, 1997)

Walker, Jonathan, *The Blood Tub: General Gough and the Battle of Bullecourt, 1917* (Staplehurst: Spellmount, 1998)

Watson, William, *A Company of Tanks* (Edinburgh: Blackwoods, 1920)

Williams-Ellis, Clough, and Amabel Williams-Ellis, *The Tank Corps* (London: Country Life, 1919)

Wilson, Charles McMoran (Lord Moran), *Anatomy of Courage* (London: Constable, 1945)

Wilson, Dale E., *Treat 'Em Rough!: The Birth of American Armor, 1917–20* (Novato, Calif.: Presidio Press, 1989)

Woollcombe, Robert, *The First Tank Battle. Cambrai 1917* (London: Arthur Barker, 1967)

Wright, Patrick, *Tank: The Progress of a Monstrous War Machine* (London: Faber & Faber, 2000)

Young, Mike, *The Army Service Corps, 1902–1918* (London: Leo Cooper, 2000)

NOTES

BL British Library; CAC Churchill Archives Centre, Churchill College, Cambridge; IWM Imperial War Museum; LA Liddle Archive, Brotherton Library, University of Leeds; LHCMA Liddell Hart Centre for Military Archives, King's College London; NA National Archives, Kew; NAM National Army Museum, London; RA Royal Archives; TM Tank Museum, Bovington; NMM National Maritime Museum, London.

Page

xxiv 'British Museum' Capt. D. G. Browne, *The Tank in Action*, p. 8

xxvii 'Who invented the tank?' H. G. Wells, 'Points From Letters', *The Listener*, 15 May 1941, p. 703

xxvii 'was too stupid' statement of claim before the High Court, 28 June 1941, Swinton papers, LHCMA LH9/28/59

xxvii 'It has been left to the Germans' *The Listener*, 15 May 1941, p. 704

xxviii 'Royal Commission on Awards to Inventors' NA MUN 5/210/1940

PART ONE

CHAPTER 1

1 'A shadow in a parapet' 'You must ferret out where they are, judging by the following signs: – Sound. Dust. Smoke. A shadow . . . etc.' from 'Tank Tips', unsigned single page typescript c. July–August 1916 in NA WO 158/834

3 'special service with the Heavy Section' NA WO 339/59279

4 'Nature, location and severity' ibid.

5 'I was asked to make' ibid.

6 'I took him as far as I might' ibid.

7 'horse show' ephemera in papers of Col. Sir Geoffrey Christie-Miller, Box 80/32/2 IWM

7 'open to officers of twelve stone' ibid.

7 'trench attack under barrage' 61st Division war diary, NA WO 95/3034

7 'exceedingly conscientious' NA WO 339/59279

8 'shot himself with his revolver' NA WO 339/59279

8 'Bullet-wound – Head' ibid.

8 'Severe types that exhibit' *Journal of Mental Science*, July 1917, pp. 400–405

8 'deeply regrets . . . died of wounds' WO 339/59279

9 fn 'Charles McMoran Wilson' C. M. Wilson (Lord Moran), *Anatomy of Courage*, p. 179

9 fn BL Oriental and India Office Collection IOR L/MIL/11/100 no. 17

9 'could not imagine why' NA WO 339/59279

9 fn 'pensions to dependants' NA T 1/12143

10 'melancholy . . . depressed' ibid.

11 'In September 1916 I happened' ibid.

12 'I am commanded by the Army Council' ibid.

CHAPTER 2

15 'the general belief that' Basil Liddell Hart, *Memoirs*, vol. 1, p. 11

15 'a troop of 450 men' Victor Huffam typescript in TM

16 'trench digging and route marches'
ibid.

16 'tough old sweats . . .' ibid.

16 'hated the OTC' Basil Henriques,
Indiscretions of a Warden, p. 110

16 'nothing more than part' ibid., p. 111

16 'killed on the Marne' *The Times*,
21 September 1914, p. 1

16 'large numbers of newly gazetted'
Henriques, op. cit., p. 112

16 'pale blue eyes' ibid., p. 112

17 'brother rifleman' C. Baker-Carr,
From Chauffeur to Brigadier, p. 12

17 'Mércèdes donated by' ibid., p. 13

19 'india rubbers and pencils' Ernest
Swinton, *Eyewitness*, p. 38

20 'a formidable enemy, well trained'
dispatch dated 18 September 1914,
Swinton, *Eyewitness's Narrative of the
War*, p. 15

21 'The [Germans] made five desperate'
dispatch dated 26 October 1914,
Swinton, *Eyewitness's Narrative of the
War*, p. 77

21 'I think [the Aisne fighting] to be
very typical' French to King George
V, 2 October 1914, quoted in Richard
Holmes, *Tommy*, p. 32

21 'The [German] infantry are holding
strong' dispatch dated 18 September
1914, Swinton, *Eyewitness's Narrative
of the War*, pp. 13–14

21 'The situation of the works' dispatch
dated 13 October 1914, ibid., p. 55

CHAPTER 3

23 'breathing space between' A. J. P.
Taylor, *War by Time-Table: How the
First World War Began* (London:
Macdonald, 1969), p. 25

23 'Before its outbreak' *Tank Corps
Journal*, no. 36, April 1922, p. 307

24 'Hiram Maxim's name' Basil Liddell
Hart, *The Real War*, p. 269

24 'What shall I do with' Baker-Carr,
op. cit., p. 80

25 'The enemy has practically' dispatch
dated 29 November 1914, Swinton,
Eyewitness's Narrative of the War,
pp. 138–9

CHAPTER 4

29 'It is essential that the men' War
Office Mechanical Transport
Committee, Interim Report for
1902–3, NA WO 33/2891

29 'the tin soldier' Frank Searle, 'From
Buses to Tanks . . .', article in
Commercial Motor, 16 March 1926
pp. 150–1

30 fn 'four-footed friends' Searle, ibid.

30 'social difficulty' 1995 conversation
with Col. Mark [sic] Dillon quoted in
Patrick Wright, *Tank*, p. 68

30 'four or five hundred powerful motor
cars' NA WO 32/7079

30 'cooperating with an unofficial' ibid.

31 'hostile force [was] threatening' ibid.

31 'There are plenty of those who
remember' McMoran Wilson, op. cit.,
p. 182

31 'not be seen laden with parcels'
Maj. R. M. Barnes, *The British Army of
1914* (London: Seely Service, 1968),
p. 38

CHAPTER 5

33 'mobile forts.' For a discussion of pre-
1914 theories of fortification see
Mallory and Ottar, *The Architecture of
Aggression*, pp. 13–33 – plus a
discursive and well-illustrated outline
of the theories of linear defence in
depth that followed. Quick-firing
guns in pre-fabricated steel cupolas
re-deployed from frontier forts started
appearing in German trench systems
in 1915 – causing great concern to
those like Swinton seeking a
mechanical means of breaking the
deadlock.

34 'I suppose we must recognise' *Off.
Hist.*: Brig.-Gen. Sir J. E. Edmonds,
*Military Operations France and Belgium
1915*, vol. 1, p. 51

38 'had instructions to give the
impression' *Off. Hist.*: Brig.-Gen. Sir
J. E. Edmonds, *Military Operations
France and Belgium 1914*, vol. 1, p. 461

38 'I formed a small administration'
W. S. Churchill, *The World Crisis
1911–14* (1923 edition), p. 321

38 'Am endeavouring to provide you'
NA ADM 116/1348
38 'attempts to use local buses failed' NA
PRO 30/57/72
38 'Steps are being taken to provide' NA
ADM 116/1348
39 'shipshape and warlike' C. R. Samson,
My Flights and Fights, p. 92
40 'On 29 September I urged Ollivant'
Churchill, op. cit., vol. 1, p. 290

CHAPTER 6

42 'wrote to the First Lord' Sir Albert G.
Stern, *Tanks, 1914–1918*, pp. 4–5
42 'Mr Churchill asks me to say' ibid.
43 'I find these irregular formations'
Kitchener papers, NA PRO 30/57/72
44 'After the fall of Antwerp' W. S.
Churchill deposition to the Royal
Commission on Awards to Inventors,
1 September 1919, NA MUN 5/394

CHAPTER 7

46 'revolving as the machine moves' NA
WO 33/2891
46 'array of fourteen to fifteen monsters'
H. G. Wells, 'The Land Ironclads', *The
Strand*, December 1903, pp. 751–4
48 'Bacon's monster gun' W. S.
Churchill, *The World Crisis, 1915* (1923
edition), pp. 72–3
49 'bearing the image' Admiral Sir
Reginald Bacon, *From 1900 Onwards*,
p. 200
49 'proposition before Mr Churchill'
ibid.

CHAPTER 8

50 'that might be of use' Maj-Gen. E. D.
Swinton, Minutes of Proceedings,
Royal Commission on Awards to
Inventors, 7 October 1919, p. 15, in
NA MUN 5/210/1940
50 'I left him on' ibid.
51 'the vast number that had' NA MUN
5/210/1940/27
51 'more and more impressed every day'
Swinton, op. cit., p. 15
51 'When we met [Brig.-]General Louis
Jackson' ibid.

52 'The remarkable deadlock' NA CAB
17/167
53 'quaint prescriptions in old books' Sir
Maurice Hankey, *The Supreme
Command 1914–18*, vol. 1, p. 229
53 'burned down his own garden hedge'
ibid.
53 'traveling armour-clad' John
Glanfield, *Devil's Chariots*, pp. 2–3, see
also the intriguing if daft Lemon's
Wheel proposal in Stern papers 1/6/
61 LHCMA and Law Report, Bentley
v. the King, *The Times*, 27 November
1925
53 'fantastic or absurd' NA CAB 17/167
54 'My dear Prime Minister' NA MUN
5/394
54 'We must crush them' Rear-Admiral
Sir Murray Sueter, *The Evolution of the
Tank*, p. 53
54 'Sent a minute to the Director'
Churchill, NA MUN 5/394
55 'It is of the utmost importance'
3 January 1915, Edmonds, op. cit., p. 65
56 fn For N. Lebedenko and the 'Nepotir'
tank see www.pravda.ru/science
56 'naval expedition would bombard'
War Council minutes of 13 January
1915, quoted in Alan Moorehead,
Gallipoli, p. 39
57 'the guiding hand of an automotive
engineer' NA MUN 5 210/1940/13
58 'the war would be over' NA MUN
5/394
59 'I am afraid I cannot' NA T 173/43b

CHAPTER 9

61 'They would never allow'
Hetherington to Edmonds, 23 October
1934, CAB 45/134
61 'Revised Hetherington Proposal' NA
ADM 116/1339
61 'woods and towns, spanning rivers'
ibid.
61 'went home determined' Churchill,
NA MUN 5/394
62 'a new type of gun carrying war
machine' NA ADM 116/1339
62 'I was ill at the time' Churchill
7 October 1919, Royal Commission
on Awards to Inventors, p. 8 NA
MUN 5/210/1940

CHAPTER 10

64 'mother's cousin' for details of this extraordinary childhood episode see R. E. B. Crompton, *Reminiscences*, pp. 8–15

67 'The British made various' Ernst Jünger, *Storm of Steel*, p. 78

70 'two wheeled armoured wagon' NA MUN 5/210/1940

70 'On account of secrecy' Churchill, 7 Oct. 1919, Royal Commission on Awards to Inventors, p. 9 NA MUN 5/210/1940

70 'Did you invite the Board of Admiralty' ibid.

71 'At GHQ at St Omer' CAB 45/134

71 'Landships were a joke' NA MUN 5/210/1940/13

71 'I am an old colonel of the Electrical' Crompton to Smith-Dorrien, 30 April 1915, NA T173/34b

71 'It is proposed' Crompton to DNC, 19 May 1915, NA T 173/34

CHAPTER 11

73 'British officers of high rank', quoted in 'Significant Individuals Behind The Development of New British Weaponry And Tactics For The Western Front', www.westernfront association.com/Foulkes

74 'arrogance – nothing can be altered' extracts from Crompton diary in MUN 5 210/1940

76 'damn idlers' Sueter, op. cit., p. 245

CHAPTER 12

77 'wholly unsympathetic' Swinton, op. cit., p. 129

77 'Crystal Palace on wheels' ibid., p. 140

77 'what seemed like a fairy tale' ibid., p. 140

77 'desirable to obtain information' MUN 5 210/1940

78 'Consultation [by the War Office] with Mr D'Eyncourt' ibid.

78 'orders then existing' NA T 173/343b

78 'a caterpillar, petrol-engined tractor' NA MUN 5 210/1940/13

78 'bosun's chairs' NA CAB 17/120b

79 'The writer should descend' NA MUN 5 210/1940/13

79 'At my own expense' Stern, op. cit., p. 23

79 'the object for which' NA CAB 17/120b

80 'There appears to be' ibid.

80 'a kind of armoured Noah's Ark' NA WO 158/831

80 'to raise enthusiasm among', Stern op. cit., p. 26

81 'like the reaping operations of a self binder' – 'Variants of the Offensive', p. 3 of typescript in NA MUN 5/210/1940

81 'His proposals gave no promise' NA ADM 116/1339

82 fn 'Col. Swinton' CAB 45/134

82 'It did not take long' Swinton, op. cit., pp. 161–2

83 'Proposal for next with equivalent' d'Eyncourt diary 23 August 1915, NMM DEY/45

83 'land cruisers or armoured' 30 August 1915, NA ADM 116/1339

84 'infinitesimally small' NA ADM 116/1339

84 'Personnel would have to be trained' NA ADM 116/1339

84 'cyanide sprayer on pedrails' CAB 17/120b

84 'a big siren or buzzer' CAB 17/120b

84 'The naval people are pressing on' Swinton to Guest, 10 September 1915, NA WO 158/831

85 'Luckily, from the point of view of secrecy' Swinton, op. cit., p. 171

85 'joyous dinner' ibid., p. 173

86 'a landship [Little Willie] had already been' NA MUN 5/210/1940/13

86 'guarded by sentries' Swinton, op. cit., p. 174

87 'proceed with the design exhibited' CID-printed memorandum in NA MUN 5/210/1940/13

87 'capable of stopping the German reversed bullet' ibid.

87 'the exact distribution' ibid.

CHAPTER 13

89 'rushing out in a yellowish' Maj. Charles H. Foulkes, *Gas!* (Edinburgh: Blackwood, 1934), p. 43

90 'It was Sunday, if it mattered'
www.firstworldwar.com/diaries/
battleofloos.htm

91 'With barrels burning hot' quoted in
Holmes, op. cit., p. 37

91 'The leading men would have been'
www.westernfrontassociation.com/
thegreatwar/articles/research/
loosbattle.htm

93 'We were no longer in a small unit'
George Coppard, *With a Machine Gun
to Cambrai*, p. 66

93 'No military pomp attended' quoted
in *The Long, Long Trail*
www.1914–1918.net/mgc.htm

CHAPTER 14

94 'Any operation on the western front'
W. S. Churchill, 'Variants of the
Offensive', NA WO 158/831

94 'They are capable of traversing' ibid.

95 'Until these machines are actually in
France' ibid.

95 'Whether the Ministry of Munitions'
*Parliamentary Debates. House of
Commons* (London: Hansard),
8 December 1915, col. 1375

95 'inventors who had hit upon' NA
CAB 17/120b

96 'It will necessitate' NA ADM 116/
1339

96 'Each member of this body' NA ADM
116/1339

97 'insect' NA WO 158/831

97 'The Tank Detachment' NA ADM
116/1339

CHAPTER 15

98 'Is anything known about the
caterpillar' Haig-minuted original in
NA WO 158/831

98 'I received instructions to go' W. S.
Churchill, Minutes of Proceedings,
Royal Commission on Awards to
Inventors, 7 October 1919, p. 7, in
MUN 5/210/1940

99 'There are two producers of
landships' Elles to Haig, NA WO158/
831

99 'A great many people' ibid.

99 'Everybody connected was sworn'
Stern, op. cit., p. 43

100 fn 'three great secrets of the war'
The Times, 2 January 1919, p. 4

100 fn 'too much talk Swinton, op. cit.,
p. 247

100 fn 'information leaking' Stern, op.
cit., p. 83

100 fn 'Major Hetherington fired' ibid.,
p. 47

101 fn 'It was more appropriate' John
Glanfield, 'Notes on the Trench
Warfare Machine', unpublished
typescript in TM

101 'enemy trenches on the Loos
pattern' Swinton, op. cit., p. 192

101 'There were Mother and Little
Willie' ibid., p. 194

101 'slug' Crompton diary, 29 January
1916, NA T 173/181

101 'Puddleduck' NA CAB 17/120b

102 'pretty mechanical toy' *The Times*,
27 November 1925, p. 5

102 'Major Ellis has been home' NA
CAB 17/120b

103 'it was a striking scene' ibid., p. 196

103 'we should order three thousand'
Sueter, op. cit., p. 91

103 'How soon can we have them?'
Stern, op. cit., p. 57

103 'Kitchener objected to it' Crompton
diary transcript, 11 February 1916,
NA T 173/181

103 'On the night of the secret' Butler to
Edmonds, 2 August 1934, NA CAB
45/132

104 'I saw the Caterpillar' RA King
George V's Diary 8 February 1916

104 'The King came a day or 2 ago and
saw it' D'Eyncourt to Churchill,
14 February 1916, original in CHAR
2/71/14–15 CAC

105 'Even if 50% were knocked out'
8 February 1916, NA WO 158/833

105 'The officers who represented me'
NA WO 32/5754

105 'Haig began, from that moment'
John Terraine, *Douglas Haig*,
p. 220

105 'I happened to meet' Swinton,
op. cit., p. 217

106 'Half a stenographer' ibid., p. 224

107 'Impossibility of Repeated
    Employment' 'Notes on the
    Employment of Tanks', edited
    version in *Off. Hist.*: Miles, op. cit.,
    1916 vol. 2, pp. 238–9 and original
    printed memorandum in WO 158/
    834
108 'The moment I mentioned' Haig
    diary, 25 May 1916, NA WO 256/10

CHAPTER 16

109 'of superior education' Swinton to
    Bird, 12 July 1916, NA WO 158/833
109 'select and warn personally'
    Burnett-Stuart to Adjutant-General,
    26 April 1916, NA WO 158/873
110 'Strictly secret and confidential'
    Huffam typescript in TM
110 'in company with three hundred
    other' ibid.
110 'Of the subaltern officers' Browne,
    op. cit., p. 24
110 'The Armoured Car' see the
    'recruiting section' printed weekly in
    The Motor Cycle magazine, May–
    August 1916. Although 'tanks' were
    not mentioned, this feature was very
    gossipy and printed long lists of
    names of those personally selected
    by Mr Smith for the new motor
    machine-gun service. Anyone with
    an inkling of curiosity might surmise
    an unusual military formation was
    in the making
111 'This officer, don't know who he
    was' Pte Phillip Page, Liddle Archive,
    Brotherton Library, University of
    Leeds
111 'capital country' Rawlinson to Col.
    Clive Wigram (King George V's
    Assistant Private Secretary),
    27 February 1917, RA Geo V
    Q2522/2 56
112 'They can be looked on as a means'
    23 March 1916, NA WO 158/833
112 'making use of our new "tanks"'
    quoted in Terraine, op. cit.,
    p. 220
112 'I hope to use "tanks"' ibid.
112 'Orders are given to the MMGS' NA
    WO 32/3274

113 'In addition to the regular' Swinton,
    op. cit., p. 220
114 'Lent to Army' *The Navy List*, July
    1916, p. B19
114 'I propose sending over to you'
    14 June 1916, NA WO 158/833
114 'I next saw Colonel Swinton . . .'
    Haig diary, 14 April 1916, NA WO
    256/9
114 'strikes and acts of God' Swinton to
    Butler, 26 April 1916, quoted in
    Stern, op. cit., pp. 77–8
114 'My dear General' Hankey to
    Robertson, 20 April 1916, NA
    CAB17/167
115 '"Tanks" 1st Aug. 150 . . . of which'
    quoted in Terraine, op. cit., p. 222
116 'friend who had just joined'
    'Memories of an Old Original',
    typescript c. 1965 by Lt-Col. Henry
    Basil Groves, in TM
116 'Do you know anything about motor
    cars?' Henriques, op. cit., p. 113
116 'would have to drive an armoured
    caterpillar' ibid.
116 'a sponson with machine-guns'
    Huffam TM
116 'It would be absurd to pretend'
    Browne, op. cit., p. 24
117 'We fired ninety-seven rounds in
    one day' Swinton to Butler, NA WO
    158/833

CHAPTER 17

118 'MMGS was full-up' *Tank Corps
    Journal*, no. 15, July 1920, p. 70
118 'Did I think they worked all' ibid.
118 'We all met after luncheon'
    Swinton, op. cit., p. 246
119 'there are a few inhabitants' ibid.,
    p. 238
119 'You can depart the United Services'
    Swinton to Butler, 16 June 1916,
    NA WO 158/833
120 'He was not pleased' Swinton,
    op. cit., p. 240
120 'the first group challenged' Groves
    TM
120 'a jug of cocoa' Edward Turner,
    Memories of a Gamekeeper's Son, p. 67
121 'not informed of the purpose'
    Swinton, op. cit., p. 244

121 'renowned for his cocktails' Olga S. Phillips, *Solomon J. Solomon, A Memoir in Peace and War* (London: Herbert Joseph, 1933), p. 172

122 'Thetford 37' NA WO 32/5754

122 'more ringed about than' Clough Williams-Ellis and Amabel Williams-Ellis, *The Tank Corps*, p. 18

122 'But as we marched in' Huffam TM

122 'countless thousands of earwigs' typescript account by Cpl H. Sanders in Tank Museum

CHAPTER 18

123 'The machines had long' Williams-Ellis, op cit., p. 18

123 'The veil was completely lifted' Huffam TM

123 'driven across country to Bernersfield' NA WO 158/833

123 'childish ailments' Swinton to Butler, 29 June 1916, NA WO 158/833

124 'actress who knew too much' Swinton, op. cit., pp. 247–8

124 'I remembered that a certain young' ibid., p. 247

124 'very minor show' NA WO 158/833

124 'Most of the officers' Williams-Ellis, op. cit., p. 20

125 'My knowledge of the internal combustion' Groves TM

125 'Medical Aspects of Tanks' by Maj. L. R. Broster RAMC, 30 October 1918, typescripts in Tank Museum, pp. 3–6

126 'There it is' Richard Haigh, *Life in a Tank*, pp. 38–9

127 'It was a hard job to turn' Daniel Hickey, *Rolling into Action*, p. 113

127 'One after the other we slide' Haigh, op. cit., pp. 57–8

128 'Solomon needs a firm hand' NA WO 158/833

128 'I have packed Solomon off' ibid.

128 'a good part of the day' Henriques, op. cit., p. 115

128 'tanks parked on the edge of a wood' *Tank Corps Journal*, no. 15, July 1920, p. 71

129 'The first batch' NA WO 95/116

129 'The men were ripe for mutiny' ibid.

129 'far ahead of the infantry' Swinton, op. cit., p. 250

129 'reception . . . was not possible' ibid., p. 251

129 'steer a course and make signals' ibid., p. 252

130 'disclose their existence' ibid., pp. 254–5

130 'No proof was needed' ibid., p. 266

131 'The paper was very short' Williams-Ellis, op. cit., p. 19

131 'Owing to the limited number' Lt-Col. J. Brough, 11 June 1916, WO 158/834

132 'These engines will be an adjunct' Burnett-Stuart to Bird, 7 June 1916, NA WO 158/833

CHAPTER 19

134 fn 'Darling – long before this' letter dated 30 June 1916 in Charteris papers, microfilm 2/2 LHCMA. That was Haig's intelligence chief's private view – the publicly expressed intention was for a climactic breakthrough. The catastrophe of 1 July was unparalleled – but modern research has questioned whether it was simply due to overburdened men plodding forward in parade ground order – the presiding image enshrined by Basil Liddell Hart in his *The Real War* of 1930 and broadly concurred with in the *Official History* (vol. 1, 1916) published two years later – which talks of 'succeeding lines . . . pressing forward heroically but blindly'. The Australian-based historians Robin Prior and Trevor Wilkinson in their persuasively revisionist *The Somme* (2005) demonstrate a significant number of battalion commanders (it was at their discretion) seeking 'many and various methods to cross no man's land to come to grips with the enemy'. The writers conclude however that the failure of the bombardment and the survival of the defending machine-gunners meant

the flesh-and-blood attackers were doomed – *whatever tactics were adopted*

135 'Although at Elveden' Swinton, op. cit., p. 259

135 'The Officer Commanding Heavy' 'Digest of decisions at a WO conference, 26 June 1916', NA WO 32/5754

136 'The Tanks should move forward' ibid.

CHAPTER 20

137 'I am pleased the news from France' Swinton to Burnett-Stuart, 1 July 1916, NA WO 158/832

137 'A Lewis gunner firing from the hip' letter from Maj. Alan Cameron, NA CAB 45/132

138 'So far I have not seen any official' Swinton to Bird, 6 July 1916, NA WO 158/833

138 'Search in whole camp for a spy' records of 3 Infantry Division in Bavarian war archives, quoted in Pidgeon, op. cit., p. 70

139 'at least twenty tanks' Burnett-Stuart to Bird, 19 July 1916, NA WO 32/5754

139 'This was where the training' Williams-Ellis, op. cit., p. 19

139 'After the last show here' NA WO 158/834

140 'moving from shell-hole to shell-hole' NA WO 158/834

140 'One huge game . . .' Henriques, op. cit., p. 114

141 'I was in a building' Groves TM

141 'Robertson, Maurice [. . .], Brough and I' Swinton, op. cit., p. 262

141 'two figures in evening dress, five in khaki' ibid.

141 'lit by the fierce glare' ibid., p. 263

141 'After three weeks, those present knew' ibid., p. 263

142 'Mr Lloyd George wore a hat' ibid., p. 264

142 'The air quivered with the roar' ibid., pp. 265–6

143 'Thursday July 21 – gala day' Phillips, op. cit., p. 172

143 'The essential fact' Swinton, op. cit., p. 267

144 fn 'tactical handling of tanks in action' NA WO 183/834

144 'It was agreed at a conference' Swinton, op. cit., p. 267

144 'I was shocked' ibid.

144 'Haig's decision to use the small number' Terraine, op. cit., p. 219

CHAPTER 21

146 'people connected' Robertson to Haig, 25 July 1916, NA WO 158/843

146 'The use of tanks in small *driblets*' ibid

146 'That to await the employment' ibid.

147 'It is not my intention to use tanks' Haig to Robertson, 29 July 1916, NA WO 158/843

147 'At a point no more than half-way round' quoted in Pidgeon, op. cit., p. 28

147 'The Royal Party returned to London' Swinton, op. cit., p. 268

147 'Col. Swinton and Col. Brough' RA King George V's Diary 26 July 1916

147 'The powers that be are beginning' Robertson to Haig, 29 July 1916, NA WO 256/11

148 'Suggested notes for officers' NA WO 158/843

149 'In my opinion the sending out' Stern to Montagu, 3 August 1916, NA MUN 4 4979 (folder 15 f. 75)

149 'sent to GHQ' J. F. C. Fuller, *Tanks in the Great War*, pp. 161–2

149 'The co-ordinating officer' p. 2 of Maj. Allen Holford-Walker typescript in NAM 2006/095

150 'Col. Brough proceeds' telegram, Wigram to Swinton, 6 August 1916, NA WO 158/843

150 'My duty was to carry out orders' Swinton, op. cit., p. 261.

150 'The whole organisation of this show' NA WO 32/5754

150 'accessories for tanks' NA WO 32/5754

150 'This is disappointing' Haig diary, 11 August 1916, NA WO 256/12

151 'Two members of the Sûreté' NA WO 158/843

151 'In order to give the railway'
Swinton, op. cit., p. 272

CHAPTER 22

152 'we could dine at the Angel' Huffam
TM
152 'We worked hard all day' Gnr Ernest
Thwaites, *Tank Corps Journal*, no. 15,
July 1920
152 'Many of the officers and men'
Groves TM
153 'Remember your orders' Swinton,
op. cit., pp. 272–3
153 'There was always healthy
competition' Williams-Ellis, op. cit.,
p. 20
153 'The whole of C Company' Swinton,
op. cit., p. 275
154 'lorry loads of men in full kit'
Thwaites, op. cit.
154 'a terrible row and noise' transcript
diary of Dvr F. S. Cutting in TM

PART TWO

CHAPTER 23

155 'Never the mind the heat' 'Tank
Tips' NA WO 158/834
157 'Heavy Section armoured cars', *Off.
Hist.*: Miles, *France and Belgium, 1916,
Appendices and Maps*, pp. 39–47
157 'expected to arrive from England'
ibid.
157 'His position in relation' NA WO
158/235
157 'The tank is a novel engine'
'Preliminary Notes' in Fourth Army
war diary, NA WO 158/235
158 fn 'There were miles and miles'
Brig.-Gen. N. Birch to Edmonds, NA
CAB 45/132
158 'Sir Douglas Haig saw me' Swinton,
op. cit., p. 277
158 'I am counting on' Haig to
Robertson, 22 August 1916, *Off.
Hist.*: Miles, *France and Belgium 1916*,
vol. 2, pp. 234–5
159 'The general objective is the same'
Fourth Army war diary, NA WO
158/235
159 'The presence of the fifty' ibid.

160 'But when we use them' ibid.
160 'Gen. Rawlinson was disposed' *Off.
Hist.*: Miles, op. cit., p. 294
160 'more of their capabilities' ibid.,
p. 243
161 'The first lot have arrived . . .'
Burnett-Stuart to Whigham,
personal, 24 August 1916, NA WO
32/5754
161 'leather helmets aroused much
curiosity' T. W. Sanders,
11 September 1957, and
reminiscences of Gnr William Taylor
Dawson, both in TM
161 'packed up like sardines' Gnr
Cutting, TM
161 'No fires allowed and food short'
ibid.
162 'we have had to wire again today'
Burnett-Stuart to Whigham,
24 August 1916, NA WO 32/5754
162 'comically complete nightmare'
Williams-Ellis, op. cit., p. 25
163 'One entered a wood . . .' Haig diary,
Saturday 26 August 1916, NA WO
256/12. The C-in-C added: 'Officers
and men have been working for the
last 24 hours without break to get
their tanks together. I commended
them on their good work and self-
denial.' Of that same demonstration
Rawlinson noted: 'On the whole I
was rather favourably impressed but
the personnel is green . . . They must
practise with live ammunt. One
officer fainted while driving. Went
into a wood well. Difficult to see
further – as only six present and two
broke down . . .' Sir H. Rawlinson's
war journal (manuscript), RLWN
1/4 CAC
163 'We are puzzling our heads'
Rawlinson to Sir Clive Wigram,
29 August 1916, RA Geo V
2552/2
163 'The official atmosphere was not
very helpful' Swinton, op. cit.,
p. 277
163 'taken aside by a senior officer' ibid.,
pp. 279–80
163 '[He] must have shown his feelings'
ibid., p. 280
163 'He probably was' ibid., p. 280

164 '3 September: I spent the' RLWN 1/
4 CAC

164 'That [Brough's] views were
unacceptable' ibid., p. 280

164 'forty-eight and looked it'
supplementary obituary signed
'Archimedes' (Brig.-Gen. Sir J. E.
Edmonds), *The Times*, 15 February
1951, p. 8

CHAPTER 24

165 'On Friday I motored' Letters of
HRH the Prince of Wales, vol. 2,
'David' to 'Papa', 3 September 1916,
RA GV/AA/598/1

165 'star variety turn of the Western
Front' Williams-Ellis, op. cit., p. 25

165 'Epsom Downs on a Derby morning'
J. F. C. Fuller, *Memoirs of an
Unconventional Soldier*, p. 78

165 'man back to England' Maj. Allen
Holford-Walker, 'General remarks
on preparations for action prior to
15th September', p. 1 of typescript
in NAM 2006/095

166 'unexpectedly issued' Henriques,
op. cit., p. 115

166 'inspecting something called tanks'
Henry Wickham Steed, *Through
Thirty Years*, vol. 2, p. 122

166 'Mr Montagu came to see me'
quoted in Gary Sheffield with John
Bourne, *Douglas Haig: War Diaries
and Letters 1914–18* (London:
Weidenfeld & Nicolson, 2005) p. 227

166 'We drove on to see the caterpillars'
Hankey diary, 7 September 1916,
quoted in *The Supreme Command
1914–18*, vol. 2, p. 513

167 'keep the tanks for an offensive' NA
CAB 17/167

167 'unsteady on his legs as he retired'
Haig to Lady Haig, 8 September
1916; Blake, op. cit., p. 164

167 fn 'proposal to expose' letter plus
enclosure from W. S. Churchill,
23 July 1926 in Edmonds pps. II/3/
17c LHCMA. The highly
personalized claim of WSC's
dramatic intervention was published
in *The World Crisis* but not in the
Official History which refers rather 'to

a fear . . . among those responsible
for the conception and production of
the tanks that they would be used in
small driblets . . . and thus sacrifice
the element of surprise to very little
purpose' (*Off. Hist.*: Miles, op. cit.,
pp. 232–33). It states that Asquith
on his mission to GHQ on 6/
7 September 'showed his personal
approval for the C-in-C's policy'
(ibid. p. 235). Asquith's feeble
deposition on 12 September to the
War Council – and their resolve to
let Haig decide – is recorded in NA
CAB 42/19/6.

Brig.-Gen. John Charteris had this
to say of the affair in his 1929
biography of Haig to whom he had
been the zealously-loyal intelligence
adviser:

It is has been argued by Mr W
Churchill and others that they
[tanks] were still only few in
number. Within a limited period a
vastly greater strength might have
been accumulated – these
considerations were all taken into
account when Haig decided to
throw them into battle. His
intelligence service [ie Charteris
himself] had already information
that showed that the Germans
were even now alive to the
existence of some new implement
of war . . . It could only be a
matter of time before the German
intelligence service would obtain
complete information and be able
to evolve an adequate
protection . . .

There was leakage at home. A
demonstration of the tanks had
been given in England at which
very large numbers of unofficial
spectators, including members of
the House of Commons had been
present. Letters taken by the
censorship had shown that full
information was being sent by one
at least of the spectators to neutral
countries, whence it would
inevitably reach Germany.
Censorship of letters from the

armies in France revealed a similar danger. Even if an inadequate defence or reply to the tanks was not forthcoming on the German side, the very knowledge of their existence would exclude the fear of the unknown, so potent a factor on the morale of an army . . .

Finally the fighting about to begin was no small battle. Even the small number of tanks available might give most potent assistance to this assault and might save many valuable British lives. It was on these grounds that Haig resolved to throw the new arm into the battle, and the decision would appear to be well justified.

Charteris, *Earl Haig*, 1929 p. 222 (footnote).

A dispassionate observer, comparing this statement with that in his next book *At GHQ* of two years later (in which he stated that knowledge rather than ignorance that the tanks were coming was the major factor in disrupting German morale on the Somme in autumn 1916) would detect a note of desperation. It might look as if the antics of the tanks – and the showing off of the Heavy Section to all and sundry in the first two weeks of September – might almost have been deliberate. Why hold back? – the secret was already out

167 'the smartness and precision' Swinton, op. cit., p. 281

168 'Most of the men' Williams-Ellis, op. cit., p. 24

168 'We had no training with' Loewe, *Basil Henriques: A Portrait*, p. 39

168 'whether his men were trained' Maj. Allen Holford-Walker, NAM 2006/ 095, p. 3

168 'fixed with no reconnaissance by any officer' ibid.

169 'Headquarters was a box van' Capt. A. G. Woods to Liddell Hart, 9 August 1957, LH 9/28/63 LHCMA

CHAPTER 25

171 'decaying suburb' John Buchan, *A History of the Great War* (London: Nelson, 1922) vol. 3, p. 201

171 'At some point' Williams-Ellis, op. cit., p. 25

172 'very different' Elles to 'Sir Archimedes' (Edmonds), 4 September 1934, copy letter NA WO 95/91

172 'The difficulty of course' 'Notes of Conference, 6 September 1916' in Fourth Army papers, vol. 6, IWM.

173 'It was desperately necessary' Prior and Wilson, *The Somme*, p. 223. Elles himself later described his role at the time thus: 'I was put on when the first tank came out in August of 1916. I was the Staff Officer and I was turned on to what was called father them . . . I had very little experience of them before they went into action.' *Royal Commission on Awards to Inventors*, 21 October 1919, p. 169.

174 'It rather reminded me of Hampstead Heath' Williams-Ellis, op. cit., p. 26

174 'became acute – stowing two gas helmets' ibid.

174 'Sixteen loaves, thirty tins of food, cheese' ibid.

175 'Two carrier pigeons, 33,000 rounds' ibid.

175 'While loading that afternoon' Huffam TM

175 'weight of metal' Basil Liddell Hart, *The Tanks*, p. 67.

175 'Bradley knew nothing' NAM 2006/ 095

176 'I attended a conference' RA GV/ AA/59B/1

176 'we should not' NA CAB 42/19/6

176 'there are rumours' ibid.

177 'following the breakthrough' Fourth Army papers, vol. 6, IWM

178 'They found themselves' Williams-Ellis, op. cit., p. 24

178 'One wanted to laugh' Stephen Foot, *Three Lives*, p. 153

178 'waddling, ambling, jolting' Lt G. Malins, *How I Filmed the War*, Herbert Jenkins, 1920, pp. 231–2

179 'meat and onions' Sanders TM

179 'clear when seen from the air' NA CAB 45/20C

179 'I and my crew' Williams-Ellis, op. cit., p. 20

179 'Having received his instructions' *Off. Hist.*: Miles, op. cit., fn p. 297

179 fn 'Even the spoken jargon of war' Baker-Carr, op. cit., p. 193

180 'Tell your men all about everything' Tank Museum, RH 86 TC 1759

180 'full of the bodies of dead Boches' Williams-Ellis, op. cit., p. 27

181 'To go ahead on foot' Henriques, op. cit., pp. 116–17

181 'switched off the engine' ibid., p. 117

181 'He came back and reported' Henriques, quoted in Pidgeon, op. cit., p. 80

181 'The Machine Gun Corps as a unit' NA WO 95/116

182 'It was only three miles or so from Green Dump' Arnold TM

CHAPTER 26

183 'Squashing dead Germans' quoted in Loewe, op. cit., p. 43

183 'It was her slowness that scared us' *Daily Mail*, 18 September 1916, p. 3

184 'White tapes had been laid down' typescript account by Gnr Albert Smith in TM

184 'Sgt Davies [the starboard gunner] was shell-shocked' ibid.

184 'We put out the flags' ibid.

185 'the Fourth Army plan' *Off. Hist.*: Miles, op. cit., p. 364

185 'attacking Germany all on his own' Maj. Allen Holford-Walker, quoted in Pidgeon, op. cit., p. 67

185 'it was decided to abandon the car' extract from handwritten account by Gnr T. H. Bernard made in October 1916, now in TM

186 'The machine [not identified] passed through' *Off. Hist.*: Miles, op. cit., p. 310

186 'As far as I know the tank' letter from Maj. A. Weymann, NA CAB 45/138, f. 280

186 'The physical, mental and nervous' Henriques, op. cit., p. 120

186 'Another authority' for a compelling investigation of the Quadrilateral affair see Trevor Pidgeon, op. cit., pp. 81–3

187 'The men . . . were very excited' letter from J. Attenborough, CAB 45/132

188 'We in the ranks' Arnold Ridley interviewed in October 1971, Liddle Archive, Brotherton Library, University of Leeds

188 'There was only one approach' *Tank Corps Journal*, no. 29, September 1921, p. 118

189 'We found the whole front' Cecil Lewis, *Sagittarius Rising*, p. 142

190 'shelled out of existence' A. E. Arnold, *Tank* magazine, vol. 45, May 1963

190 'A row of German heads' ibid.

190 'running the bearings' Hastie TM

CHAPTER 27

191 'Then a smash against my flap' Henriques, op. cit., p. 119

192 'with a smile he got back' ibid.

192 '9.00 am XV Corps Artillery' NA WO 158/325

193 'We were fired on' typescript account September 1957 by Gnr R. Reiffer in TM

193 'shouted at me from the port side' 2/Lt. J. W. Stadden TM

193 'We were within fifty yards' Reiffer TM

193 'The engine was beginning to knock' Hastie TM

193 'I saw a tank' Arnold TM

194 'You could see the clock' note from Gunner Harry Sanders, 1 September 1957 in LH 9/28/63 LHCMA

194 'Two officers only reached' W. Stadden to Liddell Hart in ibid.

194 'in seemingly unoccupied' Stadden, quoted in Terraine, op. cit., p. 225

194 'I personally don't believe' ibid., p. 228. Trevor Pidgeon gives this authoratative score card for the day. In the actions on the 15th a total of 27 tanks reached the German front line, nineteen got as far as the first

objective, eleven the second and six the third – plus a number of possibles – out of a total of forty-nine (counting the one left behind at Conteville for spares)

195 'down the road on which' Hastie, IWM sound 4126/1

196 'cruised about for a while' Arnold TM

196 'proceeded on a toilsome way back' ibid.

196 'Littered with rifles' Maj. H. Armitage letter to Edmonds, CAB 45/132

198 'It was reported' *Off. Hist.*: Miles, op. cit., pp. 331–3

199 'wanton waste of men.' Maj-Gen. Sir Charles Barter on his own account, given in a speech to a reunion dinner in 1919, was accused of such then 'dismissed with an hour's notice with disgrace from my division . . . without any attempt at investigation. My immediate appeal [for such] was totally ignored. I have been even refused official information relating to superior orders and material facts . . .' quoted in 'The Dismissal of Maj-Gen. Barter' by Col. Terry Cave, *Stand To!* no. 34 p. 15

199 'A runner explained' Lt A. J. C. Wheeler, NA CAB 45/200

200 'We shored the side up' Lt F. W. Bleumel, ibid.

200 'Away to my left rear, a huge gray object' Reginald H. Roy (ed.), *The Journal of Private Fraser, 1914–1918*, www.fordham.edu

200 'Dearest – it is no use' G. L. M. Viner, 85/11/1 IWM

201 'Darling . . . Captain Steedman's motors' Kirke papers, IWM

201 'A great battle' Rawlinson diary, 15 September 1916, typescript NAM

201 'A chap was shot while' Bernard TM

202 'became more and more haunted' Henriques, op. cit., p. 122

202 'begging to be sent back' ibid.

202 'The fine and likeable young fellow' Gnr Dawson, quoted in Pidgeon, op. cit., p. 86

202 'I regret to say however' ibid.

202 'Of my company one officer went mad' Henriques, op. cit., p. 119

202 'That it understated the horrors' M. K. Wardle to Edmonds, NA CAB 45/138, p. 276

203 'Lt. Macpherson died of wounds' war diary of D Company, appendix XII, NA WO 95/96, see also Lt G. Macpherson personal file, NA WO 339/41602

203 'It was the intention that' Anon., LH9/28/59 LHCMA

203 'can't bear to keep this' ibid.

203 'During this the first appearance' NA CAB 45/132

203 'A big grey box' Pidgeon, op. cit., p. 189

204 'If we only had a little more' Henriques, op. cit., p. 120

204 'a new type of heavy armoured car' printed on p. 1 of *The Globe* on the late afternoon of 15 September 1916, and London nationals the following morning

205 'Some of the tanks have done marvels' Haig diary, 15 September 1916, NA WO 256/13, p. 17

CHAPTER 28

206 'We commanders were ordered' Huffam TM

206 'At dawn I reported to an Australian' ibid.

206 'On a lovely morning in September' ibid.

207 'I was trapped in the wreckage' Sanders TM

207 'Men of the Durham Light Infantry' Huffam TM

CHAPTER 29

208 'Half-choked with engine fumes' Williams-Ellis, op. cit., p. 31

208 'it was in the air, rumours' Swinton, op. cit., p. 284

209 'the tanks were a great success' 18 September 1916, Charteris papers, LHCMA. At Cabinet on 18 September, F-M Robertson was asked by Grey whether the tanks had achieved as much as the

newspapers said. The CIGS replied that 'they had been a big success', NA CAB 42/20/3

209 'Although tanks had not achieved' Swinton, op. cit., p. 286

209 'Wherever the tanks advanced' Stern, op. cit., p. 96

209 'They are of an improved design' Haig diary, 17 September 1916, NA WO 256/13 p. 20

209 'in a state of great perturbation' Swinton, op. cit., p. 286

210 'It was thought desirable' ibid., p. 287

210 'After what had happened to Brough' ibid.

210 'new tanks and battered tanks' Stern, op. cit., p. 97

210 'steering and ventilation' Bacon, op. cit., p. 333

211 'steel boxes placed on copies' Stern, op. cit., p. 103

211 '[He] looked well' *The Autobiography of Margot Asquith* (Harmondsworth: Penguin, 1936), vol. 2, p. 190

211 'the heart-breaking precipitation' ibid., p. 89

212 'The Man Who Made the Tanks' *Daily Sketch*, 19 September 1916, p.1

212 'His Majesty's Land Ships: Some Facts' *Daily Mail*, 18 September 1918. Lord Northcliffe told Haig's private secretary: 'You may have noticed that directly the tanks were successful, Lloyd George issued a notice through the Press Bureau that they were due to Churchill. You will find that unless we watch these people they will claim that [the success of] the Great Battle of the Somme is due to the politicians . . .'

212 'The war is going splendidly' Northcliffe to Murdoch, 20 September 1916, BL Add. MSS 62179 f. 71

212 'a supplementary order' 'Recommendations for the expansion of the Heavy Section (Tanks) HSMGC put forward for by Maj-Gen. Butler at a conference held on 19–20 September 1916', NA WO 158/836

213 'the expansion' Haig to War Office, 2 October 1916, NA WO 158/836

213 'my superior glibly' Swinton, op. cit., p. 292

213 'Since you have been away' Butler to Elles, 22 September 1916, NA WO 158/836

214 'Swinton was probably correct' 'Talk with Martel', 29 March 1948, LH 9/28/59 LHCMA

214 fn 'Poor Hugh Elles' Letter of 4 June 1916 Charteris pps. microfilm 2/2 LHCMA

214 'Neither Col. Bradley or Martel' Letter from Lt-Col. (retd.) Allen Holford-Walker to the Official Historian, 24 April 1935, NA CAB 45/138 no. 269

215 'As you probably know, Brough' NA CAB 45/138

216 'concurs in an a further order' WO to MoM, 26 September 1916, NA MUN 4/2790

216 'Accordingly the proposed order' Army Council minutes, 27 September 1916, NA WO 33/881

216 'I can think of nothing better' NA WO 158/836

217 'This new engine has proved' Haig to War Office, 2 October 1916, NA WO 158/836

217 'very useful' NA WO 158/832

217 'of little assistance' ibid.

217 'excellent work' III Corps war diary, 29 September 1916, NA WO 95/674

218 'The tank was not at present' *Off. Hist.*: Miles, op. cit., p. 367

218 'The "Tanks" are the weirdest' Letter to Lady Hobart, 26 September 1916 Acc 1564 TM

218 'present state of development' Lt-Gen. L. E. Kiggell, 5 October 1916 in Fourth Army war diary, WO 158/236 and WO 158/832

218 '[Tanks] HQ in France' GHQ to the armies, 29 September 1916, NA WO 158/863

218 'in a certain circle' Swinton, op. cit., p. 300

219 'should be sent back with no bad mark' ibid.

219 'My intrusion was resented' Swinton to Edmonds, 22 January 1946, Edmonds papers, LHCMA

CHAPTER 30

220 'One of the officers' quoted in Johnathan Walker, *The Blood Tub*

221 'One German officer I met' *Daily Mail*, 18 September 1916, pp. 4–5

221 'I succeeded in holding out' Leut. Braunhofer writing on 3 January 1917 in the war diary of 5th Infantry Regiment Bd. 31, Bavarian Army Archives, quoted in Pidgeon, op. cit., p. 172

222 'The C-in-C has been much criticised' Butler to Edmonds, 2 August 1934, NA CAB 45/132

222 'If instead of employing' *Off. Hist.*: Miles, op. cit., p. 366

222 'vast and sprawling memoir' Swinton's entry in *Dictionary of National Biography*, vol. 53, p. 413, by Keith Grieves

222 'Various reasons have been put' Swinton, op. cit., p. 295

223 'special bullets had been issued' ibid., p. 285

224 'where records were incomplete' John Charteris, *At GHQ*, p. v

224 'loyalty of the correspondents' ibid., p. 144

224 'The Secret Service' ibid.

224 'about the tanks' ibid., p. 145

224 'It took some time before the writer' ibid.

CHAPTER 31

225 'They said they had been "warned"' section headed 'Land cruisers' in III Corps intelligence summary, 16 September 1916, signed off by Capt. W. Torr, NA WO 157/320

225 'We had heard rumours' Cedric Foley, *The Boilerplate War*, p. 15

226 'About six weeks ago' NA WO 157/320

226 'This may be a German agent's account' NA WO 157/320

226 'Friday 20 September' Charteris, *At GHQ*, p. 168

227 'in Norfolk in England' *Uber die neuen englischen Panzerwagen (caterpillar)* in History of 3rd Infantry Division Bd. 70, Bavarian War Archives, quoted in Pidgeon, op. cit., pp. 187–8

228 'egg-shaped steel housing' ibid.

229 'one or two tanks managed' ibid.

229 'Whether this weapon will be successful' ibid.

229 'Stetford' ibid.

230 'Without overestimating the effectiveness' Max Hundleby, *The German A7V Tank*, p. 13

231 'a "sergeant" who had worked' Col. Walther Nicolai, *Geheime Mächte*, p. 186

231 'He had escaped . . . from a tank' ibid.

231 'Information about this apparently' Paul Emil von Lettow-Vorbeck (ed.), *Der Weltkriegespionage*, Munich, 1931, p. 164. In his memoirs Albert Stern recalled a request from the Russian government in October 1916 for blueprint plans of tanks which he was convinced was in fact a German intelligence stunt. 'In consultation with the Ministry of Munitions and the DNC it was decided to give the Intelligence Dept. of the War Office a child's drawing and incorrect details', he wrote. 'I am convinced they found their way into the hands of the German General Staff.' *Log-Book of a Pioneer*, p. 117

CHAPTER 32

233 'It was in the summer of 1916' Julius Silber, *The Invisible Weapons*, pp. 193–6

234 'I was not interested' ibid.

234 'To go and visit the NCO's wife' ibid.

235 'The examination of prisoners' *Off. Hist.*: Miles, op. cit., p. 364 (fn).

235 'circled like an owl' Swinton, op. cit., p. 275

CHAPTER 33

237 'What kind of cars' *The Globe*, 15 September 1916, p. 1

238 'They are the caterpillar' cutting in Henriques file,' TM

238 'ignorant flapdoodle' Browne, op. cit., p. 42

238 'they became the subject of more chaff' ibid.

238 'The enemy ill-distinguished' *Daily Mail*, 18 September 1916, pp. 4–5

240 'one unbearable round of facile jest' Williams-Ellis, op. cit., p. 48

240 'This man Stern' Robertson papers LH CMA

241 'almost any design now' NA MUN 5 210/1940/10

241 'They have begun to construct in Germany' 'Russian WO Summary, 26 October 1916', MUN 4/3576

241 'The Fourth Army plan of attack gambled' *Off. Hist.*: Miles, op. cit., pp. 364–5

PART THREE

CHAPTER 34

243 'Never mind the noise' 'Tank Tips', NA WO 158/834

243 'The battle waits' NA WO 158/816

245 'voluntary transfers from' WO to OCHSMGC, 20 October 1916, NA WO 158/836

245 'Bantam battalions' ibid.

245 'Good muscular development' ibid.

246 'officers and men to volunteer for service' ibid.

246 'my son shall shoulder a rifle' Hickey, op. cit., p. 24

246 'I saw outside' ibid., p. 26

246 'He liked some of the other officers' Roy Jenkins, *Mr Attlee*, p. 77. See also Capt. C. R. Attlee's personal service record in NA WO 339/10870

247 'This is an engineers' war' quoted in Glanfield, op. cit., p. 193

248 'medieval quiet' 'Memoirs of an other rank', *Tank Corps Journal*, no. 31, November 1921, p. 159

248 'luxuriating at Auchy-les-Hesdin' William Watson, *A Company of Tanks*, p. 219

248 'Owing to somewhat strenuous times' Butler to Whigham, 25 September 1916, NA WO 158/836

248 'brooding, unsociable . . .' Anon. (Charteris), *HQ Tanks*, p. 87

249 'a man of desperate bravery' ibid., p. 7

249 'never left the Tank Corps' Fuller, *Tanks in the Great War*, pp. xiv–xv

249 'King of the Grocers' ibid.

249 'a civilian-cut' ibid.

251 'a well-appointed little man' Anon. (Charteris), *HQ Tanks*, p. 3

251 'paladin of the war' ibid., p. 15

251 'Engineers said he was no engineer' ibid., p. 18

252 'This show badly wants' Fuller, *Memoirs*, p. 87

252 'A small man with a bald head' Anon. (Charteris), *HQ Tanks*, p. 4

252 'an officer with no military' quoted in Williams-Ellis, op. cit., p. 45

253 'The inhabitants of Wool' Browne, op. cit., p. 50

253 'Lt-Col. the Hon. Claude Willoughby' History of 8th Battalion, NA WO 95/114

253 'instilled all the latest drill' Hickey, op. cit., p. 27

253 'similarly examined and instructed' NA WO 95/114

253 'A very large percentage' ibid.

254 'Apparently infantry battalion commanders' Ernest Swinton (ed.), *Twenty Years After*, pp. 836–7

254 'excellent man' NA WO 158/836

255 'to have a quiet life' Harris, *Men, Ideas and Tanks*, p. 80

254 fn 'It may interest you' RA Geo V Q977 17/60 and 19/10

255 'Little Anley is like' Fuller, *Memoirs*, p. 93

255 'He gave an encouraging tone' Browne, op. cit., pp. 49–50

255 'staff officer of tanks' Butler to Stern, 7 November 1916, NA WO 158/844

256 'The new personnel began to arrive' NA WO 95/107

257 'A man of course is ready' Haigh, op cit., p. 6

257 'I was in charge of the burying party' typescript account of 2/Lt G. E. V. Thompson, IWM 75/36/1

257 'To us in our damp' Watson, op. cit., p. 11

258 'little grizzled officer' Anon. (Charteris), *HQ Tanks* , p. 13

259 'My adjutant came from a box' Baker-Carr, op. cit., p. 206

259 'There were some good ones' Wilfred Bion, *War Diaries*, p. 8

259 'I had never seen such a band' Fuller, *Memoirs*, p. 89

260 'A pigsty' Dvr Cutting TM

260 'There were cavalrymen' Fuller, *Memoirs*, p. 89

260 'citizen force' Elles preface to Williams-Ellis, op. cit., p. v

260 'Generally a unit' *Royal Tank Corps Journal*, July 1932

262 'Pursuit of the retiring' NA WO 158/837

262 'black ones, tabbies' Haigh, op. cit., p. 74

262 'The [men] must be bathed' Fuller, *Memoirs*, p. 90

262 'the effect of wearing them' Haigh, op. cit., p. 37

262 fn 'It is difficult to convey' NA WO 95/112

263 'The heavyweight boxing champion' NA WO 158/800

263 'Every exercise and movement' Fuller, *Tanks in the Great War*, p. 69

264 'Tank Training Note number 16' Fuller papers, TS/6 LHCMA

264 'Fuller had ever actually set foot' J. P. Harris, op. cit., p. 87

264 'Tanks had nothing to fear' Fuller papers, TS/6 LHCMA

CHAPTER 35

265 'the view of the General Staff' NA WO 32/5154

265 'On the face of it the idea' NA WO 32/5154

266 'Germany is building' NA MUN 4/3576

266 fn 'The only engines available' Tritton to Edmonds, 8 May 1935, NA CAB 45/200

267 'poking their flanks with a chisel' for this extraordinary episode see NA WO 158/845, letter from Gore-Anley, 24 February 1917. Stern in his memoirs blames no individual directly – stating simply 'the military authorities decided to use sixty of these training tanks for fighting purposes', *Log-Book of a Pioneer*, pp. 148–9

267 'special guns for use exclusively' NA MUN 4/3576

267 'Special anti-tank batteries' ibid.

267 'Their failure will undoubtedly ruin' Stern to Addison, 12 March 1917, Stern papers, 1/1/6 LHCMA

267 'So far as tanks are concerned' NA WO 158/838

268 'It consisted of an awe-inspiring' Watson, op. cit., p. 41

268 'On the night of the 5th April' ibid., p. 42

269 'Stand with me at night' ibid., p. 43

269 'We had got word of trouble' Williams-Ellis, op. cit., p. 52

269 'The great thing is to go about' ibid., p. 53

270 'Zero was [set for] 5.30am' 'The Wanderings of "D" Battalion in France by a PBI (attached)', *Tank Corps Journal*, no. 22, February 1921, p. 13

271 'Our tanks lay hidden' Watson, op. cit., p. 55

271 'All my officers were assembled' ibid.

271 'Few reports arrive' ibid., pp. 57–8

271 'On 11 April 1917 near Arras' posting by R. J. Whitehead, 21 February 2003, in thread 'Tackling Tanks, the German View' on the Great War Forum www.1914-1918.invisionzone.com

272 'Any news of the other buses?' Haigh, op. cit., pp. 145–6

273 'Field's section' Watson, op. cit., pp. 62–3

274 'We were in an attack in the morning' quoted in Jonathan Walker, *The Blood Tub*, p. 106

274 'The organisation seemed to be so bad' ibid., pp. 104–5

274 'Never seen a more windy lot of officers' ibid., p. 105

274 'An Australian politician' ibid., p. 105

276 'for its scale the bloodiest' Liddell Hart, *The Tanks*, p. 104

276 'Six tanks moved forward' 'The Wanderings of "D"', op. cit.

277 'The first messages began' Watson, op. cit., p. 81

CHAPTER 36

278 'The recent battle' Haig to
Robertson, 25 April 1917, NA WO
158/845

280 'He seemed to be possessed by a
horror' Fuller, *Memoirs*, p. 114

280 'double Armstrong hut' Watson, op.
cit., pp. 101–2

280 'At a little shacky place' Maj. Philip
Hamond in LHCMA LH9/28/63–65

280 'Bathing parties were arranged' War
diary of 6th (F) Tank Bn, NA WO
95/107

281 'Each officer at this period' Watson,
op. cit., p. 92

281 'old people returning to their village'
ibid., p. 91

281 'Of the men who were in that fight'
Swinton, *Twenty Years After*, vol. 2, *A
Tank Officer Looks Back*, p. 837

281 'Church parades I am sorry to say'
Thompson, IWM

282 'Self-inflicted wounds were'
Thompson, IWM

282 'His Majesty saw the tanks' NA WO
106/291

282 'the King spoke in such a guttural'
Thomson, IWM

282 'Frequent demonstrations were
given' NA WO 95/107

283 'Tank mechanists' *The Times*, 30 July
1917, p. 6

283 'Their uniforms were new' Watson,
op. cit., pp. 108–9

284 'crack-brained – a kind of
mechanical Gallipoli' ibid., p. 118

284 'This infernal Bingham business' NA
WO 158/816

285 'a great chap' William Orpen, *An
Onlooker in France* (London: Williams
& Norgate, 1921), pp. 63–4

285 'a great bullet-headed ruffian' Anon.
(Charteris), *HQ Tanks*, p. 25

285 'On state days a pompous assembly'
ibid., p. 26

285 'Hell-bent on victory' ibid., p. 16

285 '*Gott, wie kolossal*' ibid., p. 25

286 'Greatly attached to an opera singer'
ibid., p. 35

286 'it would be disastrous if Churchill'
11 August 1916, Northcliffe papers,
BL Add. MSS 62159

287 'Before the move to Ypres' Hickey,
op. cit., p. 53

287 'On 6 July the whole Battalion' NA
WO 95/107

288 'full of squalid shops' Browne, op.
cit., p. 102

289 'like sausage meat' Beall, IWM
82/22/1

289 'The ground was so bad' Bion,
op. cit., p. 35

290 'a boy called Foster' ibid., pp. 37–9

290 'unintelligible gibberish' ibid.

291 'How are things going? Fuller,
Memoirs, p. 150

291 'that the battle was at an end' ibid.

291 'It was only by a "joy ride" ' Anon.
(Charteris), *HQ Tanks*, p. 16

291 'effervescent calculations' Fuller,
Memoirs, p. 141

292 'a ridge of hard sand' ibid., p. 161

292 'even Mr Beach Thomas' Browne,
op. cit., p. 234

292 'One commander arrived at Hill Top
Farm' Swinton, *Twenty Years After*,
vol. 2, p. 841

293 'There was an abyss of mud'
Hamond LHCMA

293 'As I neared the derelict tanks'
Williams-Ellis, op. cit., p. 98

294 'All the fighting crews' Hamond
LHCMA

294 fn Outline details of the sentencing
for desertion of Cpl. H. King and Pte
A. Morgan both of the Tank Corps
are in NA WO 213/17 and WO 213/
19

294 'inspected my few survivors'
Hamond LHCMA

294 fn 'I *like* living here I *hate* strangers'
ibid.

295 'ground . . . for which they had been
designed' d'Eyncourt to Haig,
22 August 1917, NMM DEY/43

295 'The choice of front' Haig to
d'Eyncourt, copy letter in Fuller
papers, BCI/13 LHCMA

295 'The fire was on the starboard'
typescript of Maj.-Gen. H. L. Birks in
Liddell 9/28/64 LHCMA

296 'The weather is perfectly ghastly' NA
WO 158/816

296 'When the line had advanced a little'
Watson, op. cit., p. 147

296 'We . . . must have left behind' ibid., p. 133

296 'The moral effect' Gough to Adv. GHQ 14 August 1917 (copy to tanks), WO 95/92

296 'no matter how much they proved' Anon. (Charteris), *HQ Tanks*, p. 27

296 'I hear the tanks . . .' Williams-Ellis, op. cit., p. 80

297 '20.8.17: General Capper goes to GHQ' HQ Tanks war diary, NA WO 95/92

297 'combed out for its fittest men' Fuller, *Memoirs*, p. 155

297 'I do not know – they will not let me know' 5 September 1917, CHAR 15/86a, p. 2 CAC

297 'The ideas and suggestions' 7 October 1917, NA WO 158/859

298 'Desiderata – get rid of Stern' ibid.

299 'What brought a sense of togetherness' Norman Dillon, IWM sound 9752

CHAPTER 37

301 'We had sold about' *New York Times*, 19 September 1916, pp. 1–2

304 'are a strong race and of good character' Dale E. Wilson, *Treat 'Em Rough!*, p. 12

304 'not to worry . . . people in tanks' Martin Blumenson, *The Patton Papers*, p. 423

304 'aggressive spirit' ibid., p. 427

305 'speak and read French better' ibid., p. 427

305 'like a horse' ibid., p. 444

305 'apercs to be the way' ibid., p. 432

PART FOUR

CHAPTER 38

307 'Think of your pals in the infantry' 'Tank Tips', NA WO 158/834

308 'The Army is Fighting' CHAR 15/86B CAC

309 'Battle of Albert' Fuller papers, 1/2/3a LHCMA

310 'The misuse by Sir Douglas Haig' Churchill to Edmonds, 26 January 1938, CAB 45/200

311 'From a tank point of view' Fuller, *Memoirs*, p. 170

311 'Strategically it was unsuited' *Tank Corps Journal*, no. 33, January 1922

312 'a tank officer should come' quoted in Robert Woollcombe, *The First Tank Battle*, p. 24

312 'degenerated into a plot to take Lens' Elles to Edmonds, NA CAB 45/200

313 'I was called one afternoon' Tandy to Edmonds, NA CAB 45/118

313 'Actually Sir J. Byng' Fuller papers, 1/2/3 LHCMA

314 'The Chief's main reason' Kiggell to Edmonds in LH9/28/64 LHCMA and 22 February 1946, NA CAB 45/118

315 'Eventually I decided' 'Cambrai dispatch' printed in the *London Gazette*, 4 March 1918 and *The Times*, 5 March 1918, p. 7

316 'an abomination to manhandle' Browne, op. cit., p. 261

317 'The Chinese Labour Battalion' Lt. E. F. Churchill, IWM documents 83/23/1

317 'Our Chinamen are an unknown' Elles to Capper, NA WO 158/816

317 'the two Corps commanders' Fuller, *Memoirs*, p. 189

318 'If . . . we are successful' Maj.-Gen. Louis Vaughan, 17 November 1917, NA WO 158/380

319 'We go straight in and sit on' quoted in *Off. Hist.*: Miles, *Military Operations, France and Belgium 1917, Cambrai*, p. 29

319 'usual rush of young officers' Brig. P. C. S. Hobart, *Cambrai: The Complete Narrative*, chapter VIII 'Some personal accounts of the battle by tank officers' reprinted in *Stand To!* (Journal of the Western Front Association), no. 56, p. 10

319 'As far as I can remember' ibid.

320 'swerve from its own line of advance' *Off. Hist.*: Miles, *Cambrai*, p. 34

320 'a fantastic and most unmilitary scheme' Baker-Carr, op. cit., p. 260

320 'He had laid down a system', ibid., p. 269

320 'Liaison with the Highlanders' Maj-
Gen. H. L. K. Birks, *RAC Journal*,
October 1949, pp. 202–10

321 'hilarious nights' 'The wanderings of
D', *Tank Corps Journal*, no. 30,
October 1921, p. 171

321 'blue-tinted glasses' Fuller, *Memoirs*,
p. 179

321 'False beards' see Williams-Ellis,
op. cit., p. 106, and Elles to
Edmonds in NA CAB 45/118 who
mentions Byng visiting the 'Tank
Training Office' dressed as a
Canadian. See also Foot, op. cit.,
p. 178, who mentions disguises being
adopted of a 'war correspondent' and
a 'Labour MP'. Maj. Gerald Huntbach
in a letter to Liddell Hart in 1948
however doubted these reported
stunts ever happening and said it
was merely a question of Tank Corps
personnel wearing badges of their
former regiments

321 'All unofficial discussion and
surmises' NA WO 158/356

322 'The troops made for it' Gnr
Reginald E. Beall, IWM documents
82/22/1

322 'A major in the tank corps' Watson,
op. cit., p. 168

323 'We were uncertain how much'
Williams-Ellis, op. cit., p. 107

323 'Instead of the rumble of engines'
Swinton, *Twenty Years After*, p. 843

323 'ordered out of the wood' Birks,
RAC Journal, op. cit.

324 'Tomorrow the Tank Corps'
handwritten original in NA WO
158/316

CHAPTER 39

325 'When filling with petrol' Capt. J. K.
Wilson, IWM documents PP/MCR/
1000

325 'It was a fair distance' Dillon, IWM
sound 9752

325 'It was the queerest sensation'
Coppard, op. cit., p. 122

326 'The four section cooks' NA WO
158/854

326 'a primus stove behind the engine'
Hickey, op. cit., p. 101

327 'It is really astonishing' quoted in
David Fletcher, *Tanks and Trenches*,
p. 81

327 'sleeping amid the remnants of cake'
Fuller, *Memoirs*, pp. 203–7

327 'mysterious thrill' ibid., p. 202

328 'One could hear low voices' ibid.,
p. 206

328 'huge tin thermos flasks' Maj. Philip
Hamond to Mrs Rita Hamond in LH
9/28/64 LHCMA

328 'Everyone was in jolly good trim'
ibid.

328 'Company commanders visited' NA
WO 95/107

328 'The darkness had paled' Fuller,
Memoirs, p. 206

328 'The last half hour before zero' Maj.
D. N. Wimberley, IWM documents
PP/MCR/182

329 'We moved off with the dawn' Beall,
IWM

329 'A little before six' Fuller, *Memoirs*,
p. 202

329 'I thought it would be' Bion, op. cit.,
p. 55

329 'and I laughed and laughed'
Hamond, LHCMA LH9/28/64

330 'broomhandle' Dillon, IWM sound
9752

330 'It screeched against the hull' Beall,
IWM

330 'Stunned by the devastating
precision' *Off. Hist.*: Miles, op. cit.,
p. 50

330 'The artillery barrage' Gen. Heinz
Guderian, *Achtung-Panzer!*, p. 81

330 'A side glance through' Hickey,
op. cit., p. 103

331 'quite elderly, his neck' ibid., p. 105

331 'trudging forwards with cigarettes'
recollections of Sq. Ldr A. S. G. Lee,
No. 46 Sqn RFC, *Official History, The
War in the Air*, vol. 4, p. 237

331 'A red flag stuck in the parapet'
Hickey, op. cit., pp. 104–5

331 'The fascine bumped down' J. B.
Hassall, Liddle Archive, Brotherton
Library, University of Leeds

331 'numbers of Germans being shot'
Anon. (E. Charteris), *HQ Tanks*,
p. 78

331 'Tommy drive a pick through' ibid.

332 'There was, in fact, great bitterness of feeling that day' ibid.

332 'One dugout I remember well' Wimberley, IWM

332 'Pig of a gunner!' quoted in Woollcombe, op. cit., p. 75

332 'figure with pipe aglow' typescript notes (c. 1950), 'Spearhead at Cambrai' by Maj. Gerald W. Huntbach in LH 9/28/64 LHCMA

333 'The General got out' Brig. A. E. Hodgkin diary, 20 November 1917, IWM documents P399

333 'tanks were in a queue waiting to enter' Huntbach, op. cit.

333 'foul confinement' Hickey, op. cit.

333 'a common custom if things were quiet' Hobart, *Some personal accounts of the battle by tank officers*, Chapter VIII reprinted in *Stand To!*, no. 56, p. 11

334 'A section commander's job' Hickey, op. cit., p. 101

334 'for some reason riding on the top' Hobart, op. cit., p. 11

334 'The tanks now separated' Hickey, op. cit., p. 106

334 '7:15 Crossed own front line' NA CAB 45/200

335 'and the fact that the deflector bags' ibid.

335 'Not a single battalion' *Off. Hist.*: Miles, *Military Operations, France and Belgium, 1917: The Battle of Cambrai*, p. 67

336 'As we moved forward' Coppard, op. cit., p. 124

336 'to light cigarettes' Swinton, *Twenty Years After*, p. 850

336 'standing outside the tank having a smoke' Thompson, IWM

336 'Then a most ludicrous thing' Hamond, LH9/28/64 LHCMA

337 'I returned in triumph' ibid.

337 'Several hundred civilians' Hodgkin, IWM

338 'The Boche do not seem' ibid.

338 'Operations were very successful' Haig diary, 20 November 1917, quoted in Blake, op. cit., p. 268

339 'Warning of our attack was conveyed' quoted in Woollcombe, op. cit., p. 62

340 'luckily they were rather stupid'

lecture by Gen. Byng to Canadian officers in February 1918, quoted in ibid., p. 90

340 'the danger is now understood' NA WO 158/981

340 'At 11.00pm the telephone' NA AIR 1/6/678/21

341 'old men with beards' Hobart, op. cit., p. 9

341 'Élan was discarded' Birks, *RAC Journal*, op. cit.

341 'Looting . . . slowed the infantry' Hobart, op. cit., p. 9

342 'trickled back in ones and twos' Hobart, op. cit., p. 11

342 'The battalion has been cut off' quoted in Bryan Cooper, *The Ironclads of Cambrai*, pp. 114–15

343 'It was apparent that the tanks' Birks, *RAC Journal*, op. cit.

344 'Tanks were all over the place' war diary of E Battalion, NA WO 95/111

344 'conked out with water' Wilson, IWM

344 'Climbing the slight slope' ibid.

344 'The first tank arrived . . . we fire' www.Channel4.com/history

345 'They lay there . . . in a crescent' Hickey, op. cit., p.109

345 'A shell came through' Browne, op. cit., p. 276

345 'Awarded MC. In Cambrai operations' *The Tank Corps Book of Honour* (London, 1919), p. 102

345 'Only one tank succeeded' D Bn. War Diary, NA WO 95/110

345 'It was tremendously satisfactory' Hobart op. cit., p.11

345 'on the right' '"Uncle" Harper at Cambrai: A Reconsideration', John Hussey, *British Army Review*, no. 117 – see also Bryn Hammond, 'General Harper and the Failure of the 51st (Highland) Division at Cambrai', in the *Imperial War Museum Review*, no. 10, 1995, pp. 90–100 for a more charitable assessment of 'Uncle's' role in the affair. Some retrospective analyses have sought to show that Flesquières could have only have been taken with the aid of an old-fashioned preliminary artillery pounding – and that the 51st was in

fact 'over-dependent on tank
support'
346 'surrounded by derelict tanks'
Watson, op. cit., p. 176
346 'we went up to Flesquières' Birks,
IWM sound 870/09
346 'Pigeons were half trained' *Off Hist.*:
Miles, *Cambrai*, p. 84
348 'abandon horses' NA WO 158/316
348 'British tank sergeant' *The Times*,
8 December 1917, p. 10
348 'one of the most astonishing' Fuller,
Tanks in the Great War, p. 150
348 'Albert was *en fête*', Anon.
(Charteris), *HQ Tanks*, p. 76
349 'On the appearance' Haig diary,
22 November 1917, NA WO 256/24
ff. 39–40
349 fn 'Hotblack, our military attaché'
NA CAB 45/200
349 fn 'After lunch' Capt. G. Dugdale,
Langemarck and Cambrai, p. 109
349 The hunt for the Nazi interpretation
of the lone-gunner of Flesquières
continues. Hitler's Cambrai Carpet
was reportedly featured in the art
journal *Kunst im Deutschen Reich*,
'Große Deutsche Kunstausstellung',
July/August 1940, p. 38

CHAPTER 40

350 'had been dragged about' Coppard,
op. cit., p. 123
350 'A miserable looking lot' Wimberley,
IWM
350 'And where are your reserves?'
Liddell Hart, *The Real War*, p. 374
351 'he became aware *before* the battle'
Terraine, op. cit., pp. 382–3
351 'There is no doubt that' ibid.,
p. 383
351 'We held up all the press messages'
Charteris, *At GHQ*, p. 120
351 'more details of prisoners' *The Times*,
22 November 1917, p. 7
352 'a vulgar and impertinent travesty'
Elles letter in Fuller papers, LHCMA
1/2/3a
352 'Elles made his reputation' Birks,
IWM sound 870/09
352 'wife and young daughters' see *The
Tatler*, 5 December 1917; 'shaving

cream' is cutting in Henriques
papers, TM
352 'six lorries loaded with fuel' see
account by C. Weaver-Price in *Tank
Corps Journal*, no. 31, November
1921, p. 159
352 'zig-zagging across' Hickey, op. cit.,
p. 114
353 'Hermosa' ibid., p. 118
354 'hearing English voices nearby'
Hundleby, op. cit., p. 152
354 'There were a round dozen'
Williams-Ellis, op. cit., pp. 112–13
355 'good clean tank with a good crew'
letter dated 26 January 1969
included in typescript account of
J. K. Wilson, IWM
355 'eight tanks in Indian file' ibid.
355 'white as a sheet' ibid.
355 'Near the top everyone stopped' ibid.
355 'Perhaps I'll go over to Cambrai' ibid.
356 'No change in the enemy on
Cambrai' Charteris pps., 27 Nov.
1917, LHCMA
356 'There was, of course' *Off. Hist.*:
Miles, op. cit., pp. 154–5
356 'The enemy expended his forces' NA
CAB 45/200; see also *Die
Tankschlacht bei Cambrai* in NA AIR
1/678/21431
357 'Tanks and infantry found it a
network' *Off. Hist.*: Miles, op. cit.,
p. 158
357 'Third Army's means were
exhausted' ibid.

CHAPTER 41

358 'telephone rang with the news'
Fuller, *Memoirs*, p. 217
358 'a huge man with mad blue eyes'
Watson, op. cit., p. 200
358 'The woods of Bourlon' Jünger,
op. cit., p. 205
359 'machines were mostly' Hobart
Narrative of Cambrai, Chapter V
'The counterstroke' published in
Stand To!, no. 55, p. 7
359 'I got another tank' Wilson letter in
Parsons, IWM
359 'As the tanks started to return'
Hickey, op. cit., p. 137
359 'roaring furnace' ibid., p. 138

359 'One tank had a chunk of shell' Maj. Philip Hamond to Mrs Rita Hamond in LH9/28/64 LHCMA

360 'in the interests of the cause' Haig to Robertson, 9 December 1917, Blake, op. cit., p. 271

360 'The attack upon DH is in full-swing' Charteris, *At GHQ*, p. 273

360 'The lower ranks seem to be completely' NA WO 158/53

360 fn 'One very kindly tank commander' Dillon, IWM sound 9572

360 'they were young and untrained' NA WO 158/53

361 'a torrent of rubbish' ibid.

361 'The battle of Cambrai has by now' ibid.

361 'Will the Right Hon. Gentleman', Parliamentary Debates. House of Commons (London: Hansard, 1918), 21 January 1918, col. 667

361 'I appeal . . . to the Government' ibid., 23 January 1918 col. 1102

CHAPTER 42

362 'My darling – I'm coming home' Hamond LH9/28/64 LHCMA

363 'Jan 4 1918: Southampton' Gnr R. G. Forward, IWM 93/34/1

363 'The men were given unlimited' Bion, op. cit., p. 69

363 'the Cambrai Christmas card' Fuller, *Memoirs*, p. 226

364 'fighting in Second Army zone' Hundleby, op. cit., p. 36

364 'the highest value on' conference at Bad Kreuznach, 11 December 1917, quoted in Hundleby, op. cit., p. 36

365 'After action the men have been unable' NA WO 158/854

365 'The biscuit portion' ibid.

365 'This battle of Cambrai shows' Blumenson, op. cit., p. 447

365 'Had the heavy British tanks' ibid., p. 454.

366 'a heavily armoured infantry soldier' Capt. G. S. Patton Jr, 'Light Tanks' 12 December 1917, quoted in Wilson, op. cit., p. 19

366 'those with experience of automobiles' ibid., p. 21

366 'a kind of kitchen range' Fuller, *Memoirs*, p. 232

367 'Well you goddamsonofabiches' Wilson, op. cit., p. 39

367 'look like soldiers not poets' ibid., p. 30

367 'Unless I get some tanks soon' 25 January 1918, Blumenson, op. cit., p. 477

367 'about as exciting' Wilson, op. cit., p. 34

367 'Who are the right men for the tanks?' Wilson, op. cit., p. 66

368 'parading drunkenly' ibid., p. 68

368 'We want fighters for' Ernest Hemingway, 'Six men become tankers' and 'Recruits for the tanks', *Kansas City Star*, 17–18 April 1918, www.kcstar.com

369 'I did not know a magneto from a carburetor' Wilson, op. cit., p. 33

CHAPTER 43

370 'The employment of the British Army' Fuller diary, 4 December 1917 TM

370 'From munition workers, from the USA' ibid.

370 'It would be a mistake' Fuller, *Memoirs*, p. 223

370 'Throughout the discussion' ibid.

371 'reservoirs' d'Eyncourt papers, DEY 43/pt 2 NMM

371 'Sheets of the intelligence summary' Williams-Ellis, op. cit., pp. 157–8

372 'Bovril and Vermouth' Fuller, *Memoirs*, p. 226

372 'out of uniform' NA WO 32/9288

372 'GHQ is inert and will lay down no policy' CHAR 15/86B/111–112 CAC

372 'The resources are available' quoted in Glanfield, op. cit. p. 233

373 'We were sent to Lens' Swinton, *Twenty Years After*, p. 850

373 'The sources of supply' *Tank Corps Journal*, no. 33, March 1922, p. 275

373 'No damaged part was ever' Williams-Ellis, op. cit., p.124

373 'Tanks from Cambrai' Maj. W. R. Powell-Chandler, IWM

374 'It was possible to train' *Tank Corps Journal*, no. 33, March 1922, p. 275

374 'A Scottish sergeant major' Cpl (later Sgt) David A. Pyle, 301st Tank Bn, quoted in Wilson, op. cit., pp. 53–4

374 'working with machines' Wilson, op. cit., p. 22

374 'We have got the first US officers' Capper to Elles, 22 February 1918, NA WO 158/816

375 'a great luxury, jam' *301st Battalion History* published by E. A. Wright, Philadelphia, 1919, quoted in Wilson, op. cit., p. 54

375 'They called us Uncle Sam's' Cpl David A. Pyle, quoted in Wilson, op. cit., p. 56

375 'saucy little Margarete Watkins' ibid., p. 58

376 '21.3.18 The enemy' war diary of 4th (D) Battalion, NA WO 95/110

376 'We had started a game' Thompson, IWM

377 'came back looking like burnished pewter' Hickey, op. cit., p. 164

377 'The British army were' ibid., p. 173

377 'He expected the war' ibid.

378 'At 8am as we stood on parade' Bion, op. cit., p. 78

378 'set far too low a standard' Hotblack report, quoted in Harris, op. cit., pp. 149–50

379 'I was to block the road' Hickey, op. cit., p. 195

379 'our loss in personnel' Elles to Capper, 29 March 1918, NA WO 158/816

380 'There are plenty of targets' Hundleby, op. cit., p. 114

381 'I saw to my astonishment' Francis Mitchell, *Tank Warfare*, p. 191

382 'A message dropped' *Off. Hist.*: Brig.-Gen. Sir J. E. Edmonds, *Military Operations France and Belgium, 1918*, vol. 2 , p. 393

382 'Three of the seven came back' Mitchell, op. cit., p.194

382 'Soon four Whippets had been knocked out' Hundleby, op. cit., p. 122

382 'The first major action' ibid., p. 124

383 'This tank v tank affair' Elles to Capper, 26 April 1918, NA WO 158/816

383 'We have no guarantee' ibid.

383 'The manufacture of these tanks' Tanks HQ war diary, 2 May 1918, NA WO 95/93

384 'brilliant little battle' Liddell Hart, *The Tanks*, vol. 1, p. 172

385 'General Staff could not lay down' Kiggell to Capper, 10 June 1918, MUN 5/210/1940/21

385 fn 'worshipping' *The Diary of Virginia Woolf*, vol. 1, 1915–19, ed. Quentin Bell (London, 1977), p. 131

385 'an intensely stupid man' Fuller diary, 4 June 1918 TM

385 'Tanks and their Employment with Other Arms' proof sheets in NA WO 158/832

385 'When looked at without prejudice' Harris, op. cit., p. 180

387 'There was to be no smoking' Capt. H. Smeddle, IWM 78/51/1

387 'He was ordered to support the cavalry' Fuller, *Tanks in The Great War*, p. 293

387 'I found myself to be' *Tank Corps Journal*, no. 2, May 1919, pp. 78–9

388 'after that it was minor tactics' Fuller, *Tanks in The Great War*, (1920) p. 317

388 fn 'The tanks were mechanically imperfect' for such conflicting judgements see *Off. Hist.*: Edmonds, op. cit., vol. 4, pp. iv, 156–7 and Liddell Hart, *The Tanks*, vol. 1, p. 185

389 'On Friday 16 August the tanks' Hickey, op. cit., p. 256

389 'One company had been proceeding' Bion, op. cit., p. 138

389 fn 'starters'. For an informed analysis of the number of tanks available during the last 'hundred days' of the war see 'Could the Tanks of 1918 Have Been War-Winners for the British Expeditionary Force?', Tim Travers, *Journal of Contemporary History*, vol. 27, No. 3 (July 1992), pp. 389–406

390 'In the vicinity of the embankment' Jünger, op. cit., p.261

390 fn 'The neatest idea' Mitchell, op. cit., p. 129

390 fn 'The name of [our] tank' Pte J. Laddy transcript in Liddle collection,

Brotherton Library, University of Leeds.

390 'He knew nothing about tanks' Smeddle, IWM

391 'the usual straining and grunting' ibid.

391 'As we trundled along' Bion, op. cit., p. 151

392 'The whining of the sick man' A. Jenkin, *A Tank Driver's Experiences*, p. 179

CHAPTER 44

393 'When a tank is in good condition' Report by CO 5th Tank Bde, 18 September 1918 in Fuller pps. LHCMA quoted in Harris, op. cit, p. 185

394 'The commander was almost embarrassing' Baker-Carr, op. cit., pp. 306–7

395 'literally covered with American dead' Fuller, *Memoirs*, p. 356

396 'It was the motor casing' quoted in Wilson, op. cit., p. 202

396 'The Distinguished Service Cross' General Orders no. 4, U.S.W.D., 1923 quoted in www.homeofheroes.com

398 'Four tanks crawled' Jünger, op. cit., p. 284

398 'No sooner had the battalions' Browne, op. cit., p. 502

398 'On the 5th November 1918' Elles to Edmonds, 4 September 1934, NA CAB 45/200

398 'billeted in a filthy village' Watson, op. cit. p.294

399 'Since the opening of our offensive' Elles NA CAB 45/200

399 'The comradeship of the Corps' *The Times*, 25 February 1919, p. 13

400 'vote of confidence' Hundleby, op. cit., p. 189

400 'I am pleased with the result' 7 December 1919, Edmonds papers, 2/5/1a-22 LHCMA

402 'I am commanded by the Army Council' NA WO 339/59279

402 'remembered with honour' www.cwgc.org/search/casualty= 19587

AFTERWORD

403 'native invention has been turned' *The Listener*, 15 May 1941

404 'The publication of Fuller's essay' Liddell Hart, *Memoirs*, vol. 1, pp. 88–9

404 'circumstances not likely to recur' 1919 RUSI lecture, quoted in ibid., p. 94

404 'Some enthusiasts today' ibid., p. 100

404 'these four men were all postwar recruits' ibid., p. 97

405 'armoured forces racing on ahead of the main army' Len Deighton, *Blitzkrieg*, pp. 134–5

406 'Any tank that shows its nose' Liddell Hart, *Memoirs*, vol. 1, p. 241

406 'national danger' 'Wigwam' to 'Archimedes', 28 September 1937, Edmonds pps. LHCMA.

407 'It is whispered among the initiated' LH 1/259/76 LHCMA

407 'It could only be' John Charteris, *Earl Haig*, fn. p. 222

411 'from certain papers' *Journal of the Royal Engineers*, December 1956, pp. 392–4

412 'boy admirals' Edmonds to Swinton, 14 May 1950, Edmonds papers LHCMA

412 'Tussaud's wax works' ibid.

413 'My dear Kell' NA KV 2/2410

413 'Each time I talk' LH 11/1935/103 LH CMA

413 'He was a tired' Birks IWM Sound 870/09

414 'unlikely that he no longer thinks an Allied victory' NA KV 2/2411

414 'Liddell Hart is both a Jew and an ass' Fuller to Capt. R. Gordon-Canning, 18 June 1938, mail intercept in NA KV 2/2410

414 'We who fought are corrupt' Swinton, *Twenty Years After*, p. 852

INDEX